AMERICAN APOSTLE
OF THE
FAMILY ROSARY

AMERICAN APOSTLE
OF THE
FAMILY ROSARY

The Life of Patrick J. Peyton, CSC

RICHARD GRIBBLE, CSC

A Herder & Herder Book
The Crossroad Publishing Company
New York

The Crossroad Publishing Company
www.CrossroadPublishing.com

Printed in the United States of America

This text of this book is set in 10.5/13 Sabon.
The display faces are Optima and Weiss.

Cover Art: Courtesy of Holy Cross Family Ministries, North Easton, Massachuseetts.
Cover Design: Stefan Killen Design.

Cataloging-in-Publication Data is available from the Library of Congress

ISBN 978-0-8245-2289-6
ISBN 978-0-8245-2621-4 (paperback)

2   3   4   5   6   7   8   9   10   B   16   15   14   13   12

Special thanks from
Holy Cross Family Ministries to

Tom and Erma Jean Tracy and family
The Michael and Bridget (Peyton) Gallagher family
and
Michael and Patty Smith and family

All special friends to
Servant of God Father Patrick Peyton, CSC,
Apostle of the Family Rosary

Between 1942 and 1992 Father Patrick Peyton, CSC, headed a specialized ministry that promoted family prayer through the rosary. His work would never had been possible without the support of his religious community, the Congregation of Holy Cross, and the assistance of dozens of religious who over the fifty years of Peyton's work labored tirelessly to assure success in rosary crusades, radio and television programs, and other events associated with Peyton's overall plan. It is appropriate that this first critical biography of Patrick Peyton be dedicated to those Holy Cross religious whose heroic efforts made Peyton's family prayer ministry possible.

Contents

Photographs follow page 241

Foreword

Christopher J. Kauffman

Traditional biographical studies of popular religious figures have ordinarily been contributions to hagiography composed with the intention of edifying their readers with stories of heroic sanctity. Such stories are merely two-dimensional, entirely lacking any realistic explorations of background that would provide depth to these portraits. Though the biographers may have delved into the appropriate archives, the research is not buttressed with a wide range of works in American and Catholic history. A cursory reading of Richard Gribble's biographical study of Patrick Peyton immediately reveals that this is a work written according to the canons of contemporary historical criticism: a judicious use of the primary sources, an expert command of the secondary literature in various spheres of Irish, American, and Catholic history, and a point of view that allows these sources to determine the development of the narrative and analysis. Richard Gribble's detailed story of Father Patrick Peyton is characterized by professional scholarship.

The author recognizes the complexity of the famous Holy Cross priest. Father Peyton's complexity is evident in his interaction with many notable figures in ecclesiastical, political, and entertainment spheres during a long time span replete with events that challenge Gribble's understanding of the vagaries of the human condition. Though Father Peyton's commitment to family prayer, particularly the family rosary, was demonstrated in a simple, direct, and unpretentious manner, to sustain that commitment entailed stresses and strains. Dr. Gribble captures the humanity of Father Peyton in his narrative of Peyton's experiences of distress and distraction with his staff and with representatives of the radio, TV, and motion picture industries.

To deepen the readers' understanding of Peyton, Gribble analyzes him within various contexts. This analysis entails an exploration of many

fascinating topics such as the Irish Church's religious revival in the mid-
to late nineteenth century, spirituality and popular devotionalism, trends
in family life, World War II, the Cold War, Catholic anti-Communism,
the Second Vatican Council, modern mass communications, and several
interesting areas of religion and culture. The reader's encounter with the
story of Father Peyton will yield a keen appreciation of the historical
significance of this Holy Cross priest known throughout the world for
his famous motto, "The family that prays together stays together." With
his charming Irish brogue Peyton elicited trust, confidence, and faith
among his widely diverse audiences.

Professor Lawrence Moore's historical work *Selling God* focuses on
how Protestant evangelical preachers appropriated some of the techniques of the theater and other forms of popular culture in order to
effectively market their religious messages. Richard Gribble's biographical study of Patrick Peyton tells the story of the mass marketing of a
simple message of family prayer. Indeed, Father Peyton not only appropriated the forms of popular culture but he placed his message in the
theatrical media of radio and television. The rosary crusades in dioceses
throughout the world were complex processes involving public relations
professionals, technology experts, and a team committed to promoting
a family rosary crusade through the media, in Catholic schools, and
into every corner of the diocese. The modern packaging of the traditional message was Peyton's signature style, one particularly effective in
"selling" traditional family prayers and practices.

Popular prayer and devotionalism were affected by the developments
of the Second Vatican Council, particularly those changes associated
with the liturgy, scriptural prayer, the notion of the pilgrim people of
God, ecumenism, and the Church as Sacrament. Dr. Gribble's narrative
of the self-examination and revision of the rosary crusade in light of
Vatican II includes summaries of meetings among Catholic and Protestant theologians, such as the Redemptorist Bernard Häring and Lutheran
scholar Arthur Piepkorn. These theologians suggested that Peyton intro-
duce Scripture-based meditations on the mysteries of the rosary, reforms
that would tend to generate interest among post–Vatican II Catholics
and among some Protestants. Between 1965 and 1970 Father Peyton
significantly modified the Crusade to include "Scripture, song, and spontaneous meditations." These were not entirely successful reforms, nor did
they revive the "grand public expressions" of Catholic prayer. Indeed,
there were public demonstrations in opposition to diocesan expenditures
on a crusade. Even the Latin American crusades were a disappointment.

The concluding section of this book is a balanced account of progress and conflict in the development of new programs. In the last period of his life Father Peyton was generally recognized by priests, prelates, and the pope for his many contributions to deepening the faith of millions by his eminently successful promotion of family prayer. Gribble's portrait of Peyton is a realistic account of the idealistic priest who was both a charismatic figure and a master of the media. There is a consensus that this was a graced life symbolized by the introduction of Father Patrick Peyton, CSC, for beatification in the Sacred Congregation of Causes.

Dr. Gribble's work is the first scholarly biography of Father Peyton, and no historian is better prepared for this task than this accomplished scholar. He is the author of *Guardian of America: The Life of James Martin Gillis, CSP;* of *Fulfilling a Dream: Stonehill College 1948–1998,* a history of Stonehill College in Easton, Massachusetts, run by the Eastern Province of the Congregation of Holy Cross; and of a popular work on the history of the rosary. Not only does he have background suitable to take on the biographical study of Father Peyton; he is also a Holy Cross priest who met Father Peyton and as his confrere shared with him the historical charism of the Congregation.

I have the good fortune to have been associated with Richard Gribble at the Catholic University of America both as his advisor and as the chair of his doctoral committee. It is, therefore, with a sense of personal pride and professional commitment that I recommend Gribble's book as a first-rate scholarly, candid, and readable life of Father Patrick Peyton.

Preface and Acknowledgment

On July 4, 1986, I was attending summer school classes at the University of Notre Dame. Returning to Moreau Seminary after class that afternoon, I noticed that there was a cookout in progress as part of the celebration of Independence Day. I also noticed the presence of a very tall elderly priest whose face I recognized from photos. For the first and only time I saw Father Patrick Peyton. As a seminarian in Holy Cross I was familiar with Peyton and his work, but I also knew of his life through his autobiographical account, *All for Her,* which I had read many years earlier. Knowing of his fame I wanted to meet this man, but was rather timid in seeking an introduction. Another religious, knowing of my desire to meet Peyton, literally took me by the sleeve and placed me before Peyton. "Father Peyton," he said, "this seminarian wants to meet you." Peyton was very cordial and, in fact, spent the rest of the afternoon with me, showing me videos of his latest rosary crusade in the Philippines and, of course, praying five decades of the rosary with me as we walked about the lakes that are so prominent at Notre Dame.

While this was the first and only time I encountered Patrick Peyton personally, his life's work and devotion had been part of my life from a much earlier day. A product of public schools, I attended catechism classes (religious education today) each Saturday at my home parish of St. Bruno in Whittier, California. One Saturday when I was in eighth grade my teacher invited two guest speakers who spoke to the class about Fatima and the rosary. While my mother had taught me all the basic prayers and, as best I recall, how to pray the rosary, it was not something that was part of my regular routine. However, after hearing the presentation of the two speakers that Saturday morning I made a commitment to pray the rosary each day, a promise that, with the exception of my college days, I have kept. Blessed beyond all measure because of this commitment, the rosary became a part of my life from that Saturday morning forward.

My association with the rosary and the work of Father Peyton reached its apex when I was asked by Father John Phalen, CSC, president of Holy Cross Family Ministries, the present name of Peyton's original foundation, to write a biography of the rosary priest. I was grateful for the invitation and saw the project as a way to bring the complete story of Peyton to the world and, at the same time, enhance my own appreciation for his work and the rosary, the foundation piece of his entire ministry. This project could not have been completed without the assistance of numerous people who have given freely of their time and expertise to assist in this project. The archival staffs of Holy Cross Family Ministries, Deidre McGrath and David Goodrich; the Holy Cross Fathers Eastern Province, Father David Arthur, CSC, in North Easton, Massachusetts; the Holy Cross Fathers Indiana Province, Father William Simmons, CSC, Notre Dame, Indiana; the Holy Cross Fathers Generalate, Father Hugh Cleary, CSC, in Rome; and the archivist of the Archdiocese of Los Angeles, Monsignor Francis Weber, were very helpful in allowing access to information and assisting with its retrieval. Many people assisted in reading the manuscript and making recommendations for improvements, most especially Professors Toni-Lee Capossela of Stonehill College and Christopher Kauffman of the Catholic University of America. Father Thomas Feeley, CSC, conducted numerous interviews for this project that provided significant insight from those who knew and worked with Peyton. Special thanks is extended to several Holy Cross religious, Jerome Lawyer, CSC, John Murphy, CSC, David Farrell, CSC, William Ribando, CSC, and Joseph Quinn, CSC, who worked for extended periods of time with Peyton and provided great assistance in supplying answers to numerous questions. I am also grateful to Dorothy Halloran, who worked with Father Peyton for many years, and whose review of this manuscript was very helpful. I am also very grateful for the financial support given to this project by Tom and Erma Jean Tracy.

The task of research and writing is a significant endeavor that necessitates much time and effort, but my task was made easier through the supportive environment of the Holy Cross community with whom I live at Stonehill College in North Easton, Massachusetts. I thank them for their assistance and prayers.

RICHARD GRIBBLE, CSC

Introduction

On Mother's Day, May 13, 1945, a day designated by President Harry Truman for national celebration and thanksgiving after the Allied victory in Europe, Francis Spellman, archbishop of New York, gave the introduction to a special national radio broadcast emanating from the Guild Theater on Fifty-second Street in Manhattan. The program was organized by Father Patrick J. Peyton, CSC, a Holy Cross priest who for three years had been promoting family prayer through the rosary. In his introductory welcome remarks, Spellman referred to Father Peyton as the "American Apostle of the Family Rosary."[1] The archbishop's words were prophetic for, beginning that day and continuing for almost a half-century, Patrick Peyton traversed the world many times over, a modern St. Paul, promoting a simple but profound message, "The family that prays together stays together."

The sixth of nine children of a poor family from County Mayo, Ireland, Peyton learned the efficacy and power of family prayer from his earliest days, kneeling nightly in the family's three-room cottage, following the lead of his father, and praying the family rosary. This formative experience, together with his cure from tuberculosis—which he saw as a miracle worked through the intercession of the Blessed Virgin Mary—set him on a lifelong ministry from which he would never waver. Beginning with radio, and then expanding to television, films, and most prominently an international rosary crusade campaign, Peyton set out to bring 10 million families to family prayer. Through his undying faith, herculean work ethic, and many assistants, he accomplished his original goal by the mid-1950s. His name and simple slogan became household words for American Catholics.

The contribution of Peyton to Catholic life in the United States and his worldwide influence has not yet been explored in any scholarly venue. In 1952, with Peyton's ministry receiving international recognition through its radio and television programs and the first rosary crusades outside North America, Peyton commissioned Ted Bonnet to write *The Ear of*

God, a monograph that combined a biographical sketch of Peyton and rosary devotional prayers. The book, which listed Peyton as its author, was a great success and introduced more people to the rosary priest and his ever-expanding ministry. In 1967 *All for Her,* marketed as Peyton's autobiography but actually written by Gary MacEoin, was published. *Man of Faith,* written by Jeanne Gosselin Arnold and published in 1983, was a third effort chronicling Peyton and his many successes with Family Rosary and Family Theater. However, none of these books, based primarily on interviews with Peyton and written without the benefit of access to primary sources, provides a critical analysis of his life or work.

Now that thirteen years have passed since Peyton's death in 1992, it is time for a deeper exploration of the historical record and Peyton's contribution to the Church universal. This book provides a complete chronicle of the events of Peyton's life and both the successes and the failures of his Family Rosary ministry. All archival repositories of Peyton's papers, most prominently those of Holy Cross Family Ministries and the Congregation of Holy Cross, have been used to place Peyton and his work within the context of Catholic religious, social, and political thought of his day. How was one priest with a poor record of health and few if any contacts outside his religious community able to organize, maintain, and continually expand a ministry which circled the globe and touched the lives of millions of people? The methods he used, the influential people who assisted his work, and the many conflicts which he encountered along the road must be placed into the crucible of historical analysis in order to discover the true significance of Peyton, not only as a man of prayer and devotion, but as an influence on Catholic life then and now.

Beginning his work in office space donated by Dominican sisters in Albany, New York,[2] Peyton, working almost single-handedly at the outset, slowly but steadily built his ministry of family prayer. Thousands of letters were sent to the hierarchy, priests and religious, and Catholic institutions nationwide informing them of his ministry and requesting their assistance. Peyton gave many talks and conducted Triduums in churches throughout the Northeast and Midwest. These efforts led to Peyton's first great success, the aforementioned national radio broadcast of May 13, 1945. In a whirlwind of activity over the next two years, Peyton, through his many contacts among Hollywood celebrities and radio executives, convinced the Mutual Broadcasting Company to broadcast a weekly radio show on family prayer. He wanted a show devoted to the rosary, but prudence and the advice of associates told him to take what was offered by Mutual.[3] Thus, on February 13, 1947, *Family Theater of the Air* premiered, initiating a twenty-year partnership. The program series was well received and led to several hour-long programs marking Christmas, Easter, and Thanksgiving.[4]

Success in radio encouraged Peyton to produce short films for the nascent and expanding field of television. Through his own personal magnetism, which emptied donors' pockets almost at the mere suggestion of monetary need, and the financial support of the international shipping magnate J. Peter Grace,[5] Peyton produced a series of films, generally thirty or sixty minutes, including the *Triumphant Hour,* and the *Joyful Hour,* based on holiday radio programs, and new efforts, such as the popular *Hill Number One, That I May See,* and *A Star Shall Rise.*

Peyton's family prayer ministry reached its apex through the rosary crusades. Initiated in London, Ontario, in 1948, the crusades became increasingly more complex in operation and more widespread in scope. Peyton was assisted on the crusades by a team of Holy Cross religious, Francis Woods, an Albany priest, support personnel from the Family Rosary organization, and people on the local level. By the mid-1950s Peyton's international rosary crusade had reached every continent save South America and had convinced millions of the efficacy of the family rosary.

Latin America, home to approximately one-fourth of the world's Roman Catholic population, was the great prize that Peyton, as he often stated, "wished to deliver to our Lady." The high degree of religious illiteracy among the people and the generally poor economic state of nations and the Church in this region meant that Peyton had to develop a new tool to bring his message to the people. The rosary films, a series of fifteen half-hour productions on the mysteries of the rosary, were the basic tool of catechesis that the rosary priest needed in Latin America. Filmed on location in Spain in 1956, the films were unquestionably the most significant media accomplishment of his life and produced the raw material for feature-length and shorter films that are still used.[6]

Although Peyton's Latin American crusades, conducted between 1959 and 1965, were the most significant of his career, they were also fraught with controversy. Peyton's message of family prayer continued to be preached, but with the advanced tool of the films, his missive could reach and be understood by the poor, lesser educated, and rural peoples of the region. When Peyton turned for financial assistance to his friend Peter Grace, he secured a covert economic arrangement with the Central Intelligence Agency of the United States to back the crusade effort.[7] The CIA supported Peyton's campaign because it promoted religion to a people traditionally steeped in Catholicism, thus offering an attractive alternative to the rising tide of Communist ideology in the region. Peyton reluctantly accepted the subsequent loss of his control of the campaign as a necessary consequence of the financial support he needed. The crusade's presence in Latin America at that time of political unrest, with Communists vying for control, led some to see Peyton's campaign as responsible for the toppling of Communist-leaning governments, most notably that of João Goulart in Brazil.[8]

Peyton's almost mercurial rise to international prominence was halted and even placed in retreat after the Second Vatican Council (1962–65), which initiated a new concept of Church, and most especially spirituality. The sociologist of religion Robert Wuthnow has demonstrated how the changing pattern of American spirituality from "dwelling" to "seeking" transformed religious patterns in the United States during this period away from more traditional methods of prayer to less structured forms.[9] This shift, which came about at the time of Vatican II and the political and social unrest in the United States, created a turn in American Catholicism (most prominently but also universally) away from popular devotion and piety. For many the rosary and other forms of popular devotion fell out of favor and use among a large percentage of the faithful. Additionally and simultaneously, the advent of television provided the death knell for much of radio's past programming efforts.

Peyton attempted to deal with this trying development, which he called "the rosary in eclipse," by rethinking the United States ministry, revising it in the direction of increased ecumenism espoused by Vatican II. However, the new campaign, launched in Milwaukee in 1968, was a failure and, to Peyton's great disappointment, virtually ended the crusades in the United States as they had been originally conceived. Other disappointments of the period included a fruitless attempt to reorganize the mission so that it was not so dependent on one person, and the failure of two feature films, *The Eternal King* and *The Redeemer,* made from the original fifteen rosary films. In short, the 1960s and 1970s were periods of stagnation for Peyton and his mission.[10]

From the late 1970s until his death in June 1992 Peyton's star once again begin to shine. While the crusades in the United States had ended, their resumption in Latin America and the Philippines drew great crowds. The successful 1973 television series *A Matter of Faith,* two new series of films based on the mysteries of the rosary, set both in contemporary and biblical times and featuring international personalities such as Princess Grace of Monaco and Mother Teresa of Calcutta, the completion of a Rosary handbook, and a successful "rosaries for Russia" campaign, inaugurated upon the fall of Communism and the dissolution of the Soviet Union, were also triumphs for Peyton.

The latter part of Peyton's life also included great disappointments, especially in his relationship with his religious community, the Congregation of Holy Cross. In the mid-1970s Peyton's greatest hope for a feature-length film, *The Messiah,* was an economic disaster, costing Family Rosary $2 million. More importantly, in the 1980s a new form of the crusade, Families for Prayer, initiated with great hope, ended in a flurry of polemics that pitted the rosary priest and his lay assistants against the religious superiors of Holy Cross. Nevertheless, before he died Peyton achieved the organizational restructuring that Family Rosary had sought for many years, allowing the ministry to continue promoting his plain but important message of family prayer, as it does today.

The successes and failures of Patrick Peyton, the public man of radio, film, and international rosary crusades, must be weighed against the more private religious priest. As evidenced by the historical record and the reflections of countless people he encountered during his life, Peyton left no stone unturned in his efforts to promote the family rosary. He was single-minded about his work, and his commitment led him at times to use questionable methods and ignore their consequences. Additionally, he uncritically accepted and trusted powerful and influential people who could help him achieve his goals, but who sometimes also placed him and his mission in compromising positions. In particular Peyton's uncritical confidence in Peter Grace and his associates produced more conflicts for Peyton with his Holy Cross confreres, especially his superiors in the community.

The influences that shaped Peyton's life and work were rich and numerous. In addition to formative childhood events, family values, and his illness and sudden cure, the privileges he received as a young religious also formed the man he became. New Holy Cross members were especially supportive of Peyton's mission, even though the order was severely stretched in meeting its commitments to parishes, schools, and other institutions. Provincials provided Peyton with almost carte blanche permission to do whatever he wished in promoting family prayer. Just as Peyton uncritically accepted help from any and all sources, his superiors uncritically accepted his mission, creating a vicious circle in which Peyton demanded and assumed more and more autonomy over all his projects. When after many years of operating independently, Peyton was challenged over the Families for Prayer organization, he responded confrontationally to his superiors' questions.

The chronology of this book divides logically in half. Chapters 1 through 7, chronicling Peyton's life and ministry from his birth in 1909 to the end of the Latin American crusades in 1965, describe the origins of the Family Rosary ministry, its rapid expansion, and its many successes between 1942 and 1966. During this period Peyton became an internationally well-known cleric. Through an almost superhuman drive and commitment Peyton built his family prayer ministry into an organization in which the Congregation of Holy Cross and the Church universal could take great pride. The conversion of tens of millions of families to a belief in the efficacy of the family rosary and their pledge to pray the rosary daily was an accomplishment of mind-boggling proportions. Chapters 8 through 13 relate the story of Peyton and Family Rosary in the post–Vatican II Church. Many of the successes of earlier years continued, notably the international crusades and some new film projects, but the period was dominated by the need to rethink the whole ministry in the light of the significant religious and social changes that characterized the historical period. In the post–Vatican II Church and new world situation his tried and true message did not have the appeal it once had generated. It was necessary, therefore, for Peyton and his organization to adapt. Both the man and his ministry changed externally and Family Rosary itself did seek new permanent avenues, but Peyton himself died as he lived, firmly committed to the need for family prayer through the rosary.

An epilogue that describes Peyton's spirituality, as documented by what he said and did and how others experienced him, concludes this book. Peyton was a man of indomitable faith who touched the lives of millions of people through a simple message sincerely conveyed. A product of several powerful influences, Peyton represents the very best of the human spirit of achievement and the foibles that beset all people.

Patrick Peyton truly was a contemporary apostle who traveled the world with a simple but profound message. His methods of communication were multifaceted and changed over time, but the core belief of the absolute need for family prayer never wavered. As a man who exercised his discipleship with complete fidelity and commitment, Peyton is an inspiring example to people of faith everywhere.

Chapter 1

Responding to God's Call, 1909 – 42

The green rolling peaks of the Ox Mountains in the west of County Mayo, Ireland, stand as a testimony to the beauty, faith, and tradition of a people who for centuries have identified themselves with Roman Catholicism, a religious preference and a way of life. Ireland, converted to the practice of Christianity by St. Patrick in the fifth century, has undergone great trials and many transformations of its faith practice. Poverty, domination by outside peoples, and internal dissension have plagued the Irish, but it is through such ups and downs, the agonies and ecstasies of life, that people truly bond with faith, finding it a source of their sustenance and strength. This land is the environment that produced such great people of faith as Saints Columba, Bridget, Finnian, and Colman of Cloyne. The richness of the land and the influence of the Church have worked together to create a fertile environment for the development and practice of faith.

The Nineteenth-Century Irish Church

Poverty and persecution were the dominant characteristics of the Church in Ireland prior to the twentieth century. The faith practice of the Irish people was in many ways the cause of their persecution at the hands of the British. Poverty and a sense of political and social injustice were normative for the masses; a reputation for corporal austerity in Irish Catholicism has a long history in the nation. The spiritual tradition of the nation was preserved, purified, and even enriched by people who were not only physically poor, but often identified themselves as poor for the sake of Christ. Irish spirituality in the seventeenth and eighteenth centuries was dominated by the idea that the faithful sought to be poor in order to identify more closely with the sufferings of Christ. The cruel conditions experienced by the people of the period were one reason that Irish spirituality centered about the sacrifice of the Mass, seeing in this celebration a means to become more intimately associated with Jesus' life and salvific death. The affinity of the Irish Church with the suffering Christ was distinct. The Irish Jesuit historian Diarmuid O. Laoghaire believes that the reality of the common life of the average Irish Catholic colored religious practice and was responsible for the direction taken by the Church. He concludes, "Needless to say the poverty [of the people] left its mark on the spirituality of the nation."[1]

The nineteenth-century Irish Church, still suffering from its oppressed status, was characterized by several specific traits that made it readily identifiable. First, loyalty to the pope was paramount. While disagreements with Rome were always present, the fifth-century anti-Arian slogan *sicut Christiani ita ut Romani sitis* (As you are Christians so be ye also Romans) reflected a profound Irish sentiment.[2] A second feature of the Irish Church in this period was the close association of Catholicism with the nation — to be Irish was to be Catholic. Writing in 1872, the Dominican priest Tom Burke expressed the idea in this manner:

> Take an average Irishman. I don't care where you find him — and you will find that the very first principle in his mind is, "I am not an Englishman because I am Catholic." Take an Irishman wherever he is found all over the earth, and any casual observer will at once come to the conclusion, "Oh, he is an Irishman; he is Catholic." The two go together.[3]

A third characteristic of the Irish Church was its sober and rational nature, lacking any enthusiastic or mythical element or emotionalism. The keynote for the faithful was "Let us live sober, upright, and Godly lives in this world." The dry formalism pervading the practice of the faith was especially manifest in the way people were instructed in the faith. Various catechisms synthesized Church teaching into four primary areas: an exposition of the Apostles' Creed and explanations of the Ten Commandments, the Lord's Prayer, and the sacraments. Belief was covered by the Creed, morals by the decalogue, Church order and discipline by the sacraments, and personal devotion by the Lord's Prayer.[4]

As the mid-nineteenth century approached, the face of the Irish Church began to change. The Great Famine of 1845–46 was the transformative event in the lives of the Irish men and women of the period, forcing many to emigrate and generating a closer bond among those who remained behind. Religious practice was also affected in various ways.

The eminent American historian of the Irish, Emmet Larkin, suggests that the bulk of those who emigrated from Ireland during this national crisis were the poor and less devout Catholics.[5] The new religious composition of the nation brought changes in perspective and practice. One contemporary account described the situation:

> The present sufferings of the country have greatly contributed to break down the barriers which have so long existed against the entrance of divine truth among the unenlightened portions of the people. Men are brought together by common calamity, and the gospel is now, more readily than heretofore, received from hands which have willingly administered relief to their temporal needs.[6]

The Irish Church of the prefamine period also experienced a great shortage of diocesan clergy. This situation, which was exacerbated through a significant rise in population without similar increases in secular clergy, grew progressively worse[7] and increased the significance and influence of religious communities, especially teaching orders. By 1862 the Irish Christian Brothers (founded in 1802) were administering 181 schools with an enrollment of over twenty thousand students. The Irish Sisters of Charity (founded in 1816), the Loreto Sisters (founded in 1822), and the Irish Sisters of Mercy (founded in 1827) all centered their apostolic works in education.[8]

Besides lack of clergy the Irish Church of the mid-nineteenth century experienced other problematic situations. Moral failures of clerics, although the situation was improving since the beginning of the century, were still not in check. Mass attendance was estimated at 33 percent, a state of affairs created by the lack of clergy and insufficient churches. This issue was somewhat settled before the famine through the introduction of station churches and the celebration of the sacraments in private homes, but the structures of Church organization were still insufficient at mid-century. The physical deficiencies of Catholicism were coupled with what Larkin terms an "Anglicization" of the faith in language and custom. Before the famine struck and people physically emigrated there was a psychological and cultural movement away from the traditions of the Irish Church. Thus, there was a need for the Irish to re-identify themselves as Catholics in order to again assert their national culture and self-understanding. There was a need once more to "marry" the Irish with Catholicism.[9]

Irish Catholicism in the nineteenth century was most significantly reconstructed through the efforts of Paul Cullen, cardinal archbishop of

Armagh, who between 1850 and 1878 transformed the Church, both ecclesiastically and politically, in dramatic ways. He brought order to the
ranks of the clergy by recommending quality bishops, who built a national hierarchy that was ultramontane in its theological perspective.[10]
Cullen wisely interpreted the theological winds of his day, articulated
most strongly by Pope Pius IX (1846–78), that the Church needed
to return to Rome as its theoretical and actual source of sustenance.
Theological and political ideologies of the day, including socialism, rationalism, and the beginnings of theological modernism, threatened the
authority, power, and influence of the Church, among both the faithful and society at large. Thus, working with Rome, Cullen effectively
rooted out bishops who were set in their own ways and those whose
educational, religious, and political policies inhibited the cardinal's attempts at pastoral reform; he replaced them with prelates whose thinking
was consistent with his and that of the Church in Rome.[11]

With ecclesiastical structures in place, Cullen then set out to reform
the common faith practice of the people through what Larkin calls "a devotional revolution." Devotion to the Sacred Heart, beginning with the
establishment of the Confraternity of the Sacred Heart in 1812 and the
introduction of First Friday celebrations in 1835, blossomed in the latter
part of the nineteenth century. Parish missions and preached Triduums,
organized and led by religious congregations, were introduced in the
1840s and became part of Cullen's master plan for the regeneration of
the faith. Under Cullen's guidance, Catholicism fervently embraced the
renewal of many popular devotions with origins in the Roman Church.
Benediction of the Blessed Sacrament and perpetual adoration, pilgrimages to sacred sites and shrines, processions, the stations of the cross,
novenas, and common vespers for the laity became common practices in
the Irish Church in the latter nineteenth century. These devotions were
reinforced with special sacramentals such as scapulars, medals, prayer
books, catechisms, and holy cards.[12] Larkin summarizes the contribution
of Cullen to the Irish Church:

> In the nearly thirty years that he faithfully served Rome in Ire-
> land, Paul Cardinal Cullen not only reformed the Irish Church, but
> what was perhaps even more important, in the process of reform-
> ing that Church, he spearheaded the consolidation of a devotional
> revolution. The great mass of the Irish people became practicing
> Catholics, which they have uniquely and essentially remained both
> at home and abroad to the present day.[13]

Among the many popular devotions practiced by the Irish Church during the nineteenth century and before, special emphasis has always been placed on celebration of the Mother of God, especially the recitation of the rosary. While the apocryphal tradition that Mary presented the rosary to St. Dominic in the twelfth century as a tool in his fight against the Albigensians still appeals to some Catholics, contemporary research shows that this special series of prayers developed into its present form over several centuries, gaining canonical approbation as a special devotion in the latter sixteenth century through Pope St. Pius V's bull *Salvatoris Domini* (March 5, 1572) and the establishment of the Feast of the Holy Rosary by Pope Gregory XIII in 1573.[14]

Irish devotion to Mary and the rosary has a long tradition. While the Dominicans did not "invent" the rosary, the order's influence upon this devotion was so significant, especially in Ireland, that one author has written, "Wherever our people have wandered this devotion was particularly associated with them." As early as the fifteenth century, Irish names appear in the list of the Cologne Rosary Confraternity, started by the Dominican friar Blessed Alanus de Rupe. The Sodality of the Virgin Mary, introduced by the Jesuits in the last decade of the sixteenth century, took root and became an established popular devotion in short order. The Sodality strongly advocated the rosary as a means of family prayer, so that by the dawn of the seventeenth century, its recitation in Irish Catholic homes was quite common.[15] The devotion was popular during the late seventeenth through mid nineteenth centuries, the Penal days of Irish history, most probably because this prayer could be recited in lieu of the celebration of Mass, which was made unlawful by the British authorities. By the early eighteenth century, Jeanne Miriam Johnson, CSJ, claims, "The Family Rosary was so well established in Ireland that it was often said morning and evening."[16] During the Cullen era the Family Rosary was incorporated into regular evening devotions for almost all Irish Catholic families. The Marian apparitions at Lourdes (1858), when Mary appeared to Bernadette Soubirous with a rosary in her hand, and Knock (1879), when she appeared with St. Joseph and St. John the Evangelist to a large group of people, led to an appreciable advance in the devotion.

Devotion to the rosary in the twentieth century continued to be strong and universally accepted in the Irish Church. The establishment of the Legion of Mary by Frank Duff in Dublin in September 1921, one response to Pope Pius XI's call for Catholic Action, helped rosary devotions to gain even greater acceptability through a recognized apostolate of the universal Church.[17] The recitation of the rosary as a daily devotional in families remained strong through both World Wars. It was understood to be a source of strength for families while maintaining the long-standing Irish Catholic devotion to the Mother of God. Writing in 1950 Jeanne Johnson, CSJ, concluded:

> The most tangible evidence of Ireland's age-long devotion to Mary is to be found in its love of the Rosary, an intimate part of the religious atmosphere of the country. Few and far between are the homes where this act of homage is not considered a necessary part of the day's routine.....
>
> It is to the family Rosary that Ireland owes her exceptionally wholesome family life which in turn has leavened the entire nation.[18]

In the latter half of the twentieth century, the life and mission of the Holy Cross priest Patrick Peyton was dedicated to the Family Rosary as the premier devotion to the Mother of God.

Patrick Peyton: Youth and Irish Roots

Patrick Joseph Peyton, the sixth of nine children (four boys and five girls) of John Peyton and Mary Gillard, was born on January 9, 1909, at the Peyton homestead in the townland[19] of Carracastle near Ballina in County Mayo, Ireland. He was baptized the next day at his home church, St. Joseph, in Attymass parish by the pastor, Father Walter Henry.[20] John Peyton, Patrick's father, the eldest of sixteen children of James Peyton and Bridget Ginley, was born in 1868 at the same homestead as his son. John married Mary Gillard of Rathreedane,[21] parish of Bonniconlon, who was three years his junior, in March 1899 at Immaculate Conception Church, the home parish of the bride. The Peytons and Gillards had long histories in the region. Patrick and his siblings were the fourth generation to occupy the Carracastle land, located at the foot of the Ox Mountains, but their Irish heritage went back several centuries. The Gillards, on the other hand, descended from Robert Gillard, a French soldier who remained in Ireland after the unsuccessful 1798 attempt by Napoleon's forces to free Ireland from British control.[22]

Patrick was raised in a loving family environment in a three-room thatched-roof home on a twelve-acre farm from which the family eked out a living consistent with most others in the area. John Peyton was a stonemason by trade, building many homes and stables in the region and helping the government build and repair roads. Like many Irishmen of his day, John often spent summers and autumns in England, working under extremely harsh conditions, harvesting potatoes and grains to support his family. On the farm that Mary and her children tended, the staple crop was potatoes, supplemented by a few other vegetables, plus several farm animals. When John was in England the eldest child, Bridget (known as Beatrice to her family), was placed in charge. All family members worked the bog, harvesting turf, the principal source of fuel for cooking and heat.

John Peyton, a devoted husband and concerned father, did his best to make ends meet for the family, but he suffered from a form of asthma so debilitating that by the time the last child, Kate (Kitty), was born in 1916, he was unable to do a full day's work. Eventually the need for more income forced the three eldest girls, Beatrice, Mary, and Ellen (nicknamed Nellie), to emigrate to the United States, settling in Scranton, Pennsylvania, near where other members of the Gillard family had settled a few years earlier. All the family pitched in, taking up the slack caused by the absence of John and his three eldest children. Many years later Patrick expressed his father's sentiments concerning his situation:

> My father was a man who could hold his place among men and he did until the last of us was born. He lost his health then. He had a very heavy cross on his shoulders, watching my mother trying to raise nine of us in poverty, and he could not help her, but he did not complain, and he did not tell God that He had made a mistake in taking his health from him.[23]

Like their neighbors, the Peytons did not consider themselves unfortunate or deprived, although they had much with which to contend. For instance, John Peyton's precarious health was a source of constant concern, especially because he might die and leave a widow and many children to fend for themselves. Additionally, the family suffered through many illnesses, including scarlet fever, whooping cough, and the international measles epidemic that struck before World War I. The loss of crops and death of livestock sometimes left the children without adequate food and clothing, yet the family exuded a deep and burning faith in God.[24] Francis Woods, who would later be the first cleric to join Patrick Peyton's efforts to promote family prayer in the United States, captured the essence of the Peyton domicile:

> Like all homes it had a body and a soul — the body was a Mayo body; it had no great value. Yet, this little house was alive, alive with all the faith of a Mayo heart, alive to God and Mary.... The

small door served as a sounding board to the beautiful greeting prayer of all who entered therein: "God save all here; God and Mary save you kindly." And the brick fireplace served also as the altar before which was recited each evening the Family Rosary.[25]

Despite the physical poverty of their existence, the Peytons and their neighbors worked their jobs proudly and upheld their dignity. Families were self-sufficient, but when circumstances dictated the need, all resources were shared with neighbors. The common Christian virtue of charity was present in abundance, making a deep impression on the youthful mind of Peyton.[26]

Patrick's youth was highly influenced by his maternal grandparents, who lived nearby in Bonniconlon. As was customary for Irish children during this time, Patrick twice lived with his mother's parents, Robert and Kitty Gillard, for extended periods of time, the first period before he entered school and the second when he was eight years old. The rationale for this practice was simple: at times it was realistically impossible to feed all nine Peyton children. Patrick's grandfather inspired the youth in many significant ways, but none greater than his exposition of faith. For the last twenty years of his life Robert Gillard was blind, yet despite his infirmity he demonstrated the power of faith by his intense love of prayer, particularly the rosary, and his serene acceptance of his physical condition. When others went to Sunday Mass, Robert, despite his advanced age, dressed in his finest attire, knelt down in the common room of the house, and prayed fifteen decades of the rosary. Robert told his grandson unforgettable Irish tales of the potato famine and the great generosity of its people. Possibly because of the influence of his grandfather, Patrick chose to be confirmed at Immaculate Conception Church in Bonniconlon on May 17, 1921.[27]

Peyton's childhood education was deficient. When he was five he was enrolled in Bofield School, a state-operated institution[28] less than a half mile from his home. While he resided with his grandparents he attended school in Bonniconlon parish, returning to Bofield after a few months. Peyton gained a few nicknames from his classmates, including "Pateen," an affectionate diminutive for the name Patrick, and "Leather-Bag Peyton," a name he received because of the satchel he used to carry his school books.[29] In November 1923, at the age of fourteen, Peyton left Bofield when a political dispute between his father and a teacher, Tadhg O'Leary, led the latter to strike and verbally abuse the youth. Peyton enrolled in Currower School, about a mile from his home, which was under the direction of Bernie Durkin, a friend of O'Leary. Patrick never felt comfortable in the situation and dropped out. He was stricken from the rolls on May 24, 1924, "for having been absent on thirty consecutive school days without explanation."[30]

When Peyton's formal education in Ireland abruptly ended, he worked odd jobs to assist with the family's finances. On one occasion he helped a local family with its potato harvest. While staying with the family Peyton was mortified to realize that the family rosary was not practiced. After his week's labor Peyton summoned the courage to speak to the father of the family, expressing his concern. This became his first sermon on family prayer and it was efficacious; the man initiated the family rosary in his home. Peyton's sense of fair play was tested on another occasion when he was employed as a handyman for Sandy Durkin, who although a Counselor (a government position in County Mayo) was known locally for his rather poor, even harsh treatment of workers. Peyton considered Durkin's attitude to be socially unjust and challenged him. Whether it was because of this encounter or Patrick's being caught frolicking on the job, Durkin fired him.[31]

Patrick's everyday life and his interaction with others was rather nondescript. Neighbors remember him as a handsome young man who possessed a gentle personality and was quiet, serious, and reserved. He was certainly not unsociable, however, as he frequented dances that were held in the homes of people in the area, including events hosted by his father. During his time in Bonniconlon he made the acquaintance of a young girl, Katie Cummins, although he never formally dated her. As a youth Patrick once heard a mission preacher speak of the evils of "company-keeping," prompting him to refrain from any serious relationship.[32]

Patrick's personality, described as rather shy and quiet by neighbors, did have a rough edge. Peyton's elder sister Mary described him as a youth:

> Pat had a mind of his own and was somewhat unwilling to do the will of his father, as the other members of the family were. Thus[,] for a few years he was very restless and sometimes stubborn and self-willed, much to the distress of his father.[33]

Peyton acknowledged his rebellious side: "I went through those years restless and defiant, distressing my father because of my stubbornness, locked in a prison of doubt and frustration, conscious only that the walls were higher than I could ever hope to scale."[34]

While Peyton was certainly influenced by many people, events, and circumstances, the influence of his parents was by far the greatest. Patrick's mother, Mary, was a tall woman with long silky hair, even to the time of her death. Forced by her husband's ill health to work hard during her entire married life she nevertheless possessed a quiet and unassuming manner. Peyton remembered his mother as a woman radiating peace, joy, and love of family. He once stated, "I cannot help but say that the earliest years of my life I had no other horizon, no other focus but her face, and no other sense of security except her arms that took me when I needed her." Her children confided their special secrets, hopes, dreams, and fears to her, certain that she would give them complete understanding.[35]

As was common for most Irish families of the period, Peyton's father was the dominant figure in the family home.[36] John Peyton was well respected by his family and in the local community, and was generally a demanding person. His second daughter, Mary, remarked:

We worked hard when we were young. Everything was carefully planned by father and we carried out his plans as thoroughly as was humanly possible. We did *not* [Peyton emphasis] rebel because we all realized deep down within us that we had a great man to guide us and that he must have been disappointed many times at the very ordinary children some of us were.

She continued,

Our father ... was the head of the house in every sense of the word. ... He was strict, scrupulously honest in all his dealings with his family as well as with tradesmen, businessmen, and anyone with whom he dealt. He was a devoutly religious man as well. It was he who directed all our activities.[37]

Peyton gained much from his father, including a sense of integrity and a strict work ethic, but there is no question that one central element was his living faith that he imbued in his children and expressed daily through family prayer.[38] Patrick revealed much about his father and the attitude that was given to him as a child:

I did not appreciate what it was for the heart of a man to be in love with God, but my father showed us — not by telling it to us, but by doing it — for we used to see that man on his knees in the morning, and again at four o'clock in the afternoon, and again at nighttime [sic] when he lead [sic] the Rosary. He had such living faith that he expected everybody to have the same.[39]

The family rosary was not an option for Peyton family members; rather the one "inflexible rule" was that all participated in this daily devotional, led by their father. Patrick reflected on this experience: "That nightly scene constitutes my earliest memory and the most abiding. From it I derive the entire pattern and purpose of my existence."[40] Patrick considered it a great grace to be raised in a family rosary home because it provided the foundation for a life of prayer and devotion. The daily family rosary produced the spiritual nourishment that was as necessary as daily food. Prayer was the secret weapon that allowed the Peyton family to endure the hardships of their life. Peyton clearly was grateful for his upbringing:

> As I look back over the nineteen years spent in that poor little home, I cannot recall an unpleasant moment. There were times when we had little or nothing to eat, but there were never times when we did not have our strong spirit of faith to face all the difficulties and hardships of life. Not only did my parents... teach us the great truths and virtues of our Faith by their words, but they lived these truths and virtues before our very eyes. A great spirit of charity and unity dwelt in that home; brothers and sisters never lost an opportunity to come to the aid of their parents or each other.[41]

The religious practice and home environment of the Peyton family provided a fertile field to nourish a vocation to the priesthood, a seed that was ready to germinate inside young Patrick. In addition to the daily rosary, many other expositions of Catholic practice were in evidence in the home. Devotion to the Sacred Heart of Jesus, celebrated on first Fridays, became a regular part of the Peyton faith regimen after John Peyton learned of this practice during his summer sojourns in England. The way of the cross was celebrated on most Fridays, with the Fridays in Lent being a requirement for all. Each Sunday, holy day, and first Friday Peyton family members walked the four miles to St. Joseph Church to attend Mass, in spite of the frequently inclement weather. Peyton regularly served two Masses each Sunday, that attended by his family and a second Mass two hours later. Often he spent the interval on his knees rapt in prayer. His sister Mary once commented about him, "He practiced mortification and penances to such a degree that his family was inclined to the belief that he would become fanatical."[42] Peyton understood that his faith practice was perceived to be excessive, but he had no other option:

I knew that others made fun of me behind my back and sometimes even in my presence made me the butt of sly jokes about my excessive piety. But I could not help it. I had not only become enraptured by my job as Mass server, but I had developed the secret ambition to become a priest. Soon it was occupying all my thoughts.[43]

Peyton's vocation to the religious life and priesthood, an idea not without precedent in his family,[44] was first explored at the tender age of eight. In 1917 two Redemptorist priests held a mission at St. Joseph parish at the invitation of the pastor, Father Roger O'Donnell. Two years later a similar mission was given by two Capuchin friars. Patrick was mesmerized by the stories he heard and shared his thoughts with O'Donnell, who was very fond of the youth and encouraged him in his vocation. Patrick believed that he wanted to serve God in the missions and, thus, with the pastor's blessing and recommendation, he began to inquire about the priesthood. Later in life he wrote of this experience: "It was such healthy living faith that attracted me more and more to the priesthood. I longed to become a priest by any means. I would be willing to go to the foreign missions; I longed to go to Africa, to do anything to become a priest."[45]

He first wrote to the Capuchins but received neither an acknowledgment nor a reply. O'Donnell wrote on his behalf to the Society of African Missionaries, headquartered in Cork, asking that Patrick be admitted as a scholarship student, but the response stated that Patrick did not have sufficient education to start the seminary program. Patrick was gravely hurt and voiced his frustration: "Stop this great longing within my heart — stop calling me — or show me the way. I can't go through another heartbreaking disappointment."[46] Peyton's frustration with his initial vocation investigation, coupled with his less-than-favorable prospects for success in Ireland, generated ideas that would lead him to the United States and his ultimate ministry.

An Immigrant to America

The United States, a nation built through the toil and sweat of immigrants, had by the early twentieth century experienced a long history of peoples from many lands who came to the New World seeking a fresh start and new opportunities for themselves and their families. The history of Irish emigration to the United States is long and filled with stories of triumph and sadness. Beginning in the early nineteenth century and continuing unabated until the Johnson-Reed Act of 1924[47] effectively closed the door to most immigrants, the Irish came to America's shores to escape economic dislocation and to build new lives.[48] Irish emigration to the United States was constant, but the Great Famine of 1845 increased the numbers greatly. By 1850 Catholics, who had been an oppressed minority of 1 percent of the population at the time of the establishment of the American hierarchy (1789),[49] became the largest religious denomination in the country. The Church in the United States was dominated by the Irish, especially in the episcopal ranks, where important prelates such as John England, John Ireland, James Gibbons, and Michael Corrigan served in key urban areas and effectively controlled the progress and attitude of faith practice for over a hundred years.

Economic hardship, one of the common reasons for Irish immigration to the United States, prompted members of the Peyton family to emigrate, beginning in 1920, when, in response to their father's debilitating illness, the eldest, Beatrice and Mary, left for America to look for work. They settled in Scranton, Pennsylvania, where members of their mother's family had preceded them. Beatrice met and eventually married Michael Gallagher and together they started a family. In 1923 Nellie Peyton also emigrated to Scranton, finding a job as a domestic worker in the local bishop's residence.[50]

In early 1927, Patrick, frustrated with low-paying and unfulfilling work and with the realization that he had no real future in County Mayo,[51] decided that his best option was to join his siblings in the United States. John Peyton was not fully supportive of his son's decision at the outset, but being a realist, he gave Patrick and his next older son Thomas his blessing to leave for America, asking only that they promise to be faithful to the Lord in their new land. On May 13, 1928, the anniversary of the first apparition of the Blessed Virgin Mary to the three seers of Fatima,[52] Patrick and Thomas left Ireland, never to see their parents again. After a quick stop in Boston their ship arrived in New York on May 23. The brothers immediately boarded a ferry to Hoboken, New Jersey, and then a train to Scranton where they were warmly greeted by their sisters and brother-in-law. Beatrice and Michael welcomed them into their home. Patrick was quite impressed with the United States: "I had come from the little country towns of Ireland to a city, an American city [New York], for the first time in my life. The electric lights, the street cars and everything about city life fascinated me. I thought, if Heaven looked like that, it would be wonderful."[53]

Patrick and Thomas wasted no time in seeking work after their arrival, but the pre-Depression days in Scranton did not afford many opportunities for employment. Patrick first sold American flags door-to-door, but after a very short time he secured a construction job through a family friend, Tom Manley. After only one week on the job Peyton learned that two other employees, one of whom was a family man, were to be discharged since there was insufficient work. Peyton went to the foreman and asked to be let go in place of the more senior man. Impressed with the young Irishman's totally unselfish attitude, the foreman adjusted work schedules so that neither of the two men would be discharged.[54]

Knowing of Peyton's work situation and remembering his past investigations into the possibility of the priesthood, Nellie secretly arranged for Patrick to visit with Monsignor Paul Kelly, rector of St. Peter's Cathedral in Scranton, about a position as sexton. Initially Peyton was hesitant, still reeling from his rejections in Ireland, but he eventually took the job, starting on July 1, 1928, and sharing the duties with Thomas. Patrick's close proximity to the life of the parish and his association with Monsignor Kelly, who spoke of him as "conscientious" and "capable,"[55] reinvigorated in him his former desire for the priesthood: "Being alone in the dark of that big church every morning and every night — in that holy house of God — before Jesus Christ and the blessed Sacrament — the longing to be a priest overwhelmed me."[56] After a short while Peyton told Kelly that he wanted to become a priest. The rector was pleased and, offering to pay all expenses, sent Peyton and his brother[57] to St. Thomas High School, operated by the Christian Brothers in Scranton, to begin their high school education. Close to twenty years old when he began his preparatory education, Peyton must have been impressive with his six-foot-four-inch frame and his Irish brogue, for he was elected freshmen class president on the first day of school.[58]

The future of Patrick and Thomas Peyton became more definite in the spring of 1929, when four priests of the Congregation of Holy Cross[59] conducted a mission at the Scranton cathedral. Patrick was enamored of the priests, their message, and the joy they exhibited in ministry. He spoke to the leader of the mission group, Father Patrick Dolan, CSC, and told him of his desire to become a priest, now setting his sights on Holy Cross as well as reviving his past dream of mission work. Dolan was supportive, as was Monsignor Kelly, who gave him a glowing recommendation:

In reference to his [Patrick Peyton's] application as a candidate for the preparatory work for the priesthood, I unhesitatingly recommend him. He is gifted with excellent talent, he shows visible signs of a vocation, and is anxious for the spread of the Kingdom of God upon earth. . . . I shall consider any Community or Religious Order or Congregation or Bishop quite fortunate to have his services.[60]

Patrick and Thomas finished the academic year at St. Thomas and on August 29, 1929, left Scranton for the University of Notre Dame in South Bend, Indiana, to enter the Congregation's high school seminary program.[61]

Formation for Religious Life and Priesthood

Patrick and Thomas formally entered the postulate program at Holy Cross Seminary on September 9, 1929, beginning with the second year program because of their year at St. Thomas. Patrick was very grateful that Thomas had joined his quest for priesthood. He once wrote, "He came humbly, and I know he never regretted it. He was like every other member of my family. He never refused me any sacrifice I asked of him, just as I never refused the request of them, if it was in my power to grant it." Patrick was immediately electrified by Notre Dame and the surrounding environs. He wrote, "At Notre Dame my heart filled with happiness. Here I was at home from the first instant. . . . I thanked God and His Mother fervently for welcoming me to this earthly paradise." He quickly began to learn the charism of Holy Cross, which he understood to be trifold: (1) precise obedience, (2) response to the local Church and its needs, and (3) family atmosphere and orientation.[62] He fully entered into the seminary life and was well appreciated by his peers. Raymond Cour, CSC, a contemporary of Peyton's at the minor seminary, commented, "Pat had a good sense of humor. He was very serious about studies, as he should be, [and] serious about prayer." Patrick carried out his duties, including his obedience as commissioner, which included laundry and mail delivery, with great fervor.[63]

Upon their graduation from the minor seminary, Patrick and Thomas entered St. Joseph Novitiate on campus at Notre Dame on July 1, 1932, under the tutelage of Father Kerndt Healey, CSC, who served as master of novices. In a foreshadowing of his future ministry, Peyton made his consecration to the Blessed Virgin, asking her guidance: "Take my body and my soul, take my goods, both interior and exterior and even the value of my good actions, present and future. . . . Help me to become a holy novice, a saint; I shall ask nothing more for myself." They completed the canonical year on July 2, 1933, and made temporary

three-year profession in the Congregation of Holy Cross. Patrick, because of his long desire to serve in overseas missions, took a fourth vow,
agreeing to go wherever he was needed in the Congregation's overseas
apostolates.[64] Patrick understood that his decision to profess vows meant
he was committed to his future as a Holy Cross religious:

> I firmly believe I have a vocation to the religious life in the Con-
> gregation of Holy Cross; and that I am called to be a priest of said
> Congregation. It is my unhesitating intention, with God's grace, to
> continue as a seminarian, and I have no other idea of seeking admis-
> sion to temporary profession except to proceed and at the proper
> time bind myself perpetually to the obligations of the clerical life
> in the religious state of the Congregation of Holy Cross.[65]

Despite the small volume of extant correspondence, it is clear from the
historical record that Patrick and Thomas made every effort to maintain
contact with their family, especially their father, during their time at
Notre Dame. John Peyton's health had deteriorated further during the
last several years, but the rock-solid faith that inspired Patrick remained
in place. He mentioned in letters that he prayed to the Sacred Heart,
asking the Lord's protection for his two sons and to "make them true
and faithful servants of god's Love [sic]." Patrick and Thomas had done
what they could to aid their family back home, having sent their father
all the money that they had saved from their work in Scranton, a sacrifice
for which he was grateful. In a thank-you note he reported his health
status to his sons: "I am, As usual Putting in my time as best I can since ye
sent me the luard [Lourdes] water & I made the *home Novena* in honour
of her immaculate conception. I had no attack since many thanks to Our
Blessed laidy & also to ye [sic]."[66] Their father was overjoyed to receive
a photo of Patrick and Thomas in their habits:

> Thanks be to the Sacred Heart of Jesus that *I have lived to see ye
> Bothe wearing Priests garments.* We hope and trust to god and his
> Blessed Mother that the Sacred Heart will stringthen ye [a]gainst
> any temptations that may arise [a]gainst ye & that ye will Be able
> to comply with the vows ye Have made. May god Bless & spare ye
> to wear them Right. Mother & I [are filled] with joy to see what
> god has [done] for our 2 boys [sic].[67]

The last extant letter from John Peyton to his sons, written in November 1933, closed with an expression of love, "May god Bless & spare
ye & guide ye Right & strengthen ye agains[t] all evil [sic]."[68] To the
time of his death in 1934 at age sixty-six John Peyton demonstrated the

love and faith that became trademarks of all his children, but most especially Patrick, who used these simple gifts as the base for an international ministry to promote family prayer and values.

With their high school work completed and now vowed religious in the Congregation of Holy Cross, Patrick and Thomas entered the University of Notre Dame, taking the basic classic course, including classes in Latin, Greek, philosophy, U.S. history, political science, economics, and biology. Patrick was an exceptionally gifted student who impressed both peers and professors with his academic acumen and his gentle nature. James Connerton, CSC, superior at Moreau Seminary and later Peyton's first provincial in the Eastern Priests Province, recalled his remarkable memory, calling him "a studious and prayerful seminarian aspiring to the highest in his vocation."[69] Cornelius Hagerty, CSC, who taught Patrick metaphysics at Moreau Seminary (Notre Dame), described him as a student:

> His docility startled me. What I assigned he studied carefully and earnestly; it seemed as if he committed the lesson to memory; yet he could stand examination on its meaning. He never quarreled or disagreed with me; his attitude was that of an Irish country boy toward his schoolmaster who was also a priest.[70]

Thomas Peyton agreed with Hagerty's observations: "I had to study hard for everything I learned, but Pat had a phenomenal memory. He could hear a lecture and repeat it the next day almost word for word. Or he could read something in a book and remember it."[71] During their junior year, on August 16, 1936, Patrick and Thomas made final profession in the Congregation in the Moreau Seminary Chapel. Again Patrick took the fourth vow for missionaries, promising to go "to whatever part of the world the superior general may wish to send me."[72] On June 6, 1937, Patrick and Thomas received their bachelor of arts degrees from Notre Dame, with Patrick graduating *magna cum laude*.[73]

In the fall of 1937 Patrick and Thomas began their theological training at Holy Cross College, the major seminary for the Congregation, located on the campus of the Catholic University of America in Washington, D.C.[74] While Thomas lived at Holy Cross College, where all classes were held, Patrick, because of his desire to minister in overseas missions, resided at the "Bengalese," the home for seminarians contemplating mission work.[75] Patrick's quiet and unassuming manner characterized his early days in Washington. One fellow seminarian commented, "In the seminary I would say that I didn't see anything special about him. I didn't even know that he was Irish born and had devotion to the rosary." He did

not make friends easily, but people readily recognized his goodness and
were attracted to it.[76] His religious superiors described him as "industrious, methodical, prayerful, loyal, courageous, docile, obedient, kind,
fairly refined, dependable, very contented, salt of the earth, and a good
community man." He was noted for his potential and qualities for leadership.[77] At the conclusion of his first year of theology Peyton became a
naturalized American citizen.[78]

Peyton's life took a radical turn in October 1938, when one morning
he began to spit up blood. Initially he kept his condition secret, but eventually, as the symptoms became more severe, he consulted the community
physician, Dr. John Harrington. At this time he was told that there was
no significant problem, but in a matter of weeks the spitting of blood
became a full hemorrhage. Peyton was sent to a specialist, Dr. Malcolm
Lent, who diagnosed Patrick with "advanced tuberculosis of the right
upper lobe, with consolidation and a small cavity." He was immediately
admitted to Providence Hospital, about a mile from Holy Cross College.
There he spent three months, but his condition, rather than responding
to treatment, grew progressively worse.[79]

Peyton was transferred to the infirmary at Notre Dame in May 1939
and received weekly treatments at Healthwin Sanitarium in South Bend.
Unfortunately, his downward spiral continued with little hope for recovery.[80] In October 1939 doctors offered Patrick two basic options: surgery
(thorocaplasty), a procedure that would collapse his lung but with no
guarantee of success, or prayer.[81] Medical science so far had not been
successful; the two options provided were a last resort.

Peyton was very disheartened as he saw his dream of the priesthood
beginning to slip from his grasp, but one day in late October he received
a visit from his former professor, Cornelius Hagerty, CSC, who challenged Peyton to demonstrate his faith and confidence in God and Mary
by fighting for life. Hagerty had always liked Patrick and admired his
dynamism, but now he challenged him to exercise the faith that was so
basic to his life and endemic to his character. From Hagerty's perspective
Peyton's faith was like a "keg of gunpowder" that was ready to explode,
but it needed a match to trigger the reaction. He related his conversation
with Peyton that lit the fire:

> I exhorted Patrick somewhat as follows: Pat, the Irish people have
> fought and suffered many centuries for the Catholic faith. In their
> persecutions and trials they had nothing to sustain them except
> faith in God's supernatural help. Think of the dangers, difficulties,
> enemies, persecutions, famines, pestilences they survived. Instead of

putting your trust in modern science and the skill of doctors, why don't you stir up the faith that you inherited from your long line of believing ancestors. Think of the trust they had in the Blessed Virgin, the mother of God. She is an omnipotent intercessor. What she asks for and insists on she obtains. She is always as good as her children expect her to be. She has never failed anyone who had recourse to her with faith and perseverance. Since you have faith, why don't you use it?[82]

Peyton did what his former mentor suggested and prayed to Mary for a cure. On October 31, Peyton's depression, darkness, and feeling of loneliness were replaced by lightness, freedom, and hope. He knew in his heart he had been cured. He related, "I really was in Calvary and felt that way, but just as with Christ, Easter came shortly to Him, so it came to me also."[83] Almost immediately doctors saw signs of improvement. Two consecutive treatments at Healthwin verified that Peyton's lungs had cleared; the effects of the tuberculosis were reversing themselves. The medical people had no scientific explanation for what had happened; they were understandably cautious and wanted the full six-month treatment to continue. Peyton pestered the Healthwin officials, however, who examined him completely on January 15, 1940. Finding no trace of tuberculosis, they released him from the infirmary and cleared him to resume classes at Holy Cross College, where he returned on February 5.[84] While physicians could not explain his recovery, Peyton was convinced that he had regained his health and strength through the intercession of Mary. He once stated, "When I needed her and her power and her friendship, she didn't forget that ever since I had been a little child and could open my mouth, I had used that power to say the Rosary; so when I needed her friendship, she was glad to give it to me."[85]

Peyton's return from the brink of death through a "miraculous healing" can secondarily be explained through the heroic efforts of his mother on his behalf. While he was gaining strength at the Notre Dame community infirmary, his brother Thomas told him of their mother's death on December 3, 1939. Mary Peyton had suffered a stroke in July, but aware of Patrick's condition she prayed that his suffering would come upon her. A second stroke left her in great pain, but instead of complaining, she prayed for the health of her son. After his recovery, Patrick received a letter from his aunt, Anna Gilmartin, that explained what happened:

Now your mother has got her wish, that is that God should shove Pat's sickness onto her & the two at home & send Pat back safe[ly] to his brothers and sisters. She told me these words at the beginning of her sickness. I believe some one had to go when-ever. [*sic*] . . . God has spared Pat to save souls.[86]

Peyton's sisters, Mary and Nellie, told him later that they were certain that their mother would die instead of him. She sacrificed herself for his benefit and that of the ministry he would conduct in the future.[87] His family was elated at his recovery and return to Washington. Like him they were convinced that his restoration to health was a miracle.[88]

Peyton returned to his studies in the spring semester 1940, but now as a resident and student at Holy Cross College, his dream of the foreign missions having been dashed because of his precarious health. Nevertheless, he dove into his studies with energy and a sense of thanksgiving for his new lease on life. His religious superiors continued to praise his fine qualities, although it was noted that he tended "to be over-exact with himself," "somewhat impulsive," and in possession of "no qualities of leadership."[89]

Peyton's grief over the loss of his mother was renewed when Nellie died in 1940, and neither he nor Thomas could get to her bedside. Patrick was given a note found in her room:

> I, Nellie Peyton, offer Thee, dear Lord, all my thoughts, words and actions of this day, and every day, and even life itself, for my two brothers Thomas Francis Peyton and Patrick Joseph Peyton, that if it be Thy Holy Will that they become priests that never in their priestly lives will they commit a mortal sin.

On her deathbed she told the attending priest, "Tell them [Patrick and Thomas] that if it be God's Holy Will that they become priests, I pray that they will be true priests like Jesus Christ."[90] Peyton was deeply moved by his sister's words and committed himself to a life that would honor her memory:

> I was permanently obligated to her because of the vow she had voluntarily made and gladly fulfilled to give herself, even her life, for my spiritual and temporal welfare. The least I could do in return would be to lead a life which in its intensity of love for God and His Blessed Mother and in the totality of its concentration on the work of God, would not only justify my own existence, but would leave a surplus to equal all the good Nellie would have radiated around her, had she lived a normal life span.[91]

When Peyton returned to Holy Cross College, he was a year behind his brother Tom, yet he was awarded a special indult from the Vatican to be ordained with Tom and the rest of his novitiate class. Bishop John Noll was the ordaining prelate when Patrick knelt with his brother and other classmates at Sacred Heart Church at Notre Dame on June 15, 1941, and received the ancient symbolic ritual of the laying on of hands. Patrick reflected upon that great event: "That day I gave my heart and soul in love to Mary. I promised her all the merit of my priesthood until death. The merit and glory of every action I would ever perform would be hers and hers alone."[92] The next fifty years would clearly manifest Peyton's commitment to Mary.

In the fall of 1941 Peyton returned to Holy Cross College to complete his theological training. He was warned by his provincial superior, Thomas Steiner, CSC, that he was to be cautious of his health and not risk a relapse.[93] Peyton, however, was already planning ways to meet the hope of the family that had sacrificed so much for him and to repay the Blessed Mother for interceding in his life.

Conclusion

Irish Catholic devotionalism, generated in part as a result of poverty and religious persecution over several centuries, was the basis of religious devotion from which the family rosary became an essential daily practice of the typical Irish home of the early twentieth century. Raised in an environment where his father set the example as religious leader of the family, Patrick Peyton from his earliest days experienced his faith in a way that guided the rest of his life. After emigrating to the United States in 1928, he found his vocation in the Congregation of Holy Cross. Older than his contemporaries when ordained at age thirty-two, Peyton beat all the odds in surviving tuberculosis. Convinced that his recovery was caused by the intercession of the Blessed Virgin Mary, Peyton set out, with the approval of his religious superiors, to convince others that the faith he possessed, simple yet strong and profound, could, if applied correctly, cure the ills of a society gone wrong.

Chapter 2

The Mission Begins: Family Rosary, 1942–45

Convinced that a miracle had helped him to reach his goal of ordination to the priesthood, Patrick Peyton set his sights on a ministry that would allow him to repay his friend, the Blessed Virgin Mary of Nazareth, for her intercession and favors. Peyton was certain that his return to health had come about for a specific purpose, namely, to foster devotion to Mary, but the question remained of how to achieve this goal. Once he determined the road he would take, Peyton dedicated his life and ministry to promoting family prayer and the rosary. Over a fifty-year ministerial career that would take him to all corners of the world and require his interaction with famous personalities in ecclesiastical, political, and entertainment realms, Peyton never backtracked from his purpose or goal, but constantly moved forward in a herculean effort to give his life to God's Son, Jesus, and His Mother, who had favored him with health, opportunity, and the talent to ignite a world campaign for prayer.

American Catholic Life, 1900–1940

American Catholics had become the most numerous single religious domination in the United States by 1850, but relative numbers did not equate to acceptance and prosperity within society. Nineteenth-century American Catholicism was characterized by several major trends. First, the Church was built and maintained by an influx of immigrants, starting from northern and western Europe, most prominently the Irish and Germans, and then after 1880 shifting to a massive emigration from southern and eastern Europe, especially Italy and Poland. This trend ended only with the immigration restriction laws of the 1920s, but by then Catholicism was ecclesiastically well established, with a benchmark of recognition being reached in 1908 when the United States was removed from the jurisdiction of Propaganda Fide through the apostolic exhortation *Sapienti Consilio* of Pope Pius X. Anti-Catholicism, generated most strongly through nativism and religious prejudice, dogged the faithful throughout the century, reaching apexes in the bigotry of the Know-Nothings of the 1850s, the American Protective Association (APA, founded in 1887), and the resurgence of the Ku Klux Klan (originally founded in the winter of 1865–66) in the early 1920s in the wake of the Red Scare. Anti-Catholicism helped generate what is generally termed "the Catholic ghetto," a social situation that bonded Catholics by ethnicity and religion and kept them from fully engaging American life and consequently placed them in many ways on the fringes of national society.[1]

The ghetto mentality that kept most American Catholics away from mainstream society was matched by severe conflicts within the hierarchy that created theological divisions and dropped a pall on intellectual development among scholars. The period 1895 to 1900, labeled by the priest historian Thomas McAvoy, CSC, as the "Great Crisis in American Catholic History," was the culmination of the Americanist crisis that began in earnest in 1884. The conflict pitted transformationist bishops, those with a more progressive view of theology and a more favorable understanding of Catholicism's compatibility with American life and culture, against a group of traditionalist prelates, who favored a more staid understanding of Church teaching and were more wary of Catholicism's interaction with the church-state policy of the United States. Between 1884 and 1899 the transformationists, led by Archbishop John Ireland (St. Paul) with Bishop John Keane (rector of the Catholic University of America) the idealist, Monsignor Denis O'Connell (rector of the North American College in Rome) the tactician, and Cardinal James Gibbons (Baltimore) the spiritual leader, and the traditionalists, championed by Archbishops Michael Corrigan (New York) and Frederick Katzer (Milwaukee) and Bishop Bernard McQuaid (Rochester, New York), battled publicly and privately. At issue was the question of whether Catholicism in America, which by law and custom had evolved quite differently from the European model of Catholicism, which was considered normative, should continue to meet the needs of its new home. In the early years Gibbons and his colleagues won some major victories, including averting a papal condemnation of the Knights of Labor, restoration of Father Edward McGlynn to the ranks of the active clergy, and the acceptance of a creative plan for Catholic education in the Archdiocese of St. Paul.

However, the tables turned and, after the establishment of the office of the apostolic delegate in the United States, first held by Archbishop Francesco Satolli, things turned sour for the Americanists. Keane and O'Connell were dismissed from their positions, and the 1895 encyclical *Longingua Oceani* declared that America's belief in the separation of church and state was not to be a model for Catholicism.[2] In January 1899, Pope Leo XIII, in an apostolic letter to Cardinal Gibbons, *Testem Benevolentiae,* denounced theological Americanism:

> The object of this letter is ... to point out certain things which are to be avoided and corrected ... which have arisen lately among you, and which disturb the minds, if not of all, at least of many, to the no slight detriment of peace.... We cannot approve the opinions which some comprise under the head of Americanism.[3]

The Americanist Crisis was only the first blow of what could be termed a knock-out punch to American Catholic intellectual life at the dawn of the twentieth century. Another blow was theological modernism, with roots in the European Church of the latter nineteenth century and manifest in the United States in the writings of John Zahm, CSC, John Slattery, SSJ, and William Sullivan, CSP.[4] Modernists challenged the Church's theological self-understanding by suggesting that it was intellectually unsound, especially in the wake of major scientific and industrial breakthroughs generated as a result of the Enlightenment, to believe that doctrine could not develop and that Scripture should not be studied using a historical-critical method. Led by Alfred Loisy, George Tyrrell, SJ, and Baron Friedrich von Hügel, modernists raised quite a stir in the European Church and exported their ideas to the United States, among other places. The *New York Review,* a scholarly journal of St. Joseph Seminary, Dunwoodie, New York, published between 1905 and 1908, printed several essays, including articles by Loisy and Tyrrell, that challenged the Church's traditional teaching. Challenging essays by American theologians, including Father (later Archbishop of San Francisco) Edward Hanna of St. Bernard's Seminary in Rochester, New York, and William Lawrence Sullivan, CSP, were also published by the *Review.* Modernism was condemned in a pair of encyclicals, *Lamentabili sane exitu* (1907), and most especially *Pascendi dominici gregis* (1907) in which Pope St. Pius X labeled modernism "the synthesis of all heresies."[5] The condemnation of Americanism and modernism in rapid succession placed a dark cloud over American Catholic intellectual life for some time.[6]

The ghetto mentality that characterized American Catholicism at the dawn of the twentieth century remained deeply entrenched even after World War I and the experience of the "roaring twenties." The historian William Halsey describes this period as an "era of disillusionment": "Having drawn for themselves the bleak outlines of an uncertain world out of joint, Catholics promptly set out to build their own world safe from disillusionment but wavering between the charms of innocence and the grip of paranoia." Catholicism, he suggests, was in "a constant state of cultural conflict and contradiction."[7] Similarly, the historian Anthony B. Smith has commented, "It was not until the 1930s that Catholics imagined a role for themselves within the national community." Before this period "the enormous social and intellectual implications of the large Catholic presence in America were only dimly recognized."[8]

During the interwar years, a theological thaw began: academic societies were created, scholarly publications were founded, and papal documents encouraged research and a renewal of intellectual life within the Church. In the United States several significant magazines and journals were first published, including *Commonweal* (1921), the *Catholic Biblical Quarterly* (1939), and *Theological Studies* (1940). In 1946 two important academic organizations, the Catholic Biblical Association and Catholic Theological Society of America, were founded. Pope Pius XII initiated a revival in biblical studies through the publication in 1943 of *Divino Afflante Spiritu,* considered the "Magna Carta" of contemporary biblical scholarship. This was a period of intense work in Christian anthropology and ecclesiology, based on the philosophy of Thomas Aquinas, repopularized by Pope Leo XIII through his 1879 encyclical *Aeterni Patris.*

Despite these advancements American Catholicism was not totally free of its ghetto mentality. The historian Gordon Truitt commented:

> By 1940 Catholicism in the United States had emerged as a religious institution still strongly dependent on its European roots, seemingly more interested in pastoral and pragmatic questions than in theoretical ones, and imbued with a conservatism which reflected the Church's historical origins in this country and the stories following on the Americanist and Modernist crises in the early years of the twentieth century.[9]

The defensive and apologetical posture of the American Church, often manifest in reactionary responses to change, was beginning to break down, but the effects of the ghetto mentality were clearly evident. In the same vein, in a seminal 1955 speech, later published in several forms, Monsignor John Tracy Ellis, the foremost historian of American Catholicism in the twentieth century, strongly criticized the dearth of American Catholic intellectual life and challenged scholars and institutions of higher learning to promote scholarship so that Catholics could begin to take their rightful place alongside non-Catholic scholars in the promotion and furtherance of intellectual pursuit.[10]

American Catholic Spirituality

The spirituality demonstrated by American Catholics over their history exhibited definable trends. Joseph Tetlow identifies five specific properties of spiritual practice in the United States Church. First, it is experimental. The establishment of Catholicism in a political and social environment vastly different from Europe necessitated much trial and created many errors. Next, American Catholicism has been highly experiential; Americans want a faith that matches their experience. Third, American Catholics live a democratized faith, based on their unique separation of church and state, and one that is functional, namely, feasible and expressive of the American spirit and praxis. Next, Catholics in the United States view their practice as an extension of the Church universal in its efforts to build the Kingdom of God in this world. Lastly, Tetlow suggests that American Catholics have chosen the *via negativa* through their inability to find value and adapt certain passive virtues, such as denial, rejection, and repudiation.[11] The Claretian priest and well-known lecturer John Lonzano, basing much of what he says on the life and spirituality of the Paulist founder Isaac Hecker (1818–88) articulates some uniquely American aspects to Catholic spirituality. The association of freedom with religion, the tendency to fuse nature and grace, a deeply rooted devotion to the Holy Spirit, the incorporation of national values into faith practice, and the importance of personal experience are traits readily seen in the lives of American Catholics.[12] The Benedictine scholar Jean Leclercq adds that, out of necessity, American Catholic spirituality is pluralistic in its rich diversity of approaches, trends, and unique situations.[13]

The practice of prayer through the history of American Catholicism has also demonstrated some special characteristics. As might be expected, pragmatism, expressed through rites and prayers that have proven helpful and efficacious, has been a dominant factor in the prayer life of American Catholics. Prayer for American Catholics, in a reversal of European tradition, never strongly emphasized the monastic or contemplative dimension of one's communication with God, but rather revolved around external rites and practices, especially public liturgical demonstrations of faith. The American Catholic practice of prayer, consistent with the dictum *lex orandi lex credendi,* blazed the path that the rest of theology followed.[14]

Popular devotions, commonly practiced in the Church since the Council of Trent (1545–63),[15] have always been an important element of the prayer life of American Catholics. In the nineteenth century American Catholics used devotions to saints, prayer novenas, and feast day processions as a way to express their distinctive religious character and belief. They were designed to allow people to foster their internal emotional bonds with the supernatural. These practices allowed the faithful to act, rather than having something done to them, which was the general experience of Catholics in their participation in the public liturgical life of the Church. Before the latter nineteenth century, manifestations of popular devotion in the United States were rather subdued, due in large measure to the more staid external faith practice of the dominant Irish and Germans, but with the mass arrival of new immigrants in the Gilded Age, especially the Italians, expressions of popular religiosity became highly visible and were more generally practiced by American Catholics.[16]

Marian devotion in the American Church, which became the lifeblood of Patrick Peyton, has always held a special place in the hearts and practice of Catholics. The plethora of churches and schools given Marian names, special devotions to Mary (especially the rosary), and her exceptional respect among American Catholics at large prompted one Protestant minister at the time of the Civil War to comment:

> We are prepared to believe that there is no old Catholic country in Europe, that there never has been a country, in which reverent love and earnest heartfelt devotion for the Blessed Mother of God was more deeply rooted, more ardently cherished, or more fervently and fruitfully practiced, than this same North America. It is unobtrusive, but it is real.[17]

Marian devotion might not have been "obtrusive," but it was clearly evident in every aspect of Catholic faith practice. Special feasts of the Blessed Mother, such as the Assumption, Nativity, Immaculate Conception, and Annunciation, were celebrated as holy days of obligation. Prayers and litanies were common and often collected in devotional books such as *The Imitation of the Blessed Virgin,* by Jesuit priest Francisco Arias, published in 1819. At the Second Plenary Council of Baltimore (1866) the American hierarchy recommended the institution of the "Apostleship of Prayer," a European-based devotional movement. *Ave Maria* explained that the group was "to regenerate the morbid state of society, to spread the knowledge of Mary, to glorify her [and] to give her a guard of honor against the forces of the devil."[18]

Marian devotion in the twentieth century, expanding from the strong base that had already been established, was most notable for its close association with the Fatima apparitions of 1917. Mary's message to the three children, calling for daily recitation of the rosary as a way to obtain peace and the conversion of sinners, had great popular appeal. Campus chaplains at the University of Notre Dame made their point clear in an October 1951 religious bulletin:

> Our Lady herself has told us at Fatima that "we must pray the Rosary." Will any student ignore her outright command? She promised world peace if we said the Rosary. Does any student want another world war? She promised the conversion of Russia if we said the Rosary. Will any student belittle the Russian threat?

Bishop Fulton Sheen in his popular 1948 book *Communism and the Conscience of the West* continued this theme, stating that devotion to Our Lady of Fatima would have prevented World War II and the Cold War.[19] The practice of confession, Mass, and reception of Communion on five consecutive first Saturdays, as recommended by Mary at Fatima, also became very popular. The foundation in 1950 of the lay and clerical society, the Blue Army of Fatima, by John H. Haffert and Monsignor Harold Colgan, and its rapid episcopal approbation provided more fuel to the fires of Marian devotion. The Blue Army's rapid growth is evidenced by the circulation of its organ, *Soul,* which went from a circulation of three thousand in 1950 to seventy thousand one year later.[20]

Peyton exploited the burgeoning of Marian piety to promote what would become his battle cry — the family rosary:

> Mary is just as gracious today as she was then. After God, her ways are the most constant, and so you may be sure that a family welcoming Mary under their roof today will be rewarded like the families of old. One sure means by which you can welcome Mary under your roof is the family rosary.[21]

Peyton suggested that family prayer through the rosary would eventually guide one to eternal life: "If you pray the Family Rosary Mary will bring God and special gifts to your family. . . . Ask your family to invite

Mary and her Son into their home with Mary's Rosary, and she will ask her Divine Son to invite your family into Heaven."[22]

The postwar era, besides promoting Marian devotion, also witnessed the growing popularity of contemplative prayer. This was most evident through the writings of the Trappist monk Thomas Merton, whose autobiography, *The Seven Storey Mountain* (1949), was a bestseller almost overnight. While public devotional practice remained popular, Catholics began to appreciate contemplation as a uniquely powerful method of communication with God. One commentator, speaking of prayer in the postwar period, concluded, "The nature of contemplation was the major concern of the theology of prayer in these years."[23]

While private prayer was always a part of the everyday life of American Catholics, the onslaught of World War II was the catalyst to the rapid rise of family prayer as a leading expression of their spirituality. The practice of praying together was viewed as a way to raise family members from a worldly to a divine level and to strengthen them through bonds of solidarity. *America* editorialized,

> Those activities, if they are really to keep the home the healthy and vital center of our American life, will have to include prayer — family prayer. That is one phase of family life that has fallen into decline, even among Catholics.
>
> That this Christian custom ought to be revived precisely at this time seems clear and natural. What better occasion can a family have than the presence to gather in the evening and unite in prayer for the safety of loved ones at war. Whatever silly self-consciousness we might feel at other times over praying aloud together ought surely be swept aside by the urgency of the times and the heartfelt need we all have of God's continuing and increasing guidance.[24]

After the war the promotion of family prayer continued, but its focus moved from family solidarity to religious education. Since each person learns in different ways families were encouraged to find the method that worked best for them. The important matter was to keep fixed on the goal, namely, the promotion of the family as a whole. Catholics believed that family prayer was what bound Christ to the family. Playwright and convert to Catholicism Clare Booth Luce stated, "If you are not using family prayer to generate family love and love for God you are neglecting a tremendous instrument meant to bring family happiness." She concluded, "If prayer is the 'sword of the saints,' it is also the anchor of the family."[25]

The Family Crisis in American Life

The blossoming of American Catholic spirituality, with its renewal of personal and communal prayer, and the escape of Catholic culture and intellectual life from a ghetto mentality coincided with a crisis in American family life. The Great Depression, world wars, burgeoning corporate America, fears of nuclear annihilation, the Cold War, and a general loss of traditional verities brought great concern to the family as an institution between 1930 and 1962. The magnitude of the problem was noted by the U.S. Senate in a May 1932 statement, which hinted that spirituality was needed to restore the family:

> This Congress hereby appeals to the citizenship of the United States of America who are parents, pastors, and teachers that they address themselves to serious and sustained effort to integrate within the family life of the Nation those ideas represented by the simple virtues of the homely and humble life lived in fear of God, that there be restored through the cooperation of these institutions growing out of the family — the home, the Church and the State — the balances between spiritual and material, and the remedy for these prevailing deteriorating conditions of society be effected through the inculcation in our growing youth of spirituality, morality, and good conscience toward the God of our Nation.[26]

Catholics joined their fellow Americans in their alarm and significant apprehension over the perceived breakdown of the family unit. In his seminal study of the period, the historian Jeffrey Burns shows how fears over race suicide (birth control), the proliferation of divorce, and the rise of juvenile delinquency led to the formation of many groups that aimed to aid families and resolve the crisis.[27] The Family Service Association of America (FSAA), founded in New York City in 1911, was one of the leading groups established to right the family's sinking ship. In 1938 the National Conference on Family Relations became the leading organization, with its organ, the *Journal of Marriage and Family Living,* the most prestigious in the field. For many the pinnacle event of the period that focused on the family came in 1948 when the National Conference on Family Life, referred to as the "White House Conference on Family Life," met in Washington, D.C.[28]

Suggested solutions to this massive social problem were numerous and varied. The two leading and most influential family sociologists of the 1920 to 1940 period, Ernst Groves and Ernest W. Burgess, shared

the view that the family was merely experiencing a period of dislocation, and with readjustment it would soon find itself. Groves believed
the family needed outside assistance and education. On the other hand,
Burgess, who defined the family as "a unit of interacting personalities,"
stressed the needs of the individual and personal interests, as the goal
of the family as a unit receded. Thus, Burgess argued that the family
crisis could be solved, not through social reform, but through individual adjustment. Through their combined understanding Groves offered
the chief means for restoration of the family, namely, education, while
Burgess provided the theoretical basis for resolving the crisis. The *American Catholic Sociological Review* recognized the problem[29] but was very
pessimistic toward the secular response, which basically said nothing
could be done. The journal, in contrast, suggested two possible solutions: massive state intervention or cultural revolution. Neither of these,
however, was possible from the Church's perspective; the former violated
Catholic teaching on state intervention and the latter was unlikely.[30]

American Catholics fought against the sociological mainstream of the
period and its answers to the family crisis. Catholics argued that sociologists gave in to divorce, contradicting the Church's teaching on the
indissolubility of marriage. Additionally, sociologists suggested that children were a by-product of marriage, while Catholics viewed children
as the primary purpose of marriage. Lastly, sociologists made personal
happiness the central criterion for marital bliss, an idea that violated the
Catholic teaching that marriage was a social, not an individual, institution. Catholics responded to what they perceived to be the bankrupt
ideas of mainstream sociologists by reasserting the traditions and teachings of the Church, including the belief that the primary goal of marriage
is for the procreation and education of children and that right parent-
ing is not geared toward the temporal success of children, but to their
eternal salvation.[31]

Catholic commentators of the period continued to stress time-tested
truths. James Gillis, CSP, editor of the *Catholic World* and a leading
conservative voice of the era, commented, "There is no hope for an improvement in the condition of marriage, the family, and the home except
in a return to the conviction that marriage is a sacrament." Charles Miltner, CSC, offered an equally sober response: "Love, obedience, unity of
mind and will, [and] order, these are the things we see in the Holy Family; these are the things without which no family can measure up to the
Christian ideal." Bishop Karl Alter of Toledo stressed the Church's sole
right to address the problem, but offered nothing of substance: "The ethi-
cal values and moral principles established by God concerning the family

must always remain outside the jurisdiction of any state authority."[32] In short, Catholics in many instances, while considering the forces fighting families as criminals, were long on rhetoric, but short on substance.

In the perception of some sociological professionals the solutions offered by the Church appeared lame, yet Catholics held a set of clearly defined teachings on marriage and family that gave proper direction and a sense of orthodoxy to their quest. Catholics offered four separate approaches to resolving the family crisis as it was being experienced: (1) a national bureaucratic approach, (2) a personalist sacramental approach, (3) an internal educational approach, and (4) a specialized environmental approach.[33]

Developed along a time continuum, each of the four approaches offered something unique in its method. The national bureaucratic approach, centered about the Family Life Bureau (FLB), founded in 1931 as an agency of the Social Action Department of the National Catholic Welfare Conference (NCWC), emphasized education. Operating from a supra-diocesan perspective, the FLB made policy and gave recommendations on actions, but did not perform the tasks itself. The personalist sacramental approach taught that family renewal, centered in the personalist philosophy and ideas of such giants as Emmanuel Mounier, Dorothy Day, and Paul Hanly Furfey, must be achieved through personal change, not legislation or organizational or institutional reconstruction. The internal educational approach, manifest in the Cana Conference and its associated marriage counseling centers, sought family restoration through the improvement of marriage. Lastly, the specialized environmental approach was centered about the Christian Family Movement (CFM), a Catholic Action organization that used the "observe, judge, act" approach to transform the environment in which the family lived. While Cana sought to fix the family from the inside, CFM attempted to remedy the problems from the outside.[34]

The national bureaucratic approach, manifest in the Family Life Bureau, was the one principal effort of the institutional Church to rectify the family crisis. Father Edgar Schmiedler, OSB, founder of the FLB, believed the American family was a victim of a dual revolution in industry and philosophy. The Industrial Revolution had transformed a rural agrarian culture into an urban machine culture.[35] Accompanying this shift was the philosophical movement to an individualistic and rationalistic philosophy. The priest viewed the medieval world as the "Golden Age" of the family, where rural agrarianism reigned and fixed duties and responsibilities were understood and practiced. The Industrial Revolution had undercut this ideal situation. Schmiedler described the problem:

"That our family life is showing alarming symptoms of disease and unmistakable signs of decay is apparent to all who care to see.... There is every reason, therefore, to speak of conserving the family. It is high time for action on behalf of the home. Such action to be really effective will have to seek the causes of the family's troubles and apply the remedies there."[36] The American hierarchy supported Schmiedler's work and issued the 1949 statement "The Christian Family," calling the family crisis a "present danger more fearsome than the atomic bomb."[37]

Like the American hierarchy, Peyton was appalled at the growing sense of family disunity, describing it as "the deadly sin of our age,"[38] and believed that this most basic social unit had lost its religious soul. He provided an answer to the family crisis in a 1946 radio talk:

> I do not hesitate to say that home life to become wholesome and strong and vigorous must have daily family prayer as part of its very life, and one of the reasons for the sad fact of dying homes in our age is that we threw out daily family prayer, and it must come back again if we want to save our home life.[39]

Peyton believed that the power of prayer was the fuel that set in motion the great engines of the spiritual life, most notably the virtues of faith, hope, and charity. Prayer was as essential for the family as it was for the individual. In his autobiographical book of spirituality *Ear of God,* Peyton presented his philosophy on family prayer:

> Family prayer develops decency, responsibility, and tolerance, while it diminishes their opposites, both in parents and children. It is the beginning, middle, and end of a moral education. It is the life of religion, therefore the glue to character. In this way, it is the vitality of the nation. And for these reasons, there should be a time of day or evening set aside in every home for family prayer.[40]

A crusade for family prayer was his only answer to the family crisis and the antidote to the spread of atheism in the world.[41]

Peyton held the firm conviction that family prayer would solve the family crisis; more specifically he pointed to the family rosary as "one of the most powerful weapons we have to do battle against all the forces invading the sacredness and unity of the family":

> Today more than ever there is a need of a powerful weapon to protect family life. Worldliness and worldly doctrines strike first at the family. What hope has family life against the teachings of many college professors on planned parenthood, companionate marriage,

divorce, and general immorality? The radio, newspapers, comic sheets, and magazines bring these doctrines into the home itself, lay them on the table for all to see, [and] leave them ringing in everyone's ears. Moving pictures with colour and sound attract even the wisest and wariest by scenes that make a joke of family life. Happily, God provides us with the weapon we need. It's the Family Rosary.[42]

Family Rosary, 1942–45

Peyton's desire to rectify the family crisis in America, coupled with his desire to repay Mary for her intercession on his behalf, led in 1942 to the initiation of his life work in the Family Rosary Crusade. His first idea to repay Mary was to build a beautiful shrine in her honor, but his religious superiors quickly squelched the idea as impracticable and too costly.[43] During the final semester of his academic work at Holy Cross College Peyton, while on retreat, came to realize how he could respond in a way that would fulfill what he perceived were Mary's expectations of him. In a sermon preached a few years later he explained:

> In [January] 1942, a few months after my ordination, on a Sunday morning in Holy Cross College in Washington, I made a resolution that amounts to this — to spend myself until death to bring the Family Rosary back to 10,000,000 homes in America, and not to one less than that — and to bring the Family Rosary back to home life not for the month of May or October or Lent, but for always, and to bring it about that families will not consider God as their debtor because they wish to kneel down nightly together for the Rosary of Our Lady.[44]

Peyton's dream was unquestionably a bold one for a newly ordained priest bound by his vow of obedience to go where his superior assigned him. But Peyton did not do things half way. Throughout his ministerial career Peyton demonstrated that he was not one to follow the status quo nor be satisfied with anything less than an almost heroic personal effort in his drive to satisfy his debt to Mary and make the most of his new lease on life. In a letter to his brother Thomas, he outlined the motivation that would direct the next fifty years of his ministry, "The cause of Our Lady guides every move that I make."[45] In a 1948 speech to Catholic War Veterans Peyton explained more fully:

Why am I doing it? This is the reason: I am paying back a debt to somebody. I owe a debt to some one, and I am paying it back by doing this work for Our Lady's Rosary; for the one I owe the debt to is Our Lady. She took me off the sickbed, and she put strength and health in me again; and that is why as long as I have life, I intend to use the health and strength, not in a sentimental way, but in a challenging way so that men will go down on their knees in their homes and recite the family Rosary night after night for a lifetime.[46]

Peyton's rationale for choosing promotion of the family rosary was as pragmatic as it was consistent with his personal religious experience and piety. He suggested that the family rosary would help end the war and protect loved ones in military service, but he also boldly proclaimed that the family rosary was the most "effective means of combating the evils that now beset the American home" and that it provided young people "with a weapon of self-defense against the temptations with which they are now faced."[47] He also believed that making the family rosary a permanent fixture in the United States would make Mary proud of America and bring it special favors.[48]

Peyton's great plan for the spread of the family rosary in the United States (and beyond) began in the summer of 1942 after his completion of theological studies at Holy Cross College. Peyton's superior at the seminary, Father Christopher O'Toole, CSC (who later as superior general would be a major supporter of his work), gave him permission to send out letters to those who might be interested in his family prayer project. The first letter, actually typed by a seminarian, Theodore Hesburgh, CSC, later president of the University of Notre Dame, was sent to Bishop Edwin O'Hara of Kansas City, founder of the Catholic Rural Life Conference, who enthusiastically responded, "I agree completely that the family Rosary will be the strongest safeguard of tomorrow's families. Thanks to your suggestion, I have underlined it in my program for the Confraternity of Christian Doctrine."[49]

In August 1942 Peyton met in Washington with fellow Holy Cross religious Bishop John O'Hara, former president of Notre Dame, asking his support. O'Hara, who served as bishop of the United States Military Ordinariate (and later as cardinal archbishop of Philadelphia), was happy to help and instructed all Catholic military chaplains to preach about the benefits and efficacy of the family rosary on four consecutive Sundays. He encouraged Peyton, responding, "It is hard to conceive of a better antidote to the night life that imperils the American home."[50]

Peyton's first love was to promote family prayer through the rosary, but independent apostolic ventures within Holy Cross were very rare before Vatican II. His first assignment was as chaplain to a group of Holy Cross brothers who taught at the Vincentian Institute in Albany, New York.[51] Thomas Steiner, CSC, provincial superior of the American Province of Holy Cross, did not want to place Peyton in an apostolate that would be extremely taxing and could lead to a recurrence of his tuberculosis. He wrote to Peyton, "I must . . . caution you not to take on too much work, and to be faithful to the rest period prescribed by the doctor." It is also possible that Steiner gave Peyton special privileges out of fear that the young priest had some special relationship with God. Holy Cross priests Jerome Lawyer and Patrick Sullivan believed that Steiner was intimidated by Peyton's invocations of "Mary wants it; Mary wants it." This view is even more interesting when one realizes that Steiner was a seasoned veteran, both as a religious priest and from previous experience in business.[52]

When Peyton arrived in Albany he began his ministry as chaplain to seventeen brothers after receiving faculties from the local ordinary, Edmund Gibbons. Steiner gave Peyton permission to pursue his family rosary ministry, but only after securing permission from Gibbons and so long as it did not interfere with his chaplain duties. Peyton moved into his second floor of the Holy Cross Brothers' residence on Madison Avenue. His needs were rather spartan — a bed, chest of drawers, desk and chair — but he always brought the one item that would become his trademark, a copy of Murillo's *Madonna and Child,* which he proudly displayed on the wall over his bed.[53]

Peyton dutifully fulfilled his commitments as chaplain to the Brothers, but he continued to cherish his dream of establishing the family rosary in the homes of 10 million Americans. Peyton was grateful to the Dominican sisters in Albany, who allowed him to use the unoccupied space reserved for their chaplain as his office. From this crowded setting Peyton initiated his first letter campaigns, enlisting the support of significant individuals and groups for his passionate dream. Continuing his pattern of conducting important business on Marian feasts, on November 21, 1942, the Feast of the Presentation of Mary, he sent a letter to all U.S. bishops about his proposed program. This mailing was followed on December 8 with a similar appeal for support to all presidents of national lay organizations. A third letter, soliciting the support of the 12,600 pastors of parishes in the country, was sent on February 11.[54] The letters were prepared through the herculean efforts of women students at the

Vincentian Institute and novices of the Mercy Sisters, the religious community which taught the women students at the Institute.[55] A typical letter read in part:

> Fellow-priests, then make this cause [family rosary] your own. Let your zeal and your love for God and Mary inspire the methods that you will use to assure success. Let us leave no stone unturned in our efforts to drive from the homes of our people the spirit of the world and to make way for the spirit of Mary. Raise your voice for the Family Rosary, and let this increase and make more effective that army of bishops, priests, religious, and lay persons determined to make America, the land of Our Lady, also the Home of the Family Rosary.[56]

Money for stamps arrived unexpectedly when Sister Adrian, mother general of the Mercy Sisters, and Brother John Baptist Titzer, CSC, superior of the Holy Cross Brothers in Albany, made public appeals for assistance.[57]

Peyton was encouraged by the response that he received from this initial appeal. Cardinal William O'Connell of Boston was the first to respond with an enthusiastic endorsement of the plan. Henry Althoff, bishop of Belleville, Illinois, answered: "I wish to assure you that I shall continue to promote the practice of the family rosary, and to extend this devotion in our Diocese through the cooperation of the pastors and teachers." The apostolic delegate to the United States, Archbishop Ildebrando Antoniutti, commented: "The daily practice of the recitation of the Rosary in the home will certainly be a school of prayer, an inspiration to virtue, and a powerful means of salvation."[58] Thomas Malloy, bishop of Brooklyn, was so excited that he pledged $5,000 as seed money for the Family Rosary Crusade.[59]

Peyton had been assigned to his chaplaincy position with the hope that he would curtail his activity, but he never visualized a restful life. Steiner, convinced that Peyton had been working too hard, assigned him during the summers of 1943 and 1944 as confessor to seminarians at their summer headquarters on Deep Creek Lake in western Maryland. Although the provincial cautioned him not to do too much, Peyton took with him all the responses he had received from his latest appeal to pastors, completing a fifteen-page summary report. He worked with seminarians to generate a pamphlet, "The Story of the Family Rosary," which was printed and placed in future mailings. Peyton and the seminarians also wrote over one thousand letters to bishops, priests, and other Church leaders in the United States and Canada.[60] Peyton's superiors were amazed at his progress and zeal and gave their wholehearted blessings to his efforts, convinced that this was no ordinary apostolic endeavor: The superior general, Albert Cousineau, CSC, commented, "Undoubtedly, the Blessed Virgin Mary is directing this work."[61]

The magnitude of Peyton's effort can be measured by the initial report he offered, which described the achievements between 1942 and 1944. Peyton had sent out under his signature fourteen hundred personal letters and seventeen thousand circular notes, and distributed twenty thousand posters and over 1.3 million Family Rosary leaflets. He continued to expand his circle of contacts, writing to all Catholic colleges, universities, high schools, and academies, enlisting their support as well.[62]

The success of Peyton's initial efforts combined with the support he received from those in Albany and Holy Cross in general inspired him to press forward with even greater vigor and energy. One vital key to his future success was the arrival of Father Francis Woods, who would serve from 1943 to his death in 1964 as a close confidant and full partner in the mission of the Family Rosary Crusade. Woods, a priest of the Diocese of Albany, was a member of the matrimonial tribunal of the diocese and chaplain at St. Rose College when he met Peyton in the fall of 1943. Woods was very impressed with Peyton and convinced that his crusade "was the best and simplest remedy in solving family troubles":

> Father Peyton prays knowing that all power in Heaven and on earth rests above, but he works with never a moment's lull, as though all depended on him, as though the minutes and hours of life ahead would never be sufficient to pay the debt. And work it is! Many a time I would be deeply affected and even concerned to see how tireless Father Peyton worked.[63]

Peyton, for his part, was ever grateful to Woods, who he believed could have become a bishop, had he not chosen "the vicissitudes of the gypsy for the sake of Our Lady and the sanctity of the home."[64]

The enthusiastic response to Father Peyton's initial barrage of letters prompted him to move his campaign to its next phase. Peyton sent out information leaflets and pledge cards to bishops who had favorably answered his initial call, asking them to promote drives to recruit families as "family rosary families." When clergy or religious agreed to support the crusade, he responded with a standard exhortation:

> Thanks be to God and Mary that they have made you as an apostle of the Family Rosary. I want to encourage you with the knowledge

that you are joining the ranks of countless other great men and women who are devoted to Mary and determined to spare no effort until the homes of America are homes of prayer — homes where Our Lady reigns as Queen of the Family Rosary.[65]

Peyton even wrote to Pope Pius XII in May 1945, enlisting his support and beginning a relationship with occupants of the Chair of Peter that would last until his death in 1992.[66] Peyton's purpose was to build a huge base of support for his project by informing people of his dream and asking their prayers for its success.[67] While orienting his drive for support particularly at members and groups of the institutional Church, he realized the great zeal of the laity was essential, for it was in the homes of American Catholic families that his dream would be realized.

Peyton recognized the fact that his initial success was due to the support he received in his new ministry. He was certain his endeavors were blessed by God: "The good God and His Blessed Mother must surely be pleased and, in fact, must be giving special blessing to the work."[68] More practically, Peyton had the support of Steiner: "May God bless your efforts, and may our Blessed Mother come to your aid in promoting this excellent and fruitful practice."[69]

It was not long before Peyton's crusade planted roots in Albany. As the operation expanded in the fall of 1944 Peyton hired his first secretary, Eileen Soraghan, a graduate of Vincentian Institute. The next year, needing more office space, he gratefully accepted an offer from the Sisters of St. Joseph at the College of St. Rose to move his crusade operation to an office on campus.[70] Albany artist David Lithgow was commissioned to create a lithograph depicting the family rosary. With the ecclesiastical approval of Bishop Gibbons, the work was adopted as the official campaign poster for the crusade.[71]

Established in Albany, Peyton next took his message to other eastern dioceses, with the approval of Steiner, who had given permission to preach about the family rosary anywhere he obtained the authorization of the local ordinary.[72] Between November 1943 and July 1944, Peyton expanded his campaign to Buffalo, Philadelphia, and to his beloved Scranton, speaking and preaching Triduums on the family rosary to promulgate his message and secondarily to raise much needed revenues.[73] In his talks he suggested that now was the time to fight the principal cause of the war raging in the European and Pacific theaters, namely, paganism, while bringing people back to the practice of family prayer through the rosary.[74] He argued that society was far from God and until people could reverse this course and return to a sense of values consistent with the common call to discipleship, the world would remain in darkness. The family rosary was the "medicine [that] can prevent infection from the modern disease of worldliness."[75]

Peyton's message stressed the need for prayer in the home, both personal and familial, arguing that common prayer "was the most advantageous way of exercising a positive influence for good upon impressionable children." He believed that the rosary unified families, was the primary source of their spiritual regeneration, and served as the shield against the evils of the day. He understood that family prayer, because it had fallen out of practice, was unconventional for many, but he emphasized that people were beginning to start the practice anew. He professed that his campaign would not be considered entirely successful until it was normative throughout the country.[76]

Peyton's letter campaign and active promotion through preaching and writing gained more supporters for the Family Rosary Crusade. National lay associations, led by the National Conference of Catholic Men (NCCM) and the National Conference of Catholic Women (NCCW) and including the Society of St. Vincent De Paul, the Knights of Columbus, the Ancient Order of Hibernians, the Catholic Daughters of America (CDA), and the Holy Name Society, all lent their support.[77] Peyton was able to enlist the support of the National Catholic Welfare Conference (NCWC) through Frank Hall, director of the conference's news service, suggesting that one broadcast of the nationally syndicated program *The Catholic Hour,* sponsored by the NCCM, be dedicated to the promotion of the family rosary.[78]

The Catholic press strongly supported Peyton's initiative. Editorials favorable to the Family Rosary Crusade appeared with increasing frequency in leading publications. Speaking of the Crusade, *Catholic Charities Review* commented that "success is certain," while *America* offered a plug for family prayer: "The family that prays in common is the family that loves in common."[79] One diocesan paper, speaking to the local clergy, stated,

> Please make every effort from the pulpit, through the societies and the school children to introduce the recitation of the Rosary every day in the family circle. Such a practice would not only insure the safety of our soldiers and sailors and victory for our armies, but would transform the houses of our people into true Christian homes, nurseries of virtue and of vocations to the priesthood and religious life so sadly lacking.[80]

Patrick Carroll, CSC, editor of *Ave Maria,* was a faithful supporter of Peyton's initial efforts through regular editorials, beginning in 1943. In June 1946 he wrote,

> If every Catholic family in America were to recite the rosary in a family tradition every evening, parents and children and relatives within every degree of kindred would be blessed aboundingly. And so would our nation — a much larger unit — be blessed with the protecting guidance of God's mother.

Support for Peyton's campaign was also strong among religious orders and the clergy. Women religious were especially helpful to Peyton, both monetarily and through their prayers. One typical response to his initial letter writing campaign came from the Poor Clares in Cleveland, Ohio: "Rest assured, we shall continue to pray for this wonderful work, and beg our dear Heavenly Mother to change this poor weary world, so that there will be peace and harmony, especially in Catholic homes."[81]

A major milestone in Peyton's campaign was gaining the support of Monsignor Fulton Sheen, who was becoming a household fixture in Catholic homes through the aforementioned *Catholic Hour,* broadcast each Sunday over the national NBC network. On the Third Sunday of Lent in 1945 Sheen preached a sermon on the *Catholic Hour* in support of the family rosary. He said that anyone who wished to receive a rosary and a pamphlet, *The Story of the Family Rosary,* could write to NBC. The initial estimate was for five thousand requests, but in three days alone requests were over six thousand. Eventually, fifty thousand people requested the articles.[82]

Catholic radio had been popularized by Monsignor Sheen, but the Church's efforts in this new electronic media, beginning in the early 1920s, grew progressively in dimension, popularity, and significance. One of the best-known early efforts was the inauguration by the Paulist Fathers of station WLWL in New York in September 1925. The station had low signal strength, and its authorized broadcast times were progressively cut back by federal regulators, but the station provided outstanding programming for the greater New York City Catholic community and launched the radio career of Father James Gillis, CSP, the well-known conservative journalist, editor, and commentator. The late 1920s also saw the start of the radio career of Father Charles Coughlin, often known as the radio priest, but described by his most recent biographer as "the father of hate radio."[83] In 1926 Coughlin inaugurated programs for children, but over time he became more and more political, to the point of being a staunch opponent of President Franklin Roosevelt and ultimately highly anti-Semitic in his polemical diatribes. The best-known Catholic program of the period, *The Catholic Hour,* was launched on March 2, 1930. Broadcast nationally on the NBC network, *The Catholic Hour* truly established radio as a powerful medium for communication of the Catholic message.[84] Institutional Church support for Catholic radio was officially secured in 1938 with the establishment of the Catholic Radio Bureau, sponsored by the NCCM.[85]

Catholic radio expanded during the 1940s with numerous local and national programs. *The Catholic Hour,* which aired every Sunday at 6:00 p.m. (EST) on NBC was joined by ABC's *The Hour of Faith,* and the Mutual Broadcasting System's (MBS) show *Faith in Our Time,* all nationally syndicated. All were similar in format, featuring straight talk and some music. In June 1942 NBC launched a more ecumenical program, *We Believe,* aired on Sundays at 4:30 p.m. and featuring sacred music of all faiths, plus brief readings from the Protestant, Catholic, and Jewish traditions. Local programming included more variety — music, talk, hymns, and Catholic news of interest, semi-dramatic programming, such as the life of a saint, church services, roundtable forums, and interviews.[86] The future of Catholic radio appeared to be bright: "If Catholics are progressive enough to use the increased opportunities [such as FM], there is no reason why the Church message should not be multiplied a thousandfold and in a thousand different ways through the opening of more stations."[87] The establishment of the Catholic Broadcasters' Association (CBA) in July 1948, mainly through the efforts of William C. Smith, radio director of the NCCM, cemented the Church's place on the radio airwaves.[88]

Father Peyton used the popularity of radio to communicate his central missive of family prayer through the rosary. In the fall of 1943 Francis Woods secured a fifteen-minute weekly slot for recitation of the rosary on *The Voice of St. Rose,* broadcast on Albany's WABY. Prominent local families were engaged to recite the prayers. This new venture was well received, as Peyton reported: "The weekly family recitation of the Rosary by trained students and a family ... has been so enthusiastically received by those who have heard it, that I am sure that such a weekly program would be joyfully accepted all over the nation."[89] In 1945, the show was renamed *Evening Time,* moved to the ABC affiliate WOKO, and expanded to thirty minutes, with music and short meditations added before and after each mystery. One paper described the program's purpose: "*Evening Time* seeks to elevate family life to nobler concepts of Christian living through the restoration of daily Family Prayer to the homes of its listeners."[90]

Encouraged by the success of his initial efforts, Peyton worked to institute national broadcasting of the family rosary. He first asked the NCCM to sponsor one broadcast of *The Catholic Hour,* but the request was turned down since it was perceived that rosary recitation would not be well received.[91] Peyton next spoke with George Nelson of WSNY in Schenectady, who in turn introduced him to Edgar Kobak, president of the Mutual Broadcasting Company in New York. Kobak directed Peyton to Elsie Dick, director of religious programs, but she was not initially impressed with Peyton's idea. Undeterred, he pressed Dick, who agreed to grant a half-hour national slot, originally scheduled for May 21, 1945. After speaking with Monsignor John McClafferty of New York, the liaison for radio in the Archdiocese of New York, Dick recommended rescheduling the program for May 13, Mother's Day, which President Harry Truman had declared a day of national celebration and thanksgiving, following V-E day one week prior.[92]

Now Peyton had to rapidly put together a quality program that would be well received and perhaps become a weekly occurrence.[93] Peyton booked the Guild Theater on Fifty-second Street for the event. Under the direction of George Nelson and Colonel James Healey, general manager of WSNY, who worked for free,[94] Peyton originally chose five mysteries, the Annunciation, Nativity, Crucifixion, Resurrection, and Coronation, to be prayed, accompanied by sacred music, such as the *Regina Coeli, Te Deum,* or *Ave Regina Coelorum.* Seeking national attention and, in a move to satisfy Mutual officials who wanted some "name" person associated with the broadcast, Peyton obtained the service of Bing Crosby, star of the popular movie *The Bells of St. Mary's* to speak on a special link from California.[95] Archbishop Francis Spellman of New York agreed to host the program, and the Sullivan family of Waterloo, Iowa, who had lost five sons on the USS *Juneau,* sunk in the Pacific theater, agreed to lead the rosary.

On Saturday afternoon, May 12, a full rehearsal for the program was conducted. Too little rehearsal time and the logistics of handling more than fifty participants proved too much for Peyton and Francis Woods, who assisted Elsie Dick with the program's coordination. A tape made of the rehearsal demonstrated that the production was ragged and the timing was poor, but by 11:00 p.m. the cast and crew were too tired to continue. Peyton and Woods returned to the French Hospital, operated by the Marianites of Holy Cross,[96] to rest. The next day they rose early and prayed that the day would be a great success.[97]

The May 13 broadcast was a great triumph by all accounts, despite the poor rehearsal. The stage had been carefully and colorfully decorated with a statue of Our Lady of Providence prominently displayed. After a short rehearsal the program began at 10:30 a.m. with an introduction by Archbishop Spellman, who called Peyton the "American Apostle of the Family Rosary." The Sullivan family prayed the Glorious Mysteries of the Rosary,[98] interspersed with meditations read by Monsignor Francis Shea of New York. The choir of Blessed Sacrament Church, under the direction of Warren Foley, sang hymns between the mysteries.[99] Bing Crosby's voice was heard after the rosary was completed, exhorting the radio audience:

> I want my children to pray in our home, as well as in our church. That is why I want them to believe as I believe, in the true glory and true greatness and true significance of the Family Rosary. In our home we believe in the Family Rosary as a great force working for good, working for good against evil. We believe that today, as never before, this vital force for good is necessary if we are to fashion from the holocaust of war the framework of lasting peace. As Christians, as Americans we believe in the power and the necessity of family prayer in all homes. As Catholics, we believe the Family Rosary to be the perfect family prayer.

After Crosby ended, Peyton concluded the program with a note of thanksgiving and challenge:

> I want to offer my sincere thanks to all the friends of Our Lady everywhere whose prayers and sacrifices have made this program possible for the greatest of all Mothers. I beg you to become a life-long apostle of the Family Rosary and on this day promise Mary that you will do all in your power to change the homes of the world into homes where God and Mary will be forever honored by the daily Family Rosary.[100]

Elated by the program's success, Peyton attributed it, like all his ministerial accomplishments, to the intercession of the Blessed Virgin Mary and determined to use it as a springboard for future endeavors. He expressed this quite clearly:

> We have prayed, we have worked, we have sought aid. Wherefore, if Our Blessed Mother, in whose name we strive to disseminate her devotion is pleased with what we have done, no force on earth shall prevent our reaching the good we set out to reach. But Mary has

been with us every inch and every prayer of the way, and it would be base ingratitude to harbor even a doubt that she will forsake us now.[101]

Conclusion

Patrick Peyton's ability to rise from sickness and defeat of tuberculosis was only the first of several miracles in his life. With the permission of his religious superiors Peyton began an independent apostolate, a favor rarely granted at the time, to promote family prayer through the rosary. A massive letter-writing campaign, conducted in his "spare time" and utilizing a host of volunteers, led in less than three years to a national radio broadcast featuring prominent names in ecclesiastical and entertainment circles. Dedication, commitment, and a personal drive bordering on obsession combined with fortunate circumstances and the cooperation of prominent people in the correct circles to produce a success that only Father Peyton, through his strong faith, could have achieved. Buoyed by his initial success he moved forward to bring family prayer through the rosary to the peoples of the world.

Chapter 3

Family Theater of the Air, 1945–52

A highly successful initial foray into national radio and a granite-like faith in his project and mission led to the rapid expansion of Peyton's efforts to make the family rosary as normative throughout the United States as it was in his boyhood home in Attymass. Without hesitation or hardly the blink of an eye, he set out to parlay his May 13 Mother's Day program into a weekly national radio broadcast that would promulgate his message to America and beyond. Never cowed by the high odds against such an endeavor, Peyton tirelessly and doggedly pursued his goal, never taking no for an answer. His perseverance and faith, combined with the support and assistance of many hard-working and influential people, most especially his colleagues in Holy Cross, brought the family rosary message to a national audience and became the base upon which the international Family Rosary Crusade would be launched.

Family Rosary Expands

The initial success of Peyton's family rosary campaign demanded an infusion of additional personnel and facilities. In March 1945 Peyton wrote to his provincial, Thomas Steiner, CSC, asking that additional Holy Cross religious be assigned to the Family Rosary operations in Albany. Steiner acknowledged the need: "This activity is growing to such an extent that you must have some help. You are working entirely too hard for your own physical welfare.... We will consider assigning a young priest or two to your work."[1] The provincial, however, would not make an assignment until some permanent residence for religious assigned to the ministry was secured. Thus, Peyton began to negotiate with Bishop Gibbons and his vicar general to secure a community house for those participating in the Family Rosary apostolate. Gibbons heartily supported Family Rosary, calling it a "salutary devotion," but at the outset he was reticent to allow the Congregation to be "established in his Archdiocese for any other purpose."[2] In order to satisfy both Steiner and Gibbons a compromise was struck providing a residence for religious associated with Family Rosary with the Holy Cross brothers who taught at Vincentian Institute.

On October 1, 1945, Jerome Lawyer, CSC, became the first additional Holy Cross religious to be assigned to the Crusade. Ordained in 1939, Lawyer had been destined for the Bengal missions, the ministry that Peyton himself originally sought, but he and five other Holy Cross religious, while on route to their assignments, were captured by the Japanese in the Philippines immediately after the onset of the Pacific war. Having returned to the United States in March 1945 (the Los Banos internment camp, where the religious were held, was liberated by American forces on February 23, 1945) Lawyer desired what he believed was a more active ministry, but Steiner, as with Peyton earlier, did not want to assign him to an apostolate that would overtax him physically. The provincial encouraged Lawyer to embrace his unexpected assignment: "I am certain that you will enjoy the work, and that before long you may even feel yourself fortunate to be associated with this activity."[3] Upon his arrival Lawyer was placed in charge of the Albany office, still located at the College of St. Rose.[4]

Peyton was able to obtain an independent apostolate, a rare occurrence for Holy Cross in those days, only because his ministry was supported by Steiner, who as provincial was responsible for all the Congregation's ministries in the United States. He proudly stated that "Father Peyton has something in the Family Rosary," extolling not only his work but his person:

> We are convinced he has a mission that is going to succeed, and that our country, and even the world, is going to profit immensely. Father Peyton himself is a living saint. His simplicity impresses everyone he contacts.... Several incidents in Father Peyton's life and work during this past year give evidence of supernatural intervention.[5]

Steiner, however, continued to warn Peyton not to overexert himself:

> Quite naturally I am always concerned about your physical condition. You must try and take the daily rest period as prescribed for you several years ago. Every six months or so you should get

another check-up. Above all do not over-exert yourself. Zeal is a wonderful and commendable virtue, but we have a duty to look after our physical well-being. You are doing grand and fruitful work for our Blessed Mother, but if you do not keep physically fit your activities will soon be curtailed.[6]

Peyton was grateful for Steiner's care and concern: "I surely owe a debt to you, Father. Your friendship and blessings and encouragement have, to a great extent, been the things that have made the Family Rosary cause . . . grow."[7]

The Crusade Goes to Hollywood

Seemingly oblivious to Steiner's warnings to slow down, Peyton actually increased his activity, maintaining a torturous preaching schedule of Triduums and other parish functions and accepting invitations to speak on radio. He described the rapid pace of his life:

To fulfill that resolution that I made on the Last Sunday of January in 1942, I am on the road as a salesman for Mary, with all the humiliations and the sorrows of a salesman — a man who has no home of his own, but living in trains and traveling from one city to another, and from one state to another and from one ocean to the other, trying to sell the conviction I have that in any home in any city of America, where a father and mother and brothers and sisters kneel down together nightly for the Rosary and keep that up night after night for a lifetime, that is a holy home, that is a happy home.[8]

Peyton was encouraged by those whom he contacted in his mission to press further and seek a weekly syndicated radio program on a national network.[9]

Full of confidence and with the support he needed, Peyton in late July 1945 traveled to Hollywood, California, to enlist the assistance of the stars of radio, stage, and screen in an effort to establish a permanent national family prayer program. The opportunity for Peyton to travel came about quite unexpectedly when he received a call from one of the St. Joseph sisters at the College of St. Rose informing him that "his ticket" had just been delivered. The nun had mistakenly given Peyton the travel voucher, a very rare commodity after the war, but he did not waste the opportunity and immediately set out for California.[10] As he later stated,

I went to Hollywood to sell the Family Rosary by the self-same methods that Henry Ford and other industrialists of our country use in selling cars and rubber and steel. And I went out to Los Angeles to get on my side the power house that sways public thinking one way or another.[11]

Upon arrival in Los Angeles, Peyton went to St. Vibiana's Cathedral and was hosted by the rector, Monsignor Joseph Cawley, vicar general of the archdiocese and a fellow native of County Mayo. Cawley arranged for Peyton to speak with Archbishop John Cantwell, who gave his full support, stating that family prayer had been promoted in the archdiocese since 1939. Peyton was also able to speak with Colonel Tom Lewis, founder and first head of Armed Forces Radio and now a leader in radio advertising, and his famous actress wife, Loretta Young. Both were willing to support Peyton's dream.[12] Cawley had arranged through his friend Monsignor Patrick Concannon, a native of County Galway, for Peyton to preach at his parish, Good Shepherd Church in Beverly Hills, which was frequented by many Hollywood celebrities, including Young. After the Masses Peyton met Irene Dunne, Charles Boyer, Maureen O'Sullivan, Ethel Barrymore, and several other stars, all of whom agreed to assist him. Peyton secured agreements from over thirty stars, including Bing Crosby, Gregory Peck, Don Ameche, Shirley Temple, Maureen O'Hara, and Jane Wyatt.[13]

Peyton's magnetism, a trait that would open many doors in the future and be a trademark of his effect on people, was evident from the outset in his relations with the famous stars he met. His humility and shyness were matched with a spirituality that overwhelmed most of those with whom he had contact. The actress Jane Wyatt, speaking many years after her first encounter with Peyton, commented, "He certainly hypnotized everybody in the congregation. . . . Somehow when Father Peyton asked you for something, there was no way to say no!" He was described as one with a "velvet touch. He got what he wanted but without being a tyrant, or overbearing, or anything like that." Ann Blyth, who would be an active participant in Peyton's early Hollywood productions, asserted, "I think that it didn't matter what faith or non-faith any of them [Hollywood stars] had. They were all taken with him. He had a way of enchanting even those who, perhaps, didn't believe."[14]

The special qualities that Peyton exhibited to stars were also noted by Catholic journalists. One writer spoke of Peyton: "To meet him personally is to know a man of God. Sincerity shines forth from him, and his simple faith in the value of prayer is an inspiring thing in these trouble-some times."[15] He was described as "a man of God" who demonstrated sincerity through his simple faith. Theodore Bonnet captured Peyton's spirit as manifest to those he met:

> Those acquainted with Father Peyton will, perhaps, agree that if there is one secret of his success [it is] ... that love glows and some-times blazes on [his] broad, innocent face. It exalts his plain speech, uttered in a brogue. It is equipment enough. Even those with no piety toward Mary appear to recognize and revere the love that this man brings.[16]

Before returning to New York Peyton made additional contacts with officials in the archdiocese who might be able to assist with his mission. Cantwell sent Peyton to Father John Devlin, chaplain to the Hollywood movie and radio community, who introduced him to Clarence Hutson and Robert Fennell of the public relations office of Twentieth Century Fox Productions. These men, together with script writer Fred Niblo Jr. and Pedro de Cordova, who was to act as a permanent master of cere-monies, were united in a committee, presided over by Monsignor Cawley and Father Devlin, "to think out what is the best way to hold the lis-tening audience ... and to get them to accept the message that we want to put across."[17] Peyton told Cantwell and Steiner that since he now had their support and a group of stars and producers committed to the project, all he needed was free air time.[18]

In the fall of 1945 Peyton was back in New York knocking on the doors of radio executives, requesting a free half-hour slot on a national network. He met first with Eli Oberstein of NBC, but the meeting was not productive.[19] Peyton then turned to Tom Lewis, whom he had just met in California, and asked him to intercede for him with Mutual. Lewis told Peyton he would get the air time for him. He suggested a radio drama followed by a "commercial" on family prayer, an approach that had been used successfully in the sale of all sorts of products. Lewis took his plan to Mutual chief Edgar Kobak, who agreed to give free air time, but only under four conditions: (1) Peyton would supply a first-class program, (2) the content would be nonsectarian, (3) each program would feature a major Hollywood star, and (4) Peyton would be responsible for all production costs, including orchestra and writers.[20] The stipulation of nonsectarian content was troublesome for Peyton because it would eliminate the possibility of saying the rosary on the program.

Peyton was disappointed in Mutual's offer, but he sought advice from Steiner and Fulton Sheen, both of whom recommended that he take what he could get.[21] However, Peyton decided to seek a better deal, and for almost a year he continued to search for free radio time that would permit him to include the rosary in his program. In December 1945 he reported to Steiner and Cantwell that arrangements for a national show "will soon be completed," but the agreement was never finalized. In January 1946 Peyton was offered free time from the Associated Broadcasting Corporation, but he decided to hold out for one of the top national networks.[22] Jerome Lawyer pragmatically concluded, "Things do not look too bright for our radio program."[23]

In the spring of 1946, after many failed attempts to secure the air time he needed, Peyton formed an advisory committee to help create a quality radio program along the lines dictated by Mutual. Fulton Sheen, who was "very enthusiastic" about the project, joined the committee, as did Clare Booth Luce. Sheen advised Peyton to stand clear of NBC and to accept Mutual's offer.[24] Seeing the wisdom of taking what he could, Peyton accepted Mutual's offer, which gave Family Rosary a half-hour of free air time on any one evening, Monday through Saturday between 8:00 and 10:30 p.m. for a twenty-six-week trial run. When the contract was signed in January 1947 Peyton was forced to agree that the words "Protestant," "Catholic," "Jew," "interfaith," "interdenominational," "denominational," and "nonsectarian" would not be used in any of the scripts.[25] Peyton was satisfied and ready for the challenge, informing Archbishop Cantwell, "If we can prove ourselves during these 26 weeks, they will never put us off the air."[26]

In the fall of 1946 Peyton began preparing in earnest for his proposed program series, which could start anytime after January 15, 1947.[27] He returned to Los Angeles to work with Tom Lewis, who had been convinced by his wife, Loretta Young, to organize the programs. They decided to initiate the format popular in radio "soap operas," with short and simple comments inserted into dramatic plots to sell the idea of family prayer. Production costs, which were Peyton's responsibility, were estimated to be $2,000 weekly. Al Scalpone, a Hollywood public relations agent, was responsible for the "commercials," the two most famous being, "The family that prays together stays together," and "A world at prayer is a world at peace."[28] Alfred Lord Tennyson's famous comment "More things are wrought by prayer than this world dreams of" was another popular "commercial" expression. Peyton wisely arranged for Kobak to meet with Lewis and the planning team before the programs commenced. The Mutual chief was highly impressed with the group's organization and spirit and told Peyton he hoped that in the near future all 380 Mutual stations would be carrying the broadcasts. Peyton too was pleased with the future prospects: "The way things are shaping [up] I have no fear to say that this program will rate among the best on the air, and that it will accomplish its purpose."[29]

National Catholic periodicals, such as *Our Sunday Visitor,* and various press releases advertised that Family Theater's purpose "is to sell Daily Family Prayer to America as a basic help to a richer life at home, at work and at play, and to make the Daily Family Rosary an evening sacrifice in every Catholic home."[30] Peyton himself was very optimistic about his debut: "I hope it [Family Theater] will be the best program on the air and will restore to the homes of the nation family prayer which is so necessary at the present time."[31] Peyton's high hopes were further buoyed by Mutual's decision to postpone the first broadcast, moving it from February 6 to February 13. What others might have seen as frustrating delay, Peyton interpreted as yet another sign of divine intervention.[32]

Family Theater of the Air — *Beginnings*

On February 13, 1947, *Family Theater of the Air* debuted at 7:00 p.m. (PST) with "Flight from Home," starring Loretta Young and Don Ameche and narrated by James Stewart. The program, written by True Boardman and with music conducted by Meredith Wilson, was broadcast from Mutual's Los Angeles affiliate KHJ and dedicated to the family "with the hope that families everywhere will always be together and that your home will be a happy one — with the conviction that prayer, simple prayer, will keep it that way."[33]

General reaction to the first Family Theater programs was quite positive. Peyton acknowledged that the nonsectarian nature of the programs was not attractive to some Catholics, but the overwhelming tide of opinion was highly favorable. Peyton reported to Steiner that the phone switchboard was jammed after the first show with hundreds of calls, including a local auxiliary bishop of Los Angeles, expressing excitement and offering congratulations.[34] One religious superior was so impressed with the program that he sent a check for $8,000 "to help you to continue the splendid work of the Family Theater broadcasts."[35] Jerome Lawyer, CSC, informed Albert Cousineau, CSC, the superior general of Holy Cross, "The Family Theater series of weekly broadcasts from Hollywood have been a great success. The letters from people all over the United States have proven to us that through this most beautiful program on family prayer they have come closer to God, and have already begun the Family Rosary in their homes."[36] Edgar Kobak was so pleased with the programs that in August he extended the free air time indefinitely and began to speak of special half- or full-hour programs for Christmas and special holidays.[37]

Family Theater was a team effort, but it was clear to all that the personality, drive, and complete dedication of Peyton was the glue that kept the organization focused and united and the fuel that fed its overdrive engine. Many noted his simple and unassuming manner, but *L'Osservatore Romano* captured the essence of Peyton's contribution:

> The merit for these [first broadcasts] is to be attributed to the tenacious will of the priest who, in his deep devotion to God and His Virgin Mother, found the strength to overcome discouragement which would have fallen upon anyone who would have had to face so many difficulties and set-backs.

Peyton's devotion to Mary was so strong that he made her a visible reality to many, who, inspired by his demonstration of love for the one who had interceded for him at his time of need, were more than willing to recite the daily family rosary.[38]

Little time elapsed between the humble beginnings of Family Theater and its transformation into an established program. Ed Kobak, who was determined "to place a campaign of propaganda behind this program," encouraged Mutual stations to carry the broadcast. He was also elected chairman of the Advisory Council that Peyton had organized in the spring of 1946.[39] By July 1947 *Family Theater of the Air* was being carried by 300 Mutual stations (out of 380) in the United States, 16 shortwave stations directed across the Atlantic and Pacific, and Armed Forces Radio.[40] Captains of industry joined the Family Theater sponsoring committee, which Peyton organized in early 1948.[41]

Unquestionably the greatest key to Family Theater's initial success was the vast array of Hollywood stars and other well-known American personalities it featured. The list of stars on the broadcasts reads as a "who's who" of Hollywood. Besides those enlisted during his 1945 summer trip to California, Peyton obtained the services of Walter Brennan, Van Heflin, Ozzie and Harriet Nelson, Vincent Price, William Holden, Robert Young, Roddy McDowell, Bob Hope, Ronald Reagan, Donna Reed, Alan Young, Barbara Stanwyck, Jack Benny, Peter Lawford, and Richard Basehart as feature stars. Program hosts included Dana Andrews, Edward G. Robinson, Gary Cooper, Jack Haley, Nelson Eddy, Cesar Romero, Fred MacMurray, Ricardo Montalban, Ray Milland, Notre Dame football coach Frank Leahy, and FBI director J. Edgar Hoover. Over the years the list of stars continued to expand.[42] Peyton was fully aware that his Hollywood connection was crucial to his success. "These stars are the foundation. If they break with me, I am done for; the entire structure will fold."[43]

Less visible to the public than its impressive star roster, but just as crucial to the program's success, were its talented writers. Father Timothy Mulvey, OMI, a prominent writer for *The Catholic Hour*, was first retained in July 1946 to work for Family Theater full time.[44] He was joined by True Boardman (writer of "The Flight Home"), Budd Leser, Jon Slott, Fred Lipp, Margaret Lowery, Richard Broderick, and Dan Johnson, who collectively wrote the majority of the scripts during Family Theater's first year. Mark Kearney, Bob O'Sullivan, John Kelley, and Fred Niblo Jr. were some of the talented writers who joined the program after the first year.

Frequently plagued by last-minute crises procuring scripts, actors, hosts, and financing, somehow the show was broadcast every week, aided by an occasional rerun. Some of the most notable and well-received programs included Fred Lipp's "The Hound of Heaven," based on Francis Thompson's epic poem, first broadcast on October 2, 1947; "God and a Red Scooter," written by Timothy Mulvey and reprised five times; "The Littlest Angel," by Charles Tazewell; "Stolen Symphony," written by James Reuter, SJ, and Mark Kearney, and "Passion and Death," the work of Jon Slott.[45]

Because of its popularity and through the efforts of Edgar Kobak, Family Theater programs were picked up by more and more stations. In December 1947 a Family Theater press release listed the coverage as 338 stations on the Mutual Network, plus an additional 269 stations throughout the world on Armed Forces Radio. Rapid expansion had by October 1948 given Family Theater "the distinction of being the largest sustaining program on any network in the world."[46] Exactly one year later Peyton claimed that the programs were being carried on 432 stations in the United States, plus Armed Forces Radio and in Canada through the Canadian Broadcasting Corporation (CBC). By 1954 Family Theater was aired on 450 Mutual stations, plus 300 foreign stations and the Voice of America, which broadcast shows to Australia, China, New Zealand, Canada, Philippines, Hawaii, Puerto Rico, Japan, Korea, Ireland, France, Germany, Italy, and throughout South America.[47]

Family Theater's rapid expansion, though a strain on resources, was welcomed by the general public and greeted with rave reviews. Without underestimating the significant contributions of his many assistants, Peyton felt the product itself explained its popularity: "If you have a good product and are honest and sincere when you tell people about it, they'll buy it. If your product is any good they'll keep buying it. On our program we have the best product in the world, PRAYER. Through Family Theater we advertise it."[48]

Family Theater drew great applause for its selection of shows and their originality, including adaptations of biographical histories, famous short stories, novels, and legends. It was the magic of Father Peyton himself, however, that continued to mesmerize those with whom he came in contact. One writer's praise was filled with a challenge to her readers, "His [Peyton's] untiring zeal in getting this fine series on the air and keeping it there has now become legend. The product of that zeal is still very much of a reality, and if you and your family are not devotees of the program give it a hearing." The personal cause that Peyton avowed was also noted:

> He is literally "a salesman of Our Lady" bearing humiliations and labors, living out of a suitcase, traveling by land and air. No sacrifice is considered too great; no demand too trivial when there is an opportunity to preach and work for the restoration of the daily Family Rosary in every home.[49]

Family Theater Comes of Age

The backing of Edgar Kobak, who considered Family Theater the "prestige program" of the Mutual Network,[50] and the immediate success of the series in many circles led to special broadcasts almost immediately. The first special program, titled "The World's Greatest Mother," was broadcast on Mother's Day, May 11, 1947. Originating from New York, the program featured a recitation of five mysteries associated closely with the motherhood of Mary: Annunciation, Nativity, Finding of Jesus in the Temple, Crucifixion, and Coronation (the same set originally scheduled for the May 13, 1945, program). Ethel Barrymore narrated the program with Irene Dunne, Ruth Hussey, Rosalind Russell, Loretta Young, Don Ameche, Charles Boyer, Pat O'Brien, Bing Crosby, Charles Murphy, and Margaret O'Brien reading the prayers.[51] The program's high ratings prompted Peyton to approach Kobak requesting a similar show for Christmas. "The Joyful Hour," which aired on December 20, 1947, and originated from Mutual's station in Los Angeles, featured eighteen Hollywood stars in a recitation of the Joyful Mysteries. The program was so well received that it was reprised on Christmas Day.[52] *Variety* gave the broadcast high marks:

Rev. Patrick Peyton, C.S.C., progenitor and director of "The Family Crusade" series on Mutual brought this year's efforts to a highly inspirational climax last Saturday night with an hour's Christmas presentation entailing the services of 18 film and radio names. Even those outside the faith couldn't have helped but be deeply impressed with the subdued devotion, the fine dovetailing of dramatic narrative with music and the overall insinuating cadence of the program. The general effect was a thing of aural beauty and ritualistic power.[53]

Piggy-backing on the success of the Christmas show, an Easter program, "The Triumphant Hour," was broadcast on March 28, 1948. This dramatic presentation of the Glorious Mysteries featured another all-star cast, including such regulars as Ann Blyth, Ruth Hussey, and Don Ameche, teamed with some newcomers, Fibber McGee and Molly, Jerry Colonna, and the Dionne quintuplets from Canada. The *Boston Post* described the program as "a solemn and stirring reenactment of the glorious resurrection of Christ . . . one of the most inspiring observances of Easter ever presented."[54] Programs for Mother's Day, Christmas, and Easter became annual events in the late 1940s and early 1950s. On May 8, 1949, a special Mother's Day program in honor of Our Lady of Fatima, with Charles Boyer, Ann Jamison, and Loretta Young, was aired. The first "Thanksgiving Hour," which Jerome Lawyer, CSC, extolled as "one of the best of all programs," was broadcast on November 22, 1950, and starred Richard Widmark, Pat O'Brien, Ezio Pinza, Ann Blyth, and Jo Stafford.[55] Reviewers continued to be amazed at Peyton's ability to draft stars for his shows. The *Hollywood Reporter* commented, "The actor–producer–writer list [for Family Theater] looks like it was copied from the motion picture and radio yearbooks."[56]

Rather than relying on their star power, Peyton promoted the special programs through a barrage of advertisements and mailings. For the May 8, 1948, "World's Greatest Mother" program Peyton sent to every parish in the country thirty colorful and attractive posters giving the date and time of the broadcast. Similarly a photo-offset of an April 11, 1948, *New York Times* story on Peyton in Hollywood was sent to all Catholic parochial schools, private schools, and academies. National organizations such as the Knights of Columbus, Catholic Daughters of America, NCCM and NCCW local affiliates, Knights of St. John, Notre Dame alumni, and the St. Vincent de Paul Society were contacted and encouraged to promote the program.[57]

In addition to high ratings, Family Theater's quality programming resulted in many accolades, both inside and outside the Church. In 1947 and 1948 the California Congress of Parents and Teachers, Inc., presented its annual Radio Award to Family Theater "for outstanding public service to the welfare of the family." The Ohio State University awarded Family Theater its religious division prize for three consecutive years (1948–50) noting "its wide appeal and fine presentation of the value of religion in everyday living." The anniversary issue of *Radio and Television Life Magazine* lauded Family Theater as an "outstanding new program series"; the General Federation of Women's Clubs awarded its 1950–51 radio prize to Family Theater for "best network program for adults." *Radio Annual* selected *The Joyful Hour* as one of the five "Outstanding Broadcasts of 1947." In 1949 the Council of Catholic Women for the Archdiocese of Milwaukee presented its highest award to Family Theater for its "outstanding and compelling influence in the restoration of family life to its proper dignity."[58]

Even more gratifying to Peyton than these awards was recognition from the Holy Father. In a personal letter Pope Pius XII lauded Peyton and his ministry:

> You may, therefore, count with confidence, beloved son, on the continued encouragement and prayerful support of the Common Father of the sore-tried universal Christian household, in the measure that your radio broadcast of the Good Tidings, avoiding the perils of mere showmanship with programs of reverent and becoming instruction, song and story, gives ever fuller and more genuine expression to one of Our heart's deepest desires.[59]

In spite of its large audience and numerous awards, Family Theater was still financially insecure. The free air time provided by Mutual and the donated services of the Hollywood celebrities reduced costs to approximately one-tenth the norm, but approximately $2000 weekly was required to pay script writers, directors and office personnel, musicians, and other production fees.[60] From the outset Peyton organized massive letter-writing campaigns soliciting donations. Letters were sent with a brochure that read, "SUPPORT FAMILY THEATER—IT'S YOUR PROGRAM." With a mailing list that grew to thirty thousand by late 1946, Peyton was able to meet his needs, but not without much consternation on the part of all associated with the apostolate. Steiner told Peyton that individual donations were inherently insecure since they were based solely on audience appreciation, pragmatically pointing out, "Looking at the activity from a business viewpoint, it does not seem to be too stable."[61] The new archbishop of Los Angeles, James Francis McIntyre, also was concerned about Family Theater's financial stability since it appeared to him the operation was not well organized. The vice-provincial of the newly formed Eastern Priests Province of Holy Cross, James Connerton, CSC,[62] tried to assure McIntyre that donations were adequate and the ministry was more secure than it might appear.[63] However, the program would not enjoy the security of predictable financial support until 1969 when the "All for Her Fund" was established.

Peyton's lack of financial acumen did not mean he could not deal shrewdly with the whole issue of economic backing for Family Theater. In the summer of 1946, while on a postordination trip home to Ireland, which had been delayed by World War II, Peyton met the shipping magnate J. Peter Grace, initiating a relationship that would last until the priest's death in 1992. Grace over the years was a source for loans and outright gifts, but his financial acumen and influence were even more helpful. In late 1948 Grace suggested tactics to get Mutual to pay the majority of the production costs that were out-of-pocket expenses for Family Theater. The first step Grace recommended was to stall paying overdue bills to Mutual. Jerome Lawyer, CSC, explained Family Theater's position:

> Our purpose for stalling and asking for cancellation [of our debt] is part of a well-conceived and well-advised plan to get Mutual to undertake payment of Family Theater's production expenses. This plan was suggested by high persons in radio circles who feel, as we have felt for some time, that Mutual is getting the lion's share of benefits from Family Theater without contributing anything to the support of the production costs.
>
> Mutual recognizes the great reputation of Family Theater. The network has no other dramatic program that will compare with it, either from the excellence of purpose, scripts, acting — or what Mutual brags most about — the great array of radio and screen stars on the program. . . . While we realize that we are getting a lot of benefit in the way of getting publicity and putting our message across — we do not overlook the fact that Mutual is profiting greatly from our free advertisement and the consistently favorable [to Mutual] publicity that Family Theater offers. I know of no program that has received such wide and universally aclaimed [sic] recognition.[64]

The stalling tactic worked: by 1949 Mutual began to assume the expenses for the orchestra, musical direction, and production management.[65]

Family Theater had become a fixture on weekly radio and was expanding its operations, but no formal structure for the whole Family Rosary organization (Albany and Hollywood) existed. As early as December 1946 both Lawyer and Steiner realized the need for incorporation to safeguard the operation, help its fiscal stability, and give it legal status. At the outset two stipulations were mandated: (1) the provincial be president of the board and (2) the organization remain nonprofit. Family Theater was incorporated on February 25, 1947, with Thomas Steiner, CSC, as president, Christopher O'Toole, CSC, as vice president, and Patrick Peyton, CSC, as secretary-treasurer. As the years passed the composition of the board changed, based principally on changes of leadership within Holy Cross.[66] Family Theater's two principal purposes were:

1. To prepare, produce, and broadcast a series of radio programs to inspire listeners to institute family prayer as a conventional and consistent activity of family life and to perform each and every act necessary or convenient in connection with the preparation, production, and broadcast of such radio programs.

2. To publicize and promote family prayer as a conventional and consistent activity of family life and to educate and inspire the general public to institute family prayer in their homes.[67]

The establishment of a board brought some structure to Family Rosary, but it was the work of numerous others that kept the day-to-day operations functioning smoothly. In 1948 Bob Fennell, whom Peyton had met in 1945 during his first trip to California, became the first business/production manager and guided Family Theater operations for its first two critical years until Joe Russell took the production reins in February 1950. Clerical assistance was provided by two of Peyton's nieces from Scranton, Catherine and Mary Gallagher. Accounts and finance in California were handled by Richard Rowe. In Albany an army of volunteers from the College of St. Rose, the Vincentian Institute, and Holy Names Academy handled the mass mailings.[68]

Peyton was in almost constant contact with his provincial, requesting that additional Holy Cross religious be assigned to the Family Rosary ministry. Recognizing that Connerton, his former mentor, would bestow his "protection, love, and guidance"[69] on the ministry, Peyton nearly always asked for those who were newly ordained, considering it "so essential that [they] be docile, humble, and full of fire for Our Lady and for the Rosary." It seems likely that Peyton wanted men from the seminary because they would be more docile and willing to submit to his control. On his side, Connerton, although eager to assign more priests to Family Rosary, and even establish a religious foundation in Albany, could not move immediately, however, for personnel and financial resources were scarce in the fledgling vice-province.[70]

Between 1946 and 1950 several Holy Cross religious were assigned to Family Rosary. In the fall of 1946, when the Mutual free air time was secured, Francis Gartland, CSC, was sent west to Hollywood to assist with future publicity needs. The next January Raymond Finan, CSC, was also assigned to Hollywood to help write scripts. In January 1948 Albert Heinzer, CSC, was sent to Albany to take over the parochial duties at St. Madeleine Sophie parish in Schenectady, freeing Francis Woods to work full time with Family Rosary.[71] Gartland and Finan stayed with Family Rosary only a short time, but Heinzer would play a major role as overseer of operations in Hollywood. Although Peyton was still technically the chaplain to the Holy Cross brothers, his work took him away from Albany much of the time, so Jerome Lawyer, CSC, picked up the slack while supervising the Albany office.[72] Additional personnel to join Peyton's team included John Murphy, CSC, in 1949 and Joseph Quinn, CSC, and John Corr, CSC, in 1950. Murphy and Quinn would serve for many years in key positions, especially in the international crusades inaugurated in 1948.

As the commitment of the Congregation to Peyton's apostolate increased, so did the conflict between Peyton and the personnel assigned to him. It was clear to those community members assigned to Family Rosary that Father Peyton was "in complete charge" and that all "decisions . . . are subject to change by him." John Murphy, CSC, commented, "Peyton made it clear to all that he and he alone dictated policy. He did not allow another to be placed in a position that would allow one to dictate any form of policy for Family Theater or Family Rosary."[73] Often Peyton would arrive from one of his countless trips and begin to dictate orders. Lawyer once explained,

> Father Peyton has been with us the past few weeks. You yourself know how hard it is to get anything done when he is around. He had us spend most of our time writing sermons and preparing a little booklet on how to say the rosary. I don't think Father realizes that there are everyday chores that have to be taken care of.[74]

Peyton often seemed unconcerned with office routines, forcing personnel to adapt to his schedule when he visited. He routinely appeared oblivious to the needs of his fellow Holy Cross religious as well. Lawyer and Murphy often commiserated about their mutual frustration. With a comical twist Lawyer wrote, "Don't work too hard. You simply can't do everything Fr. Pat suggests and stay, at the same time, away from the grave.... Remember, I have the first priority on cracking up." But Lawyer had to admit, "The work is being accomplished even if it is accomplished the difficult way. So keep up the spirits and just smile when tempted to swing."[75]

In addition to the friction within the apostolate, the newly arrived archbishop of Los Angeles was a source of external tension. McIntyre raised questions concerning the canonical status of Family Theater and Family Rosary, especially with respect to finances. Because he feared that financial problems with the Hollywood operation might harm the archdiocese, he wanted written assurance that the Congregation of Holy Cross would assume all responsibility for the policy and financial obligations of Family Theater. The archbishop was correct in stating that Peyton was "expending large sums of money... without any close check by Holy Cross."[76] He also wanted to know if canonically the local operation came under his jurisdiction. McIntyre was wary of the control Peyton seemed to enjoy and asked that "the Community... have more direct and immediate supervision of the organization." He observed Peyton as a loose cannon in his domain, a situation which McIntyre would not tolerate. Peyton attempted to mollify the archbishop by thanking him for his support of Family Theater programming. While McIntyre was not wholly satisfied, the conflict eventually died away with the erection of permanent organizational and better financial structures for Family Theater.[77]

The archbishop was also concerned that Family Theater had no permanent base of operation. When Peyton first came to Los Angeles he was hosted by the Immaculate Heart of Mary Sisters who operated Immaculate Heart of Mary College on Franklin Avenue in Hollywood. The Sisters were happy to provide for Peyton's needs, but as Family Theater's operations expanded it became obvious that a permanent location was needed.[78] As would be the case countless times in the future, Father Peyton's need was satisfied quite unexpectedly through the generosity of a benefactor who had met him, was enamored of his personality, and became a disciple in his ministry. In early 1948 Jacoba Buchenau, a nurse anesthetist who had profited from canny real estate investments, offered Peyton a large home that she had recently acquired at 7201 Sunset Boulevard. Buchenau had met Peyton through her membership in the Tabernacle Society at Marymount High School, which Peyton often visited when he was in California. The house and property, worth approximately $60,000, needed repairs and still had a mortgage, but Buchenau promised to present the property in a ready condition free of all encumbrances. Peyton secured the proper permissions from Holy Cross and Archbishop McIntyre to accept the gracious benefaction, and the first permanent home for Family Theater was blessed by McIntyre on December 8, 1948.[79]

Family Theater and Films

Family Theater's triumphant entry into the electronic medium of radio was followed by a successful debut in the increasingly popular instrument of television. In May 1949 Family Theater sponsored its first television film, a twenty-minute short titled *The Road to Peace,* starring Bing Crosby and Ann Blyth, and produced by Twentieth Century Fox studios.[80] The film depicted the evils of the world and suggested that they could be solved through daily prayer. Positive reviews encouraged Peyton to press forward with a series of films under the guidance of Jerry Fairbanks Productions.[81] In April 1950 a star-studded cast, including Pat O'Brien, Maureen O'Sullivan, Jane Wyatt, Don Ameche, Roddy McDowell, and Jack Haley, was assembled for *The Triumphant Hour,* a film version of the successful radio show that depicted the passion, death, and resurrection of Christ. The production was broadcast on CBS, NBC, ABC, and the Dumont networks, plus some twenty-seven independent stations across the country.[82] The film's success[83] led to the production of *The Joyful Hour,* featuring Ruth Hussey, Nelson Leigh, Lloyd Corrigan, and Pat O'Brien, for the Christmas season later in the year. The production, which aired on ninety-two stations on its debut, was called "a notable contribution to television" and praised for its message: "Father Peyton ... follows in his video film the precepts which have guided his FAMILY THEATER. His cast and his productions are thoroughly professional, and he enriches his religious presentations with a knowing appreciation for dramatic values."[84]

Success drove Father Peyton to produce more quality films conveying the need for family prayer. *Hill Number One,* also produced in 1951, depicted the story of Golgotha and the resurrection as told by an army chaplain on the battlefield to a disgruntled artillery crew hurling howitzer shells at an enemy hill. This film, starring Ruth Hussey, Joan Leslie, Leif Erickson, Jeanne Cagney, and Gene Lockhart, and featuring the debut of James Dean, was one of the most popular ever produced and received rave reviews. The *New York Times* commented, "One of the most nearly perfect performances ever seen on TV, mixing dramatic import with compelling simplicity."[85] This was followed by *That I May See,* the story of Bartimaeus, the blind beggar (Mark 10:46–52), which featured Jeffrey Lynn, Ruth Hussey, Richard Hale, and Raymond Burr. The *Hollywood Reporter* rated the film "as the producer's finest effort and certainly one of the finest films ever made for the medium."[86]

In 1952 Peyton delivered three more successful film productions. *The World's Greatest Mother,* described as "another epic in Father Peyton's films of Biblical lore," followed the important events in the life of the Blessed Virgin Mary. Later in the year *The Hound of Heaven,* following on the successful radio program of the same title and starring Rosalind Russell and MacDonald Carey, and *A Star Shall Rise,* which featured Raymond Burr, John Crawford, and Richard Hale as the three wise men who discovered the Christ child, were well received. These films and those produced earlier were reprised over the next several years by stations across the country.[87]

The general reaction to Peyton's films was very positive. Jack Gould, the leading critic of the *New York Times,* extolled Peyton and his products:

> The leading producer in this field is the Rev. Patrick Peyton, a Catholic priest of Hollywood, who has made a number of superb religious films with top-flight motion picture stars. He almost alone has seemed to recognize that with a mass media the mode of presentation is every bit as important as the message.[88]

Al Scalpone, a Hollywood public relations giant, echoed similar sentiments: "Every single program — radio or TV — produced by the Crusade, has received praise from the public and press. They are programs of which any member of the Church can be proud."[89]

Positive comments like these did little to assuage the anxiety of Edmund Gibbons, Peyton's ordinary in Albany, who warned that working with Hollywood celebrities constituted "playing with fire." The bishop was especially upset when the *New York Daily News* published a photo layout of Mona Freeman, who had participated in one of Peyton's productions, "with her breasts fully exposed and her seductive smile." He stated, "I cannot for the life of me see how you can expect the blessing of the Immaculate Mother of God on your Rosary crusade when you risk your reputation by securing the theatrical services of brazen women with shady reputations." He concluded, "No doubt, you have plenty of advisors. I do not intend to be one but merely to voice what I know to be the sentiments of a good many that the Crusade for Mary can get on very well without the expensive and sometimes disedifying aid of the Hollywood stage."

Peyton acknowledged that there was much worldliness in Hollywood, but defended his use of celebrities: "The Hollywood stars, our own brothers and sisters, created by God, and destined for Heaven as all of us, are grateful from the bottom of their hearts for an opportunity to use their talents for the advantage of God rather than for the advantage of the world."[90]

Television's ability to widen the reach of Peyton's family prayer mission was matched by the increased costs of film production. Before the production of films, records show that assets always met costs with some surplus remaining, but additional costs for films, office personnel, plus the required assessment paid annually to the Eastern Province, necessitated some plan.[91] While Peyton continued to speak at Triduums and the base of his financial appeal letters grew greatly, it was clear that the ministry could not continue forward without some financial base from which to operate.

The key to financial stability for Family Rosary was, almost from the outset, centered about J. Peter Grace, president of the W. R. Grace Company, who met Peyton, as previously mentioned, onboard the SS *Washington* during the priest's trip home to Ireland in July 1946. One year earlier Grace had become head of the multimillion-dollar international corporation started by his great-grandfather William Russell Grace in 1854. The company made its name in shipping, with special interest in Latin American operations.[92] It is clear that the relationship between Grace and Peyton was one of mutual admiration and respect, with each influencing the other in various ways over their long friendship. Jerome Lawyer, CSC, claims that Grace was the greatest influence in Peyton's adult life, but that the inspiration was mutual: "Pat tried to be Peter Grace and Peter tried to be Pat Peyton."[93] Grace firmly believed in Peyton and his work: "It has been a great thrill to have any part in the Family Rosary Crusade. As I tell everyone I meet when I can buttonhole them for a minute, the Family Rosary seems to me to be the only answer to the situation in which we all find ourselves today."[94]

Peyton expressed similar sentiments: "All the burdens I feel upon my shoulders, be they big or little, I can take to Peter Grace and he does not begrudge his precious time to lend his mind and his heart to face those problems and make the decision that is always the right one."[95]

Film costs, which ran from $20,000 to $40,000 per program, were Peyton's immediate concern. Through a series of "loans" contracted with the Grace National Bank in New York the necessary funds were obtained. Each new film was financed through a separate loan account bearing the name of the production.[96] While technically Grace had loaned Family Rosary money for the various films, it is common belief that the debts were never paid, most probably at the request of Grace himself.

Grace also worked with Peyton to create an overall permanent financial plan for the expanding Family Rosary operations. Grace believed that Peyton's great contribution to Family Rosary was his spiritual guidance, not his financial development efforts:

> Father Peyton has reached what appears to be the end of his development road for no other reason than a financial obstacle. It seems to us imperative that this famed apostle of Christ be permitted not only full time on the spiritual work required but also that the financial worries which are so handicapping any attempt to plan for the future, be taken away from Father Peyton and his associates.[97]

In the fall of 1951 Grace began to speak with Family Rosary officials about approaching five hundred wealthy individuals and institutions that would annually donate $500 to the apostolate, thus forging a solid financial base. Less than a year later Grace expanded his idea, suggesting that any reasonable source of funds should be explored. In response the Family Prayer Foundation, under the direction of Father John Lynch, CSC, was established in February 1952. Four categories of contributors were targeted: Group 1: five hundred people contributing $500 annually ($250,000); Group 2: one thousand people contributing $10 per month ($120,000); Group 3: five thousand working young women and housewives contributing fifty cents per week ($130,000); Group 4: four thousand schools contributing $15 annually ($60,000). It was believed that the annual contribution of $540,000 would pay for all Family Rosary and Family Theater endeavors.[98] When the plan languished, the firm of Rich and Associates was hired to handle promotion and development. When this relationship also foundered, Peyton entrusted all the major financial decisions of the organization to Grace.[99]

The need for financial stability did not obviate the fact that Family Theater had achieved great success and recognition. By the close of 1952 the organization had been launched, had expanded into two media, radio and television, and had been well received by secular and ecclesiastical individuals and groups. Al Scalpone, a marketing executive for the media, encouraged Peyton to keep on the offensive with his campaign: "With radio and television you can accomplish — nay, *are accomplishing* — the objective of the crusade on a scale never dreamed possible before the age of electronics."[100] Thomas O'Neill, chairman of the board of Mutual, praised Peyton's accomplishments:

> I am happy to be privileged to join with your many other friends at this time in paying to you my sincere and everlasting tribute for your stimulating and inspirational work in bringing to millions your theme that "The family that prays together — stays together." . . . It is our cherished hope that for many years to come it may be our privilege and pleasure to participate with you in bringing to millions of American families these now nationally known [and] worthwhile programs.[101]

Support and the conviction that Family Rosary was needed by the society and the Church was also voiced by members of Holy Cross. The superior general, Christopher O'Toole, speaking of the rapid expansion of the crusade, asked "that all Provinces and Vice-Provinces give their support as much as possible" to its efforts.[102] More personally James Connerton, CSC, whose reelection as provincial at the 1952 Eastern Province Chapter was received with great joy by Family Rosary personnel, wrote to Peyton, "All I can say is that you have my full confidence and I hope Our Lord and Our Lady may lead you to even better and bigger things for their sakes."[103]

Conclusion

Patrick Peyton's successful debut on national radio in May 1945 was only the first of many triumphs in the use of public media. During the latter 1940s and early 1950s this contemporary apostle of the rosary, through his own initiative and a few minor "miracles," was able to generate a national following through his promotion of family prayer on radio and television. His charismatic personality drew disciples from many corners, but most prominently the stars of stage, screen, and radio in Hollywood and, in the person of J. Peter Grace, a lifelong friend and source of significant influence and financial acumen. Adding to the list of "miracles" was the gift of thirty minutes of free radio time each week over the leading network of the day, the Mutual Broadcasting System. With his twofold ministry, Family Rosary and Family Theater, established on opposite ends of the country, Patrick Peyton was poised to unify and expand his operation as the heyday of American Catholicism took hold in the 1950s.

Chapter 4

The Crusade for Family Prayer, 1952–60

As the 1950s rolled along, the name Patrick Peyton, through his dual works of Family Rosary and Family Theater, was becoming a household word. While Bishop Fulton Sheen dazzled audiences and attracted a following through his routine appearances on NBC's *The Catholic Hour*, and especially his *Life Is Worth Living* television series (1952–57), Peyton and his ministry were also being recognized as evidenced by the popularity of the slogan, "The family that prays together stays together." This decade, the heyday of American Catholicism, saw the national and international expansion of Peyton's work, through the establishment of a solid financial base, the constant support of the Holy Cross community, and national recognition in ecclesiastical and secular circles. The national development of his Crusade for Family Prayer became the solid base that marked Peyton's ministry as an established institution and the foundation from which his life's work was generated.

American Catholic Life in the 1950s

Emerging from its "ghetto mentality," Catholicism in the United States during the 1950s reached its apex in participation and popularity, approaching full acceptance in American society. The end of the immigrant Church, coming as a result of the immigration restriction acts of 1921 and 1924, led to greater Catholic assimilation. While national churches continued to function, their ethnic solidarity began to break down as the continued infusion of new immigrants dissipated. After World War II Catholics entered colleges and universities in greater numbers than before, mostly due to the Servicemen's Readjustment Act, the so-called GI Bill. Moving forward economically and socially, Catholics no longer felt

73

the need to apologize for their faith; instead they became more vocal about its expression.

During the postwar period, American Catholics evolved in their personal and communal theological understanding and faith practice. Before this period most Catholics viewed their faith as a combination of private ritual practices, personal moral behavior, and affirmation and adherence to Church teachings. The public practice of the faith was not heavily emphasized in the practical experience of most American Catholics. After the war, and especially during the decade of the 1950s, the ritualistic understanding of Church practice gave way to a more "public Catholicism."[1] One significant characteristic of the period was a greater sense of unity. Will Herberg in *Protestant — Catholic — Jew* argued that Catholics in the 1950s began to view their faith as a proper way to be American; there was no longer a need to hide one's faith. He explained, "Religion has become the primary symbol of 'heritage' and church membership the most appropriate form of 'belonging' under contemporary American conditions."[2] The historian David O'Brien agrees that the period was one of greater unity, but argues that solidarity was generated as a reaction to the continued presence of anti-Catholic forces. The united front in defense of the faith and refutation of the anti-Catholic contentions of Paul Blanshard in *American Freedom and Catholic Power* (1950) illustrates O'Brien's point. Catholicism's more visible presence was a second shift in Church practice. During the decade the Catholic population rose from 27.7 to 40.8 million; 4 million children attended Catholic schools, double the number in 1920. Seminaries and convents were filled with candidates for the priesthood and religious life. Sunday Mass attendance was 78 percent, an all-time high.[3]

The Church in the United States in the 1950s can be described by some clearly definable characteristics. The noted historian of American religion, Robert Wuthnow, describes a spirituality of indwelling, common for all religious practice in the period, that stressed God's presence in sacred places. One of these sacred places was the home, where families prayed, children read and played games, and domestic tranquility reigned. The home became sacralized; it was "where spirituality was primarily located."[4] Parish-centered Catholicism, a second characteristic of the period, is consistent with Wuthnow's spirituality of indwelling. Geographic parishes, generated in large measure by suburbanization, replaced ethnic national churches. The pastor was a unifying symbol for the community and the leader of parish spiritual, recreational, and social activities; his authority was paramount. People were not averse to this situation, but rather were generally content to simply "pay, pray, and obey." The Church was the center of life for the average Catholic in every significant and visible way.

Along with Americans in general, Catholics strongly opposed Communism and supported all efforts to root out any of its vestiges. Catholic opposition to Communism and Communist nations was constant, beginning with the Red Scare of 1919, moving to the denunciation of Franklin Roosevelt's recognition of the Soviet Union in 1933 and support for Franco's forces in the Spanish Civil War, then culminating in the events of the 1950s, especially the polemic of Senator Joseph McCarthy and his protracted but unsuccessful attempts to identify Communists in the American government and military. Along the road some notable people carried the banner of American Catholic anti-Communism, including the aforementioned James Gillis, CSP, Patrick Scanlan, editor of the *Brooklyn Tablet,* Father John O'Brien of Notre Dame, and most especially Cardinal Francis Spellman, the archbishop of New York, who in his powerful position as leader of the American Church and personal friend of Pope Pius XII assisted all who stood against the tide of atheism promoted by Communism.

The 1950s also produced a fertile environment for the revival of Catholic conservatism in the United States. As described by Patrick Allitt,[5] a conservative Catholic force was created from a coalition of anti-Communists, disillusioned ex-Communists, and opponents of liberalism. Catholic conservatives banded together and went into battle in order to challenge the specter of Communism, both foreign and domestic, and to provide an alternative to the liberal response, which was considered too weak and lacking conviction. Capitalism received mixed reviews from these Catholic conservatives, but not so Communism, which was considered an evil that threatened to dominate the world. The revival of conservatism was deemed necessary if Christian civilization, with the United States now its chief guardian, was to be preserved. Allitt summarizes the prevailing conservative approach:

> The Catholic conservatives took a militant anti-Soviet and anti-Communist position.... They understood communism as a Christian heresy, viewed the events of the cold war in religious terms, and believed themselves to be the new defenders of the heartland of Christendom, defenders of God's truth, while showing a special solicitude for the Christians of the "captive nations" behind the Iron Curtain and the "Bamboo Curtain." Many of them believed the final struggle of the world was imminent, that a third world

war, heavy with theological as well as political significance, had, in effect, already begun.[6]

American Catholics became upwardly mobile in certain visible ways but continued to languish in intellectual endeavors and positions of power and prominence. Better education and general economic prosperity aided Catholic efforts to succeed in business as well as the legal and medical professions, but in 1955, as stated in chapter 2, John Tracy Ellis, the dean of American Catholic historians, asked why a dearth of Catholic intellectual life still existed in America.[7] Despite their numbers American Catholics also remained underrepresented in the decision-making positions of education, politics, and business.

The family crisis that began in the 1920s continued in the decade of the 1950s to be manifest in various ways, and thus Catholics renewed their efforts to define the problem and to seek answers. The Jesuit sociologist John L. Thomas suggested that the Catholic challenge was how to maintain its distinctive understanding of the family within a society that saw no great value in its basic precepts:

> Complex and changing American culture neither supports nor explicitly opposes Catholic goals. It provides a more or less tolerant climate. But at the same time it provides ideals and concepts that are either strong pressures against our reaching our goals or stable modes of wearing us down.[8]

The Dominican priest Gerard Meath, who suggested that a false distinction was being made between the secular and the sacred in society, advised families to see themselves more as a Christian unit that should seek its solidarity through corporate worship, especially the Mass and other sacraments.[9]

Family life during the 1950s was experienced differently compared with the past. The common view that the 1950s was the last gasp of traditional family life before the revolution of the 1960s ushered in a significant shift in values has been challenged by the sociologist Elaine May, who suggests the 1950s brought, "the first wholehearted effort to create a home that would fulfill virtually all of its members' personal needs through an energized and expressive personal life." Arlene Skolnick agrees with May on the uniqueness of the decade, but suggests that the period was a false front, "the topsoil that protected the seed of rebellion that was germinating below."[10]

The American Catholic hierarchy voiced its opinion on the decade and its family crisis, describing it as a "present danger more fearsome than the atomic bomb."[11] Karl Alter, archbishop of Cincinnati, in a 1951 address to the Family Life Conference, signaled the call to reform in order to save society:

> It is obvious and, therefore, it may seem unnecessary to declare that the well being of the family is the measure of our national well-being. What is obvious, however, can easily be forgotten. Since the family is the primary social unit, it should be evident that if family life disintegrates the stability and welfare of the nation as a whole will suffer.[12]

Richard Cushing, archbishop of Boston, concurred with Gerard Meath, suggesting that families must return to more "frequent reception of the sacraments and sacramentalizing our daily lives."[13]

As expected, Peyton continued to plead for the family rosary as the solution to the family crisis. He proclaimed,

> For a family to operate together daily, to be constantly aware of their dignity and their mission on earth to keep alive within themselves the truth that they are God's children — ...there is something more needed in that home than, let us say, the material furnishing of that home.... There is needed in the family something spiritual that will hold them together — and that thing is family prayer. To bring into that family's life the completeness and perfection they need — the Family Rosary is needed.[14]

The Crusade for Family Prayer Organizes

The expansion of Family Theater into television, its continued weekly radio broadcast, and the initiation by Family Rosary of the international rosary crusade (chapter 5) strained the efforts of personnel, and thus Peyton pressured his superiors for more religious to join his ministry. As in the past, efforts centered around obtaining men who had just been ordained. Competition for personnel was strong, since all the apostolic endeavors of the Eastern Province were on the rise and the number of men available, while steadily increasing, could not meet all the expanding needs. In 1952 Lawyer informed Peyton that Father Baker High School, a new ministry of the province in Buffalo, New York, would receive the new personnel Peyton had hoped to receive. In a resigned tone Lawyer reported, "At least we aren't losing any. Next year we will be able to get two, I'm sure. And from then on several a year."[15] The next year,

Peyton, in his usual manner of associating his work with that of the Blessed Virgin, wrote to Connerton:

> Dear Father Provincial, I do hope that you won't forget us when you are assigning your newly ordained priests. I do hope and pray, dear Father, that you will lighten the load on our shoulders by giving us one of the best. I know your love for this work and for Our Lady will always prompt you to do what is best for us.[16]

Peyton's requests did bring Holy Cross men to his ministry, including John Lynch and Archibald McDowell in 1951, John Corr and James Mannis in 1953, and Philip Higgins in 1956.

The bid for additional personnel for Family Rosary was only one part in a general campaign to improve the organization's structure. Incorporation of Family Rosary was an important legal maneuver that satisfied requirements for nonprofit status and allowed contributors to donate to a registered institution, but clearer and more effective canonical organization was needed to mollify the Church at large and the Congregation of Holy Cross specifically. Connerton had to walk a tightrope, bringing structure to Family Rosary and thus meeting the objections of Archbishop McIntyre in Los Angeles on the "loose" organization of Family Theater, while simultaneously giving Peyton sufficient freedom to operate in his unique apostolic position within the Congregation. In December 1948 Connerton appointed Jerome Lawyer, CSC, "religious director," a position similar to a local superior.[17] The vice-provincial explained, "This appointment is designed so [as] not to hamper Father Peyton or any of you in the work you have been doing, and, on the other hand, to give religious character to your operations."[18] By 1956 both Connerton and the superior general, Christopher O'Toole, CSC, had suggested establishing a formal *domus formata* for the collective Family Rosary/Family Theater operation, but the Eastern Provincial Council rejected the plan, stating that the present organization must be maintained, "unless we want to curb and possibly destroy or stifle Father Peyton's work." The council viewed Peyton's work as "far in advance of the Church's and canonists, who have not caught up with the channels of religious propaganda, namely, TV, Radio, Press, and Outdoor Advertising." The councilors concluded with a biblical reference, "to pour Father Peyton into the mold of [the] 1918 [*sic*,–1917] conception of Canonical establishments would be like pouring new wine into old bottles."[19]

One question that continued to linger, especially because of physical logistics, was the relationship of Family Rosary to Family Theater.

The erection of the Eastern Province of Priests in 1948 placed Family Theater in an awkward position, since the ministry operated within the geographic confines of the Indiana Province.[20] In addition, the rapid expansion of Family Theater operations in both radio and television, the name recognition that came with this success, and disagreements on methods and programming associated with *Family Theater of the Air* created a strained relationship, in the minds of some, between Hollywood and Albany. John Murphy, CSC, director of the Albany office, tried to mend fences between the two offices in a letter to Robert Fennell, business manager in Hollywood:

> Father Pat told me that he may have given you the wrong impression that there were strained relations between the two offices. There have been times when we here in the Family Rosary headquarters have criticized some of the Family Theater broadcasts and even some of the methods and policies of running Family Theater, but I assure you, Bob, that those criticisms were raised because of our deep interest and devotion to Family Theater. We have always tried to be objective in our criticism and to give credit whenever credit was due.
>
> I hope, Bob, that the wrong impression will be corrected. Should it continue, it would certainly harm the work of Family Theater and Family Rosary. After all we are working toward one end for Our Lady and family prayer. It would be a shame if after preaching family unity and family harmony we did not have these qualities in our own family relations.[21]

The perception of a strained relationship and the logistical problem of having offices at opposite ends of the country brought two different suggestions for a resolution. When the Eastern Vice-Province was established in May 1948, it was suggested that the Hollywood operation be placed under the direction of the Indiana Province. Jerome Lawyer, CSC, strongly objected to this idea:

> I cannot see how the Family Theatre can be separated from the Family Rosary. The Family Theater has always been and is an essential and integral part of the Family Rosary activity. If the Family Theater is placed in the western [Indiana] province, I am afraid we are going to have a house divided against itself. I am afraid it will create another of those situations where we have a dual superiorship.[22]

The second proposal, suggested by Peyton, was to centralize operations in Hollywood, because of its name recognition and recent successes, and close down the Albany office. However, Lawyer, Murphy, and other Holy Cross religious associated with the operation disagreed, suggesting that increasing the identification of Family Rosary with the glitter of Hollywood was the wrong message to send, and the public in general and Catholics specifically would be much more accepting of a program headquartered in the conservative region of Albany.[23] The eventual solution was to create "The Crusade for Family Prayer" as an organization encompassing the work of both offices under the common banner of family prayer. The Crusade was incorporated as a nonprofit religious organization in the state of New York, "for the purpose of encouraging, through the use of mass media of communication, the habit of daily family prayer in this country and abroad."[24]

The controversies and disagreements over organizational matters did not distract Peyton and the Crusade workers from continuing to promote family prayer, specifically the family rosary as "the great weapon against all the evils of family life."[25] Peyton was appreciative and encouraged by his success as evidenced by the many bishops, priests, and nuns who joined the cause and helped bring countless numbers of families to the practice of the family rosary, but he never forgot that he was only the vehicle. Mary drove the family rosary engine: "I think it is wonderful that Our Blessed Lady has chosen Holy Cross, which is dedicated in a special way to her, as the leader in the crusade to restore the Family Rosary to all the homes of the country."[26]

Peyton's eagerness to emphasize the simplicity and accessibility of family prayer sometimes gave his remarks an anti-intellectual cast. He suggested that the concept "The family that prays together stays together" was not learned from libraries or books, but rather from one's lived experience. It was from his convictions and not some theory that he came to know of the power of the rosary in his life. Once he proclaimed, "All the universities and all the colleges and all the classrooms and all the professors in the whole of the earth are nothing in comparison to the tremendous things that . . . the Rosary can teach a man."[27]

Father Peyton gained even wider notoriety and made many converts to his cause through the publication of two books in the early 1950s. *The Ear of God,* published in March 1951 and written with the assistance of Theodore Bonnet, a seasoned journalist, was an autobiographical account of Peyton's childhood, which he combined with spiritual meditations on the rosary. The book was well received, distributed widely, and promoted through a series of book signings, especially in Hollywood, whose celebrities continued to contribute to the success of his family prayer ministry.[28] In 1953 the first edition of *Father Peyton's Rosary Prayer Book* was published. Consisting of a series of meditations upon the mysteries of the rosary, the book was written upon the suggestion of Rear Admiral Edward J. Hemphill, Navy chief of chaplains, who told Peyton that sailors and soldiers had requested a simple and practical book on the rosary for use onboard ship or in the field. Peyton worked on the book with the Trappist priest M. Charles Fiddler. It was widely distributed to service personnel in a pocket-sized edition and later became an effective tool of the Family Rosary Crusade.[29]

Besides his own personal advocacy, books, and supporters, Peyton also used advertising to blanket the nation with his message. The popular *Family Theater of the Air* commercials appeared on large billboards throughout the country. The Outdoor Advertising Association of America, headquartered in Chicago, pleased with Peyton's efforts to promote the family through prayer, provided free billboard space (sixty feet by sixteen feet) throughout the country. People traveling on the major roads, especially in urban areas, often saw the slogan "The family that prays together stays together" displayed before them.[30]

The efforts of Father Peyton, through Family Rosary and Family Theater and the use of advertisements, continued to draw strong support from groups and individuals throughout the country. The Friends of Father Peyton and His Crusade, a Pittsburgh-based group that supported Peyton through annual donations and daily recitation of the rosary, was one of several groups that arose in Pennsylvania, New York, and Florida. The Apostleship of Prayer promoted the family rosary as "serving the principal ends which our Association seeks to achieve." The group urged "all Associates not only to adopt the practice of the Family Rosary, but also to participate in the rallies which will be held in this country."[31] Patrick Carroll, CSC, editor of the weekly *Ave Maria,* continued to predict a bright future for Peyton's work:

> Today, not all American Catholic families recite the Rosary; but many do, and more will. Father Patrick Peyton has made his good start, has put his hand to the plow and has not turned back. He is humble, and so the Blessed Virgin likes him. So do Hollywood's Catholic screen actors. So does everybody who admires the brave adventure to get people to pray. His great apostolate will succeed.[32]

The general applause for Peyton's efforts was summarized well in *America:*

Legends have grown up around Rev. Patrick J. Peyton, CSC, the zealous Irish priest who began the Family Rosary Crusade ten years ago. In sober fact, however, his accomplishments have been more legendary than the folklore.[33]

In 1952 Peyton was presented with the Marianist Award from the University of Dayton "because of [his] extraordinary success in fostering devotion of the Family Rosary." In 1954 he won the George Washington Honor Medal for his essay "Don't Be Afraid to Pray," which the citation called "an outstanding achievement in helping bring a better understanding of the American way of life during 1953." In 1956 he was granted honorary membership in the Fourth Degree of the Knights of Columbus, an award given only three times previously in the history of the Order.[34]

In addition to domestic success, Peyton enjoyed the continual endorsement of the Holy Father throughout the 1950s. In 1951 Pius XII published *Ingruentium Malorum,* an encyclical that promoted the practice of the family rosary:

> But it is above all in the bosom of the family that we desire the custom of the Holy Rosary to be everywhere adopted, religiously preserved and even more intensely practiced. In vain is a remedy sought for the wavering fate of civil life if the family, the principle and foundation of the human community, is not brought back to the norms of the Gospel.[35]

Peyton was obviously elated at the encyclical's publication: "This is the greatest milestone — it is assurance that the Family Rosary Crusade is blessed by God because Christ's Vicar without reservation pleaded most emphatically for it."[36] The pope prayed for God's blessing to come upon Family Rosary so it "may continue to be enthusiastically received by an ever-increasing number of Catholics."[37] In 1955 the pope, as part of the Marian year celebration, granted special indulgences to those who practice the family rosary, calling it the "antidote to the secularistic spirit of the present day." He called upon his fellow bishops and ordinaries "to assist in the conduct of the Family Rosary Crusade."[38] Pope John XXIII, shortly after assuming the Chair of Peter in 1958, continued the tradition of his predecessor in praise of Peyton's efforts:

> When parents and children gather together at the end of the day in the recitation of the Rosary, . . . [i]t is certain that they will meet with greater facility the problems of family life. Homes will thereby be converted into sanctuaries of peace. Torrents of divine favors will

come to them, even the inestimable favor of a priestly or religious vocation.[39]

The Crusade for Family Prayer Expands

International operations of Family Rosary had been initiated in 1948 with the first rosary crusades in Canada (see chapter 5), but no efforts to date had been made to start a foreign foundation for the organization. In 1950, however, Peyton entered into negotiations with James Connerton, CSC, Albert Cousineau, CSC, and Christopher O'Toole, CSC, to expand Family Rosary's operations into South America. Peyton had learned that an Argentine group, La Comisión Pico-Templo, Nuestra Señora de Fátima, headed by Celia Ruiz-Guinazu, was prepared to erect a shrine to Our Lady of Fatima near Buenos Aires. Father George DePrizio went to Argentina to review the situation and reported that Ruiz-Guinazu's group wanted "the shrine to be given to [a] group of priests performing valuable work in support of the rosary." Ruiz-Guinazu was very enthusiastic about Father Peyton and his Family Rosary ministry and hoped that Holy Cross would take administrative control of the proposed shrine.[40]

In mid-July 1950 Peyton traveled to Argentina for a three-week personal assessment of the situation. The original site for the shrine, about forty-five miles southeast of Buenos Aires, was considered "not practical" because of its distance from the capital city. The Comisión proposed a second location at Quelmes, only eight miles from the capital, and on a major highway. The site, which was offered by the Redemptorists because they lacked personnel to sponsor it, was home to a thousand-seat church, Our Lady of Lourdes, a building with thirteen classrooms, five bedrooms, and a good-sized kitchen, a garage, and servants' quarters. Near the property was the summer residence of the apostolic nuncio and other buildings owned by ecclesiastical authorities. On July 31 Peyton met with the archbishop of La Plata, Juan Carlos Solari, who offered the church to Holy Cross. The Comisión requested four religious (at least three priests) be assigned and agreed to pay all expenses for Family Rosary, should they set up an office in Buenos Aires, until such time that the operation could become self-sufficient.[41] Peyton excitedly reported his enthusiasm for the proposal: "Father, I am thrilled with the possibilities that exist in Argentina for the propagation of the Family Rosary through South America. The things that happened during those three weeks are so great that I hesitate even to tell you in this letter."[42]

Peyton's enthusiasm over the project was echoed by that of the new superior general, Christopher O'Toole, CSC, who wrote to Connerton,

"I would like to do everything I can for the Family Rosary cause," and suggested that George DePrizio, CSC, and Joseph Quinn, CSC, be assigned to the project. He hoped that within a year a priest from the Indiana Province might join the team. He also wrote to Laurent Lapalne, CSC, provincial of the French Canadian Province of Priests, asking that Gerard Le Blanc, CSC, be released for the Argentine foundation, arguing that given the tense political situation in the country,[43] "any sacrifices we can make to remedy the situation are now in order." O'Toole informed the Comisión, "Be assured that we will do everything possible to hasten the day when the Family Rosary Crusade will be launched vigorously in South America."[44]

Connerton was much more wary of the proposal, fearing that the scarcity of personnel to man existing apostolic commitments made the initiation of a new effort unwise. He believed the vice-province "was too weak to sponsor a dependent" organization and there were insufficient religious to take on a new assignment without harming present obligations. Ultimately, in February 1951, after many letters and discussions, Connerton informed the general,

> We wish to withdraw all offers to undertake the [Argentine] responsibility, feeling that after trying as hard as we did to offer some workable plan, our first position was the best; that such a project is inadvisable for us.... We feel it would be wiser to consolidate what foundations we already have rather than to expand at this particular time.[45]

However, Connerton's decision did not stop Peyton from continuing his efforts to establish Family Rosary in Argentina. He continued to be buoyed by the support of O'Toole: "I have found great enthusiasm for the Family Rosary as a result of your visit here. There is no doubt that the Family Rosary Crusade will be a success apart entirely from the question of the Shrine."[46]

Peyton thus wrote the general (a very awkward and unorthodox move without permission from the provincial), acknowledging difficulties with the Argentine political situation, and asked for a Spanish-speaking priest to interact with local ecclesiastical officials. The spark of O'Toole's previous support for the Argentine foundation was reignited by Peyton's request, causing the general to speak with Theodore Mehling, CSC, provincial of the Indiana Province, about the possibility of assigning a priest to Buenos Aires for Family Rosary. Mehling, who had visited Argentina and was aware of the political situation, assigned Archibald McDowell, CSC, to the Argentine mission.[47]

After spending a few weeks at Family Theater in Hollywood brushing up on his Spanish, McDowell arrived in Buenos Aires in July 1951. O'Toole explained, "Father McDowell is going to Buenos Aires to take some preliminary steps for the advent of the Family Rosary Crusade in South America and in Argentina in particular."[48] The local ordinary, who "desire[d] that the spread of the Family Rosary may be efficacious," agreed that McDowell could lodge with the Passionist Fathers during his stay in Buenos Aires. McDowell established a small office in the basement the headquarters of La Comisión Pico-Templo, Nuestra Señora de Fátima.[49] He reported a few accomplishments, including the translation of the leaflet "To Save the World," produced a new leaflet on what the pope and Cardinal Santiago Luis Copello of Buenos Aires said about the rosary, and aired a few of the Family Theater television films.[50]

Significant problems arose with the Argentine foundation almost from the outset. The establishment of the Family Rosary office in the headquarters of the Comisión was interpreted as a sign that the shrine proposal was still being considered by Holy Cross. O'Toole told McDowell to make it clear to the Comisión that Holy Cross had made no personnel commitment to the shrine.[51] The political situation worsened with Argentina being described in correspondence as a police state no better than Hitler's Nazi regime. McDowell reported to the superior general:

> If, with God's help, I am able to go unperturbed by the present political fiasco, you can expect some pleasing results. If, however, by a strange but not impossible turn of events the Family Rosary Crusade is considered a political maneuver of the "Religious of the Dollar" — as one write-up referred to us [North Americans], then anything can happen, including the persecution of the Church, which is not infrequently mentioned.[52]

O'Toole agreed "that Buenos Aires is not a propitious place for North Americans at the present time."[53] Holy Cross officials concluded that unless Peyton brought his international rosary crusade to Argentina soon it was not wise to keep McDowell in place. McDowell obtained permission from Cardinal Copello, archbishop of Buenos Aires, to have the crusade in September or October 1952, but Peyton could not meet the deadline, so McDowell left Argentina in May 1953 for a new assignment.[54]

The expansion of Family Rosary operations in California and on the international front brought more personnel to the ministry and required bigger and better facilities in Albany. The College of St. Rose had served as host to Family Rosary since 1945, but now Family Rosary needed to establish its own home and identity. In 1954 the provincial asked John Murphy, CSC, director of the Albany office, and Frank Quinn, CSC, to look for a building that would serve both as office space and a residence for the Holy Cross religious. At 773 Madison Avenue Murphy found a three-story building, an annex to the Vincentian Institute, being offered by the Diocese of Albany. The asking price was $35,000, but Murphy, knowing that the structure needed $22,000 worth of major repairs before it could be occupied, offered $20,000 to Auxiliary Bishop Edward Magnin; the deal was accepted. On October 18, 1954, the title of the building was given to Family Rosary. Murphy, working with some lay associates, had the first floor refurbished and it was blessed by Bishop William Scully on December 8. Refurbishment of the second floor, housing a chapel and more office space, and the third, with rooms for religious, was completed by September 1955.[55]

New Horizons in Radio and Television

The 1950s saw a rapid shift from radio to television as the principal entertainment medium, a change Peyton capitalized on with a successful series of short films, beginning in 1949, and continuing throughout the decade. Nevertheless, radio continued to be a prominent part of Family Theater and even saw expansion in various ways. The challenge to radio made by television was great, but one commentator stated,

> There is a place for radio. There is a need for it. Radio can never be what it was. It can never return to the dominant place it once held any more than silent film can replace today's moving picture. But it can find its proper place in the overall scheme of things . . . and that's exactly what it is doing . . . and doing well.[56]

Catholic radio shows in the mid- to late 1950s continued to be aired through national and syndicated broadcasts. Besides *Family Theater of Air,* broadcast by Mutual, *The Catholic Hour* (NBC), *The Christian in Action* (ABC), and *Church of the Air* (CBS) were weekly programs. Many additional shows were syndicated and aired widely, including *The Ave Maria Hour* (Society of the Atonement), *The Sacred Heart Hour* (Jesuits), *The Hour of St. Francis* (Franciscans), *Hour of the Crucified* (Passionists), and *Lamp Unto My Feet* (NCCM).[57] Programs specific to the rosary were aired as well. By 1953 the Catholic Broadcasters' Association reported twenty-six stations in the United States were broadcasting a daily program of rosary recitation that could be heard in five thousand cities and towns; forty-two stations carried a similar weekly program.[58]

Family Theater of the Air continued its quality programming of contemporary dramas that preached the message of family prayer. Original programs were the norm, but beginning in 1957, due in large measure to tight finances, the reprising of programs became more frequent.[59] Nevertheless, the quantitative accomplishments of Family Theater in the radio medium were statistically remarkable. From the opening broadcast in February 1947 until 1961, *Family Theater of the Air* broadcast 462 original half-hour programs, about 220 of which were written by staff writers with freelance writers supplying the rest. Additionally, 23 hour-long presentations were broadcast on special holidays (Mother's Day, Easter, Thanksgiving, and Christmas), plus a special tribute to Pope Pius XII aired shortly after his death in October 1958.[60]

Family Theater could justly be proud of its record, which was noted by various groups with awards throughout the decade. In 1953 the conservative and patriotic Freedom Foundation of Valley Forge, Pennsylvania, honored Family Theater "for bringing about a better understanding of American life." Two years later the Thomas Alva Edison Foundation gave its National Mass Media Award to Family Theater as "the radio program best portraying America." The Catholic Audio Visual Educators (CAVE) Association presented Family Theater its communication arts award in 1956. On its tenth anniversary in February 1957 Family Theater was recognized by the American Legion for upholding the principles of American society.[61]

A new venture in radio for Family Theater was initiated in 1952 through the economic support of the Catholic Daughters of America (CDA). The Daughters gave $25,000 to produce fifteen half-hour dramatic presentations of the mysteries of the rosary. The programs, written by Fred Niblo Jr., one of Family Theater's best staff writers, were produced by Family Theater, but financed by the CDA. As was his custom, Peyton secured numerous Hollywood celebrities to donate their time and expertise in these productions, including Bing Crosby, Anna Maria Alberghetti, Eileen Farrell, Ann Blyth, Jeff Chandler, Jimmy Durante, Gigi Perreau, and Ricardo Montalban.[62] Peyton wanted to parlay this gracious gift into more name recognition for Family Theater by having the shows broadcast nationally. He reported to Connerton as "almost definite" an arrangement where the glorious mysteries would be aired on *The Catholic Hour* (NBC), the sorrowful mysteries on *Christian in Action* (ABC), and the joyful mysteries on *Church of the Air* (CBS). He concluded, "If it does work out it would be wonderful because then Our Lady and the Family Rosary would have all the major TV and radio networks of America propagating the Family Rosary."[63] Peyton's plan did not materialize, however, so the programs debuted on Cleveland radio stations as a prelude to the local Rosary Crusade between May 31 and July 5, 1953. Eventually the programs, which were well received, were made into records and became a staple of the publicity used in international crusades.[64]

Peyton, pleased with his new success, pressed forward to bring his message to the international air waves. In October 1952 he met with Charles Wilson, an official with the Crusade for Freedom and sponsor of Radio Free Europe. Wilson directed Peyton to Bill Rafael, the man in charge of the fourteen Munich stations that broadcast to Iron Curtain countries. Rafael, a Catholic who had attended one of Peyton's Triduums several years earlier, granted fifteen minutes of free air time, to be used by Peyton during unscheduled periods. Peyton's request to the Voice of America, which broadcast (among other places) to South America, also resulted in a gift of limited free time.[65] Family Theater programs were also broadcast via Armed Forces Radio plus local stations in Australia, New Zealand, Mozambique, the Philippines, and most of East Africa.[66]

The relationship between Family Theater and Mutual grew stronger in early 1956, when the president and chairman of the board, Tom O'Neill, announced a special sixteen-week series of shows on Saturday evenings dedicated to broadcasts of the mysteries of the rosary. Each program presented a dramatization of a mystery, followed by a song or two by stars such as Bing Crosby or Jo Stafford, and concluded with recitation on one decade of the rosary. The fifteen mysteries were scheduled to end on St. Patrick's Day; the sixteenth show would be dedicated to Mary as the "World's Greatest Mother." Peyton was elated about the program series:

> I can feel that through this tremendous opportunity Our Blessed Mother has received from the Mutual Broadcasting Network, we would betray her if we don't use it to reach the hearts of millions — and through her most appealing program convince them to pray the Rosary as we would have them to.

Peyton, who was always thinking of additional ways to promote the family rosary, hoped that Mutual's gift would lead eventually to a weekly Saturday evening recitation of five mysteries of the rosary. He intended to obtain international figures, including church and state officials, even the pope, to give a message at the end of each broadcast or, even better, lead a decade of the rosary.[67]

Mutual's support of Peyton's apostolate expanded when on December 8, 1956, "Bernadette of Lourdes," the first program of a new weekly half-hour series called *Marian Theater*, was aired. The series, broadcast each Sunday "to illustrate practical applications of the rosary mysteries to everyday life," was "strictly Catholic and religious," as opposed to *Family Theater of the Air*, which was intentionally and strictly nonsectarian. The series was paid for by Tom O'Neill, who was also responsible for its genesis.[68] *Marian Theater* produced thirty-seven original programs between December 8, 1956, and September 11, 1957. Some of the better-known episodes were "Keeper of the Inn" (Christmas 1956), "Prisoner of War," "Vocation," "Martyrdom of Isaac Jogues," and "Herod's Pact." The CDA rosary mystery series was broadcast on *Marian Theater*, with two shows in April 1957 and the remainder broadcast between September 7 and December 21, 1957. Additionally in 1958, *Marian Theater* programs were aired in Spain, under the title of the *Family Hour*, and Mozambique. On January 11, 1958, *Marian Theater* began reruns of Family Theater productions with "The Hound of Heaven." In total *Marian Theater* ran for 198 shows, ending on September 25, 1960. The need to supply both weekly programs from past *Family Theater of the Air* broadcasts was a constant problem and led to the cancellation of the series.[69]

While Catholic radio in the 1950s slowly lost ground despite national and syndicated programming, television was rising rapidly in popularity. Unquestionably the most prominent personality in Catholic television of the period was Fulton Sheen, who graduated from his premier position with NBC's *The Catholic Hour* to national television prominence with his show *Life Is Worth Living* (1952–57). Sheen was the archetype for the movement of the Catholic tradition into mainstream America; his show demonstrated the Americanization of Catholicism after World War II. Every Tuesday at 8:00 p.m. Sheen drew great audiences to his programs, even when it went head-to-head with "Mr. Television," Milton Berle.[70] Sheen, like Peyton, held a very traditional understanding of the family, where respect for law and appreciation of authority were fostered through a structure that placed the father in the essential role of authority and justice and the mother as representative of the essence of love and mercy that leavened the discipline of the law.[71] Other popular Catholic TV shows, following in the footsteps of earlier radio programs, included: *The Sacred Heart Program*, *The Christophers*, *Hour of St. Francis*, *Chalice of Salvation*, plus the NCCM's array of shows: *Look Up and Live*, *Lamp Unto My Feet*, and *We Believe*. Later the NCCM added two special series, *Rome Eternal*, first aired in January 1958, and *The Holy Sacrifice*, a comprehensive explanation of the Mass, broadcast in October 1959.[72]

Family Theater kept pace with the rapid expansion of television with new original programs. *Trial at Tara,* the story of how St. Patrick brought Christianity to Ireland, was released in 1953. That same summer Family Theater produced a series of twelve one-minute films, broadcast on television during sign-on, sign-off, and station breaks. Each film in the series, titled *Inspiration Please,* featured a great figure in Church or secular history, such as Abraham Lincoln, Thomas Jefferson, Franz Josef Haydn, Louis Pasteur, and St. Teresa of Avila, speaking on the meaning and value of prayer in their lives. The series was underwritten by Joseph P. Kennedy, former U.S. ambassador to England, with scripts by Fred Niblo Jr. and John T. Kelley, veterans of the Family Theater ministry.[73] One publicity flyer read, "We at Family Theater feel that this series of affirmations can offer solace to the world, testimony to the power of faith and prayer in our time." Arthur J. Connell, national commander of the American Legion, commented on the series:

> I believe that your television spots on prayer, prepared for free distribution to the television stations, will help, by bringing God into the home, to restore family prayer and wholesome family life, with the consequent return to old-fashioned honesty and decency, and love of God and country.[74]

During the 1950s Family Theater also obtained for its use several Spanish film productions. Through the intervention of Bishop Angel Herrera of Málaga, the Spanish government granted Peyton free use of *Alma de América* (Soul of America), a film that portrayed Catholicism's role in the discovery of America. With only slight modifications the film, retitled *Dawn of America,* was syndicated throughout the United States. In 1959 Peyton obtained rights to two other Spanish films, *The Kiss of Judas* and *Our Lady of Fatima.*[75] Peyton was very shrewd in his dealings for these films. He reported,

> The Catholic Daughters of America have pledged us 30,000 dollars for [the] Our L[ady] of Fatima picture. This information, however, I do not want publicised and nothing should be left undone to try to get Our L[ady] of Fatima for nothing and like the Christopher Columbus [film, *Alma de América*] for all time. The Judas picture I feel we can also get eventually and at a much cheaper price than they are asking — and for nothing perhaps.[76]

All the Family Theater films were widely circulated and broadcast throughout the country. Some of the most popular, as measured by the number of screenings, were *A Star Shall Rise* (1,860 screenings),

Trial at Tara (1,151 screenings), *The World's Greatest Mother,* (979 screenings), *That I May See* (937 screenings), *Dawn of America* (864 screenings), *Hill Number One* (707 screenings), and *The Triumphant Hour* (650 screenings). By 1961 Family Rosary films had been broadcast over 8,500 times.[77] In addition to television, the films were distributed through rental agencies to parishes, schools, and other institutions. Coordinated by Family Theater's business manager, James Ambrose, a cadre of thirty-eight distributors rented films for private and public functions.[78]

Family Theater's movement into the world of television films, together with the continued operations of *Family Theater of the Air,* led to the need for more personnel and equipment. The small house given Father Peyton in 1948 by Jacoba Buchenau was now too small. The need became more acute in September 1958 when the Building and Safety Commission of Los Angeles, after a thorough inspection of the premises, recommended that a new building be constructed or a building at a different site be purchased, since the needed repairs on the present building would be cost prohibitive.[79]

Peyton and his associates decided that an existing building might not have the needed space and facilities and, thus, they began to appeal to community and Los Angeles ecclesiastical officials for permission to construct a new building at the original site. Albert Heinzer, CSC, director of Family Theater, supervised the erection of the new building, which was estimated to cost $175,000. He was able to receive permissions from the Eastern provincial and General Councils of Holy Cross, and from James McIntyre, the archbishop of Los Angeles, who had been given a red hat in 1952.[80] Heinzer suggested three possible plans to finance the new building: (1) use of on-hand funds from offices, totaling $176,000, (2) an appeal to the Jacob Raskob foundation for a grant, (3) use of $45,000 in sterling on deposit in Ireland for Family Rosary, plus a capital drive.[81] Peyton personally lobbied Robert Raskob of San Francisco to finance the project. Raskob agreed to the request and told Heinzer and Peyton that he would ask the Raskob Foundation to underwrite the building. Family Rosary received $175,000 from the foundation for the construction. The building rose rapidly and was dedicated by Cardinal McIntyre on August 15, 1961.[82]

Patrick Peyton's Work Ethic and Relationships

By the close of the 1950s Patrick Peyton had become a well-known and established figure on the national scene through a series of great triumphs achieved in the media of radio and television. This success was accomplished through much hard work and the loyal support of many people. Peyton's personal motivation for his ministry was articulated time and again as twofold: (1) repaying a debt to the Blessed Mother for his cure and (2) saving the family which was in crisis. Peyton explained how his debt was related to the family crisis in the United States:

> The family was meant to be the cradle of religion, and religion the soul of the family. In America, family prayer and scripture reading used to be general customs. They are no longer. They have not been for some years. The family is the weaker for it. There are broken homes in every street. The nation is the poorer. But the family that prays together stays together. Restore to the family its religious soul and you enrich the country, you strengthen civilization. If enough families pray, they can save the world.[83]

Peyton's dedication to cause and devotion to Mary and the family rosary were noted by all with whom he came in contact. Mary Jane McQueen, the eldest daughter of Jacoba Buchenau, the benefactor of the Sunset Boulevard headquarters for Family Theater, knew Peyton for many years and commented,

> Fr. Peyton's sense of his own mission led him to make a total commitment to his work, and he pursued that with a holy passion every moment of his life, even when he was resting and not working. He was totally engrossed in fulfilling his mission. It was his reason for being.[84]

Ann Blyth, one of the first Hollywood stars to join Peyton's radio and television mission, put it simply, "Mary was his passion. . . . He had the innocent deep belief that she would always be there. And she always seemed to be."[85] His dedication sometimes took a toll on his health, as he ignored his friends' warning to slow down. He once wrote to his sister, "We are working hard, and I just can't take the advice of anyone who tells me to rest."[86] Peyton was obsessed with his ministry, a reality that bore much fruit but over his career raised significant problems when blind dedication triumphed over rational thinking.

While Peyton's methods may have raised some concerns of others, the strong support he had enjoyed from Holy Cross from the outset continued throughout the 1950s. In 1953 the superior general, Christopher O'Toole, CSC, writing to the Congregation of Holy Cross worldwide, recognized the accomplishments of Peyton's work and asked for more community assistance: "The Family Rosary Crusade has done more to stimulate devotion to Our Lady and especially the Rosary than any movement in modern times. . . . I urge all Religious to make every effort to assist the work of the Family Rosary Crusade."[87] James Connerton's support through the assignment of personnel, approval of new endeavors, and serving as Peyton's chief cheerleader was critical to the success of Family Rosary and its founder. The provincial once called Peyton a "divine tool in the spread of devotion to Our Lady and her Rosary," so strongly did he believe in the merit and efficacy of the work and the holiness of Peyton himself.[88] Peyton fully acknowledged the contribution Connerton's support brought to Family Rosary: "I try with my Masses and prayers to pay back the debt that the Family Rosary Crusade owes you. Your friendship and backing and authority have given the Crusade its security, and made possible its growth and richness."[89] Jerome Lawyer, CSC, also acknowledged Connerton's faithful assistance: "He is truly a great friend of Family Rosary. It is through his encouragement, interest, and at times, heroic patience, that Family Rosary has been able to make the rapid strides it has made during the past years.[90]

Provincial support for Peyton's Family Rosary Crusade did not miss a beat when George DePrizio, CSC, assumed the reins of the province in 1956. DePrizio, recalling conversations with Peyton about his great dream when they both were students at Holy Cross College in Washington, acknowledged, "It has all come true and is one of the great miracles of our time." The provincial was proud of his relationship with Peyton and pledged his "fullest support" after his election. Through the suggestion of DePrizio the 1958 Eastern Province Chapter highly commended "Father Patrick Peyton and his present associates in the Family Rosary–Family Theater apostolates for extraordinary accomplishments in their various fields of activity."[91]

The great success and progress achieved by Family Rosary from the outset and the support Peyton received from the leadership of Holy Cross could not hide the fact that some significant personnel conflicts existed within the organization, but most especially between Peyton and those Holy Cross religious who worked directly with him.[92] A review of the extant data and interviews with many who worked with him closely indicates that the primary source of this conflict was the independence Peyton enjoyed from the very outset. Connerton's undying and seemingly uncritical support for Peyton's efforts produced an environment where the rosary priest believed he could operate almost with impunity and without external authority. The provincial admitted to the superior general that the situation was unsatisfactory, even hinting that he was afraid to act against Peyton:

As you perhaps know I have recognized the need for considerable freedom for Father Peyton to operate successfully and have not imposed my authority upon him.... Father Murphy feels that too little authority has been exercised over Father Peyton both by the Director and Provincial and I, for one, think he is right since I value the observance not only of the vow but also the spirit of the vow. I might say that I would have attempted to exert more authority over the Family Rosary had I felt that I was entirely free to do so and that I would not interfere with its progress.[93]

One month later Connerton again wrote the general, hinting that Peyton's independent attitude was irritating him: "Father Peyton came here for a visit. That is something of a triumph in itself along with the many other victories he talks about. His visit was very informative, helpful and, of course, a bit oppressive."[94]

Peyton's unusual independence as a religious coupled with his perceived need to repay a debt to the Mother of God while simultaneously solving America's family crisis brought millions to prayer, but produced an attitude that demanded that people comply with his wishes. Those who "were not onboard" or were unable to understand his superhuman devotion and dedication were cast aside, ignored, or severely chastised.

Holy Cross religious who worked with Father Peyton over the years have expressed the view that he felt confined by the restrictions, rules, and procedures of religious life in the Congregation because such controls made the accomplishment of his goals more difficult. Jerome Lawyer, CSC, believed that as the years went by Peyton drew further and further away from the Congregation. He wanted the freedom to get things done, to move on projects without the delays that normal procedures, especially obtaining permission, required. John Murphy, CSC, often expressed his frustration at not being informed by Peyton of what he was planning to do, causing consternation and often embarrassment to co-workers. He expressed his frustration to Lawyer: "I am beginning to understand what you went through when you were here, that is, with regard to being kept in the dark about a lot of things that were going on."[95] Fellow workers have commented that Peyton's certain belief in his personal commission from the Blessed Mother to spread devotion to her through the rosary "transcended all other obligations." To the irritation of his fellow religious Father Peyton justified his violation of community regulations by associating his work with the will of the Virgin Mary. His passion for ministry blinded him at times to the needs of others.[96]

The relationship that developed between Father Peyton and his fellow religious might well be described as one of love and hate. Community members respected Peyton for who he was and what he had accomplished. They marveled at his energy and dedication and were grateful for the multiple gifts he possessed and shared in his promotion of family prayer. Fellow workers were extremely loyal to him and wholly dedicated to the ministry, but they were often disheartened and at times angered at the way they were treated. Unquestionably Peyton was more dedicated to the work than to his fellow religious. He was grateful to Holy Cross, as expressed constantly to provincials and superiors general, for providing the opportunity to engage in a specialized apostolate, but often he overlooked the contributions of others. One fellow religious commented, "I think he took his own community members for granted. Maybe in his mind this was our obedience...and we were duty bound to support him and his work."[97]

Patrick Peyton was a man with whom it was difficult to work, but former colleagues all agree that any problems that arose did so not from malicious intent or ill will, but rather from a level of dedication and single-minded devotion that was incomprehensible to others and blinding to himself. Peyton was a hard taskmaster with those who shared his work and seemingly assumed that others were willing collaborators in all aspects of the day-to-day operations of Family Rosary. For Peyton there was no privilege greater than advocating devotion to Mary. One of Peyton's classmates accurately summarized the feeling of many:

> He would be so intent on what he was doing and the importance of what he was doing for the welfare of the Church that he could be neglectful of people around him....I don't think that would be deliberate on his part. He would think that they [Holy Cross religious with whom he worked] were privileged in being allowed to do this for Our Blessed Mother.[98]

Patrick Peyton's relationship with Jerome Lawyer, CSC, and John Murphy, CSC, because of the frequency of their close contact, positions held in the Family Rosary organization, and common Holy Cross membership was unique compared with others. Both men cherished the opportunity to participate in the work and to have known Patrick Peyton, and they recognized his holiness and contribution to Holy Cross and the Church, but their frustration was readily apparent as well. They felt that Peyton was often "out of control," especially when he would arrive home from his countless trips and, like a whirlwind, whip the office (Hollywood or Albany) into chaos with his demands for immediate attention on matters of great import to him. Office workers were more tolerant, but the community bonds and higher expectations of brother-hood held by Holy Cross religious, especially Lawyer and Murphy, created much friction and left a very rough edge on their personal relationship.[99]

The many laymen and laywomen who worked closely with Father Peyton over the years echo the sentiments of Holy Cross religious, but without the feeling that their work was not appreciated. Co-workers stated of Peyton, "He is exasperating, but interesting and holy. He has used everyone, but he never abused anybody."[100] Working in the Family Rosary organization required selfless devotion and complete dedication to the work. As one worker put it, "If you had a personal agenda or any agenda, it wasn't going to work here." Yet, those who knew him best claim that co-workers understood that the demands would be high if the work was to be accomplished. Dennis Roverato, who joined Family Theater in 1973, commented, "He could be very demanding and some-times unreasonable, but that came with the territory. I think all of us who worked so long for him and with him realized that our work wasn't for him. It was for the Blessed Mother, so you could forgive him."[101]

The work ethic that Peyton set for himself was also demanded of those who shared his ministry. Fed by activity, Peyton expected others to re-act in a similar way. A day's work in the office often became fourteen hours when Peyton visited. Still, most co-workers admired his dedica-tion, persistence, and devotion, and, thus, overlooked the demands that were placed upon them.[102]

Peyton was often blind to the needs of others; he could not compre-hend how his enthusiasm and zeal for ministry was hurtful to many, most especially his fellow Holy Cross religious. He was appreciative of the efforts of others and realized the many sacrifices that people made for the work, even though he often failed to acknowledge it. He made every effort to make amends when his blindness to the mission caused hurt or frustration to others. This was especially true in his relation-ship with his brothers in Holy Cross. In letters of apology he praised the efforts of those who shared his life and asked others to overlook his actions when crudeness or lack of patience led to misunderstanding and anger.[103] Peyton summarized his attitude in a letter to Family Rosary personnel:

> As you are all aware the demands of the Crusade are overwhelming and as dear Father Jerry Lawyer has often said the one great fault in me is my lack of expression of appreciation. As I have often

said this apparent lack of appreciation on my part is not real. To all those who stand beside me so selflessly devoting their bodies and souls to our Blessed Mother and her advantage in the Family Rosary Crusade, I say that not a day goes by without my pleading in prayer for that reward from God and Mary, which is your due, to fall upon you.[104]

Peyton was blinded by his passion for the ministry and his certain belief that his labor was the work of the Blessed Virgin, but according to the comments of many who worked with him closely, he was not one who intentionally neglected another, forgot to say thank you, or made unreasonable demands.[105] His dedication and commitment to the cause of family prayer was on such a high plane that others, while giving their all, were still often not able to perform at the level, intensity, and duration that Peyton believed necessary to accomplish the tasks he set for himself and the organization. His independence of thought is understandable when he was allowed by his religious superiors, almost from the outset, to set his own agenda and navigate his own course in religious life and priesthood. The consistent affirmation and support from Connerton, while being helpful to the mission, may have been hurtful to his development as a religious. The comments by others that Steiner, a strong-charactered man, was somewhat cowed by Peyton, and Connerton's fear of restricting him, demonstrates that his strong personality, dedication, and the perception that he could not be deterred from his objective dominated others. Father Peyton was not the easiest person in the world with whom to work, and he often failed to demonstrate appreciation for co-workers, but his heart and mind, always centered on his dream of spreading family prayer throughout the land, reveal a true man of faith.

A review of Peyton's work ethic and Holy Cross relationships serves as an introduction to some discussion of his whole personality (the epilogue is more expanded), which on the surface was manifest in simple ways, but on a deeper level was more complex. Unquestionably Peyton's family life in Ireland and his faith experience there and in the United States were the two primary building blocks upon which his personality was constructed. These two forces were integrally linked, creating in Peyton a man of indominatable faith, expressed most notably by his insistence upon the need for family prayer. His experience of the efficacy of this daily regimen in uniting families convinced him there was no other proper way for a family to live.

Peyton's conviction that families must pray together and his life experience, most especially his firm belief that he was saved from death to promote his family prayer ideals, created a man who found himself on a heavenly mission that needed the cooperation of all with whom he associated. On the surface Peyton appeared to most outsiders as calm, prayerful, simple in expression, and patient — a man of faith in every way. The calmness, simplicity of his public message, and patience were, however, less evident to insiders. The passion of his commitment to the family prayer mission he headed did not allow him to be calm, simple, or patient, but rather, almost necessitated a more aggressive approach to bishops, fellow priests and religious, and many others closely associated with his ministry. Peyton could not be patient nor passive in his work, for he firmly believed that his work was truly that of the Virgin Mary; he was the central vehicle for its actualization. The significant work of Family Rosary and Family Theater would never have blossomed and produced such a significant impact on Catholicism through a passive and less energetic approach to the work. When it was necessary Peyton had the ability to stand tall, talk tough, and be highly directive. This led to some conflicts among his peers, but any other approach would not have generated the outward success of the crusade over the years. In some ways it can be said that Peyton was two men, the calm and more sensitive person visible to the millions and the tougher more business-like man who ran an international organization for the promotion of family prayer. The former was more natural; the latter a result of life experience and the conviction and passion in which he held his ministry.

Conclusion

The heyday of American Catholicism during the 1950s witnessed the solidification and subsequent expansion of Peyton's Crusade for Family Prayer. The organization of Family Rosary and Family Theater with the Crusade for Family Prayer, the addition of several Holy Cross religious to the mission, and the expansion of its radio and television ventures brought national recognition to the organization and to Father Peyton. Heard over the airwaves and seen on television and on highway billboards, Peyton's simple message of the need for family prayer made significant inroads into American society. The time was right and the environment ready for the expansion of the Crusade to an international audience.

Chapter 5

The International
Rosary Crusades, 1948–59

The media of radio and television, combined with significant publicity, support from the Catholic press, and his own charismatic personality had made Patrick Peyton, Family Rosary, and Family Theater nation ally known in the United States. Throughout the country people listened to *Family Theater of the Air* and *Marian Theater* and they watched a growing number of films, made for television, that promoted Peyton's basic message of the need for families to return to prayer as a solution to the many difficulties they faced in contemporary society. The goal that Peyton set for himself in January 1942 as he contemplated his response to his miraculous recovery of health, namely, that "ten million families and not one less" would begin to pray the family rosary, required a method to encourage this practice more directly than his radio and television ventures, which promoted family prayer generally. Thus, beginning in 1948 and continuing until a few years before his death in 1992, Patrick Peyton circled the globe many times over, preaching his simple but effective message in a series of international rosary crusades. He achieved his goal and much more while moving his ministry from national to international spheres.

The Revivalist Spirit in American Christianity

Christian history in the United States has been replete with talented and inspired preachers of God's word. Americans have been fascinated by those who proclaim the Gospel and explicate its meaning for the faithful by preaching from church pulpits, town squares and parks, and countryside camp meetings. The value and efficacy of this specialized ministry has not gone unnoticed, but rather has been recognized most

99

especially in the fact that the practice continues today in various ways and settings. The foundation of America's national values on Christian principles demonstrates the attraction of Christ's message and mission to the people of this land.

Revivalism in the United States holds a special place in the overall history of preaching. The value of the itinerant preacher has been well known since the early thirteenth century in Spain. Dominic Guzman, in an effort to root out the heresy of Albigensianism, founded a religious congregation (Order of Preachers — Dominicans) dedicated to preaching God's word from town to town. In the early eighteenth century, reaching its peak in the 1740s, the American colonies experienced a "Great Awakening," the general revival of evangelical religion. Led by Congregationalist theologian Jonathan Edwards (1703–58) and manifest most profoundly through the Methodist minister George Whitefield (1714–70) and the Presbyterian Gilbert Tennent (1703–64), this general revival released a religious fervor and passion never before seen in this country. Whitefield was an event in himself as he raced from town to town, from vacant lot to crowded church, from open field to busy market in his efforts to proclaim God's boundless grace. The intensity of the religious renewal wrought by the Great Awakening was replayed a little over a half century later during what has been labeled "The Second Great Awakening." Disciples of Edwards, gathered under the title of the "New Divinity Movement," sought to establish churches on strict principles of regenerate membership and sharply defined standards of doctrinal membership. Led by such champions as Lyman Beecher (1775–1863) and Charles Finney (1792–1875), this second significant national revival was characterized by camp meetings in rural areas led by itinerant preachers who drew thousands to week-long gatherings.[1]

American revivalism in the latter nineteenth and early twentieth centuries in the United States was dominated by three dynamic preachers: Dwight L. Moody, Billy Sunday, and Aimee Semple McPherson. Beginning in the 1870s and continuing to his death in 1899, Moody (1837–99), together with musician and composer Ira Sankey (1840–1908), worked from Chicago to organize a national and eventually international revival campaign. Vast crowds assembled to hear Moody preach what the *New York Times* labeled the "electric revival," accompanied by hymns, written and performed by Sankey. The Moody Memorial Church and Moody Bible Institute of Chicago continue his work today. Billy Sunday (1862–1935), a former professional baseball player who was converted to Christ by a street preacher in Chicago, served as the prototype for Sinclair Lewis's protagonist Elmer Gantry.

Sunday began his preaching during World War I in army camps and dominated the revivalist scene for the next twenty years. What he lacked in professionalism and sophistication he more than compensated for in sensationalism, high drama, and a coarse style that reflected the limits of his background. McPherson (1890–1944), a Canadian native, launched her American preaching career through a series of national tours. She eventually settled in Los Angeles and drew tens of thousands to the Angelus Temple, where she preached regularly.[2]

Catholic revivalism in the United States, well described by the historian Jay Dolan,[3] took the form of parish missions, usually conducted by religious orders. The Jesuits, Redemptorists, and Paulists were the best known for this specialized ministry. A typical mission would begin on Sunday evening after the event had been advertised at the morning Masses. Sessions in the morning and evening were scheduled with the main sermon of the day at night. Mission preachers celebrated daily Eucharist and provided numerous opportunities for sacramental confession. The goals of these missions were nothing less than personal conversion and the overall transformation of society. A strong moral code was a hallmark of most missions as evidenced by the temperance pledge, which was generally evoked.

Beginning in 1892 the Congregation of Holy Cross conducted its "mission band" ministry with community members generally traveling in pairs to various parishes to conduct two-week missions, one week for men and one for women.[4] Missions opened on Sundays with an explanation of the event at all the morning Masses. Beginning the next evening and running through Saturday band members gave talks on the love of God, sin, death, judgment, hell, the crucifixion, and the mercy of God, and finished with a holy hour. Confessions were heard and benediction celebrated every evening. It was just such a traveling mission band team that captured the attention of Patrick and Thomas Peyton in the spring of 1929, leading them to Holy Cross and the priesthood.

The revivalist spirit flourished most profoundly in the mid-twentieth century when the preaching of the Protestant evangelist Billy Graham made his name almost a household word. Born in North Carolina in 1918 and raised on his father's dairy farm, Graham in 1934 was inspired by Mordecai Fowler Ham, a Kentucky revivalist. Graham traveled about, preached his first revival in 1939, and was then ordained a Baptist minister. He initiated his formal preaching career in 1947, but his first significant success came two years later in the Los Angeles crusade. Graham's crusade technique was very systematic. Two months ahead of time, a front team would arrive, blanketing the area with publicity

and mobilizing the local Protestant churches. Then Graham would arrive and launch a series of revival meetings in athletic stadiums or large
auditoriums.[5]

In addition to being Peyton's contemporary, Graham bore some obvious resemblances to him. Beginning in 1950 Graham inaugurated a
weekly national radio program, *The Hour of Decision,* which by 1954
was reaching 15 million people over a thousand stations. His patented
sign-off was well known: "And now, until next week, good-bye, and may
the Lord bless you real good." He also wrote a newspaper column, "My
Answer," that was syndicated in almost a hundred dailies throughout
the country.[6] He was best known, however, for his international evangelical crusades that sought the personal conversion of nonbelievers and
the transformation of those who already professed Christ as their Savior.
Graham's arrival on the scene fueled the religious revival that characterized the 1950s.[7] A humble servant of God, Graham described himself
and his ministry: "I'm no great intellectual, and there are thousands of
men who are better preachers than I am. You can't explain me if you
leave out the supernatural. I am but a tool of God."[8] By 1954 his ministry had made him "the best known, most talked-about Christian leader
in the world today, barring the Pope."[9]

The International Rosary Crusades Begin

The spirit of revivalism endemic to American Christian culture became
the international trademark for Peyton in the natural progression of his
mission to reinvigorate the practice of the family rosary to the world. The
Mother's Day broadcast of May 13, 1945, coupled with the inauguration
of *Family Theater of the Air* less than two years later made Peyton a
well-known figure in North American religious circles, but it was the
initiation of his famous rosary crusades that spread his fame and message
to the world. His purpose in organizing the crusades was articulated in
different ways. First, he saw the crusade, in historical perspective, as
an act of evangelization for parishes and schools through a publicity
campaign that harnessed the power of the mass media. The crusade was
also a way to respond to the call from Mary for prayer and penance.
Lastly, returning to a basic parameter of his mission, the crusade was to
defend the family "in its darkest hour by means of daily family prayer,
the daily Family Rosary, the centuries old practice of the homes and
families of yesteryear."[10]

Peyton's international rosary crusades began almost by accident. In
the early fall of 1947 Peyton, while attending a Marian Congress held in

Ottawa, Canada, and advertising his Family Rosary and *Family Theater of the Air,* met Father John T. Maloney, who invited him to preach a Triduum at his parish, St. Mary's in London, Ontario, on September 21–23. On the last evening of the Triduum Maloney gathered together some clergy friends to discuss organizing a diocesan family prayer drive. When Peyton said he would hold a crusade if the bishop approved, the group went to the ordinary, Bishop John T. Kidd, who supported the prospect fully and appointed his auxiliary John Cody as liaison with Peyton and diocesan director of the crusade.[11] When Thomas Steiner, CSC, heard about the plan he wrote to the ordinary: "Here in the United States this work has been attended by most phenomenal results, and I am sure that your Excellency will experience the same good effects in your Diocese."[12]

On Maloney's recommendation the family prayer crusade was modeled on a highly successful diocesan financial drive that had just been completed. The six-week development drive used all possible methods of advertising — billboards, trailers, movie theaters, special radio programs, and commercials — to inform the faithful of the diocese of the economic need. When the enthusiasm for the drive had reached its peak, then a door-to-door canvass of every home in the diocese was conducted. Teams of two laymen, organized through the local parish, were sent to homes to obtain pledges.[13]

Formal planning and organization of the crusade began almost immediately after Bishop Kidd had given Peyton's idea his blessing. Peyton's first opportunity to publicize his future crusade came one month later when Father Andrew Mahoney, who had attended the St. Mary's meeting and was vicar general of the Diocese of London, Ontario, arranged for Peyton to speak at two diocesan clergy conferences to be held on October 30 and 31 in London and Windsor respectively. He wrote to Peyton,

> We shall give the entire afternoon session of each conference to this matter and you will have an opportunity to take as much time as you wish to explain and enthuse the clergy at first hand, as you did [for] the few who heard you at St. Mary's Church here.

He continued,

> You will find all the Clergy of the Diocese just as receptive and anxious to cooperate to the full in this providential work of sanctifying and restoring the Catholic Home as were the few priests you had a chance to meet while in London.[14]

Preparations began in earnest as the calendar year drew to a close. On December 9, 1947, Peyton met with Bishop Cody and started to work out the details for the crusade. The dates were set for March 28 to May 9, 1948. Peyton led the crusade activity but brought with him a strong supporting cast including Francis Woods and Patricia Spanbauer, his crusade secretary from Albany, Raymond Finan, CSC, from Hollywood, and two French-speaking Holy Cross priests, Adrien LeDuc and Gerard LeBlanc, both stationed at St. Joseph's Oratory in Montreal.[15] While Peyton and the other Holy Cross religious donated their services, salaries for lay personnel, plus costs for advertising, printing, housing, food, and other special needs were assumed by the diocese. Bishop Kidd wrote to his priests to encourage them and ask their cooperation just prior to the initiation of the crusade:

> This Crusade, dear Fathers, is your crusade.... We [Bishops Kidd and Cody] realize that many families are already saying the Family Rosary. But if all the families in the diocese are to be won to the practice of the Family Rosary, it is your zeal and love for Mary that will accomplish it.[16]

In a pastoral letter he expanded his ideas,

> I wholeheartedly agree with Father Peyton that the most effective means of keeping families united under God and Mary is the daily and fervent recitation of the Family Rosary. Our aim, therefore, will be to have every man[,] woman and child who can say the Rosary, pledged to its daily family recitation.[17]

The crusade itself, the first of its kind, was also different from those conducted by Peyton during the next forty years. The crusade was formally announced in every parish on March 21 and began the next Sunday, March 28, with clergy asked to preach on the subject of the rosary and family prayer for the next five Sundays.[18] Immediately after the official opening, dinner meetings were held for deaneries on March 30 in London (London and Stratford) and March 31 in Windsor (Essex and Kent). The meetings provided a second opportunity (besides the past October clergy conferences) for Peyton to explain the crusade, including its purpose and most importantly its method and plan for the next five weeks. Pastors were then asked to come to a separate meeting, accompanied by two laymen from their parish, for an explanation of the pledge drive to be held at the end of the crusade. To generate more interest a pulpit exchange was arranged in adjoining parishes on the second and third Sundays of the campaign.[19] The London, Ontario, crusade was also unique to Peyton's ministry because it involved no massive rallies. Instead Peyton gave thirty individual presentations between April 3 and May 2, including an address on April 18 to a crowd of fourteen thousand at the Capital Theater in London.[20]

Support for the crusade came from many sources. The *Canadian Register*, published in Kingston, Ontario, agreed to publish five special issues promoting the crusade, beginning on the opening day of March 28.[21] Similarly, during the latter stages of planning, the crusade organizers decided that the publication of a weekly newspaper, promulgating information about the crusade, plus many articles on family prayer, the rosary, and various other family-oriented areas of Catholic life would be beneficial. Thus, *The Time for Family Prayer* was established and published on the six Sundays of the crusade. Peyton was able to get significant Church personalities, ecclesiastical and secular, to write essays, which appeared over and over again, for *The Time* as the crusade moved from region to region within a country and internationally.[22] The second issue of the paper contained a feature article by Cardinal Francis Spellman of New York in which he lauded the crusade by invoking Peyton's signature expression:

> In this hour of world crisis, the Crusade for Family Prayer with the Rosary in your diocese is most edifying, helpful and urgent. The spirit of prayer can bring peace on earth. Family Prayer is one of the surest means of keeping the family, both of individuals and nations, holy and united. Indeed, the family that prays together stays together. Those nations that pray together will never go to war. May our Lady of the Rosary intercede at the Throne of Mercy for the world to win a triumph for Christianity over Godless Communism by the power of prayer.[23]

The most crucial part of the crusade, the one to which all other efforts were directed, was the pledge drive conducted during the final week. Organization of this massive door-to-door campaign was its key to success. The pledge drive of six thousand laymen volunteers was organized by John J. McHale Sr., diocesan co-chairman of the crusade, and Colonel Paul Poisson, M.D. The initial meeting headed by the pastor and two volunteer laymen became the core committee for the pledge drive. From this core, one chairman was selected for each one hundred homes in the diocese. The chairmen in turn selected five team captains, one for each twenty homes; team captains recruited three other volunteers, creating a team of four. This team split into two so that each pair visited ten homes, with the goal of obtaining signed pledges to faithfully pray the family rosary. This method became the model used in crusades throughout the world.[24]

Besides seeking pledges from those physically able to participate in the family rosary, Peyton from the outset canvassed those who were ill or infirm, asking them to make the following "heroic pledge": "To our Lady of the Rosary, I offer all my pains and sufferings, even death itself, that all families of the London Diocese and of the world may have the grace and courage to make the daily Family Rosary pledge and keep it faithfully."[25] Extant stories of men and women who signed such pledges for the success of the crusade abound, demonstrating the influence Peyton's message of family prayer had on all.

The London, Ontario, crusade was a great success in many ways. For Peyton the demonstration of faith was most vivid during the pledge week when over eighty thousand families, 95 percent of the diocese, signed the pledge to faithfully pray the family rosary.[26] The crusade set the basic pattern for duration, format, and method of future crusades. Francis Woods, writing for Peyton, acknowledged gratitude to Bishop Cody, noting what the future might hold for the Family Rosary Crusade: "Both Father Peyton and I feel that we will never in this world be able to thank you sufficiently for what you are doing for Our Lady, not only on a diocesan basis, but on a worldwide basis."[27]

There was a long way to go, but Peyton had made the first inroads in his original plan to bring the family rosary to 10 million families. His great success in London, Ontario, was followed by three additional crusades in Canada between 1948 to 1950 that covered almost all of Canada. Between late July and early September 1948 Peyton was in western Canada giving talks and preparing the way for a rosary crusade.[28] From September 19 to October 31, 1948, Peyton, Woods, and Finan conducted the crusade in the province of Saskatchewan, thereby advancing from one diocese in London, Ontario, to the Archdiocese of Regina, the Dioceses of Saskatoon, Gravelbourg, and Prince Albert, plus the *abbatia nullius* of St. Peter.[29] Archbishop Michael O'Neill of Regina was the crusade sponsor. In additional to covering several dioceses, the Saskatchewan crusade was the first to feature rallies, which eventually became the trademark and staple of Peyton's international rosary crusade over the years. On September 26, 15,000 attended the first outdoor rally at the Benedictine Abbey of Our Lady of Mount Carmel. A total of twenty-six rallies were held in the province, with the greatest attendance of 25,000 registered at Regina on October 17. The crusade was again a great success as 150,000 families pledged to pray the family rosary.[30] Philip F. Pocock, bishop of Saskatoon, heralded prophetic words at the end of the campaign: "I am confident that the Family Rosary Crusade can sweep the world if it is given a chance."[31]

From Saskatchewan the crusade moved to northwest Canada, expanding in scope from a province to a geographic region. From September 4 to October 16, 1949, Peyton brought his forces to the four archdioceses of Vancouver, Edmonton, St. Boniface, and Winnipeg, five dioceses, two Ukrainian exarchates (Central and Western Canada), and seven apostolic vicariates. The crusade also expanded in terms of personnel, with the arrival of newly ordained John Murphy, CSC, who joined Peyton, Woods, Finan, and Gerard LeBlanc (from the London crusade). Both Peyton and Lawyer expressed their gratitude to Connerton for Murphy, who, it was hoped, "could organize [the crusade] in a business way" and be "a gold mine for the Family Rosary work."[32] Of the thirty-two rallies on this crusade fourteen were attended by Peyton. A total of 224,000 people attended, with 70,000 and 60,000 at Winnipeg and Edmonton respectively.

Father Peyton's family rosary crusade made some intervening stops in the United States before returning to eastern Canada and the province of Ontario between April 30 and June 4, 1950. Peyton, Woods, and Murphy headed the team that conducted twelve rallies for 115,000 people covering the Archdioceses of Toronto and Kingston and their two suffragan sees of Hamilton and Peterborough. Later that same year, September 3 to October 7, a special crusade conducted by French Oblates of Mary Immaculate (OMI) was held in eastern Ontario, Quebec, and New Brunswick provinces. Peyton spoke at rallies held in Ottawa, Cap de la Madeleine, Quebec, and St. John's, New Brunswick.[33]

The Crusade Organization and Program

Peyton's first few crusades taught many lessons and generated a program and organization that, with minor variations, depending on circumstances, became standard in crusades worldwide throughout the 1950s. Peyton analogized the phases of the crusade to tactics used by armies on the battlefield. The first phase, the employment of the mass media to advertise the future campaign, was described as an aerial bombardment to soften the ground. The next phase, the crusade itself, resembled the movement of troops to capture the objective. Last, the follow-up campaign, including the establishment of permanent diocesan parish and school organizations, was depicted as "occupation forces to maintain the victory."[34] The military-like assault was conducted against several specific groups, including parishes, neighborhoods, colleges and universities, elementary and high schools, hospitals, prisons, and the armed forces.[35]

Along with an understandable orientation favoring Catholic prayers and traditions, Peyton's crusades also fostered from the outset an ecumenical spirit, a rarity in the period. In Saskatchewan he stated: "The main idea of the Family Rosary Crusade is to have all Catholics recite the Rosary daily in their homes; the secondary objective is to bring the people of all faiths to a realization that prayer is absolutely necessary in these troubled times."[36]

The crusade made every effort to appeal and reach out to people of faith regardless of denomination, even non-Christians. The ecumenical message reached people as evidenced by the presence of a not insignificant number of non-Catholics at rallies wherever the crusade was held. Support for the crusade came from all sides as well: "Ministers of every creed have praised and supported Father Peyton's work just as actors and musicians of differing beliefs have been unanimously generous in contributing their time and talent."[37]

Crusades usually ran for eleven weeks, the first five of which were preparation. Once Peyton set dates with local ordinaries,[38] a front team was sent to the headquarters city five weeks before the official opening day. The team consisted of at least one priest (at the outset often it was Francis Woods and/or John Murphy; later Joseph Quinn took this position) and generally two lay secretary assistants. Patricia Spanbauer, who assisted the crusade in London, Ontario, was joined by Dorothy Kahl in 1949, when the campaign first came to the United States in Scranton. The front team set up the crusade office, often in the local chancery, arranged for rally sites, obtained advertising, and promoted publicity by sending literature to all parishes and schools. Radio spots that featured the half-hour radio CDA programs on the mysteries of the rosary were arranged. Press conferences were also used to promote the crusade. Meetings with the clergy as well as various institutions and constituencies that the crusade targeted were arranged as well. Generally Father Peyton would attend these preliminary meetings, especially when opportunities arose to address fellow clergy. His speech was often key to generating the required initial inspiration to get the campaign going on the local parish and school level. These were long and arduous days (generally twelve to fourteen hours of work daily) for these dedicated men and women, many of whom labored "behind the scenes" for the success of the crusade.[39]

The last part of the preparation was the responsibility of the local bishop. A local diocesan director was appointed to work with the front team and those who would actually conduct the crusade. The bishop then formally announced the crusade through the publication of a pastoral letter which was read one Sunday at all Masses. Peyton asked the local ordinaries to take their own personal pledge, "to do all in [their] power so that the family Rosary will be recited in EVERY CATHOLIC HOME in my diocese."[40]

The work of the front team to create a receptive environment was critical to the success of the whole operation. Supporting materials that informed and excited people, as well the necessary instructional manuals for those on the local level who participated in key aspects of the crusade, most especially the pledge drive, were of great importance to the overall campaign. *The Time for Family Prayer* was used in most English-speaking crusades, especially in the United States and Canada. The paper ranged from twelve to thirty-two pages and contained essays about the local crusade, including the sponsor bishops, essays that introduced Peyton and his mission (this was always a feature of the first issue), and articles about the rosary, family prayer, and family issues confronting contemporary life. During the five to six weeks of its publication certain standard essays and articles were routinely published. "Atom Bomb and the Rosary" was an editorial that claimed the rosary would keep war at bay; "Something Is Terribly Wrong in the World" was written by Peyton, suggesting that the rosary will solve the problems of the world.

One standard feature of *The Time* that attracted many was the number of essays written by Hollywood celebrities and other well-known Americans. Loretta Young and Louella Parsons contributed regularly; J. Edgar Hoover and Clare Booth Luce also wrote essays that were often published in the paper. Hoover echoed many of Peyton's own themes in his essay for *The Time*, which was often republished in Family Rosary literature:

> We must return to the days when family life was simple and sincere. We must return to the beautiful and refreshing custom of family prayer. The family that kneels together in common prayer builds a fortress against the angry waves of evil and temptation. I am convinced that evil in the world will be reduced to the realm of insignificance [*sic*] if families return again to the simple, old-fashioned practice of daily prayer.[41]

In a similar tone H. I. Phillips, columnist for the *New York Sun,* wrote:

Family prayer, developed in full spiritual beauty through the Rosary, can do more to restore the brotherhood of man, tolerance, a proper concept of duty, and a determination for world peace than all the United Nations' bodies, diplomatic sessions and Big Four meetings on earth. . . . The return to family prayer in the spirit of our ancestors is a crying need of the hour.[42]

In addition to *The Time for Family Prayer,* each campaign published its own *Crusade Handbook* explaining procedures and organization and providing general information for Peyton's crusade at large and for the local campaign specifically. Handbooks were also printed and distributed for teachers, clergy, and pledge leaders. Parish kits containing posters, prayer cards, the necessary handbooks, and pledge cards were sent to all pastors before the crusade formally began. All campaigns adopted a common graphic that showed a family praying the rosary together. Above the family was the slogan, "The family that prays together stays together." Below the family was the exhortation, "Rosary Day — Every Day. In Every Family Circle." A crusade prayer and hymn were adopted.[43] Radio and television were also valuable assets in the promotion of the crusade message. Crusade personnel sought to saturate the region with radio and when available television coverage of the crusade. The radio recordings of the fifteen mysteries, sponsored by the Catholic Daughters of America, were a staple after their introduction in 1953. The growing number of films produced by Family Theater also advertised the crusade when they were aired on local stations.[44]

The crusade itself generally ran for five or six weeks, beginning with the reading of the local ordinary's pastoral letter in the parishes of the diocese. Peyton often commented that the crusade's purpose was to mobilize the movement for family prayer, but it "is not just a spectacle, it is a penetration so extensive and intensive that God's grace perdures throughout the diocese." The rally, while being a high point for the whole crusade, was only the culmination of several weeks of preliminary work.[45] The work of the formal crusade began with a series of dinner meetings where pastors were told their important role in the campaign and were encouraged to promote the crusade in their parish in all conceivable ways. Schools and teachers were also organized to promote the crusade. Local ordinaries called meetings, generally held at a local theater or similar large auditorium, at which Peyton would explain the crusade, emphasizing the teacher's specific role. Teachers were given a manual and instructed to decorate their classrooms with posters, pray and sing hymns each day for the success of the crusade, give talks to the children about the rosary, family prayer, the apparitions of Mary at Lourdes and Fatima, and most importantly hold an essay contest that gave awards to students. As mentioned previously, Sunday sermons on the subjects of family prayer and the family rosary specifically were made available to local clergy for delivery during the formal crusade period.[46]

The crusade rally was the highlight of the campaign in gathering people from the entire region into a central location for a service of prayer and, most importantly for most people, the opportunity to hear Peyton give a talk on his favorite subject. The rally, organized by a local committee set up by the crusade front team, was generally held in a large athletic stadium, park, or public meeting place. Often rallies featured children who formed a living rosary on the field. Programs featured song, recitation of the rosary, comments by the local ordinaries and dignitaries, with Peyton's passionate and stirring talk as the finale. Rallies were major events for the local community and drew people from the entire region. Heroic accounts abound that detail how people traveled sometimes for days, often walking (especially in third world nations), to attend a local rally.

Peyton was the crusade's focal point and charismatic leader whose energy drove the campaign, provided the event name recognition, and furnished inspiration to the local people who assisted the Family Rosary regulars. He was amazingly effective in getting people, groups, and institutions to donate time, service, or material things to the crusade. Even in lands where Christians were a (sometimes insignificant) minority Peyton was able to obtain free advertising in daily newspapers or have announcements of crusade events printed gratis. Many who encountered him commented, "I could not refuse him."[47]

Peyton's charismatic personality and presence at the rally were crucial to the success of the crusade, but his time physically present during the actual five to six weeks of the crusade was rather limited. He made the initial contact with local ordinaries, setting dates and parameters for the crusade, and he generally met with clergy and teachers at the preliminary meetings at which the crusade was explained (often with the assistance of another crusade priest) and given its initial shot of adrenalin through the passionate way he presented his ideas. As explained by a long-time fellow crusade worker, Joseph Quinn, CSC, Peyton's role in the crusade ended here: "[He] mostly talked at the rally. He would put all his efforts into that. He would help us at the beginning to get some of the people for publicity, television owners, and that sort, but [he] never took part in the physical preparations."[48] While his co-workers labored to prepare a fertile field for the rally and his message, Peyton traveled to schedule future crusades, as well as overseeing the ongoing operations of Family Theater and Family Rosary.

The rally, which raised fervor about the crusade to a fever pitch, was a perfect introduction to the pledge drive, the final event of the crusade. The teams organized to canvass the region by a door-to-door campaign were given valuable instructions in the *Handbook for Crusade Leaders,* which had been distributed during the preparation period. First, pledge workers were encouraged and challenged in their special task:

> You are to be spiritual salesmen of the Family Rosary. A salesmen must know his product thoroughly, and plan in advance various methods of effective approach. You must know this perfect family prayer, The Family Rosary, study the best approach and be ready to meet all possible objections.... You will convince others in the measure in which you, yourself, are informed and convinced.[49]

The booklet suggested certain techniques for countering the most common objections to practicing the family rosary: (1) lack of time, (2) the family is never together, (3) private recitation is sufficient, (4) some in the family refuse to participate.[50]

At the insistence of Peyton, the actual pledge drive was always and exclusively conducted by men. John Murphy, CSC, explained: "Our theme in those days was that God made man the head of the home and it was his responsibility to give spiritual leadership to the family.... To have men go out asking for prayers to the Blessed Mother had an impact that only they could create."

Families were told that the pledge did not bind compliance under the pain of sin, but rather that it was a commitment to setting aside time daily when most members of the family would be present to recite the rosary. Additionally, pledge workers told those they visited that those family members not present on a given day and those who lived alone fulfilled their agreement by private recitation. The crusade pledge read: "To obtain peace for the nations of the world and the love and protection of God and Mary for myself and the members of my family, I promise to recite the daily Family Rosary."[51] Pledge workers also asked the aged and infirm for a heroic pledge of prayers for the crusade's success.

The pledge drive ended the formal crusade, but important matters still required the attention of Peyton and his staff. After every crusade Peyton wrote letters to every bishop in the United States, and at times prelates overseas, described the recent campaign, and encouraged them to consider a crusade in their diocese. This personal contact with members of the hierarchy was one of the keys to his success.[52] The final step of the crusade was finalizing its costs. At the outset Peyton made it his policy not to make the crusades a source of revenue for his other projects. He explained, "There is no element of profit whatsoever ... in the crusades. It is merely necessary that we don't go in debt."[53] Beginning in 1952 in the New Orleans crusade, however, Peyton did, when the situation presented itself, ask wealthy people for monetary assistance, arguing that he would rather obtain significant amounts from a few benefactors than small amounts from many. Crusade costs were borne by the local ordinaries, who shared expenses based on the percentage of people serviced in a diocese compared to the whole crusade region. Peter Grace, who had backed many of Family Theater's film projects, believed that the crusades needed a solid financial base and thus suggested to Holy Cross officials that a priest be assigned as a full-time development representative. Such a position was not created until 1968, when Robert Rioux, CSC, was appointed executive director of the Albany office and director of development.[54]

During the 1950s the Family Rosary Crusade and its parent bodies, Family Rosary and Family Theater, were blessed with many people who came to the ministry, labored long and well, and through their efforts allowed the crusade to reach millions and achieve Patrick Peyton's goal of gaining 10 million families for the family rosary. Joseph Quinn, CSC, joined the Albany team in 1950, but in late 1953, after John Murphy was severely injured in a car accident, he became the leader of the crusade front team and remained in this position until 1967.[55] In Hollywood Albert Heinzer became director in 1955, succeeding Jerome Lawyer, who was sent to Spain to direct the production of fifteen half-hour films of the mysteries of the rosary (chapter 6). John Murphy replaced Quinn and led the Albany operation from 1953 to 1959. The Family Rosary/Family Theater team also grew with lay assistance in both locations, including a host of volunteers, especially women from the College of St. Rose.[56]

Peyton was blessed with many loyal and dedicated colleagues who aided him in his quest to bring the message of family prayer through the rosary to the world, but it was his personality, dynamism, zeal, and personal commitment that drove the movement's engine and was the great attraction to the millions who heard his message. Peyton presented himself to others as "a quiet, unassuming priest radiating sincerity and humility." His six-foot-four-inch frame and proportionate breadth notwithstanding, most people experienced him "almost diffident, ... yet there was something about him far beyond these. It was his utter child-like simplicity."[57] Peyton was a positive person who respected the goodness of humanity and recognized human weakness, but he often had difficulty acknowledging human limitations for himself and others. One journalist described him as "a never-to-be-forgotten experience, a spiritual uplift that leaves one happy and contented as never before." Using the same metaphor another writer described him "as an experience so unusual that it is unlikely most of us will ever see his like again in our life-time."[58]

Peyton became a naturalized American citizen in 1938, but, of course, he never lost many of the Irish qualities that formed his life of faith and became so attractive to people worldwide. He never lost his brogue, which helped make him somewhat distinct, but it was the more fundamental values he learned as a child that carried him forward in his specialized ministry in the promotion of family prayer. Peyton never forgot the integral role his family played in his spiritual and personal development, and he never skipped an opportunity to acknowledge his family and give them gratitude. John Murphy wrote to Peyton's sister Kitty, "Father Pat never forgot for a minute that he owes everything that he has ever accomplished to his wonderful family."[59]

Peyton's Irish heritage also imbued him with the belief that family was the basic element of society and faith and that its restoration to a place of prominence in contemporary life was essential. It was not time for theorizing about the ills of society and family; there was a need to act now, "to restore that daily family prayer which for centuries has brought unity, understanding and happiness to the families that practiced it faithfully — the Family Rosary."[60] Peyton observed a great weakness in the family in its contemporary tendency to separate individual members of nuclear families, making the home merely a place for eating and sleeping. Recalling his Irish roots, Peyton suggested that his past experience, if lived today, could save the world:

> God let me be born in a Rosary Home, and so with my own eyes I saw what its power is. In my childhood the Family Rosary let me see every night my Mother and Father kneeling beside each other in adoration and love of God as they recited out loud the tremendous sentences of the Rosary. What that meant for a little child... was like wax to be molded! In childhood the Rosary in the Home gave me great leadership — a great sense of security, a great feeling of peace — in adolsescense [sic] it gave me a Home to live in that was anchored to God — and in young manhood it sent me into the world fortified with a bright light of Faith to show me where the way was safe or dangerous.[61]

For Patrick Peyton the solution to the contemporary family crisis was not complex, and it had been learned in the three-room thatched-roof house in Carracastle: family prayer through the rosary would save human society.

Tall of stature and passionate in his message Peyton nevertheless serves as a classic study in contrast when we analyze his style and eloquence as a speaker and his efficacy as a communicator. By all accounts and standards Peyton did not possess great gifts as a public speaker. Unlike his popular contemporary Fulton Sheen, who dazzled audiences on radio and television with oratorical eloquence, Peyton broke every rule of syntax, provided nothing of great intellectual merit or persuasive argument, and was described by Bishop Thomas Flynn of Lancaster, England, as "quite artless, unstudied, [and] simple." Loretta Young said he was "a terrible speaker — very unsophisticated."[62] Yet, despite his style Peyton effectively communicated his message. One observer of the Hexham, Newcastle, crusade of 1952 commented,

> The doubtful became certain, the lukewarm became fervent and the strong were strengthened. . . . Fr. Peyton is no orator, but his words are straight from the heart and he had the men in the hollow of his hands. They would have done anything he asked of them. He converted the shy, the awkward, the diffident and the indifferent into enthusiastic apostles who were willing to go out and canvass for the Family Rosary, no matter what opposition they might have to meet.[63]

Peyton's unsophisticated yet heartfelt message captivated audiences everywhere. When Peyton spoke, there was a stillness "that was to be experienced rather than described."[64] His message was essentially the same wherever he went, describing his life in Ireland, his cure through the intercession of the Blessed Virgin Mary, and the need for the family rosary. People were convinced of his complete sincerity and readily became disciples in his army. His simple style was a great asset, rather than a detriment, precisely because people believed what he said. He possessed "a different kind of eloquence that captured you, that made you hang on to what he was saying because the sincerity was there."[65] He struck no dramatic poses and used no theatrical gestures, but "he is proving through personal experience what the love of God can achieve for the humblest to the highest in the land."[66]

The impact that Peyton had on people was truly remarkable and demonstrates why he was so successful despite the obstacles and pitfalls he encountered in planning and preparing his family rosary ministry.

Through his simple yet sincere words he whipped crowds into a frenzy
of faith. One writer commented, "He's the closest thing to the flames
of Pentecost in 20 centuries."[67] He was viewed by contemporaries as a
humble and sincere priest who stood at the head of a great movement,
possessive of a faith "that is moving mountains, and more than mountains."[68] People were deeply affected by Peyton's spiritual presence; his
emotional energy when injected into people at crusades most especially
was real and quantifiable. One account written after Peyton spoke at a
rally in Singapore is illustrative: "Without hesitation I would say not a
single person left that field this evening the same as when he entered it.
Even if one didn't understand the language he [Peyton] was speaking in,
there was something in the speaker himself."[69] Peter Grace summarized
how and why Patrick Peyton made such a deep impact on others: "I
don't see how anyone could work closely with Father Peyton and not
have a very strong faith, as it seems to me that a number of small miracles occur almost each week."[70] Patrick Peyton was able to succeed when
rational thought may have considered it impossible.

The Crusades in the United States, 1949–58

The experience gained and the success enjoyed in the first three Canadian crusades in 1948 and 1949 paved the way for the first American
rosary campaigns, the first two of which were held in locations with
special significance in Peyton's life: Scranton, Pennsylvania, where he
emigrated in 1928, and the Midwest, where he spent eight years in religious formation at Notre Dame. The Family Rosary Crusade came to
Scranton between October 16 and November 20, 1949, at the invitation
of Bishop William Hafey, whose relationship with the Congregation of
Holy Cross had born fruit through the establishment of King's College
in Wilkes-Barre, Pennsylvania, in 1946.[71] Hafey wrote to his diocese: "It
is our fervent hope that all ... families, recognizing the desperate need in
our times for a return to family prayer, will find the grace and courage
to sign their daily Family Rosary pledge and keep it faithfully."[72] The
crusade featured five rallies, the largest of which drew fifty thousand in
Scranton. James Connerton observed his first rally and "was thrilled to
death with it."[73]

The American crusade moved to the Midwest in October 1950, with
a campaign encompassing the archdioceses of Louisville and Indianapolis and their four suffragan dioceses. The campaign was in some ways
another homecoming for Peyton, most especially on October 22, when
thirty-five thousand people poured into the Notre Dame football stadium

to hear him speak. The student publication the *Scholastic* commented, "The marked contrast between the pomp and color of the rally's procession and the simple message given by Father Peyton hit home."[74] After drawing fifty-two thousand to a rally in Indianapolis, Peyton took his campaign to Crookston, Minnesota, between October 15 and November 19. Francis Woods made all the arrangements, allowing Peyton to concentrate on the Midwest crusade. He did come to Crookston on November 5 to address fifteen thousand in the only rally of the campaign.[75]

A geographically extensive crusade, covering nine archdioceses and dioceses along the mid-Atlantic coast from Baltimore to Atlanta, was conducted between September 30 and November 4, 1951. Francis Woods and John Murphy, CSC, led the front team, disseminating information through eight local Catholic newspapers, including the *Catholic Standard* of Washington, D.C., the *Catholic Review* in Baltimore, the *Providence Visitor*, and the *Bulletin*, published in the diocese of Savannah-Atlanta. Peyton spoke at all eighteen rallies, addressing seventy thousand on October 28 in Washington, D.C.[76]

As the engine of Peyton's family rosary crusade gained more steam with the advance of time, the rosary crusader took on larger and larger projects. In 1952 the crusade was conducted in the South, centered at New Orleans, and in the archdiocese of New York. Between January 13 and February 17 Archbishop Joseph Rummel of New Orleans hosted the crusade. Twenty rallies were held in cities of the dioceses of Alexandria, Lafayette, Little Rock, Mobile, and Natchez, with the crowd of 110,000 at New Orleans on February 3 setting a new record for the crusade. The New Orleans crusade was supported not only by Rummel and his suffragan bishops, but by some significant government officials, including Sid McGrath and Hugh White, governors of Arkansas and Mississippi respectively. Mayor deLesseps S. Morrison of New Orleans declared February 3–10 as "Family Prayer Week" in the Crescent City.[77]

The crusade next moved to the archdiocese of New York between September 14 and October 19. Of the five rallies held by far the most spectacular was the one at the Polo Grounds on October 12, attended by seventy-six thousand. Cardinal Francis Spellman echoed Peyton's message in his talk:

For many years past the spirit of the world has been seeping into homes, dampening family spirit, disrupting family ties and destroying family virtues. The inevitable result is, our nation is nearing the brink of disaster. For as the family goes, so goes the country. To restore and to preserve the integrity, the sanctity and the peace to our homes, and thus save our nation's life, is the high duty that devolves upon us all, impelling us to be faithful in the daily recitation of the family Rosary for these intentions. For it has been demonstrated that the family which prays together stays together, bound together by the holy ties of faith in Mary, hope in Mary and love for Mary.[78]

Another highlight of the New York crusade was the first appearance of Joseph Quinn, CSC, on the front team; unfortunately it was also the first campaign where financial difficulties arose. Woods negotiated with Monsignor Joseph McCaffrey on the budget for the crusade, which was set at $30,000. McCaffrey, however, was under the impression that the budget was $15,000 and, thus, when the archdiocese was given a bill for $30,000 he refused to pay. After some negotiations both sides agreed to pay half of the disputed figure. The experience generated a discussion on the use of written contracts for financial responsibility, but the idea was never implemented.[79]

Because the mid-1950s were dominated by international crusades, the domestic crusades were, for the most part, rather small. The Cleveland crusade, held between May 31 and July 5, 1953, was most notable for its introduction of the fifteen mysteries of the rosary radio broadcasts that were sponsored by the Catholic Daughters of America. These radio shows became standard in American crusades and later worldwide after their translation into Spanish.[80] In October 1955 Peyton accepted the invitation of Bishop Edwin O'Hara to conduct a crusade in Kansas City to celebrate the diocesan diamond jubilee and the bishop's silver episcopal anniversary. Peyton was happy to accept, remembering that O'Hara had helped him launch his Family Rosary operation in 1942. Three rallies were held with the October 30 Kansas City event the best attended. The crusade then moved to the Pacific Northwest, first in the Diocese of Juneau, Alaska, and then in the various vicariates of the region from July 22 to September 6, 1956.[81] The campaign then moved south to the archdioceses of Seattle and Portland and their six suffragan sees from September 9 to November 2. Bishop James Byrne of Boise expressed his appreciation to the superior general of Holy Cross for Peyton and his work:

I do not need to tell you, Father O'Toole, how impressed I was by the sincerity and singleness of purpose of Father Peyton.... Having the opportunity of watching him for the past five days that I was with him during the week, I could not help but feel that God is using him to do a very important work.[82]

The final stop for Peyton's rosary crusade in the United States in the 1950s returned to the nation's heartland. As early as 1953 Peyton had been in contact with Bishop P. W. Bartholme of St. Cloud, Minnesota, who asked that the crusade come there that fall. Peyton responded that he could not meet that schedule, that he hoped to be able to conduct a crusade that would encompass Minnesota and the Dakotas, and to that end he had been in contact with Archbishop Aloysius Muench of St. Paul, the metropolitan of the region.[83] Denis Sughrue, CSC, joined Joseph Quinn on the front team for this last American crusade of the decade. The campaign was eventually planned for September and October 1958, beginning with a rally in Minot, North Dakota, on September 7, and concluding with the largest rally to date, in St. Paul on October 5, when nearly 225,000 people were in attendance. The pledge drive was also the most successful to date, with 96 percent, totaling over 1 million families, signing the pledge.[84]

The International Crusades in the 1950s

The first international venture outside Canada was a series of campaigns in England in 1951 and 1952. Father Peyton first met Bishop Thomas Flynn of Lancaster in August 1949 at Lourdes when the prelate addressed a group of pilgrims at the Marian shrine. Flynn, who possessed a lifetime devotion to the Blessed Virgin, told Peyton that he was very interested in a crusade in his diocese. One year later Francis Woods visited Flynn and scheduled the crusade to begin on February 11, 1951, the Feast of Our Lady of Lourdes.[85] Peyton realized the significance of this crusade: "I feel that this is a most important Crusade because it will in all probability open the door to all Europe to our efforts to bring peace to the world through Family Prayer."[86] For his first European venture he set the lofty goal of one million written pledges.[87]

This first English crusade was most noteworthy for its support from the local ordinary and because it provided the needed introduction for Peyton to the Church throughout Europe. John Murphy, CSC, along with his dedicated secretaries, readied the scene for Peyton, who spoke at the six rallies in the region between February 25 and March 11. Peyton spent almost every other waking moment making contacts for future crusades. Bishop Flynn was highly proactive in his support and outright advocacy of the rosary crusade. In reflecting upon the campaign he commented:

> I wish to say that his [Peyton's] visit to the Diocese has been a stupendous success.... Everywhere he has inspired the greatest enthusiasm for the Cause of the Family Rosary. Clergy and laity alike have taken him to their hearts and have responded with the utmost zeal to his appeal. I look for a great spiritual revolution in the Diocese as a result of this man's work. I am convinced that nothing greater has happened in my time.[88]

Similarly Murphy acknowledged the inspiration that Peyton brought to the diocese: "Right now they are all on fire. They have completely forgotten the slogan they have lived for centuries, 'It's never been done before,' and they are going all-out to stage the biggest rallies ever held in Lancashire."[89]

Peyton's initial foray into England was well received, especially considering the rather skeptical attitude held by most local people toward Americans. This success spurred Peyton to a full assault upon the Church in England beginning in the region of Newcastle, Hexham, and Middlesbrough between April 20 and May 25, 1952. During the Lancaster crusade Peyton had met Bishop Joseph McCormick of Hexham and Newcastle, who invited Peyton to conduct the campaign. The bishop was very high on Peyton and his credentials: "In Father Peyton I have found a priest who has devoted his life to this apostolic work. He has experience; he has understanding; he has the Holy Father's personal commendation and blessing."[90] Again John Murphy blazed the trail, but he realized that Peyton was the main event: "All I can say is that I have done my best to get the fires started but everyone here is waiting for you to kindle the sparks into a conflagration. That you alone can do!"[91] This crusade exploited the Family Theater films that had gained such accolades in the United States. *The Road to Peace, Hill Number One, That I May See, The Joyful Hour,* and *The Triumphant Hour* were shown in parishes and schools and generated much interest for the crusade and especially the rallies that culminated with one hundred thousand in attendance in Newcastle.[92]

The English assault moved south to Birmingham between May 25 and June 29. The fourteen rallies, including eighty-five thousand in attendance at Birkenhead on June 1, were successful, but it was the "conversion" in heart of Archbishop Joseph Masterson that was most noteworthy. Uncertain of Peyton at the outset, the aging prelate later remarked:

I thought he [Peyton] might be a high-powered American salesman such as I have seen at the cinema, [but] when I met him I found he was a very humble and holy man.... I became one of his greatest admirers and I am delighted he has been able to come to this diocese. The world so badly needs family prayer. Fr. Peyton I regard as an ambassador of Our Blessed Lady.[93]

Masterson's sentiments were shared by others who experienced the crusade as an event that touched people's hearts and buoyed their faith. One writer captured the feeling of many: "The Family Rosary Crusade has stirred this diocese such as nothing else has done in history.... God be praised for this great apostolate which goes right to the root of the matter by introducing God and our Blessed Mother into the family circle."[94]

The English campaign culminated in the London crusade (Archdiocese of Westminster) extending to the surrounding regions in the south between June 29 and August 3. The crusade received an added bonus when the pope wrote to Cardinal Bernard Griffin, archbishop of Westminster:

We earnestly exhort those of Our beloved children toward whom the [Family Rosary] Crusade has been directed to regard the joint recitation of the Rosary in the family circle as a most important collective act in their daily lives and a most certain way of obtaining the spiritual and temporal favors of which they stand in need.[95]

The crusade began well with one hundred thousand in attendance at a rally in Hyde Park, a crowd unprecedented in the memory of local residents for a religious gathering. Bishop Thomas Flynn of Lancaster, who was the first prelate to invite Peyton to England and had been such a great advocate in 1951, continued to sing his praises: "Here is our modern David, carrying a sling with five stones, each a decade of the Rosary. And he is bidding the world to imitate and use that sling effectively — with a faith and singleness of purpose which reflect David's confidence and sureness of aim."[96]

The London crusade reached its apex on July 27 with a massive rally attended by eighty-three thousand at fabled Wembley Stadium. A living rosary of youth conducted in mime assembled on the athletic field, hymns were sung, and the rosary was recited. Cardinal Griffin urged the crowd to make home life an experience promoting prayer, creating a condition that is helpful and efficacious to both the church and the state. Peyton's message impressed people by its "simplicity as much as by his supernatural enthusiasm for a cause which he believes can save our society from shipwreck by winning for God the family, society's basic unit."

Peyton made a big impression on the crowd and the nation: "Britain will long remember the American Rosary Priest with the hint of an Irish brogue who is such a fighter for the Family Rosary."[97]

During and after the English campaign, Peyton returned to Canada, where his great crusade for family prayer began a few years earlier. Peyton first brought the crusade to the archdiocese of Halifax and its suffragan sees in Nova Scotia between May 1 and June 10, 1951. A total of ten rallies were held, but most were small, except for the sixty thousand in attendance at Halifax on June 3. The strain of the crusades on Family Rosary personnel was significant. While Peyton never gave evidence of exhaustion until it was too late, others were less heroic. In a comical tone John Murphy wrote to Joseph Quinn back in the Albany office, "I have been bearing up well under it all—but I think it will not be long before they put me in a cell with a butterfly net—a fishing line and a gold-fish bowl."[98] One year later, in late August 1952, following the London and New York crusades, Peyton went even further east in Canada to Newfoundland. Several Family Theater films, including the popular *Hill Number One* and *That I May See,* were shown in local parishes, schools, and rented theaters; *Family Theater of the Air* broadcasts were aired on local radio stations. The largest of three rallies, held in St. John's, drew fifteen thousand people.[99]

At the invitation of Bishop John Cody, who was now the local ordinary, in 1956 Peyton returned to the place it all began, London, Ontario. To guarantee a successful reprise Cody assigned one of his priests as the diocesan family rosary director. This was the precursor of what became the postcrusade format in the 1960s.[100]

His resounding success in Lancaster, England, encouraged Peyton to seek similar engagements in other lands. In November 1951 he accepted the invitation of Archbishop Daniel Mannix of Melbourne, Australia, to speak at a special jubilee year celebration. Since this was not a formal crusade, a local priest, Gerard Coghlan, made the necessary arrangements. The large reception that Peyton received in Melbourne, when eighty thousand heard him speak, inspired him to promise a full crusade in 1953.[101]

The interim period was occupied with crusades in the United States and then his first foray onto the European mainland in Málaga, Spain, and the British dependency of Gibraltar. In July 1952, during the London crusade, Peyton met Bishop Angel Herrera of Málaga, who invited the crusade to his diocese. To overcome the language barrier,[102] Peyton obtained the services of Marcos McGrath, CSC, an Indiana Province Holy Cross priest (like Archibald McDowell in Argentina), who was fluent in

Spanish from his Panamanian heritage. Peyton, who was reticent about speaking Spanish, learned the language well enough to speak at the rally, so convinced were Woods and other co-workers that his presence was vital to the success of the operation. There were six rallies with an estimated one hundred thousand in attendance in the city of Málaga. From Málaga the crusade moved the short distance to Gibraltar at the invitation of Bishop Richard J. Fitzgerald. The campaign, which was held from January 25 to February 28, 1953, was conducted almost simultaneously with the Málaga endeavor. Connerton congratulated Peyton on his Spanish campaign: "I just want to say to you that we are very happy over your present crusades and join you in thanking God and His Blessed Mother for this further blessing upon the work of spreading prayer among families throughout the world."[103]

The major effort of the rosary crusade in 1953 was the five-month campaign in Australia. Peyton's triumphant reception at his jubilee year presentation in Melbourne made his introduction to the "land down under" not as necessary as in other places. The whirlwind campaign covered twenty-six dioceses, centered in the north, east, and southeast sections of the nation: Queensland, New South Wales, and Melbourne. Queensland, covering the archdiocese of Brisbane and its four suffragan dioceses, was the first stop, from August 23 to September 27. John Murphy, CSC, Francis Woods, Dorothy Kahl, and Kathy Holther, a secretary from the Hollywood office, who replaced Pat Spanbauer due to a family emergency, made all the preliminary arrangements for the campaign. Family Theater films and various radio programs, most especially the Catholic Daughters of America series, were used as publicity. Nineteen rallies were held, all of which were relatively small, save in Brisbane when 85,000 gathered to hear Father Peyton speak. In New South Wales twenty-four rallies were held between October 4 and November 8. A massive throng of 110,000 crowded the Sydney rugby stadium to attend the rally.[104]

The Australia campaign reached Melbourne, the site of Peyton's initial triumph in the nation, on November 20 and continued until December 20. Peyton was hosted by Archbishop Daniel Mannix, through whose influence the crusade was invited to the various regions and dioceses of the country. Large crowds were present at several of the twenty rallies held in the region, with 150,000 present in Melbourne and 60,000 in Adelaide. Sadly the Melbourne crusade was the last for John Murphy, who was involved in a serious automobile accident during the campaign. After his recovery he was reassigned as director of the Albany office, and

Joseph Quinn, CSC, who had tasted the crusade life in New York a year prior, became the chief front man for the international crusade.[105]

March and April 1953 found the crusade on the island nation of New Zealand. Francis Woods did the preparation work, with the transition between John Murphy and Joseph Quinn still in process. The crusade, which encompassed the entire nation through its four dioceses, featured eleven rallies, with the best attended at Auckland (33,000) and Wellington (25,000).[106]

The great triumph of the Australian and New Zealand crusades provided a jumping-off point for return to Europe. On April 25, four days after completing the campaign in New Zealand, Peyton arrived in Tuam, Ireland, to begin a four-month campaign. The rapidity of the trip, a miracle of travel in those days, was a sign to many that the crusade was blessed from the outset. He was joined by Francis Woods and Joseph Quinn, CSC, who came from Albany as a full-time replacement for John Murphy. Members of the Irish hierarchy collectively had not extended an invitation to their native son, but Peyton was confident that with the support of Archbishop James Walsh of Tuam and the enthusiasm that the crusade had generated in other places he would be able to make the circuit of most of the Irish Republic and parts of Northern Ireland.[107] The Tuam rally was a great success and demonstrated the faith of the local people. The town of four thousand hosted twenty thousand at the local football (soccer) stadium, including some two hundred from the Aran Islands, many of whom had never seen an automobile or heard English spoken.[108]

The Irish crusade was special for Peyton in many ways. Certainly the return to his native land had to bring satisfaction, but to return as an international celebrity, promoting a devotion so instrumental to Irish Catholicism, must have been that much more significant. The campaign conducted twenty-one rallies, including one at Belfast on June 13 that drew one hundred thousand people, but Peyton's return to his beloved County Mayo and most especially to Ballina, the town adjoining Attymass, probably brought the most satisfaction. The local football field was crowded on June 6 with fifteen thousand who braved rain to come and pray the rosary and hear Father Peyton speak. The event and the person of Patrick Peyton made deep impressions on all present.[109] One local journalist commented:

> In my more than twenty years in Irish journalism... never had I come face to face with a man so humble, so saintly, so sincere, so unostentatious, so absorbed in his noble ideal and single-hearted

purpose, and so preeminently equipped with the qualities of mind and heart for his glorious global mission as Fr. Peyton.[110]

Fellow Holy Cross religious were appreciative of his work ethic during his whirlwind campaign, but worried about his health:

> The rallies take a good deal out of the poor man and hehas [*sic*] been completely exhausted during the past few days. It takes episcopal orders to get him to rest. He is so gentle and selfless that he insists upon seeing everyone who wants to see him, the more humble the suppliant the more insistent he is that he see the person.[111]

The international crusades in 1954 closed with a return to Spain and the dioceses of Vitoria, San Sebastián, Bilbao, Tarragona, and Santander. With the assistance and support of high government officials, including the prime minister and Francisco Franco's right-hand man, Luis Carrero Blanco, and minister of justice Antonio de Oriol, the two main rallies at Bilbao and San Sebastián were very successful, drawing over 120,000 people each.

Although Peyton's crusade had covered many lands by the end of 1954, the succeeding year would prove to be the busiest in the decade for the rosary crusade. From mid-November 1954 until September 1955 Peyton kept a torrid schedule of rallies and personal appearances that was never equaled. This drive began with a four-month crusade in fifty-nine archdioceses and dioceses of the nations of India, Pakistan, Burma, Ceylon (Sri Lanka), Malaysia, and Siam (Thailand). In early 1954 Peyton sent Francis Woods to India to speak with Cardinal Valerian Gracias, archbishop of Bombay, about the crusade. Gracias suggested that the crusade could be linked with the Marian Congress to be held in December. The idea won instant favor from the Indian hierarchy.[112] Thus, the crusade began on December 8 when Peyton addressed seventy-four bishops and one hundred thousand others during the closing session of the Congress, challenging the nations to whom the crusade was coming to obtain 5 million pledges for the family rosary.[113]

The crusade proceeded from diocese to diocese and nation to nation over the next four months. Peyton's schedule was not for the faint of heart. During the period he spoke at thirty-seven rallies and made sixty-two appearances in all. The largest gatherings were in Bombay, India, and Colombo, Ceylon, where crowds of two hundred thousand and one hundred thousand respectively, composed of Christians, Hindus,

Moslems, Sikhs, and Parsis, came to hear Peyton's message. This ecumenical spirit was present throughout the campaign but was especially prominent in Burma, as noted in a secular newspaper, the *Nation*:

> Last week, there came to Burma a good man, a holy man, a man of God. In a few days he was gone, and the manner of his going was as unobtrusive as his coming. But he left implanted in the minds of several thousand people a tiny seed destined one day to grow into something reaching the very sky.[114]

Quinn was elated about the crusade's success and wrote the superior general:

> It [the crusade] made a tremendous impression on all, Catholics and non-Catholics alike. The Buddhist papers have been enthusiastic in spreading the message and taking as their slogan that "the family that prays together stays together," and one of them reminded [us] that "it is indeed welcoming in these days of materialism and strife that there is still so much faith and hope in spiritual values."[115]

A postcrusade report sounded a similar note: "Succeeding where the politicians have failed, Father Peyton has forged a SEATO [South East Asia Treaty Organization] (in the spiritual sphere) embracing even the neutralist Indians, Ceylonese, and Burmans."[116] A souvenir booklet, the first of its kind, outlining in photos and prose the highlights of the crusade, was published to celebrate the campaign's great success.

The crusade next moved to the African continent, beginning with the South African campaign, which covered thirty-one archdioceses and dioceses. Peyton had been invited by Archbishop Owen McCann of Cape Town, a member of the Administrative Board of the South African Catholic Bishops Conference, who had been impressed by the Family Theater films. A total of eight rallies were held, with the highest attendance of twenty-eight thousand at Johannesburg on April 10. One local pastor, "enthralled to meet such a holy man," wrote to James Connerton about his experience of Father Peyton:

> There can be no possible doubt that Father Peyton was a phenomenal personal success here during his African Family Rosary Crusade. There can be no doubt either, about the burning sincerity, the tireless energy, the simple but convincing eloquence, the quite indescribable hold that he had over extraordinar[ily] diverse audiences here.[117]

The South African crusade was followed immediately by the commencement of the East Africa campaign, running from May 14 to September 24. Peyton had been invited to the region by Archbishops Celestine J. Damiano and J. R. Knox, the ordinary for Nairobi and apostolic delegate respectively, as well as the other bishops of the region. The campaign was the largest undertaken to date, comprising seventy-four archdioceses and dioceses in six East African nations: Kenya, Tanganyika, Rhodesia, Nyasaland, Uganda, and the Sudan. Besides speaking at all thirty-two rallies, Peyton also visited Catholic institutions of all sorts, especially hospitals, giving support to thousands who were sick, crippled, or handicapped.[118] The crusade took a toll on Peyton as he succumbed to severe heatstroke,[119] but this did not diminish his effectiveness:

> Father Peyton certainly gained overwhelming victories for Our Blessed Lady in South, East, and Central Africa. From every territory glowing reports have come from archbishops, bishops, priests, and religious testifying to the phenomenal success of the crusade and its lasting results.[120]

As in India, a thirty-six-page souvenir book was published relating the story of the campaign in photos and words.[121]

The torturous schedule which Patrick Peyton kept in 1955 probably explains the reduced international crusade activity for the remainder of the decade. During his crusade in India, Peyton made contacts for his future activities. In Calcutta he met Cardinal Fernando Quiroga y Palacios, archbishop of Compostela, Spain, who extended an invitation for the crusade to come to his archdiocese and the four other dioceses of his province. The crusade returned to Spain, beginning in Santiago Compostela in February 1956.[122] One year later Peyton brought his rosary campaign to the dioceses of Salamanca, Badajoz, and Albacete. These crusades were significant for the introduction to the crusade of the Spanish *misioneros,* women who lived in community much like religious but wore no habit. The assistance of the *misioneros* was helpful in Spain, but their presence would be critical in the Latin American crusades of the 1960s.[123]

Two more European crusades closed out the decade. Upon receipt of an invitation from Archbishop Mario Macrionitis, SJ, of Athens the crusade was conducted in Greece between October 7 and December 15, 1957. Finally, Peyton brought the crusade to the diocese of Brugge, Belgium, beginning on April 27, 1959, and closing on June 18. Four rallies were held with sixty-five thousand in attendance at Kortrijk on June 7.

It was during this final European crusade of the decade that the fifteen half-hour films depicting all the mysteries of the rosary, filmed in Spain in 1956, were first used.[124]

Peyton's international rosary crusade closed a highly successful decade by coming to the Philippines following the Belgium campaign. Philippine ecclesiastical officials had been in formal communication with Father Peyton about a crusade in their country as early as 1953. Originally Peyton planned to bring the crusade as a precursor to a Marian Congress, scheduled for January 1955 (as he did in India), but changes in the dates for the Congress to December 1954 combined with commitments previously made in other locales ended the crusade possibility for the time.[125] After a lapse of almost five years, formal dates for the crusade were set between November 1 and December 10, 1959. Providentially the international crusade reached its apex as the decade ended. Four rallies were held, with 1 million in attendance at Cebu and 1.5 million at Luneta Park in Manila, despite torrential tropical rains that preceded Father Peyton's address. The rosary priest was overjoyed at the reception he received: "Never in all the history of the crusades have I come to an area or country that is responding like the Philippines. No one is holding back."[126] Almost 1.2 million pledges were signed as the crusade closed, leading Joseph Quinn, CSC, to comment, "The Crusade in Manila was without doubt the greatest we have had in any part of the world." The great success of the crusade led to the establishment of the first permanent international Family Rosary office, with Father Bienvenido Lopez appointed as its first director.[127]

Evaluation of the Crusade Effort

The breadth of the Family Rosary Crusade and the energy demonstrated by Patrick Peyton and his faithful co-workers was characteristic of a work ethic that the fabled rosary crusader always manifested. Peyton truly believed that his mission in life was to work ceaselessly for Mary, and he communicated this message to all with whom he worked. Writing to all associated with Family Rosary, he declared:

> Let us all face the jobs ahead of us and grasp all the opportunities that fall from the heavens, compensated in so doing by the knowledge and assurance that we have a great privilege that is peculiarly our own, of wearing our lives out — I mean that literally — for our dear Blessed Mother and her work.[128]

Peyton stopped at nothing in order to promote the Family Rosary Crusade, and he believed that others must be equally dedicated. He was never content to allow even one possibility to pass that might advance the cause:

> I cannot help but put down here what Our Blessed Mother must often think in her heart, even now, as She sees what could be done if the effort was put forth for Her, and as She sees what is left undone because of fear or pride, or any other motive or laziness. The best way to summarize what must be often in the heart of Our Mother as well as frequently in my own is: "The saddest words of tongue or pen are the words that might have been."[129]

Unable to acknowledge his human limitations, Peyton sometimes drove himself to the point of exhaustion and ill health. From the time of the first crusade in London, Ontario, co-workers noted that his schedule would greatly tax anyone, yet Peyton gladly pushed himself to promote devotion to Mary. Fellow Holy Cross religious recognized the strain under which he labored, felt it themselves, and often pleaded with him to slow down. John Murphy once cautioned him,

> Father Pat, please get what rest you can for the couple of days before you come to England. If God spares you the health to live through the first ten days after you arrive, it won't be so bad — but the Lord help you for the first part of the crusade — it will be awful.[130]

Even the superior general suggested, "I urge you again to take reasonable care of your health, because if you do that you will be able to do much more in the long run. Do not hesitate to take time out for a rest now and again, that can be offered up to God, as you know."[131] Fellow workers often asked his family to intercede when their efforts were unsuccessful.[132] Rarely would Peyton recognize his need for rest, but even when he did, any respite was not for personal enrichment, but for the betterment and promotion of his work.[133]

The single-minded devotion to Mary through promotion of the family rosary characterized the life and mission of Father Peyton. He often identified his will with that of the Virgin Mary — an attitude that did not sit well with his confreres. Rather than identifying himself as under obedience to religious superiors of Holy Cross, Peyton often voiced the idea that his obedience was to Mary, who gave him his orders as well. One fellow religious commented about this belief, "We really didn't like that."[134] Father Peyton believed in the promotion of family prayer, but its seems little else was of importance to him. An Australian journalist noted the phenomenon: "He [Peyton] is literally obsessed with the idea that the restoration of family prayer is the root of the matter."[135]

Father Peyton's independent and almost autonomous operation combined with his strong commitment, superhuman energy, and single-mindedness of purpose continued to feed the strained relationship between the crusader and his fellow Holy Cross religious who worked with him. John Murphy, CSC, and Joseph Quinn, CSC, have voiced the opinion that Peyton seemingly had no concept of the needs of his fellow workers. Quinn commented:

> He [Peyton] often disregarded the needs of the people who were working for him — the priests, brothers and sisters and secretaries. If we were hungry at night, we would keep going right through supper time. We would not stop for things like that. That was hard to handle. I think he lost his temper when he didn't get his way. In general I think he was kind, but sometimes I wondered if he had any real concern for us.

Some Holy Cross religious concluded that Peyton was somewhat insecure with community members as manifest in an inability to relax in their presence and in seldom being able to express gratitude for a job well done.[136] When rallies concluded, he insisted that the whole staff observe a holy hour immediately in thanksgiving for the event's success. The timing was poor, and the efficacy of such a prayer was lost on all but Father Peyton.[137] Unable to recognize his personal limitations, it was equally difficult for him to see the boundaries of others; he was demanding of the time and dedication of all.

Despite his one-track mind and his many conflicts with Holy Cross co-workers, strong support for Peyton and his ministry continued from the community and outside sources. The superior general, Christopher O'Toole, CSC, and the provincials, James Connerton, CSC (1948–56), and George DePrizio, CSC (1956–64), continued to provide their support through circular letters and the assignment of personnel. One co-worker suggested, "He [Peyton] was held in high esteem by all the members of the Province.... He was a marvelous apostolic figure for all of us."[138] *America* magazine noted Peyton's contribution:

> The Rosary Crusade is a crusade for peace and life for all men. It is charged with the disarming simplicity and unusual charity of Father Peyton, who pledged himself when menaced by a seemingly mortal illness to obtain 10 million pledges of the daily recitation

of the rosary. The faith of American Catholics will surely prompt them to carry out their part in fulfilling this promise to the Mother of God, especially since she is our national patron.[139]

Conclusion

The introduction of the international rosary crusade in 1948 in London, Ontario, and its system of massive public rosary rallies and a door-to-door pledge system was the last link, after establishment of Family Rosary and Family Theater, of Peyton's tripartite system to return the family rosary to American Catholic homes. By the statistics that his crusade team kept the initial goal was achieved in 1957, but Peyton continued on in attempts to win more people to his family rosary philosophy of life. Peyton had crossed the oceans and found success on every continent save South America, a place rich in possibility because of its predominantly Catholic population. He believed, however, that the South American crusade needed one additional tool not present in the 1950s: a series of films depicting the fifteen mysteries of the rosary. The story of Father Peyton's life thus must turn to the production of these films and their use in the Latin American crusades.

Chapter 6

The Rosary Films, 1953 – 60

Patrick Peyton's efforts to restore family prayer through the rosary had reached five continents, and his goal of bringing 10 million families to the practice of this special devotion had been achieved, but for this tireless priest and servant of Mary the main goal of Latin America, home to over one-third of the Roman Catholics worldwide, still remained to be conquered. While ostensibly Catholic, Latin Americans, mainly because of poor social conditions in their native lands, were not adequately catechized to appreciate and gain spiritually from the rosary crusade as it had been originally conceived and practiced in other nations. A specialized tool was needed, therefore, to evangelize and educate Latin Americans in the basic teachings of the faith. During the age of discovery Franciscan and Dominican friars brought picture books to the native peoples of Latin America to teach them about Jesus' life, His salvific death and resurrection, and the precepts of the Catholic faith; but the twentieth century required something more sophisticated.

Technology in the middle twentieth century provided more advanced methods of catechesis through radio and most especially the miracle of film, which allowed viewers to witness events and instantly receive the Christian message. Peyton had already used the varied media of radio and film to promote and sustain his popular adage, "The family that prays together stays together," and thus he found it natural to use similar ways in crusades in Latin America. However, the project that Peyton conceived, producing fifteen films to relate the story and tradition of the mysteries of the rosary, was gargantuan. But once he determined that the project was necessary to "win Latin America to the family rosary," he was undeterred by the finances and resources it would require, and he pressed forward, bringing to fruition the most significant project in the history of Family Theater.

The Idea Is Born

The films developed against the background of the Cleveland crusade of 1953. The premiere in Cleveland of the fifteen half-hour radio programs based on the rosary mysteries and sponsored by the Catholic Daughters of America[1] gave Peyton the idea that something similar could be done in film for broadcast on television. This idea was reinforced in his mind from talks he had conducted during the Málaga crusade the previous January with film executives in Europe, who suggested that the success of the first films produced by Family Theater was an indication of the direction that should be taken with respect to media operations.[2] Peyton justified the work that would be involved by outlining four benefits of the films: (1) They would turn American home televisions into classrooms where peoples of all faiths — Protestants, Jews, pagans, and Catholics — could learn about the divinity of Christ and His great love for humankind. (2) They would help bishops in foreign missions to assist with the conversion and catechesis of local peoples. (3) They would show what rich food for mind and heart is found in the rosary. (4) They would be a worthwhile and practical gift to Our Lady to honor the centenary of the declaration of the dogma of the Immaculate Conception (proclaimed by Pope Pius IX on December 8, 1854). He concluded: "With this gift [the films] She will be able to use the medium of television to bring the millions of people all over the world lessons of love and peace that She has come to the earth so often herself to tell us."[3] In his mind, based on his last objective Peyton set a goal to complete the project by December 8, 1954.

In his usual style of never taking no for an answer and with the belief that all was possible if sufficient effort was applied, Peyton began to plan the format of the films and the logistics for their production. He suggested that each film should consist of three parts. The dramatic portion would depict the historical facts of the mystery, but also its implications and applications for the lives of contemporary people. For instance, the Gospel evangelists' report that the crucifixion of Jesus gave the prisoner Barabbas a second chance means that Christ will give a second or third chance to all who call upon him. Each film would feature appropriate music sung by a well-known artist as well as a short segment of the prayers of the rosary, recited in an inspirational setting. Peyton believed his Hollywood connections would permit him to obtain much of what he needed either gratis or inexpensively. He immediately asked friends for blank film and costumes gratis. He then planned to hire fifteen major Hollywood directors and script writers to work on the films, which he hoped would be produced at the sound stage of Holly-wood legend Mary Pickford.[4] It would soon be evident, however, that the scope of this project was so vast that both the timetable and hopes for a minimal budget were not realistic.

With the dream cemented in his mind, Peyton hit the road in search of monetary sponsors, either groups or individuals, most especially reli-gious congregations, who would put up $25,000 to cover the costs of one film. He realized at the outset that this amount might not be sufficient, but he proclaimed, "With this much guaranteed for each, I have every confidence that I will be able to receive the remainder."[5] On May 31, 1953, Peyton, with great confidence that Mary would guide his work, went on the road in quest of sponsors. That first day was a great triumph as in a whirlwind of travel, talk, and arm twisting he was able to secure sponsorship pledges from the Dominican sisters in Adrian, Michigan, the Sisters of the Immaculate Heart of Mary in Detroit, and the School Sisters of Notre Dame in Milwaukee.[6]

Peyton's international travels as the apostle of the family rosary pro-vided him with the perfect pulpit from which to solicit film sponsors. His magnetism and charismatic charm overwhelmed almost everyone as religious societies and communities throughout the world opened their coffers to support the project. Peyton was overt and unabashed in his style of imploring peoples throughout the world to financially support this project. Undeterred by his failure to obtain as many free services as he had hoped, and realizing that his original estimate of $25,000 was too low, he continued to seek funds in sometimes creative ways. At the Marian Congress that preceded the crusade in India, Peyton con-vinced two religious orders of nuns to co-sponsor a film. His 1954 return to Ireland also produced a sponsor through the joint efforts of various congregations of sisters.

The Australia crusade of 1953 provided Peyton with significant if di-verse support. John Murphy, CSC, the local director of the Australian crusade, reported, "Father Peyton is doing his best to raise a lot of money over here for the proposed fifteen half-hour moving pictures."[7] Peyton convinced four congregations of nuns, the Good Shepherd Sisters, the Sisters of Mercy, the Brown Sisters of St. Joseph, and the Presentation Sisters, to each sponsor a film for $20,000.[8] Additionally, the cardinal archbishop of Sydney, Norman Thomas Gilroy, speaking on behalf of the hierarchy in Australia, agreed to sponsor the Ascension mystery. The four bishops of New Zealand were engaged to financially support the Annunciation. The sacrifices made to support the rosary film project were noted by those in the Family Rosary organization. Edmund Murray, CSC, marveled at the generosity of smaller religious communities: "It appears that the smaller the community and the less obvious [is the] possibility of large donations from these poor and tiny groups, the greater their sacrifices and the higher their contributions."[9] Peyton noted the worldwide aspect of the appeal of the project, 60 percent of which was financed by sources outside the United States:[10]

> As this project has developed, sacrificing contributions have risen up, not only in the United States and Australia, but Canada, New Zealand, France, Ireland, Spain, and Pakistan. Truly, this seems to be an example of the Mystical Body of Christ in action with so many countries cooperating to help produce this gift for the Mother of God.[11]

Although Peyton was not shy about requesting help from the Congregation of Holy Cross, the bulk of his support from that direction came as a result of a coordinated effort orchestrated by Christopher O'Toole, CSC, superior general of the men, and Sister Mary of St. Rose, CSC, superior general of the Sisters of the Holy Cross, who each pledged $25,000 to sponsor the Crucifixion and Carrying of the Cross mysteries respectively.[12] This early planning period for the films within the Holy Cross community also produced additional evidence that the films could function in more ways than merely being broadcast on local television stations. The superior general was informed:

> We are engaged in producing fifteen half-hour films on the Mysteries of the Rosary, primarily for television use in the United States. However, the films are being made in such a manner that they may easily be dubbed into all foreign languages. They will thus be available for all foreign mission countries where Communism is making headway — Asia, India and Africa.[13]

Planning the Films

The need to secure financing for the rosary films was an ongoing effort with which Peyton had great expertise and familiarity, but he realized from the outset that he would have to secure key personnel to oversee and run the project since his schedule would not allow his personal supervision. He chose Jerome Lawyer, CSC, the first Holy Cross religious to join Peyton's team in October 1945, and the director of Family Theater in Hollywood since 1950, as executive director of the film project. As was his custom to buoy the confidence of his lieutenants in the crusade, Peyton wrote Lawyer,

> This is a little note to tell you how extremely happy your letter written from Hollywood has made me and how thankful to God and Our Blessed Mother I am that they have you to protect their interests in these 15 films — that they have you to generously and affectionately and warmly not sparing yourself to make sure that every one of the great benefactors that God and Our Lady has given this project will have their interests protected 100 percent, but most of all that they have your mind and heart and humility to guarantee that nothing will be left undone to give them 15 films that will be worthy of them.[14]

In January 1954 Peyton met with an advisory committee of twenty-two supporters and colleagues in the office of Joseph I. Breen Sr. Breen, former head of the movie industry's Production Code of Morality, had agreed to chair the advisory committee and to plan the overall project. As a result of the meeting, and in consultation with Lawyer, Peyton engaged Joseph Breen Jr. to coordinate the script writing in order to maintain continuity of story and format. The younger Breen was eventually made project director, not only because of his familiarity with the scripts, but also on the basis of his Hollywood track record, particularly his role as director of the 1952 film *The Miracle of Fatima*, which Peyton much admired. Breen saw the project as an "opportunity to make these pictures for Our Lady really Catholic, and yet in a way that will appeal to non-Catholics, Jews and others, to make Our Lady, we hope, better understood and loved by them."[15] John Kirby, former vice president of W. R. Grace and Company, was named as financial advisor and business manager for the project.

The production team's first challenge was to select a filming site, keeping in mind Peyton's primary goal of professional filming "in Hollywood or wherever a great job can be guaranteed and most economical at the same time."[16] Joseph Breen Sr. suggested Spain, articulating several reasons for his choice. First, Spain is a nation steeped in the Catholic tradition and possessing a strong overall religious atmosphere. Geographically the nation is similar to the Holy Land and the people in appearance possess physical features that are very Middle Eastern in quality. Spaniards have a long history of religious plays and several recently released religious films were produced there. Lastly, production costs would be considerably less than in Hollywood. In July 1954 John Kirby and Peter Grace met with General Francisco Franco, ruling dictator in Spain, who "expressed great interest in the project," viewing it as a spiritual dimension to his military campaign for Catholicism.[17] Lawyer expressed initial reservations with Spain, noting that control of operations would be difficult, the language barrier was significant, and the quality of facilities was uncertain. Lawyer convinced the rosary priest initially, but after the conclusion of the African crusades Peyton, working through Francis Woods, asked Lawyer to visit Spain and reconsider its advantages.[18] Eventually Spain was chosen for the production for the reasons outlined by Breen, with the factor of lower costs being predominant. The superior general was ambivalent about the decision: "Father Lawyer will find many difficulties in making the films in Spain. The Latin mentality is a bit different from our practical Anglo-Saxon outlook. However, from the religious and artistic point of view, the films made in Spain should certainly be superior."[19]

While the site was being debated, efforts to produce fifteen quality scripts was proving even more difficult. Between 1953, when Peyton first conceived of the idea, and 1955 the scripts were written and rewritten, rejected, accepted, and then rejected a second time. The rush to complete the project by Peyton's original target date of December 8, 1954, "really loused things up" according to Lawyer, who realized that quality scripts would require more time.[20] The script editor, Joseph Breen Jr., was assisted by Fathers William Robinson, CSC, who consulted on the final versions of the scripts, and Francis Bennett, a priest from the diocese of Dunedin, New Zealand, whose task was to keep scripts theologically and biblically sound. Twenty Catholic writers were originally contracted for the project, but the final scripts were produced by only six writers.[21] Peyton was concerned about the quality of the scripts and wondered if more money would enhance them, but none was forthcoming.[22] The scripts, completed by mid-year 1955, were approved by Lawyer, who described them as "real heartbreakers."[23]

Proximate preparations for the film productions took a major step forward when Lawyer, John Kirby, and a few support staff arrived in Madrid on September 27, 1955, to begin the on-site preparations. Peyton came to Madrid for a team discussion between October 6 and October 10. At this point, the pressures of the project, particularly those imposed by Peyton, were clearly beginning to weigh on Lawyer, whose past experience, pastoral skill, and qualifications did not include producing Hollywood films. Francis Woods tried to mollify Lawyer:

> I might mention that Father Pat is very happy over the way you are handling this project and he is in a mood now so that he really does not care how long you take for he fully realises [*sic*] that every

change you make and every delay in date is for the better, so Father Jerry, do not feel that you must push this beyond what you think is the best. If your strength and health holds out just keep after it until you feel that you have exactly what everybody wants. Father Pat is completely relaxed about it and is one hundred percent confident in every change and everything you are doing.[24]

During the next six months, Lawyer and his associates worked feverishly to begin filming. They confronted many hurdles, described in their correspondence as "red tape," concerning imported equipment, international transfer of funds, and the intricacies of Spanish procedures and customs. Lawyer negotiated contracts for constructing sets and arranged housing for the production team. He made the difficulty of the task clear in a letter to John Murphy, "This is not a glamorous life — it's Hell."[25]

The most pressing task before filming could begin was securing the final support personnel and actors for the key roles in the films. Edwin DuPar, one of Hollywood's top cameramen, who had worked with Joseph Breen on The Miracle of Fatima, was hired to be the chief cinematographer. The total support staff of sixty-five included Bill Persons, the project's production manager, Gerald Turney-Smith, the film editor, and Mary Jane Buchenau (daughter of Jacoba Buchenau), the production secretary. Javier Echenique, a Spanish priest, assisted Francis Bennett as religious consultant and censor. The key roles in the films were filled with Spanish actors, led by Antonio Villar, the "Bing Crosby of Spain," who played St. Peter and Pontius Pilate, Virgilio Teixeira, who played St. John, and Maruchi Fresno, who played the Sorrowful Mother beneath the foot of the cross. The most elusive role and by far the most important was that of the young Mary.[26] In an attempt to find the best person 175 women were interviewed, but the right match was not discovered until Lawyer received a tip about a young woman living some distance from Madrid who had the perfect face for the role. The woman, Dolores Cantabella, was a peasant who could not walk completely erect and knew little about city life or movies, but her simplicity and beauty were exactly what the role required.[27]

Production and Film Premieres

True to Peyton's custom of the past, the rosary film project was formally inaugurated on March 25, 1956, the Feast of the Annunciation, with a Mass celebrated by Javier Echenique, religious advisor on the films and a representative of the Propagation of the Faith in Rome. The event, attended by Christopher O'Toole, CSC, was followed one week later on April 2 with the first day of filming on outside sets. This continued until August 28. Peyton visited the Madrid set on April 6 and declared, "The pictures are off to a wonderful and blessed start."[28]

The day-to-day production of the films, as one might expect, experienced many small obstacles and surprises. Director Breen, Lawyer, and the rest of the production staff had to deal with the temperamental actors, including the production's major star, Antonio Villar, who often failed to show up on the set with the precision Americans take for granted. Weather was always a problem, forcing Breen to rearrange the shooting of scenes to make them more consistent with the environmental conditions, or even the hour. The scorching heat and sudden rain of the Spanish summer made production at times a guessing game. A major power outage on July 17 forced more rescheduling. The daily schedule varied greatly due to these vagaries, but shooting days were long, almost always twelve hours, and the production team worked six days per week. There were times when filming ended at 2:45 a.m. and reporting time for the next day was 7:00 a.m.[29]

To simplify production, scenes requiring similar sets and climatic conditions were shot together, even if they came from different mysteries. To the outsider the method might appear haphazard and disjointed, but Breen was an accomplished Hollywood director, who efficiently worked to bring the project to completion as professionally, economically, and rapidly as possible. Peyton's intention to dub the films into multiple languages for various uses prompted Breen to shoot the films with the actors mouthing the words in a form of pigeon English, because the translation and dubbing process into English would be easiest, an important detail since the American audience would be the most critical. Rather than use Hollywood facilities, each day's film was flown for processing to Denham Laboratories in England, to expedite its return and lower costs.[30]

Visitors to the Madrid studios were rare, but certain Holy Cross religious did make prominent calls on the set. Father Peyton came infrequently, but his presence was always marked by two distinctive reactions — a sense of uneasiness on the part of the director, who believed his presence simply interrupted his plans, and a sense of wonder on the part of the actors who, although unable to understand much of anything that Peyton said, were, nonetheless, so powerfully struck that they were often brought to tears by simply listening to him speak. One observer noted, "His [Peyton's] tone, his expression and mannerisms were so compelling that in themselves they commanded the attention of everyone present."[31] Visiting at different times, Christopher O'Toole, CSC, and George DePrizio, CSC, the newly elected provincial of the Eastern Province of Priests, were quite impressed with the project. DePrizio was thrilled to observe the filming in progress and congratulated Lawyer on "doing an excellent job." O'Toole also lauded the project and its leaders: "Everything seems to be very well organized. Certainly Father Lawyer and John Kirby have done a magnificent job. These films will be without question the finest films in existence on our Blessed Mother."[32]

Filming moved inside after August 28 and continued uninterrupted until September 20. From September 20 to 27 the crew shot the final scenes in the province of Murcia and the village of Guacerma, appropriately the home of Dolores Cantabella. The final day of shooting was September 27, one year to the day since Lawyer and Kirby had arrived in Madrid to begin preliminary work on the production of the films.[33] Peyton praised Lawyer for his efforts in completing this major stage of the project: "Great have been your accomplishments these five months! I feel as I said in the beginning that no motion picture ever made will come near to what you have done. . . . Your work is the key to bring the family rosary to heights never dreamed of before."[34]

The completion of filming was followed by the large and significant task of editing, dubbing, and mixing the films with music. Lawyer, who continued as overall supervisor of the project, was told by Peyton "not [to] spare the horses" in obtaining the best dubbing and music that was available. The first priority was to append Peyton's rejoinder to pray the family rosary, filmed in Spain at the very end of production. The films were fully edited and then, using six thousand feet of recordings, obtained by Joseph Breen from the Vatican Library, music was inserted into the films.[35] The films were first dubbed into English, French, and Walloon (for the Belgium crusade) with Spanish and German following. Eventually the films were also dubbed into Portuguese, Italian, Flemish, Japanese, Korean, and the Bolivian and Peruvian Indian dialects of Aymara and Quechua.

The film production costs can be measured on quantitative and qualitative levels. Peyton's initial estimate of $25,000 per film almost tripled to nearly $70,000, after production and postproduction costs were factored into the equation, raising the overall project to slightly over $1 million. The qualitative cost in the life of Father Lawyer may have been more significant, especially in terms of its effect on his relationship with Peyton. Once again Lawyer confided his thought to John Murphy stating that he was "fed-up" and "at the end of my rope in F[amily] R[osary]." Still in Spain as overseer of the final editing phase of the project, Lawyer reported, "If any of us live through 1958 — it will be another miracle —

or as Father Peyton will say — another milestone in Family Rosary history — because we will then have [spiritual] martyrs in heaven for the cause."[36]

Even before the films were ready, however, Peyton, with his gift of forward thinking, was planning premieres. His first idea was to show an edited feature-length version of the films at Lourdes to celebrate the centenary of Mary's appearance to Bernadette Soubirous in 1858. In early 1957 Peyton approached Pierre Marie Theas, bishop of Tarbes and Lourdes, seeking permission to show the films during the centenary. His first idea, presented in March 1957, was to build a separate theater for the presentations, but this was scaled back by December to a request to show the films in the Basilica of Pius X or, if not feasible there, outdoors in a field across from the grotto. He wished to have a Triduum presentation February 8–10, 1958, to prepare for the February 11 celebration, and then to show the films every Saturday throughout the year.[37] An international centenary committee approved the general idea of showing the films, but Peyton was unable to secure the February dates and eventually the whole plan collapsed.[38]

While Lourdes negotiations were in progress, Peyton was making arrangements for the world premiere of the films, appropriately in Madrid. The local archbishop approved Peyton's plan to launch a "Mission of Mary" campaign by showing the sorrowful mystery films at local theaters during Holy Week. Peyton had originally envisioned showing the films in a football stadium in Madrid, but realized that only the stouthearted would brave the elements to see them. Instead, using the local ordinary's idea, Peyton secured thirty theaters on the Gran Via to premiere the films. During the week over one hundred thousand people attended the films with the response being very favorable. One local reviewer wrote:

> The noble intention which animated Father Peyton has resulted in one of the best representations of the Passion of Christ which we remember. A true account, a model of order, carried out with perfect naturalness. There is nothing theatrical or exaggerated; everything is calm and true. A true representation with perfect coloring, the perfect casting of all parts; the sequence of narrative; the work of composition, in fact, everything shows a realization of the plan, as if the daily elements which went to complete it were of divine inspiration.[39]

The "Mission of Mary" in Madrid was the first public screening of the films, but two important private screenings were held earlier in February.

Four films, *The Scourging, The Crowning with Thorns, The Crucifixion,* and *The Descent of the Spirit,* were shown to General Francisco Franco and his wife. Peyton reported, "The Generalissimo was actually moved emotionally and his wife was crying." A special screening of all fifteen films was provided for Pope Pius XII. In response the pontiff, who was very pleased with the films, wrote to Peyton,

> These films have an apostolic character and value beyond their technical and artistic perfection. They open up the book of God's revelation to man; they turn the pages of a divine love story for those to read who will, and reading to understand the infinite yearning of God for the creatures of His omnipotence.... Blessed will the faithful be who have the good fortune, let us rather say the precious grace, to see these films. We simply hope their number will be legion.[40]

The success of the Madrid premiere did not prevent Peyton from regretting the missed opportunity to reach larger audiences at Lourdes. Thus, when Javier Echenique suggested that the upcoming World's Fair in Brussels would be a suitable venue for the films, Peyton promptly contacted the superior general Christopher O'Toole, CSC, concerning the possibility. The general thought it was a great plan and suggested that the films be shown at Civitas Dei, the Vatican Pavilion at the fair. O'Toole contacted Count Enrico Galeazzi, governor of Vatican City, who also liked the idea and met with Peyton in Rome. Peyton convinced Galeazzi of the plan's merit, and thus the governor sent him to Paul Heymans, commissioner of the Holy See and representative of the Holy Father at the fair. Some caution was offered since plans for construction of the Vatican Pavilion were well under way, but creative thinking produced a plan to add a separate theater to the original plan, which did not impinge upon the proposed design. Peyton and Heymans agreed on the plan.[41]

Even after receiving Vatican approval for the World's Fair showing, Peyton still had to arrange the financing. Heymans explained that the cost of the pavilion addition, estimated at $60,000, would have to be borne by Family Rosary, since the Vatican budget had been spent on the pavilion itself. Heymans also insisted the films be dubbed in Dutch,[42] another unanticipated expense, to accommodate the World's Fair attendees.[43] Eventually Peyton was able to negotiate down the pavilion estimate to $40,000, then to $30,000. For that price he was able to obtain a three-hundred-seat theater, projection room, and four conference rooms.[44] Peyton then called upon Harry John of the DeRance Foundation, who provided $40,000 for the building and the purchase of screens, projectors, and auxiliary equipment.[45]

Peyton's plan was now in motion, but his style of negotiating deals and signing expensive contracts was not well received by his religious superiors, who were cut out of the decision process. John Murphy, CSC, informed Peyton that both the superior general and provincial insisted that Family Rosary follow canonical procedures regarding the expenditure of funds.[46] Peyton, however, saw the opportunity to show the films to an international audience and, thereby, assist the work of Mary as much more important than any procedure:

> But, to me personally, there is still a more sacred and more taxing responsibility — this is the responsibility of being aware every second of my working hours that Our Blessed Mother is alive; that She is real; that She is not a theory; that She is somebody's daughter and that She has Our Incarnate God as Her Son. Once she granted me a great favor . . . it is the remembrance of that that drives me to the ends of the Earth for Her, for Her interests and for the accomplishment of Her holy will in regard to the Family of to-day. Her interests are the driving motivation of my hour to hour — day to day — and year to year decisions and actions, labors and sufferings.[47]

The Brussels Universal and International Exhibition, open between April 17 and October 19, 1958, allowed the world to view the fruits of Peyton's greatest endeavor to date. A special press screening was arranged on April 29, with the theater open to the public from May 1 to October 19. Daily screenings, from 12:00 noon to 8:00 p.m. continuously, were held in English, Spanish, Walloon, and French. Additional screenings were periodically held in the larger twelve-hundred-seat convention hall and at outdoor sites. A survey showed that viewers responded most positively to the sorrowful mysteries, with the glorious and joyful next in ranked significance.[48]

The Brussels World's Fair provided Peyton with opportunities beyond the promotion of his rosary films. He hoped that many world leaders and other highly influential people would see the films and, thus, become apostles of the Family Rosary in their native lands. In Brussels Peyton met Bishop Leo Josef Suenens, auxiliary to Cardinal Van Roey in Malines and Bishop Emile Josef de Smedt of Bruges, both of whom became great champions of Church renewal and leaders at Vatican II. These meetings led directly to the crusade in Bruges conducted between April

and June 1959. Peyton also met Archbishop (later Cardinal) Rufino J.
Santos of Manila, initiating a long and highly productive relationship
between Family Rosary and the Philippine people that was formally
inaugurated with the first crusade conducted there in November and
December 1959.[49] The success of the Brussels World's Fair was crowned
when Peyton, Lawyer, and Peter Mueller, CSC, received the Pro Ecclesia
et Pontifice award from Pope John XXIII in November 1959, granted
in recognition of the positive effect of the films on the peoples of the
world.[50]

Before he considered international distribution, Peyton brought the
film series back to his own community. The assistant provincial, Bernard
Mullahy, CSC, arranged a special screening of five of the films at the
University of Notre Dame for Holy Cross religious, priests, brothers, and
sisters, in the greater South Bend, Indiana, region. The event, attended
by Peyton, was a great boost for the local community and for some one
thousand nuns, participants in the summer Institute of Spirituality, who
were also invited to the screening.[51]

The Use and Distribution of the Films

The rosary films had not been completed before the question of their
use and distribution was debated. Peyton's original idea — that the films
be syndicated for viewing on local television stations — began to evolve
into a larger vision. He knew that he wanted to maintain control of distribution but was undecided about the details: should they be distributed
privately or commercially? He realized that the religious orders who had
contributed to the production of the films had a right to use them, and
that this method of distribution would not require costly advertising. On
the other hand, he also realized that commercial distribution would generate more money to recoup production costs. He wrote to Lawyer, "In
our determination to hold on to the Films we would be imposing upon
ourselves the impossible task of exploiting them ourselves — a task more
impossible than reaching the moon."[52]

In the absence of a definite distribution plan, proposals for use of
the films proliferated. Breen recommended developing a feature-length
film for commercial theatrical release prior to television viewing. Peyton proposed to "sell" the films to Propaganda Fide for international
distribution through an authorized Church office to mission dioceses
throughout the world. Additionally, working with Peter Grace and John
Kirby, he investigated how the films could be distributed commercially in

Latin America.[53] These ideas became grist for the mill of Peyton's ever-active mind that was always geared toward the promotion of family prayer through the rosary.

Peyton continued to vacillate on the questions of private versus commercial distribution and the overall purpose and use of the films in the greater scheme of his future objectives for the Family Rosary Crusade. He began to sell the films to religious communities for $15,000 a set, with a discount to $250 per film for congregations that were less financially secure and those orders that had contributed so generously to their production. Later, he pulled back from this practice, even canceling purchases, because he feared his control on the use of the films would be compromised.[54] Still conflicted on how to proceed, Peyton in late August and early September 1958 asked Joseph Breen to arrange a screening in New York for a select group, Ray Mackland, photo editor, and Sam Welles, religion editor for *Life* Magazine, Tom O'Neal and Donald Henderson of Twentieth Century Fox, and Peter Grace. Despite positive reactions from all present Peyton did not press any commercial venture at the time as he believed the doctrinal message of the films might be watered down or even lost. Lawyer agreed with the decision, stating that the films had never been intended for a commercial end.[55] The films could be distributed locally through the Albany and Hollywood offices.

The decision to avoid commercial distribution was short-lived when, at the request of Donald Henderson, chief financial officer at Fox, several Fox executives attended a private screening to determine the commercial potential of the films. Their reactions were mixed, but most concluded that the filmmaker would lose a great opportunity if it failed to distribute a well-edited feature-length version of the film. Because of their religious subject, Ulric Bell, executive assistant to Spyros Skouras, president of Fox, believed, however, that their appeal would be limited, so it would not be wise for the company to enter this venture when it was in the midst of production and distribution of *The Greatest Story Ever Told*, a film with a story line almost identical to that of the rosary films.[56] While the general reaction was extremely positive, Breen offered caution. He knew that Fox had invested $1 million in *The Greatest Story Ever Told* and a second film, *The Day Christ Died*, and he warned that the filmmaker might purchase the rosary films and then promptly shelve them to eliminate competition with their own projects.[57]

Skouras, even with input from his top advisors, kept postponing his decision. He asked Peyton to view more footage, and thus on December 13 he watched four additional films. In January Skouras informed Peyton that Fox would not take the films for distribution, citing the "inability to arouse sufficient support in his company to distribute the films."[58] Peyton was "crushed" at the decision, lost all hope with film companies, and began to fear that even television would not want the films.[59]

After the great disappointment with Fox, an opportunity arose for their distribution and financial gain through Cardinal Richard Cushing, archbishop of Boston. In July 1959 Cushing met with Peyton at Notre Dame and offered to show the films in Boston with all the proceeds to benefit Peyton's forthcoming work in Latin America, an area of the world that was dear to the heart of the archbishop. He told Peyton, "To back these pictures for Our Blessed Mother is the happiest thing I can do. I have built colleges and hospitals, I have sent missionaries abroad, but to give myself to the work of helping distribute these films of grace and divine life will be the most compensating gift I ever gave." Thus, Cushing pledged to contribute $1 million toward Peyton's mission to Latin America.[60]

Cushing, who was widely known for his numerous and significant benefactions, immediately initiated his plan for local screening of the films. He purchased the old Loew Theater in Back Bay for $1.25 million and renamed it the Donnelly Memorial Theater. One local paper commented that Cushing's move had an additional purpose: "The theater will be an instrument in warning Catholics in Latin America against the false prophets of Communism — until more priests and nuns can be sent to those countries."[61] On October 1, 1959, the Joyful Mysteries were premiered with two shows daily. Cushing's enthusiasm for the project waned, however, when after six weeks of good attendance, interest began to dissipate. Peyton worried that Cushing's disappointment might lead the archbishop to give a second thought or even retract his million-dollar pledge.[62]

Father Peyton made several more attempts to distribute the films in individual countries, but he was far too busy and spreading himself too thin to effectively supervise any formal distribution program. Moreover, he remained uncertain as to what he really wanted, a situation which placed others, most especially Father Lawyer, in poor, even compromising positions, when Peyton made proposals half-heartedly and then summarily removed them with little or no consultation with his field people. Lawyer was often frustrated at the indecisive way Peyton approached the whole distribution issue. He commented, "What I do hope is that some definite plan is established about the distribution of these films. It is so difficult working on national distribution when you have the feeling that anytime Fr. Pat is going to send you a letter telling you to get out of the contract."[63]

Distribution of the films remained a tenuous question for several years, and thus the other major question, namely, the creation of a feature-length film for commercial distribution, came to the forefront. Ideas concerning a commercial venture began to circulate during the shooting of the films in Spain and continued during their final production and premieres. As mentioned earlier, Joseph Breen believed a commercial film would yield "a great financial return."[64] Most assuredly Peter Grace, the financial backbone and decision maker of the crusade, was ready to take every opportunity to advance economically Peyton's work. He wrote,

> When one considers the fantastic sacrifices that were made, mostly by orders of nuns and converts to get the original pictures made, and the extraordinary quality that was obtained for the money that was expended, I am more than ever convinced that some way must be found to cash in on the Fifteen Mysteries movies that were made in Spain.[65]

Francis Woods's communications with Hollywood people also had convinced him that a film could be made and "shown for a period of weeks at premium prices." The financial angle was certainly not unattractive to Patrick Peyton, but for him the great benefit was the promotion of the whole crusade: "If the effort to transform the 15 twenty-five minute films into one full length masterpiece is successful, there is a chance that the Family Rosary Crusade can crash the heights of the Ten Commandments, Ben Hur . . . and other similarly renowned religious masterpieces."[66]

It was the promotion of his crusade that ultimately led Peyton to take the lead in producing a commercial movie with an established Hollywood filmmaker. In October 1958, while Twentieth Century Fox was debating the possible distribution of the rosary films, Peyton pressured Spyros Skouras to make a feature film:

> The world in turn is waiting for the hope, comfort and strength that these pictures edited into a major feature have the power to impart. This is the purpose for which they were made — to reach the souls and the minds and hearts of the masses across the earth. Now that they are ready for such re-editing into a major feature, it is my grave responsibility not to delay.[67]

In the spring of 1960 Peyton resumed talks with Skouras about the production of a feature-length film. Skouras probably approached Peyton about the project to avenge what he considered a double-cross by a rival filmmaker. *King of Kings,* produced by MGM, was released at the same time as Fox's *The Greatest Story Ever Told.* Angered at the infringement of first privilege, Skouras promptly resigned from the Motion Picture Producers' Association and immediately contacted Peyton about the films' availability.[68] Ignoring Skouras's dubious motives and swallowing his earlier disappointment with Fox, Peyton responded with enthusiasm. Lawyer, however, had serious reservations, noting that Family Rosary had been burned before in such a process. He was not adverse to a good financial return so long as it could be done "without sacrificing too much of our independence and the apostolic nature of the films." But he had serious problems with "the hate and revenge motive on the part of Fox," a reality that could not be denied.[69] Nevertheless, on August 24, 1960, Family Rosary and Fox signed a contract for the production and distribution of a feature-length film titled *The Eternal King.* Fox was responsible for the editing, with Family Rosary people present for cutting and splicing. The film was slated for release in December 1960 or January 1961.

There were problems with the project from the outset. Christopher O'Toole, CSC, voiced his displeasure that Peyton had again exercised options outside his purview, signing a contract that involved alienation to the rights of the film, which by Canon Law belonged to the Congregation of Holy Cross.[70] Even more immediate was the overtly negative response to the films from the Jewish community, who considered them anti-Semitic. Cardinal Cushing noted this in an earlier letter to Peyton:

> Confidentially, I know by the underground and many sources that we are going to be in trouble with the films of the Rosary in the United States, Europe and probably in South America. I have not seen the Sorrowful Mysteries but International Judaism is organizing against this film. As far as I can gather, the reaction against it in this country is nationwide and it is becoming evident that our own people are supporting the Jews in their opposition.[71]

Despite these problems *The Eternal King* was premiered in two different versions in separate locations. On October 1, 1960, Boston's Donnelly Memorial Theater screened a three-hour edited version that was not well received. After being pared to two hours and ten minutes, it was shown in Stamford, Connecticut. Most viewers were very impressed with the film, but the accusation of anti-Semitism was again raised by a few.[72] Later in 1961 Peyton discussed with George DePrizio, CSC, and John Meehan, a member of Peter Grace's inner circle, the possibility of showing *The Eternal King* at the Venice Film Festival. All agreed that it was too much of a risk to test the film in such waters, and the idea was dropped.[73]

Lackluster response to *The Eternal King*'s premieres and the threat of problems from the Jewish community prompted Fox to cancel its contract with Family Rosary on March 20, 1962. Tensions between Family Rosary and Fox had been brewing from the outset, but they escalated after December 1960, when Fox's response to questions and requests became so sluggish that Peyton began to doubt the studio's commitment to the film. Family Rosary contemplated a lawsuit against Fox but backed off for several reasons. First, litigation would further delay the film's release. Second, if Fox was ordered to compensate Family Rosary, the studio might retain rights to the film and it would never be viewed. Third, Family Rosary had nothing to gain from lengthy litigation, especially if the court judged the film to be anti-Semitic. Lastly, Peyton did not want anything to jeopardize Family Rosary's access to the film.[74] Peyton accepted Fox's settlement offer of $100,000: $25,000 in cash and $75,000 in prints of the film.[75]

With Family Rosary's second debacle with Fox now settled, Peyton was free to seek other distribution options. He considered several options, making formal contact with Astor Productions, distributor of the popular film *La Dolce Vita,* and United Artists. Finally, he sought advice from Lawyer, whose role as former executive director of the films made his opinion valuable. Peyton reluctantly decided that in its present form *The Eternal King* could not succeed. For the time being the idea of a feature-length film on the life of Christ was shelved.

Conclusion

The accomplishments achieved through the efforts of Patrick Peyton and those who supported his Crusade for Family Prayer, through the use of radio and television films and a whole series of rosary crusades that had been conducted in all continents save South America in the 1950s, were augmented greatly through the production of fifteen films depicting the mysteries of the rosary. Conceived in Peyton's mind in 1953 from the inauguration of the radio programs on the mysteries and sponsored by the Catholic Daughters of America, the project became reality beginning in 1956 when, under the guidance of Jerome Lawyer, CSC, the films were completed on location in Spain. Once completed, however, a protracted debate ensued as to how these films could best be used, not only to advance Family Rosary's message of family prayer, but also to generate additional revenue that could be used for future endeavors of the organization. The most important use of the films, however, their utilization in rosary crusades in Latin America, was still to be realized. Providing a whole new dimension to the crusade through catechesis, the films became the backbone of the popular mission and the effort to win Latin America to the cause of Mary and her family rosary.

Chapter 7

The Latin American Crusades, 1959–66

The Family Rosary Crusade, first organized and conducted in London, Ontario, in 1948 traveled the world during the 1950s, landing in every continent save South America. Patrick Peyton's initial dream of bringing 10 million families to the practice of the family rosary was secured in the 1950s and the crusade became well known throughout the Catholic world, but for Peyton the great prize of bringing the crusade to Latin America, home to over one-fourth of the world's Roman Catholics, still eluded him. Armed with his new weapon of the rosary films, Father Peyton was now poised to bring the crusade to a land that was steeped in the Catholic tradition but mired in a state of religious illiteracy due to social instability, a paucity of educational opportunities, and a dearth of clergy. Peyton continued to preach his principal and basic message of family prayer through the rosary, but in South America he also used the crusade to fight Communism, at a time when the escalating Cold War and the creation of a Soviet outpost in Cuba, only ninety miles from the mainland, caused Americans to fear the spread of Communism and seek its demise at any cost.

Church and State in Latin America

Catholicism in Latin America, planted by Spanish and Portuguese missionaries in the sixteenth through eighteenth centuries, was in a state of crisis in the post–World War II era. The three most prominent problems were a serious shortage of priests and religious caused by a dearth of vocations, the need to instruct a generally religiously illiterate population, and the need to implement a vast Catholic social action program throughout the region. These problems led to the formation of the

151

Consejo Episcopal Latinoamericano (CELAM), during the International Eucharistic Congress held in Rio de Janeiro in 1955. Formed along lines similar to the National Catholic Welfare Conference in the United States, with headquarters in Bogotá, Colombia, CELAM's aim "was to develop common policies and co-ordinate action on education, social affairs, information, youth, and other matters." Ronan Hoffman, OFM, a leading figure in Latin American Church affairs and professor of theology at the Catholic University of America, commented concerning CELAM: "The importance of this Council can scarcely be exaggerated."[1]

Reigning pontiffs recognized the critical situation in Latin America. On April 19, 1958, Pope Pius XII established the Pontifical Commission for Latin America to study the basic problems of Catholic life in Latin America and, in cooperation with the various Congregations of the Roman Curia, to help solve them. On November 14, in a written address to the third annual CELAM conference, the pope expressed "deep interest in the problems of the Church in Latin America."[2] Pius XII's successor, Pope John XXIII, was even more strident in his call for renewal of the Church in Latin America. He wrote to various national conferences of bishops asking them to support the Church in Latin America by improving social standards and sending workers to the region.[3] On December 8, 1961, he addressed a message to all Latin America prelates: "Unmask those who deceive with facile opinions and false teachings.... Do not give enemies of the Church the chance to accuse the Church of not concerning itself with the temporal needs of men."[4]

The mandate for the Church to act was strengthened by its acknowledgment as a significant voice and force in the region. Experts inside and outside the Church agreed that the struggle was social and economic as well as spiritual, and thus the Church's response must be on various levels and in multiple ways. The Church was viewed as a key player in finding solutions. David Lawrence, writing in the *New York Tribune*, stated, "The Catholic Church has tremendous influence in every country in Latin America — each of which is predominately Catholic in its religious affiliation." Ronan Hoffman, OFM, went further in describing the wide scope of Catholicism's influence:

> The fact is that the Catholic Church in Latin America is organized on a continental and national basis, is actively at work, and is even in the forefront of the social and economic development of the people. A number of people are of the opinion that if one is thinking

in terms of getting things moving in Latin America, it is impossible to overlook the Catholic Church in an area overwhelmingly Catholic.[5]

Statistics from the period indicate the scope of the religious problems. One commentator claimed that 70 percent of Latin American Catholics were ignorant of the basic fundamentals of the Faith. While 95 percent of the people were baptized, only one-third of this number had received their first communion and approximately 6 percent of men and 12 percent of women regularly attended Mass. Hoffman argued, "Until a new more broadly-based social, economic, and political equilibrium is achieved, Latin America will remain an area of turmoil."[6]

While religious illiteracy was a concern of many, the overriding issue and the one which needed to be solved in order to right the direction of the Church in Latin America was the need for social reform. Commentators and Church officials argued that the Church needed to break with the social elite and their conservative theological outlook to prevent people from turning to Marxism or Communism. Bishop Manuel Larraín of Talca, Chile, stated in an interview: "Only one possibility exists today of improving living conditions in Latin America: a rapid and radical transformation of its economic and social conditions to bring them in line with the principles of Christian social teaching."[7]

At its 1960 meeting in Fomeque, Colombia, CELAM issued a statement calling the state of underdevelopment and hunger in Latin America "a serious sin and the greatest danger of our time."[8] Some feared that Latin America would abandon its Catholic faith entirely and slide precipitously into agnosticism and amorality. Archbishop Dom Helder Camara, auxiliary in Rio de Janeiro, summarized the thinking of many ecclesiastical officials: "It [Latin America's need for social reform] is indispensable for the sake of all Christianity. A continent that is Catholic in name must be Catholic in fact. There is grave danger that the people of Latin America may cease to be Catholic or even Christian."[9]

Various national episcopal conferences issued statements reflecting the Church's response to South America's problems. In a 1962 pastoral letter the Chilean bishops, writing at a time of political transition in their country, argued against Communism, stating that it did not have the answers to the social problems the people experienced. The letter concluded that the time was now and the Church possessed the necessary message:

The hour in which we are now living is the hour for action; and because it is the time in which a new country is being created we want the voice of the Church to reach you. We have the right and duty to intervene, indicating the moral, natural and religious fundamentals which must guide you in these difficult circumstances.[10]

That same year the Brazilian episcopal council issued an emergency plan warning against Communism and Capitalism, suggesting the need for "freedom and the resources that respond to a dignified system of life." The Peruvian bishops in a letter of May 1, 1963, emphasized the Church's task to enlighten its people and to form in them a genuine social conscience. In a joint communique the bishops, echoing Peyton, appealed to the electronic media to transmit their message: "Only through the press, the radio and to a lesser extent the camera and television ... can we keep contact with the great mass of our fellow citizens."[11]

In the United States, the Church responded by sending personnel and economic aid. As mentioned in chapter 6, Cardinal Richard Cushing of Boston responded to the pope's call for workers to go to Latin America by establishing the St. James Society in 1959.[12] The call of Popes Pius XII and John XXIII to action in Latin America led to a 1959 meeting at Georgetown University between representatives of CELAM, episcopal conferences in the United States and Canada, and emissaries of the Holy See. This meeting led to the reestablishment of the Latin American Bureau of the NCWC.[13] The Bureau identified six areas for action in Latin America: (1) development of new clergy and religious, (2) construction of a religious education program that would eventually eliminate religious ignorance, (3) the strengthening of Catholic education, (4) creation of an adequate Catholic religiosocial and socioeconomic program, (5) a stronger place for the Church in the press, radio, and movies, and (6) a substantial increase in the lay apostolate.[14]

The Congregation of Holy Cross also responded to the call to aid the Church in Latin America. Foundations were made by Holy Cross in Chile in 1943, in Brazil and Haiti in 1944, and Peru in 1963, by which time there were eighty Holy Cross religious ministering in Latin America. In his first circular letter, published in 1963, the superior general, Germain Lalande, CSC, recognized the pressing need in the region:

> Latin America is undergoing a tremendous change. Her political and social structures have to be completely revamped. It is evidently not the task of the Church as such to direct this process of reconstruction. But hers is the responsibility to train militant Christians, basically interested in the material and spiritual needs of the people. These Christians should be the ones inspiring reorganization and, in certain cases, courageously taking the lead. If such Christians are

not available, then the evolution will be achieved independently of Christian principles, and the people of Latin America will face the danger of turning against the Church.

The General Chapter of 1962 suggested that Peyton's Family Rosary Crusade was a particularly suitable response to the South American problem.[15]

The call for priests and religious to come to Latin America also met the need to challenge the rising tide of Communism, which found its way to this region as early as the 1920s, with party groups present in Cuba, Mexico City, and Montevideo in that decade. The historian Robert Alexander claims that Communism in the region reached its apex immediately after World War II, but during the 1950s its influence began to ebb, partially because party leaders followed the Soviet Union in turning almost violently against the United States. This was a direction that liberal Catholic elements, who might have been sympathetic if Communists were fighting the Nazis, were unwilling to pursue.[16] Other factors working against Communist dominance in the region were the emerging highly nationalistic middle class, which was more disposed to exploit Communist assistance than to adhere to its ideology and discipline, and the absence of revolutionary zeal among the urban population.[17]

However, other expert observers of the situation in Latin America agree that Communism actually became more pervasive in the 1950s. Tactics used by Communist sympathizers were very elastic, adapting to the need of the region or people. One major effort, promoted by Nikita Khrushchev, premier of the Soviet Union, was to export Fidel Castro's Cuban revolution to South America. Trained in eastern bloc nations, mainland China, and other Communist strongholds, professional revolutionaries began to infiltrate labor unions and agrarian parties, attempting to transform their political and social ideas. Harry Schwartz, a reporter for the *New York Times* and specialist in Soviet affairs, warned: "If Communism is not now a major force in Latin America, it is an appreciable one, with potentialities that are not underestimated in Moscow and should not be underestimated by us."[18] South America was certainly ripe for Communism: its poverty, mushrooming inflation, anti-Americanism, and inequitable land distribution were mirror images of the social conditions in Cuba at the time of its revolution. Reports stated that between one hundred thousand and two hundred thousand workers in Latin America were Communist sympathizers (compared with ten thousand in the United States), and twenty-five newspapers and magazines, including a few dailies, were Communist organs.[19]

According to the experts, the Communists' immediate goals in South America were to foment anti-Americanism, frustrate all democratic remedies to the social dilemma, and neutralize the region for a Communist takeover. Long-range goals included replacing the influence of the United States in the region with that of the Soviet Union, obtaining political control, and ultimately establishing a Soviet form of Communism on the continent as had been implemented in Eastern Europe after World War II.[20] Another important design of the Communists was to undermine the influence of the Catholic Church by identifying it as sympathetic to and supportive of the traditional social structures which generated the present situation. One contemporary report commented, "Bent on destruction of the Catholic Church, [Communism] has launched a vigorous offensive to gain control of this strategic area."[21]

Communists in Latin America did not operate without opposition. The need for social reform was clear to all contemporary observers and was being addressed by both church and state, but there was a need to overtly and effectively stand against the onslaught of the Communist ideology and its supporters through institutions that were recognized locally and had the strength to produce a positive result. Juan Dora-Duque, a Cuban Jesuit priest, argued that Communism could be effectively defeated only through a counterideology, namely, Catholic social teaching. Victory in Latin America required capturing the imagination of its peoples, and as the historian Arnold Toynbee argued, religion is the key to imagination:

> The West has erred because it has chosen to fight Communism with Communism's own materialist weapons. As long as the battle is fought in these terms, the Communists will keep on winning. Western democracy must base its appeal on more than freedom, more than property; it must base its appeal on religion. Only in this way can democracy turn the tables on the Communist assailants. The grace of God might bring about this miracle.[22]

The belief that religion must be a major player in combating Communism throughout the world was noted by historians and contemporary observers. Communism was aided in lands where religious practice had diminished and places where large numbers of people were highly religious by culture and tradition but possessed little knowledge of their faith. This phenomenon was noted not only with Christianity, but in lands where Islam was the cultural religion. In contrast one commentator observed, "A country which is strong in its religious beliefs is one which has as effective a barrier against Communism as you can find in the modern world."[23] Experts argued that organized religion was the grave enemy of Communism for it promoted moral and spiritual values against which the Soviet ideology had no response acceptable to the people. One observer, hopeful for the future, commented, "With continual effort it is not overly optimistic to foresee the full power and organization of the Church being brought to bear for the solution of Latin America's grave problem."[24]

Roman Catholicism's religious and cultural domination of Latin America required that it play a leading role in opposing the spread of Communism in the region. The call to action for the Church was well stated in 1955 by a non-Church organization, the American Institute of Management:

> There is currently a great need for the revival of true spiritual fervor in the world. As the American Bishops of the Roman Catholic Church have proclaimed, "Christianity faces today its most serious crisis since the Church came out of the catacombs." While the Moslem threat in previous centuries was certainly no less severe than the present danger of Communism, the Moslems were by no means without a full appreciation of spiritual values. The Communists are the Godless ones.[25]

Richard Armstrong of the *Saturday Evening Post* viewed the Church "as a major anti-Communist force in Latin America."[26] The need for the Church to act was echoed by Ronan Hoffman, OFM: "The situation is this: if the Latin American Catholics of today (not of tomorrow) do not remake Latin American society in accordance with the social teachings of the Church, the Communists will remake it (and they are already active in remaking it) in accordance with their concept of life and man's destiny."[27] As the only institution firmly established in every South American country, the Catholic Church, with its organization and formidable strength, was the obvious choice to lead the charge against Communism.

The challenge to act in Latin America was also heard by the U.S. government as the world moved away from World War II and became embroiled in the Cold War. Although George Washington in his farewell address to the nation in 1796 had advocated an isolationist position,[28] from 1898 forward the United States often became embroiled in Latin American affairs.[29] Communist infiltration and influence in Latin America was a growing concern to American officials after World War II. Vice President Richard Nixon, after completing an eight-nation tour of Latin America in 1958, commented, "For Communism to come to any one of the republics is the very foreign intervention which is incompatible with ... [America's] principle of non-intervention."[30] Most observers suggested a measured response, arguing that the United States should help establish political democracy by providing economic support and promoting social reform in the region.[31] The historian James Garneau has accurately summarized America's response to Latin America:

> In the post–World War II period, the political, cultural, and religious future of Latin America was of increasing concern to the United States government, to the Catholic Church in the United States, and to the Holy See.... Their principal concern was the advance in Communism and its growth in Latin America. The prevention of its spread was an important goal for the Church at all levels, and for various governments within the capitals of Latin America as well as Washington, D.C.[32]

From the outset of his administration, President John F. Kennedy advocated a proactive stance toward its Southern neighbors. In his January 30, 1961, State of the Union Address, Kennedy, speaking of the people and governments of Latin America, stated, "The United States stands solidly at their side to help them block off the inroads of Communism and build a better life for themselves and their children in a secure atmosphere of freedom." The president labeled the situation in Latin America "very critical," and "the greatest challenge which the United States now faces, except for the direct matter of our dealings with the Soviet [Union]."[33]

Kennedy's call for action led directly to his creation of the Alliance for Progress, established at the Inter-American Conference held at Punta del Este, Uruguay, in August 1961. The program set up $2 billion per year of external financing to Latin America over ten years. An additional $8 billion per year in development was to be provided by Latin American nations themselves over the same time period. The goal of the Alliance program was to increase the gross national product of the region by a minimum of 5 percent per year. The United States agreed to supply $1.1 billion annually in loans and outright grants.[34] The Alliance, similar in conception to the Marshall Plan of 1947, was called "a patchwork that satisfied nobody" by its opponents. Political commentator Daniel Friedenberg labeled the Alliance "a desperate attempt on the part of the Kennedy administration to return to the earlier stage of the Good Neighbor Policy [that] evolved under Franklin D. Roosevelt, subordinating the protection of U.S. business investments to the goals of peace and the avoidance of revolutionary transfers of political power."[35]

The fear of Communism expressed by Kennedy was deeply rooted in American political history. In 1938 the House Un-American Activities Committee (HUAC), commonly called the Dies Committee after its Texas Democrat founder, Representative Martin Dies, was formed and began investigations into Communist influence in the United States. In 1954 through 1956 the committee received new life under the chairmanship of former FBI agent Harold H. Velde, whose motto was "Get the Reds out of Washington and Washington out of the Red." In 1947 President Harry Truman established the Loyalty Review Board to search for Communists among American government employees. The English historian Michael J. Heale has labeled the Republican offensive of 1948 to 1952 against Communists in the United States and anti-Communism in general the "second red scare." Republicans seized upon the evolution of the Cold War, the "fall" of China, Soviet development of nuclear weapons, and the Korean War as harbingers of Communist activity in the United States. In January 1950 the conviction of Alger Hiss of perjury (in effect convicting him of being a Soviet spy) convinced many Americans that Communist operatives were active in the United States. The Hollywood blacklists only added fuel to an already raging fire of fear.[36]

During the 1950s the principal organs of government, major political parties, trade unions, leading religious officials, and many public and private institutions across the nation agreed that Communists had no legitimate role in American society. The polemic of Senator Joseph McCarthy of Wisconsin between 1950 and 1954 galvanized the nation against Communism. McCarthy became "the personification of American anticommunism," holding the nation spellbound through a series of accusations against high-ranking government officials without one shred of serious evidence.[37]

No federal agency was more committed to the eradication of Communists from America's shores than the FBI, led by J. Edgar Hoover and his obsessive fear of subversion. In May 1950 Hoover told a radio audience:

Communists have been and are at work within the very gates of America. There are few walks in American life which they do not traverse.... Wherever they may be they have in common one diabolic ambition: to weaken and to eventually destroy American democracy by stealth and cunning.[38]

Hoover and the agency he headed searched for Communists in all avenues of American life. Hoover regularly contributed copy to *The Time for Family Prayer,* stating here and elsewhere that a God-fearing, stable family life was a powerful bulwark against Communism.[39]

American religious leaders joined with political figures to oppose the incursion of Communism in the United States. In 1933, when President Franklin D. Roosevelt initiated negotiations to recognize the Soviet Union, the National Catholic Welfare Conference, *Commonweal,* and *America* all argued strongly against it. The Paulist priest James Gillis, editor of the *Catholic World,* wrote that it was not ethically sound to do business with "a crafty, unprincipled, conscienceless, murderous group."[40] Parallels were often drawn between the way American Catholics viewed Communists and how the Inquisition viewed heretics. It was a battle of good versus evil, light against darkness, the friends of God pitted against the friends of Satan. Led by the Jesuit priest Edmund Walsh, founder of Georgetown's Foreign Service School and labeled by one historian as "the most influential Catholic anti-Communist in the country,"[41] Catholics argued against Communism, not because it was un-American, but because it was considered atheistic, anti-religious, and ultimately anti-human. Jeremy York, a freelance writer of the period, described American Catholics as the "most militantly anti-Communist" and claimed, "It is virtually an American Catholic dogma that peace can only be achieved by a national policy of militant ant-Communism."[42]

American Catholic anti-Communism reached its apex in the mid-1950s and continued for another ten years. Events in Europe, most prominently the incarcerations of Cardinal Josef Mindszenty in Hungary and Archbishop Aloysius Stepinac in Yugoslavia, became popular "martyr" causes for American Catholics. Members of the hierarchy, especially Cardinal Francis Spellman of New York, the foremost Catholic anti-Communist spokesman of the post–World War II period (and a strident supporter of Senator McCarthy's polemic), Archbishop Richard Cushing of Boston, and the popular television and radio personality Bishop Fulton Sheen were at the forefront of the American Catholic anti-Communist drive. American Catholics generally supported government efforts, such as those led by Senator McCarthy, Vice President Nixon, and J. Edgar Hoover, to root out Communists, paving the way for God and democracy.[43]

American Catholics took great pride in the Church's uncompromising stance against Communism, believing that the world had turned to the United States to protect Catholics from the Soviet ideology. The historian Richard Gid Powers, who labeled American Catholics as the "backbone of American anticommunism," described the American Church's stance on two levels: "Their anticommunism may have been a religious obligation for American Catholics, but it was also something of a status symbol, a mark of social respectability that demonstrated their superior patriotism in their competition with Jews and old-stock Protestants."[44] The advent of the 1960s and the election of a Catholic, John F. Kennedy, as president, led to a dampening of American Catholic anti-Communism as the need to be perceived as a superpatriot subsided.

The anti-Communist message was also preached by American Protestants. Fundamentalist groups, such as the American Council of Christian Churches, led by its founder Carl McIntyre and the Christian Crusade and organized by Oklahoma evangelist Billy Hargis, denounced Communism and launched drives to save America from the Red menace. The most prominent spokesman for American Protestantism in its campaign against Communism was Billy Graham, who congratulated Congressional committees for "their work of exposing the pinks, the lavenders, and the reds who have sought refuge beneath the wings of the American eagle." Graham preached that it was only through a return to Jesus Christ and the nation's acceptance of Him as its Savior could the nation stave off the spread of Communism. He challenged the United States to renew its dedication and commitment to what made it strong:

> They tell me there are only 3 or 4 million Communists in Russia now. How do they do it [control the country]? Dedication. We're going to have to become dedicated to the things our country believes in and stands for. And one of those things, and one contributing factor, has been religious faith that made this country great.[45]

As one might expect, Patrick Peyton spoke out stridently against Communism, offering his ever-present message of Marian devotion through the rosary as an offensive weapon. In a series of radio addresses in June 1946 he gave two reasons that the rosary would destroy Communism. First, he claimed that if the family rosary was practiced throughout the United States Mary would look favorably upon the nation and ask the Father that nothing harmful happen to it. Second, he stated that reciting the rosary itself would save America because Communism has no concept of God while those who pray the rosary believe in God. He concluded his last talk in the series: "The rosary is the offensive weapon that will destroy Communism — the great evil that seeks to destroy the faith."[46] Peyton's role in the defeat of Communism was acknowledged by one priest as early as 1951: "Fr. Patrick Peyton, CSC, [is] a twentieth

century knight [who] rides out to meet the devil of Communism with
the flashing sword of the Rosary."[47]

The Family Rosary Crusade in Latin America — Background

After eleven years of conducting crusades throughout the world and
now armed with the special tool of the rosary films, Father Peyton stood
poised to enter Latin America. He explained his long desire to bring the
crusade to this region:

> Since 1953, when we went to Spain and became acquainted with
> the Spanish language and tempermental ways, I always felt that Our
> Blessed Mother permitted me to work in Spain and be accepted
> by the Spanish people in order to prepare me by that novitiate
> experience for the day that would come when Her beautiful will
> would have me here [in Latin America].[48]

The importance of the Crusade in Latin America was recognized by
others. Both Jerome Lawyer, CSC, and James Mannis, CSC, described
the work in Latin America as the most important the Family Rosary
Crusade had contemplated.[49] With the Crusade ready to enter Latin
America, Pope John XXIII wrote to Peyton: "Our spontaneous wish is
that your mission today — wherever the ordinaries will call you — may
in like manner penetrate the depths of hearts and the intimate circles of
families and leave many lasting fruits of salvation."[50]

On the verge of its South American mission, the Family Rosary Crusade was viewed by many as an active warrior in the battle against
Communism in the region. In a 1950 master's thesis, Sister Jeanne
Miriam Johnson, CSJ, placed Peyton's Family Rosary Crusade at the
forefront of a rebirth of Catholicism that must stand against "the power
of Russian Communism." Two years earlier the national commentator
James Gillis, CSP, declared that the family rosary was the weapon that
will "sweep the world of Communism."[51] A radio broadcast editorial
commented:

> With Khrushchev and Communism threatening to destroy the
> world, the work of Father Patrick J. Peyton becomes of greater
> importance to every individual living today. And when Commu-
> nism is overcome...as it will be...one of the great factors in the
> triumph of religion and freedom and decency will be the work of
> this humble priest who is convincing mankind that...the world
> that prays together stays together.[52]

Another writer stated, "He [Peyton] is our best bet against Russia."[53]

A private report, "United States Security and the Power of Prayer,"[54] noted the efficacy of the Family Rosary Crusade against Communism in three ways. First, the Crusade operated under the auspices of the Catholic Church, which was the most dedicated and effective anti-Communist force in Latin America. Second, the Crusade organized the laity as its central core of workers, an effective method in a land lacking clergy. Last, the Family Rosary Crusade used "a minutely planned and proven technique of infiltration, employing indigenous organizations, communications and peoples to penetrate Communist strongholds in depth in Latin America with a weapon Communists cannot fight on equal ground." The report concluded, "There is no other organization available which can mobilize local forces in Latin America on such a mass basis to accomplish these objectives."[55] However, from the outset of the Latin American crusades some were aware of the disadvantages of associating it with anti-Communism. Norman Carignan voiced his concern to his boss Peter Grace:

> It would be seriously damaging to Father Peyton's Crusade in Latin America if it became publicized in the United States as an anti-communist crusade because that would immediately place a political tag on it with all that that entails in the politically volatile situations in Latin America.[56]

The Crusade's potential in Latin America and its efficacy against Communism were noted by many in Holy Cross. Peyton — like many others in Holy Cross — saw no such problems; rather he underscored the Crusade's potential for countering Communism, stating that the purpose of the Crusade was "to revive their [the people's] hope and faith which are the only means that will save them from falling into the clutches of Communism."[57] In 1950 the superior general, Christopher O'Toole, CSC, wrote to his provincials asking them to support the work of the Family Rosary Crusade, stating that it will "save the world from the threat of Communism." Noting that the work of the Family Rosary Crusade in Latin America "cannot be over-emphasized," O'Toole's successor, Germain Lalande, CSC, wrote to the Congregation worldwide, "Since the Family Rosary Crusade can reach the popular masses rapidly by the use of its own special methods, it can be regarded as one of the most effective means of preventing peoples of Latin America from sinking rapidly into materialism and becoming the prey of Communism."[58]

Peyton's new understanding that the rosary could be a useful tool in the fight against Communism in Latin America never derailed his original mission of family prayer, but rather was an added application. For Peyton the basic message of his crusade and his ministry as a whole, that families and therefore society would be saved through the family rosary, never wavered. At times the message's proclamation may have taken on additional causes, but the rosary priest's single-minded vision of Marian devotion was never compromised.

The belief that the Crusade would be an effective weapon to smash Communism in Latin America was only one of a series of important and unique aspects that separated the Latin American crusades from those previously conducted. The religious illiteracy of a people otherwise steeped culturally in Catholicism required a new approach that was satisfied by the introduction of the "popular mission," which advertised its goals: "to preach the Gospel message of the Incarnation of Christ, [and to gain] our Redemption and Justification through His Death and Resurrection."[59]

During the production of the rosary films in Spain Peyton viewed them as a potentially powerful catechetical tool, especially in rural areas, to educate people about Christ and spread Marian devotion and family prayer. He wanted the films to be quickly dubbed into Spanish and Portuguese and made available for the popular mission as an antidote to Communism: "We are determined to wage a prayer and catechetical offensive — a real positive answer to the Communist exploitation of our brothers and sisters in South America."[60] Even with good translations, the poor infrastructure of Latin America required some sort of transportation system for the films and all the projection equipment. Originally Peyton proposed that trailers be equipped to serve double duty, carrying all the film and projection equipment, and housing the trained laity who would serve as catechists and projectionists. In 1956 Peyton approached Harry John and Peter Grace about his idea, but both men had reservations. Peyton was disappointed and voiced the new efficacy of the films beyond their catechetical value: "These Rosary films [will] do a great work in South and Central America to counteract the efforts of Communism and to be one remedy towards the solution to one of the greatest crises in all South and Central America, namely, the shortage of priests."[61]

Grace's lack of enthusiasm regarding Peyton's transportation scheme did not deter Peyton, after consultation with his film production team, especially business manager John Kirby, from sending Jerome Lawyer to the shipping magnate seeking financial assistance. Grace was asked to sponsor the films in Peru, Chile, and Colombia, three South American nations that were significantly important to the business interests of

W. R. Grace and Company. Peyton reported that Grace agreed to finance $500,000 toward a project that would bring the films to the poor and illiterate in South America.[62]

Grace agreed to support the mission in Latin America, but his true "conversion" to Peyton's plan came in 1958 when he viewed the films at the Brussels World's Fair. Grace was so moved that he almost overnight became a great advocate for using the films in Latin America. Peyton reported that Grace "pledged that he would spare no effort in order to get financial help for us to cover Latin America with these films." In a privately published booklet, Grace, quoting Senator George Smathers of Florida, hinted at his proposed target area for the films: "The slums . . . of this hemisphere not only disfigure the cities; they disfigure the souls of the people who inhabit them; they . . . are the favorite territory of Communist agitators, the breeding ground of maggots which bid to destroy society."[63] With Peter Grace onboard Peyton was assured that his new venture would receive the attention and financial backing it needed.

With occasional adjustments to local conditions and needs, the basic format for conducting the popular mission was consistent throughout South America. At the outset the team divided the area into sections based on population and the number of film and projection sets available. The on-site crusade director, Joseph Quinn, CSC, met with local pastors to explain the popular mission and to determine film projection sites, such as public squares and athletic fields, which had to be accessible and not identified with a parish church. In a move that foreshadowed the new and more active role of the laity in the post–Vatican II Church, pastors then provided a list of laymen to be trained as instructors and technicians. These men were brought together within the next few days for brief instruction about the nature of the crusade and their role within it. Then the catechists attended fifteen consecutive days of instruction about contemporary applications of each mystery of the rosary, while technicians received training appropriate to their duties. Women volunteers, who would go door-to-door inviting people to attend the films, were given four training sessions. Two weeks before the first film was shown the region was flooded with advertising, including handbills distributed by the women volunteers, billboards, and cars with loudspeakers, besides the normal channels of radio and television. Finally, the films were shown on eight consecutive nights, two films per evening. A special closing ceremony with a midnight Mass generally substituted for the second film on the last evening.[64]

The popular mission was the central feature of the Latin American crusades and one of the principal reasons for their ultimate success. Each popular mission team consisted of at least four people: the team leader, an instructor, a technician, and a driver. The popular mission drew great crowds that increased dramatically as the days of the films' screenings passed. The mission drew people of varied religious backgrounds, including many indifferent Catholics who, as a result of the mission, returned to the practice of the faith. The films achieved their emotional effect on all without respect to educational level or cultural status. Popular mission techniques were also applied effectively in schools, hospitals, prisons, and military outposts.[65]

Besides the addition of the films, a second innovation in the Latin American crusades was the use of secular missionaries as members of the Crusade team. In 1956, while engaged in the crusade in Compostela, Spain, Peyton met María Camino Gorostiza, foundress and superior general of Las Misioneras Seculares (Institute of Secular Missionaries). Peyton asked the nuns, who did not wear religious habits, to assist in the work in Spain. After a successful partnership Peyton asked Gorostiza and her members to become part of the crusade team in Latin America. The two agreed verbally to a plan that would bring "as many missionaries as we may need" to work with the Family Rosary Crusade. Peyton was grateful, writing to the Missionaries: "I cannot exhaust in words what is in my heart in security, in strength, in wisdom, in good judgment, in triumph and victory and, most of all, unbounded love, for the future, because of the personnel of the Crusade."[66]

The Missionaries, like the popular mission, became an integral cog in the Family Rosary Crusade machine in Latin America, participating in all crusades, although their numbers varied from one crusade to another. Although no formal agreement was made with the Institute until 1963, the relationship between Peyton and these women was mutually amicable and helpful. Eventually two teams of Missionaries worked with Father Peyton's overall operation, one on the crusade front and a second as staff assistants with the Hollywood personnel of Family Theater.[67]

The popular mission, rosary films, and use of secular missionaries were all elements of Peyton's outreach program to Latin America. He was ahead of his time in seeing the need to reach out in a preferential way to the poor and marginalized peoples of the world. He understood that economic poverty was often closely linked with spiritual illiteracy. The newly produced rosary films were the perfect material to meet the special needs of the poor by providing for them a resource that would not only allow them to gain knowledge of the faith, but equally importantly to clearly demonstrate that their personal needs were recognized as important and that they would be met by the Church.

The Family Rosary Crusade in Latin America Begins

Patrick Peyton's concept of the popular mission sounded good on paper, but it required a pilot program to determine its efficacy. Because of its spiritual poverty, extremely mountainous terrain, and the presence of many Communist organizations, Peyton identified Bolivia as an excellent place to test the popular mission with its use of mobile film units. In 1957 and 1958, therefore, Peyton contacted several bishops in Bolivia, outlining his plans for the popular mission and asking what needs existed in their dioceses for such a program. He also advertised the fact that "one of the great business leaders of North America [Peter Grace] had seen the films at Brussels [and] feels they are the ticket to get into South America."[68]

Five bishops responded to Peyton's overture, requesting that the popular mission come as soon as possible.[69] Carlos Brown, MM, auxiliary bishop of Santa Cruz, enthusiastically described what the mission could do for his people:

> If God blesses this plan that you and your friend [Peter Grace] have conceived and we are able, thanks to your help [to] reach all of our people with the message of the Rosary, that devotion will become even more profound and real and will bring untold fruits for the good of the Church here in Bolivia and all Latin America.[70]

Bishop Thomas Danehy, MM, administrator apostolic for the Diocese of Pando, wrote that the mission would turn the tide against Communism and Protestantism, which were competing for the loyalty of his flock. Bishop Jorge Manrique of Santa Cruz viewed the films as "a possible way of combating Communism and the method acceptable in this hard atmosphere."[71]

Next Peyton went after funding to properly equip vehicles with machinery and personnel. In July 1958 he asked Harry John, who had donated $40,000 for the construction of the theater in Brussels, to outfit two mobile units for the Diocese of Santa Cruz in Bolivia to test the popular mission, scheduled for October in union with a Marian Congress. Within a month of the request John agreed to supply the required $22,000, but because he was not able to provide it until the next year, the pilot program was placed on hold.[72]

In late 1958 Peyton's pilot program and the whole of the Latin American crusade effort took a dramatic turn when Peter Grace became integrally involved with the financing. From the moment that Grace first viewed the rosary films at Brussels he saw their potential use in Latin

America, a region of the world that was important to him for several reasons. W. R. Grace and Company's significant business ventures in South America[73] would be adversely affected by the Communist infiltration of the region. Like most American Catholics, Grace valued the need to spread the faith, especially in a land where Catholicism was in trouble, but undoubtedly the most important catalyst to Grace's involvement with the Family Rosary Crusade was his firm belief in Father Peyton and the work he did. Grace observed how Peyton was able to saturate an area with his crusade in a short amount of time, a condition that would be devastating to the Communist camp while lifting the spiritual poverty of the people. He wrote to a business associate: "I personally believe that the long range effects of Father Peyton's work are the best possible defense that we have against the Communist menace in Latin America."[74]

In addition to supporting the Rosary Crusade, Grace also actively promoted U.S. involvement in Latin American affairs. He believed at this moment in history there was "no area more essential to us [the United States] than Latin America," an opinion he shared in an address to the World Trade Week Council in 1958: "I think it is unfortunate and almost disastrous that we in the United States have failed to realize completely just how we stand in this troubled world of ours, how dangerously we are exposed to the Soviet threat [in Latin America] and how by helping others we are actually helping ourselves."[75]

He applauded his friend Richard Nixon on his 1958 Latin American tour,[76] but cautioned that this venture demonstrated the problems in the region, especially with respect to Communism. Grace believed the United States needed to become more involved in the region and be a better neighbor. He stated, "There is some urgency about this because many Latin American people have become accustomed to think that we take them for granted." He advocated a policy of private investment and supported economic and social advancement in the region. Since Latin America was the key to the national security and economic well-being of the United States it should be of top priority in our policy of foreign relations.[77]

Grace's belief that the present situation in Latin America constituted a grave danger to the security of the United States and the Church was the foundation upon which he advocated a strong program to fight Communism in the region. He suggested an immediate, vigorous, and positive campaign of psychological warfare, promoting the American ideals of freedom and justice for the individual and democracy in government, as the solution to the economic and social problems that plagued the area.

Grace believed the films should be accessible to the less educated, those confused or misled by Communist propaganda, those ignorant of what the United States represents in the contemporary world, as well as the spiritually deprived. He promoted a loan program to meet the immediate need for more housing and an intensive teacher training program to help rectify the high rate of illiteracy.[78]

Grace strongly supported President Kennedy's Alliance for Progress by serving as its commerce committee chairman and encouraging the U.S. business community and individuals to consider investment in Latin America, even if this required some change in policy. He realized that economic need must come first in any program of social reconstruction:

> In its simplest terms, our goal in Latin America should be to help nations of the area grow economically while they retain internal political freedom and thus remain part of the Western community of nations. Without economic growth the other goals will be much more difficult — if not impossible — to achieve.[79]

Grace firmly believed that there was an urgent need for the American government and its people to act now before it was too late.

In April 1958 Grace asked Vice President Richard Nixon to organize a meeting of American business leaders with significant holdings in South America, including Walter Donnelly, director of South American Operations for United States Steel Corporation, David Rockefeller, vice chairman of the board of directors for Chase Manhattan Bank, Juan T. Tripp, president of Pan American World Airways, Inc., and W. E. Knox, president of Westinghouse Electric International Corporation. Nixon liked the idea and called the meeting after his return from his eight-nation tour of the region. Grace used the meeting to build an alliance of business colleagues with common interests for his fight.[80]

Grace fully believed that the greatest source of strength in Latin America was the Church, and he had complete faith in Peyton and his Family Rosary Crusade, but he still was in a quandary as to how to finance such an operation in the region. In July 1958 he wrote to John Moore, a friend and business associate who was chairman of the Business Advisory Council and one "in a particularly powerful position to influence government policy":

> What I would like to know from you is how we can get a movement similar to that described by Father Peyton financed — whether it be through the C.I.A., through Franco, or through some foundation. There is no easy answer to this question, but even a smart selfish

non-Catholic could see the merit of this idea if the situation got rough enough and we were indeed, as we may well be, forced to place major reliance only in the Western Hemisphere.

Grace asked Moore to speak to Senator John Kennedy and Representative John McCormack,[81] and he informed Peyton of his plan.[82]

On November 24, 1958, one week after a meeting between Grace and Allen Dulles, director of the CIA, a formalized plan and proposal was made to the intelligence chief in a twelve-page letter. Grace outlined Peyton's earlier life and then presented details on his rosary crusade and its efficacy in nations across the globe. He told the director:

> When one considers, Mr. Dulles, that this priest came here from Ireland at age nineteen and went to Hollywood in 1945 with nothing but his faith and a dedicated will to win the world to family prayer and unity, with no previous experience with or education in the entertainment field, I think it is pretty clear that when one gets behind this man, one is backing a proven winner.

He went on to outline the dangers of Communism in Latin America and argued, "He [Peyton] can continue to deliver for our side." Grace, after stating that the strongest bulwark against Communism was religion, offered the films as the necessary weapon:

> I believe, Mr. Dulles, that these [rosary] films measure up to the greatest successes that Father Peyton has had in radio and television and that, if the wherewithal is provided to show them throughout the South American continent, they can be the strongest weapon against the Communist menace.

Grace concluded his letter asking for $500,000 "in order to get these films in the field." He suggested that any money be given through an intermediary group, and said he looked forward to meeting the next week with the vice president on this matter.[83]

On December 3, 1958, Grace met with Allen Dulles and Vice President Nixon at the White House to discuss the Latin American proposal.[84] Dulles, who had been friends with Nixon since 1947, had great respect for the vice president. Grace, as mentioned previously, also supported Nixon. The three men discussed Grace's proposal and Nixon approved the plan, asking only if Communists to date had tried to disrupt the films in any way. The vice president was very interested in meeting Peyton, saying to Grace, "Bring him by the office — must be fantastic." A few weeks later Grace wrote Nixon thanking him for his support and informing him that "activities will commence on a pilot basis in three or four months."[85]

Immediately after Nixon approved the pilot program, Peyton informed his Holy Cross superiors. He first wrote to his provincial, George DePrizio, CSC, including in his letter a copy of Grace's proposal to Dulles. He also wrote to the superior general, Christopher O'Toole, CSC, described his plan for South America, and acknowledged his great debt to Grace. Rather naively the general responded, "As you know he [Grace] is the soul of generosity and his only desire is to be of help."[86]

The ease with which Peter Grace took financial control of the crusade and the uncritical acceptance of his plan by Peyton and others in Holy Cross were consistent with the relationship between the shipping magnate and rosary priest. Grace, a strong Catholic who would lead the U.S. chapter of the Knights of Malta during the presidential administration of Ronald Reagan, was convinced that Peyton and his crusade were the solution to Communism in Latin America.[87] On the other side, Peyton, who was able to obtain money from benefactors but knew nothing about finances, trusted Grace implicitly, both from their friendship and the great influences which the tycoon commanded throughout the United States.[88] Peyton acknowledged that Grace was "the Champion, the Defender and the Protector of the Family Rosary movement since the beginning"[89] and that he was absolutely necessary in the Family Rosary Crusade scheme of operations:

> Of all the men in the entire world Peter [Grace] is the one, and the only one to whom we can look for the financial protection, defense and security of the Crusade. To be away from Peter for many months is to be away from the very source that enables us to continue financially.[90]

The single-minded and, therefore, partially blind approach of Peyton to his basic message of Marian devotion created an uncritical trust with Grace. For the rosary priest what was important was the message of family prayer through the rosary; he left the specifics of fund raising to others.

The rapid and unexpected series of events that gave financial backing to the crusades in Latin America led to a sudden shift in plans, especially with respect to logistics with the pilot program. On January 6, 1959, the films were shown at Grace's Manhasset, New York, home to "the man assigned in the highest circles [of government] to make the decision regarding the South American program," who afterward met with Grace, two of his top officers, and John Kirby to map out a strategy for the crusade in South America. The crusade was given $20,000 "as the budget to make the proving." Peyton commented after the meeting, "We all feel, and even our friend [government official], that if this proving goes through there will be more help forthcoming to help us become efficient instruments to advance the wishes and will and person of Our Blessed Mother in that continent."[91]

Government financing of the crusades in Latin America forced Peyton to share control of the location and timing of events, a shift from his normal mode of operation, but one he apparently did not mind so long as his Marian message remained at the forefront. This shift became evident when Peyton's Bolivian pilot program was scrubbed and the town of La Serena, Chile, three hundred miles north of Santiago, was chosen.[92] Arrangements were made to equip test vehicles for the pilot program, which was originally scheduled to begin on March 25. Although Peyton had three fully equipped station wagons ready by March 20,[93] the March 25 deadline was extended at the government's request, causing Grace to almost reach "the point of giving up," but the test program was eventually conducted successfully in September.[94]

Meanwhile, in late February 1959 Peyton journeyed to Rome to solicit support for the popular mission in South America. Cardinal Domenico Tardini, secretary of state, and Archbishop Antonio Samore, secretary of the Sacred Congregation of Extraordinary Ecclesiastical Affairs, supported his cause, but warned him not to enter South America with an attitude of superiority, but rather with kindness and charity. They also counseled him to seek invitations from local ordinaries rather than foisting the crusade upon a particular nation, region, or diocese. Peyton also received the encouragement of the pope for his popular mission program.[95]

The involvement of the CIA in the Family Rosary Crusade in Latin America was consistent with the agency's aims and history. Founded in 1947 the agency, through the publication in 1948 of NSC Directive 10/2, was given power to conduct independent covert operations against foreign countries. It defined itself as "a clandestine operation designed to influence foreign governments, events, organizations, or persons in support of United States foreign policy; it may include political, economic, propaganda or para-military activities."[96] In Latin America the agency sought to protect state governments from local insurgents. In support of such an effort the CIA used transnational corporations, churches, and religious organizations. A former CIA agent, Mansfield Sprague, reported that in 1960 the agency supported clandestine operations "with nongovernmental organizations in education, labor, publishing and other fields." These programs "were essential at the time to counter the threat of Communist activity which was preventing the establishment and threatening the existence of the institutions everywhere, particularly in the so-called less-developed areas."[97]

The CIA's involvement with religious groups was quite extensive and was manifest in two separate areas: the use of missionaries as informants and direct financial aid to missionary apostolates, which were perceived to be tools in the anti-Communist struggle. During the Cold War U.S. missionaries routinely collaborated with the CIA, providing the Agency with information about Communist activities in Latin America.[98] In 1974 the director of the CIA, William Colby, told Senator Mark Hatfield (R-Oregon) "that the CIA had used missionaries in the past for political and intelligence gathering reasons and would continue to do so."[99] This policy continued into the 1970s, prompting church and state officials to question the practice. In July 1975 Donald Ehr, SVD, chairman of the Conference of Major Superiors of Men's Mission Committee of the U.S. Catholic Mission Council, complained about the co-opting of missionaries:

> It is a widely held belief, both among indigenous Church personnel in the third world and among many U.S. missionaries, that the CIA has, over a long period of time and in many countries, routinely sought the cooperation of missionaries in tasks that are wholly inconsistent with the evangelizing and pastoral mission of the Church.
>
> It appears that in some instances the cooperation was sought and sometimes regrettably granted — with full knowledge that the CIA was involved.[100]

Less than one year later George Bush, director of the CIA, issued new regulations on the relationship of the CIA to missionaries: "In light of the special constitutional concern with Church-State relationships, [the] CIA shall establish no secret, paid or unpaid, contractual relationship with any American clergyman or missionary."[101] Yet, despite this edict, the problem persisted in the administration of President Jimmy Carter, who sought ways around the new policy in order to continue the flow of information.[102] The journalist Penny Lernoux summarized the situation:

> The CIA attempted to play God in Latin America, deciding who should be President, who should be eliminated, how the people should live and whom they should have as allies and enemies. Foreign missionaries and local religious groups were among the many

means used to achieve these ends, but because of what they believed and taught, their manipulation must be viewed as an act of calculated cynicism.[103]

The CIA also provided financial backing to various Church organizations in Latin America and elsewhere. Thomas Quigley, director of the Division for Latin America of the USCC, stated,

> The prime targets for C.I.A. contact were precisely such pragmatic liberals sent in large numbers during the period to Latin America from the United States churches — the "concerned" missionaries from the mainline Protestant churches and from Catholic societies like Maryknoll and the Jesuits.[104]

Former State Department employee John Marks, in his book *CIA and the Cult of Intelligence*, claimed that "30 to 40 percent of the churchmen he [Marks] interviewed... knew of CIA Church connections."[105] The Belgian Jesuit Roger Vekemans, working for the Centro Bellarmino in Santiago, Chile, "reportedly had obtained substantial remuneration from the CIA" to support anti-Communist labor unions.[106] In February 1967 the *New York Times* reported that the National Council of Churches had received financial assistance from foundations allegedly linked to the CIA. Another report, claiming that the agency supported the Blue Army and Opus Dei, besides Family Rosary, concluded, "An infiltration of Church organizations by the American government and the world of American business for political objectives is certainly nothing new."[107]

On a second front, the CIA also supported humanitarian efforts that frustrated Communist ideologues. The historian James Fisher, for example, describes the CIA's involvement with the missionary doctor Tom Dooley in Southeast Asia and his Medical International Organization (MEDCO) in the 1950s.[108]

With government funding of the pilot program in place, Grace and Peyton continued their development efforts. Peyton met with Cardinal Richard Cushing at Notre Dame in July 1959, and the Boston prelate promised the crusade $1 million for its work in Latin America. In January 1960 Cushing's contributions began to pour in, but his total gift was only $160,000, barely 16 percent of his promised benefaction. Cushing explained that his income had dwindled, but it is likely that the archbishop, using the rationale that Grace would find the financing from other sources, may have felt less committed to his pledge once Grace in essence was given control of the crusade's finances.[109] Peyton, without the knowledge of his Holy Cross superiors, also tried to raise money from local ordinaries in the United States, asking them to recognize the Family Rosary Crusade in Latin America as a missionary effort that would entitle it to send speakers to parishes for mission appeals. This ploy backfired when the superior general, Germain Lalande, CSC, ordered Peyton to withdraw his appeal, saying that it conflicted with the Holy Cross Foreign Mission Society's annual parish appeals.[110]

At the same time, Peter Grace made overtures to his friends in the business world. On the same day in November 1958 on which he wrote Allen Dulles, Grace wrote a similar letter to John Madden, chairman of the board of Emigrant Industrial Savings Bank in New York, asking for $500,000 of support, although it is not clear whether he was asking for a loan or a gift.[111] Early in 1959 Grace planned a dinner for "a group of the top men of the American companies in South America to donate to a fund to make this South American program work in the hinterlands there."[112] He also convinced Charlie Miller of Miller Brewing Company and Harry John of the DeRance Foundation to support, at least in principle, the crusades in Latin America.[113]

The Crusades Begin in South America

With his financing secure and the pilot project successfully completed, Peyton was ready to begin his crusade in Latin America, starting with Chile. In the fall of 1959 he wrote to the bishops of Chile, informing them of his desire to conduct crusades in the country. Both Peyton and Grace met with Manuel Larraín, bishop of Talca, who used his influence to open the nation to the crusade.[114] Peyton eventually set up crusades encompassing the entire nation along its more than twenty-seven-hundred-mile length. On August 15, 1959, Peyton and two secular missionaries, María Luisa Luca de Tena and Begona Díaz, arrived in Santiago. These three were later joined by Joseph Quinn, CSC, Carmen Amann, Fuensanta Gonzalez, and Margarita de Lecea.

Once personnel were present the crusade began to organize. A headquarters was set up in Santiago through the benefaction of Dr. Eduardo Cruz Coke, a prominent physician and politician who was then serving as Chile's ambassador to Peru. The necessary equipment was transported to Valparaiso via the Grace shipping lines. Besides its primary message of the family rosary, the crusade focused on anti-Communism, manifest best through the popular mission. It was believed that "the influence of Communism will be directly attacked in all those families that adhere to the message of the Crusade."[115]

The rosary films were first used in Chile in a commercial venture that was to publicize the upcoming crusades in the nation but also to raise as much revenue as possible. Peyton secured the Astor, the foremost movie theater in Santiago, to debut the films. Two benefits were held, the first on October 17 for the hierarchy and a second on October 20 for priests and religious in the area; regular screenings commenced on October 28. For the first performances the Scourging at the Pillar and the Crucifixion were shown back-to-back for the first half of the program and the Resurrection and Ascension were shown after a short break. In lieu of the normal intermission the house lights were raised only slightly and on the screen was projected a huge white cross. Most in the theater stayed in their places as classical music, such as Bach's "Toccata and Fugue," was played in the background. One observer commented, "It was impressive; you could tell the pictures had their effect."[116] In Santiago the films were shown in the Ducal Theater for five weeks, but they were screened only for a few days in other locales. In total the films were shown in eighteen cities and fifty-four theaters with more than 110,000 in attendance.[117]

The most important use of the films was for the popular mission. Fifty projection teams were sent into the field with the result that each night the crowds increased as word spread and people "eagerly returned for the next instalment." The crowds that attended the mission were enormous, and the effect on the people was even more noticeable. One report stated, "One has only to be present in the slums of Santiago and see the expressions of the innocent poor to recognize the import that the movies have in areas where Communism has been thriving for many years." Joseph Quinn, CSC, reported how the diocesan clergy in the area had never seen a response by the people equal to that received by the films.[118]

Lessons from earlier crusades were effective in Chile, especially with respect to advertising, which Peyton suggested "is not only a means but an end."[119] In the Chilean crusades some of the most popular *Family Theater of the Air* broadcasts were translated into Spanish, recorded in Chile by local radio and television personalities, and aired on local stations, where they were well received. A crusade poster, with a caricature of Peyton's face, designed by a local artist, Jorge Delano, was found on almost every street corner, on buses and other public transportation vehicles, and on huge banners that hung from buildings and in public parks and squares.[120]

After the popular mission ended, the crusades began in the central section of the nation, with, as usual, the publication of a pastoral letter by the local bishop, five weeks of parish homilies, and assorted meetings with parishes, schools, and other institutions. Before the first rally, however, Peyton returned to the United States to attend a meeting on April 24, 1960, with Peter Grace and government representatives to review progress and future funding. Peyton wrote to Jerome Lawyer, CSC, in veiled language about his previous arrangements: "There are things that have gone on between Peter [Grace] and myself that will have such far reaching consequences for the Crusade, but that I am not able for the moment to convey to you."[121] Later he reported in a diary:

> On Sunday April 24 [1960], at the Carlton Hotel in Washington with Peter Grace, Frip Flanagan and another great friend of the Family Rosary Crusade and myself, a new crossroad for the Family Rosary Crusade was reached. I am very grateful that as a result of Sunday's meeting we will have the finances that may reach five times what we received for entrance into Chile, for the entrance into another Latin American country with films, projectors, screens, jeeps, machinery, etc. We have to pursue this some two or three steps further but at least the basis has been established and the hopes are high that Our Blessed Mother will realize this opportunity.[122]

Rather blindly, Peyton seemed unconcerned about the source of his funding; his profound faith in Mary, proclamation of the message of family prayer, and sufficient money to carry the crusade throughout Latin America were his primary concerns. Peyton was financially set for the remainder of the Chilean crusade as well as his next venture, whatever that might be.

The crusades in Chile moved first north and then south, covering the full length of the country in less than a year. The central crusade peaked with a series of seven rallies, the first in San Felipe on May 1. Rallies in the port city of Valparaíso and Rancagua drew 80,000 and 60,000 respectively, but the largest rally was conducted at Cousino Park in the capital, Santiago, on May 15 with 550,000 in attendance. The reaction of one participant at the rally was highly descriptive: "The Apostle of the Rosary World Crusade spoke in Spanish tinged with an English accent — what supernatural fire emanated from his simple words."[123] Clearly Peyton's message was as efficacious as ever.

In the northern region five rallies were held between June 26 and July 24. Quinn reported, "This crusade for Family Prayer has been a great success in the center and northern parts of Chile."[124] Between September 25 and November 15 ten rallies scheduled in the south were sparsely attended, but since the region had recently been devastated by an earthquake, the courage of the people in the wake of such a tragedy made any attendance heroic. In Valdivia, for example, a city 80 percent destroyed by the temblor, fifteen hundred attended the rally, while in Concepción, a city known to be "a breeding ground for Communism," forty thousand attended the same event.

Members of the Chilean hierarchy were very appreciative of the crusades. Bishop Francisco Valdés of Osorno, a city in the south where thirty thousand attended the rally, commented, "Without [a] doubt the visible result of the Family Rosary program must correspond to the invisible spiritual fruit that it has produced." Bishop Manuel Larraín of Talca, whom Peyton and Grace had visited to arrange the whole campaign before the crusade began, wrote to the superior general in appreciation of Peyton:

> I want to thank you . . . for the immense good that dear Father Peyton has accomplished among us with the Family Rosary Crusade. It has been like an explosion of dormant faith — the awakening of which has enabled so many straying souls to find God again. It is the great victory of Mary, who has always loved these Latin American lands in a special way, and who, by means of this crusade, has once again manifest her love.[125]

After a break long enough to permit the transfer of equipment and a short rest for the secular missionaries and Father Quinn, the crusade headed for Venezuela and established its headquarters in Caracas on April 1, 1961. Extant data does not reveal how and when it was decided to move the crusade to Venezuela, but based on what transpired in Chile and later crusades, it is likely that the U.S. government was a significant player in the decision process. The political situation in South America changed drastically after the April 1961 "Bay of Pigs" debacle, when a planned U.S. government invasion of Cuba ended in disarray and defeat. Pro-Cuban sympathizers were active in Venezuela and were hostile to any American-based entity, including the rosary crusade. Acknowledging the difficult road ahead, Peyton gave his own rationale for the move to Venezuela: "Caracas was chosen for a crusade because it was another Havana, ready for revolution, very restless and disturbed."[126]

Peyton's staff claimed that he was building "an organization composed of Americans and Venezuelans to fight Communism."[127] He contacted several politically connected people who assisted him with the Venezuelan crusade. The most important person in the area was Walter Donnelly, a former ambassador to Costa Rica (1947), Venezuela (1947–50), and Austria (1951–52), and now the representative of United States

Steel in Venezuela. From his previous experience Donnelly was well connected in Washington and served as the local contact for the government money flow. He once wrote to Peyton, "If you want help you need only to ask me to do it and I shall cooperate with the greatest pleasure."[128] Peyton recognized Donnelly as "an extraordinary friend and champion" of the Venezuela crusade: "He has taken the Missionaries and myself to his heart and home, and is giving the crusade his complete dedication."[129] Besides Donnelly, who arranged his schedule so he was in Caracas for the duration of the crusade, Peyton received the support of two other American businessmen in the area, Jim Gorman, vice president of Grant Advertising, and Ted Mulvehy, president of Sinclair Oil, both Notre Dame alumni.

The political situation was so tense that Peyton had to get government permission to screen the rosary films during the popular mission, which targeted three specific groups: the poor and religiously uninformed, youth in schools, and parishes. The popular mission was interrupted on a few occasions from Communist sympathizers in the region. The extreme poverty of certain areas became breeding grounds for Communists with the result that the mission was at times welcomed with people throwing stones and tomatoes resulting in some minor damage to equipment and in some cases stopping the films on a particular night. Despite the incidents Donnelly reported to Grace, "These minor attacks will not deter Father Quinn and the missionaries from carrying on the campaign."[130]

The crusade in Venezuela also included the extensive use of Family Theater television films produced in the 1950s. American films were very popular in the country, and the publicity value of Hollywood stars was a great boost to the crusade. Joseph Quinn, CSC, obtained free air time from several local television stations to broadcast in Spanish *The Road to Peace, Hill Number One, A Star Shall Rise, The Triumphant Hour, The World's Greatest Mother,* and several segments from the *Inspiration Please* series.[131]

Despite efforts by Communists to disrupt the event, including a bomb threat and ripping down banners and posters across the city, the rally held in Caracas on July 16, 1961, with six hundred thousand in attendance was successful. Attempts to sabotage Peyton's work failed as noted by a local news story: "As an antidote to the type of disorder that has been occurring in Venezuela, the demonstration was heartening. It showed that the political disturbances are the work of a tiny minority, and do not reflect the feelings of the people."[132] More importantly for the future of the crusade, reports to the U.S. government also noted the efficacy of the rallies in Venezuela:

This was a tremendous blow to the Communists and the Castroites and if the momentum and organization initiated by Father Peyton's Crusade can be maintained it seems to me that this might be the turning point in the struggle between the Communists and the forces of democracy in Venezuela.[133]

The need for Grace to report the results of the crusade to his Washington contacts is evident from Peyton's correspondence: "Peter Grace asked me to work out a report that would be ammunition for him to win our mutual friends for another crusade."[134]

The efficacy of the crusade, namely, its lessening of the people's spiritual poverty and especially its success "in breaking through Communist opposition," was emphasized by Grace and his assistants in writing to Peyton's provincial and superior general: "Father Peyton has demonstrated that he can saturate an area in a few months in a manner which is devastating to the Communist cause merely by turning the attention of the people to their God and their Faith, which Communism must, of course, destroy in order to win victory." Norman Carignan, vice president of W. R. Grace and Company, claimed that Peyton's form of Catholic Action "can become the most effective anti-Communist organization in the country" and be "the turning point in the struggle between the Communists and the forces of democracy in Venezuela."[135] Christopher O'Toole, CSC, agreed with Grace's assessment: "Certainly you are right when you say that Father Peyton, with the technique he uses, can saturate in a few months and so deliver a telling blow against the Communist cause."[136]

Peyton's crusade in Venezuela was heralded by church and state officials as well as by his immediate associates and supporters. Theodore Moscoso, U.S. ambassador to Venezuela, commented:

> I believe this stimulation of Christian solidarity [the crusade] must have a tremendous spiritual impact on the people of this country who have been besieged by Communist subversion for so many months.... I wholeheartedly recommend that Father Peyton be encouraged to continue his crusade throughout the free world and wherever democracy and Christianity are threatened by Communist aggression or subversion.[137]

Humberto Quintero, cardinal archbishop of Caracas, in thanking Peyton expressed what had been accomplished by the crusade:

> We are living in a grave moment, threatened by the repeated and astute attempts of Marxian atheism to inflitrate into the minds of

our people. Against these impious and dividing ideas, your Crusade of prayer constitutes a powerful barrier. For this reason I consider your Crusade to be a Providential work.[138]

One of Quintero's suffragan bishops, Alejandro Fernández-Feo, reflecting on the success of the rally in the face of great odds, wrote, "I believe that what has occurred is a miracle of God through the intercession of the Virgin Mary."[139] Peyton also noted his great victory: "The Family Rosary Crusade has shaken the Christian conscience in Caracas, from the highest level to the lowest.... The triumph of the Family Rosary has coincided with the decline of Communism in Caracas and Venezuela."[140]

It was not clear where the crusade would go after the movement's triumph in Venezuela. Peyton, Grace, and Donnelly wanted to move to Colombia. Christopher O'Toole, CSC, recommended Brazil, the largest country on the continent, which he also saw as the Church's most important target, given Brazil was home not only to more Catholics than any other South American nation, but also represented a significant concentration of Communist influence.[141] However, the decision seems to have been vested with the federal government personnel who controlled the crusades' finances, and who insisted on examining the potential crusade sites. Donnelly explained to Peyton, "The priority will be determined after considering all the facts received from the field with which I agree, even though the country we discussed [Colombia] is desperately in need of relief."[142]

In late October 1961 Peyton's team received word that Bogotá, Colombia, would be the site for the next crusade.[143] The delay and uncertainty created by the federal government's partial control left a bad taste in Peter Grace's mouth, as he viewed Peyton's main objective might be compromised. Thus he asked Peyton to prepare a complete plan and definite program for how the Family Rosary Crusade could accomplish its goals if it were free from the financial plan in place.[144]

The crusade in Colombia began on December 8, the Feast of the Immaculate Conception, when Peyton and his staff set up their operation in Bogotá. The popular mission, which began in January 1962, was unmarred by the disruptions experienced in the Venezuelan campaign. Because the Crusade began with only $60,000, some $20,000 shy of the normal budget, Peyton and Grace had to scramble for benefactors in the United States and Colombia to make up the shortfall. Only in March 1962 was the Bogotá money made available.[145] Despite the money difficulties, the rally held in Bogotá on March 25, the Feast of the Annunciation, drew 1 million people, the largest crowd to date in the South American campaign.

The Crusades in Brazil

Control of the destination of the Family Rosary Crusade continued to be an issue at the end of the Colombia campaign. Peyton, ever concerned with the promotion of the message of family prayer, reported to Grace that while the Bogotá crusade was in progress he was looking to move to Ecuador and then Buenos Aires, but, "an abrupt change in our plans took place at the end of the Bogotá crusade when it was decided that all plans had to be postponed and the Crusade effort should be immediately concentrated in Recife and Rio de Janeiro [Brazil]."[146] Christopher O'Toole, CSC, who had promoted the idea of Brazil before Colombia, was pleased about the selection:

> I am so happy that you are now working in Brazil. God knows that now is the time to exert all the influence possible to counteract the evils of Communism in that country. At last the hierarchy and the clergy of Latin America are becoming aware of the fact that it is not Protestantism they have to worry about but Communism.[147]

The Brazilian clergy also welcomed the Crusade with enthusiasm: "I believe the Crusade is a remarkable medium for combating Communism in a peaceful way, not so much because it is a crusade for the Rosary, but because it is a crusade for the Rosary *prayed* as a family."[148]

The political situation that greeted the crusade was the most tenuous so far. In January 1961 Janio da Silva Quadros, thought by some observers to be a very eccentric man, was democratically elected as the president of Brazil, but after serving only seven months he resigned under severe pressure, making Vice President João Goulart his successor. Goulart was not a Communist, but it was clear that his direction was to the left, since he surrounded himself with advisors and aides who were Communists or leaned in that direction. Under Goulart inflation remained high,[149] corruption was rampant, and unrest spread throughout the nation. Robert McNamara, the U.S. secretary of defense, questioned Brazil's professed neutrality in foreign policy, arguing that if a nation was not committed to the West then it could easily fall into the Soviet camp.[150] Peyton called the political situation in Brazil a "crisis," describing the problem as the "present form of government . . . making desperate efforts to maintain itself in the country against a dictatorial regime of a Communist nature which is endeavoring to take over the nation."[151]

The abrupt change of plans, at least in Peyton's mind, that sent the crusade to Brazil did not allow for any break for weary personnel who moved to Recife, the capital city of the state of Pernambuco in northern Brazil in June 1962. They found a region plagued with economic, political, and religious problems. Food and housing shortages, arising from the dire poverty of the region, brought Communists to the area in great numbers. Due to these problematic social conditions Mass attendance was down significantly. Peyton understood the importance of the Recife effort and placed it, as was his norm, in the hands of Mary:

> All this...can spell out nothing more for anyone with faith than the fact of how serious in the mind of Our Queen is this battle. She is compelled from what I have described to give an extraordinary intervention in order to surround this effort in Recife with a defense so great it is impregnable.[152]

The popular mission began in Recife in late July 1962, but it was clear before this date that there were a few obstacles to negotiate before the crusade could commence. First, major difficulties were found in importing the projectors and other pieces of equipment, and a satisfactory place for dubbing the films in Portuguese was not available locally, forcing the use of American facilities. Even more problematic, the Recife campaign overlapped with one in Rio de Janeiro, thus requiring duplicate equipment. This need prompted a meeting on April 4, 1962, between Walter Donnelly and the Washington contact that approved a higher budget of $115,000 for the campaign.[153] Through the diligent work of his faithful staff, most especially Joseph Quinn, CSC, Peyton was able to obtain the necessary equipment and conduct both the popular mission and the other aspects of the crusade without further complication.[154]

The crusade in Recife proceeded without complications and was well received by the local people and greatly appreciated by Church officials. Although Communist opposition was present in the form of small gatherings of sympathizers and several incidents of vandalism, the main rally, held on September 16 with five hundred thousand in attendance, was a great success. Calling the crusade the "greatest triumph of any Catholic movement in our cities for decades," one local newspaper declared: "The Crusade pushed back tremendously the Communist forces."[155] The success of the Recife crusade inspired Peyton, who declared that it "has been needed for a long time," to produce a twenty-five-minute documentary, *Smile of Recife,* for use in future popular missions.[156]

The Recife campaign marked a major shift in how a crusade's success was measured. In the past the major measurement of success for Peyton was the number of pledges signed by the end of the campaign. In Latin America, however, extant records rarely include pledge numbers, although the statistics were kept. The CIA's mark for success was measured in the campaign's efficacy as an anti-Communist tool. Interiorly, however, Peyton never deviated from his own measure of success, namely, the promotion of the family rosary. He was fully aware of how the films made the mysteries of the rosary come alive for the people.

When the crusade moved from Recife to Rio de Janeiro, problems centered around the issue of control. In late July and August 1962 Peyton, Grace, and Donnelly were in communication about the budget for the Rio de Janeiro crusade, which apparently had not been approved by the government contact as previously thought. Peyton reported to Grace that Donnelly had "received assurances that the Rio budget...would be forthcoming in July,"[157] but monies would not be provided until Washington completed its review of the Recife campaign. This delay and the demand for verifiable evidence on the efficacy of the crusade was irritating to Peyton, who complained to Donnelly:

> I feel that it would be wonderful if you and Peter could actually meet our friends before the Recife Rally and get them to approve the budget for Rio without having to wait for the outcome in Recife. As I said to Peter last night, they do not have a one hundred percent batting average, so why are they so demanding on the Family Rosary Crusade to have a one hundred percent batting average all the time. You also said to me that our friends put our team in the hardest battle field.[158]

The delay and uncertainty frustrated Peter Grace as well. Peyton, speaking for himself and Grace, wrote to Donnelly, "It is too difficult to be told to go to a certain place, especially when crusades take lots of planning and then after a crusade to sit idle for long periods of time waiting for a decision to be made regarding our next move." Extant correspondence indicates that those in control of the Crusade's destination sought verifiable proof of the campaign's effectiveness in fighting Communism, such as losses of Communists in elections and small attendance figures at Communist functions versus the crusade attendance.[159] Grace met with Donnelly in early September 1962 in New York to map out a strategy for developing with the government a more definite policy concerning the handling of the crusade. Later that same month Grace, after attending a twentieth anniversary benefit for Family Theater in Hollywood, met with his senior vice presidents and then called his Washington contact, who guaranteed him "a whole day if necessary" and possibly an hour with "an even higher source" to discuss the issue. Peyton contacted Donnelly and asked him to attend this meeting, which helped iron out some of the past communication difficulties.[160]

The financing uncertainty did not impede the progress of the crusade, which moved into Rio de Janeiro in early August 1962. The need for extra equipment, which Peyton had articulated earlier, became even more critical in Rio, where thirty mobile units proved inadequate for a population of 3 million. It was suggested that the crusade time could be extended to accommodate the need, but Peyton responded that the crusade schedule would not allow extra time in one area and that the general time pattern of crusades had worked well in the past. Grace spoke to Donnelly, who requested additional funds from "our benefactor." Peyton reported to Grace, "Our friend in listening to Walter grasped the problem and quickly recognized that we would require for Rio twice the equipment needed in Recife and twice the number of films." Approval of the additional funds was given.[161]

The Rio de Janeiro campaign was the largest undertaking of the Family Rosary Crusade to date. In his pastoral letter of November 11, 1962, Cardinal Jaime de Barros Camara welcomed the Crusade as his antidote to ideologies contesting God: "The world's spiritual renewal cannot conform to the spirit of darkness. Cuba and Berlin are two poles around which world peace wavers. So the rosary crusade comes at a most appropriate hour to face the wave of evil which Satan wants to hurl upon us."[162]

The huge area presented organizational challenges, but eventually the city was divided into four sectors with two separate crusade offices to control operations. To serve the large population, the films were shown on local television (as well as in the parishes, schools, hospitals, and other institutions) on fifteen consecutive evenings. On December 8 the citizens of Rio were given a special present: an illuminated rosary thirty meters in length, with a cross eight meters high, adorning the famous Cristo del Corcovado, which overlooks the city.[163]

The rally in Rio, held on December 16, was the largest gathering of people in the history of the crusade so far: 1.5 million came to pray the rosary and hear Peyton deliver his patented message. Besides Church officials, the event was attended by President João Goulart. Dom Helder Camara, auxiliary archbishop of Rio de Janeiro, expressed the desire of many in commenting after the rally, "God willing, the Family Rosary Crusade will never leave Brazil. It is a movement that finds a deep echo in the Brazilian soul."[164]

Unlike the campaign in Colombia and the initial move into Brazil, where delays were experienced, Peyton on January 25, 1963, wrote Walter Donnelly that he had received word from Tom Doyle, an associate of Peter Grace, that Crusade's next destination was Salvador in the state of Bahia.[165] For the next few months, however, before the crusade commenced, several meetings were held between Peter Grace and his assistants, Walter Donnelly, and the Washington contact, with respect to the future direction of the Crusade. Peyton was obviously very interested in the progress of the meetings and asked Donnelly to use his influence to obtain permission "that would put this campaign into action." As in the past Washington demanded reaction to the previous campaign in Rio de Janeiro, but Peyton, maintaining his overt focus on the crusade's original objective, commented, "I have a feeling that if our friends say that they cannot do it we must still do everything to make that 'no' into a 'yes' in one way or another."[166] In early June Grace, Donnelly, Peyton, and the Washington contact met in New York City and worked out a mutually agreeable plan that would keep the Crusade in Brazil for the next two years. Despite Peyton's presence at the meeting, it seems that he was more of a pawn than a player in the decisions made on the direction of the Family Rosary Crusade.[167]

The crusade in Salvador was conducted between April 8 and June 6, 1963. The crusade was met with more hostility here than in other areas of Brazil. One report stated: "A certain hostility towards everything 'American' exists to a greater degree than we noticed in other Brazilian regions. In some sectors of the crusade they have charged that 'the American stigma is endeavoring to create an unfriendly atmosphere.' " The rally was held on June 2 with Don Augusto Alvaro da Silva, the cardinal primate of the country, the governor of the state of Bahia, and the mayor of Salvador in attendance. The gathering ended with the six hundred thousand faithful waving a "sea of handkerchiefs," as an expression of popular affection for Peyton.[168]

The crusade in Salvador was conducted almost simultaneously with one in Belo Horizonte, the capital of the state of Minas Gerais, located in the east-central zone of the nation. The team arrived on February 28, 1963, and set up an office in mid-March, but the popular mission did not commence until early April. The films were shown in the three parish sectors, then in schools, hospitals, prisons, and military barracks with over 2.1 million in attendance. As in Rio de Janeiro, the films were also shown on local television. The rally was held on June 16 and drew some five hundred thousand including local civic and Church officials.[169]

Crusade personnel took a short respite before moving to Porto Alegre, beginning on September 3 and concluding on December 21. The popular mission, which was plagued by inclement weather, including unusually cold days and lots of rain, aroused the interest of residents to the films and their message. One local journalist commented, "This effort of Father Peyton can be called, from a motion picture club standpoint, the most fantastic Motion Picture Club in the history of humanity."[170] The rally, held on December 15 and attended by three hundred thousand, was another in the long line of successes in the Latin American crusades. One member of the local hierarchy was pleased with the crusade's ability to transform people and spur their faith: "I think that the movement has a wonderful motive and an enrichment of doctrine, and it [is] carried out in an active way. I am certain that the Crusade here will also bring many people to God, through the hands of Our Lady."[171]

The close of 1963 marked another milestone in the Latin American crusades with the introduction of the Family Day celebration on December 8, the Feast of the Immaculate Conception. Following the Bogotá crusade a special celebration, broadcast on local television, featured the recitation of the rosary in the local cathedral along with music. In Brazil, however, the commemoration was led by the President João Goulart, who declared December 8 Family Day throughout the country. Joseph Quinn, CSC, put together an hour-long television special that originated from Rio de Janeiro, but was broadcast throughout South America. Among the personalities on the show were Pele, the famous soccer star, Sarita Montiel, a famous Latin American singer, Bing Crosby, who sang "Ave Maria," Agostinho dos Santos, the bossa nova king of Brazil, who sang a Samba version of "Ave Maria," Cantinflas, the Mexican entertainer, and Lenny Eversong, the Kate Smith of Latin America. A television strike in Rio threatened to ruin the show, but Quinn and a technician worked round the clock to get the program ready by air time. The program reached the single greatest audience in Family Rosary's history.[172]

The Family Rosary Crusade in Brazil was highly successful and had certainly made its mark in the nation, beginning in 1962, but the campaign found its high point and place of greatest conflict in São Paulo, the largest metropolitan area in the nation. The scope of the task that Peyton's crusade was to accomplish can be grasped by realizing that São Paulo was the largest archdiocese in the world with approximately 6 million people who were served by only 225 secular clergy. Thus, it was obvious from the outset that a severe test awaited Peyton's Holy Cross assistants and the secular missionaries. Additionally, the number of laymen and laywomen needed to lead the popular mission and other crusade functions was staggering. The crusade was conducted between July 19 and August 23, 1964, with the popular mission beginning on April 6.

The political and religious situation that greeted Peyton's crusade was highly unstable. Quinn warned Peyton that many groups wanted to use the Crusade to advance their own political position and ideas, but that to avoid the danger, Peyton must keep the crusade independent of any particular group or political position:

> One of the greatest problems here in São Paulo is the political sit-
> uation at this moment. There are attempts to use the Rosary as
> a means to further the political aims of some groups and for this
> reason the Cardinal has asked us to hold up any publicity until this
> sentiment blows over. He does feel that in the great battle for the
> Crusade we must be very careful and very cautious, so that the spir-
> itual aim of the Crusade is maintained at all times. The situation
> is very delicate here but I hope the Crusade will help the people
> during this great crisis.[173]

William Belyea, CSC, a Canadian Holy Cross priest who joined the crusades in Latin America, echoed a similar message, warning, as the superior general, Christopher O'Toole, CSC, had earlier, "I think the danger we must avoid is that of permitting any political party to identify itself with us."[174] Brazil's national stability became even more volatile when the local ordinary, Cardinal Carlos Motta of São Paulo, suddenly resigned.

The political situation boiled over beginning on March 31 when a military coup, led by the army chief of staff, General Castelo Branco, overthrew the Goulart government. Unrest had been brewing for some time with middle-class anti-government rhetoric, harassing by journalists of Goulart and his lieutenants, and the campaign of "Women for Democracy," which publicly spoke against the reigning regime. People were not asking for a new leader, but rather that the president remove some of his associates who, it was perceived, were leading the country down the road of chaos and possible civil war. When on March 13 Goulart called for significant government reforms that included legalization of the Communist party and granting landless peasants property held by the government, moves made without the consent of the Brazilian legislative branch, the military, which was generally anti-Communist and mistrusted Goulart, began to take action. The coup was over by April 1.

Branco was proclaimed president and was inaugurated on April 15. Lincoln Gordon, U.S. ambassador to Brazil, said of the coup, "Future historians may well record the Brazilian revolution as the single most decisive victory for freedom in the mid-20th century."[175]

Neither the political turmoil nor the uncertainty in Church leadership deterred the crusade from moving forward. The popular mission began shortly after the coup on April 6 and ran until August 5, the added time made necessary due to the population of the area and the many institutions to whom the mission was sent. An estimated 4.3 million people attended the films, shown on 80 projector sets in 7 parish sectors and employing the services of nearly 700 projectionists and 470 catechists. The rally, described by Peyton as an "extraordinary triumph,"[176] was held on August 16 and drew 2 million, the largest crowd ever to attend such an event in the history of the Family Rosary Crusade. Reactions to the event accented what the crusade would produce for the future: "We thank God as well as Our Lady for the privilege of having Father Peyton with us. May the fruits of the Family Rosary campaign unite all the families of this archdiocese in the service of our God and our country."[177]

The role of the Family Rosary Crusade in the political revolution in Brazil was much debated during the final days of the crusade in São Paulo and for some time after. It was clear to all that the crusade possessed the ability to generate great religious fervor among the people and provided the organization and taught the skills necessary to maintain this enthusiasm and use it to penetrate Communist strongholds. Additionally, the crusade created a broad psychological effect by giving heart and courage to those same people and their leaders who were previously uncertain and possibly fearful of Communism. The crusade, as previously discussed, was also perceived by many in and out of Church circles, the learned and the common person, to be an antidote to Communism.[178] Some people, such as the noted columnist Victor Reisel and the auxiliary archbishop of Rio de Janeiro, Dom Helder Camara, went further, however, attributing the fall of Goulart to the work of the crusade.[179] The comment of the new president, Castelo Branco, however, was most significant: "I admire the Crusade. Since the Great Meeting [reference to the rally] in Rio de Janeiro, I give it credit for the formation of the public opinion of the Brazilian people in order to have the valor to bring about the revolution of March 31."[180]

The Holy Cross community accepted that the crusade had been a catalyst in precipitating the revolution. Peyton, as might be expected, regaled in the association of his work with the downfall of the government which he believed was red tainted:

> As you are aware...much credit is given by great leaders in the Church and the State in Brazil to the Family Rosary Crusade in the overthrow of the Goulart Government that was moving the country rapidly into Communistic control. Overnight the situation was changed without a drop of blood. The credit is being given by great leaders...to Our Blessed Mother and the Family Rosary Crusade for having done this.[181]

Richard Sullivan, CSC, who assumed the reins as the provincial of the Eastern Province in April 1964 and attended the São Paulo rally, reported a similar message in a benign tone to the superior general:

> More than once I heard it said that the success of the Revolution which saved Brasil [sic] from Communism was due in great part to Father Peyton and the Rosary. One secular paper editorial stated that in history this revolution would take its place along side Lepanto's victory through the Rosary.[182]

The reactions of acceptance and even glee expressed by Peyton and his immediate superior were not shared by the superior general, Germain Lalande, CSC, whose broader view allowed him to understand the possible ramifications of the crusade's association with politics in general. After receiving Sullivan's report of the São Paulo crusade, Lalande asked the provincial to tell Peyton to be more prudent, "in order that the Crusade, in the mind of the people, may not be interpreted as having political overtones." In a meeting with Peyton, Quinn, and Belyea, Sullivan told them of the general's concerns. He then responded to the general in defense of the crusade, but with a hint that Peyton was somewhat naive about the issue: "In the efforts to combat atheistic Communism, it might be easy (and is easy) to get involved in the politics of a country. It would be the last thing that Father Peyton would want—but it is the goal for the Crusade that he avoid the possibility that politics use him."[183] Peyton rallied behind the predominant anti-Communism ethic of the day, but it was never his principal concern.

The connection made between the Family Rosary Crusade and political events in Brazil was significant, but the recognition that the almost three-year campaign garnered came from all fronts. Cardinal Carlo Confalonieri, president of the Pontifical Commission for Latin America, commented, "The Pontifical Commission greatly appreciates your work among the Latin American peoples and considers your mass apostolate to be an effective contribution to the progress of Catholic life in these countries."[184] Many sources continued to applaud the crusade for turning the tide of religious faith, tilting the balance of power away from Communism and toward greater cooperation and social justice, and creating a "powerful lay apostolate": "In South America, in the short space of five years, the Crusade has shown itself a most powerful means of catechizing masses of people whom the conventional structures of the Church do not reach because of the shortage of priests."[185]

Observers of the crusade were the most avid voice in its praise. One São Paulo journalist wrote, "I observed, from the commencement of the Family Rosary Crusade in Recife until now, the great influence which it has on the conscience of Brazilians. Before the revolution, one slept with pistols in our beds [but] now, thanks to the influence of the Crusade, we can sleep in peace." Another writer commented, "And the Rosary brought about the miracle of the cohesion of all forces, brought their spirits together, unified their wills, consolidated the ties which existed between the people's aspirations and the patriotic vigilance of the Armed Forces."[186]

The Congregation of Holy Cross proudly boasted of the merit of Peyton and the crusade as paragons in response to the call of the Holy Father for action in Latin America. In 1961 George DePrizio, CSC, provincial of the Eastern Province, urged his members to join Peyton's crusade, thus answering the Vatican's call for missionary help in Latin America. He extolled Peyton to the general:

> Anyone who says that Father Peyton's crusade work is merely a superficial and emotional stirring of the people aroused just for the occasion simply does not know what he is talking about. I have never seen such a vital demonstration of faith before in all my life and I am convinced that only God knows the wonderful things that are wrought through it.[187]

Lalande was equally generous when responding to the provincial:

> I thank God for the good He chooses to accomplish through the instrumentality of Father Peyton. In these decades Father Peyton is to your province and the Congregation as a whole what, in his time, Brother Andre was to Holy Cross in Canada and to the whole Congregation. These are men whose message and influence escape geographical bounds.[188]

The Crusades under a Cloud

The association of the Family Rosary Crusade in the minds of many with the revolution in Brazil and Peyton's dependence upon the U.S. government for its financial backing in Latin America caused those in positions of authority within the Congregation of Holy Cross to exhibit grave concern for the future of the family prayer ministry. Superior general Germain Lalande apparently was aware that Peyton was receiving money from the CIA[189] and worried about what would happen if the financial arrangement was publicly known. He wrote to Richard Sullivan, CSC,

> I might add that you should make sure that Father Peyton is very prudent in matters of accepting funds for the Crusade. He should most certainly not accept money from government or para-government sources which, if they were known, would most likely endanger seriously the work of the Crusade. . . . It is better to be satisfied with less than to have at our disposal large sums which, later, might jeopardize our work. The more our work is free from political influences the more advantageous for the Church.[190]

Sullivan repeated Peyton's argument that without financial support the crusades would be restricted to wealthier dioceses. The provincial implied that he was willing to support Peyton even if it meant taking a risk:

> No one wishes to harm the Church, the Congregation or the Crusade work. The purpose is to bring people to God and the Church. It would be disastrous if the opposite should happen. The two problems you raise [political involvement and special funding] indicate risks. The question is: should the risks be taken or should we limit the work to a scale which might be ineffective?[191]

The stakes grew higher and fear greater when Theodore Hesburgh, CSC, president of the University of Notre Dame, wrote to Lalande informing him about the financing arrangement set up by Peter Grace. Hesburgh related a conversation, held on October 6, with Grace, that centered about the Latin American financial arrangement, including Grace's involvement and the recent development of Lalande's serious concern about the agreement. Hesburgh was alarmed and stated, "a number of people were talking about it [the financial arrangement]." He continued:

> I cannot alter my opinion that this situation is extremely dangerous. This is not to deny the good work that has been done by the Family Rosary, but I believe that all of the good would be destroyed, as well as many other innocent works, if the facts of this matter ever came to light. I am also reasonably sure that many of the American hierarchy would be horrified at the thought.[192]

Lalande replied stating that he too was concerned about possible repercussions, in Latin America and most especially with Notre Dame, which might be cast in a negative light since Grace was chairman of the board of trustees.[193]

On October 24, 1964, Peyton, Lalande, and Bernard Mullahy, the assistant general, met at the Holy Cross Generalate in Rome to review the situation. Peyton reported that Lalande had been informed about the financial arrangement from "a letter from America" and this had led the general in turn to write Richard Sullivan about his concerns. Peyton also revealed that Grace, after viewing the rosary films, had gone to his top lieutenants to seek their support for the Family Rosary Crusade's entrance into Latin America, but that the aides had rejected the plan, leaving Grace to seek other sources. Grace then went to the CIA, which also was not initially interested. Ultimately he went to Allen Dulles, who liked the plan and then became the intermediary with Vice President Nixon to obtain final approval. John McCone, who succeeded Dulles as CIA director in November 1961, believed "that the crusade could help them in the fight against Communism."[194]

At first Lalande stridently opposed the whole operation, fearful of the damage that it could inflict upon the Congregation of Holy Cross and Family Rosary Crusade should the events become public knowledge. The general wrote, "It is absolutely necessary, therefore, that the crusade slowly become free of this source of revenue and that it only undertake the work that is possible from other sources of revenue that are more normal." Peyton defended his actions, arguing that the U.S. government channeled massive food and material aid to Latin America through church agencies, that other church leaders and institutions received money from the same source, and that after five years the financing details would no longer be newsworthy. He protested that the general's decision to cease all contact with the CIA and its financial resources would impoverish the Eastern Province by destroying one of its principal ministries, and that for Family Rosary the "source of support is indispensable for the survival of its Latin American apostolate." Peyton also emphasized the crusade's efficacy against Communism, suggesting that the government's position was "identical with the conscience [and] the objective of the Church: the destruction of Communism." He continued, "The calculated risk taken by the Family Rosary Crusade is, in my opinion, 95 to 5 percent safe. North Americans, were it to become known, would, except for the fanatical fringe, be happy that the Family Rosary Crusade was efficacious enough against Communism to merit such trust." Peyton concluded his defense by stating that the crusade had been receiving help for so long and so much that "what advantage would there be in stopping it now?"[195]

In the end, the general implemented a compromise. The Family Rosary Crusade would continue its funding policy, but would exercise extreme caution to avoid any identification with the U.S. government. Lalande allowed Peyton to continue to receive government support, "but [the Crusade] must break away when it is provided with another source." Lalande told Peyton that he should make every effort to find another source as soon as possible.[196]

The general, however, continued to voice his concern, this time to Richard Sullivan, through a series of letters, which eventually led to a meeting between the two men in Rome in February 1965.[197] Lalande's concern was now more focused: he feared chastisement from the Holy See "for not acquainting it with the set-up and the consequences for the Church which could result from such a state of affairs." He told Sullivan that Peyton "does not see the difficulties and dangers" and suggested that "all the means at our disposal . . . cannot be used indiscriminately. Some risks we simply cannot take." Lalande implored Sullivan to join Peyton in finding another source of financing for the Crusade.[198]

In the first days of July 1965, Lalande met three times with his assistants, who suggested that "a few high-ranking and trustworthy Vatican officials," known to be balanced and practical, be contacted for advice about the Latin American situation. These officials believed the issue so serious that the pope should be informed immediately. Thus, on July 9 Lalande met privately with Pope Paul VI and explored the entire issue, including the involvement of Peter Grace as the intermediary with the CIA and the efficacy of the crusades, and concluding by telling the pontiff that the possibility of public disclosure was minimal and that if the money supply was cut off it would likely mean the end of the Family Rosary Crusade in Latin America. Lalande reported to Sullivan that the pope, after listening, did not hesitate to tell the general that in the future "the Family Rosary, for any reason whatsoever, should absolutely not accept funds or help from the source you are acquainted with or any other source which could jeopardize the work of the Crusade or the over-all apostolate of the Church." The pope concluded, "Please tell Father Peyton that it is the Holy Father who wants the question settled in this way and that the Holy Father has understood the problem very well."[199]

When the general met with his assistants on July 23 it was decided that Peyton was not to accept funds, directly or indirectly, from the CIA, that a detailed report listing monies received, from whom, and approximate dates of reception, was to be written by October 30, and that future decisions regarding dealings with any government financial source would be left to the provincial and superior general. Lalande concluded, "It is our conviction that these decisions will greatly benefit the Family Rosary Crusade and that they will contribute to its stability and its apostolic impact."[200] Lalande notified Peyton and his provincial of the decisions and then wrote to the pope regarding the matter. He told the pontiff that Peter Grace had obtained "certainly more than one million dollars" from the CIA for the operation of the Family Rosary Crusade and he affirmed that other Catholic organizations had or still were receiving funds from the same source, "but we do not believe that this is a reason to do the same."[201]

On September 15 Richard Sullivan met with Peyton, Quinn, and William Belyea, CSC, to discuss the general's instructions. They all accepted the general's directives; however, Sullivan found himself in a bind, because $200,000 had been formally accepted on July 2, 1965, for crusades in Ecuador and postcrusade work in Chile, Colombia, and Venezuela. Believing that the ramifications of canceling the crusade would be too great, he told Lalande that the bishops had made commitments to the scheduled events, that Family Rosary would have no adequate reply when people asked why the crusade had been canceled, and that a huge television postcrusade production, slated for December 8 and scheduled to be shown throughout Brazil, Colombia, and Venezuela, could not reasonably be canceled. Lalande reluctantly gave permission to proceed with the plans, admitting "simply to drop the whole thing would require a number of explanations which we simply cannot give."[202] Once permission was given, Peyton wrote Paul VI, accepting the pope's directive as the will of Christ and his Virgin Mother.[203]

Lalande's capitulation seemed only to heighten his fear and consternation. He asked Sullivan to "keep a close eye on the Crusade, especially the funds received for its apostolate." The general's concern peaked in mid-October when he was summoned by Archbishop Angelo Dell'Acqua, in the office of the secretary of state, Cardinal Amleto Cicognani, to answer the pope's questions about the crusade's progress in ending government funding.[204] Lalande wrote to Sullivan:

> I'm not sure Father Peyton is fully convinced that he must not make use of such funds for the Crusade. He keeps insisting that there is no fear that the same source providing these funds will become known. On the other hand, I wish to point out very emphatically that I made it clear to Father Peyton that if he does not carry out the wish of the Holy See, which is also mine, and if I ever find out, directly or indirectly, he's receiving funds from the source mentioned in previous letters, I shall be forced to ask all of our Provincial Superiors to call back to their respective Provinces their religious engaged in the apostolate of the Crusade, and I shall be forced to acquaint the bishops of South America with the situation of the Family Rosary Crusade.[205]

Lalande accurately concluded, "One thing is also clear, Father Peyton does not see very clearly in all of this and he has a blind and exaggerated confidence in Peter Grace."[206]

The high-level discussions concerning the financing of the crusades did not slow Peyton's Latin American campaign, which, still using government funding, was directed toward the Dominican Republic. In late July 1964, during the São Paulo crusade, Grace met with his high-level assistants "regarding the next moves for the Crusade and Post Crusade in Latin America." The new director of the CIA, Admiral William F. Raborn, wanted to use the crusade in the Dominican Republic as a test to see if money should continue to be given to the operation.[207]

The crusade in the Dominican Republic was scheduled to coincide with a Marian Congress beginning on March 25, 1965. Rather than crusades for specific dioceses, a nationwide campaign was planned, centered in the capital, Santo Domingo, with satellite crusades conducted simultaneously in the country's other four dioceses.[208] Because Peyton had assigned Joseph Quinn, CSC, to be both director of the postcrusade in South America and on-site leader of the crusades in Spain, William Belyea, CSC, became the on-site leader in the Dominican Republic. As in Caracas and Recife, the popular crusade, beginning in mid-February 1965, was marred by rock throwing and even a couple of Molotov cocktails. This hostility to the Church could be traced, at least in part, to the government of Juan Bosch, now in exile in Puerto Rico. Although six film showings were disrupted by acts of vandalism, the films were shown to over 2 million people.[209] The crusade was capped with six rallies, the largest in Santo Domingo drawing 250,000 on March 21.

The conclusion of the crusade was marked by two diverse events: a political revolution in the country, and Peyton's first meeting with Cuban bishops. The revolution, which pitted Communist loyal constitutionalists against the reigning loyalist civilian junta, prompted U.S. intervention against the Communist forces. U.S. involvement received some degree of hemispheric approval when a peace force, gathered by the Organization of American States (OAS), supplemented U.S. attempts to restore peace. Secular missionaries from the crusade were enjoying a two-week vacation at Boca Chica Beach when the revolution broke out and was reported over the radio. They were evacuated to Puerto Rico only after they obtained new passports with the assistance of local friends of the crusade and of the U.S. government.[210] After the crusade Peyton and Joseph Quinn met with José M. Domínguez, bishop of Matanzas, and Fernando Azcarate, auxiliary bishop of Havana, about the possibility of a crusade in Cuba. The Cuban prelates told Peyton that because the Communist government allowed the Church to operate in religious matters within its own confines, a modified crusade must be conducted on Church property. Grace wrote his Washington contact, "I believe we now have sufficient information on hand so that, at least, you can give it preliminary consideration."[211]

As a test case for future funding of Peyton's work, the crusade in the Dominican Republic was not considered a great success. The nation was probably the most religiously illiterate nation that the Crusade had entered, a legacy of thirty-one years of Church repression under the regime of Rafael L. Trujillo. When the statistics did not compare favorably with previous crusades, Washington became uneasy, prompting Grace to attempt to explain what had happened and why. He claimed that the Dominican Republic was "the greatest challenge we have yet faced." He argued that the campaign could not be judged solely on numbers; it was necessary to look at the sacrifices of many campesinos who walked long distances to view the films and attend the rallies, and the many whose hearts were converted.[212] Although the "friends in Washington" did not seem overly pleased by the results, equipment and personnel were transported to Panama, the site of the next Family Rosary Crusade.[213]

After a very short break Belyea arrived in Panama on May 3 to prepare for the crusade there. The reception of the crusade by the local bishops was rather muted, but the major concern, as in other nations, was the presence of Communists. Belyea reported to Peyton, "As you probably know from the newspapers, the Communists are becoming more active here as well as in other Latin American countries. From many quarters I hear of the dangers of new riots in the near future. Many will be hoping we can bring some tranquility to the country and should be disposed to co-operate."[214] As in the Dominican Republic, the crusade was conducted on a national level from June 20 to August 1, 1965, beginning with the popular mission. In an effort to improve on the low attendance encountered in the Dominican Republic, Peyton told Belyea to bombard the area with advertisements and to obtain press coverage for every aspect of the crusade. For one week, August 1 to 8, a mini-crusade was held in the Canal Zone, including the television broadcast of the films. The national crusade culminated on August 11 when 250,000 attended the rally held in Panama City.[215]

From Panama the crusade returned to South America, specifically Ecuador. Both Richard Sullivan, CSC, and Germain Lalande, CSC, were concerned about the political unrest in Ecuador, as well as the importance of preventing any semblance of association with politics. Archdiocesan officials in Quito vacillated on the commencement of the crusade, but once a September 1965 start date was arranged a local team was built, including Jim Raaf, the local representative of Peter Grace. The Quito crusade concluded on February 27, 1966, after holding six rallies, the largest of which was attended by 100,000 in Quito on February 13.[216]

The crusade then moved to Guayaquil, a place Peyton originally had been invited to in May 1964. Once again the Family Rosary Crusade encountered religious apathy and even indifference in Guayaquil, a sign of latent hostility toward the Church from political forces. In reporting to Peyton that "the word rosary is beginning to create an immediate apathy among the many, even the militant members of spiritual organizations," Belyea suggested substituting "Family Unity" for "Family Rosary" in their advertisements.[217] Nonetheless, the major rally, held in Guayaquil on August 14, 1966, was attended by 220,000, a figure reported by a local paper as "unprecedented in the history of Guayaquil." Peyton related, "Given the past history of Catholicism in Guayaquil and its present state, I judge the Rally to have a significance that I had not noted in past Rallies."[218]

The conclusion of the campaign in Ecuador brought to a close the Family Rosary Crusade efforts in Latin America for the immediate future. The Institute of Secular Missionaries, which Peyton discovered in 1956 and which had played such a significant role in the Latin American crusades, chose not to continue with Peyton's work. In the spirit of *aggiornamento* that was characteristic of the Second Vatican Council, the Institute decided that individual members should be free to choose their apostolates, rather than being assigned. This new policy, coupled with the past experience of the difficulty of the crusade apostolate, made it impossible to recruit sufficient members to build a team for the crusade.[219] A second blow, which also contributed to the crusade's suspension in Latin America, was the loss of William Belyea, CSC, who chose to return to Canada to study psychology, leaving the team no qualified Spanish-speaking member.[220]

Peyton could certainly boast of the efficacy of the crusades in Latin America. Between September 1959 and October 1965 the crusades were conducted in 42 dioceses with a total population of nearly 28 million people. More than 23 million attended the films, which were shown by over 2,600 technicians and a similar number of catechists, 9 million attended the rallies, and over 200 radio and television stations aired Family Rosary commercials, Family Theater shows, and various films.[221] Most importantly for Peyton, his message of family prayer through the rosary had now been proclaimed on every continent.

With the end of the South American campaign, Peyton's work continued, shifting to a postcrusade mode in a number of locations that had been the sites of full-fledged crusades. The spirit generated while a rosary crusade was in progress was tangible and significant, but as with all religious fervor, it began to wane with time. Peyton wanted to maintain the spirit of the crusade, especially his principal goal of the recitation of the family rosary, long after the crusade had ended. The postcrusade was intended to accomplish this goal and to establish a system for continuing Catholic Action in the area.[222]

The postcrusade organization was standardized under the general direction of Joseph Quinn, CSC. A local diocesan director, generally a priest, assisted by two lay executive assistants, a council, and a board of advisors, manned a local permanent crusade office and was the overseer of five divisions. The Control division organized and coordinated activities and plans. The Mobile crusade educated Catholic lay leaders and took the message of the crusade to all institutions, including parishes, hospitals, orphanages, prisons, and military posts. The division of Mass Media used mass communication to remind people of the need for family prayer. The Public Affairs office maintained contact with individuals and organizations who were able to collaborate efficiently and effectively in the development and realization of the postcrusade plan. Lastly, the Youth Division delivered the message to all educational institutions.[223] Peyton himself articulated three goals for the postcrusade: acquisition of the films by local dioceses for their use, distribution of rosaries at special liturgical events such as confirmations, marriages, and first communions, and the organization of an annual Family Day in each diocese.[224]

The postcrusade was designed to imitate the original crusade, but rather than put all energy into one concentrated time period, the maintenance of the spirit of prayer was the goal. As with the original crusade, films were shown in parishes, priests periodically gave sermons on family prayer through the rosary, and parish visitation teams continued to help form family-based Christian communities. In schools the films were combined with periodic poster contests and assignments on the rosary. A five-year plan emphasized specific themes, thus revitalizing the basic message.[225] The single greatest manifestation of the postcrusade effort was the promotion of Family Day, first initiated on December 8, 1963, in Brazil. In 1965 a similar celebration was broadcast on radio and television throughout South America. Organized through the efforts of Joseph Quinn, CSC, this program featured recitation of the rosary, a brief dramatic program, "When a Life Is a Prayer," comments on Vatican II and its emphasis on family prayer, and a brief talk by Peyton.[226]

The end of the crusades in Latin America provided the opportunity to terminate the crusade's association with the U.S. government. Sullivan wrote to Peyton in January 1966 reiterating the superior general's warning that the operation would be scuttled if any further association between the Family Rosary Crusade and the CIA were revealed. Yet the provincial jumped to the rosary priest's defense in a letter to the superior general, asking that the postcrusade offices remain open and that fifteen projectors and sets of films be sent to Cuba, since they had been requested by the local hierarchy. Lalande approved both requests, but wondered how the offices could be financially maintained once the federal funding had been exhausted.[227]

On April 25, 1966, Lalande met in Montreal with Richard Sullivan, CSC, Jerome Lawyer, CSC (now serving as assistant provincial), Joseph Quinn, CSC, and Philip Higgins, CSC, to find a final workable solution. Lalande said he was amazed to discover the extent to which the crusades were controlled by the government. When he learned that the CIA hoped to continue its funding, he was adamant that the connection be formally severed, setting June 30, 1966, the last day of the fiscal year, as the final day that government funds would be accepted.[228] Peyton, realizing that the government arrangement would soon be lost, asked that Cardinal Francis Spellman of New York serve as an intermediary between the CIA and the crusade, but Lalande responded that if he heard of such an arrangement he would inform the pope directly. By late August Sullivan reported to the general, "He [Peyton] assured me that the matter was concluded and over."[229] In the end, Peyton was obedient to his superiors and followed their instructions.

The six-year relationship between the U.S. government and the Family Rosary Crusade raises many questions. How did a program whose only goal, as articulated by Peyton himself, was promoting family prayer, get involved with covert money from the CIA, thus placing itself in a situation that necessitated the intervention of the Holy Father? The answer is twofold. First and most important was Peyton's single-minded thinking, creating a personal blindness that was readily apparent to those who knew him well, and that had often created friction with co-workers. He simply could not see anything save the promotion of the family rosary and devotion to Mary. Jerome Lawyer, CSC, speaking of the association of the crusade with the CIA summarized it well: "It was simply another way to get money, and Pat would do anything to get money for Our Lady."[230] Second, Peyton placed far too much trust in Peter Grace, consigning financial matters to him without asking significant questions. Peyton's uncritical confidence and undying support for Grace, an attitude that was totally reciprocal, allowed the latter, who was well connected in business, government, and religious circles, to run the financial affairs of the Family Rosary Crusade almost without constraint.

The historical context also helps explain the Crusade's association with the CIA. The specter of Communism was so feared that any act that would assist in its removal was considered not only a patriotic move for Americans, but an act of Catholic devotion. To root out Communism served both church and state: for the church it eliminated a significant source of atheism and for the state it removed a great challenge to democracy and laissez faire capitalism. As Peyton saw it, the ability of the Family Rosary Crusade to assist in the downfall of Communism, while simultaneously converting people to the need for family prayer through the rosary, was a double victory for God. Since the objectives were perceived to be good, the means of achieving them were not of any great significance, especially since no one was being hurt.

The historical record shows that in some countries the Family Rosary Crusade coincided with revolutions that moved governments away from Communism and toward political policies supported by the United States. While no extant data specifically links the efforts of the U.S. government funding of the crusade with efforts to secure Latin American allies, it would be naive to deny that federal officials believed that Peyton's campaign was an efficacious weapon in the fight to remove Communism from Latin America. And while Peter Grace, as a faithful Catholic and loyal American, desired the downfall of Communism for religious and patriotic reasons, the elimination of the Red menace would also benefit his significant business operations that were historically linked to South America.

Conclusion

The production of the fifteen mysteries of the rosary films and the grand desire to bring the Family Rosary Crusade to the one continent it had not entered, one populated with over one-fourth of the world's Catholics, led Patrick Peyton to Latin America. This new round of crusades was similar in many ways to those conducted in the late 1940s and the 1950s, but the needs of local Catholics, a people of low economic means and poor religious training, demanded new techniques, including the popular crusade, the participation of lay collaborators as catechists and technicians, and the use of secular lay missionaries from Spain. The additional features of the crusade, the poverty of the region, and the tenor of the times that supported almost any effort to eliminate Communism led Peyton, through the prompting and assistance of his loyal friend Peter Grace, to accept U.S. government funding for the crusades. While the crusade's role as a government tool to eliminate Communism was a far cry from its original purpose of promoting family prayer, Peyton never lost focus on his priority and continued to foster the family rosary through discipleship to Mary as fervently and zealously as before. The 1960s would allow Peyton to continue championing the cause of family prayer and Mary in multiple venues throughout the world.

Chapter 8

An Understudy Role: The Family Rosary Crusade, 1960–65

The Family Rosary Crusade reached its apex of international fame and publicity through the crusades in Latin America, the last continent to receive Peyton's campaign, conducted between 1959 and 1965, but as was always the case the rosary priest had several irons in the fire at one time in different locales and with varied aspects of his specialized ministry for the promotion of family prayer. Peyton's great triumph in Latin America, made especially significant because of the initiation of the popular mission and the use of secular missionaries, was one of the main events of his career, causing other accomplishments to receive less recognition, but regardless of their understudy role, the other events of Peyton's ministry were noteworthy to the peoples and regions he served. American Catholicism's heyday of the 1950s continued into the new decade with the election in 1960 of the first Roman Catholic president John F. Kennedy, and the first visit to the United States by a reigning pontiff, Pope Paul VI, in 1963. The aura associated with the personality and ministry of Patrick Peyton continued as his international rosary crusade retraced its steps in the Philippines and Spain and broke new ground in the United States.

The Rosary Crusades, 1961–66

From the outset of his ministry in 1942 Patrick Peyton continually stated that his one goal was to get people to pray the family rosary, but to achieve his goal he used many means, including the mediums of radio and film and his international rosary crusades. It was the crusades, however, that were specifically structured to invite people to accept the challenge of Peyton's message and sign a pledge to pray the daily family rosary. The crusades, successfully conducted on all continents, reached their apex in Latin America in the early 1960s. Simultaneous operations in other locales brought Peyton's message and charisma to new and familiar spots. The crusade, last conducted in the United States in St. Paul in October 1958, now came to San Francisco in the fall of 1961 through the invitation of Archbishop John J. Mitty.

The San Francisco crusade was arranged through correspondence between Peyton and Bishop Hugh Donohoe, an auxiliary in San Francisco, who acted for the ordinary due to the latter's ill health. Peyton met with the bishop in February 1961 to work out all relevant details. The crusade was centered in the City by the Bay but also included, at the insistence of Joseph McGucken, bishop of Sacramento, the state capital and other regions of Northern California.[1] The crusade front team, headed by Joseph Quinn, CSC, arrived in San Francisco in August 1961 and immediately started to prepare for the forthcoming campaign. Archbishop Mitty issued his pastoral letter, which was read on September 3 in all parishes:

> You recognize the need for spiritual rejuvenation in this time of strife, world-wide confusion and conflict — this period of moral decadence and religious persecution — this age of escapism and skepticism. A distraught world seeks peace, while prating but not practicing piety. The Rosary as a family prayer and a prayer for peace answers the need.[2]

The crusade in the dioceses of San Francisco and Sacramento progressed as earlier efforts, without the use of the popular mission, and culminated with a grand rally held on October 7, 1961, at the Polo field in San Francisco's Golden Gate Park. Among the five hundred thousand present were several dignitaries, including auxiliary bishops Donohoe and Guilfoyle and Governor Edmund (Pat) Brown. Peyton delighted his audience with his simple but powerful message and concluded with a special prayer written specifically for the event.[3] The event was recorded on film, which served as a tool to popularize the crusade. Successful smaller rallies, held in Sacramento, Redding, and Eureka in the latter half of October, provided a fitting conclusion to Peyton's return to the American crusade scene.[4]

The San Francisco triumph brought Peyton's ministry to a new audience, but the bulk of the crusade effort during the first half of the 1960s consisted of returns to earlier crusade sites. Peyton's initial crusade visit to the Philippines in 1959 had been highlighted when more than 1.5 million people braved torrential rain to attend the great crusade at Luneta Park in Manila. Shortly afterward nine archbishops and bishops petitioned Peyton to return and bring his crusade at his first opportunity. Such encouragement prompted him to take a break from the campaign in Chile in February 1960 and visit the nine original Philippine dioceses as well as one additional that by this time had also requested the crusade. Peyton assigned Joseph Quinn, CSC, and Bienvenido Lopez, a local Filipino priest who worked closely with Peyton's team, to head the organizational effort. Peyton originally set the target dates for the crusade as December 1960 to May 1961.[5]

In July 1960 planning for the proposed crusade began in earnest. Quinn expressed optimism: "We have been hoping to go to the Philippines — ever since leaving there last December — and hope that we will be able to carry on the crusade in all the 10 dioceses as scheduled previously."[6] Lopez took the lead in contacting diocesan officials and making all proximate arrangements, but only four of the dioceses could commit financially to the campaign; the others felt the pinch of a nationwide ecclesiastical fund drive for the construction of a Filipino College in Rome.[7] The financial situation was severe enough that Lopez suggested that the crusades be delayed until the financial picture was brighter, and that Peyton should come to the Philippines in January 1961 for the annual bishops' meeting, when the monetary drive for the Filipino College would be over. Peyton heeded Lopez's suggestion and attended the meeting. He then visited with the bishops in their locales working out the specifics for the proposed crusade. By the fall of 1961 all ten original dioceses were back in the fold and ready to receive the crusade, which would begin in November.[8]

The crusade effort in the Philippines was accompanied by a simultaneous effort to inaugurate radio and television broadcasts along the lines of the productions of Family Theater in Hollywood. While visiting the Philippines Peyton had contacted Jesuit Father James Reuter and asked him to produce television shows for Family Theater in Manila. Reuter secured air time, obtained scripts for programs, and offered his first program on October 27, 1960, but Peyton and his assistants were wary of the direction he was taking. Rather than being supervised by Family Theater, Reuter worked directly under the cardinal archbishop of Manila, Rufino Santos. Peyton, believing the situation to be important, instructed Albert Heinzer, CSC, director of the Hollywood office, to threaten Reuter with legal action unless he signed a document guaranteeing Family Theater full control of his media efforts.[9] The mis-understanding was resolved when Reuter came to Family Theater in March 1961 to review procedures and products for future use in the Philippines. Rerun programs of *Family Theater of the Air* and *Marian Theater* were broadcast on one hundred stations in the Philippines beginning in March 1962 at the conclusion of the crusade.[10]

Joseph Quinn, CSC, and Francis Grogan, CSC, together with Bienvenido Lopez and two members of the Irish Auxiliaries, Gertie Lally and Pearl Buckley, prepared and conducted the Philippine crusades, with Father Peyton present for the rallies, as was his normal mode of operation.[11] Once again the crowds at the rallies were phenomenal with 200,000 present in San Fernando on January 28, 1962, 2 million at Cebu on March 4, and 500,000 in Naga (Archdiocese of Caceres) on March 11.[12] A total of fourteen rallies were documented in the Philippine souvenir booklet published in May.[13]

Because the Philippine crusade was so successful, even with the absence of a popular mission, Peyton sought funding for a postcrusade popular mission. He sent Francis Grogan, CSC, to San Francisco to speak with Robert Raskob, whose foundation had guaranteed $175,000 toward the construction of the new Family Theater building in Hollywood. Grogan met Raskob on February 18, 1963, and reported, "I can say that I left with great assurances within myself that Robert is behind our popular mission all the way."[14] Peyton asked the foundation for $80,000 to cover costs of films, projection equipment, and generators for field use, but only $40,000 was granted.[15] Nevertheless, Peyton reported to Cardinal Santos that financing for the mission was in hand.

Because the popular mission coincided with efforts in the United States to distribute *The Redeemer* (see chapter 9), Peyton showed his feature-length film as a prelude to the fifteen mysteries. Bienvenido Lopez and a second Filipino priest, Jose Borces, planned to start the popular mission in Manila as soon as the proper equipment arrived, but delays were many and significant. In June 1964 Lopez wrote to Peyton asking that copies of *The Redeemer* be sent so that it could be shown in Manila in July, allowing the popular mission, which was originally scheduled for September and October, to proceed as planned.[16] The film was eventually premiered in Manila on October 25, 1965, over one year later than scheduled. It was shown from November 12 to 22 but received a very lukewarm response, as it had in the United States. Lopez suggested that the film had hit stiff competition from films in other theaters and that it might have done better if shown during Holy Week instead of the pre-Advent season. Nevertheless, Peyton was disappointed with the film's lack of appeal. Despite the lackluster response, the popular mission commenced in January 1966, starting in Manila, reaching all the dioceses visited in the previous crusade within one year.

The Philippine crusades of 1962 became the catalyst in setting up a factory for the mass production of rosaries, a goal that had been in the mind of Peyton for several years. As early as 1961 Peyton and Lopez had been in communication about manufacturing great quantities of rosaries for distribution during crusades. Two years after the Philippine campaign ended the discussion became more formal when Jose Yulo offered Peyton a plot of land for the site of a rosary factory. The plot was adjacent to a technical school run by Salesian priests who, it was thought, could assist with and support the factory.[17] However, since Peyton's original discussions with Lopez a similar endeavor had been started in Dublin through the generosity of Peter Grace. Grace's offer was more appealing, since it included a building and the money to buy a specialized machine for producing the rosaries. Peyton ultimately opted for the Dublin site, explaining that it would not be efficient to divide rosary production between two sites so distant from each other. The Dublin factory, supervised by Bridie Doherty, an original member of the Irish Auxiliaries,[18] sent rosaries to Latin America, the Philippines, and later to Milwaukee in 1968 for what would be the first crusade following the Second Vatican Council.

The triumph in the Philippines inspired Peyton to go next to Spain, the site of another successful crusade, but even dearer to Peyton's heart because of its role in the rosary films. The invitation to return to Spain came not from ecclesiastical officials as was usually the case, but from Antonio Oriol, the former Spanish minister of justice, who had welcomed the crusade in 1954. Oriol and Luis Carrero Blanco, ministers to General Franco, contacted Peyton in January 1963 asking that the crusade return to mark Spain's twenty-fifth anniversary of "liberation" from Communism. Oriol agreed to finance an extensive and extended popular mission that would bring the fifteen mysteries of the rosary films to all the people of Madrid.[19] The Spanish government also volunteered to finance Peyton's effort, a fact unknown to Church officials at the time, but a cause of consternation in the Vatican when it was revealed in 1965 at the height of the controversy concerning government involvement with the Latin American crusades.[20]

The popular mission in Spain differed significantly from popular missions elsewhere, because Peyton wanted to repay Spain for its assistance in producing the rosary films. Peyton informed the superior general, Germain Lalande, that he anticipated the mission lasting two full years, since he hoped that every Spaniard who wanted to see the films would be able to do so. Francis Grogan, CSC, and Robert Pelton, CSC, suggested to Peyton that since he planned a very extensive campaign he should show the films not only to the poor, the target groups in Latin America and the Philippines, but to the wealthy as well. The films were shown in the drawing rooms of prominent Madrid residents, leading to greater support for the crusade and inspiring some to become catechists to members of their class.[21] Peyton was excited about the popular mission and its possible ramifications: "The Madrid possibility is great! A triumph in Madrid will mean successes in other areas."[22]

The popular mission was conducted in Madrid between May 1963 and June 1964. The region was divided into fifteen sectors, with two films shown per night for eight nights. Peyton firmly believed in the efficacy of this effort, expressing his basic creed of bringing Christ to the masses: "By means of the films the Crusade has developed an extraordinary force and power to penetrate the hearts and minds of the poor, the religiously uninformed, the masses lost to the Church and her sacraments."[23]

The extensive popular mission in Madrid was followed by the crusade, conducted between March and May 1964 using the standard methods and time frame. The ongoing Second Vatican Council and its more open and ecumenical understanding of the Church prompted Francis Grogan, CSC, to suggest that the campaign change its name to Crusade for Family Prayer in an effort to generate greater name recognition (the generic term "prayer" compared with the specific term of "rosary"), a more ecumenical environment, and, thereby, greater overall success. The idea was not accepted at the time, but it planted a seed for the future direction of the crusade ministry.[24] The Madrid crusade reached its climax with the rally held on May 31, 1964, and attended by an estimated 1 million people. Bernard Mullahy, CSC, assistant general, who witnessed the rally, lauded Peyton and the Family Rosary Crusade in a letter to the provincial, Richard Sullivan:

> I never felt prouder of Holy Cross than I did when I witnessed the tremendous work it accomplished in the Archdiocese of Madrid. Holy Cross has indeed been singularly blessed by having had this apostolate confided to it, and your province in particular is especially fortunate to have this extraordinary opportunity to carry on a world wide apostolate of such intensity and impact.[25]

Peyton too was pleased with the Crusade's great success, attributing it to Mary: "In 22 years of working for her, I will consider that Sunday [crusade] as one of the outstanding examples of Her intervention to guarantee to the Family Rosary Crusade one of its greatest victories."[26]

From Madrid the crusade traveled to Barcelona, where a rally was held on February 28, 1965, and then on to the Canary Islands for a series of rosary campaigns under the field direction of William Persia, CSC. From September 1965 to December 1966 crusades were conducted in Las Palmas, Santa Cruz de Tenerife, and Palma de Mallorca.[27] The efforts of the core crusade team were aided by the addition of members of the Focolare movement, a lay and clerical group, headquartered near Florence, who performed many of the functions previously carried out by the secular missionaries.[28]

The successful return of the Family Rosary Crusade to the Philippines and Spain was overlapped with investigations into the possibility of expanding Peyton's ministry to new lands and peoples. In October 1961 Holy Cross bishop Vincent McCauley in Uganda was authorized to write Peyton on behalf of forty-eight bishops in five African nations — Uganda, Tanganyika, Nyasaland, Northern Rhodesia, and Kenya — inviting the crusade to the sub-Sahara region, using techniques that were proving so successful in Latin America. McCauley said he would supply the personnel, who would be trained by the crusade team, if Peyton could supply the equipment.[29] In 1962 an invitation was received from Hong Kong. Francis Grogan, CSC, and Bienvenido Lopez, working on the Philippine crusade, journeyed to the city-state and were "impressed by the militant Catholic spirit prevalent in the...diocese."[30] It was hoped that the Raskob Foundation could again be tapped for $40,000 to fund a Hong Kong campaign. In 1968 Peyton visited Vietnam, said Mass for American troops in the field, and visited with Archbishop Van-Binh of Saigon, who was enthusiastic about a crusade. Unfortunately, none of these prospects — Africa, Hong Kong, and Vietnam — ever came to fruition.[31] Nonetheless the crusade could proudly boast that since its inception in 1948 it had visited 34 countries and conducted crusades in 317 dioceses, and that more than 22.8 million had attended rallies. Additionally, foreign offices for the Family Rosary Crusade were operating in Madrid, Dublin, Roselare (Belgium), Caracas, Sydney, and Manila.[32]

Triumphs and Tribulations

The understudy role of the non–Latin American crusades of the early 1960s in no way detracted from their efficacy nor was it a sign of the crusade's waning popularity, since several significant triumphs occurred during this period. The most significant event was the twentieth anniversary celebration for Family Theater, organized by its Hollywood friends and attended by dignitaries of Church, state, and the entertainment world. In December 1961 Jack Haley and Rosalind Russell, who had been involved with Peyton's Family Theater ministry almost from the outset, volunteered to head a committee to organize a special dinner to honor Peyton and the Crusade. A series of meetings was held, leading to Haley emerging as the general chairman, with Russell, Loretta Young, Irene Dunne, and Louella Parsons as co-chairs. At a February 8, 1962, luncheon, the "Friends of Father Peyton Committee" was formed and a tentative date of May 15 set for the celebration. Over one hundred sponsors, individuals and couples, were engaged to get the project organized as a fundraiser with a goal of $150,000, to be reached by attracting fifteen hundred to the $100-a-plate banquet. Due to schedule conflicts the original date was shifted to September 8.[33] Peyton approved the benefit at a meeting with over eighty Hollywood celebrities in May 1962.

The banquet, truly a gala affair, was attended by sixteen hundred in the International Ballroom of the Beverly Hilton Hotel, the largest celebration to date in the facility. Danny Thomas presided as master of ceremonies over an evening of musical entertainment from the stars, including Anna Maria Alberghetti and the Lennon Sisters, headliners on the Lawrence Welk Show, whose rendition of "Ave Maria" drew a tear from Peyton. Verbal tributes were given by many of the dignitaries in attendance, including representatives from Holy Cross, Germain Lalande and George DePrizio, Hollywood stars Ann Blyth, Raymond Burr, Loretta Young, and Irene Dunne, J. Peter Grace, Luke Hart, Supreme Knight of the Knights of Columbus, and former Vice President Richard Nixon, who stated, "I was honored to be invited to participate in helping such a fine cause."[34] Telegrams from Pope John XXIII, President John F. Kennedy, and California governor Edmund Brown were read. Possibly the finest tribute was given by the superior general, Germain Lalande, CSC, who noted that Peyton's ministry had friends in high places: "It is clear that Father Peyton's vocation cannot be explained by mere human reasoning. It is obviously a mandate from God Himself.... We offer Father Peyton our homage, our respect, and our prayers for continual success in all that he is doing for God, Our Lady, and family life."[35]

During the 1960s many personal and ministerial awards came to Patrick Peyton for his life's work. As had been the case with Pope Pius XII, both John XXIII and Paul VI wrote to Peyton, praising his ministry and congratulating him on his accomplishments. Paul VI was especially gracious in his comments in recommending the Family Rosary to all Catholics:

> We are pleased to note that in the past twenty-one years, the Family Rosary Crusade has carried the message of family prayer to the peoples of thirty-two countries. . . . We cherish the prayerful hope that the zealous endeavors of the Family Rosary Crusade may be productive of even more abundant spiritual fruits.[36]

Besides recognition from pontiffs Peyton and his work were honored locally. In June 1962 the rosary priest was awarded an honorary doctorate of letters from Stonehill College, sponsored by the Congregation of Holy Cross in North Easton, Massachusetts. In April 1964 the California Federation of Women's Clubs (CFWC) recognized Peyton for his work in "encouraging a greater recognition of the contribution of religion and spiritual values to family stability."[37]

In the mid-1960s Peyton's work was honored by three additional events. In 1964 the first edition of *Family Prayer*, published by Benziger Brothers under Peyton's name, was made available to the public. The book contained three sections: (1) prayer, (2) family prayer, and (3) the family rosary, plus an appendix of congratulatory letters from Popes Pius XII, John XXIII, and Paul VI. This volume was intended to complement the rosary meditation book that had been in circulation for some time. One year later an effort was started to generate a full biography of Father Peyton. Although Ted Bonnet, who had written *The Ear of God* in 1952, was not interested in the project, Tom Lewis, working for Family Theater, was able to retain Gary MacEoin, a Dublin-born author, to research and write Peyton's life story. Peyton furnished documentation and sat for twenty hours of taped interviews for the book. Published as an autobiography in 1967, *All for Her* provided Peyton with a monograph which told his story as well as that of Family Theater and his international rosary crusades.[38] In 1967 Peyton's friends and associates in Albany, not to be outdone by Hollywood, hosted a twenty-fifth anniversary dinner on November 21. Although the glitz of Hollywood was absent, nonetheless seven hundred guests gathered to honor Father Peyton. Although not in attendance, President Lyndon Johnson sent a congratulatory telegram.[39]

Peyton reveled in the success of his ministry, not for himself, but for its promotion of the family and devotion to Mary, but like all people his highs of ecstasy were coupled with the periodic depths of despair. On February 19, 1964, Francis Woods, the Albany priest who was the first to join Peyton's crusade effort, died. In a letter of praise to his local ordinary, Bishop William A. Scully, Peyton described Father Woods as the "perfect priest, fervent champion of Our Lady, [and] outstanding promoter of the Family Crusade." Death struck even closer to home one year later when his brother-in-law, Michael Gallagher, husband of Peyton's sister Beatrice, died while he was in the Philippines attending to details concerning the ongoing popular mission. Peyton was close to his whole family, but the fact that Michael and Beatrice had provided a home for him and his brother Tom upon their arrival in Scranton was a kindness he never forgot. Peyton wrote to console his sister:

> Now that your dear partner has gone home ahead of you, you must feel very lonely dear Beatrice. But thanks to our father and mother, who gave to us all — their children — the equipment, the training, and the faith to enable us to walk roads to their end — you are fortified to accept and respond to this wish of God.[40]

The death of his brother-in-law caused Peyton to reflect on his family, whom he loved but rarely saw, because of the demands of his work. He had expressed this reality to his sister Mary, earlier telling her that what he accomplished for the Blessed Mother did not allow him time to write, but he hoped her "delicate heart and soul understood this." He did not want his family members to think he was neglecting them. He counted on their continued understanding that the demands of his work "do not give me the time to do justice to the love that I owe to my own sisters and brothers and their families."[41] Peyton truly loved his family, but as was the case with other members of his religious community, the work he pursued and his devotion to the Mother of God took precedence over his personal associations with people.

Peyton was also plagued by health problems during the 1960s. His breakneck pace, lack of exercise, overeating, and single-minded devotion affected his health on several occasions, as his associates observed. James McArdle, a Pittsburgh attorney who headed his local "Friends of Father Peyton" organization, suggested that Peyton's provincial be told so he would "take off for at least a week or two from the grueling and killing pace." Peyton's personality, lifestyle, and extra weight led to severe hypertension, and he also developed diabetes and heart irregularities, a situation that his provincial, Richard Sullivan, CSC, called a "cause for apprehension."[42] At the end of 1968 he was ordered to take six months off, and he lost sixty pounds. Although he described the period positively, saying it provided "peace and quiet to revitalize myself both soul and body,"[43] he was eager to get back to work, telling Grace that with medication, "I will be able to continue as in the past, working without let up."[44] However, by the end of the decade he was admitted to the hospital for hernia surgery, and the doctors ordered another two months of total rest.

The Sarita East Case

Peyton's uncritical and questionable reliance on Peter Grace, which had contributed to the crusade's problems in Latin America, surfaced again in 1960 when what started as an innocent personal association ballooned into an international civil litigation whose complications lasted almost twenty-two years. Sarita Kenedy East, a wealthy Texas widow, owner of half of the oil-rich La Parra Ranch and a great benefactor to Catholic causes, began in late 1959 to review her will with the assistance of Brother Leo (Christopher Gregory), a Trappist from Spencer, Massachusetts, and Peter Grace, who met East through Leo. Brother Leo had become a spiritual advisor to East in the mid-1950s and had secured significant donations from her for Trappist foundations in South America. The association became more formal when East asked Grace to serve as her legal and financial advisor. On January 22, 1960, East, following the advice of Grace, executed a new will, prepared by Grace's personal attorney, that invalidated her 1948 will and set up a trust, The John G. and Marie Stella Kenedy Memorial Foundation. She placed the bulk of her fortune, estimated at the time to be $20 million, in this foundation. Those listed as members of the foundation included Bishop Mariano Garriaga of Corpus Christ, East's local ordinary.[45]

The establishment of the foundation was a clear indicator that East wished to leave the bulk of her fortune to the Catholic Church, but in the mind of Peter Grace, the primary Church benefactor, the Diocese of Corpus Christi, represented a far too narrow use of her estate, prompting him to suggest that the Church universal should benefit more substantially.[46] Brother Leo was also concerned that the foundation arrangement would diminish financial assistance to the South American cause. Peyton, who first met East in 1952 when engaged in the New Orleans crusade, was drawn into the affair when both Leo and Grace asked him to speak with East and help her to see that the needs of the universal Church outweighed those of the Diocese of Corpus Christi. Peyton wrote Jerome Lawyer, CSC, explaining that Leo had asked him to visit East in Texas, "to encourage her and to help him in his efforts to get her to make her money benefit the wide world instead of just the Corpus Christi area." Peyton, who knew from Leo that East "has great regard for me and a great love for our work," actually met with her first in Buenos Aires in

May 1960 and then on June 1 in Texas.[47] Peyton hoped "at least 25 percent of the income of that Foundation" would come his way.[48] He spoke
to East about his dream for a weekly television show, similar to *Theater
of the Air,* that would be a great teaching tool for American Catholics.
The obvious implication was that her monetary resources could fund
such a project.[49]

On June 2, 1960, after the previous day's meeting between East, Leo,
and Peyton, the three went to New York to meet with Peter Grace at his
Manhasset, Long Island, home. Peyton understood that the stakes were
high and action was necessary now for the membership of her foundation
to be changed. He wrote, "Time was essential. Sarita is old and might
die at any moment. And if she did what an opportunity would be lost."
At Manhasset East broached the possibility of adding a codicil to her
will that would change the foundation membership. Leo had hoped that
members of the Latin American Bishops Conference (CELAM), such as
Bishop Manuel Larraín of Talca, would be made managers of the foundation, but East was not ready for such a move. Grace was more direct
and suggested that Leo, Peyton, and a Sister Loretta from St. Vincent's
Hospital, who knew East well, be made members. In the end East decided
that Grace was more appropriate than Sister Loretta, but she agreed with
the selection of Leo and Peyton.[50] Peyton was pleased that the change
had been made, calling it "a day to be remembered in the history of the
Family Rosary Crusade," but at the same time advised that no one outside the group should know of the codicil.[51] Naively Peyton said later,
"My participation in that Foundation was for Our Queen and to advance her will and wishes."[52] Jerome Lawyer, CSC, washed his hands of
the whole matter when he learned the details: "I had some fragmentary
information on the Sarita Trust. I did not, however, suspect that Peter,
Brother Leo, and Fr. Pat were trustees. This is one of those things that
can very likely turn into an international Schwartz affair. I want no part
of it!"[53]

For the next few months Peyton corresponded with East on several occasions, thanking her for her benefactions and inviting her to witness the
Chilean crusade in progress. She came to La Serena so she could see first
hand the Crusade's efficacious work. Peyton additionally asked Grace
to lobby the widow to see if she would finance the construction of two
homes, one for crusade priests and a second for the secular missionaries
in Manhasset.[54]

In November 1960, while visiting Argentina, Mrs. East was diagnosed
with throat cancer, a condition which was verified upon her return to
the United States. Grace arranged that she be transported to New York

City for hospitalization. There she was regularly visited by Grace, Leo, and Peyton before she died on February 12, 1961. When her will was read and the codicil became public it was not long before the document was contested by Lee H. Lytton Jr. as agent for Bishop Garriaga and the others removed from the foundation membership list. The suit stated that undue pressure had been placed on East in the addition of the codicil. Peyton was listed on the suit as "a nominal alleged co-conspirator."[55]

Grace immediately sprang into action to ward off the scandal of a public trial. On April 27 a meeting was held at the Holy Cross generalate in Rome between the superior general, Christopher O'Toole, CSC, his assistant Bernard Ransing, Peter Grace, and Patrick Peyton to discuss the Sarita East case. Grace assured Edward Heston, CSC, procurator general for the congregation, that he used "every legitimate means . . . to accomplish the expressed desire and intent of Mrs. East to benefit the Church universal." He also stated that should immediate and definitive action on the resolution of the foundation's assets not take place, "we can only blame ourselves for our inactivity and indecision."[56] Grace wished to enlist the assistance of the apostolic delegate, Archbishop Egidio Vagnozzi, to convince Garriaga to back off before the public hearing scheduled for May 25. O'Toole asked Peyton to speak with Garriaga and Grace to speak with the delegate.[57] The rapid response and cooperation desired did not happen as neither the bishop nor the delegate were contacted, prefiguring future case proceedings. Even Vagnozzi himself was not able to convince Garriaga to back down and allow the Vatican to intervene and settle the case.

The case only became more tangled with time. The Vatican took its first action in August, calling a meeting at the Congregation of the Council, headed by Archbishop Pietro Palazzini, to seek a compromise as the only viable solution. All the principals in the case except Peyton were present. The discussion focused on seeking a compromise as the only viable solution. Palazzini was especially eager to settle the case since he interpreted the documentation to mean that Grace had significantly influenced East's decision to change her will. He was told in a memorandum, "Mr. Grace cannot deny having used persuasion, encouragement, and influence, etc. on Mrs. East to induce her to recast her testament in order to make the Universal Church the beneficiary. . . . If the lawsuit follows its normal course, Mr. Grace will have to tell the truth . . . and the simple truth will cause the Church immeasurable harm."[58] While Peyton remained on the periphery of this battle publicly, he kept abreast of events at all times.[59]

Both sides wanted a compromise, but neither would agree to any of the proposals that were made. Christopher O'Toole, CSC, simply wanted an "honorable solution" since he perceived that a Texas court would never rule in favor of the defendants, including Peyton.[60] Eventually the Texas litigants proposed an 80 percent to 20 percent split of the foundation, the former portion, estimated to be $14.4 million, to be placed in a separate foundation, The Sarita Kenedy East Foundation, and to be administered by the New York principals, headed by Peter Grace. Initially Grace balked, calling the proposal insufficient, since new information had recently revealed that East's fortune was much greater than had been originally estimated. Others pressured him to accept the offer in order to avoid scandal and a public trial.[61] The proposal had not been fully evaluated when, as in the summer of 1962, members of the East family filed a new suit, claiming that the 1960 will and the foundation it established were invalid, and that the original will of 1948, leaving her fortune to her children, was still in force. The additional complication placed any settlement on hold.

The Vatican continued to make every effort to resolve the case between the two parties. In February 1962 Pope John XXIII appointed Archbishop John Krol of Philadelphia as apostolic visitor with "plenary power to take such measures, including canonical penalties, as he deems to be necessary to remedy the regrettable situation that has developed in the matter of the Kenedy Foundation."[62] While Krol worked the American scene, representatives of John XXIII offered a 70 percent to 30 percent division, the larger portion to go to the named benefactors (Grace et al.), but this time Garriaga balked. In the end the proposed ecclesiastical solutions were disregarded, with each side holding out for a greater slice of the monetary pie.[63]

The case came to some resolution in February 1968 when Judge William Edwards of the 79th District Court in Texas ruled "that undue influence flows in the execution of the entire 1960 will and its codicils."[64] The ruling, however, was appealed repeatedly throughout the 1970s, especially by Brother Leo, who, although canonically removed from the Trappists in 1966 by his abbot, Thomas Keating, OCSO, believed that he could obtain his share of the East estate. In 1983 Rene Gracida, who had been recently appointed bishop of Corpus Christi, promptly brought closure to this case of mistrust and wounded ambitions by cleverly rearranging the membership of the foundation board, which had changed over the years, giving himself control. He quickly liquidated the foundation monies according to the 1962 compromise that gave Grace's Sarita K. East Foundation $14.4 million. Almost immediately Grace began to funnel funds to Family Rosary for its apostolic endeavors.[65] Today the East Foundation, administered in New York, continues to regularly assist the work of Holy Cross Family Ministries.

Conclusion

The flurry of activity that characterized Patrick Peyton and his Family Rosary Crusade continued unabated in the 1960s. Unquestionably the majority of time, personnel and economic resources, and energy was placed on the crusades in Latin America and the new approach of the popular mission, but the understudy status of other projects did not in any way negate their efficacy in the rosary priest's overall mission to promote family prayer through the rosary. Using techniques and methods that had proven successful throughout the world in the 1950s, plus the new opportunities provided by the rosary films and their feature-length product, *The Redeemer,* the rosary crusade returned to places of previous triumphs and blazed a return to North America. The decade was a time of great triumph as Family Rosary was recognized by hundreds of celebrities in a 1962 dinner celebrating the organization's twentieth anniversary, but the period was also marked by significant trials for Father Peyton personally through faltering health, the deaths of close colleagues and family, and most problematically his name and the organization he founded and loved mired in a protracted legal battle of which he was highly conscious, but played a rather insignificant role. The decade was also a time for the Crusade for Family Prayer to rethink its organization, method of operation, and projects. It is to this reorganization and the new projects of the 1960s we must now turn.

Chapter 9

Reorganization,
Restructure, and Frustration:
Family Rosary and
Family Theater, 1960 – 69

The crest of popularity and recognition enjoyed by American Catholicism in the late 1950s and early 1960s was also experienced in Peyton's Rosary Crusade. Yet the latter's success was achieved without the definitive structure of the Crusade, both as an entity in its own right and within the framework of the Congregation of Holy Cross. At the crossroads of the 1960s, Peyton was forced to look at the overall structure of his ministry and to evaluate its future direction. This assessment was prompted by the movement of Family Rosary away from its emphasis on Family Theater, coupled with the ongoing transition from radio to television as the primary media form. The great successes of the 1950s for Family Theater, in radio and its early films, was reversed, due in large part to Peyton's physical absence from Hollywood and his concern with the Latin America crusade effort. From the outset the campaign had been wholly associated with Peyton's persona, a reality that all knew, but one that became increasingly problematic as the operation's complexity increased. Thus, beginning in the latter 1950s and continuing through the next decade Peyton, Holy Cross, and the Family Rosary Crusade sought better organization while enhancing its self-understanding and inaugurating new projects to revitalize Family Theater. The results were mixed as Family Theater emerged from the decade shorn of much of its former prowess and still looking for a solid base for its media ministry within the ever-changing and expanding world of Hollywood.

218

The Family Rosary Crusade
and the Congregation of Holy Cross

From its very outset in 1942, the specialized family prayer ministry of Patrick Peyton, manifest in its two primary branches of Family Rosary and Family Theater, enjoyed the support of provincials and superiors general of Holy Cross in the form of personnel and financial resources. One report in 1960 stated: "From the beginning Father Peyton's superiors in the Congregation of Holy Cross have lent support way beyond what one would ordinarily expect for a new work of this nature which was nothing more than a gleam in Father Peyton's eyes when it started."[1]

When the Family Rosary Crusade was established, Thomas Steiner, CSC, was provincial of the American Province of the Congregation, but when the Eastern Province was founded in May 1948, Peyton was forced, like many Holy Cross religious, to make a choice as to which province he would join.[2] His selection of the Eastern Province placed his family prayer ministry under the jurisdiction of a fledgling religious body that, like all nascent organizations, struggled to survive financially and searched for personnel in order to achieve stability.

As described previously, James Connerton, CSC, the founding vice-provincial (provincial after 1952), was a strong supporter of Peyton and his work. The Family Rosary Crusade's value and efficacy were also recognized by Connerton's successors, George DePrizio, CSC, and Richard Sullivan, CSC. Peyton appreciated the Congregation's constant support:

> The Family Rosary Crusade has enjoyed this great blessing, security and protection from two Superiors General and three Provincials. It is precisely because of this that the Family Rosary Crusade enjoys a status in the Catholic Church and is accepted, trusted and used by Bishops the world over as a worthy instrument capable of effective service and accomplishment.[3]

But the Congregation's support could not compensate for the fact that Peyton's ministry was poorly organized and, except for the formal boards that governed Family Rosary and Family Theater, lacked the structure required by a constantly expanding operation. Thus, as the 1960s dawned, it became clear to Peyton and his superiors that the Crusade needed a formal organizational base.

Besides the poor organizational structure, the ministry continued to suffer, silently to the outside observer, from the often tenuous relationship between Peyton and his fellow Holy Cross religious. George DePrizio, CSC, admitted to the superior general, "I have been aware for some time of a growing unrest and uneasiness among Father Peyton's staff."[4] Over the years battles between Peyton and his confreres in Holy Cross were numerous and often significant, yet these disagreements stemmed not from personal pique, but rather varied understandings of how the ministry should proceed, and Father Peyton's superhuman energy and enthusiasm for his work, a condition which was hard for his brothers in the community to understand. Jerome Lawyer, CSC, accurately summarized the situation to Peyton personally:

> I know that you will permit me to be frank with you to the point of not sparing you in my remarks. I need not remind you of the many battles we've had during the past fifteen years. Although I lost my temper and you yours, I don't think either of us ever considered these battles anything personal. We never held grudges. Even to this day, although I can remember the places and times of historical battles, I cannot in most cases remember what the battle was about. The point I'm trying to make is that only the Cause mattered, that the Cause was bigger than both of us.

Lawyer understood that Peyton's "uncompromising stand on excellence" in any and all endeavors associated with the family prayer apostolate was one of the great sources of dissension, coming about through varied abilities and levels of commitment.[5] Peyton was not naive to these problems, often commenting that the work was too dependent upon him. He realized he needed others as he often wondered what would happen to his work after his death.

Specific suggestions for improved organization were first raised in the mid-1950s. The provincial, James Connerton, CSC, and the superior general, Christopher O'Toole, CSC, discussed designating the Family Rosary Crusade a *domus formata,* a canonical term that referred to a religious house of at least six professed members, at least four of whom had to be ordained, with Peyton appointed as superior. But neither the Albany nor Hollywood houses met the canonical requirements, so the idea was dropped.[6] All agreed that the Crusade needed far more personnel, a situation complicated by the fact that since the ministry was assigned to the Eastern Province of Priests, access to a broader spectrum of religious was restricted. In 1960 it was suggested that Peyton's mission be shifted organizationally, placing it directly under the superior general, a move that would widen the personnel pool to Holy Cross religious worldwide.[7] Peyton was urged on several fronts to act promptly, not only to organize the operation, but to assure that he was placed in charge:

We feel it is essential to urge you to use every effort possible within the rules of the Congregation of the [*sic*] Holy Cross to have the Family Rosary effort given a separate and distinct organizational status. We are convinced that only if you are able to persuade the Provincial and/or Superior General to have yourself appointed a religious superior akin to an abbot, with the direct authority over the Holy Cross personnel assigned to your organization, can you operate a tight, well-knit, coordinated effort.[8]

Despite the prompting Peyton gained no further personal control over the personnel issue.

The first significant response to the personnel crunch came in 1963 when the new superior general, Germain Lalande, wrote a circular letter to the Congregation asking provincials to supply religious to the Crusade in an unselfish way. Lalande told the Eastern provincial, George DePrizio, CSC, responding to the need for personnel for the Crusade, "You may rest assured that I will cooperate as fully as possible."[9] Lalande's ability to provide personnel remained limited, however, as religious were assigned to ministries by their provincials.

The lack of organization apparent in the Family Rosary Crusade was in many ways attributable to the personality and mode of operation of Patrick Peyton. He spread himself very thin and was physically incapable of supervising diverse operations in many parts of the world simultaneously. During the height of the crusades in the 1950s and early 1960s, Peyton was seldom seen in Albany or Hollywood.[10] Besides his lack of physical presence Peyton was "infamous" for making decisions in what was perceived by others to be a haphazard mode of operation. Often days of planning for an event would be wiped out in an instant when Father Peyton, after taking the matter to prayer, would announce to his co-workers that Mary, the Mother of God, had directed the crusade in a direction opposed to that which had been planned. While no one could fault Peyton for the spirituality of his decision process, the often contrary opinions made others feel that their input was of little significance. Lack of consultation was another consistent problem that plagued relations between Peyton and his co-workers and led to disorganization. Many times only Father Peyton knew and understood what was planned and the method to achieve stated goals. Jerome Lawyer, CSC, spoke for many when he wrote to Peyton expressing the need to change how the Crusade operated on a day-to-day basis:

So much up to now has been haphazard, there's been groping; there has been indecision. And all these tendencies hurt the very purpose of our existence. I am not opposed to the haphazard, indecisive mode of operating if I know what I'm operating for — ... but I feel that having passed through the adolescent stage the Family Rosary should know the facts of life — what it's here for.[11]

Father Peyton's desire to personally control the Crusade's work and direction was above all the issue that kept any formal organization from being pursued with any urgency. On February 2, 1961, DePrizio met with Lawyer, Quinn, John Corr, and James Mannis on how the Family Rosary Crusade could be better integrated into the fabric of the apostolic work and constitutional framework of Holy Cross. It became clear that many of Peyton's Holy Cross religious co-workers were wary of his independent attitude and its unfortunate results: unorthodox financial procedures, neglecting to consult the Provincial Council on important matters, and failures to obtain required permissions per the Constitutions of Holy Cross for certain activities. The provincial believed that the awe which some had for Peyton caused them to fear standing in his path in any way. While all agreed that he had good intentions, Peyton often overlooked the fact that those assigned to the ministry had rights and obligations as priests and religious who felt duty bound to work within the framework of their vows, especially obedience and poverty, which they felt were often abused by Peyton. DePrizio admitted that the rosary priest's independent mode of operation had to be curtailed:

I myself feel personally that unless something quite definite is done once and for all [concerning Peyton's *modus operandi*] we face some very serious situations both as regards the [Holy Cross] men [assigned to Family Rosary], and as regards the work.

The February 2 meeting produced a manual of operation for Family Rosary, but DePrizio informed the general, "We feel that without your approval we can never get Father Peyton to follow it closely." He further concluded, "Perhaps the time has come to re-evaluate the situation radically both for the sake of Father Peyton and the future of his work, as well as the sake of CSC."[12]

The superior general was equally concerned about the situation and desired a more clear organization and decentralization of the ministry away from Peyton. He understood that in the past religious had been chosen to work in Family Rosary "who would not edge in, so to speak, on Father Pat's domain," yet, he continued, "if he does not allow someone else to do some of the things that he is now doing, there is little chance for any true leadership to develop."[13] In line with earlier suggestions O'Toole told DePrizio, "Sooner or later the Family Rosary staff must submit to a more careful organization in harmony with Canon Law and the Constitutions [of Holy Cross]."[14]

Peyton's independent apostolic method was created through a series of factors. Unquestionably his single-minded devotion to his self-appointed task, namely, the promotion of the Family Rosary, trained his mind in one direction. His passionate belief in the need for family prayer was laudable, but it created a sense of blindness to any other ministerial needs and most importantly to methods used to achieve his goals. Peyton's personality was in many ways governed by the adage, "If you want it done right, do it yourself." This perspective forced him to take control as much as possible. He was not a good delegator, but rather held the reins of control tightly, fearful it seems that his goals could not be met in any other way.

Peyton's personality and devotion to his cause were factors in his autocratic manner, but another factor was the Congregation's nearly carte blanche approach to his ministry. Since few if any restrictions were placed on Peyton from the outset of his specialized ministry, he grew accustomed to having things done his way. Thus, while Peyton's own drive and personality may have created a tendency toward his observed leadership style, it was his superiors in Holy Cross who actualized this behavior by their failure to notice and curb certain practices until they became ingrained as a standard operational method for the Crusade.

Lack of organization, unrest between members of Holy Cross, and the fear that Peyton's independence were growing problematic prompted Richard Sullivan, CSC, who took the reins as provincial of the Eastern Province in June 1964, to initiate a serious review of the Family Rosary Crusade. Sullivan sought advice from Bernard Mullahy, CSC, assistant general, about how to proceed. Mullahy told him that the General Administration was concerned over reports of Peyton's health problems and tendency to overwork, especially expressing fear about the continuity of the ministry should something happen to him. He wrote, "I am sure that one of the major concerns of your Provincial Administration will be to provide the necessary structure and the adequate manpower both numerically and qualitatively, which will insure the future development of this extraordinary apostolate."[15] Sullivan acknowledged the need to stabilize the Crusade and believed from his review of past difficulties between Peyton and members of Holy Cross that problems arose when Peyton balked at prior suggestions for improved organization and structure. Additionally, Sullivan hinted that one serious problem could be attributed directly to Peyton himself: "You speak about qualitative manpower in the Crusade; the fact that it is presently not better is due, I think, to Father Pat himself. When one considers that he had in his organization men as Father Frank Gartland, Father John Murphy, Father Lawyer and Father Corr, it is evident that he had the best men in the province. Such men are hard to replace."[16]

Sullivan then appointed James Connerton, CSC, and Jerome Lawyer, CSC, to explore how the Crusade was associated with the formal structures of the Holy Cross Community and suggest a way to guarantee the Crusade's permanence.[17] Lalande was pleased with this move: "The problems of the Family Rosary Crusade are serious and require serious and thorough study. I am very happy that you thought it best to create a committee in order to study the whole question and, if possible, to reach solutions which will be beneficial to the Crusade."[18]

Connerton and Lawyer conducted the study by means of a series of letters written between September and November 1964. Lawyer inaugurated the correspondence study by stating things that were obvious to most. He stated that the Family Rosary work was so integrally bound to Peyton that it was impossible to speak of one without the other. He observed that although the community's rule mandated that religious follow certain procedures for conducting ministry, "Peyton is convinced that the Constitutions of Holy Cross are holding back his work." Lawyer's fifteen years of experience in the Crusade convinced him that Peyton wanted complete control on the movement of personnel, as well as authority to solicit funds for any of his multiple projects and to excuse the religious assigned to his work from "monastic rule," substituting a holy hour for common religious exercises.[19] Lawyer also described Peyton's obvious difficulty with authority:

> In the matter of delegation my impression of Father Peyton is that he personally wanted practically all power delegated to him but did not relish delegating authority to others. This has always led to a bottling up of power and authority with the result that jobs could not be done because on the spot decisions could not be made independent of Father himself.

He admitted that the uniqueness of Peyton's ministry deserved accommodation from the community, but insisted there must be a simultaneous shift in Peyton's thinking.[20]

Unquestionably the most strident criticism of Peyton's mode of operation with the Family Rosary Crusade was his perceived difficulty with authority. Again Lawyer wrote, "I've always felt that Father Peyton had a constant fear of higher authority — a fear that they [community supe-riors] would in some way place obstacles to 'his plans.' He always felt the need to condition them — to win them over by subtle persuasion and even a bit of pressure." Lawyer stated that Peyton often believed superiors were trying to thwart his work. When a conflict arose Pey-ton often claimed greater loyalty and obedience to the Blessed Mother than his superiors, a situation which prompted Lawyer to state, "He [Peyton] should develop the healthy attitude that superiors exist to help and encourage him while at the same time trying to protect him from mistakes."[21]

Lawyer then zeroed in on the seemingly constant difficulty that ex-isted between Peyton and his close associates in the Crusade. It was a mystery to Lawyer that Peyton, who demonstrated such persuasive and inspirational power to millions of people around the world in his multi-faceted ministry would irk rather than inspire his small group of religious and lay collaborators. Clearly mistakes were present on both sides, but Lawyer asked, "Should not he who is so conscious of the importance of public relations (even bending backwards to maintain such relations) be equally or more conscious of the need of bending backwards to inspire and maintain the loyalty of his own small group of lay and priest as-sociates?" He wondered at the time how many members of Holy Cross would join the Crusade if a new structure were established allowing vol-unteers across the Congregation to participate. There was no doubt in Lawyer's mind that errors existed on many fronts and that despite all human shortcomings the Crusade had accomplished great things, yet he concluded, "If we are to make it [the Crusade] work more effectively now and guarantee its continuance in the future, then all and everything must be re-examined and many changes made — one of which I deem very important is the psychological attitude of Father Peyton."[22]

James Connerton, CSC, whose experience with Father Peyton and the Crusade was from a different perspective than Lawyer's, concurred with many of the latter's observations. He had experienced Peyton's tendency to act independently and had heard numerous stories of the tension that existed between the Crusade team, yet, as had always been his attitude, the former provincial believed in the rosary priest and his work. He sug-gested in his letters that granting the Family Rosary Crusade the status of a district, which Canon Law and the Constitutions of Holy Cross al-lowed, would impose structure on the community, guaranteeing proper reporting procedures, and simultaneously give Peyton greater indepen-dence to operate without violating canonical restrictions.[23] Lawyer, who had from the outset of this discussion suggested several possible canonical structures for the Crusade, agreed with Connerton's assessment: "I agree with your idea of a District. I feel that such a homogeneous group working together for a common goal would stimulate greater enthusiasm and also make more efficient the operation of the Family Rosary Crusade."[24]

Connerton and Lawyer's study gave Richard Sullivan ammunition for more formal discussions with the General Administration of Holy Cross on the reorganization of the Family Rosary Crusade within the community. Sullivan met with the superior general Germain Lalande, CSC, in February 1965 to discuss the matter. Lalande made it clear that organizational solutions must be found within the juridical structures of the Congregation and that "it is absolutely out of the question to think that the general administration will at any time take over direct control of the Crusade." He admitted as well, after reviewing the correspondence between Lawyer and Connerton, "The problem of Fr. Peyton and the Crusade is even graver than we were led to believe."[25]

In April Sullivan called a meeting with Lawyer, Connerton, and Peyton "to suggest a new structure which will enable Family Rosary to operate more efficiently and guarantee its perpetuity." All agreed that the Crusade needed greater freedom to send people anywhere in the world and to undertake any activity that would further its mission. Additionally, those assembled stated that the Crusade needed to solicit funds for the ministry without having to obtain special permission from the provincial or general. The group suggested the Crusade be made into an "operational and functional" district, as opposed to a territorial entity, an act that would award Peyton's work the same kind of recognition from the Congregation that it had received from the Church universal.[26]

The results of the correspondence study and the April 13–14, 1965, meeting were brought to the Eastern Provincial Council, which met in special session on April 19 to review all that had been done to date and make recommendations to the superior general on reorganization. The council looked at three options: the *domus formata,* vice-province, or operational district. Since the local Crusade configurations in Albany and Hollywood did not meet the criteria for *domus formata,* and the council found vice-provincialship too bold a move, the operational district proposal won by default, and the council further recommended that Peyton be appointed superior, with Joseph Quinn, CSC, as his assistant.[27]

When the General Administration of Holy Cross met on July 23, 1965, the members refused to approve the Eastern Province's recommendation of an operational districtship. Lalande reported, "We fail to see how giving the Family Rosary Crusade district status could be advantageous to its growth and stability."[28] He was concerned about setting up an "operational" district without the consent of a General Chapter of the Congregation, arguing that such an entity "could very well result in serious friction between the Family Rosary Crusade and the various Provinces." While not approving an operational district Lalande and his staff recognized that the finances of the crusade needed to be administered along the norms of religious life in Holy Cross. Additionally, Lalande was clear that Peyton had to be able to work with other religious, especially his councilors, should he be appointed superior of the Crusade team. He warned, "If the above mentioned items are neglected, we fear that when Father Peyton is no longer in a position to take an active part in its apostolate, the Crusade might be on the verge of collapse."[29] Through all the discussion the canonical status of the Crusade within the Congregation of Holy Cross remained the same.

Reorganization of the Family Rosary Crusade

The effort to clarify the relationship between the Family Rosary Crusade and the Congregation of Holy Cross occurred while a similar review sought to create new structures within the Crusade organization itself. Peyton himself articulated the need for better structure: "It is my firm belief that our worldwide movement has reached the point where it must now be organized along clear cut lines."[30] During the Christmas season of 1960 Peyton met with Peter Grace and hammered out a formal organizational schema. The program was presented and discussed at a meeting between Peyton, Lawyer, John Corr, CSC, Al Scalpone of Family Theater, and John Meehan, Grace's attorney. All agreed to the general plan and prepared to implement it.[31]

The plan centralized the operations of the Hollywood and Albany offices under one general director, Peyton, but it also created five separate departments, each of which had a supervisor who reported to Peyton. The rosary priest understood the need for more people to be involved in supervision: "During the 19 years of its [Family Rosary] history, it has been . . . all too dependent on one man. The continuance of this is, to say the least, a danger to the future of the Crusade."[32] A house council, consisting of Holy Cross religious and a lay board of advisors, provided counsel to the general director. Personnel and legal matters were overseen by the assistant director, who reported to Peyton. A management committee, headed by the director of one of the standing departments, coordinated the activities of the five departments. The committee was to meet monthly to act upon matters submitted by the departments. Each department was responsible for a specific element of the over-all Crusade effort. The Control Department handled budgets, general correspondence, product distribution, and purchasing. Mass Media of Communications was responsible for films, radio recordings, public re-lations materials, mobile crusade necessities, and educational initiatives. The Public Relations Department dealt with public relations and fund raising. The Mobile crusade handled scheduling and planning, execution of crusades, and establishment of postcrusade offices. The Office of Pen-etration was responsible for the youth program and the coordination of all affiliated offices.[33]

Implementing Grace's formal organizational scheme was postponed when Albert Heinzer, CSC, argued that the Crusade's offices should be centralized in Hollywood and the Albany office closed. Such a move, he said, would result in better policy and fiscal control, eliminate dupli-cation of operational expenses and capitalize on Hollywood's superior facilities.[34] Opinions on the centralization question varied among the Holy Cross religious assigned to the ministry. Philip Higgins, CSC, claimed that Peyton wanted to centralize operations in California, but the rosary priest himself believed the two-office system worked well by aiding fund raising and being an incentive to recruiting Holy Cross men for the apostolate. He further stated that closing the Albany office would jeopardize stability and be an admission that the Crusade had been operating incorrectly from the outset.[35]

The failure of Family Rosary to definitively address the reorganization issue, especially after a formal plan had been presented, triggered an un-usually strong outburst by Peter Grace against his friend Patrick Peyton. In February 1966 Grace wrote a harsh twenty-eight-page letter to Peyton listing ninety-five questions about the lack of organization of the Family Rosary Crusade and criticizing Peyton for wasting money. He argued that the Hollywood office was an economic drag on the entire operation, suggesting that it might be better to close it. His rancor against the Albany office was equally tart; the office, he said, raised money simply to keep the facility running, a purpose that made no sense. He railed against placing the burden for finances of the whole operation on him: "Your answer to this [financial] predicament is that I should call the shots, but I don't have the knowledge that is required, and I don't have the time."[36]

Prompted by Grace's strong letter and the insistence of his fellow Holy Cross religious, Peyton commissioned two separate centralization stud-ies. In June 1966 a consulting team from William E. Hill & Company, Inc., after a thorough review of the operations and records of Family

Theater and Family Rosary, concluded, to the surprise of none, that the international crusade operation was the central ministry of the organization, while Family Theater had become a financial drain on the mission. The consultants suggested that the Crusade be divided into two separate wings: the home crusade, directed by Joseph Quinn, CSC, which would be charged with maintenance and building further the crusade concept in areas of greatest geographic promise, and the television crusade, led by Peyton with another priest and secretary. The Hill Report further suggested that the Albany and Hollywood offices be consolidated into "an appropriate New York City location."[37]

A second study, initiated by the Eastern Provincial Council and approved by Peyton, was conducted in house by Al Scalpone, who had been with the Family Theater operation in Hollywood almost from the beginning. Scalpone conducted a series of interviews, inspected facilities, and reviewed all records in detail. His report concluded that unless the Crusade became institutionalized, using an organizational structure broader than one controlled by Peyton, "it will most assuredly die with Father Peyton." The report stated, "There is no doubt that at present the F[amily] R[osary] C[rusade] is not organized. The objectives and the functions have been determined primarily by one man. The responsibility for these functions has been centered on one man. And the authority too. And Father Peyton is that man." As Scalpone saw it, the primary need was to centralize offices, and he threw his support behind a West Coast location, stating, "It is my recommendation that the Family Rosary Crusade headquarter in Los Angeles. And I urge that the physical move be made just as soon as a satisfactory religious house is in being."[38]

Despite efforts on several fronts to actually inaugurate and place in action a plan of reorganization for the Crusade, operations continued as normal. As with the failure to make any canonical change in the relationship between Family Rosary and the Congregation of Holy Cross, so the internal workings of the Crusade remained in their state of haphazard uncertainty. The inaction present in both of these separate but related endeavors demonstrates an unwillingness, in the long run, on the part of Father Peyton to change. His strong will and determination had guided the Crusade since its inception with all significant decisions made by him. Peyton could not control the actions of the General Administration in its decision to refrain from giving the Crusade district status, but it is apparent that if Peyton had wanted to change or reorganize the inner workings of the Family Rosary Crusade it would have happened. The staid operation of the Crusade was indicative of Father Peyton's mind-set that refused to relinquish control of a work he so dearly loved.

Family Theater, 1960–70: Triumphs and Tribulations

The most apparent manifestation of the need for renewal in the Family Rosary ministry was found in the sagging work of Family Theater. The great success that Peyton had enjoyed with his weekly national radio program, *Family Theater of the Air,* began to wane in the early 1960s. The ascendency of television left radio in its wake. One indicator of this shift is that radio advertising revenues dropped 75 percent between 1947 and 1960 while television advertising during the same period rose 3000 percent.[39] Another signal was the growing popularity of religious television, as demonstrated by the work of the Paulist priest Ellwood Keiser. Beginning in 1960, his weekly program, *Insight,* which offered dramas on religious themes, much like *Family Theater of the Air,* was broadcast until 1983.[40] Family Theater in particular was also affected by the troubles of its Mutual Broadcasting partner, which went into bankruptcy and changed ownership twice in the late 1950s.[41] Finally admitting that it was folly to continue investing in a dying industry, Peyton ceased production of original *Family Theater of the Air* programs in 1962, although reruns continued until 1968.[42] Peyton, writing in 1960, acknowledged the need for Family Theater to change its focus:

> If the Family Rosary Crusade rests on its radio laurels, it will go backwards through no fault of its radio presentations, but merely because of radio's ever growing obsolescence. It is urgent, therefore, that the Family Rosary Crusade faces up to this problem and adopts new methods which will permit it to have the same position on the television networks as it has today on the radio networks.[43]

Although Peyton felt that success on television would lead to triumphs in other media, he also realized that TV presented significant financial hurdles. The radio broadcasts, after deducting donated air time and the services of the Hollywood stars, ran approximately $1500 per week. A similar weekly show on television, even with some projected cost savings from similar donations, ran between $20,000 to 30,000 per episode. Peyton outlined the problem and its solution:

> The hurdle that has to be overcome is obvious. A commercial entity has to be convinced of the excellence of the Family Rosary Crusade presentations, of the extraordinary prestige value of sponsoring the Family Rosary Crusade message, and of the cost savings available so that it will finance the continuation of the Family Rosary Crusade presentations switched from radio to television.[44]

At the same time he was pursuing television funding, Peyton tried to increase Family Theater's press exposure, which lagged behind that of other religious ministries, the Billy Graham Crusade in particular. Peyton got stories about Family Theater published in newspapers and magazines, including *Time,* the *New York Daily News,* and the *New York Daily Mirror.* Additionally, in February 1960 Peyton launched *Family Fortress,* a syndicated column reporting Family Theater activities distributed by King Features.[45]

Peyton also explored two other ways to increase Family Theater's national exposure. He attempted to produce two pilot films, at a cost of $60,000 each, featuring Hollywood stars and promoting family prayer, but was unable to obtain financing.[46] He also petitioned Cardinal Spellman to set up an office in New York City "to harness the power of Madison Avenue and complement and supplement the Hollywood office in facing the tremendous challenge ahead of us in regard to a weekly TV program of high caliber." Peyton reported that the Raskob Foundation would donate $150,000 toward the construction of a New York City office. Peter Grace offered free space on the twelfth floor of his newly constructed company headquarters on Manhattan's east side. However, Spellman's Diocesan Board of Consultors rejected the request, stating that the Albany office already provided sufficient Eastern coverage.[47]

Peyton not only realized that Family Theater's star was falling with the rise of television, and thus there was a need to adjust; he also believed the organization required rejuvenation on all fronts in order to "leave an impact upon the heart and mind of America as it did in the late 40's and 50's."[48] One method to reinvigorate programs was with new personnel. During the early 1960s María Luisa Luca de Tena, one of the Spanish secular missionaries, Tom Lewis, and Raymond Cassel, CSC, joined the Family Theater team. Peyton investigated new projects for his extended team to tackle, but the basic philosophy and direction of his ministry never changed. He wrote, "We must come to the moment of truth and quickly, so that we are square and sincere with ourselves as to what is the purpose of Family Theater — to advance Mary, to bring Mary as a leader before the public of America and the world."[49]

In spite of all his efforts, however, the mass media were clearly slipping away from Peyton. Peter Grace, writing in February 1966, acknowledged that five years earlier Peyton had stated that Family Theater was in danger of extinction, and stated, "I am [now] afraid you are extinct."[50] Peyton himself was forced to concede, "Family Theater Productions, after extraordinary success in radio and in the first days of television, has not, for the past few years, made any real impact on the radio and television public."[51]

Regardless of the nonoptimistic forecast, Peyton still needed to raise money to keep his ministerial ship afloat and sailing in smooth waters. In the 1960s mass mailings continued and expanded, always with the hope that the charisma and appeal of Father Peyton himself would bring in the necessary revenues. This direct solicitation method expanded over the years with the list exceeding 100,000 by the middle of the decade.[52] Numerous local groups held benefits and formed special associations to assist Peyton's cause financially. In the fall of 1960 Peyton reinitiated contact with past New York State benefactors, asking them to restart a series of "Dinnerman's Meetings," which had been inaugurated in 1955. The plan was for Peyton's friends to hold fundraising events to be held wherever the crusades had been conducted, an ambitious strategy calling for events in thirty-two states and the District of Columbia.[53] In 1962 the Kitty O'Grady Family Rosary Club, started originally in 1949, held its first dance fundraiser in Cleveland. In October 1964 John Timothy Smith, a prominent Syracuse attorney and active Catholic, died suddenly from a heart attack. Over the next few years Smith's family and friends organized the John Timothy Smith Memorial Benefit to promote the work of Family Rosary, which he had loved.[54]

Two national fundraising efforts were the Society of M and the Family Prayer Century Club. The Society of M was an organization of local groups of fifteen men each, who agreed to contribute $1000 per person annually to promote the Family Rosary Crusade. Each member also pledged to recite one decade of the rosary daily. While each group consisted of only fifteen official lifetime members, the club was also open to associate members who agreed to the monetary contribution and rule of prayer.[55] In 1966 Peyton wrote to major superiors of religious orders asking them to contribute $100 annually (or a lifetime membership of $1000) to a new national fundraiser called the Family Prayer Century Club. The successful program was ultimately extended to auxiliary members for $50 per year.

Individual benefactors continued to be of great importance to the Family Rosary Crusade. Harry John of the DeRance Foundation, who had paid for the theater in Brussels to show the rosary films, gave $10,000 in 1959 for radio broadcasts in Spain. In the early 1960s he made two significant contributions, totaling $95,000, to purchase real estate lots for investment near Family Theater headquarters in Hollywood.[56] Peyton always counted on his friend and number-one benefactor, Peter Grace, who continued to assist with his advice and personal contributions, including one sale of stock options in 1965 that netted Family Rosary over $166,000.[57]

Family Theater was, unquestionably, in a period of organizational uncertainty in the 1960s, but *Family Theater of the Air* and *Marian Theater* continued during the decade. Besides the two weekly shows aired in the United States, Canada, and via Armed Forces Radio to various foreign lands, Radio Madrid and its affiliates in Spain and Radio Cooperativa, a national network in Chile, offered weekly Family Theater broadcasts. *Marian Theater* featured a special broadcast on September 2, 1962, titled "The Story of Father Patrick Peyton," starring Marvin Miller and narrated by Dan O'Herlihy. This was the last significant event for this series, which aired its last broadcast on February 3, 1963.[58]

Peyton's normal radio broadcasts continued, but not without encountering a disagreement with the American Federation of Television and Radio Artists (AFTRA). Over the years Peyton had always managed to meet all of his financial responsibilities with respect to radio, but it was seldom without a struggle. However, in 1960 Peyton was informed that he owed back royalties to script writers for Family Theater reruns, as well as back payments to a 5 percent welfare and pension fund, which had been inaugurated by the union in 1956 — a fact of which Peyton was unaware. Back payments of this union fee coupled with royalties for programs reruns threw Family Theater into a financial crisis.[59] Peyton sought advice and received two opposite responses. Al Scalpone advised Peyton to state his ignorance and appeal to the sympathy of those requesting payment. Jerome Lawyer, CSC, recommended that Peyton object to the request. Peyton, however, chose a middle route by writing to Family Theater's creditors asking that after their back payment or royalty had been received, the parties would return the same amount to the Crusade as a donation.[60] Many, sympathizing with Peyton's dilemma, did precisely what he asked.

Although the 1960s was not a time of great innovation for the radio side of Family Theater, a few new projects were completed. The Spanish language series *A Search for Peace* included fifteen radio spots, of thirty-second or one-minute duration, on the theme of seeking peace in the midst of the ongoing Cold War. The *Prayer Series* consisted of twenty-six invocations from famous prayers composed over the centuries that were recorded by famous personalities. *Stories of Our Savior,* a series of scripturally based reflections on the life and ministry of Jesus, were nationally syndicated.[61]

New international radio efforts were also inaugurated during the early 1960s. Thirty-five-minute rosary meditation scripts were written for and broadcast by Radio Free Europe in English and Polish. The same station broadcast "Our Lady's Peddler" as an Easter special in 1961. A series of 150 five-minute radio programs, each emphasizing one practical moral point for day-to-day living, was released in Latin America in an effort to translate the fervor of the ongoing crusades into a way of life.[62]

The *Family Theater of the Air* radio ministry ended in 1968, but not without a final blast of nostalgia. On Christmas Eve 1966 a new hour-long *Joyful Hour* was broadcast, featuring Gregory Peck as narrator, the singing of Bing Crosby, Perry Como, Ann Jamison, Dennis Day, and Jo Stafford, and starring Ann Blyth, MacDonald Carey, Jeanne Crain, Ruth Hussey, Ricardo Montalban, Pat O'Brien, and Maureen O'Hara among others. Holy Week 1967 featured a Good Friday program based on the Catholic Daughters of America *Carrying the Cross* radio show, and a reprise of the 1950 *Triumphant Hour* on Easter Sunday.[63] Speaking of *Family Theater of the Air,* one commentator said in praise of Peyton's efforts, "No one can deny that Father Peyton's radio venture was a success."[64]

Family Theater's endeavors in the realm of film in the 1960s were, as might be gathered from previous comments, more numerous than those in the radio medium. In 1964 Peyton lobbied strongly to have the original fifteen rosary films shown in the Spanish Pavilion at the New York World's Fair. Although he was confident that he could accomplish this goal, he overestimated his persuasive powers, lamenting when his request was denied that the fair "is quite Protestant."[65] This same year Peyton made a significant effort to have the rosary films shown in Lourdes, where he had tried and failed in 1958. On February 11, the Feast of Our Lady of Lourdes, Peyton and Francis Grogan, CSC, were present, together with local dignitaries, when the Annunciation, Crucifixion, and Coming of the Holy Spirit on Pentecost were shown in the Cine Bernadette.[66] Peyton used this modest triumph as the starting point for a grandiose plan to purchase land near Lourdes and construct a permanent theater for showing the films. As with many of Peyton's hastily conceived plans the Lourdes project never got off the ground. However, between 1965 and 1967 Peyton was able to show the rosary films in the Cine Bernadette in German, Italian, French, and English.[67]

Recall that from the time the rosary films were made, Peyton kept alive the idea that a feature-length film for profit could be made from them. The first such effort, *The Eternal King,* was never shown in theaters because of a distribution dispute with Twentieth Century Fox and because of unfavorable reviews which labeled the film as anti-Semitic. In 1963 the film was reedited, with a new prologue and epilogue, and given the title *The Redeemer*. After unsuccessfully approaching MGM, Peyton, once again, went to Twentieth Century Fox and its president Spyros Skouras, who agreed to release the reedited film as competition for Samuel Bronston's production, *King of Kings*. However, fears that the film was still anti-Semitic and therefore defamatory caused Skouras to balk. The film was again reviewed when Fox was sold to Daryl F. Zanuck, but it was thought at the time that no amount of editing could remedy the situation.[68] The film was premiered, however, by Family Theater in a private screening for two hundred. The general reaction was quite positive, but some viewers had misgivings about its commercial potential.[69]

The Redeemer was then acquired for release by Dale Robertson of United Screen Arts, who arranged to show the film in the National General Corporation's theaters in San Francisco and Oakland, beginning on March 2, 1965. In December 1964 the film was previewed by the Film Advisory Committee (FAC), an information agency that presented its opinion to film studios about various Jewish questions. Speaking on behalf of the committee, its chairman, Allen Rivkin, stated that the group's purpose was neither to approve nor disapprove films, since it was not a classification or censorship body. His rejoinder notwithstanding, Rivkin, evoking the ecumenical sentiments of the ongoing Second Vatican Council, called *The Redeemer* the most "inflammatory [and] disgusting thing I've ever seen," claiming that the reediting had done nothing to correct the film's anti-Semitic bias.[70] Criticism of the film would not stop, however, as evidenced by the comments of Lester Gutterman, chairman of the Jewish Community Relations Council: "We are deeply disturbed by the prospect of an impending national commercial distribution of 'The Redeemer.' The film perpetuates the old myth of the Jews as deicides and, therefore, furthers anti-Semitism."[71]

At first United Screen Arts continued with its plan to premiere the film in San Francisco. Peyton was encouraged, commenting to a secretary, "All stops must be pulled out to make 'The Redeemer' a triumph."[72] But as the premiere drew closer, United Screen Arts became increasingly wary of sponsoring a film that was causing controversy even before its release. Finally on February 23 the company exercised its option and canceled its distribution contract with Family Rosary.[73]

The hostile reaction to *The Redeemer* by the Jewish community forced Peyton to lower his expectations on the film's distribution and commercial value. Peyton began to realize that his only option was selected local distribution. In the summer of 1965 Family Theater entered into contract with Empire Pictures of Dallas, Texas, which agreed to release the film city by city.[74] Raymond Cassel, CSC, became advertising chief for the film and also contacted newspapers, radio, and television, local clergy and dioceses, theater companies, and schools. Cassel's efforts were complemented by Robert Rioux, CSC, who was sent by Peyton as a front man to speak with local ordinaries promoting the film, especially by encouraging release time from parochial schools for students to view it. The anti-Semitic label continued, however, negating most of Cassel's and Rioux's efforts. *The Redeemer* opened in Corpus Christi, Texas, on November 4, 1965, and in two theaters in Dallas on November 12. In all, *The Redeemer* was shown in twenty-eight cities in Texas, eleven cities in New Mexico, four in Massachusetts, and two in Connecticut, between November 15, 1965, and February 1, 1966.[75]

Reviews from Texas, New Mexico, Massachusetts, and Connecticut screenings were generally very good. The film was described by one reviewer "as an intensely moving experience." He continued, "For the over-all accomplishment, we owe a note of thanks to Empire Films, the Holy Cross Fathers, especially Father Patrick Peyton, for giving us a genuinely spiritual film that rises repeatedly to high artistic quality."[76] The film was even lauded on the floor of the U.S. Congress by Representative James A. Burke, who extolled the film's technical excellence and its wholesome religious entertainment: "At a time when so many of our motion pictures that are being shown have an adverse effect, particularly on young people, it is welcome news to learn that efforts are being made to have presented a film which has a meritorious effect on people."[77]

The film's American premiere and first showings were followed by international distribution when it served as a prelude to the popular mission in the Philippines in 1965. It was also distributed in Ireland, Mexico, Guatemala, Ecuador, Colombia, Venezuela, Greece, Singapore, and Malaysia.[78]

The rosary films were also spun off into several new projects for Family Theater in the 1960s. "The Promise," first aired through syndicated stations on Christmas eve 1963, was a half-hour adaptation of the Joyful Mysteries.[79] Beginning on December 10, 1967, and continuing for the next six weeks, television stations across the country broadcast Family Theater's latest release, a series of six half-hour films, called *The Prince of Peace,* constructed from the original fifteen mystery films, *The Promise,* and *Smile of Recife,* probably the most popular of the documentary films made from the crusades. Each *Prince of Peace* film addressed specific religious themes and featured a short concluding conversation between Peyton and a Hollywood personality. The series was well received and "garnered raves from television stations and their public."[80] The original rosary films were also shown on local stations from Los Angeles to Boston. The films were generally broadcast in a series with the Joyful Mysteries aired during the Christmas season and the Glorious during Easter being the most popular formats.[81]

Family Theater also produced a few original programs in the 1960s. Beginning in 1962 and continuing for two years Family Theater produced many ten-, twenty-, thirty-, and sixty-second television spots called *The Family Unity* series. These brief segments were intended for public service announcements and contained inspirational messages on family prayer by some of Hollywood's leading artists, including Peter Falk, Ann Blyth, Margaret O'Brien, Terry Wilson, Herb Anderson, and Jack Haley. A similar endeavor featured Peyton more directly and was titled "A Minute of Family Prayer with Father Peyton."[82] Family Rosary documentaries highlighting crusades in San Francisco ("This Is the Hour"), Recife, and Milwaukee (1968), plus a general film on the operation of the crusade, *The Key to Peace,* were also produced at this time.[83]

The Psalm series, a group of five-minute films based on the biblical psalms, was the most significant new television effort for Family Theater during this period. Maria Luisa Luca de Tena was placed in charge of this project that began to take shape in early 1963. A pilot series of four psalms was prepared and premiered at the Twentieth Century Fox building in Hollywood on February 15.[84] Hathaway Watson, president of RKO Broadcasting, was interested in the new series and agreed to pay one-third of the production costs and get them shown on television stations across the nation. Originally Luca de Tena suggested that fifty films be made, but Watson counterproposed an initial run of fifteen to twenty. They compromised on thirty,[85] with the first film of the series completed in September 1963.[86] The first twenty-four films were packaged in groups of six and syndicated as *The Song of the Ages.* Some of the more popular films were *The Escape* (Psalm 1), *The Solitary Man* (Psalm 6), *The Find* (Psalm 21), *The Lord Is My Shepherd* (Psalm 22), *The Soldier* (Psalm 41), *The Mask* (Psalm 61), and *The Game* (Psalm 132).[87]

The Psalm series garnered awards for Family Theater and served, as had the rosary films, as a source for the creation of longer and more saleable films. *The Soldier,* which introduced William Shatner to the Hollywood scene, won a bronze medal at the 1964 Venice Film Festival in the category of dramatic short subject.[88] *The Search,* which synthesized five Psalm series films, starred Raymond Burr and William Shatner, and used the songs and lamentations of King David to explore the human search for self-discovery, was awarded first prize by the International

Catholic Communications Association (UNDA) at the International Film Festival at Monte Carlo. Three other half-hour films, *The Find, The Ful-fillment,* and *Somewhere Along the Line,* a sequel to *The Search,* were made from the Psalm series.[89]

Peyton was hopeful that the excellent reception and awards for the Psalm Series would lead to some financial gain. He acknowledged his difficulties in harnessing the television market and hoped that this new series would help him to obtain a corporate sponsor "that would give us the financial resources for a continued efficacious Apostolate, through the medium of TV."[90] Peyton met with officials at RKO and NBC in efforts to explore practical ways that the series could be used and to convince them that free broadcast time should be made available so the Psalms could be aired in stations across the country. Tom O'Neal at RKO agreed to look at the issue, but nothing materialized. Edward Stanley, an NBC executive, was impressed with the "the unique charac-ter and . . . the remarkable and highly-skilled production techniques" of the films, but explained that it was extremely difficult to carve out five-minute slots from regular programming in order to insert the Psalm films. Additionally, Stanley was wary that although the Family Theater iden-tification with the films was modest, other groups might ask for similar consideration. In the end NBC also turned down Peyton's proposal.[91]

The decade of the 1960s was a time of much frustration for Father Pey-ton and his Family Theater ministry, but his ever fertile mind continued to produce ideas for ways that his overall message of family prayer could be promulgated through the now reigning medium king of television. As the decade of the 1960s dawned Peyton entertained many possibilities for the television market. In conversations with his Family Theater team sev-eral options were raised, including public service spots using Hollywood stars, a weekly show, the continuation of past efforts in the production of religious films, and documentaries from the footage shot at crusades.[92]

Many times Peyton expressed the desire to start a weekly television program similar in content to his popular *Family Theater of the Air* broadcasts, yet he knew that an estimated cost of $40,000 to $60,000 per program would require corporate sponsorship. Peter Grace believed in the efficacy and potential of a weekly program and told Peyton that if a pilot could be made he was sure supporters would appear.[93] In 1961 officials at Standard Oil offered to loan Peyton $30,000 to produce a pilot program, which the priest hoped to sell and then use to obtain corporate sponsorship from Standard Oil. At about the same time Pey-ton's Hollywood friends Rosalind Russell and Jack Haley organized a committee of their peers to look seriously at a weekly Family Theater television show.[94] Although neither the pilot nor the sponsorship materialized, Peyton continued to work on the TV project. He mapped out thirteen half-hour shows treating problems contemporary families faced. The programs were to allow the audience to "see" the formulation of these problems and to realize that any sound answer was not obtainable without reference to one's religious dimension. Subjects were to include faith, evil, suffering, death, family, sin, poverty, war and peace, grief, riches, science and technology, freedom, and love. Significant figures in politics, religion, philosophy, literature, and science would appear in each program, which a Hollywood celebrity would narrate. In spite of Peyton's creative ideas, the project never materialized.[95]

Another project Peyton came up with during the 1960s was the Moral Series. As early as December 1957 Joseph Breen had suggested that a series of films on the Ten Commandments made, not from the Jewish Old Testament perspective, but from a more positive angle emphasizing "Thou shalt" rather than "Thou shalt not."[96] In 1963 this idea was resurrected when Peyton reported that the Lewis Foundation gave Family Rosary $35,000 for a preliminary study on a film series based on the Decalogue. Family Rosary was to present a formal report including: (1) prospective audience for such a series, (2) distribution, (3) an appealing format, (4) names of accomplished writers who could provide good scripts, (5) suggested stories and plots, and (6) possible production problems. Peyton was excited about the project, stating, "If we succeed, then we are almost sure that [the] Foundation and its leadership will see the Series through to the end."[97]

Development of the possible series, titled *The Encounter Series*, continued between 1963 and 1967. The programs were to show the relationship between God and humanity from a moral perspective. Each episode, set in Palestine at the time of Christ, would develop a character from the Gospels who encounters Christ. The climax of each story was the encounter with Christ and how that event affected the character's moral behavior.[98] The needed scripts could be obtained from past unused material that could be adapted, starting from scratch through the development of a format and concept and following it for all ten films, or contacting professionals in all areas, including writers, directors, and actors, and getting an outside group to supervise the whole project.[99] While several scripts were completed, this ambitious project, like the weekly television show, was never realized.[100]

In the spring of 1966 Peyton began working on a Christmas television special featuring recitation of the Joyful Mysteries of the rosary, with famous stars participating in prayer and song. Jackie Gleason, who

was very interested in producing the show,[101] wanted the program to include the celebration of Midnight Mass with famous choirs, such as the
Sistine Chapel Choir, singing Christmas music. Famous stars would be
engaged to read passages from Scripture relevant to the Joyful Mysteries,
and after each reading a famous artist would sing an appropriate hymn
accompanied by a world-class orchestra. The recitation of the mystery
would be accompanied by shots of ethnically and socially diverse families throughout the world. The last decade of the rosary would be recited
by the Holy Father.[102] Peyton saw the program as a way to promote the
image of the rosary in the post–Vatican II Church:

> To do something for the rosary today, to present it in a new dimen-
> sion, to glorify and glamorize it, to show it to the masses in depth,
> to demonstrate its paraliturgical essence and to prove its power to
> enrich the intellectual is the need of the hour. Who more than FRC
> could be expected to raise a voice in its defense.[103]

Planning for the program continued despite the uncertainty of the
pope's participation, an element that Peyton saw as key to its success. Peyton asked permission from his Family Rosary Council[104] to spend between
$500,000 and $700,000, saying he was certain that the Lewis Foundation
and several wealthy friends, including Harry John and James McArdle,
would provide the bulk of the money.[105] CBS informed Peyton that it was
willing to assist in its underwriting and transmission to many nations simultaneously via satellite. Peyton informed the pope of the progress he
had made in planning this television spectacular, but Paul VI, claiming he
had too many commitments, chose not to participate in the program.[106]
Peyton was obviously disappointed in the pope's inability to be part
of the program, a reality which would necessitate a shift in direction,
but he continued to believe the show could still be aired. The focus of
the program was changed completely, from a recitation of the rosary to
a ninety-minute program *Prayer for Peace*. The new format called for
twenty-five world leaders to be filmed expressing in their own words
or prayers a desire for peace. Walter Cronkite, the distinguished CBS
news anchor, was slated to host the program, which was to feature a
panel discussion with Protestant, Catholic, Jewish, and Orthodox religious leaders.[107] The lateness of the hour with respect to Christmas
obviated any possibility to air the show in 1966. Peyton was hopeful
that the program would be shown in 1967, but the energy that accompanied the original concept was not transferred to the *Prayer for Peace*, and
thus like other endeavors of the decade at Family Theater, the Christmas
program was never completed.

As the decade of the 1960s closed it was evident to all that the period had not been friendly to Family Theater and there was a need to change in order to right the ship that was sailing in rough waters. John Gurley, CSC, who joined the Crusade for its return to Latin America after Vatican II, believed Family Theater had the potential to be a powerful force in religious broadcasting, but commented, "It is in need, perhaps, of a more unified and determined program — a sharper focusing on its real reason for being and an integration of its efforts into an overall program of religious broadcasting."[108] Peyton admitted that "Family Theater was the loser" through his neglect, a situation created because of his concentration on the Crusades, especially in Latin America. The 1970s would bring new life and opportunities to the worldwide Rosary Crusade Peyton loved so dearly.[109]

Conclusion

The great success and the notoriety that characterized the Family Rosary Crusade in the 1950s, continuing into the next decade in Latin America, became elusive goals for Father Peyton's operation in the United States. Many factors contributed to Family Rosary's decline as a notable contributor to American popular religiosity during this period. The decline of radio and the subsequent rise of television as the media of choice for Americans was a transition that was not well negotiated by Family Theater. Lack of funds, but most especially insufficient direction from Father Peyton, caused Family Theater to fall from its status as a household word for most Catholics. Reorganization efforts, including a proposal to centralize operations at the Hollywood office, were aimed to provide others in the organization with the authority to make decisions to prepare for a future without Father Peyton, but these ideas were never fully implemented. Thus, the status quo of a haphazard approach to business, dependent almost totally on the personality and decisions of Father Peyton, continued with the consequence that Family Theater failed to reclaim its former glory. The inability of Family Theater to satisfactorily reorganize or bring to fulfillment any significant television specials during the period illustrates the ministry's stagnant status. Family Theater had the potential, the contacts, and the ability to reclaim its position in the Hollywood market, but it would take time and much effort in a world that was transformed in the 1960s, culturally, socially, and religiously. It would be the great challenge of the Family Rosary Crusade to find itself, adapt, and then reconnect to God's people in the postconciliar age.

1. Peyton family photo. Patrick is front row right side standing.

2. Patrick Peyton as a seminarian
at Holy Cross College,
Washington, D.C.

3. Lithograph of the Family Rosary by David Lithgow.

4. Patrick Peyton on the day of his ordination, June 15, 1941, University of Notre Dame.

5. Students at Vincentian Institute, Albany, New York, assist with early Family Rosary mailings, 1943.

6. Family Theater of the Air: Standing: Pedro de Cordoba, Roddy McDowell, Dennis Day, Ricardo Montalban, MacDonald Carey. Seated: Jeanne Crain, Father Peyton, Maureen O'Sullivan, Joan Leslie, Ethel Barrymore. December 20, 1947.

7. Family Theater of the Air live performance.

8. Holy Cross Religious discuss Family Rosary projects: Left to right: Francis Woods, Jerome Lawyer, CSC, Albert Heinzer, CSC, Patrick Peyton, CSC.

9. Family Rosary Crusade team previews rosary films: Left to right: Joseph Quinn, CSC, Philip Higgins, CSC, Patrick Peyton, CSC.

10. Family Rosary team discusses future plans: Left to right: Patrick Peyton, John Murphy, Francis Woods.

11. Patrick Peyton preaching
at a Family Rosary Crusade.

12. Patrick Peyton preaching at a parish Triduum under
the watchful eye of Our Lady of Divine Providence.
Long Beach, California, 1948.

13. Family Theater, 7201 Sunset Blvd., Hollywood, California.

14. First permanent Family Rosary Headquarters, 773 Madison, Albany, New York.

15. The original Family Theater building donated by Jacoba Buchenau.

16. Family Theater in Hollywood, California.

17. Patrick Peyton preaching at Family Rosary Rally, Barcelona, Spain, February 1965.

18. Patrick Peyton preaching at Family Rosary Rally, Rio de Janeiro, Brazil, December 1962.

19. Patrick Peyton in front of Family Theater in Hollywood with his famous billboard slogan in the background.

20. Albert (Hap) Heinzer and Father Peyton stand before one of several posters used in billboard campaigns, beginning in the 1970s.

21. Billboard announced the weekly *Family Theater of the Air* radio broadcasts.

22. Billboard announcing the Family Rosary Crusade in New York City, October 12, 1952.

23. Patrick Peyton with the Murillo Madonna and Child, his favorite depiction of the Blessed Virgin Mary.

24. Members of the cast and staff on the set of the Rosary mystery films, Spain 1957. Left to right: Mary Jane Buchenau (McQueen), Antonio Vilar, Ann Rossetti, Joseph I. Breen, Jerome Lawyer, CSC, Edward DuPar, and John T. Kirby.

25. Father Peyton leads cast and crew of Rosary mystery films in a moment of prayer.

26. J. Peter Grace, the shipping magnate who was instrumental with the Family Rosary Crusade, as financial backer and friend of Patrick Peyton.

27. J. Peter Grace and Father Peyton meet with Pope John Paul II.

28. Father Peyton and
Sister Mary Buckley.

29. Patrick Peyton
and John Gurley.

30. Jerome Lawyer, CSC.

31. Patrick Peyton discusses film plans with Princess Grace of Monaco.

32. Patrick Peyton discusses ideas with Mother Teresa.

Chapter 10

Renewal and New Directions: The Family Rosary Crusade, 1964–75

The decade of the 1960s, described as "a revolutionary moment" by the Jesuit Church historian James Hennesey, witnessed significant social, cultural, and religious change throughout the world. The United States was especially susceptible to the vicissitudes of the period because of a number of factors: the long-standing existence of freedom of expression, the efforts of the American civil rights movement to create true equity, and the country's embroilment in an unpopular war. These factors heightened tensions and made liberal and radical ideas more visible and, in the minds of many, more suspect.

For the Church the monumental event of the period was the Second Vatican Council, which met in four fall sessions between 1962 and 1965. Called by Pope John XXIII and continued under his successor, Paul VI, the council transformed the face of Roman Catholicism through the promotion of *aggiornamento*, ecumenism, and the advent of a more pastoral approach to living the faith. The Vatican Council was a defining event for the Family Rosary Crusade, as it was for the whole Church, and served as the rationale behind the new direction that Father Peyton's work would take.

The Second Vatican Council, the 1960s, and American Catholicism

In the history of Roman Catholicism ecumenical councils have been called for two basic reasons: to root out perceived or acknowledged heresy and to define significant Church doctrine or dogma. The first

242

council, held in Nicaea in 325, served both purposes: first condemning the theology of the priest Arius, who viewed Christ as a *tertium quid,* one not fully human or divine; second, formulating the Nicene Creed, which was modified into its present form at Constantinople in 381. Vatican I, the twentieth council, held during 1869 and 1870, defined the dogma of papal infallibility in its document *Pastor Aeternus.* In the interim, eighteen other councils, including the famous gatherings at Constance in 1415, which ended the Great Western Schism, and at Trent (1545–63), which presented the Catholic response to the Reformation, gave direction, corrected abuses, and defined teachings in the Church.

The Second Vatican Council was called by Pope John XXIII in a speech at St. Paul's Outside the Walls on January 25, 1959, the last day of the annual week of prayer for Christian Unity. John had been elected just months before his announcement, and partly because of his age — seventy-six — was considered an interim pope, so his dramatic announcement came as a great surprise to the entire world, especially the Catholic Church. The pope called for a diocesan synod for Rome, a revision of Canon Law from the 1917 Code, and an ecumenical council of the world's bishops. He also stated the council's three principal purposes: to promote ecumenism, to bring the Church into the modern world (he used the word *aggiornamento*), and to be pastoral in nature and work.

Preparations for the council began almost immediately when the pope asked over eight hundred theologians, the hierarchy, heads of male religious orders, and the faculties of thirty-seven Catholic universities worldwide to provide suggestions for what the council should address. A relative oasis of calm in the midst of secular Cold War upheaval and the Church seemingly free of both heresy and uncertainty about doctrinal matters indicated that there would be minimal response to the pope's call for action. However, over two thousand individuals and institutions provided ideas for possible study by the council. Cardinal Alfredo Ottaviani, prefect of the Holy Office, put in charge of organizing the council, was a strong theological conservative wary of modernization in any form. He used his influence and position to "pack" the preparatory commissions with only "safe" theologians who would not move the Church from the position it had maintained with barely an inch of movement since the time of Trent. The twelve commissions that were established wrote seventy schema for possible debate by the council fathers, including revelation, moral order, the deposit of faith, family, liturgy, the media, and Christian unity. All the draft documents were neo-scholastic, juridical, and moralistic in tone and content.

The council was formally convoked with the document *Humanae Salutaris* of December 25, 1961. In this document Pope John used the terms "sign of the times" and *aggiornamento,* expressions that would prove significant for the future direction of the council's work. The pope's comments reversed the long-standing edict proclaimed at Lateran V (1512–17), which said "men must be changed by religion" to "religion must be changed by men." With the pope leading the way, shortly after the first session of the council opened on October 11, 1962, the bishops voted to move away from the rather staid tone of the preliminary schema, substituting a more open view that would allow the bishops themselves to determine the council's direction. Ottaviani and his conservative forces had been routed at the outset, setting the tone that would be carried through to the council's conclusion on December 8, 1965.[1]

The four sessions of Vatican II produced sixteen documents, more than all the documentation of the twenty previous councils combined, that were divided into three areas of descending significance. Four constitutions, including documents on liturgy, revelation, the Church, and the Church in the modern world, were the council's crowning achievement. Nine decrees, including important treatises on ecumenism and the lay apostolate, and three declarations — including the one document with a distinctively American tone, the Declaration on Religious Liberty — were published. The net effect of these important documents was the emergence of a new self-understanding for Roman Catholicism, exemplified most significantly in the rise of collegiality, the increased role of the laity, ecumenical dialogue, and a complete updating of the liturgy, including the use of the vernacular language. The importance of Vatican II in the history and direction of the Church might best be stated in the work of the Jesuit theologian Karl Rahner. In his division of Church history into epochs, Rahner provides three: the apostolic era, 30–49, the era of the Church, 49–1962, and the era of Vatican II, 1962 to the present.[2]

As important as it was, the Second Vatican Council was only one episode in an era of dramatically shifting traditions and social and cultural value shifts, especially in the United States. Beginning in 1954 with the famous *Brown v. Board of Education* Supreme Court ruling, which reversed the 1896 *Plessy v. Ferguson* decision of "separate but equal" schools and effectively ended racial segregation in public education, the American civil rights movement marched forward. Led by Martin Luther King Jr. and his Southern Christian Leadership Conference (SCLC), as well as the more militant Malcolm X and Stokely

Carmichael, the movement peaked in the 1960s, effecting legal change and social transformation.[3]

The 1960s was also a period of great disillusion for many Americans. Beginning in the late 1950s under President Dwight Eisenhower, American involvement in the war in Vietnam escalated, expanding to other nations of Southeast Asia. Although the United States had been embroiled in several armed conflicts in the twentieth century, including two world wars and Korea, the nation had never found itself engaged in such an unpopular and misunderstood conflict, creating dissension on all fronts and breaking the personality and lives of so many, including President Lyndon Johnson, who prosecuted and escalated the war throughout his tenure in office.[4] The 1960s also witnessed the assassinations of leading Americans, including President John F. Kennedy in 1963, and Martin Luther King Jr. and Senator Robert Kennedy within two months of each other in 1968. Social unrest, the desire of freedom and autonomy that characterized the "counterculture," and a general distrust of traditional structures created an environment of disillusion.

Christianity in the United States, which enjoyed popularity and acceptance in the 1950s, was also experiencing a period of confusion and transition. The sociologist of religion Robert Wuthnow suggests that in the 1960s spirituality and organized religion in America found themselves running in opposite directions. Many Americans continued to participate in organized religions, but young people often sought spirituality in different venues, opting for freedom of choice in lieu of specific confessional denominations. Wuthnow summarizes his understanding of the period:

> Americans in the fifties chose largely to remain where they were, opting for security rather than risking their faith in a genuine search for spiritual depth; however in the 1960s many Americans, having learned that they could move around, think through their options, and select a faith that truly captured what they believed to be the truth, took the choice seriously, bargaining with their souls, seeking new spiritual guides, and rediscovering that God dwells not only in homes, but also in the byways trod by pilgrims and sojourners.

He further contends that the ease with which the shift from indwelling to seeking occurred indicates that the strength of the indwelling model during the 1960s has probably been overrated by previous scholars.[5]

American Catholicism also found itself in a period of great internal upheaval, confusion, and uncertainty. The historian Philip Gleason, using the word "disintegration" to describe this era in the Church, wrote,

"The strongest sense I had was of a Church, a religious tradition, that was undone, breaking apart, losing its coherence."[6] Symptoms of disintegration included a massive exodus from the priesthood and religious life, the falloff in vocations, the closing of Catholic schools, a breakdown of respect for ecclesiastical authority, and the sexual revolution.[7] The chaos felt by many American Catholics during this period was accentuated when people recalled the great sense of unity that dominated the Church between 1920 and 1960. The disintegrative impact of changes in the postconciliar Church was especially troublesome to those whose faith had been formed during the comparatively peaceful period between 1920 and 1960.[8]

Mindful of the ancient Church dictum *lex orandi lex credendi* (the law of prayer is the law of belief) it is important to review how the American Church's prayer life was affected by Vatican II and the general turbulence of the period. The priest-sociologist Andrew Greeley noted six areas of transition and change for the spiritual life of American Catholics. First he speaks of the movement from devotional acts to objective virtue. Before the 1960s the average Catholic in the United States considered the spiritual life and devotions to be synonymous. After Vatican II the practice of devotions was subjugated to the practice of virtue. Next is the transition from the Eucharist as a devotional act which was sometimes received before, after, or outside Mass, to the Eucharist as public worship in liturgical form, inextricably connected to the Mass. Third, Greeley speaks of the shift from concentration on the individual to concentration on the whole. He claims, "The communitarian emphasis can be found in almost every dimension of the emerging Catholic spirituality." One drawback in this transition was a tendency toward worldliness and secularism.[9]

Next Greeley discusses the movement from what he terms "monastic to secular," in his description of the sense of the faithful that priests and religious no longer had any special corner on the market of spirituality. Marriage gained equal footing with the religious state. Greeley next notes a different strategy in approach to the spiritual life. In the past people sought spiritual perfection and, when attained, they acted upon it, but the postconciliar Church stressed commitment and action as ongoing efforts throughout one's faith journey. Lastly, Greeley suggests that there was a noticeable shift in emphasis from the theoretical to the functional, particularly in the movement away from spiritual traditions of the past, perceived to be no longer relevant, to a more functional and action-oriented mode of operation. Even with the new schema that Greeley proposed, he was clear that there was never a complete break with the past.[10]

The postconciliar Church certainly began to march to a different drummer, but the need for family prayer remained central to the common Christian life. Karl Rahner, SJ, considered by many to be the most significant Catholic theologian of the twentieth century, wrote, "If the family were no longer able to pray together, neither would the Church community any longer be genuinely capable of doing so." Echoing the sentiments of many others, Rahner continued, "If there will always be a praying Church, then the domestic sanctuary of the Church — the home — will likewise remain, and with it the hope of preserving the Family Rosary."[11]

The status of popular devotion, which Greeley and others[12] identified as endemic to the pre–Vatican II Church, became uncertain after the council. Some believed that Vatican II obviated the need for personal devotions. The Constitution on the Sacred Liturgy (*Sacrosanctum Concilium*) suggested a more critical treatment of popular devotions, stating that their purpose was to lead the faithful toward the celebration of the Eucharist since "in fact the liturgy [the Mass] by its very nature is far superior to any of them."[13] The theologian Carl Dehne suggests that liturgists in the postconciliar Church viewed popular devotions as "subjective" since they contained almost no Scriptural base and had originally been developed only as a substitute for the Mass. Devotions waned in the wake of the council because there existed "no popular theological reason for the celebration of any service except the eucharist and other sacraments."[14] Greeley offered a more positive interpretation: "Far from being opposed to the liturgy, popular devotion can prepare people for participation in the liturgy and even point the way to the further development of the liturgy itself."[15]

The rosary, a significant popular devotion for centuries, found itself attacked on several fronts. Stories abound of priests in the pulpit breaking rosaries before their congregations with the admonition, "The rosary is no longer relevant." However, the rosary also had its staunch supporters. For instance, the Dutch Dominican theologian Edward Schillebeeckx presented an intellectual argument in its favor:

> The Rosary is a synthetic Christological Creed, a *symbolium* or compendium of dogma and doctrine, in the form of a prayer of meditation, a summary in prayer of the whole of the dogma of the Redemption. Because its use has become so widespread, the Rosary

is clearly a most important weapon in the instruction of the Church community in Christian dogma.[16]

The Irish writer Gary MacEoin presented a more measured and popular opinion on the rosary:

> As long as there are masses of people with low levels of religious instruction and formal education, it will have a value in substantially its present form. For more sophisticated believers, bored by its repetitiveness, it will evolve into a variety of more scriptural, more personal and more liturgical forms.[17]

Predictably, Peyton voiced his continued belief in the efficacy of the rosary, particularly within the family unit. He noted that the pope continued to call for family prayer as "the sure defense and unfailing protection of the family," and that since his crusades had won millions to the practice of the family rosary there was no need to change now. He continued to argue,

> The Family Rosary Crusade is dedicated to the Family, its unity and its sanctity. Family Prayer, especially The Family Rosary, is the simple but powerful means the Crusade proposes and propagates as practical, possible and efficacious, for the family to use in order to maintain its unity and foster its sanctity.[18]

Vatican II and the Family Rosary Crusade

In spite of his traditionalist approach to theology — a result of both his home life and his training for the priesthood — Peyton was intelligent and perceptive enough to see that the Vatican Council would have a profound impact on the Church in general and his crusade in particular. He promptly began lobbying the bishops in attendance for their approval of his work, going to Rome frequently between 1962 and 1965 and making sure that he was present for the entire final session, between October and December 1965. During this period he met with the council fathers, asking their opinions on family prayer and their guidance on the future of the crusade, as well as lobbying strongly for writing a section on family prayer in the final council documents.[19]

Peyton's chief allies in his effort to include a family prayer statement in the documents were Cardinal Leo Josef Suenens, who had been the auxiliary bishop of Malines-Brussels in Belgium when Peyton first showed the rosary films at the Brussels World's Fair and when the crusade came to the region in 1959, and Mark McGrath, CSC, bishop of Santiago de Veraguas in Panama, who introduced Peyton to many of the bishops. Peyton also worked with Arthur McCormack, a Mill Hill Father, Robert Pelton, CSC, and the Redemptorist priest and famous theologian Bernard Häring. With McGrath and Pelton, Peyton drafted a statement for inclusion in "Schema 13" which became the Pastoral Constitution of the Church in the Modern World, or *Gaudium et Spes*. He also asked Cardinal Suenens to urge the bishops to include a statement on prayer in "Schema 13."[20] Suenens supported the proposition on the council floor: "In order to strengthen the sense of God in the intimacy of the family, that prayer by which all its members in faith and love worship God and receive His most fruitful blessings is especially advantageous."[21]

Efforts were also made to include some statement on family prayer in the Decree on the Apostolate of the Laity. Peyton received an unexpected boost in this effort from Bishop Erbert Bednorz of Poland, who spoke on the council floor promoting family prayer and mentioning both Peyton and his crusade. Bednorz stated that the family could be a domestic sanctuary of the Church only through the spiritual piety of its members and through common prayer. His comments then turned more specific, "Family prayer — which in our times Father Peyton of the Congregation of the Holy Cross stresses with such insistence in his crusades — so intrinsically unites the family that the children most willingly turn to it: nowhere else are they more at home in a good Christian family."[22]

Peyton succeeded in having statements on family prayer included in both these highly influential documents. *Gaudium et Spes* states, "Inspired by the example and family prayer of their parents, children, and in fact everyone living under the family roof, will more easily set upon the path of a truly more human training, of salvation, and of holiness."[23] The Decree on the Apostolate of the Laity states, "The mission of being the primary vital cell of society has been given to the family by God himself. This mission will be accomplished if the family, by the mutual affection of its members and by family prayer, presents itself as a domestic sanctuary of the Church."[24] The superior general, Germain Lalande, CSC, reported to Richard Sullivan, CSC, Peyton's provincial, that the rosary priest's significant efforts in lobbying the bishops had paid off. He concluded, "He was for us a source of comfort and a splendid example of hard dedicated work and [a] profound spirit of prayer."[25]

Peyton also exploited the council to show the rosary films whenever possible. He was pleased when any bishops viewed them, but was most interested in attracting bishops from missionary countries, hoping that they might purchase the films for use at home or even request a crusade.

The films were shown on a published schedule in English, French, Spanish, and Portuguese between November 12 and December 4, 1965, in the San Pietro Cinema of the Vatican. While all 2,500 bishops were sent invitations to the screenings, only 160 attended.[26]

Cardinal Suenens urged Peyton to build on his triumph at Vatican II by publishing a book, *Family Prayer and the Council,* consisting of essays written by ten to fifteen giants of the council, on the subject of family prayer in the postconciliar world. The timing of the book would coincide with the end of the council as the well as the twenty-fifth anniversary of Family Rosary. Among those enlisted to make contributions were: Bishop Mark McGrath, Bernard Häring, CSSR, Edward Schillebeeckx, OP, Cardinal Leo Josef Suenens, Yves Congar, OP, Henri de Lubac, SJ, and Barnabas Ahern, CP. The book was to be edited by Robert Pelton, CSC, and Renato Poblete, SJ, a sociologist from Chile. Several publishers were approached, including Doubleday, but interest in the project was minimal, and so the book project collapsed.[27]

Self-Examination and Revision of the Crusade

Although Peyton had scored a major victory with the inclusion of the prayer statements in two of the council's key documents, he realized that his crusade needed thorough review and revision if it were to be relevant to the postconciliar Church. As Richard Sullivan, CSC, proclaimed, "All of these things and others put together convince us all, including Father Peyton and his superiors, that it would be wise to put the spotlight of *aggiornamento* on the Family Rosary Crusade." He went on to say that unless the Crusade sought renewal it would in a few years become passé, in a Church which now emphasized liturgical, catechetical, and biblical movements.[28] Peyton hinted at his openness to change, suggesting that family unity was the primary work of his ministry and not devotion to the rosary. Still, Robert Pelton, CSC, has suggested that while Peyton may have been open to modifications of his ministry, "ideologically it would have been almost impossible for Pat to adjust to Vatican II."[29]

Prompted by McGrath and Pelton, Father Peyton engaged the Jesuit sociologist Renato Poblete from the Bellarmine Center for Sociological Research in Santiago, Chile, to conduct a thorough study of the Family Rosary Crusade.[30] He wrote Sister Mary Buckley, president of the Sisters of Mercy in Albany, "We are . . . undertaking a study to specifically find the place of the Family Rosary in the post-conciliar world."[31]

The review was conducted between October 25 and November 27, 1965, during the last session of the council, while Peyton lobbied the bishops. The study looked at three specific questions: (1) How does the Crusade fit into the renewal of the pastoral work of the Church? (2) In what way does the Crusade answer the religious needs of the people? and (3) How do bishops look at the crusade — its positive and negative elements? The two primary vehicles used in the study were a review of the literature and reports from the crusades, including interviews with forty bishops who had hosted crusades. The participants, chosen by Peyton and McGrath,[32] were given questionnaires "to determine those aspects in which it [the Crusade] should renovate its viewpoint and methods in order to enter into the full stream of the council, its doctrine, its spirituality and its pastoral methods."[33] Poblete also conducted four separate meetings with a group of theologians, including John Courtney Murray, SJ, Jean Daniélou, Yves Congar, OP, Bernard Häring, CSSR, and sociologists, Emile Pin, SJ, Francis Houtart, and Isaac Wust, concerning the crusade.[34]

On November 11 two meetings associated with Poblete's study were held at the Belgian College and at the Holy Cross generalate. The first, held in the morning and hosted by Cardinal Suenens and attended by Peyton, welcomed twenty-seven participants, including bishops, theologians, and five religious women, who focused on the place of popular religiosity (the Family Rosary Crusade being one example) in the postconciliar Church. Because of Suenens's personal interest and the ongoing Poblete study, attendants also discussed the organization of the future Crusade.[35] The ideas from the morning meeting became the subject of an evening session at the generalate attended by Peyton, Poblete, McGrath, Pelton, and the Mill Hill Father Arthur McCormack. Here it was decided that Peyton's entire crusade team should gather at the University of Notre Dame the following March "for a careful examination of the Poblete Report" and to continue discussing the role of the Family Rosary Crusade in the postconciliar world.[36]

The Poblete Report outlined both positive aspects of the crusade and areas that required improvement. There was no question that the crusades had helped families to become communities of prayer and to show them how to provide service to others. The participating bishops unanimously described the crusades as well-organized, effective in the use of mass media, and successful in giving the laity a heretofore unknown sense of purpose. In particular they praised the efficacy of the rallies and the popular missions.[37]

On the negative side was, first of all, the need for better follow-up, since great resources of manpower and money were expended on the

crusade, but insufficient means were disbursed for follow-up and maintenance. The report suggested that while Peyton's talks during the crusades
were "extremely good for sincerity, honesty, and conviction of present-
ing one idea,...the crusade itself [and] Father Peyton's sermons lack
a deeper sense of theology." The report stated that Peyton needed to
broaden his talks beyond devotions, especially to Mary, embracing the
whole meaning of Christian life with its spiritual and social implications.
This was especially important in underdeveloped regions of the world,
where the Church's social doctrine needed to be preached more openly.
The rosary, the report indicated, should not be presented as a magical po-
tion that guarantees success to those who use it. The report concluded,
"Probably it would be better to present family prayer instead of just
praying the rosary." Poblete stated that the crusade, as all already knew,
was too closely linked with the charism and person of Father Peyton.
Lastly, the report suggested that training of the laity, although valuable,
was too rapid and superficial.[38]

To solve these problems the Poblete Report recommended that the
crusade take a number of steps. First, it should review its pastoral mission and its connection to popular devotion in the wake of Vatican II.
Second, it should review all literature, sermons, and other materials, updating them to correspond to the new concept of Church generated by
the council. The lay catechists should provide deeper and more theologically sound explanations of the mysteries in their popular mission
sessions. Next, the crusade must be more team driven; Peyton needed to
learn to operate in a more decentralized mode with respect to decision
making. Lastly, the report warned Peyton that he must be aware of the
ulterior uses that some might have for the crusades:

> The directors of the crusade should be aware that political extreme
> rightists, especially in Latin America, would like to use the Cru-
> sade for their own political purposes....Although the Crusade is
> completely apolitical the director should be aware that they may
> be used in some places for this purpose.[39]

The principal recommendation of the November 11, 1965, meeting
between Peyton and his trusted advisors at the Holy Cross Generalate
gave rise to a conference held at Notre Dame the ensuing March. Between March 20 and 26, 1966, Notre Dame hosted a conference where
many of the world's leading theologians discussed significant theological issues raised at Vatican II. Among the participants were Godfrey
Diekmann, OSB, Yves Congar, OP, Henri de Lubac, SJ, Bernard Häring,

CSSR, Karl Rahner, SJ, Walter Burghardt, SJ, and John Courtney Murray, SJ. Peyton and his Family Rosary Crusade team also attended the sessions.[40] Immediately after this conference Peyton held his own meeting, between March 26 and 31, to discuss the role of the Crusade in light of the theology just discussed by the assembled experts. Some of the experts stayed on and were joined by the team that had assisted Peyton in Rome, namely, Mark McGrath, CSC, Renato Poblete, SJ, Robert Pelton, CSC, and Arthur McCormack, MHM. Peyton also invited a few Protestant pastors and theologians to bring a more ecumenical view to the discussions.[41]

Discussions during Peyton's conference ranged far and wide in an attempt to reshape a ministry with many past successes, making it more relevant to a Church that had significantly shifted direction since the crusade began. Speakers commented that the specific end of the crusade, namely, family unity through prayer, must be maintained, but the base of the crusade needed to expand to embrace social and liturgical references and other apostolic works that would promote Christianization of the family.[42] Bishop McGrath stated, "The aims of the Crusade should be more ambitious in depth and less in extension." In short, the conference participants collectively stressed that the Crusade had to use family prayer to foster liturgical prayer and social action.[43] Bernard Häring, CSSR, cautioned that although the fixed formulation of the rosary was fine as long as people understood it, "we must break away from magical mathematics and mechanical indulgences." He suggested using other "forms" of the rosary and was seconded by Rev. Arthur C. Piepkorn of Concordia (Lutheran) Seminary in St. Louis, who noted that Protestants welcome prayer that is scripturally based, such as meditations on the mysteries of the rosary, and might be attracted to a more generic approach.[44]

The conference concluded with several recommendations for action. A fundamental change adopted was to alter the name to Crusade for Family Prayer as opposed to Family Rosary Crusade in an effort to provide a wider context and audience for the Crusade's mission and message.[45] It was also agreed that a study should be done to evaluate uniting the Albany and Hollywood offices (the William Hill and Al Scalpone studies mentioned in chapter 9) for more efficient operations. Participants agreed that the Eastern provincial should be provided with a five-year plan for the Crusade's operation so that appropriate numbers of personnel could be obtained for the proposed projects. Lastly, the conference suggested that Albert Heinzer, CSC, remain as the director of the Hollywood office while James Connerton, CSC, and Philip Higgins, CSC, share duties in Albany.[46]

The March 1966 Notre Dame conference became the catalyst to events that prepared the Crusade to meet the postconciliar world with a new and updated format. From January 7 to June 30, 1967, Peyton sent Joseph Quinn, CSC, William Persia, CSC, Robert Rioux, CSC, John Gurley, CSC, George DePrizio, CSC, and William Belyea, CSC, to a pastoral institute in Madrid, sponsored by the University of Salamanca. Quinn explained Peyton's rationale:

> The purpose of sending the men to Madrid would be that Father Peyton believes this institute would help the Family Rosary Crusade to update itself in line with the thinking of the Second Vatican Council. He also feels sure that the Pastoral Institute will enrich the Crusade for tomorrow.[47]

Besides creating a whole new package of crusade literature, Peyton hoped that the Institute would reestablish the Crusade in the Spanish mass media, including weekly television, Family Theater radio, and screenings of *The Redeemer,* and thus win back the secular missionaries to the Crusade team.[48]

After the institute ended, Joseph Quinn, CSC, Robert Pelton, CSC, Renato Poblete, SJ, and some of his colleagues from the Bellarmine Center in Santiago, Chile, met in Spain during July and August 1967 to review and revise the Crusade's literature in light of the Second Vatican Council. Peyton supported this endeavor fully: "I feel very strongly about the fact that the more points of view we have for the literature we are preparing for Milwaukee the better."[49]

Vatican II and the significant effort made by Patrick Peyton in its wake to review and update the Family Rosary Crusade gave his work new direction, yet it was not clear what that focus would be. The need to change had been recognized and recommendations for modifications made through the Poblete Report, the Notre Dame conference, and the Pastoral Institute, yet his colleagues in the ministry and brothers in Holy Cross realized that it would be very difficult for him to navigate safely in these new postconciliar waters. William Persia, CSC, worried that Peyton was using the rosary as an end and not the means to achieve family prayer. James Mannis, CSC, commented concerning Peyton's reaction to popular devotion's fall from prominence after the council, "I don't think it ever lessened the . . . conviction that he had carried with him for years. I don't think he liked the new attitude, but I don't think it affected him at all."[50] The postconciliar age was present; it was now up to Peyton to welcome or reject it.

The Family Prayer Crusade, 1968–75

The newly updated and renewed Family Rosary Crusade made its first stop in the postconciliar period in Milwaukee in 1968. Archbishop William Cousins first requested a crusade in 1959, after Peyton's great triumph in St. Paul, but the rosary priest's commitments to Latin America and his hopes to work in Asia delayed the Milwaukee crusade.[51] The Vatican Council and Peyton's decision to update the Crusade further delayed its arrival in Milwaukee, but Cousins saw this as a benefit: "Postponement [of the Crusade] has actually worked to our advantage. We shall be the beneficiaries of a complete updating of the campaign in line with the Conciliar Decrees."[52]

The Milwaukee crusade occurred from April 14 to May 26, 1968, with Peyton assisted by Joseph Quinn, CSC, Robert Rioux, CSC, Raymond Cassel, CSC, and John Gurley, CSC. Peyton understood the importance of this, his first venture after the Vatican Council. In a talk to the local Serra Club he stated, "I'm grateful to Milwaukee because it was here — the first city after the Council — that God allowed us to come. So that the result of Milwaukee's love, Milwaukee's leadership, Milwaukee's fire, will be felt across the nation."[53] To emphasize its new approach, Peyton advertised his crusade in a different way, dividing it into three phases: (1) orientation/preparation phase, (2) realization phase, and (3) postcampaign phase. The packaging was slightly different, but the basic program remained: establishing an office, preliminary meetings, and the popular mission as precursors to the actual crusade, which began with the bishop's pastoral letter, included the parish, school, and institutional campaigns, and ended with the rally and pledge drive. The postcrusade, which had been noted in the post-Council renewal to need more time and resources, was to be formalized and institutionalized.[54] Joseph Quinn, CSC, summarized the Crusade's renewed appearance and direction:

> The overall objective of the Crusade would remain the same, namely, prayer in the family for peace and unity and love in the family. The new dimension regarding the objective would be the aspect of the family reaching out as a testimony to the community at large of their faith in God and their example for the family of today.[55]

Although its basic format remained unchanged, there were some significant innovations in the Milwaukee crusade. The most obvious change was the name, "Crusade for Family Prayer," moving away from the use of the word "rosary." Cousins explained the move to his clergy:

> We repeat this is a Campaign of Family *Prayer*, leaving the Rosary to the countless thousands who find in it the traditional values, the comforts and consolations of earlier days, and opening up at the same time the whole broad vista of family prayer in *all* of its forms, not omitting family participation in the great sacrificial prayer of the Mass.[56]

The Crusade also promoted neighborhood home Masses to coincide with the more open and pastoral approach of Vatican II. Innovative ways of praying the "traditional" rosary included the use of Scripture, song, and spontaneous meditations. Peyton also suggested that the pledge drive include a questionnaire about family prayer life. Lastly, while not necessarily innovative, Cousins made provision to supply every home in the archdiocese with a rosary.[57]

Both Peyton and Cousins supported a major thematic innovation of the Milwaukee crusade — its emphasis on ecumenism. Peyton told Quinn he wanted "a practical, efficacious, operational program that you could sell to the Anglican Bishop, to the Methodist leader [minister] and to the Jewish rabbi."[58] Reflecting the unusually wide embrace of the crusade's interconfessional approach, Cousins asked "all people of good will" to participate in the Campaign for Family Prayer. The Reverend Kenneth Knoespel, president of the Greater Milwaukee Council of Churches, encouraged local pastors to participate in the crusade: "Because this [church unity] is a goal in which we all believe, surely there is an ecumenical potential to their campaign that merits consideration."[59] In further gestures of ecumenism, the non-Catholic religious schools were invited to participate in the school program, and a new prayer book with prayers from various Christian traditions was introduced.[60]

Although Peyton fully supported the more ecumenical approach, he objected to any reduction of Marian devotion. He voiced his perennial message in a more generic way, "This is my heart, this is my belief, this is my love, this is my fire, this is what I try to say to all peoples: Muhammadan, Hindu, Jewish, Protestant and Catholic: 'pray — pray with your family and learn from experience the meaning and value of this — the family that prays together stays together.' "[61] This new, more open view did not lessen his devotion and direction to Mary:

Far from de-emphasizing Our dear Mary, I strike out for Her with all the enthusiasm that ever I had. If there was ever a truce [*sic*] charisma, this is mine: To get the world aware of Mary's essential relationship with Christ, our God incarnate, in saving Mankind. When you destroy Mary, you destroy the Incarnation mystery and when you destroy the Incarnation mystery, Christ is gone.[62]

Father Peyton was not ready or able to move from his central message and hope; in his mind there was absolutely no need for a new direction, only new methods.

The popular mission which had been inaugurated in Latin America but never tried in the United States was introduced in Milwaukee with the unfortunate name of "Ghetto Crusade," the target population being inner-city blacks, Hispanics, and poor whites. In keeping with the ecumenical spirit of Vatican II, Quinn met with Protestant bishops and rabbis, at the invitation of Archbishop Cousins, asking them to encourage their congregations to attend the films that were part of the Ghetto Crusade. The rosary films and *The Prince of Peace* series were used in parishes while *The Redeemer* was shown in schools.[63] The Ghetto Crusade was funded through a $21,000 Raskob Foundation pledge.[64]

The rally was much less successful in Milwaukee than in previous crusade sites. Approximately 35,000 people came on May 12, Mother's Day, a disappointing turnout for Peyton, who had hoped to gather 250,000 for the event.[65] Many factors were responsible for this poor showing. First, Mother's Day was not a good date since many families celebrated this event at home. Additionally, Danny Thomas had been announced as master of ceremonies far in advance of the event, but had to cancel suddenly. Even though his replacement, Don McNeill, was well known as host of the popular *Breakfast Club* radio show, Thomas's cancellation was a disappointment. Finally, a group of protesters from a local social justice group asked people to boycott the event, arguing that financial support of the crusade could have been better used to help the poor of the area.[66]

Like other aspects of the crusade, the rally had a truly ecumenical flavor. Instead of the traditional use of five separate families to lead the decades of the rosary, Peyton chose five families from various religious traditions, two Catholic, two Protestant, and one Jewish, to say prayers of their tradition. One report stated the families "explained the meaning of family prayer in their lives and offered typical prayers."[67] Phil Bengston, head coach of the local National Football League heroes, the Green Bay Packers, recited one decade of the rosary, and the team's defensive captain, Willie Davis, recited the Twenty-third Psalm.

The Milwaukee crusade, the first exemplar of Peyton's postconciliar approach, received a good deal of criticism. One priest commented that the timing was all wrong, suggesting that racial matters were much more important than a family prayer crusade.[68] The most severe criticism, however, came from those who were not pleased with the new-look crusade. Critics claimed that the campaign's name change and the substitution of general prayer for the specific rosary prayers effectively de-Marianized the event. Others objected to the ecumenical slant and a questionable "new theology of prayer." One priest spoke for many in stating,

> Having been confronted with the ominous and disquieting news that Father Peyton's crusade has been "completely updated" and will involve significant changes and deletions, we now have doubts and grave misgivings about the "Campaign for Family Prayer," and feel, to put it in backyard slang, that we are being gypped.[69]

Archbishop Cousins countered the criticism by stating that he believed "the Crusade gave prominence to the Rosary and re-established a devotion that was being unfairly ridiculed by those of the modern school."[70]

The legacy of the Milwaukee crusade was preserved on film. From the outset of the campaign Peyton was interested in making a film so the crusade could be seen for its new innovations. Through a $5,000 gift from Archbishop Cousins, a ten-minute documentary titled *Turning On* and narrated by Danny Thomas was produced.[71]

After its U.S. debut, the postconciliar Crusade for Family Prayer went to Latin America, where the preconciliar Family Rosary Crusade had been so wildly popular. The crusade team changed dramatically in the postconciliar period. Joseph Quinn, CSC, who had served the ministry almost continuously since his ordination in 1950 and was the backbone of Peyton's efforts, left the crusade as did Robert Rioux, CSC, and William Belyea, CSC.[72] John Gurley, CSC, became the cognizant Holy Cross team player, joining the effort formally in 1967. Richard Sullivan, CSC, told Peyton that Gurley was the crusade's hope for the future:

> Father Gurley is the one hope for its [Crusade for Family Prayer] continuation and for its possibility of attracting other young men

into the work; he sees the importance of the apostolate and is willing to work for it in a selfless manner. As you well realize Father John could choose and be very successful in other apostolates.[73]

Gurley was pleased to join the Crusade, and especially to participate in Latin America, where he felt the mental and spiritual needs of both the region and the peoples matched the crusade so closely.[74]

In another significant staffing change, for the first time non–Holy Cross personnel took the lead roles as local overseers. Two priests from the region, Luis Armijos Valdivieso, OP, from Guayaquil, Ecuador, and Reinaldo Pol Yparraguirre from San José, Costa Rica, were assigned by their local superiors to work with Peyton's crusade throughout Central America and Mexico. Peyton praised his new team: "Fathers Gurley, Armijos and Pol have been the catalyst for Our Lady's overwhelming success.... These men are my hope for the future leadership of the Crusade. They are performing a truly miraculous job.... I believe I have never been so happy, uplifted and hopeful for the future of the Crusade as I am now."[75]

As with the Milwaukee campaign, the Crusade's return to Latin America was marked by some modifications along the lines of the themes of Vatican II. The preparation, realization, and postcampaign phases were followed as in Milwaukee. The parish homilies emphasized generic family prayer rather than the rosary in particular. In these crusades the rally was generally not the last major event, but rather was scheduled in the middle of the crusade, with often two or three weeks of homilies, plus pledge week, now referred to as family week, following.[76]

Attempts to incorporate Vatican II's new pastoral approach were a joint effort between the local churches in Latin America and the crusade leadership. In August 1966, the Central American hierarchy met in Panama City and established a Central American Permanent Commission to direct this joint pastoral effort. As a first step toward mass evangelization, the bishops requested that Father Peyton's crusade be brought to the six republics of Central America, beginning in 1967. Peyton responded, however, that the crusades had been suspended so the ministry could be reviewed and updated. Additionally, Peyton had promised Archbishop William Cousins of Milwaukee that the Crusade would come there first.[77]

The Crusade finally returned to Latin America in October 1969, in response to a formal invitation from Cardinal Mario Casariego of Guatemala City. As with the highly successful efforts in South America, the crusade was initiated with the popular mission. An estimated

1.2 million attended during the eight nights the movies were shown. Gurley captured the moment, "The Popular Mission program is very powerful and efficacious — and this is readily seen by anyone who has an eye and interest for the pastoral needs of the faithful."[78] A pastoral letter from the Guatemalan bishops endorsed the crusade's postconciliar posture:

> The Crusade for Family Prayer, which we begin today, is an effort of the entire Church in Guatemala — bishops, clergy and the faithful. The Church directs this effort toward all of the families of the country without exception. We make a united call to every family, Catholic or non-Catholic, inviting them to pray for a holier family and a happier world. And in this way, every true Christian should become an authentic promoter of justice and peace.[79]

The rally in Guatemala City was held on December 7, 1969, in the spacious Campo de Monte. The event, attended by one hundred thousand of the faithful plus forty bishops, was a great success and marked a return of the crusade to prominence after the less than successful effort in Milwaukee. Cardinal Archbishop Mario Casariego preached at the rally and extolled the crusade and Father Peyton: "Guatemala will be as one great family praying together. Here we will always pray as Father Peyton has taught us — Father Peyton — the modern prophet of family prayer, the humble apostle sent to us as another Elias [Elijah] to bring down upon us the blessings of Our Lady of the Rosary."[80]

The Crusade moved from its triumph in Guatemala to Costa Rica, where it was directed by Reginald Pol. Difficulties in transporting the film equipment turned out to be a blessing in disguise, since it postponed the start of the crusade long enough for tensions between the local clergy and the hierarchy to abate.[81] The popular mission was conducted in three cities between May 4 and July 12, 1970. The principal rally was held in the capital city of San José on August 2 with fifty thousand in attendance.

The crusade continued to gain momentum as it moved to El Salvador and Honduras. A central office was established in San Salvador in September 1970 with Luis Armijos, OP, John Gurley, CSC, and the local auxiliary bishop, Oscar Romero, as local directors. The crusade in El Salvador was conducted between January 7 and March 10, 1971, with the rally held on March 6 in San Salvador's Liberty Park.[82] The Crusade immediately moved next door to Honduras between May 3 and July 11, 1971.

The crusades in Central America were especially efficacious in raising questions on the need for the Church to assist the poor. The combination of the Crusade's appearance and the teachings of Vatican II created a new atmosphere among Church officials. Robert Rioux, CSC, reported this new mentality to the superior general: "We [the Crusade] have been successful in convincing some of the power structure in these countries that they have an obligation to alleviate the poverty of the people."[83] The social justice side of the Crusade for Family Prayer was now prominently displayed.

Mexico played host to the Crusade for Family Prayer longer than any previous nation, with crusades conducted intermittently between the spring of 1970 and the end of 1974. Thanks to the presence of Pol, Armijos, and Gurley, the crusade could be conducted simultaneously at several sites, significantly extending the ministry's range. The Crusade first landed in Mexico at Mérida on the Yucatan peninsula in April 1970. Under the direction of Father Armijos (Pol was with Gurley in Costa Rica) the crusade proceeded smoothly, with the rally held on May 31, 1970, with fifty thousand in attendance. The Crusade visited eleven separate areas from Oaxaca in the south to Tijuana in the north, with stops in the large cities of Guadalajara, Hermosillo, and Obregón in 1972, and Mazatlán and La Paz in 1973. Between January and June 1974 the Crusade was conducted in Mexico City, under the direction of Luis Armijos, OP, climaxing on May 31 with a grand rally that was followed by a successful pledge campaign.[84]

In addition to the ambitious Latin American crusade efforts, Peyton also brought his crusade to the Holy Land in the 1970s. Although Gurley had some reservations about this project, which took him by surprise, Peyton pursued his ambition of reaching all Christians in the Holy Land between February and May 1971. Peyton placed Robert Rioux, CSC, in charge of preparation for a pilgrimage to Israel. Over four hundred people, including eight Holy Cross priests, participated in an international rosary pilgrimage,[85] with rallies held in late May in Nazareth, Bethlehem, and Jerusalem.[86] The Crusade's efficacy was noted by one observer: "Your visit to the Holy Land has strengthened the belief of our people in [the] Virgin Mary and her Son Jesus Christ. Your words and your preachings has [*sic*] strengthened the faith of all of us and has impressed on our heart so much: if we were not believers, we became believers."[87]

Conclusion

The socially volatile 1960s was also a period of religious uncertainty through Vatican II and its revolutionary approach to renewal in the

Church. *Aggiornamento* and its application became the rally cry for Church reform in liturgy, ecumenical dialogue, increased role of the laity, and a greater pastoral approach to the needs of God's people. Patrick Peyton was forced to critically examine the Family Rosary Crusade, updating its approach and theology to conform to the council documents. Although Peyton energetically sought renewal through self-study and conferences, he continued to preach his simple yet profound message, that families needed to pray together in order to survive. Peyton's renewed ministry, the Crusade for Family Prayer, continued to bring his message to people in the United States and Central America, but the vast crowds and the apparent hunger for the message were beginning to wane. It was a new world and a new Church that Peyton would face in the 1970s and beyond.

Chapter 11

Patrick Peyton and the Rosary in Eclipse: The Crusade for Family Prayer, 1970–80

Father Peyton's specialized ministry of family prayer was not a good fit with the post–Vatican II world in general, or with the socially and politically turbulent United States of the 1960s in particular. The fallout from the council — changing attitudes toward ecclesiastical authority, the mass exodus of priests and religious from ministry, a significant downturn in religious vocations, a general loss of institutional religious practice, and a lack of enthusiasm for the rosary and other forms of popular religiosity — severely impacted Peyton's ministry. In spite of its continued success in Latin America and numerous attempts to shift direction, the Crusade for Family Prayer sustained minimal growth in the 1970s, in essence maintaining a holding pattern. Peyton believed that his ministry would move through this eclipse and emerge with some of its old vigor restored.

American Catholicism in the 1970s

Driven by its heyday of the 1950s and the first years of the 1960s, American Catholicism "arrived" as an acceptable group in American society, but this significant accomplishment and new status also made the faithful more subject to the general trends of the nation. Most observers agreed that Catholicism in the United States participated in the generic malaise that followed the revolutionary moment of the 1960s. The end of the cultural revolution and American involvement in Vietnam, the post-Watergate loss of confidence in government, liberalized attitudes toward sex and the general acceptance of divorce, together with a declining economy, made Americans feel that their star was descending. The crisis for Catholicism was multifaceted with its manifestations seen in varied opinions on Church authority, faith, leadership, and identity. Many wondered to what degree the postconciliar Church would be able to bridge these divisions and place Catholicism on the road to wholeness. One commentator wrote about the situation, "Beyond question . . . in the United States at the present time, transcendent religious belief finds itself engaged in a direct contestation with a secularistic, humanistic worldview, which rejects supernatural religion and absolute moral values."[1]

Reasons for the malaise and proposed solutions were proffered by leading Catholic voices in various fields. People in general experienced a loss of Catholic identity when it was perceived that the American environment was influencing Catholicism much more than the faith was swaying national trends.[2] Most commentators saw the problem as a reaction to the transformation effected by Vatican II and the consequent need for American Catholics to abruptly face modernity, but some believed the crisis would have occurred, with or without the teachings of the council. The Jesuit sociologist of religion John Coleman believed that soon after John F. Kennedy's election signaled American Catholicism's escape from the ghetto and from its apologetic as a persecuted minority, there was a sudden short burst of the new Catholic presence with people such as Eugene McCarthy, James Groppi, the Berrigan brothers, and Sargent Shriver making headlines, but the rising star was soon eclipsed. Coleman wrote,

> Soon, however, this ever so brief Catholic renaissance exhausted its shallow roots as disillusionment, institutional setbacks measured in terms of the falling rate of Mass attendance, declining numbers of pupils in parochial schools, a drastic drop in vocations to the priesthood and religious life and a sapping of communal identity became the indices of the import of *aggiornamento* on Americanization.

As a solution Coleman recommended implementing the social teachings of the Church from a more pluralistic and ecumenical viewpoint.[3] The crisis brought many opportunities for new ideas, but the possibility of failure, brought about through a gradual erosion of institutional relevance and personal commitment, was very real.[4]

The dean of American Catholic historians, John Tracy Ellis, identified a host of mostly external factors that had contributed to the crisis. His list included secular humanism, as exemplified in the mass media, the rise of individualism, the breakdown in church and state authority, a resurgence of hedonism, and a craving for change embodied in the national frenzy to always be "with it." Ellis, echoing his famous 1955 call for Catholic intellectuals to assert themselves, commented, "But if all the complex congeries of causes could be objectively weighed and measured, it would be found, I believe, that the environment and atmosphere of mundane pursuits and goals would have played as influential a role as any other." For Ellis Catholics had simply allowed Richard Neuhaus's "Catholic Moment"[5] to slip through their hands.[6]

American Catholicism's intellectual vacuum of the pre–Vatican II period was matched by a dramatic shift in Catholic spirituality and popular piety in the wake of Vatican II. Rather than publishing a separate document on Mary, the Council Fathers placed their teaching on the Mother of God in the last chapter of *Lumen Gentium,* which emphasized her role as Mother of the Church. Immediately after the council, devotion to Mary went in two opposing directions. Many "progressive" Catholics, as noted by the priest-sociologist Andrew Greeley, dropped all devotion to Mary. But the years after the council also gave rise to several very conservative and even radical Marian groups. Both *Fatima Crusader,* edited by Father Nicholas Gruner, and *Immaculate Heart Messenger,* edited by Father Robert J. Fox, were vehement in their anti-Communism and cynical in their worldview.[7]

Although Peyton seriously attempted to reformat the Crusades in response to Vatican II, his devotion to the rosary and Mary was immutable. He realized that with the ascendancy of social activism in the Church, personal devotions such as the rosary would almost surely be on the wane, but he was confident that the rosary would someday become popular again. He explained, "It is exactly that, an eclipse. The Rosary is like the moon. When the eclipse is over it will be all the brighter." The eclipse did not stop Peyton from proclaiming the rosary's efficacy for his life: "The Rosary has been my secret. It has been my life, my security, my spirituality. It has been the motor which has driven me. It has given me everything a man could want."[8] He gave lip service to a more open attitude toward alternative forms of prayer, but he obviously found the rosary the most efficacious prayer of all, particularly for families.[9]

I have always said that the Rosary is the prayer FRC must strive to have families pray. For me the Rosary makes the difference. We cannot say our work is done when we have won a family to pray spontaneous prayers, grace before and after meals, shared prayer,

[or] readings from Scripture. We must never stop having and setting our sights upon educating, motivating and inspiring a family to reach the heights — to make the traditional Rosary their family and favorite prayer. . . . It goes without saying then that we must advocate Family Prayer — but cannot stop there. We must do all in our power to lead the family to pray the Rosary.[10]

Family Theater in the 1970s

The dawn of a new decade brought new possibilities and hope to Family Theater, but it was clear to all that success was possible only with renewed efforts to reverse the lackluster performance of the Hollywood office in recent years. The radio programs that brought prominence to Family Theater officially ended in 1968 when the rise of film and television made successful radio programming almost obsolete. Raymond Cassel, CSC, who believed that Peyton had not redirected his ministry boldly enough, recommended that Family Theater's efforts be shifted to film projects. He commented on the rosary priest's recent efforts in Hollywood, "If it doesn't talk the language of film to 1971 America it shouldn't be promoted." He suggested that Peyton was overemphasizing fundraising and ignoring new projects:

> The fearless leader is now mounted rearward on his horse while yelling "charge." The dough is in the rear, but God's power is in the front. The God of his youth somehow got him the dough when he was a young man chasing spiritual objectives mounted on his horse frontward. Now that his obsession is going directly after the dough somehow the spiritual dimension eludes him. He's fumbling for the way, and won't listen to anyone who might show him the way. He might well end up ten years from now with 10 million bucks which he will use partly to store 1,000 prints each of "The Psalms," "The Rosary Mysteries," "The Kiss of Judas," mounted on gold reels.[11]

Peyton acknowledged that the productive juices of Family Theater had not flowed well in recent years, but as usual he attributed the problem to personnel. John Gurley, CSC, who had joined the Crusade during the post–Vatican II Latin American crusades, cautioned Peyton that any sweeping changes in personnel would be problematic and suggested privately that the rosary priest's personal control might be more the culprit.[12] Nonetheless, Peyton's will prevailed, and in 1972, Mary

Buckley, RSM, whom Peyton first met in 1942 when he arrived in Albany, was made manager of Family Theater, in an effort to make the operation financially self-sufficient.[13] Raymond Cassel, CSC, who began to work in Hollywood in 1965, was assigned in 1968 to a new operation, "Family Theater East" at Manhasset, and put in charge of dubbing and distributing the films.

Despite frequent conflicts between personnel at Family Theater, the Hollywood office did generate some new programs as the 1970s progressed. In January 1971 a new series of one-minute radio spots was broadcast over the Mutual network, stressing the value and need for family prayer embodied in the popular slogan, "The world hasn't got a prayer...without yours." After their debut on Mutual the spots were carried on independent stations and broadcast overseas in local translations.[14] In addition to these spots, seven new fifteen-minute programs featured members of the hierarchy describing their understanding and relationship with the Virgin Mary.[15] The fifteen mysteries of the rosary, which had been edited earlier in the two films, *The Eternal King* and *The Redeemer,* were once again repackaged into three ninety-minute films, *The Savior* (Joyful Mysteries), *The Redeemer* (Sorrowful Mysteries), and *The Master* (Glorious Mysteries). The advent of international television live broadcasts, made possible through the use of satellites, created a new market for Family Theater. Pope Paul VI's Christmas Midnight Mass, sponsored by Family Theater, was broadcast live from St. Peter's in Rome in 1972. The ninety-minute special, aired on 131 stations in the United States, brought a new degree of national exposure to Peyton's mission. Similar broadcasts, funded by the DeRance Foundation and other smaller benefactors, were held at Easter and Christmas in 1973, each concluding with a personal message by Peyton.[16]

The most significant new project for Family Theater during this decade was the *A Matter of Faith* series. The inability of Peyton to bring to fruition his 1966 idea for a spectacular Christmas program, especially after such extensive planning, was a great disappointment to him, but out of the ashes of failure arose a new idea to bring to television the ideas on faith and prayer of one hundred of the world's most influential people in all areas of society — politics, business, religion, etc. In 1968 Peyton visualized a ninety-minute one-time documentary of clips of interviews with these giants of world society that would be a testimony to the faith present in contemporary society. By late 1969 the basic idea was complete and arrangements had been made for Family Theater to produce the program in partnership with Metromedia Producer's Corporation.[17] Suggestions for titles included *This I Believe* and *I Believe in God,* but *A Matter of*

Faith was ultimately chosen. The program was "designed to recapture and refocus the spotlight on eternal values that once held it [the world] exclusively, and in so doing to reassure many that they are indeed on the right track if they believe in God, prayer and the corollaries to these."[18]

Peyton's idea gained support within Family Theater with plans, therefore, moving forward, but it was felt after some time that the originally planned ninety-minute format would not adequately allow presenters to articulate their ideas nor viewers to comprehend their message. Thus, the format of the program was shifted to a series of half-hour interviews that would be aired weekly in a special series. Besides the perennial questions of funding and a medium for broadcast, this series also required that a system be created to choose those to be interviewed for the program. Peyton asked elite American personalities, including Mr. and Mrs. Bing Crosby, Father Theodore Hesburgh, CSC, the Apollo astronaut Colonel Frank Borman, and Hubert Humphrey, to serve as a committee to select the one hundred people to be interviewed for the series.[19] A list of two hundred candidates generated by Peyton and his associates was provided to the committee which selected one hundred from which those to be interviewed would be chosen.

The *A Matter of Faith* series was broadcast initially over the CHEX Television Network of Canada from April 29 to July 22, 1973. Thirty-nine shows were planned schematically and twenty interviews were filmed, but the broadcast series featured only eleven interviews, one per show, sandwiched between an initial program that introduced the series with clips of future programs, and a concluding show that chronicled the life and accomplishments of Father Peyton. The Mother's Day show, broadcast on May 13, was by far the most publicized, and featured Fulton J. Sheen, long retired from the popular *Life Is Worth Living* television series but still a formidable influence among American Catholics, by virtue of his best-selling books.[20]

The success of *A Matter of Faith* was advanced through an extensive billboard advertising program directed by Albert Heinzer, CSC. Through the generosity of the advertising firm of Foster and Kleiser, Family Theater's famous slogan, "The family that prays together stays together," first appeared, in 1947, on a few billboards in Hollywood, including the busy thoroughfare Wilshire Blvd. The first major advertising program was launched in 1960 with four thousand smaller posters distributed nationwide. Similar programs were conducted in 1963 and 1965.[21] Beginning in 1972, Heinzer, under Peyton's direction, worked with Frank Cawl, president of the Outdoor Advertising Association of America, Inc., on a nationwide billboard slogan campaign promoting family prayer. Cawl wrote to numerous outdoor advertising firms seeking their assistance in a new program, to begin on Ash Wednesday, February 16, 1972, and featuring varied slogans under the headline "The family that prays together stays together." The purpose of the program was "to keep before the traveling public the importance of wholesome family life as part of our American heritage."[22]

The renewed billboard campaign was launched as scheduled in February 1972. Consistent with the Association's previous "Religion in American Life" program, space was donated while posters were obtained at a reduced fee. A poster designed by Dailey and Associates was printed gratis the first year by Kubin-Nicholson of Milwaukee, "because of their belief in [the] work." During that year, billboards advertising Family Theater's message were erected in 215 cities in 42 states, plus Ontario, Canada. The next year 220 advertising companies erected 2,830 posters with the slogan, "Pray Together. You'll Stay Together."[23]

In 1976 a more ambitious three-year billboard project was launched, a short slogan to be followed by the Family Theater trademark phrase. The lead-in expressions were, in consecutive order: "God Makes House-calls," "God Listens," and "God Answers." During the first year of this campaign almost 3,000 posters were erected in 177 cities in 38 states. Space continued to be donated, and Kubin-Nicholson printed the posters at a reduced cost. Peyton applied to various foundations for funding, but he also continued to rely upon Peter Grace, who could be counted on to provide funds when other sources had been exhausted.[24] Advertisers were generally more than happy to provide free space. A typical response was sent by the Lubbock (Texas) Poster Company: "The poster is lovely and just the type of message we like to display whenever space is available for donation."[25]

The billboard campaign was so successful that it was renewed for a second three-year period, beginning in October 1978. At the same time promotional kits containing a series of ten-second spots were sent to 342 television stations. A survey conducted later showed that 69 stations in 22 states, ranging from Baltimore in the East to Orlando in the South and St. Louis in the Midwest, used the advertisement. A similar promotional mailing was conducted in 1979, but the survey afterward revealed that only 34 responding stations had used the spots.[26]

Family Rosary in the 1970s

The nature of the Crusade for Family Prayer and the history of its evolution had generated over time a specialized ministry that from the outset was closely allied with the personality of Peyton. This basic fact, manifest most visibly through his need for control and his inability to adapt, made progress in creative directions more difficult in an American Catholic environment that was already, as outlined previously, in a state of crisis. Those who worked closely with Peyton commented that his penchant for control never wavered over the years. Some voiced the opinion that his need for personal involvement in every aspect of the work and his overriding influence in every decision became detrimental to the ministry's ability to move forward and find new areas for growth. His Holy Cross co-worker Raymond Cassel, CSC, expressed his frustration: "Peyton is still holding every single facet of this [ministry] firmly in the palm of his hand to the point where he can squeeze it away in an instant. That's why everything is so screwed up and would be even if governed by intelligence rather than emotion."[27]

The other significant area that held back progress, in the minds of many associates, was Peyton's inability to adapt adequately to the post–Vatican II Church. It is clearly evident, as seen in the process used to refocus and recast the Crusade in the wake of Vatican II, that Peyton made significant outward efforts to change with the time. Additionally, his attempts to place more pastoral emphasis on evangelization and the need for significant catechesis and ecumenical efforts attest to his desire for change. Yet, as the failure of the Milwaukee crusade of 1968 demonstrated, one could legitimately ask whether his efforts to update were efficacious in any significant way. Could others relate to the changes that were effected? Peyton's efforts to transform the external aspects of his work were apparent, but it is equally evident that internal change was extremely difficult for him. His efforts to change the Crusade were not transferred into his heart. Father Frank Fahey, an Irish secular priest who worked with Peyton for a short period in the early 1970s, accurately expressed what many believed and experienced concerning Peyton: "I suppose he couldn't be but himself and when he'd go to speak himself, no matter what changes we made, he would come out with the same thing: the rosary, the rosary, and so he went into that groove. He would try and change, but he couldn't."[28] Despite his more staid understanding of the Church, Peyton never lost the admiration of those who walked the road with him. This is certainly true for Peter Grace who called Peyton "our good friend and apostle" and "the most productive and holy priest I have ever known."[29]

In addition to the problematic aspects of Peyton's personality, the crusade continued to suffer from financial insecurity, which Peyton sought to remedy by obtaining a permanent endowment. In 1969 the actor Jack

Haley, one of the first Hollywood personalities to pledge his assistance to Peyton in the 1940s, suggested that fifty individuals, groups, or institutions, one for each Hail Mary in the rosary, each pledge $100,000 to raise a perpetual endowment of $5,000,000. This sum, to be known as "The All for Her Fund," would generate interest to fund daily operation of the Crusade; the basic $5 million was never to be touched.[30] Peyton explained the nature and symbolism of the Fund:

> The fifty founders have a symbolic meaning for me. They represent the fifty Hail Marys of the Rosary. The fifty will constitute a living and unique Rosary that will guarantee the perpetuation of the Family Rosary Crusade and its affiliates, the Family Theater and the Crusade for Family Prayer — all dedicated to the family and its unity through prayer and [the] Family Rosary.[31]

The All for Her Fund was established, but obtaining not only pledges but actual contributions was much more difficult than the project's initiation. As per usual Peyton went not only to his wealthy friends but to those whom he knew from previous experience had influence upon others. Among others he contacted Walter Donnelly, who had been so helpful during the South American crusades of the 1960s, and asked him to assist in securing people for membership in the fund. Other key supporters with connections to the past included Antonio Oriol, the Spanish government official who had assisted during the production of the rosary films, and Peter Grace, who pledged $100,000. Oriol agreed to sponsor five Hail Marys, although he was not sure he could generate the funds to meet his pledge. Cardinal Rufino Santos of the Philippines pledged three Hail Marys. As with the financing of the rosary films some religious communities were willing to assist by pledging one Hail Mary.[32] Fundraisers were organized by Archbishop Joseph T. McGucken of San Francisco and the Lewis Foundation.[33] Peyton also approached his own order for funding, but his request was not brought to the floor of the General Chapter of 1980,[34] an omission that Peyton took quite personally, exacerbating the tension between him and some members of the order.

A finance committee to oversee the operation of the Fund, chaired by Peter Grace, was established in 1978. Even with the committee, contributions from those who pledged continued to be received slowly, with some who pledged never contributing anything. Peyton's report, which stated that by 1980 only forty committed individuals or groups had pledged

to give $100,000, was indicative of the difficulty he had in securing the
$5 million endowment he desired.[35] After ten years of contributions and
interest the fund stood at close to $2.5 million.[36]

At least partly motivated by the Crusade's financial problems, Peyton turned to Latin America, where the Crusade had always thrived,
and outlined a new vision for that region. In addition to the staffing
problems caused by Peyton's age and Joseph Quinn's departure, Peyton
identified three challenges that the Latin American crusade would have
to address: the need to make the Crusade permanent, to organize lay
leaders who would implement the Crusade's social action mission, and
to train local leaders who would extend the Crusade's range into new
territories. To meet these challenges, Peyton recommended an ongoing
catechesis program based on the rosary films, the mass media, and visits
to homes, schools, hospitals, and prisons, and expansion of social action programs such as Young Christian Workers (YCW), Catholic Youth
Organization (CYO), St. Vincent de Paul, Pax Romana, Legion of Mary,
and the Knights of Columbus.[37]

In the past Peyton had often referred to the concept of the mechanical priest, a mobile unit consisting of a jeep or similar vehicle loaded
with all the equipment needed to show the rosary films. Similar units
had been effectively used in the 1960s in South America. Now Peyton
saw the mechanical priest as the method par excellence for Latin America, especially considering the dwindling pool of Holy Cross religious
actively engaged in crusade work. The German hierarchy provided a
grant of $85,000 through its Adveniat Foundation to be used in the de-
velopment of the popular mission, using the mechanical priest, in Latin
America.[38]

Buoyed by the prospects of future good fortune and now with financial security, Peyton was ready to return to South America, beginning
in Argentina in 1974. This visit was long overdue, since Peyton had
gone to Argentina in 1951, in response to an invitation to conduct a
crusade and oversee a shrine to Our Lady of Fatima. The project had
never materialized, but in 1972 Archbishop Adolfo Tortolo of Paraná
renewed his invitation to bring the crusade to his archdiocese, and possibly to the rest of the country. This time Peyton refused the invitation
because of commitments extending into 1974. John Gurley responded
that the crusade was "disposed to collaborate with you in whatever way
possible to make this a reality," but concluded that present commitments did not allow the possibility of a crusade in the area until at least
1974.[39]

Peyton promptly began preparing for the crusade. Two local priests, Luis Pedro de Fornari and Enrique Imperiale, attended a six-month training course so they could operate and supervise the crusade. Luis Armijos, OP, who was working with the crusades in Mexico, traveled to Argentina in August 1973 to assist the two local clerics and plan a national crusade.

The crusades in Argentina began in July 1974 and continued on a semi-continuous basis until December 1982, reaching nineteen dioceses and attracting over 5 million people to the rallies. Beginning in the Diocese of San Martín, the crusade moved to Paraná in September 1974, Buenos Aires between April and December 1976, Santa Fe between April and July 1977, Tucumán between April and December 1981, and ended in Morón in an extended campaign between March and December 1982. Father Peyton spoke in Paraná in December 1974, but health problems and other commitments made additional appearances impossible.[40] Even so, the Crusade was well received, indicating there was more to the ministry than simply the charism of Patrick Peyton. Juan Rodolfo Laise, bishop of San Luis, Argentina, lauded Peyton and his work: "Its [the crusade's] fruits have been outstanding and self-evident; and we are sure the Lord will reward you for all the benefit that the *películas* [films] of the Rosary have done for the souls."[41]

Like Argentina, Bolivia had previously caught the attention of Peyton, but the Crusade had never been conducted there. Peyton's original plan called for the pilot program for the popular mission to be conducted in Bolivia, but when Peter Grace arranged for U.S. government financing of the Latin American operation, plans changed and the pilot mission was conducted in La Serena, Chile. In August 1974 the Bolivian bishops invited Peyton to conduct a crusade, beginning in May 1975, as part of the national celebration of 150 years of independence. The need to train local clergy to operate and oversee the crusade, the need for additional personnel, plus significant delays in the procurement of equipment and the dubbing of films into the local Indian dialects of Quechua and Aymara resulted in the Crusade being initiated in La Paz, the national capital, only in March 1979. Luis Armijos, OP, worked with local clergy to conduct the Crusade,[42] which ran from March 25 to May 6, 1979, with a grand rally held on April 15. The Crusade then moved to the archdioceses of Santa Fe in October 1979 and Sucre in January 1980, and the diocese of Tarija in December 1979.[43]

Mexico, the site of a series of Crusades between 1970 and 1974 that utilized local people under the leadership of John Gurley, CSC, Luis Armijos, OP, and Reinaldo Pol, again hosted the Crusade when it returned in 1981. Popular missions were conducted in the Dioceses of

San Luis Potosí between March and July 1981 and Querétaro between July and December 1981.[44] As with his previous visit, rallies were well attended in both regions, marking another success in Latin America.

The return of the Crusade to Latin America was only one of two major examples of *déjà vu* experienced by the Crusade for Family Prayer in the 1970s. The extensive discussions and plans generated for the possible reorganization of the Crusade for Family Prayer and its connection with the Congregation of Holy Cross worldwide in the 1960s were renewed in the ensuing decade. The rationale for the Crusade for Family Prayer, articulated in its 1954 incorporation document, namely, to promote "a program of prayer, particularly family prayer, in order to develop the mental, moral, and spiritual well-being of all peoples and in conjunction therewith to educate, restore, and preserve the individual family as the basic unit and true foundation of society," never wavered, but the organization's ability to achieve this goal also seemed elusive.[45] In 1971 three separate corporations — Crusade for Family Prayer, Family Rosary, Inc., and Family Theater — existed with officers common to all three. In 1975 the provincial of the Eastern Province of Priests, William Ribando, CSC, called for a more formal organization, partly because he wanted the province to be fiscally protected from any financial liability incurred by Family Rosary or Family Theater.[46] One year later he offered a proposal making the Crusade for Family Prayer the parent corporation, with Family Rosary and Family Theater as subsidiaries. The Crusade's corporate board would be elected through a process approved in the by-laws, with Peyton and the standing provincial as *ex officio* members. Family Theater and Family Rosary were to have their own boards of directors, chosen by the corporate board.[47] When nothing was done with the proposal, the provincial in May 1977 appointed a committee to study the Crusade's organization and recommend structural changes, but this effort also bore no fruit.[48]

The previous effort to place the Crusade under the jurisdiction of the superior general, championed by Richard Sullivan, CSC, was renewed by friends and associates of Peter Grace in 1980. Charles Miller and Thomas Doyle in a communique with the superior general, Thomas Barrosse, CSC, argued that it was now necessary to place Peyton's ministry under the General Administration. The perennial problem of autonomy of the Crusade would be solved as it would stand alone. Additionally, it was stated, referencing Ribando's concern that any financial burdens of the Crusade not ill effect the province, that such an independent structure would relieve the provincial of such economic worries. This proposal, however, like all others in the area of reorganization, fell on deaf ears with no action being taken.[49]

A Film Gamble Goes Awry—The Messiah

In July 1973 Father Peyton, Peter Grace, and Al Scalpone, who had been affiliated with the Family Theater office since its first radio days, began to discuss the possibility of sponsoring a major motion picture on the life of Christ. The failures of *The Eternal King* and *The Redeemer* to achieve wide public recognition and appeal had always been a great disappointment to Peyton, who wanted to produce a significant film on Christ, as one aspect of his career still unfinished. The three men agreed that the project must go forward and Peyton should use his Hollywood contacts to secure a first-class director and support staff for the film. Thus, he elicited the advice of the actor and director Gene Kelly and director Michael Frankovich who suggested Francis Ford Coppola, Fred Zinnemann, David Lean, Sir Carol Reed, and Robert Wise as possible directors. Arthur Miller and Tennessee Williams were suggested as prospective screenwriters.[50]

The advice received and names proffered for the prospective film seemed of little significance in the fall of 1973 when Peyton met the famous Italian director Roberto Rossellini on a trip to Athens.[51] When Peyton described his plans for the film, to be titled *The Messiah*, Rossellini quickly agreed to direct it and head the production team. Peyton explained his motivation: "I had to have a superb motion picture made on the life of Christ and his mission. I was determined it would happen; I was driven to it. I had a list of five filmmakers, but when I met Rossellini I threw the list away."[52]

Rossellini submitted an eighteen-page summary to Peyton describing his ideas for the film. He originally envisioned a two-part film, each half two to three hours in length. Part 1 would cover the Old Testament story from the covenant with Yahweh to the coming of Christ. Part 2 would encompass Christ's life. Although the plan was pared down to one two-to-two-and-a-half-hour feature, both Peter Grace and Al Scalpone were wary of Rossellini and advised Peyton to go with another director after reviewing Rossellini's work. Dennis Roverato, director of the film department, also recommended the director be dropped, suggesting fellow Italian Franco Zeffirelli in his place.[53] Peyton, however, commented, "I did not take their advice. I felt that Rossellini was the man I was looking for. I decided that I would fly blindly with him." Gene Kelly concurred with the decision, praising Rossellini as "head and shoulders above the Hollywood film-makers."[54]

Peyton's motivation in making the film went far beyond his desire to erase the memories of past failures. Initially he articulated a threefold purpose: (1) to serve as a method of catechesis for the masses, (2) to spread the Gospel message, and more practically (3) to produce revenue for the Crusade.[55] Peyton believed that religious ignorance of the day could best be erased by enlisting the media on the side of Christ. He commented, "Lack of knowledge of Christ in today's secularized and de-Christianized world prevents there being an option to choose His teaching instead of following the persuasively presented isms and ologies of our permissive society. To make this knowledge available to the widest possible audience we must avail ourselves of the means provided by the scientific and technological developments which characterize our time."[56]

Peyton further hoped that the film would make Christ understandable, "regardless of a person's religion."[57] He expressed his dream to Rossellini, "My prayers are ever beseeching our Blessed Mother that 'The Messiah' will be all that you and I are hoping for.... Within me are excitement, enthusiasm and a sureness that 'The Messiah' will be a source of hope and uplift for all men everywhere."[58]

Peyton's original plan was for Family Theater to have overall responsibility for the film, with Rossellini producing and directing, but when the Italian filmmaker suggested that his planned feature would cost $4 million Rossellini and Peyton struck a deal to supply $2 million each. Peyton's half entitled him to distribution rights in the Western hemisphere and all other nations where English was the national language; Rossellini's money gave him distribution rights in all other lands. On May 11, 1974, a letter of intent was signed and on July 2 a formal distribution agreement finalized. Peyton reported, however, that "no part of the $2,000,000 shall be paid until the motion picture is completed and delivered in form ready for distribution." The contract stipulated that an English version would be delivered to Family Theater by December 8, 1975.[59] Peyton was pleased with the agreement, believing that the film would become "a monument for insuring the permanence of his work."[60]

In order to raise his $2 million Peyton immediately approached Harry John of the DeRance Foundation, which had supported many of Peyton's former endeavors, beginning with the special theater at the Brussels World's Fair of 1958. Peyton asked for a $1.5 million loan, but several reservations to the funding were raised from the outset. First, concern was raised over the lack of control in the production of the film, with Family Theater forced to accept what Rossellini would create. Fear was also present about committing to a film that had not already been made. Lastly, John was skeptical that Rossellini could make the picture he claimed for only $4 million when a similar production in the United States would cost in the range of $25 million. John Miller, attorney for Harry John, summarized DeRance's concern: "We know of no way that DeRance, Inc. can make a realistic appraisal of the investment aspects of this transaction prior to the actual payment of funds."[61] Despite the reservations DeRance agreed to provide the funds for the film.[62]

Peyton next went after the additional $500,000 for the film, writing to a list of wealthy individuals provided by Peter Grace, and writing to groups including the Hearst, Lewis, Ahmanson, and Raskob Foundations and to the Lilly Endowment. Peyton also solicited the financial backing of the American and Canadian bishops, American pastors, major superiors of religious congregations, and Catholic fraternal orders, but the response from these groups, as well as from individuals and foundations, was lackluster.[63] Thus, pressured by Rossellini to guarantee his half of the money, Peyton made up the difference from Crusade funds as well as a $150,000 contribution from Peter Grace's daughter Mary.[64]

Once he had secured the funds Peyton began negotiating for *The Messiah*'s distribution. Even before the financial package had been finalized Peyton had been queried about distribution rights in the Far East. In September 1974 the Canadian Broadcasting Corporation contacted the rosary priest for distribution rights in Canada, but he responded that Family Theater was negotiating a worldwide distribution program. Peyton himself contacted several major film companies, including Warner Brothers, Twentieth Century Fox, Allied Artists, Walt Disney, Columbia, and Paramount, but no formal distribution agreement was made.[65] Peyton was told that he needed to obtain sound advice from his Hollywood contacts and make a decision on distribution.[66]

Production of *The Messiah* took place in 1975, but not before Peyton was forced to undergo a period of supervised rest after suffering complete exhaustion. Peyton's efforts to push the film, which he claimed would be the crowning achievement of his thirty-three years of ministry, coupled with advancing age and other activities landed him in the Sacred Heart Clinic in Rome when he arrived in December 1974, fresh from the Paraná, Argentina, crusade rally. Doctors ordered three months complete rest to control the effects of his exhaustion, as well as complications from his diabetic condition.[67] The episode was a wake-up call for Peyton and a precursor of what lay down the road. One of the nuns attending him reported, "He is only 66 years old but is an OLD 66. He has driven himself mercilessly all these years and it has taken its toll physically and this unexpected 'marking time' of the past three months has given his body time to tell him a few things!"[68]

Returning to work after his hospital stay, Peyton went to Tunisia where *The Messiah* was filmed, using a cast of unknowns and a script that was suspect from the outset. In order to assure orthodoxy in both acting and dialogue Peyton arranged for Father Carlo Martini, president of the Pontifical Biblical Institute, and Fathers Stanislaus Lyonnet and Jean Gallot of the Gregorian University in Rome as advisors.[69] Peyton felt obligated to stay at the site of production, not only to satisfy his perennial need for some control, but to assure that enthusiasm for the project be maintained as Peyton found Rossellini's moodiness problematic in setting the tone for the film. He commented,

> I have seen him [Rossellini] at times, since my arrival[,] under tension. *Now,* I am sure, more than ever of my need to be near him all through the filming of "The Messiah." I have seen him also exhibit an enthusiasm for the film that is extraordinary. You can understand, therefore, why I must keep that enthusiasm alive at any sacrifice.[70]

The script was written by an Italian screenwriter, Silvia d'Amico, but this was not an area of great concern to the director, who felt confined by a prepared script. Failure on the part of Peyton and Family Theater to insist upon a preapproved script proved problematic.[71]

Filming concluded in September 1975, with dubbing into Italian and French completed almost immediately thereafter. Peyton praised the film as "a diamond mine," regretting his doubts about Rossellini, but his remorse turned out to be premature.[72] In the first week of November the film was shown to one hundred Italian bishops and superiors general of religious communities. Peyton, who attended with his superior general, Thomas Barrosse, CSC, was impressed, calling it "so very moving — so very simple — so very true," but he had been unable to understand the Italian dialogue and thus made his comments without full knowledge.[73] Following this preliminary showing Rossellini informed Peyton that he was out of money and, therefore, the promised English version could not be made without Peyton's funds. Against the advice of his associates and attorneys Peyton on November 21, 1975, signed a contract with Orizzonte 2000, Rossellini's production company, agreeing to turn over the $2 million, less $150,000 held back for the production of the English version. Thus, without a film in hand, Peyton delivered his only bargaining chip to assure compliance with the original agreement, namely. an English version film delivered on or before December 8. The monies were released to Orizzonte on December 24.[74]

The first public screening of *The Messiah* was held at Trinity Church in Paris on February 18, 1976. Reactions to the film were mixed, but the praise was muted. *Variety* commented, "It is an inspiring work, a film by a religious man, and at times visually stunning as well as shocking." Another reviewer wrote, "The scenes are very good and the action smooth. I believe we have a good product, and no reason to think otherwise."[75] French reviewers were not impressed. *Le Monde* commented, "The whole idea of God is missing. The leading character seems to have no center of gravity." The article criticized the film's dialogue: "There is a river of words with no relation to what is going on. It is like some interminable commentary to which finally nobody listens." While the *Herald Tribune* labeled the film "a singularly uninspired experiment," the harshest comment came after the film's performance at the Tehran Film Festival:[76]

> Roberto Rossellini's "The Messiah" is, in this reviewer's opinion, the greatest disappointment of the entire festival. An unbelievably amateurish retelling of the story of Christ, one can hardly believe that it carries the imprimatur of the once-inspired Rossellini. The casting is atrocious. The title role is played (?) by a young man without an ounce of acting talent — just another pretty face of the type one sees any night by the score on the Via Veneto. All of his dialogue consists of quotes straight out of the Bible and he rattles them off like a grocery list. The young lady playing his mother looks and acts about 14 years old at the time Jesus is born — which is fair enough — but she still looks and acts about 14 years old when he dies 33 years later — which is carrying immortality a bit far. Her face registers all of the emotion on Mt. Rushmore. Rossellini must have phoned this one in — over a bad connection.[77]

The negative reviews were the beginning of an avalanche of problems with the film that would plague Father Peyton for some time. It was discovered that Rossellini had not obtained the promised $1.5 million from the Italian government for the film's production, forcing the director to take cost-cutting measures, one of which was shooting much of the film in silence. Dialogue was later added, but the ability to dub in English became highly problematic. Additionally, Rossellini's total control of production allowed Peyton no voice on script or translation. Other

significant areas of concern about the film were: (1) characters uniden-
tified, (2) scene sequences not bridged, (3) few if any close-ups, (4) an
almost nonexistent musical score, and (5) sound effects so poor they
would have to be redone.[78] Peyton and his associates wondered with all
the apparent cost-cutting measures where the monies expended on the
project had gone and, thus, desired an audit to be done, but this request
infuriated Rossellini, who staunchly refused to cooperate.[79] Rossellini's
failure to meet his contractual agreement to deliver an English version
of the film seemingly did not bother the veteran director.

Peyton's most significant problem and gravest concern was the production of an English version of the film. He worried greatly that unless
an English version was made soon the reputation of the Crusade for
Family Prayer would be damaged. This overriding fear precipitated his
decision to go against the advice of his associates and release his procured
monies to Orizzonte before the English version was received, as promised
in the original agreement. However, Orizzonte was to deliver all that was
necessary for the English version to be made by Family Theater, but the
company failed on this agreement as well. Peyton's problems mounted
when the DeRance Foundation, irritated that nothing had been received
for the monies given to Orizzonte, demanded that Peyton pay interest
on the money, starting from the date he released the funds in late December 1975 and continuing until an English version was delivered. Still
confident that the English version would be produced, Peyton agreed.
This was a great risk since his Hollywood technical advisors said that
the film was so flawed that it could never be commercially viable without major alterations. To make matters worse, under the terms of the
contract modifications could be made only with the express consent of
Rossellini, who would not cooperate.[80]

With *The Messiah* embroiled in controversy and no easy and swift solution forthcoming Peyton was forced to write his financial supporters
to explain the situation and articulate his reservations with the film.
He directed his secretary, Patricia Spanbauer, to place the following
explanation in a generic letter to be sent to all on the donor list:

> I am disappointed in the picture as it now stands. It must be
> changed. Presently we are negotiating, through legal counsel, with
> the production company and the laboratory in Rome to obtain the
> rights necessary to make the required changes. And, as you know,
> all legal procedures seem to take forever. This is why no release
> date for "The Messiah" has yet been determined.[81]

Peyton articulated his reservations more specifically to another religious: "I am far from satisfied with the film in its present state. It leaves much to be desired. It is my determination that the English version of 'The Messiah' will highlight, above all, the divinity of Christ and clearly portray His mission and message."[82]

Peyton and Family Theater personnel met with Peter Grace and his associates to try to salvage the film before all was lost. They agreed Orizzonte had broken the original contract, and thus monies lost and products not delivered were Rossellini's responsibility. The group concluded that Orizzonte should be sued for (1) delay in delivering a distributable film, (2) contract violations, and (3) placing the work of the Crusade in jeopardy. Additionally, the group suggested that Family Theater must be given complete freedom to remake the film as necessary.[83] Before legal action was taken, John Gurley, CSC, was sent to Rome in March 1976 to meet with Rossellini and officials from Orizzonte to see if the impasse could be negotiated, but both sides were unbending.[84]

Rossellini suddenly went on the offensive and initiated his own legal action to keep Peyton from modifying the film. On April 16, 1976, a Roman magistrate ordered both Orizzonte 2000 and Family Theater "to bring no changes to the cinematographic work, 'The Messiah' ... without the previous consent of Roberto Rossellini." Nevertheless, Rossellini brought Family Theater to trial in January 1977, accusing Peyton's organization of tampering with *The Messiah* without permission. The case was protracted and was eventually settled out of court in November.[85]

The Cross of Ill Health

Despite the pain and disappointment with the failure of *The Messiah* Peyton continued to be recognized for his accomplishments. Pope Paul VI continued to support the rosary as an efficacious method of family prayer. In 1974 in *Marialiis Cultus* he wrote, "But there is no doubt that, after the celebration of the Liturgy of the Hours, the high point which family prayer can reach, the Rosary should be considered as one of the best and most efficacious prayers in common that the Christian family is invited to recite." One year later in *Evangelii Nuntiandi* the pope echoed Peyton's policy of utilizing mass media as an agent of evangelization: "Mass media put at the service of the Gospel is capable of increasing almost indefinitely the power in which the word of God is heard. The Church will feel guilty before the Lord if she does not utilize these powerful means." Peyton also celebrated the Crusade for Family Prayer's thirtieth anniversary with a Mass and gala banquet, and its thirty-fifth with the publication of a booklet highlighting special crusade events. In 1979 he received the Pro Piis Meritis cross for his dedicated service to the Church from the Knights of Malta.[86]

The 1970s was the decade when the whirlwind pace of operation kept by Peyton and the advance of years manifested themselves in serious illness. In 1969 Peyton had been diagnosed with diabetes and ordered to lose significant weight and to eat better. As described previously complications from the diabetes and his hectic pace landed him in the hospital for three months at the outset of 1975. One year later, while attending the forty-first International Eucharistic Congress, held in Philadelphia as part of the nation's bicentennial celebration,[87] Peyton suffered a heart attack, although he did not realize it at the time. He addressed the delegates despite feeling poorly and later went to Denver for another engagement before he saw a physician and the condition was diagnosed.[88] Peyton was ordered to cease all activity for six months, a cross that he attempted to bear more gracefully by interpreting it as a rest imposed by the Blessed Virgin.[89]

Peyton's heart condition continued to be problematic, necessitating a quadruple bypass operation in May 1978. The surgery was performed at Good Samaritan Hospital in Los Angeles, allowing him to convalesce at the Little Sisters of the Poor in San Pedro, thus initiating a relationship that would last until his death. Peyton's recovery was prolonged by two bouts with pleurisy. Doctors reported that his heart was enlarged and there was some damage, but that after a sufficient period of recovery he could resume his normal activities, provided he paid better attention to diet and rest.[90]

After his initial convalescence Peyton returned to Albany, where two Filipino women, Josefina Bayot, a wealthy benefactor, and Benny Belangue, a nurse, assisted him. Peyton was very grateful for the care he received from these women. By October Mary Buckley was able to report, "He's just like his old self, bouncy and animated. It has been a long illness but he has come through in great style."[91]

Conclusion

The decade of the 1970s was a period of searching and adjustment for American Catholicism and Peyton's Crusade for Family Prayer. It was clear to Peyton that the postconciliar era and changes in society had brought the rosary and, thereby, his ministry into a period of eclipse.

He knew that adjustment was necessary, but rooted in his basic belief in the family rosary, change was always difficult to both conceive and attain. The result for the Crusade for Family Prayer was a period of minimal activity, especially compared with the remarkable successes of earlier days. Accomplishments in the production of the series *Matter of Faith,* a significant expansion of the outdoor billboard campaign, and the return of the popular mission to Latin America was matched with the embarrassing failure of *The Messiah.* A series of personal health problems that slowed his activity prompted Peyton to utilize innovative ideas and revised methods of operation, yet in his heart the family rosary remained the solution to all the woes of society. Nonetheless, the need for modernization led in the 1970s to the development of a new branch of the Crusade, "Families for Prayer." It is to the details of this momentous episode in Father Peyton's life that we will now turn.

Chapter 12

Families for Prayer, 1973–89

The rapid changes in Church and society that characterized the post-conciliar period suggested new ways to bring Father Peyton's message of family prayer to people throughout the world, but especially in the United States. Crusades conducted after Vatican II at Milwaukee and throughout Central and later South America were received in different ways, necessitating varied approaches. The more traditional method of the 1950s, emphasizing the rosary as the staple of family prayer and the use of the popular mission, was effective in Latin America, but dissatisfaction with the Milwaukee campaign in 1968 indicated that American Catholics had to be approached in a new way. In the first years of the new decade, Peyton sought a strategy and technique that would succeed with postconciliar American Catholics but still communicate the timeless idea that family prayer was a powerful antidote to secularism. Peyton invested his hopes in Families for Prayer, created in 1973, and saw its administrator, John Gurley, CSC, as the man who would continue the mission beyond Peyton's lifetime. Unfortunately, the Families for Prayer program not only failed to meet its expectations, but it brought pain to Peyton and many others, and eventually resulted in more frayed relationships between the rosary priest and some members of the Congregation of Holy Cross.

The Campaign for the Seventies

The need for a new direction in the U.S. crusades was reflected in a 1970 report, which concluded, "One fact that does seem certain...is that without major adaptations it would be most difficult to have a successful and effective crusade in an American diocese today." Eager to attract young Americans, Peyton began to make the crusade more catechetical, sensing a loss of the traditional beliefs and practices that had been central to Catholic life before the council.[1] During the Crusade's thirtieth anniversary celebration, Peyton announced a new program, "Campaign of the Seventies," which would concentrate his efforts in North America. Peyton publicly offered the idea that, in the wake of Vatican II, there was a need to promote prayer in general and to be more ecumenical in an effort to embrace all families in the United States.[2] He explained that the Campaign for the Seventies "is an effort to help our families save themselves — to encourage them to pray, to show them how to pray, not only for their own well-being, but for the well-being of the society in which they live."[3]

Contemporary needs of people coupled with the new theological and ecclesiastical approach of Vatican II were the main factors that led Peyton to create the Families for Prayer Crusade beginning in 1972. Basing much of its technique on the need and efficacy of family prayer as articulated in *Gaudium et Spes* and in the Decree on the Apostolate of the Laity, the new program placed emphasis on family and group prayer in any format, including the discussion of Scripture, spontaneous prayer, typical morning and evening prayers, and even grace before and after meals. In spite of the fact that the printed guidelines continued to recommend "particular emphasis to the family rosary," the new approach emphasized the fact that the act of praying, rather than a particular form of prayer, was paramount.[4] Daily prayer, the primary vehicle in one's relationship with God, should be as natural as eating, sleeping, working, and relaxing, with each family choosing the type of prayer that suited its needs and situation.

In organizational terms the Families for Prayer Crusade of the 1970s resembled earlier crusades. Each crusade had three phases — orientation, realization, and follow-up — which flowed one to another. After the establishment of a central office a survey of the diocese would be conducted and then a series of organizational meetings. The orientation phase differed in time depending on local conditions, but generally ran about two months. The realization phase of five weeks was still inaugurated with the local ordinary's pastoral letter, after which a series of sermons was given in local parishes. But within these organizational boundaries, there were important differences in the new crusade. First, the program was ecumenical, with members from the three great Western religious traditions asked to participate in the concluding rally. Families were asked not only to pledge, but to proudly display in their homes a commitment plaque to remind them of their need to pray as a family. The follow-up phase included quarterly mailings to all homes to sustain the family's commitment and make suggestions on new ways to pray.[5]

The Families for Prayer Crusade's realization phase centered its efforts in parishes and schools, with the concluding rally now called a Festival of Prayer. Families were encouraged to form small prayer groups; neighbors and friends were asked to gather at least weekly, using a prayer format they found helpful. While the desire to reach out to all people of faith was unquestionably a new emphasis, home Masses were promoted for Catholics as a way to bring local people together in prayer. Individuals and groups were urged to visit shut-ins, the sick, the infirm, and others with special needs.[6] In schools the rosary films, formatted as the *Prince of Peace* series, were shown and used as a vehicle for class discussions. In addition to poster contests as done in the past, teachers were encouraged to assist their students by inviting guest speakers and leading class conversations on the importance of family life and its need for unity. The concluding rally was a mass gathering of people from the whole diocese at which people were given the opportunity to witness publicly the importance their neighbors and fellow parishioners placed on the family and family prayer. Similar in large measure to rallies of the past, there were nonetheless some important innovations. While the rosary was always a preferred option the prayer form used at the festival might be more scripturally based and more ecumenical, with members of various faiths participating. Contemporary music, such as songs from the popular Broadway musical *Godspell,* was also frequently utilized.[7]

The Families for Prayer Crusade was budgeted for $2 million its first year, with $1.5 million earmarked for a new television campaign advertising the Crusade. The Rullman and Munger advertising firm was hired to direct the ad campaign, which would "sell" family prayer much the same way conventional advertising sold products and services. The spots, to be run in local areas where the Crusade was being held, were also geared toward encouraging families to request a commitment plaque and family prayer aides.[8] One spot ran:

> Whatever a family's faith is, all families should be exhorted to pray frequently together in their homes, and in the manner best suited to each family. A national prayer program for families would not be effective if it was pointed to only one faith. It is essential that an ecumenical spirit prevail in all its efforts. Therefore, the specific what and how of prayer is left up to the individual family. The why of prayer is what Families for Prayer is all about.[9]

The new Families for Prayer Crusade was formally launched in Providence, Rhode Island, between August and December 1972. Bishop Louis Gelineau welcomed Peyton and his team as part of the diocese's centenary celebration. Peyton realized the importance of the revised Crusade's debut: "The vision I have and am trying to reflect in this memorandum is such that I feel Rhode Island is the heart of the whole campaign for the seventies — that it is the key that will unlock the door."[10] The crusade emphasized positive suggestions and innovative techniques rather than dwelling on family problems, and to this end local prayer groups and home Masses were especially promoted. The Festival of Prayer, held on November 24 in the Providence Civic Center, drew an estimated nine thousand and was described as giving "witness to the power of prayer to bring peace and unity to the family and the community."[11] Peyton was optimistic that the Providence campaign had placed the Campaign for the Seventies on the road to success:

Our program for family prayer in Rhode Island, rather than wasting time with what is wrong with the family, concentrated on motivating the family to positive action — the spiritual renewal of the family. This crusade to turn things around through prayer — family prayer — family rosary — that received such a warm acceptance from the families of Rhode Island is not just a light in the night that will go out. This campaign is but the beginning.[12]

Next, the Crusade moved west, with campaigns in Juliet, Illinois, St. Louis, Missouri, and South Bend, Indiana, between August 1973 and May 1974. As in Providence, the Crusade in Joliet, held between August 22 and November 3, 1973, was part of the diocese's silver anniversary celebration. The crusades in St. Louis and Joliet were conducted simultaneously; the campaign in South Bend was held in April and May 1974 with the concluding Festival for Prayer program held on May 17 on the campus of the University of Notre Dame.[13]

The final crusade of the Campaign for the Seventies was held in Puerto Rico in 1976. Holy Cross Bishop Alfred Méndez of Arecibo first inquired about the crusade in October 1973, but a crusade office was not established until January 1975, with the assistance of Luis Armijos, OP. Although a territory of the United States, Puerto Rico, because of its Hispanic culture, was perceived as more receptive to the traditional crusade format of the past. Therefore, the innovations of the Families for Prayer Crusade were utilized in local parishes, but the basic format of those crusades ongoing in South America was followed. The crusade itself was formally held between January and August 1975, but the concluding rally was not conducted until December 5, 1976.[14]

Families for Prayer

While Peyton may have believed that the Providence campaign proved the effectiveness of the revised Crusade for Family Prayer in the United States, the crusades in Joliet and St. Louis made it clear that the original diocesan-wide approach no longer had appeal for North Americans in the postconciliar era. Irish secular priest Frank Fahey, who joined Peyton in Joliet, offered the opinion that the Crusade's method, even as it had been modified, was simply not in touch with the attitudes and ideas of America in the 1970s.[15] Fahey developed a modified version of the crusade, also parish oriented, that gave more freedom for individuals and groups to initiate their own prayer forms and frequency of meetings.[16] Thus, in 1973 Peyton gave John Gurley, CSC, who liked Fahey's idea, permission to initiate "Families for Prayer" (FFP) as an outreach program activity of the Crusade for Family Prayer. Peyton's approval, however, had a catch: the program would have to be self-supporting from the beginning, and it would eventually have to be reoriented toward Mary and the rosary and shifted from a parochial to a diocesan orientation.[17] As with all his projects over his long career, Peyton always prominently voiced his clarion message that emphasized Mary and family prayer.

From the outset, both Peyton's motivation and his attitude toward FFP were puzzling. Sister Mary Buckley, RSM, claimed, "Father Peyton was never enthusiastic. He reluctantly permitted it with the proviso that it would be a wedge to open the door for Mary and the rosary."[18] This explanation, however, is inconsistent with Peyton's general method of operation. He never entered ventures in which he did not believe, and his penchant for control required that he possess absolute say in the direction of a program and the actions of its personnel. It was clear to all in a position to know that the diocesan crusade in the United States had seen its day. The 1960s and Vatican II had created a new America and thus, in order to meet the need presented, Peyton was forced to inaugurate new programs. While it might not have been the optimum plan, Peyton approved its establishment under prescribed rules because at the time he had generated nothing from his own creative mind to substitute for it.

Unlike the Campaign for the Seventies, which was more or less old wine in new bottles, Families for Prayer proposed an entirely new approach to Peyton's mission. The program's purpose was clear:

> Families for Prayer, [the] newest aspect of Family Rosary, is a 5-week family-centered parish renewal program to promote the unity, spirituality, mission, and vocation of the family through daily prayer. The program aims to help families through sharing and praying together, to become more aware of Christ living among them and strives to deepen each member's relationship with one another through Him. At the same time the program seeks to develop an awareness of mission within the family, and thus helps to facilitate the renewal of the entire parish community, of which the family is the center.[19]

The program sought to create small groups of families who not only would be committed to family prayer and the family rosary but also would spread the practice throughout the parish and beyond. For instance, parishioners were encouraged to minister to each other, particularly by forming prayer groups consisting of several families, who would not only pray together using biblical, liturgical, and personal prayer, but also spread the practice throughout the parish and beyond. Another innovation was an emphasis on the ecumenical nature of prayer, a goal that was promoted by inviting members of various faiths to serve on the FFP board of directors in order "to achieve our goal of ecumenism in our work among the families of America regardless of religious affiliation."[20]

The FFP program ran five weeks with different themes and emphases of prayer. During the first week "The Family: Growth in Love and Understanding" was the theme. In the second week the focus was "Prayer: Encounters with God, Self, and Others"; the third week centered more specifically on "Family Prayer: Response to Christ among Us." The latter two weeks were more evangelical, stressing "Vocation and Mission: Bringing Christ to the World," in week four, and ending with a week centered on "Commitment: Celebrating Family and Eucharistic Community."[21] Each parish received detailed program materials on these five themes in specialized formats for liturgy, education, and youth programs.

Families for Prayer was initially directed by John Gurley, CSC, who had been Peyton's protégé since his outstanding work on the Latin American crusades. Peyton praised Gurley as the future leader of the Crusade for Family Prayer:

I thank God and Mary in a special way for you. Since I met you in Rome a few years ago and asked your cooperation to make the most of the moment there, your generosity, your ability, your conscientiousness to perform thoroughly a job that you promised to do impressed me so much that I longed for the Crusade to be enriched by your presence. Through God's holy providence that has happened and you have not disappointed me. As I look into the future I see your leadership, your totality in giving of yourself and your worldwide vision as one of the great guarantees that our Blessed Mother will have a champion to help her perpetuate this God-given concept to help the family save itself. May she implement my wishes, my longing to give you a worthy thanks.[22]

Gurley worked with Sister Angelita Fenker, SFCC, as associate director, and Frank Fahey, who briefly assisted the program by visiting parishes to speak with pastors about FFP. In 1979 Ken Silvia, CSC, took over as director of Families for Prayer, allowing Gurley to head up the Albany office of Family Rosary.[23]

Families for Prayer was inaugurated in the fall of 1974 with a pilot program that ran in two parishes. The program grew slowly but steadily reaching 270 parishes and over 250,000 families by the summer of 1981. The trend, with the exception of the period June 1978 to June 1979, was always up, with more parishes involved in the spring, most probably because of the Lenten season.[24] Gurley could report that he was "very pleased with the way things are going." Peyton too was pleased:

Our Families for Prayer parish programs are reaching tens of thousands of families throughout the country with the message of family prayer and the family rosary. Not a day goes by without our becoming involved in some new program or some new activity to help strengthen family life.[25]

As more parishes began to use FFP, expanded organization and facilities were needed. Initially the program operated out of the Albany office at 773 Madison Avenue, but once programs were operating in many widely scattered parishes simultaneously, regional offices were necessary. When Family Rosary purchased 775 Madison in 1975 Families for Prayer moved its central operation there. By 1980 local offices were operating in Birmingham, Boston, Dallas, Evansville (Indiana), Joliet, Kansas City, Los Angeles, Oakland, Plainfield (New Jersey), Portland (Oregon), St. Paul, Washington, D.C., and Wheeling (West Virginia). Beginning in 1979, in response to the announcement by the National

Conference of Catholic Bishops (NCCB) that 1980 would be celebrated as the "year of the family," Families for Prayer began to publish its organ *Together for Prayer,* a four-page weekly bulletin containing information on FFP activities, a reflection on the Sunday Mass readings, and general encouragement for families to pray and be ministers of service.[26]

The initial success of the Families for Prayer program, as noted by both Gurley and Peyton, was certainly welcome and good news to the provincial, William Ribando, CSC. He told Gurley that he had received much spontaneous good feedback from various pastors and others associated with the program. The provincial was pleased with *Together* and congratulated both Gurley and Silvia for their efforts. In a missive to Gurley he wrote, "You and Ken are to be cordially congratulated on the way the whole apostolate is going. It really sounds great. I know the program is having a tremendous effect on families throughout the country." Ribando called Families for Prayer "the most promising work among [Peyton's] present apostolates."[27]

The success of Peyton's latest endeavor did nothing to solve his financial problems; on the contrary, it was an additional drain on the already strained finances of the crusade's resources, since it had no independent funds on which to draw. Extant records show that as the years of FFP operations continued, even with an expanding parish base, the negative cash flow from the program only grew worse. In 1976, the first year of FFP's financial records, the program lost $26,035; by 1980 the accumulated operational loss was over $350,000.[28]

Ribando realized that FFP was not profitable, but he was not overly concerned. Many fine apostolic ventures, such as the Holy Cross mission effort in Peru, were not economically self-sustaining. Other apostolates, such as higher education, however, were highly profitable, keeping province finances in the black.[29] Nevertheless, FFP's financial problems triggered a serious dispute between Peyton, Ribando, and their respective allies over the viability, operation, and control of the Families for Prayer program. Peyton felt that the monies had been raised for the work oriented toward Mary and the rosary. But he felt Families for Prayer was straying from its original ministerial objectives which were clearly outlined when the program was initiated in 1973.[30] He commented to a benefactor: "Families for Prayer and the bulletin *Together* were to have been adjuncts of the Family Rosary Crusade. In themselves they are praiseworthy and perform an effective service to the stricken family. Unfortunately they have not developed as I expected — Marian and Rosarian in essence."[31]

Peyton's objections to FFP became personal as well as professional when he began to feel that Gurley's commitment to family prayer of any kind was irreconcilable with Peyton's preference for the family rosary.[32] Peyton called Gurley "incompetent for the job he holds" and concluded "He *must be removed* and *replaced* [emphasis Peyton's] but how is the big issue."[33] Peyton wanted to reassert control so that his principal Marian message would remain clear, but was in a quandary as to how to proceed. Peyton also resented the tensions that arose between Gurley and Sister Mary Buckley, who returned in 1980 to take charge of the operations in Albany after eight years as head of Family Theater. It is highly probable that Peyton, who was grateful for Buckley's long service and most assuredly was told about the conflict, was sympathetic to her concern and wanted to assist her in achieving some sense of peace in her new position in the East.[34]

Gurley responded to Peyton's concerns by claiming that the real problem was that the rosary priest was not center stage in the Families for Prayer program. He wrote to the provincial:

> What then is the basis for Father Peyton's objections and displeasure? I believe it is that Father Peyton sees Families for Prayer (and *Together*) not as his thing, but as my thing; not as his idea but as my idea, not as his success but as my success. Because he believes that Families for Prayer and *Together* are not his, he won't buy into them. Every one of the many CSCs who have worked for Father Peyton and with whom I have consulted are very sympathetic to if not wholly accepting of this line of thinking.[35]

Gurley rejected the idea that FFP was taking money from the Crusade and using it for purposes for which it was not intended, namely, a program that was not sufficiently Marian or rosarian in its orientation. He pointed out that many of Peyton's prize projects, such as *Family Theater of the Air,* the *A Matter of Faith* series, the Psalm films, the outdoor billboard campaign, and most recently *The Messiah,* were not oriented toward Mary or the rosary.[36]

The conflict peaked in February 1981 when Peyton, feeling "morally bound to stop monies from F[amily] R[osary] going to FFP," spoke to the superior general, Thomas Barrosse, CSC, and told him that he planned to remove Gurley from his position as head of the Albany office and from the Crusade for Family Prayer. Barrosse, in turn, told Ribando of the planned action, thus setting in motion a series of events that would cause a great furor. The provincial sought advice from his Council and then on March 6 wrote the general describing his plans.[37] First, Peyton would be directed to immediately make arrangements to restore control of the board of directors of the Crusade for Family Prayer to the Congregation. Second, Peyton was not to interfere in any way with the direction of the work of Families for Prayer or *Together*. Lastly, there must be no attempt to "fire" John Gurley. Any such action would result in the provincial's removing Peyton and "retiring him to [the community infirmary at] Notre Dame." He concluded, "John Gurley has faithfully directed the practical administration of the entire worldwide [Family Rosary] apostolate for 15 years. His removal from the work would be a disaster not only for the Families for Prayer but for all the other aspects of these apostolates."[38]

On March 22, 1981, Peyton met with Ribando at the novitiate for the Eastern Province of Priests and Brothers in Waterford, New York. At this time the provincial hand-delivered a letter that outlined the three demands determined upon when the council met earlier in the month.[39] After this fiery meeting, on March 30 Ribando sent a second letter to Peyton stating, "It is most important for you ... [to] cooperate fully with Fr. Gurley and Fr. Silvia. This would mean that Families for Prayer and *Together* must be accorded everything necessary for these programs to continue and develop."[40]

Peyton, sensing a deviation from the intended direction of FFP, as well as loss of personal control, immediately informed the other directors of the Crusade for Family Prayer about the situation, prompting an angry response from Peter Grace, the priest's great champion. Grace's attachment to and support of Patrick Peyton was well known, and thus it was not unexpected that he would rapidly come to the aid of his friend whom he perceived to have been wronged by his religious community.[41] On April 3 Grace and Dr. Charles Miller, chairman of the board of directors for the Crusade for Family Prayer, met with Barrosse in Halifax, Nova Scotia. The pair challenged each of Ribando's three demands, backed Peyton's contention that FFP had improperly used monies not designated for it, and described what they considered "the strange anti–Family Rosary alliance between Father Ribando and Father Gurley." Grace also told Barrosse that the provincial's demand that the board of directors of the Crusade for Family Prayer be reconstituted and given back to Holy Cross was illegal. He later wrote, "I insist, dear Father General, this cavalier treatment is personally insulting to these laymen and is totally unjust and less than Christian." Grace recommended that the general rescind the orders of the provincial and immediately divest Families for Prayer from any connection with the Crusade for Family Prayer.[42]

Following the meeting, Grace sent the provincial three letters on April 2 criticizing his judgment.[43] The provincial replied to Grace by posing a series of questions. Ribando asked why Peyton had suddenly changed his mind regarding the efficacy of FFP and Gurley's leadership, which only a few years previously he had praised. He was also curious to know why, if the situation with Families for Prayer was so grossly out of control, he had not been informed before and had come to know of the severity only when informed by the superior general of Peyton's plans. Grace was asked why board meetings for Family Rosary, Family Theater, and the Crusade for Family Prayer had been held in the past and he and other Holy Cross board members were not informed. Lastly, echoing Gurley's earlier comment, Ribando asked why Families for Prayer could not be financed by the Crusade for Family Prayer when other expenditures, such as the $2 million spent on the debacle of *The Messiah* and $70,000 expended on a proposed commissioned biography of Peyton, were never questioned.[44]

Familiar with Grace's habit of drawing on his powerful connections, Ribando made a preemptive strike, writing to Grace's friend Cardinal Terence Cooke of New York and asking him to consult with Ribando or the general before contacting Roman officials about the matter. Ribando also wrote to Archbishop Pio Laghi, apostolic pro-nuncio to the United States, indicating that he would be most happy to provide any information concerning the Families for Prayer controversy for review by the Holy See.[45]

The Provincial Council also entered the fray in support of its embattled provincial. Writing on behalf of the council, Joseph Callahan, CSC, argued,

> As for Families for Prayer, we feel John Gurley has done a great job and has sought and received approval for all his budgets and all expenditures. Further we feel, in fact, Families for Prayer is the one work which will carry Fr. Peyton's charism into the future. . . . We feel that preserving Families for Prayer is a way of insuring a legacy for Fr. Pat.

On another level Callahan told the general, "We also feel you should resent the intrusion of Peter Grace as a defender of Fr. Peyton in and before his own community."[46]

John Gurley wrote to the provincial to present his side of the conflict. He told Ribando that Grace "exaggerated this whole situation out of all proportion and has thus aggravated it greatly." Gurley believed that Grace's response was typical for his position:

Mr. Grace's solution is typical of what is generally conceded by many to be the traditional big business attitude: the bottom line is profit; if a company or an activity is incurring a deficit or not making enough money, cut it loose, without the slightest thought and regard for the suffering this inflicts on others.

Gurley maintained that FFP had every right to exist as a viable and active apostolate in the Church and Holy Cross.[47]

Gurley also presented the provincial with his own plan to resolve the controversy. Consistent with Ribando's thinking, he recommended that members of the Eastern Priests Province of Holy Cross form the majority of the board of directors of the Crusade for Family Prayer. Second, he proposed that Families for Prayer and *Together*, as legitimate expressions of the general objectives of the Crusade, continue to function and grow within the limits of approved budgets. Lastly, he argued that the Albany mailing list should no longer be regarded as the personal property of Peyton but rather should become the basis for financial support for the entire apostolate.[48]

Movement toward resolution of the Families for Prayer controversy began almost as soon as Peyton received Ribando's three demands. Thomas Barrosse first asked Ribando to rethink his request that the board of directors be reconstituted, arguing that such a move would be inconsistent with Vatican II's insistence on increased lay participation. He suggested that the board membership be changed more gradually, since it was not possible to achieve the required three-quarters vote with the current lay members, many of whom resented Peyton's being "stepped on."[49] Barrosse also had to admit his frustration in dealing with Father Peyton: "Both Bill Hogan [former provincial and now procurator general] and Ted Hesburgh are convinced that, just as Pat has always operated on his own — board or no board — he will continue to do so; he does not seem capable of doing otherwise and can hardly be expected to change much at this point in his life."[50]

On May 8, a full seven weeks after the fateful March 22 meeting, Peyton finally responded in writing to the provincial's demands. He first asked for clarification, pointing out that the March 21 letter had told him to have nothing to do with Families for Prayer, but the March 30 letter had asked him to do all he could to assist the program. More pointedly, however, Peyton explained that when he tried to carry out the provincial's directive to return control of the board to Holy Cross, the lay members had objected, stating that the by-laws could only be changed by a three-quarters majority of the board and that under its present makeup, such a vote would not achieve the desired result.[51]

Barrosse offered a reasonable compromise solution to the controversy in late May. Prior to this he met with Grace, Charles Miller, and Thomas Doyle at the generalate and listened while Peyton's friends continued to plead their case. On May 27 the general offered a four-part plan to resolve the crisis, allowing all to save face as much as possible. The plan called for the legal separation of Families for Prayer and the Crusade for Family Prayer under the following terms:

1. A three-year progressive 25 percent per year cutback to the subsidy given Families for Prayer by the Crusade, creating financial independence for FFP by June 30, 1984.

2. A separation of facilities, with Families for Prayer and *Together* utilizing one Madison Avenue house and Family Rosary the other.

3. Separate fundraising, with mailing lists to be shared until a mutually agreeable arrangement could be worked out: Peyton's name would not appear on either the FFP letterhead or the masthead of *Together.*

4. Continued directorship of the Albany office by John Gurley for the next three years, with Gurley supervising the move toward eventual separation.[52]

Before the particulars of the proposed compromise could be readily studied by both sides, the conflict erupted again when strong protests were lodged from many fronts about the contents of the weekly bulletin *Together.* In its September 22–27, 1980, issue *Together* supported both INFACT's boycott of Nestle's infant formula and the Roman Catholic Liaison, a group that supported the boycott of J. P. Stevens's products because the company was not unionized. Peter Grace, echoing Peyton's chief complaint, protested that funds intended for Marian devotion should not be used to promote causes, unless they were approved by those who supplied the funds.[53] An even greater controversy was created by an essay in the June 15, 1981, issue, challenging the real presence of Jesus in the Eucharist. In response to Jesus' statement in the Scriptures (John 6:55), "For my flesh is true food and my blood is true drink," *Together* stated, "It's important to remember that flesh and blood are not meant to be taken literally. The bread and wine are vehicles by which Jesus communicates to us his total life and all that it means." The July 27 to August 1, 1981, issue similarly challenged the authenticity of the words of institution proclaimed by Jesus at the Last Supper.[54]

Reaction against *Together*'s perceived heresy was strong and swift. One angry response from a priest was sent to Peyton directly:

Neither Luther nor Calvin could ever have written something more against the dogma of the "Real Presence" of Our Lord on the Most Blessed Sacrament!!! It is pure heresy in the fullest sense of the word!! How can an article of this kind be published in *Together*, the publication of Families for Prayer which has your name under President on its first page???[55]

Besides the perceived challenge to the real presence, the *Together* essay was also criticized for its perceived denigration of Christ: "It is well to remember that a divine person cannot communicate to us 'His total life.' This would make the finite equal to the infinite, the creature equal to God."[56]

The conflict's final resolution remained elusive for six more months while the various parties traded blows in a mental boxing match. Not to be preempted, Peter Grace landed the first blow in a letter to the superior general. Grace believed his task was to protect the special relationship Peyton had with the worldwide community and to oppose any efforts in name or by alleged sponsorship to change the message of Marian devotion through family prayer that Peyton had preached to tens of millions of people. He concluded, "If we allow them [the faithful] to be scandalized by publishing under Father Peyton's aegis, views on subjects not connected with him or by impeding or harassing his apostolate, we run a grave risk of perdition and, for this reason, I am trying to help him to be able to continue his work of the past 40 years."[57]

The board of directors of the Crusade for Family Prayer met on August 21, 1981, to discuss the compromise, listening to arguments on both sides. Peyton claimed that he had no choice but to act as he did:

In view of my many years of seeing my assistant [Gurley] become independent and using Family Rosary money unilaterally — to do his own thing — the Families for Prayer — the *Together* and in short to overstep his role as assistant, I had no choice after many efforts alone with him ... but to bring it out in the open and to the Superior General himself.[58]

Peyton blamed himself for giving Gurley $75,000 from the "All for Her Fund" and, thus, exacerbating the problem. Ribando pushed the members for a vote to accept the May 27 so-called Roman Compromise, but the board refused to take definite action, thus prolonging the battle. Board member Bartley MacPhaidin, CSC, president of Stonehill College in North Easton, Massachusetts, was told to arrange a meeting with Gurley and Peyton and reach a common understanding before the board's next meeting.

Before this meeting was held, however, the Provincial Council met with Peyton on November 13, reasserting its support for Ribando and warning Peyton that should any attempt to fire Gurley or to remove him from any of the boards upon which he sat be made Holy Cross would pull its sponsorship from Family Rosary. In a heated reply, although not surprising considering the magnitude of the conflict and Peyton's single-minded devotion to his mission, the rosary priest asked the provincial and his councilors whether he was free to search for new Church sponsorship and canonical status apart from Holy Cross. The provincial expressed his openness to such an exploration.[59]

On February 2, 1982, the board of directors for the Crusade for Family Prayer met to consider the separation agreement that Gurley and Peyton had worked out when they met with MacPhaidin, as directed, on November 19. Under the terms of the agreement, the Crusade's subsidy for FFP would be gradually reduced, the organizations would share mailing lists, FFP would be given the Madison Avenue headquarters, with ten years to repay its value, and FFP would rent all satellite offices. The board's affirmative vote in theory brought the controversy to a close.[60]

It took a couple of months for Peyton to sign the agreement, but on July 1, 1982, Families for Prayer, Inc., became a separate organization from the Crusade for Family Prayer.[61] Gurley was made executive director and Patricia Spanbauer became the Albany office manager. In its certificate of incorporation, Families for Prayer stated its function and goals:

> The purposes for which the corporation is organized are to promote the spiritual well-being of the family through programs, publications, and other services meant to enhance the quality of family life especially through the encouragement of daily family prayer; and, in furtherance thereof to use such effective means as the Board of Directors may deem necessary or advisable to carry out the objectives of the corporation.[62]

Families for Prayer was now a separate body, but its connection with Peyton and the Crusade for Family Prayer was not severed completely for a few more years. Initially FFP had to arrange a series of lease agreements with Family Rosary for everything from office space to computers to a fleet of automobiles for its regional offices. FFP also had to repay Family Rosary its debt of almost $225,000.[63]

The Roman Compromise mandated that the Crusade for Family Prayer subsidize FFP for three years, for a total of 150 percent of FFP's fiscal loss for the operational year 1980–81. The subsidy figure amounted to $218,811. The first year's subsidy, paid in 1982, was to be 75 percent of the 150 percent total, 50 percent in 1983, and 25 percent in 1984. Toward the end of Families for Prayer's first year under the compromise plan Peter Grace was once again questioning the superior general, saying that he was "less than pleased with the compromise" and reporting that after its first year FFP's fiscal loss had exceeded the subsidy by $72,413 or 66.2 percent. In Grace's mind the financial situation would not recover. The fiscal loss for FFP from 1976 had reached almost $1.4 million, prompting the shipping magnate to write to the general:

> I, as a layman with long involvement in legal matters by reason of the position of fiduciary responsibility I hold as an officer, director or trustee of many public industrial and commercial corporations, ... am appalled (to say nothing of being scandalized) by the cavalier attention paid to the *diversion* [emphasis added] of almost $1.4 million. ... I consider such diversion illegal, dishonest and scandalous.

He concluded his comments by stating that he would initiate action to recoup the $218,811 that the compromise had promised to Families for Prayer.[64]

Barrosse responded by questioning Grace's motivation, stating that according to new provincial, Joseph Callahan, CSC, Grace's strategy aimed less to recoup the financial loss than to force Families for Prayer into bankruptcy. Barrosse feared that this incident would start Peyton off on the wrong foot with his new provincial, and that Peyton should, therefore, speak to Callahan and set things right. He commented, "I only wish I were present to speak with you [Peyton] myself. I fear a heavy cross is being prepared for the end of your life which I am convinced can be avoided."[65]

Between 1982 and 1989 Families for Prayer continued to operate as usual, but its downward financial spiral only accelerated. The fiscal loss in 1983 was $188,815 and in 1984 $187,686. In October 1983 and again in January 1985 the Eastern Province loaned FFP $20,000 to print its literature. Callahan became very concerned, telling Gurley in 1985 that this would be the last loan and informing him that FFP was not to take on any new commitments for at least one year.[66] Cost-cutting measures were implemented and FFP sought to break its dependence upon Family Rosary by exercising its option and purchasing its office at 775 Madison, yet the parent body was reluctant to sell. Eventually Families for Prayer secured a $100,000 loan and purchased the property.[67]

Families for Prayer was in a death spiral that would end only in 1989. An audit completed on September 8 reported that the organization was over $800,000 in debt. More problematic, however, was the audit team's conclusion: "The Company's [FFP] recurring losses from operations and net capital deficiency raise substantial doubt about the entity's ability to continue as a going concern."[68] In response the new provincial, David Farrell, CSC, ordered the dissolution of Families for Prayer effective immediately. FFP owed the Crusade for Family Prayer $198,913. As partial payment of the debt, the FFP office at 775 Madison was transferred to the Crusade.[69]

Immediately upon the dissolution of Families for Prayer the provincial was deluged with payment demands from creditors. While during its last few years of operation Families for Prayer had managed to repay some of its debts, during its final year its overall indebtedness was $800,000, a staggering figure that the Eastern Province did not want to liquidate. Thus, Farrell went to Peyton and the board of directors for the Crusade for Family Prayer stating that the Crusade and not the province had fiduciary responsibility for FFP. In the end, Peyton, through the influence of Farrell, agreed to pay the debt, a calculated move by the latter to help the rosary priest patch up his relationship with his fellow religious. The debt was paid in 1989.

The conflict that arose between Peyton, the Crusade for Family Prayer, and its associated allies and John Gurley, Families for Prayer, and its allies presents a sad and sobering chapter in the lives and careers of Peyton and Gurley. Strong evidence leads to the conclusion that Gurley was not a good businessman and should not have been placed in charge of a fledgling operation that had no source of financial backing other than revenues from parishes and the support of the Crusade for Family Prayer. Gurley admitted that he made many errors in his leadership of Families for Prayer, and it is clear that the program should have been better financially managed. If FFP had been under better financial supervision things most probably would not have gotten out of control and the firestorm that ensued could have been prevented. Additionally, Families for Prayer never achieved the three conditions that Peyton mandated in 1973 when he placed Gurley in charge of the new ministry.

Gurley's errors and the questionable viability of the Families for Prayer program do not negate his efficacy as a priest nor remove the fact that Peyton's attitude and actions contributed to the controversy. It is clearly evident that Peyton was not pleased that his control over the Families for Prayer operation was limited. He continually argued that the reason Gurley should be removed and Families for Prayer placed under his supervision was that monies expended were not being used as designated by benefactors. Peyton was not simply concerned that FFP lost money, but more especially that this money was being lost in an endeavor that was not oriented along the Marian and rosarian lines that were the central themes of his ministry.

Blinded by his tunnel-vision devotion to Mary and the promotion of family prayer in her honor, Peyton, as often happened in his career, could not understand why his fellow religious did not see what seemed so obvious to him. His absolute need to further Marian devotion was the card that trumped all hands. As in the past the rosary priest's single-minded devotion resulted in strained relationships in the Holy Cross community. Still, one cannot ignore, as pointed out by both John Gurley and William Ribando, that no question was asked when many projects of the past went forward with little or no association with Marian devotion. Most of these endeavors, such as *Family Theater of the Air,* the Psalm films, and more recently the *A Matter of Faith* series, were economically solvent, but Peyton's greatest economic failure, *The Messiah,* had no more connection to Mary and the rosary than Families for Prayer. It could easily be concluded, therefore, that operational control was of equal concern as economic viability. As Families for Prayer gained the approval and satisfaction of the province membership, Patrick Peyton's penchant for control placed him in conflict with Gurley. His unidirectional thought in ministry was a mark of his greatness, yet its misunderstanding among peers periodically brought heartache.

The Families for Prayer controversy was not a highlight for anyone concerned and errors were made on both sides, plus there were failures in the leadership of Holy Cross. Possibly, however, the impressions of William Ribando, CSC, given almost twenty years after the events, are most enlightening:

Fr. Peyton was a man who did great things and whose effects are still felt very greatly, but a man who was very suspicious of his community, very intent on tying down financial resources so they could not be used in any apostolic way different than the exact way he envisioned. In theory he was happy for others, including provincials, to play a role, but [he] wasn't ready to be challenged.[70]

The single-mindedness of Peyton's thought was often beyond the reach of others.

Conclusion

At the beginning of the 1970s Peyton was optimistic that his new ideas for the Crusade for Family Prayer, based on the changes wrought by Vatican II, would succeed, but by the end of the decade his innovations had failed. When the Campaign for the Seventies floundered a radically new parish-based program, Families for Prayer, was created. While Peyton's support for the program was not wholehearted, he did believe in John Gurley, whom he had groomed over the years. When Peyton realized that the program would never be financially solvent he tried to change leadership. His plan, however, was thwarted when, for the first time in any significant way, he ran into conflict with his Holy Cross superiors. The almost blank check that Peyton enjoyed from the outset of his ministerial endeavors was challenged, initially by his provincial, William Ribando, CSC, supported by the superior general, Thomas Barrosse, CSC, and continuing with future provincials until the Families for Prayer experiment ended in 1989, when it was clear the organization could not attain economic solvency. However, a brighter side to the decade of the 1980s was present as Family Theater once again gained notoriety and brought renewed prominence to Father Peyton and his international ministry for the promotion of family prayer. It is to this story we must now turn.

Chapter 13

Renewal and Encores: The Crusade for Family Prayer, 1980–92

The sense of social and spiritual stagnation that plagued American society in the 1970s, due in large measure to the physical proximity to the tumultuous decade of the 1960s, was gradually transformed in the 1980s into renewal on many fronts. The new decade saw movement to a more centrist position, as seen through greater appreciation for traditional family values and the return to acceptability of certain trademarks of religious piety, including the rosary. The 1980s were certainly not a return to the preconciliar Church, but that decade provided an environment that allowed the work of Patrick Peyton to find renewal and new beginnings. Provided a new lease on life through his successful heart surgery, Peyton expanded his family prayer crusade through Family Theater, a continuing billboard campaign, and a new project, the international Crusade for Family Prayer. And at long last, the ministry was successfully reorganized, as the rosary priest and his associates prepared for his death and a transition to new leadership.

American Catholicism in the 1980s

The spring 1979 meeting of the American Catholic Historical Association, held at the University of Notre Dame, featured a session that in many ways characterized the two prominent and opposed ways American Catholics viewed the state of the Church during the decade of the 1980s. In his paper "The Loss of History," James Hitchcock of St. Louis University maintained that Vatican II's concept of *aggiornamento* had dampened the faith. He stated, "Instead of doctrinal development there was doctrinal contestation. Instead of seeking how new insights might be reconciled authentically with traditional teaching, the latter was indirectly assaulted."[1]

The historian David O'Brien agreed that there had been a downturn, but suggested that this decline in American Catholic life in the 1970s was caused by two converging factors. He stated that the past close association of Catholics with American culture became problematic for the Church when flaws in society were revealed and many associated these imperfections with the Church, since accommodation to the American way of life had always been part of American Catholicism. The second cause O'Brien suggested was the collapse of the American Catholic subculture.[2] O'Brien was optimistic, however, that precisely because of its history of accommodation, the Church would follow American culture at large as it began to recover.[3]

The priest-sociologist Andrew Greeley also saw a more favorable future. He perceived a movement of American Catholics away from an institutional and ecclesiastical base to a noninstitutional and non-ecclesiastical foundation for their faith practice. This was viewed by Greeley as a positive sign, for it demonstrated a greater sense of self-awareness and thus a more mature attitude toward the practice of the faith.[4]

The more optimistic attitude on the direction of Catholicism in the United States was also articulated by the hierarchy. James Malone, bishop of Youngstown and president of the NCCB, believed the American Church had emerged victorious from the doldrums of the 1970s to a renewed consciousness of the active presence of God and the renewed mission of the Church. He wrote, "The Catholic Church in the United States is a vibrant, struggling, learning, diverse community trying to put the word of God and the teaching of our Church to work in our lives, in our communities and nation."[5] The publication by the American bishops of two major pastoral letters, "The Challenge of Peace: God's Call and Our Response" in 1983 and "Economic Justice for All" in 1986, demonstrated the vitality of the bishops' voice and the dawning of a more forceful presence in American society. The bishops by their action went on record that they would not shy from, but rather would tackle and state their opinion on the important societal issues of the day.[6]

The preeminent manifestation of the new face of Catholicism in the United States had been in generation since World War II, but in the 1980s the presence, importance, and influence of Hispanics in the Church burst out in a spectacular way. Unquestionably the massive influx of immigrants from Latin America changed the American Church, with 23 million Hispanics in the United States by 1980. The Jesuit social theologian Allan Figueroa Deck noted, "The second immigrant experience promises to be every bit as significant, if not more significant, than the first one." Some Catholics, especially those long-established ethnic groups who had built the Church in the United States, perceived the Hispanic migration to be problematic, but it was clear that Latin Americans would continue to emigrate and to stay. Archbishop Patrick Flores answered such criticisms: "The Hispanics of our country are not a problem to be solved; they are a people to be loved and a people to be respected. The challenge before us is to regard ministry to Hispanics as an opportunity for growth and for learning."[7]

The reality of the Hispanic presence in the United States necessitated a reevaluation of the pastoral approach to these newly arrived peoples. For several generations Hispanics were ignored and their spirituality underappreciated, causing in large measure a significant loss of Latin American peoples from the Roman Catholic Church to a whole host of evangelical Protestant groups, including the many "storefront" churches that appeared better able to meet the personal needs of individuals and especially families.[8] The practice of popular religiosity that is so basic and important to Hispanics, having been considered sentimental and unorthodox by many, must, on the other hand, be viewed as a viable and acceptable understanding of the Church. The American Catholic bishops considered the challenge significant enough that in 1983 the NCCB issued "The Hispanic Presence: Challenges and Commitment," a document that expressed the significant opportunities brought by the cultural presence of Latin Americans.[9] Father Peyton's Family Theater operation was conscious of the Latin American population and thus as early as the 1960s made significant efforts in the translation of literature and the dubbing of films for use in the Hispanic community.

One aspect of the Church in the 1980s that was attractive to the burgeoning Hispanic population was a new emphasis on the family. The year 1980 itself was marked in three significant ways with respect to family life: the United States bishops dedicated the year to the family, the United Nations declared 1980 the year of the child, and a Synod of Bishops met to discuss problems associated with the Christian family. The American bishops had earlier spoken of the need to revitalize family life:

Family life is a basic theological and religious reality. It is in our families that most of us come to a knowledge born of religious love and that we first become aware that the movement of love is always and everywhere toward the creation of values, not merely their reproduction. As pastors we know that without a renewal of family life, there will be no genuine or extensive renewal of the wider life of the Church.[10]

Peyton echoed these sentiments, offering the family as the solution to the multiple problems of society:

No nation — no society whose family life is in dissonance has ever held together and prospered. Renewed family life is at the heart of this nation's survival. This is not one religion against another, this is go no go for our society — for everyone regardless of race, creed or culture.[11]

Peyton brought his views to the 1980 Synod of Bishops in Rome and contributed significantly to its work. Before the bishops convened, several prelates, including Archbishop John Quinn of San Francisco, petitioned Peyton for information about his family rosary crusade, knowing of its past efficacy in the promotion of family prayer. Peyton provided a thirty-page report summarizing his work to date and providing quotes from favorable letters and other documents.[12] Peyton lobbied freely with the bishops, both individually and in groups, hoping that the family rosary would be given "an explicit and powerful recommendation for Catholic families the world over." The Philippine primate, Cardinal Jaime Sin, lauded Peyton for his efforts: "I personally saw him motivate the Synod of Bishops gathered in Rome in behalf of the Christian family in the modern world to adopt a resolution of the need and power of the Family Rosary to spiritualize the family."[13] Peyton's lobbying efforts were successful: the Synod endorsed the rosary as a form of family prayer: "In fulfilling these tasks the family will be, as it were, a 'domestic church,' a community of faith living in hope and love, serving God and the entire human family. Shared prayer and the liturgy are sources of grace for families."[14]

Family Theater in the 1980s

The 1980s was a time of renewed life for Peyton as manifest with the support of the new Pope, John Paul II, who from the outset of his reign gave his blessing to the rosary priest and his Crusade for Family Prayer. While still archbishop of Cracow, Karol Wojtyla had given his support to Peyton's work, and this was renewed shortly after he assumed the

Chair of Peter in October 1978. On February 17, 1979, Peyton met in a personal audience with the new pontiff. At this time John Paul II called Father Peyton a "man of faith." The pope publicly proclaimed the rosary to be his favorite prayer and agreed to pray this devotional the first Saturday of each month over Vatican radio.[15] John Paul II, like Father Peyton, hoped that the eclipse of the rosary would soon end and that "once more [it would] become the accustomed prayer for the 'domestic Church' which is the Christian family."[16] Through letters and personal contact the pope remained Peyton's close and constant ally.

For Peyton, the pope's support was only one indication that the Church was emerging from its eclipse into a period of great opportunity. Peyton announced his vision:

> With the years remaining to me, the health that has just been re-stored to me, the decade of the 80s — the fifth decade of years the Lord has allowed me to work for Our Lady — I intend with all my might to make the decade of the 80s be like the fifth glorious decade of the Rosary — the crowning years of those five decades spent in Her service.[17]

The decade possessed the potential for greatness for those of faith and daring; Peyton was not going to allow the occasion slip by without his best effort.

Another person who recognized the promise of the new decade was Al Scalpone, long associated with Family Theater, who had previously criticized Peyton for allowing Family Theater to stagnate. Now he urged Peyton to respond to the spirit of the times by creating new programs and projects.[18] Buoyed by his own renewed optimism and challenged by Scalpone's call for renewal, Peyton, "as a last hurrah," planned to make a new series of films, based on the fifteen mysteries but using contemporary settings and images. Originally the plan called for a series of television programs that would illustrate how a typical family could find union and strength through family prayer.[19] It quickly became apparent that since there was no funding, the TV series would be impractical, but a single film about the Nativity, *The Most Joyful Mystery*, was completed before Christmas 1980 and made available to any station that would give it free air time. The program, which starred the Tony Award–winning actor Barnard Hughes and featured Peyton along with cameos by Bob Newhart, Danny Thomas, Ricardo Montalban, Pat O'Brien, and Anne Lockhart,[20] aired on seventy-three stations in the United States, thirteen in Canada, and four in the Philippines and was well received.[21]

The Nativity film cost $340,000 to produce, so the film project would obviously be expensive: it was estimated that the remaining films would be just under $6 million, with a projected completion date of 1985.[22] A special fund was set up in April 1981, and Peyton began to write to various foundations seeking their assistance for the project. He asked the DeRance Foundation, which had been so helpful to Peyton in the past, for $500,000 and the John D. and Catherine MacArthur Foundation for $4 million. Extant records do not indicate the amount received, although both foundations provided some support.[23]

Peyton's new project gained momentum when Princess Grace of Monaco agreed to participate in three films. In 1981 she narrated *The Greatest Mystery,* filmed in London and featuring the popular English music sensation Petula Clark, the Irish folk group the Chieftains, and the London Players depicting how Easter is celebrated by various cultures throughout the world. The following year Princess Grace hosted *The Seven Last Words,* filmed at the Vatican museum and featuring a dramatization of the crucifixion by the London Players, and *The Nativity,* filmed at the altar of St. Peter's Basilica and depicting the birth of Christ.[24]

Peyton also obtained the services of Mother Teresa of Calcutta and the fabled actress Helen Hayes. *The Visitation,* the mystery chosen by Mother Teresa, was narrated by Bob Newhart and shot in 1981 in Washington, D.C., London, and the campus of the University of Notre Dame. Besides the words of Mother Teresa, the film featured selections by the Notre Dame Glee Club. *The Annunciation,* starring Helen Hayes, Tony LoBianco, Eli Wallach, and Barnard Hughes and featuring the singing of Irish tenor Robert White and opera diva Renata Scotto, was filmed at St. Patrick's Cathedral in New York and released in 1983.[25]

The last six films of the series (a total of twelve were made) were supervised by Bob Stabler. Two of this group, *The Assumption* and *The Coronation,* were filmed at the Old Tucson Studios in 1984. One year later *The Ascension* and *The Descent of the Spirit* were shot at Old Tucson, but these two films, both featuring seasoned veteran actors Stuart Whitman, Joseph Campanella, and Judy Geeson, re-created the biblical events, abandoning the more contemporary line used in the previous films. *The Presentation,* starring Carol Lawrence and Doug McClure, and *The Finding,* featuring June Lockhart, Margaret O'Brien, and Tom Poston, were both filmed in Vancouver, Canada, and returned to contemporary settings. The film project was capped in 1987 with a television special, *The Joyful Mysteries of the Rosary,* hosted by Loretta Young.[26]

Peyton's new films won many awards. The Southern California Motion Picture Council presented its Golden Halo Award to *The Greatest Mystery, The Seven Last Words, The Nativity, The Annunciation, The Finding, The Presentation, The Descent of the Spirit, The Ascension,* and *The Joyful Mysteries.* The International Film and TV Festival of New York presented its bronze award (1981) to *The Greatest Mystery* and its silver award in 1982 to *The Visitation.* The Award for Excellence from Religion in the Media was presented to *The Nativity* (1983), *The Finding* (1986), and *The Presentation* (1987).[27]

Crusades in the 1980s

As described previously the formal crusade effort in the United States ended when the attempt to rejuvenate the campaign, beginning in Providence in 1972, failed to generate sufficient interest. The end of formal crusades in North America did not mean, however, that Father Peyton was not active. Quite to the contrary, throughout the decade of the 1980s he was a speaker in high demand at various conferences and events. In 1982 he was the featured speaker at a rosary rally in Albuquerque and preached a Triduum, as he had so many times in the early days of his ministry, at the La Salette Shrine in Attleboro, Massachusetts. In May 1983 he returned in triumph to St. Paul where he had brought the crusade twenty-five years previously. He preached another Triduum at the dedication of the Immaculate Heart of Mary Shrine in Santa Clara, California, and ended the decade in October 1989 as the honored guest of the annual Rosary Sunday Celebration held by the Diocese of Phoenix.[28]

The original crusade format may have lost its relevance in North America, but it continued to appeal to Catholics in other countries. During the 1984 Eucharistic Congress in Lima, Peyton reinitiated the popular mission in Peru, which he financed through a grant of $300,000 from the Sarita Kenedy East Foundation, which was managed by Peter Grace.[29] The request provided money for films, projectors, generators, and all the accessories necessary for the popular mission that began in the Archdiocese of Cusco in May 1984. Moving about the country, the mission, under the direction of the Peruvian Dominican Javier Ariz, was held in the Archdioceses of Lima and Trujillo as well. The crusade enjoyed its customary popularity in Latin America. One report stated, "The results so far have been excellent in surpassing the expectations of the leaders."[30]

The success in Latin America was reminiscent of the crusade's great triumphs of the 1980s in the Philippines. From his first visit to the

island nation in 1959 Patrick Peyton and his ministry became sym-
bols of Catholic faith practice. In March 1978 a seven-year campaign,
conducted semi-continuously, was initiated in Manila and directed by
Bishop Bienvenido Lopez, who had previously worked with Peyton.
Many hoped the Philippines would be the springboard for a crusade
throughout Asia. Cardinal Jaime Sin of Manila formally announced the
new "Family Rosary Crusade" in his see city, and the campaign was initiated by Peyton in the region of Tondo, "the most notorious slum area
of the entire Philippines."[31]

The campaign was conducted somewhat differently in that teams of
crusade participants gave seminars to local peoples, instructing them on
how to conduct the crusade. Peyton realized that this was not the optimum operational method, saying that it "falls short of how thoroughly
it was pioneered in Latin America," but he was confident that the campaign would be successful, mostly because of his own presence, which
recently had not been much in evidence, as a result of his poor health.[32]
In fact, Peyton spoke at several rallies in May and again in October
1981. The magical flair and charismatic charge that Peyton gave to the
crusade was once again being exhibited and experienced.[33]

The apex of the seven-year crusade campaign began with an invitation from the Philippine hierarchy for Father Peyton to conduct a grand
crusade as part of the Marian year of 1985. In December 1984, at the
outset of the year, Peyton met with local bishops in Cebu, San Fernando,
Davao, and Caceres to discuss a nationwide crusade during the ensuing
year.[34] He expressed his hopes for the future:

> I [have] the great hope that the Bishops of the Philippines will unite
> and through them, their priests, teachers, and lay leaders to make
> the most of the extraordinary opportunity to implant deeply in the
> hearts and minds of the Filipino people, the need of Mary and the
> power of the Family Rosary to help them cope with the problems
> of today.[35]

Peyton made the Philippine crusade his top priority, believing the potential to be great for a massive crusade from September to December, of
the Marian year.[36]

In July, the Crusade, which was captured on film, began with the
appearance of billboard and radio advertisements. Peyton reported, "I
have an hour a day [on radio and television] for at least a year so give
them everything we have — black and white, color, short and long, new
and old."[37] In an unusual move from past crusades, Peyton was present
in the Philippines for the entire period of the campaign, September 8 to

December 8, having come even earlier to supervise the preparations. He considered this the greatest opportunity of his ministerial career:

> Never in all the forty three years of working for Our Lady have I experienced such an opportunity as this for the Family Rosary Crusade. Never was there a whole nation with all the bishops of its sixty-seven dioceses, its twenty hundred parish priests and its forty four million Catholics committed to an all out three month effort for the Family Rosary.[38]

The rally held on December 8, 1985, at Luneta Park attracted 2 million people in one of the most powerful displays of faith experienced by Peyton in his life. In his typical fashion Peyton preached his patented speech about his life and the importance of the family rosary, but on this occasion he concluded his message with some challenges to believe in Mary's efficacy to overcome the forces of evil. He ended his talk with his patented message: "Will you offer to pray the Family Rosary every day, at best with all the members of your family, if not, with some, or alone if necessary?"[39] One report of the rally succinctly captured the significance of the event in Peyton's mind: "Father claims that never in the 43 years of the Crusade has he experienced such an unusual intervention of Our Lord and never has he had such an awareness of our Lady's presence, prayer, and guidance."[40]

In a postscript strikingly similar to events twenty years earlier in Brazil, Ferdinand Marcos, who had ruled the Philippines in a form of dictatorship from 1965 to 1986, was overthrown in a bloodless coup that some attributed to the recently completed rosary crusade. One free-lance journalist agreed that there was more to the revolution than was physically present: "The revolution had come at just about the right time. One cannot help but see the hand of God in the events that took place, brought about by the preceding year, 1985."[41] On February 25 forces loyal to Corazon Aquino, armed with rosaries, held off a squadron of Marcos's tanks. Peyton commented about the chain of incidents: "The miraculous events of those four days in late February have left in the hearts and minds and homes of millions an awareness of their Spiritual Power—a power engendered by the rosary. It will make history. It will be told by parents to their children through ages to come."[42]

Notwithstanding his success in the Philippines, Peyton realized that the Crusade needed a new direction if it was to continue. He explained the situation:

I feel I may not, on account of ill-health and advancing years, be
in a position to direct the Crusade for much longer and it may not
be possible to have all the features of the Crusade which my team
and I have been able to provide for the bishops in whose dioceses
are preached the crusade.

Wishing to leave as his legacy the ideas that had shaped crusade efforts
in the past,[43] he devised the concept of a rosary handbook, a "do it
yourself kit" which he hoped would be "a catalyst to enable bishops to
organize diocesan crusades anywhere in the world."[44] Peyton asked the
Sarita Kenedy East Foundation for a grant of $200,000 per year for five
years to cover the cost of printing, translating, and shipping one hundred
thousand copies of the handbook around the world.[45] The foundation
agreed, however, to give one lump sum of $200,000.

The handbook provided guidelines on every facet of the preparation,
organization, conduct, and follow-up of a successful eight-week crusade.
There were sections on organizing the crusade, an exegetical summary
on the mysteries of the rosary, theological and spiritual source material
from the foremost architects of Vatican II, a teachers' source section,
and an appendix of sample crusade materials including posters, pledge
cards, and pledge certificates. The handbook described the roles of all
participants, from the local ordinary to those who were slated to visit
individual homes. The handbook was accompanied by supplementary
aides, including the rosary prayer book, audio and video cassettes on the
mysteries of the rosary, and a documentary video on Father Peyton.[46]
Peyton wrote of the handbook's purpose, "It is not a question of just
one more good devotion or movement. Here is offered to a diocese a
powerful help for the renewal of faith and prayer in the family, [and]
therefore in the Church."[47]

Peyton attempted to imbue the handbook with an ecumenical spirit.
The Methodist minister and Peyton devotee J. Neville Ward contributed
an essay on the ecumenical aspect of the family rosary. Peyton himself
suggested alternative forms of the rosary that might be used, especially
abbreviated ones such as an Our Father and three Hail Marys per decade.
He stated, "The real essence of the rosary is the prayerful recitation of
the actual prayers that are said combined with thinking about one aspect
of a mystery."[48]

The former provincial, George DePrizio, CSC, was asked to coordinate the massive distribution effort, but Peyton stayed close to the
project. The manual was translated into Spanish, French, German, Italian, Polish, and Portuguese and sent with the package materials in a

monumental mailing to eight hundred of the world's bishops. Peyton hoped that the publication and promulgation of the handbook would bring "new horizons and undreamed of potentialities," but disappointingly only 25 percent even responded to the invitation to consider a locally organized crusade. This lackluster response was very hurtful to Peyton.[49]

When direct mailing did not work, Peyton decided to go on the road to "sell" his handbook to the world's hierarchy. His first stop was the Bishops' Synod of 1987 in Rome. Lobbying for his project one-on-one and in groups, Peyton used his special gift of persuasion to gather much support. As in the past Pope John Paul II endorsed the handbook as an excellent means for the local Church to promote family prayer. Peyton secured several proclamations from various contingents of bishops in support of his new endeavor. One such declaration stated, "We, the undersigned, express heartfelt encouragement for Father Peyton's current efforts to promote diocesan-sponsored Family Rosary Crusades throughout the world, as a proven means of spiritual renewal and a concrete and effective instrument of catechesis and evangelization."[50]

Encouraged by his accomplishments in Rome, Peyton continued to travel and lobby the bishops for the handbook. He described his new role:

> My priority in these final years of my life is to search out bishops in all parts of the world who will sponsor the Crusade — who will go all out, and not count the cost — to preserve for us and for future generations the magnificent heritage and treasure of our Catholic faith, the family rosary.[51]

In November 1987 he went to Nairobi, Kenya, and met with Cardinal Maurice Otunga, who agreed to distribute the handbook to all the bishops of East Africa. Back in the United States Peyton enlisted the support of several influential American prelates: Cardinals Joseph Bernardin of Chicago, Bernard Law of Boston, and John O'Connor of New York, Archbishop John May of St. Louis, and Bishop Howard Hubbard of Albany, who signed a declaration similar to that obtained at the Bishops' Synod earlier in the year. He journeyed to Ireland in February 1988 at the request of Cardinal Tomas O'Fiaich, archbishop of Armagh, to speak to the annual bishops' meeting at Maynooth. In May 1988 he traveled to Lima, Peru, to attend the Marian and Eucharistic Congress, also enlisting support from many Latin American bishops. Returning to the United States, Peyton's road show to "sell" the handbook found him on the East Coast in November 1988 and a West Coast swing from California north to Alaska the next February. One year later in March 1989 he traveled to Australia and New Zealand to gain more supporters.[52]

Reactions to the handbook were generally positive, but few bishops used it to conduct a crusade. In October 1989 eleven members of the Mexican hierarchy signed a pledge "to encourage [our] brother priests to promote the Family Rosary Crusade as an efficacious means of evangelization."[53] Archbishop Bernardino Pinera of La Serena, Chile, announced that he would conduct his crusade using the handbook, describing it as "a masterpiece of doctrine and wisdom." Archbishop Joseph Cassidy of Tuam, Ireland, also voiced his support for the program and his plans to use it. Archbishop Roger Mahoney in Los Angeles, on the other hand, while acknowledging Peyton's good intentions, believed the program was unrealistic and impractical.[54]

The first U.S. crusade to use the manual took place in Stockton, California, whose bishop, Daniel Montrose, described the merits the crusade had brought to his diocese during April and May 1988:

> I really do feel that there has been a change in attitude in the minds and hearts of many of our priests and they are much more favorably inclined toward the Rosary than before. . . . I think the parishes that have really tried to promote the Rosary Crusade are going to be very thankful in the days and years ahead. I am grateful to you for having urged me to do the Diocesan Rosary Crusade; it is a great blessing for our Diocese.[55]

Other sites of domestic crusades were Palm Beach, Florida, in 1990 and Sacramento, California, in 1991.[56]

Other Crusade Activities in the 1980s

The successful billboard campaign that was launched in 1947 and had been so successful in the 1970s continued throughout the 1980s. The second three-year program, following the successful 1976–79 campaign, ended in 1982 with impressive statistics. During the six-year period almost eighteen thousand billboards displayed the family prayer message, and more than sixty-three hundred television spots were aired. Slogans used included "God Makes House Calls," "God Listens," "God Answers," "Ask God," and "Use Your Hot Line to God." The billboard campaign was financed to a large extent through regular (usually annual) contributions from the Grace Foundation.[57] In 1984 Peyton's billboard campaign won the Wilbur Award from the Religious Public Relations

Council, Inc., headquartered in Chicago.[58] The billboard campaign continued into the new decade with one new slogan, "Don't Give Up. Pray. It Works!" being added to those used.[59]

The desire for new beginnings and the ongoing controversy over the Families for Prayer issue prompted a move by the Albany office to a new location. In May 1983 the headquarters for Family Rosary was moved from 773 Madison to Executive Park, a section of Stuyvesant Plaza. At this same time Josefina Bayot, the Filipino woman who had served as a financial assistant to Peyton since his open heart surgery, purchased a home on Cortland Street in Albany for Father Peyton and other Holy Cross religious engaged in the ministry. The home was occupied by Peyton and his assistant Benny Belangue, who cooked his meals, did his laundry, and assisted with routine errands.[60]

During the 1980s Peyton received numerous personal awards. In 1980 the combined boards of the Crusade for Family Prayer, Family Rosary, and Family Theater authorized $70,000 to commission a biography of Father Peyton, an update from *All for Her,* published in 1967. The book, written by Jeanne Arnold, was published in 1983.[61] On his seventh-fifth birthday (1984) the city of Scranton celebrated "Patrick Peyton Day" with a Mass celebrated by Bishop (later Cardinal Archbishop of New York) John O'Connor in the cathedral, where Peyton had served as sexton so many years before.[62] In 1988 Peyton was honored by his native Ireland as "Mayo Man of the Year" with a presentation made at the Burlington Hotel in Dublin. The decade closed in grand style with Peyton being awarded the initial St. Maximilian Kolbe Award, given by Father James McCurry, OFM Conv., national director of the Militia Immaculate, an organization founded by Kolbe. Conferred on October 6, 1989, the award was granted to Peyton for his "authentic understanding of the Blessed Virgin Mary in the theology, spirituality, and apostolic life of the Church."[63]

Crusade for Family Prayer in the 1990s

Finding a replacement for the now-aging Peyton became even more pressing in the 1980s. Dennis Roverato of Family Theater commented,

> I think he felt tremendous anxiety about what would happen with the work after he passed on. . . . He was exhausted, his body was exhausted, and I think deep down he knew that he had done as much as he could do. But his main concern that followed him through the

years that I worked with him, was that the work would continue after his death.[64]

For over twenty-five years Peyton had been grooming young priests as possible successors, even providing lists of Holy Cross religious who might be approached. The most promising person in Peyton's mind was John Gurley until the Families of Prayer conflict soured their relationship, contributing to Gurley's early death.[65]

In May 1983, the provincial, Joseph Callahan, CSC, sent out a generic call for a successor, stating that Peyton was willing to provide an internship. The qualifications he gave were very general: "Naturally a gifted preacher and motivator is required and a person deeply committed to the rosary as a contemporary means of spiritual growth."[66] Peyton himself weighed in with his own selection, Peter Grace, who he said would "preserve the purity of purpose with which the Crusade began — the Family Rosary, pure and simple." Peyton's suggestion demonstrates where his loyalty lay, both in people and the overall direction of his work.[67]

Reorganization efforts, another long-standing project, also continued into the 1980s. In 1990, at the mutual suggestion of the provincial, David Farrell, CSC, and Peyton, Sister Gerald Hartney, CSC, an accountant who was knowledgeable about Canon Law and experienced in working with Church officials in Washington, D.C., to shore up the archdiocese's sinking fiscal ship, was asked to assess the financial structure of the organizations and make recommendations for restructuring. She expressed her understanding of the Crusade's contemporary aim:

> My own interpretation of your goal at this stage is to insure that funds donated in Mary's name will have the legal safeguards, careful stewardship, and professional management necessary to continue and expand your special mission in any continent until the end of time.[68]

Sister Gerald reported that the Crusade seemed to be operating outside the confines of the Church, with no oversight of spending and no accountability to the local ordinary or other ecclesiastical officials. What organization existed, she said, was haphazard, with Peter Grace in effect managing the finances while his associate Thomas Doyle conducted the day-to-day activities as treasurer.[69]

In June 1990 Hartney presented her reorganization plan. She recommended a two-tier structure with a corporate board serving as overseer to the two basic corporations, Family Rosary and Family Theater. The All for Her irrevocable trust would combine the investment portfolios for both New York–based corporations (Crusade for Family Prayer and Family Rosary)[70] as well as the investments for Family Theater and would serve as the basic economic resource for the overall corporation. Both Family Theater and Family Rosary would have their own boards of directors who reported to an executive director, a new position to be filled by a layman, Robert Klein.[71] She offered three principal reasons for the restructuring plan:

1. The need to monitor investments required constant oversight at a board level, and existing annual meetings for Family Rosary and Family Theater were inadequate for such oversight.

2. Funds donated to Family Rosary were funds donated to the Catholic Church; a two-tiered corporate structure would provide the accountability required by the church and state laws.

3. To perpetuate Peyton's work beyond his lifetime, a trust with an active board of directors is needed.[72]

A plan devised by William Hogan, CSC, was implemented with Hartney's assistance during the summer of 1990. In June the boards of directors for Family Rosary and Family Theater met, and the new corporate board structure was created. The plan designated the corporate board to consist of four Holy Cross religious, two of whom were the superior general and Eastern Province provincial, and two additional lay board members to be appointed by the four religious. The corporate board in turn appointed the boards of directors for Family Rosary in Albany and Family Theater in Hollywood.[73] The plan gave control of the Crusade's operation to Holy Cross, a situation that had been desired but elusive since 1980, when William Ribando, CSC, requested a similar change during the Families for Prayer controversy. By 1990 Peyton had come to agree to the need for Holy Cross support in his ministry. The superior general, Claude Grou, CSC, eased the priest's possible apprehension:

> We certainly share your concern since we all want to make sure that the work you have started will continue. We all agreed that the active support of the Congregation of Holy Cross will be the best guarantee for its future and we were glad to tell you of our desire to provide this support.[74]

The restructuring effort prompted Sr. Mary Buckley, RSM, who first met Peyton in 1942 at Vincentian Institute, to retire from Family Rosary. She told Peyton that she had been receiving signs that it was time to retire but that the reorganization made the decision easier. The rosary priest praised Buckley for her many dedicated years of service: "Only the thanks of God and Mary would be adequate for the gift given to the Crusade and myself in you and all that you are in excellence, competence, dedication, consecration, and loyalty."[75]

The reorganization of Father Peyton's Family Rosary operation was conducted as the Hollywood operation pressed forward with new projects in the 1990s. In 1991 two new films were released: *The Annunciation* and *The Rosary Around the World,* the latter depicting how the rosary was celebrated at Marian shrines around the world.[76] This same year Peyton, again having conceived of a grand project to create a new series of fifteen films (pared down to five) aimed at youth and placing biblical messages in contemporary settings, entered into an agreement with the "Witnessing to God's Love Foundation," headquartered in Holland, for a $1.4 million grant to finance the films.[77] Peter Thompson, the producer of the popular television program *Quincy* and the *Ann Jillian Story,* was engaged as producer. The first, *The Choice,* reflecting the theme of the Annunciation, was completed in the fall of 1991 and premiered at the Santo Domingo Film Festival in February 1992.[78] The other four films, *The Visit, The Search, The Hero,* and *The Journey,* were filmed in July 1992 and premiered together in October at the Television Academy of Arts and Sciences in North Hollywood.[79] The five films, which served as a bridge from the rosary films of the past to future endeavors, received numerous accolades, including the Golden Halo from the Southern California Motion Picture Council in 1994 and the Award for Excellence from the Film Advisory Board the same year.[80]

In 1991 and 1992 Father Peyton marked two highly significant anniversaries, the Golden Jubilees of his ordination and the foundation of Family Rosary. He celebrated his anniversary of ordination with celebrations at Notre Dame, North Easton (Massachusetts), Albany, Chicago, Philadelphia, San Pedro (California), and throughout Ireland, all places of significance for him over his years in Holy Cross. The Golden Jubilee of Family Rosary was noted by numerous dignitaries of church and state, including Pope John Paul II and Mary Robinson, president of Ireland. The pope wrote, "I give thanks to God for the many gifts bestowed on the Church through your tireless and persevering efforts during this half century. . . . I pray that all Christian families may discover the treasure of the Family Rosary in order that their family life be strengthened and blessed."[81] One writer observed, "Father Peyton's accomplishments are not always in the forefront of our national memory today. In the eyes of some, his style of piety harkens back to another era. Yet his important place in the history of Catholic media seems secure."[82]

Exhibiting his lifelong penchant for opportunism, Peyton capitalized on the collapse of the Soviet Union in 1989 and the gradual restoration of the Church in Eastern Europe by inaugurating his "Rosaries for Russia" program. In Detroit on October 6, 1991, he announced his intention to collect 1 million rosaries that would be sent to Russia, the Balkans, and former Eastern bloc nations for distribution by local ordinaries. By June 1992 over eight hundred thousand rosaries had been collected and sent overseas and Peyton's goal of 1 million was exceeded within a year of his call.[83]

In spite of his enthusiasm for the growth and expansion that occurred in the 1990s, it was apparent that Peyton's time was running short. He was comparatively healthy in the 1980s but by the 1990s his heart ailment became more troublesome, necessitating a pacemaker in 1987 and angioplasties in 1990 and 1992. He was hospitalized three times for congestive heart failure: in December 1991 as well as February and April 1992.[84]

After a few months of failing health Father Peyton's life began to slowly ebb away. Throughout his illness he remained faithful to the recitation of fifteen decades of the rosary and, when possible, his daily Mass. On the evening of June 2, 1992, he could not finish his rosary, but was told by the staff members at the Little Sisters of the Poor in San Pedro, California, that they would finish the prayer for him. Patrick Peyton died peacefully at 5:20 a.m. on June 3. His last words were, "Mary, my queen, my mother." Statements of condolence and praise were received from peoples and groups around the globe. Archbishop John Foley, president of the Pontifical Commission for Social Communication, wrote, "The death of Father Patrick Peyton is a loss which will be deeply felt. He touched the lives of millions of people through radio and television with the simplicity and sincerity of his life and of his message." The superior general of Holy Cross, Claude Grou, CSC, commented:

> As he departs for his final reward, Father Peyton leaves to us all a mission to persue [*sic*]. We, who have seen the importance of his work, need today to join hands and renew our commitment to pursue the task for which he has given us his life. And, as we persue [*sic*] this work, we know that we can count on his support and protection.[85]

Father Peyton was buried on June 8 in the Holy Cross community cemetery at Stonehill College in Massachusetts following a funeral at which David Farrell, CSC, presided and George DePrizio, CSC, preached. At his wake service the night before, John Murphy, CSC, who had worked with Family Rosary for ten years, praised Peyton's contribution: "Father Pat was unique — he was charismatic — he was seemingly tireless, and in his lifetime, he did more to inspire devotion to Our Lady and the rosary than anyone in history." Possibly the most fitting testimony to Peyton came from William Ribando, CSC, who, twenty years after his conflict with the rosary priest, stated,

> His influence as an apostle was truly enormous. He brought a type of public spirituality to people that you saw in few others except maybe Mother Teresa or Dorothy Day. He was in his own way a hero of the era, and I think he had a God-given grace to be a true apostle and priest.[86]

Conclusion

It was appropriate that Patrick Peyton and his international Crusade for Family Prayer once again returned to a degree of prominence in the 1980s and early 1990s, capping a family prayer ministry that spanned five decades and visited every habitable continent. Emerging from the societal and ecclesiastical doldrums of the 1970s, Peyton's Crusade for Family Prayer experienced a renewal of its earlier crusade successes with a return to the Philippines and garnered numerous awards for a series of new films based on the mysteries of the rosary. Peyton also prepared as much as he could for the transfer of his ministry by restructuring the Crusade for Family Prayer, creating a "do it yourself" crusade program handbook, and making overtures for one to take his place before his death. Even as he arranged to transfer his ministry Peyton promulgated his message through his Rosaries for Russia Program.

Patrick Peyton's life began in the humble setting of Attymass in County Mayo, Ireland, and ended in the simple home of a group of Roman Catholic nuns, but in between his ministry took him around the globe numerous times and put him in the company of leaders of Church, business, and state. But Peyton never forgot his spiritual roots, which went back to the main room of the family home when all gathered nightly and prayed the rosary, with his father as the leader. This scene was Peyton's earliest and strongest memory, and it provided his lifelong raison d'être. Patrick Peyton beat all the odds, rising from obscurity and defeating tuberculosis, but he knew that his special journey was not for him but for the promotion of devotion to the Mother of God. People today could learn a new lesson from an old playbook — The family that prays together stays together.

Epilogue

Patrick Peyton's Spiritual Odyssey

During a ministerial career that spanned more than half a century, Father Peyton became internationally well known through television films, his popular half-hour weekly radio program *Family Theater of the Air* (1947–68), and his international rosary crusades, which began in London, Ontario, in 1948 and continued to the late 1980s. Through this specialized and individual apostolate Peyton touched the lives of countless people, most of whom were mesmerized by his charism, sincerity, and sense of purpose. Peyton was not sophisticated in speech, nor did he demonstrate great intellectual acumen, yet he easily met his original goal of persuading 10 million families to say the family rosary by the mid-1950s, using his simple but profound message, "The family that prays together stays together."

This biography of Patrick Peyton would not be complete, therefore, without a description and analysis of his spiritual journey and how it was experienced, perceived, and understood by those he encountered along the road of life. Peyton's message to the world was quite simple, but as the methods used to communicate that missive were complex, so too the personality and spiritual understanding of the communicator were multifarious. Single-minded in his devotion to Mary, because of his Irish roots and his conviction that his defeat of tuberculosis came as a result of Mary's intervention on his behalf, Patrick Peyton, the Apostle of the Family Rosary, exhibited a devotion and sense of commitment rarely seen. It is appropriate, therefore, that this book close with such an investigation.

Peyton's Theology of Prayer

Patrick Peyton's personal understanding of the Blessed Virgin Mary was central to his prayer life and the conduct of his ministry. Mary of Nazareth was the driving force in Peyton's life; in a very real way he dedicated his life to her and the promotion of what he believed was her work on earth. He once wrote, "It's not a cause or theory which drives me, it's a person. I feel an awareness of Mary, a driving sense of her humanity, her personality, and all she has lavished upon me." On another occasion he stated, "To Mary, Mother of God, I dedicate myself, and I shall do my all to do this daily and every day of my life."[1] Peyton's attraction and devotion to Mary began when he was a child, but unquestionably his cure from tuberculosis also put his life on a course from which he refused to deviate. When his life was in crisis Mary had not abandoned him but rather provided him a privilege that for Peyton was a debt he could never adequately repay. He knew then that the rest of his life "would be a continuous act of repayment to her." Mary was his defense and strength; she was the one who would guide him through the highways and the detours of life. In a speech he once commented, "Mary is my strength; she is my spirituality; she is my peace; she is my prayer; she is my purity; she is my sureness; she is my defense, my protection."[2]

Peyton did not perceive Mary as an unapproachable person in the heavens, but rather as immanent and real in every conceivable way. He often spoke of Mary being alive, the daughter of Saints Anne and Joachim, a woman who understood suffering because she had faced poverty, deprivation, and sorrow. Mary's power to intercede was unexcelled:

> Mary is omnipotent in her power of prayer. Mary is omnipotent in her power of intercession with her Son. Mary can do anything God can do. The only difference is the way they do it. God does it by His Holy Will; Mary, by her holy prayers. God wills something and it happens; Mary prays to Him for something and He does it.[3]

Because Mary was real and efficacious in her prayers, Peyton could think of no greater honor than to serve Mary. He wrote, "To do work for Mary is indeed a blessed and wonderful privilege."[4]

Peyton's sense of Mary's immanence explains his confidence that she was in charge of the Family Rosary ministry. He often wrote and spoke to others about how Mary not only blessed the work, but guided every aspect of what happened; she was the one who ran the ministry, "the brains of the crusade." He once commented, "From the beginning, I have relied on Mary to be the leader and the decision maker of the Family Rosary Crusade and all its activities. So far she has not failed me."[5] Peyton often asked Mary to intercede in order to win victories for the crusade. He also believed that it was Mary who had brought about the conversion of South America, turning people away from Communism. He stated, "From her hands will come the answers to the terrible problems of the day. To her alone has God given the answer to Communism."[6]

Mary was not only in charge of the crusade; she was in Peyton's mind the person for whom he worked. He referred to her periodically in letters as "our superior."

> Our Blessed Mother is our Superior. The intense consciousness and awareness of that fact that our Blessed Mother IS [emphasis Peyton's] our Superior and that her wishes are ours, and that to accomplish them we will do everything in our power, will be the soul of the Family Rosary priests and sisters and people. Because Our Blessed Mother is our Superior I will beg and plead with her daily to fill the hearts of those of us who are her instruments with an extraordinary love of each other, an extraordinary co-operation with each other. Your fervent prayers, devotion, spirit of sacrifice and love for Our Blessed Mother will do a lot to bring this about in all of us.[7]

His belief in Mary's guidance of the crusade helps in understanding why he often ran afoul of members of Holy Cross who could not comprehend his motivation. The discipline of religious life prior to Vatican II that almost commanded obedience to rules and regulations was not the drummer to which Patrick Peyton marched. Rather, firmly believing that Mary's will was of more consequence than that of his religious superiors, Peyton often acted in ways contrary to accepted norms of the day. Often he rebelled when asked to send his annual assessment to the province, claiming that he could not take Mary's money. His resistance to requests of religious superiors was surely tainted with a sense that he did not want his autonomy jeopardized, but more fundamentally it was rooted in his sure conviction that Mary's will must be done.[8] He was more than content to surrender himself to her love and will. Crusade colleagues often spoke of how Peyton referred to himself as Mary's donkey, being led to do whatever she needed or wanted done.[9] One observer noted, "I just think his overriding love for our Blessed Mother took precedence over his own personal comfort. Whatever he wanted to do was secondary to accomplishing what he wanted to do for her. His attention to our Blessed Mother always came first."[10] John Murphy once stated, "Every moment of his life was lived for Mary, and his love for her, and his zeal to inspire others to love her was contagious. His entire life was dedicated to doing more and better things for our Blessed Mother."[11] In many ways Peyton was blinded to all other possibilities or realities in his life. The title of his "autobiography," *All for Her,* was illustrative of how he and others perceived his relationship to Mary and the purpose of his life.

The personal dimension of Peyton's relationship with Mary was also apparent to those who shared his life and ministry. He often told friends and colleagues that he spoke with Mary as one would speak with a spouse or lover. One person commented, "I soon learned that his dedication of every minute of every hour of every day of his life to Mary was not a meaningless pledge."[12] The actress Loretta Young, the first Hollywood personality to befriend Peyton, succinctly captured the personal dimension of Peyton's relationship with Mary: "I don't think I've ever seen a man ever, in this world anyway, in love with a woman the way he [Peyton] was with her [Mary]. There was no pretense about it. You could see him just glow when he would talk about her."[13] Peyton's feeling was not sophisticated, but rather was manifest in a simple, almost childlike spirit, which was real.

Peyton's devotion to Mary, important as it was to his spiritual life, did not rule out other influences. Francis Grogan, CSC, observed, "I always said he was well balanced in his spirituality. He had great devotion to our Lady and to the rosary, but he also had great esteem and love for the Mass, and he made a holy hour every day. He was a man of prayer, and a man of great love of Mary."[14] In line with orthodox Roman Catholic theology and praxis, Peyton argued that Mary was the way to Christ, her Son: "The real reason [for devotion to Mary] is that no man, or woman, or family can have a sincere love for Mary without having convictions about Her Son in the Blessed Sacrament and in the Mass, and be willing to live these convictions."[15] Peyton believed that in loving Christ we are called through baptism to be the presence of Christ to others, and that we would therefore experience hardship, suffering, and pain, just as Jesus did. He wrote,

> God does not like pain for its own sake. Pain is in our lives to serve us as a stepping stone to heaven. It was in His own life in the Garden of Gethsemane. He has always shown us the way and has never asked us to say "yes" to a hardship that He has not borne Himself but with a hundred times more intensity.[16]

Peyton described the difficult path which he saw as the only way to eternal life:

And so my dear people, the life of Christ in you is a grand life. And if it is healthy there is agreat [sic] spirit of sacrifice in you, a great spirit of self-denail [sic], and self-surrender. [F]or the essence of the Christian life is only this — the spirit of sacrifice. There is no other way to bridge the gap between heaven and earth except by the narrow way of the cross.[17]

Peyton saw prayer as the essential aspect of spiritual life — an aspect that one must experience internally and then externalize in the form of virtuous action. For him ministry was only a manifestation of what must be happening inside. He wrote, "Prayer is...above all an event — an experience — an initiative — a decision that takes place interiorly. What happened exteriorly is also prayer, but only in so far as it expressed the interior attitude of the soul." He understood prayer as "an intimate experience between the man who prays and God, a living communication between two free beings based in love."[18] One observer noted that Peyton's personal prayer was "the source of the overwhelming power that people recognize in him."[19]

The three most obvious externalizations of Peyton's inner prayer life were the Mass, the rosary, and devotion to the Holy Spirit. Friends and colleagues have noted the importance of priesthood to Peyton and the celebration of the Eucharist as the central act of that vocation. Many commented that when he celebrated Mass people felt they were in the presence of God in a special way. As one observer put it, "He just had a touch that was different." Peyton did not take Mass intentions, but daily offered the Eucharistic sacrifice in thanksgiving to Mary for granting him life and opportunity. Thus, while his private and liturgical prayer was highly significant to him, Peyton continually centered his spirituality in Mary, whom he loved and for whom he daily labored in spreading the message of family prayer.[20] Still, Peyton often vocalized prayer to the Holy Spirit whose active presence in the world guided the Church and society.

Just as the central object of Peyton's spiritual devotion was Mary, the central message of his spirituality was the need for family prayer through the rosary. To Peyton, the rosary itself was the key that would unlock the chains which kept society and especially the family away from God. In Peyton's view, the power of the rosary came, not primarily from the prayers, but from meditation on the mysteries, the essential activities in the drama of Salvation History, which Peyton believed would soften the hardest heart. As Mary was the way to Christ, the rosary was

the "pavement which enables you to get there."[21] Peyton spoke of the
rosary's efficacy in leading one to Christ:

> The person with the rosary in hand has the key to learning the most
> important of all lessons: the love of God for us, the destiny he has
> in store for us and the way he is helping us to reach that destiny. In
> other words, the rosary, by its very essence, tells a person who uses
> it wisely and well who Christ is, what he has done for me, [and]
> what he has a right to expect of me.[22]

Even more important than its efficacy for individuals seeking a mean-
ingful inner life was the rosary's role in the spiritual life of the family unit.
From the outset of his ministry Peyton bemoaned the state of upheaval
that characterized the average family in the United States after World
War II. In an earlier era the Industrial Revolution had, in Peyton's esti-
mation, done a disservice to the family by replacing the common family
business with factories. World Wars I and II also splintered families by
"forcing" women to work and causing great dislocation through death
and injury. In the succeeding years Peyton identified new family problems including addictions, runaway and rebellious children, divorce, and
most prominently materialism. He once stated of American culture:

> It's *the* [emphasis Peyton's] sin against the first commandment —
> the false god, materialism — that really enslaves people. Talk about
> slavery — it's man's mortal enemy, gripping him, provoking him
> to want four cars, hold two jobs, and in the process, rejecting
> tradition.[23]

Since social sanity could be restored only through a renewal of family-
based unity, the family must seek that unity through family prayer. He
once stated, "The restoration of family prayer is a basic need and if it
is given the chance it will prove itself to be the most efficacious and
powerful protection against the dangers of our age."[24] Family prayer
was the vehicle that would bind families together, make more bearable
the crosses and vicissitudes of life, and help people to better recognize
their absolute dependence upon God.

Peyton's promotion of family prayer found its apex in the idea of the
family rosary. Ingrained in his person and spirituality from childhood,
he understood it to be the greatest of all prayers that a family could
recite and the one to bring resolution to the present family crisis that
was evident to all. He commented, "My work — and I pray to persevere
in it until my last breath is drawn — is to urge families throughout the
world to pray united as families so that they can experience the Family

Rosary for what it is, a powerful prayer to bring joy, peace and unity to troubled homes."[25] Peyton believed the family rosary was efficacious in bonding families, warding off evil, and initiating personal renewal in people and nations. He suggested the United States could learn a lesson from the family rosary:

> Patriotism and a sense of social responsibility are worthy motives with which to evoke family action. In its misery, its helplessness, the world admits that it is in need of a leader; our country, particularly, holds out its hands in supplication. What better instrument for self-recovery could be placed in those hands than the Rosary, the recitation of which will gain the aid of Mary, the Mother of God?[26]

Father Peyton told the world that the family rosary was the answer sought by families. The rosary had the ability to restore the vitality that society had slowly drained from families over a period of time. He wrote, "There is no better way to insure the happiness and safety of your family now and forever than to begin at once the daily family prayer of the Rosary. It will give you your share of peace and happiness here below, and the promise of eternal joys." He suggested that the family rosary would aid parents to carry out their familial duties. Peyton did not believe the rosary was a panacea or a magic formula, but if prayed faithfully it can be "the light in [the family's] darkness" and will "assure the constant and loving protection of God for the family."[27] Although Peyton himself believed that the family rosary was the most forceful prayer, he did promote, especially later in his life, a more ecumenical and broader message that family prayer of any type was highly desirable.[28]

Patrick Peyton's Personality and Philosophy of Life

The multiple aspects of Patrick Peyton's philosophy of life all stem from his single-minded commitment to Mary, the Mother of God, and to the rosary, the special prayer of devotion to her. All who knew and worked with Peyton described him as single-minded and possessed by tunnel vision, a reality that he readily acknowledged: "My call has always been to Mary and to her rosary and I don't think I would have the motivation sufficient to continue if I lost my focus on the rosary and on Mary."[29] He seemed unable to readily relate to others except through the rosary. People were very conscious that he was close to Mary, but it was equally clear to most that he had little knowledge of current events or other relevant news. One example of this limitation was Peyton's inability to engage people in table conversation. Many who knew him have stated that he was quiet and even sullen at meals until the conversation changed to Mary. Then, as if a lightbulb had been turned on, he became vocal and animated.[30] His colleagues on the crusade wished he would read a news magazine so they would have something about which they could converse other than their work.[31]

Driven by the perception that he needed to repay Mary for her favor to him, Peyton found acceptable anything that advanced the cause of Mary and her rosary. This almost obsessive concentration made Peyton blind to the consequences of decisions such as the financing of the Latin American crusades and his general blank-check attitude toward Peter Grace. His single-minded devotion, while providing the discipline needed to give direction and support to his ministry, created problems and controversies. William Ribando, CSC, summarized the situation: "Pat possessed a sincere desire to do God's will, but he took a blind line at times."[32]

Peyton's single-minded approach to life and ministry translated into a personal work ethic that few were able to match. His day-to-day activity was conducted as if there were no tomorrow. People may not have always understood his motive nor been clear on what he was trying to accomplish at a specific time, "but it was clear that their impression was of a very dedicated man." Peyton never stopped reaching for goals that others perceived to be impossible and, remarkably, he often achieved them, because he was clear that Mary was with him in every endeavor.[33] One lay observer of Peyton's whirlwind approach to his work commented to him,

> I am still somewhat dazed by the magnitude of your vision and still more impressed with the obstacles you have overcome in spreading your message of Family Prayer around the world. Each segment of your work would be a full job for anyone else. I can frankly say that I don't know how you ever had and still do have the energy to accomplish so much.[34]

Peyton demonstrated absolute dedication to purpose and was not content with his personal effort unless the will of Mary, as he understood it, was being satisfied.

Father Peyton's personal dedication led, however, to an often unrealistic and over-demanding attitude toward fellow workers. Peyton made no apologies for his high expectations:

> It must be a fundamental and indispenable [*sic*] assumption that each and every one working for FRC considers his primary objective to be: to serve Our Blessed Mother for the spiritual well-being of families everywhere through prayer, family prayer, the Family Rosary.[35]

Both religious and lay co-workers agree that Peyton's perfectionism placed great demands on others. Dorothy Halloran, who before her marriage traveled with Peyton on the international crusades, commented, "If he [Peyton] wanted something done, he wanted it done and done his way because he thought that was the right way."[36] All agree that one had to be selfless to work with Peyton; it was simply impossible to do all that he asked.[37] At times his demanding nature manifested itself in stubbornness, but this quality was often to the betterment of the mission; he was unwilling to accept anything but the best from individuals and institutions, especially when it came to satisfying the will of Mary.[38]

Peyton's relationship with members of his religious community, the Congregation of Holy Cross, was also determined by his single-minded nature, even though Holy Cross was highly supportive of Peyton's efforts from the very outset. The rare privilege afforded the rosary priest by the provincial of the American Province, Thomas Steiner, CSC, namely, the establishment of an independent apostolate, was indicative of support he would receive from succeeding provincials. Superiors general were also supportive of Peyton's work, although not directly.[39] The priests who worked the crusades with Peyton were very loyal and supportive of his efforts as well. John Murphy, CSC, stated,

> We loved Fr. Pat. We were extremely devoted to him. He never realized how devoted we were, how dedicated we were to the work. The best friends he had in the world were the priests who worked with him. We were loyal, we were faithful, we would do anything for the work and we really worked very, very hard, but he was never one to express gratitude to the Community members, the priests who worked with him.[40]

In spite of this general support, Peyton's high expectations and his single-mindedness created friction with his fellow Holy Cross religious. Most disagreements arose because Peyton's colleagues "could not see the purpose of his work and resisted him."[41] From Peyton's perspective, the Congregation seemed to have little interest in his work.[42] More profound than these differences in perspective, however, was a fundamental disagreement between Peyton and his confreres about how to lead a religious life. From the outset of his apostolic life Peyton participated in an independent apostolate and in many ways was fully autonomous. Because of his unusual mission and the extraordinary degree of support he received, Peyton came to think of himself as unique, so he was naturally frustrated by attempts to limit his activities and by demands that he follow regulations by which others were bound. On the other hand, it is also easy to see how other religious, who, although part of Peyton's ministry, worked under the guidelines of a more standard religious life model, might not comprehend his ways.

Peyton's philosophy of life and ministry were highly influenced by his single-minded devotion, but so too were some aspects of his personality. Opinions vary on the degree to which control was a tool used by Peyton in the daily work of Family Rosary. The actress Ann Blyth observed that although Peyton always possessed opinions on how things should be done, in those areas where his expertise was weak he bowed to the knowledge of others. Dennis Roverato, on the other hand, argued that Peyton would often hire people to do a certain job, but then would refuse to listen to what they had to say.[43]

This writer finds the evidence overwhelming that Peyton was reluctant to relinquish control in any aspect of his work. The most persuasive proof of his reluctance was the failure of one reorganization attempt after another. Only when Peyton knew his death was imminent did he accept a restructured organization that would safeguard the considerable Crusade funds he had accumulated. Peyton's preference for malleable young priests as crusade recruits was another symptom of his desire for control, as was his habit of making decisions by seeking guidance from Mary, who spoke only to him.

As with his conflicts with Holy Cross religious the control which Peyton demonstrated was, in large measure, generated over time by the decisions of superiors who allowed Peyton to operate independently and thus by default possess large measures of control. The degree of autonomy he was given meant that the rise or fall of the Crusade for Family Prayer was basically up to him. Thus, in order to secure success Peyton took control and guided the Crusade in a direction that he believed would bring the best results. Possessing such a high degree of control from the outset, it would have been difficult for any person, including Patrick Peyton, to easily or readily divest him from such autonomy.

Peyton was fortunate to possess many personal qualities that attracted people to his message and work. The simplicity of Peyton's rural Irish roots never left him. He was not a well-spoken nor a famous orator; on the contrary, it was the simplicity of his message which was attractive to people. His simplicity was often manifest in a childlike humility that was noticed by all. He was not a man who chose the limelight; rather it chose him. While he associated freely with the rich and famous, he always maintained his simple, sincere, and humble countenance. Peyton has been described as a naturally shy man who never luxuriated in the great crowds and the media attention, but rather took on the immensity of the world as a task given him by Mary in the promotion of the family rosary.[44] He would have been content to stay home and do his work, but his calling required that he be more outward and charismatic. Peyton made no attempts to exalt himself; what he did was truly out of love for Mary, for in his mind it was her work.[45] He believed himself to be the vehicle chosen by the Mother of God to promote family prayer, but he did not wear this distinction on his sleeve as some mark of holiness.

Numerous people have commented about the generous spirit that Peyton demonstrated with others. He never refused an invitation to pray with another person, whether it be over the phone, as often happened, or when someone simply asked for some of his time. People with varied problems often called and asked Peyton to pray with them. His favorite response was the Memorare. On the street he often stopped, shook hands with people, and always had something pleasant to say. People's status was of no consequence to Father Peyton; he treated all the same.[46]

Other highly attractive aspects of Peyton's personality were his sincerity, nonjudgmental manner, and sense of humor. His physical appearance (six feet four inches) was certainly an asset when he first met people, but it was his sincerity that won them to his cause. Peyton was able to command attention when he spoke, not because of his eloquence, but rather his sincerity; listeners were convinced that he firmly believed what he said.[47] Peyton also possessed the rare quality of being able to present ideas without making others look unenlightened or ill-informed. He possessed an excellent sense of humor and loved to tell jokes and to hear them.[48]

One of the qualities that assisted Peyton most in his ministry was his power of persuasion. Few people could resist when Peyton asked a favor. One associate commented, "He just had that magic about him."[49] He often couched his request in a way that may have made some uneasy, suggesting "Mary wants it" with certain requests. The strong faith that Peyton held makes it clear, however, that he believed his exhortation; he was not trying to make others feel guilty or put on airs. His persuasive power allowed him to complete many tasks that the average person would never attempt. Patrick Peyton knew with complete certainty that the Mother of God was directing his efforts. Thus, he always went forth with complete confidence that even the most seemingly difficult tasks could somehow be met.

Holiness and Influence on Others

People of faith define holiness in many ways, but regardless of one's personal understanding of the concept, people in varied ways expressed the belief that Patrick Peyton was a man who exhibited holiness. Many people experienced a special presence, often described as an aura, in the person of Father Peyton. The actress Gigi Perreau commented,

> You knew that you were in the presence of a holy man. There was an aura about him that never left. It was not something that came and went on occasion. Wherever he went, whatever the circumstances, you knew that you were in the presence of someone extraordinarily special and holy.[50]

Numerous people use the word "holy" when speaking of Peyton, saying on occasion that he was touched by the hand of God.[51] Associates also were overwhelmed by his goodness, which manifest itself through the holiness and righteousness others demonstrated from their association with him. He made others feel better about themselves, their faith, and the Church.

Peyton cast a large shadow that was seen in the positive influence he had on others. People were touched by his presence; they simply wanted to be around him, feeling certain that they would be better persons because of the encounter. The actor Joseph Campanella stated, "His influence was good on everybody. . . . I think he made everybody want to be a little better."[52] His special influence was noted by George DePrizio, CSC, during his time as provincial:

> Anyone who says that Father Peyton's Crusade work is merely a superficial and emotional stirring of the people, aroused just for the occasion, simply does not know what he is talking about. I have never seen such a vital demonstration of faith in all my life and I am convinced that only God knows the wonderful things that are wrought through it.[53]

Gigi Perreau also noted Peyton's singular presence: "He had an extraordinary charisma that you really don't know how to explain. He really is, I would say, the only man that I have met that has ever had this quality to such an extraordinarily powerful degree, more than anyone else."[54]

Besides the intangible influence which Father Peyton brought to count-less people, there are also numerous reports of his action or words restoring health or faith to individuals. Once while in Chile Peyton was told that the niece of the rector of the diocesan seminary in Santiago was in a hospital with incurable cancer. The child's mother asked Peyton to pray the rosary for her daughter, which he happily did with the woman on the spot. On the next visit her daughter was much better and even-tually she recovered fully. During a trip to Rome, Peyton visited Bishop Thomas Flynn of Lancaster, England, who had suffered a stroke and was completely paralyzed, blessing him with a relic of St. Maria Goretti. At once the prelate was able to move a finger; later he recovered fully. Albert Heinzer, CSC, reported that on a crusade in 1957 a nun asked Peyton to pray for her brother, who was a fallen-away Catholic. He complied and the man attended the rally, received the sacraments, and returned to regular practice with the Church.[55]

As stated at the outset of this epilogue it is not the task of the historian nor the theologian to judge the sanctity of a person, but it cannot be denied that many people who knew and worked with Patrick Peyton have called him a saint. Many describe him as a "saintly man" while others saw him as a "saint in contemporary times." The actor Joseph Campanella offered a succinct summary of his impressions of Peyton: "I don't want to call anybody a saint on earth, but if anybody came close it would be him. The saints perform miracles. What he was able to do was miraculous. And the feeling he gave I think was awesome." Interestingly, Peyton did not shy away from the label, but gave credit for his life where it was properly due: "I am not afraid when people call me a saint. I am. But who made me so? I am a saint because my mother and father and all people around the world made me so. I am not afraid to say I am holy."[56]

Conclusion

During a ministerial career that spanned half a century, Patrick Peyton through radio, film, and most especially an international rosary crusade campaign, touched the hearts of millions through his simple yet sincere and profound message: "The family that prays together stays together." He was born and raised in a rural section of County Mayo, Ireland, and his first spiritual experiences of life occurred when his family nightly gathered to pray the rosary. This initial prayer experience became the seed from which his whole life blossomed and was the seed to the mes-sage that he repeated countless times during his life. Father Peyton's message and manner were never complex and his speech was not eloquent, but, convinced of a miracle in his life, he never ceased to use every sophisticated means and take full advantage of every opportunity to tell people of the necessity of family prayer. People who heard and saw Peyton only once, plus those who worked with him closely, agree that it was his sincerity that attracted others. All knew in their hearts that Peyton believed what he proclaimed with every fiber of his body. In our contemporary world that experiences so much rhetoric in political and ecclesiastical circles, it is easy to see how one whose integrity was solid and whose words were believable would leave a significant impression on others.

Patrick Peyton's message was simple but, like the methods he used for its promulgation, his personality and spirituality were deep and complex. The Blessed Virgin Mary was the center of his life and the one to whom he gave credit for any and all of his accomplishments. Many people, especially members of his religious community, the Congregation of Holy Cross, were not able to adequately understand his dedication nor the depth of his need to respond to the heavenly favors granted to him. Peyton was an independent operator, surely rare for a religious of his day, but the nature and breadth of his ministry could not be conducted any other way. At times his judgment and blind trust in others were faulty, but his motivation, sincerity, and dedication could never be questioned. From humble beginnings Patrick Peyton became an internationally recognized personality, associating with the rich and powerful, but he never forgot his spiritual roots. His life and legacy serve to illustrate well the challenge of Jesus in His "Sermon on the Mount": "Enter through the narrow gate; for the gate is wide and the road is easy that leads to destruction, and there are many who take it. For the gate is narrow and the road is hard that leads to life, and there are few who find it" (Matt. 7:13–14).

Notes

*A list of abbreviations used in the notes
can be found on page 433.*

Introduction

1. Text of Mother's Day Radio Program, May 13, 1945, P 98 arm, Archives Holy Cross Generalate (hereafter AHCG), Rome, Italy.

2. Peyton began his ministry in Albany while serving as chaplain to the Brothers of Holy Cross who taught the male students at Vincentian Institute. The female students were taught by Dominican sisters who gave Peyton some vacant space in their convent as his first office. Later he moved to the College of St. Rose, sponsored by the Sisters of St. Joseph of Carondolet, where his family rosary ministry was resident for several years.

3. Peyton's original idea was a nationwide weekly broadcast of the rosary, but colleagues, supporters, and those who knew the business well, such as Fulton Sheen, advised Peyton that if given the opportunity to go on national radio he should take what was offered, even if that meant not fulfilling his original idea. *Family Theater of the Air* was a weekly series of dramatic shows that promoted the concept of family prayer generically. Peyton was not allowed by the sponsoring company, Mutual Broadcasting, to focus on the rosary.

4. The first of these hour-long programs, called *The Joyful Hour,* aired during the Christmas season of 1947. This program and similar ones broadcast for Easter, Mother's Day, and a few years later at Thanksgiving, were more specifically religious in their content and included decades of the rosary, most often led by leading personalities of stage and screen.

5. Peyton met J. Peter Grace, head of the W. R. Grace Shipping Company, in 1946 when the former was traveling to Ireland for his postordination trip home, an event delayed due to World War II. The two men struck up an instant friendship that ended only with Peyton's death in 1992.

6. These fifteen films were completed in one year with Jerome Lawyer, CSC, as the driving force behind the project.

7. The entire story behind the involvement of the CIA as financial assistants to Family Rosary is long and complex. It is detailed in chapter 7 of this book.

8. While the influence of the rosary crusade cannot be denied, the historical record does not support the position that CIA assistance was provided to assure Goulart's overthrow.

335

9. Robert Wuthnow, *After Heaven: Spirituality in America since the 1950s* (Berkeley: University of California Press, 1998), 1–18. Wuthnow says the increasingly complex social and cultural environment for Americans is probably the principal cause for this shift. Americans became more people of personal spirituality and were not as interested in seeking organized religion to solve their problems. He says that this shift was caused by a "conversation" with the past. The present emphasis on seeking and negotiation is a reaction to how Americans perceived the past and was shaped by historical events.

10. In many ways the decade of the 1960s was a stagnant period for Family Rosary Crusade, especially considering its great strides in the previous decade. Peyton was also filled with ideas, but few during this period produced any significant fruit toward the promotion of family prayer.

Chapter 1: Responding to God's Call

1. Diarmuid O. Laoghaire, SJ, "Traditional Irish Spirituality in Modern Times," in *Irish Spirituality,* ed. Michael Maher (Dublin: Veritas Publications, 1981), 123. See also Peter O'Dwyer, *Towards a History of Irish Spirituality* (Blackrock, Ireland: Columba Press, 1995), 221–25.

2. This expression of faith is attributed to St. Patrick.

3. Quoted in Desmond Keenan, *The Catholic Church in Nineteenth-Century Ireland* (Dublin: Gill and Macmillan, 1983), 28.

4. Ibid., 19–28.

5. Emmet Larkin, "The Devotional Revolution in Ireland," *American Historical Review* 77 (1972): 651.

6. Quoted from the *London Standard* in O'Dwyer, *Towards a History of Irish Spirituality,* 227.

7. Larkin, "The Devotional Revolution in Ireland," 626–27.

8. O'Dwyer, *Towards a History of Irish Spirituality,* 270–71, 223–25.

9. Larkin, "The Devotional Revolution in Ireland," 630–49.

10. It should be noted that Cullen's theological position was consistent with that of Pope Pius IX and was reinforced at Vatican I with the triumph of ultramontanism in the definition of papal infallibility.

11. Larkin, "The Devotional Revolution in Ireland," 640, 648.

12. Keenan, *Catholic Church in Nineteenth-Century Ireland,* 149–52; Donal Kerr, SM, "The Early Nineteenth Century: Patterns of Change," in *Irish Spirituality,* ed. Maher, 140–41; O'Dwyer, *Towards a History of Irish Spirituality,* 229–31; Larkin, "The Devotional Revolution in Ireland," 644–45.

13. Larkin, "The Devotional Revolution in Ireland," 625.

14. The evolutionary history of the rosary and its place in popular devotion is detailed in Richard Gribble, *The History and Devotion of the Rosary* (Huntington, Ind.: Our Sunday Visitor, 1992).

15. Helena Walsh Concannon, *The Queen of Ireland* (Dublin: M. H. Gill & Son, 1938), 129–35, 146.

16. Jeanne Miriam Johnson, CSJ, "Education to the Family Rosary" (MA thesis: Catholic University of America, 1950), 11, 12, 14.

17. In 1922 Pope Pius XI in *Ubi Arcano* called for the initiation of Catholic Action, which he defined as the work of the laity in support of the apostolic efforts of the Church hierarchy. The Legion of Mary was an immediate success, through

its mission of regular prayer and visits to the poor. The Legion spread quickly and within twenty years was established on five continents. See O'Dwyer, *Towards a History of Irish Spirituality,* 260–61.

18. Johnson, "Education to the Family Rosary," 4, 18.

19. Townlands were units of a land system developed during the period of British rule in Ireland. A few townlands or villages were under the ecclesiastical jurisdiction of one parish.

20. Patrick Peyton Baptismal Certificate, Church of St. Joseph, Attymass, County Mayo, Ireland.

21. Rathreedane is commonly known by the local people as Gillardstown because the town is habitated almost exclusively by members of the Gillard family.

22. Gillard Family Reunion Book, 1998, Property of Robert Gillard, Bonniconlon, County Mayo, Ireland. See also "Peyton Family Direct Line," Patrick Peyton Papers, 06–11, Archives Holy Cross Family Ministries (hereafter AHCFM), North Easton, Massachusetts. Robert Gillard escaped from the battle with the British and journeyed alone to the region of the Ox Mountains in Mayo. There he was taken in by a family named Neary. He married one of the Neary daughters, Bridget, and they had four sons. Patrick Peyton's mother, Mary, was the granddaughter of Robert Gillard. Group Interview, June 4, 2000, Patrick Peyton Memorial Centre (hereafter PPC), Attymass, County Mayo.

23. Patrick Peyton, Sermon III, n.d. [1946], 09–17, Family Theater Papers, AHCFM.

24. Patrick Peyton, Family Biographical Notes; Peyton, "Autobiography," 09–17, Family Theater Papers, AHCFM.

25. Francis Woods, "Bound by Gold Chains," 14, unpublished manuscript, n.d. [1946], found in PPC, Attymass, County Mayo.

26. Group Interview, June 4, 2000, PPC, Attymass, County Mayo.

27. "Material Requested by Father Pat for his book, 'Thoughts About My Grandfather' "; "American Educator in the Family Rosary," Papers found in 09–17, Family Theater Papers, AHCFM; Patrick Peyton Data Sheet, Peyton Personnel File, Archives Holy Cross Fathers Eastern Province (hereafter AHCFE), North Easton, Massachusetts; Woods, "Bound by Gold Chains," 19.

28. State schools in Ireland at the time would have been equivalent to parish parochial schools in the United States of the same era. Religion was a regular part of the curriculum, and the local parish pastor was the principal figure responsible for the hiring of teachers and administrators.

29. Group Interview, June 4, 2000, PPC, Attymass, County Mayo.

30. Patrick Peyton, *All for Her* (Hollywood, Calif.: Family Theater Publications, 1967), 8–9, 19–20; Jeanne Gosselin Arnold, *A Man of Faith* (Hollywood, Calif.: Family Theater, Inc., 1983), 10; Biographical Data, Patrick Peyton Personnel File, AHCFE.

31. Peyton, *All for Her,* 26–27; Arnold, *Man of Faith,* 20–22; Group Interview, June 4, 2000, PPC, Attymass, County Mayo; Woods, "Bound by Gold Chains," 29–30. Peyton and Woods describe how Patrick was asked by Durkin to prepare a local hall for a St. Patrick's Day dance. Durkin caught Peyton and a fellow worker, Pat Boyd, dancing with brooms rather than cleaning.

32. Group Interview, June 4, 2000, PPC, Attymass, County Mayo; Peyton, *All for Her,* 24–25; Woods, "Bound by Gold Chains," 26. Peyton once told a fellow

Holy Cross religious, Albert Heinzer, that "he was madly in love with Katie Cummins." He often wrote her name in whitewash on the Peyton family cowshed, an act his mother considered crazy. Katie died at the age of twenty from tuberculosis. See Albert Heinzer, CSC, Questionnaire, May 13, 1961, 09–17, Family Theater Papers, AHCFM.

33. Mary Peyton, Written Testimony, July 23, 1959, Property of Rev. Bill Melody, CSC, Notre Dame, Indiana.

34. Patrick Peyton, *All for Her,* 25.

35. Ibid., 7, 32; Mary Peyton, Written Testimony, July 23, 1959; Robert Gallagher, Interview with Thomas Feeley, CSC, November 3, 1998; Patrick Peyton, CSC, Interview with Karen Swanson, January 1979, 09–17, Family Theater Papers, AHCFM.

36. Liam Ryan, "The Changing Irish Family," *Furrow* 45 (April 1994): 215. Ryan states, "The traditional Irish family gave the father a powerful means of authority over his children and wife. It was a system in which children contributed to the family home much more than they ever received in return."

37. Mary Peyton, Written Testimony, July 23, 1959.

38. Each evening John Peyton recited the following prayer: "O most loving Jesus, who by thy ineffable virtues, and by thy example of thy domestic life, didst consecrate the family which thou didst choose on earth, in thy clemency look down upon this household humbly prostrate before thee and imploring thy mercy. Remember that this family belongs to thee, for to thee we have in a specific way dedicated and devoted ourselves. Look upon us in thy loving kindness. Preserve us from every danger. Give us help in time of need. And grant us thy grace to persevere to the end in imitation of the Holy Family, that having revered thee and loved thee faithfully on earth, we may bless and praise thee eternally in heaven. O Mary, most sweet Mother, to thy intercession we have recourse, knowing that thy divine son will hear thy prayers. And do thou, O glorious patriarch St. Joseph, assist us by thy powerful mediation, and offer by the hands of Mary, our prayers to Jesus. Jesus, Mary, and Joseph, enlighten us, help us, and save us. Amen." Peyton Family Biographical Notes, 09–17, Family Theater Papers, AHCFM.

39. Patrick Peyton, Sermon III, n.d. [1946], AHCFM.

40. Patrick Peyton, *All for Her,* 5–6.

41. Patrick Peyton, "I Talked to Mary," *Extension* 43 (June 1948): 11. Peyton left the following description of his home environment: "Two villages, my mother's and my father's, were my world. Poetry and song would be inadequate to tell what those two villages said to me during my growing. Within sight were the Ox Mountains. In summertime they were a blanket of purple flowers. At night little fires starred the mountains from the overheating heather. From another direction I heard the moaning of the gigantic waves of the Atlantic Ocean coming to their death on the shores of Enniscrone miles away. What a lesson of how all earthly things, no matter how mighty and powerful, will come to end like all those waves. Indelibly impressed in my memory is the bog of my mother's village. As a child sitting on the heather, when I looked as far as my eyes could see, the sky met the earth. Nearer to me neighbors in family groups harvested the turf. For them and for me lunch time was a daily picnic. The streams, rushing down from the mountains, could not be stopped by the biggest boulders as they made their way to the ocean. It was an experience of mystery, togetherness, joy and happiness. It was a glimpse of heaven!"

See Patrick Peyton, "My Magnificat," n.d. [1980], PPC, Attymass, County Mayo, Ireland.

42. Mary Peyton, Written Testimony, July 23, 1959.

43. Patrick Peyton, *All for Her,* 16.

44. Each branch of the Gillard family had been blessed with at least one and as many as five religious vocations. It was generally thought that Patrick's gentle manner, derived most probably from his grandfather Robert Gillard, was the proper disposition for priesthood. See "Material requested by Fr. Pat for his book — thoughts about his grandfather," 09–17, Family Theater Papers, AHCFM.

45. Patrick Peyton, Autobiography, Part I, 09–17, Family Theater Papers, AHCFM.

46. Quoted in Mary Peyton, Written Testimony, July 23, 1959. Peyton himself wrote of his disappointment, "As a result of that letter I became so discouraged that I threw up the vocation. I didn't want to be a priest anymore." See Patrick Peyton, Autobiography, Part I, 09–17, Family Theater Papers, AHCFM.

47. In 1921 the Johnson Act mandated that only 3 percent (based on the 1910 census) of any particular national group could enter the country annually. The National Origins Act, also known as the Johnson-Reed Act of 1924, lowered the percentage of any national group to 2 percent based on the 1890 census. It was clear to Catholics that the act was passed in an effort to eliminate Eastern and Southern European peoples, many of whom were Catholics, from entering the United States.

48. The Irish emigrated to the United States from the outset of the nation, but the Great Famine of 1845–46 was the stimulus that brought millions to America's shores. The Irish had the advantage of being English-speaking, but they were generally less skilled and poorly educated compared with other immigrants, especially Germans, making their welcome less than cordial. The infamous slogan, "Irish need not apply," was often invoked by employers. They generally settled in eastern cities and worked in factories. Many fine books have been written about immigration to the United States and specifically about the Irish. Two well-known general monographs on the topic are: Roger Daniels, *Coming to America: A History of Immigration and Ethnicity in American Life* (New York: HarperCollins, 2002), and John Higham, *Send These to Me: Immigrants in Urban America* (Baltimore: Johns Hopkins University Press, 1984). Two books more specific to Irish immigration are: Edward Laxton, *The Famine Ships: The Irish Exodus to America* (New York: H. Holt, 1997), and Kerby A. Miller, *Emigrants and Exiles: Ireland and the Irish Exodus to North America* (New York: Oxford University Press, 1985).

49. John Carroll, "The First American Report to Propaganda on Catholicism in the United States," March 1, 1785, in *Documents of American Catholic History,* ed. Michael Maher (Wilmington, Del.: Michael Glazier, 1987), 1:148.

50. Peyton Family Biographical Notes, 09–17, Family Theater Papers, AHCFM.

51. Patrick had angered some local employers, especially when the news of his clash with Sandy Durkin became common knowledge. More importantly, it was the common practice of the day that a family's homestead would be given to the eldest son. Thus, knowing that his brother Michael would be given the family farm, Patrick believed his best option was to seek his future in the United States.

52. On May 13, 1917, three Portuguese children, Lucia dos Santos and Francisco and Jacinta Marto received the first of a series of six visions of the Blessed Virgin Mary, in a field near their village of Fatima. Peyton's departure on this special day of

Mary was the beginning of a pattern of always doing important matters on Marian feast days, a practice that would continue throughout his priestly career.

53. Woods, "Bound by Gold Chains," 35.

54. Ibid., 25; Patrick Peyton, *All for Her,* 37.

55. Paul Kelly to "To Whom it May Concern," July 9, 1929, Patrick Peyton Personnel File, AHCFE.

56. Robert Tracy, "Life of Father Peyton," n.d. [1980], Essay found in PPC, Attymass, County Mayo.

57. Patrick had spoken with Thomas who, impressed with the life at the cathedral, came to the realization that he too had a vocation.

58. Woods, "Bound by Gold Chains," 40.

59. On March 1, 1837, a formal pact was made between the Brothers of St. Joseph, founded by Father Jacques Dujarie in 1820, and a band of auxiliary priests of the diocese of LeMans, France, under the direction of Father Basil Anthony Mary Moreau. The union formed the Congregation of Holy Cross, a religious congregation of clerics and lay brothers. On May 13, 1857, Pope Pius IX granted canonical status to the Congregation by acceptance of its constitutions. Holy Cross first came to the United States in 1841 when a band of religious under the leadership of Father Edward Sorin, CSC, established themselves in Vincennes, Indiana. Disagreement with the local ordinary precipitated Sorin's move to South Bend and the establishment of the University of Notre Dame in 1842. From its inception the Congregation has served to meet the need of the local Church. Even today its major apostolic works remain higher education, parochial ministry, and missions. Today the Congregation has seventeen hundred priests and brothers working in fourteen countries.

60. Paul Kelly to "To Whom it May Concern," July 9, 1929, Patrick Peyton Personnel File, AHCFE.

61. "American Educator in the Family Rosary," 09–17, Family Theater Papers, AHCFM.

62. Patrick Peyton, *All for Her,* 43, 44, 46–47.

63. Raymond Cour, CSC, Interview with Thomas Feeley, CSC, June 1999, AHCFM.

64. Letter of Admission to Profession, May 21, 1933; Vow Formula, July 2, 1933, Patrick Peyton Personnel File, AHCFE.

65. Patrick Peyton, CSC, "Statement," October 15, 1932, "Request for Admission to Vows," May 10, 1933, Patrick Peyton Personnel File, AHCFE.

66. John Peyton to Thomas and Patrick Peyton, May 9, 1933, and June 4, 1933, Patrick Peyton Papers, Family 6–11, AHCFM.

67. John Peyton to Thomas and Patrick Peyton, September 7, 1933, Patrick Peyton Papers, Family 6–11, AHCFM.

68. Ibid., November 7, 1933.

69. Report on Visit to the University of Notre Dame, October 21–23, 1963, 05–01, Correspondence, Connerton, AHCFM.

70. Cornelius Hagerty, CSC, "Rev. Patrick Peyton, CSC," in Anecdotes, 06–03, Patrick Peyton Papers, AHCFM.

71. Quoted in Arnold, *Man of Faith,* 17.

72. Vow Formula, August 16, 1936, Patrick Peyton Personnel File, AHCFE.

73. Notre Dame Student Transcript, 06–08, Patrick Peyton Papers, AHCFM. Patrick graduated 29 of 469 with a 91.58 percent average. Tom Peyton graduated 30 of 469.

74. In 1887 Bishop John Keane, the first rector of the Catholic University of America, issued an invitation for religious communities to establish their theologates on or near the grounds of the fledgling university. The idea was to centralize graduate educational opportunities for those in formation for priesthood. The Paulists were the first to establish themselves on campus. Holy Cross moved its theologate to Washington in 1895, with John Zahm, CSC, as superior. For details on the early years of the university see Patrick Henry Ahern, *The Catholic University of America, 1887–1896: The Rectorship of John J. Keane* (Washington, D.C.: Catholic University of America Press, 1948); Peter Hogan, SSJ, *The Catholic University of America, 1896–1903: The Rectorship of Thomas J. Conaty* (Washington, D.C.: Catholic University of America Press, 1949), and Colman J. Barry, OSB, *The Catholic University of America, 1903–1909: The Rectorship of Denis J. O'Connell* (Washington, D.C.: Catholic University of America Press, 1950). An overview history of the university is found in C. Joseph Nuesse, *The Catholic University of America: A Centennial History* (Washington, D.C.: Catholic University of America Press, 1990).

75. The "Bengalese" was a five-minute walk from Holy Cross College. In 1968 the Congregation of Holy Cross moved its major theologate to Moreau Seminary at Notre Dame. Seminarians take courses at Notre Dame, but reside at Moreau Seminary. Today the former Holy Cross College is O'Boyle Hall at Catholic University; the "Bengalese" was sold and now houses a ballet academy.

76. Roman Ladeweski, CSC, Interview with Thomas Feeley, CSC, June 20, 1999, AHCFM.

77. "Report on the Qualifications of Seminarians," August 4, 1937, Patrick Peyton Personnel File, AHCFE.

78. Biographical Resume, 06–08, Patrick Peyton Papers, AHCFM.

79. Patrick Peyton, *All for Her,* 48–50.

80. House Chronicle for the Community Infirmary, 1934–72, Archives of the Congregation of Holy Cross, Indiana Province (hereafter AHCFI), Notre Dame, Indiana.

81. Johnson, "Education to the Family Rosary," 27.

82. Cornelius Hagerty, CSC, "Rev. Patrick Peyton, CSC," Anecdotes, 06–03 Patrick Peyton Papers, AHCFM.

83. Robert Tracy, "Life of Father Peyton."

84. Patrick Peyton, *All for Her,* 57–61; John A. Most to Patrick Peyton, CSC, January 8, 1940, 10–04, Publications, AHCFM. Most, a physician at Healthwin, cleared Peyton to return to classes but cautioned him to go slow in his activity.

85. Patrick Peyton, CSC, Speech to Catholic War Veterans, May 1948, 09–17, Family Theater Papers, AHCFM.

86. Anna Gilmartin to Thomas and Patrick Peyton, n.d. [February 13, 1940], 06–11, Patrick Peyton Papers, AHCFM.

87. Mary Peyton to Patrick Peyton, January 9, 1940, 06–11, Patrick Peyton Papers, AHCFM.

88. Michael Peyton to Patrick Peyton, January 30, 1940; Mary Peyton to Patrick Peyton, January 19, 1940, 06–11, Patrick Peyton Papers, AHCFM.

89. "Report on the Qualifications of Seminarians," February 19, 1940, Patrick Peyton Personnel File, AHCFM. It is interesting that before his bout with tuberculosis he was labeled by superiors as one with great leadership ability. The change in attitude is not readily explainable.

90. Patrick Peyton, *All for Her,* 61–62; Nellie Peyton, Prayer, n.d. [1939–40], 06–07, Patrick Peyton Papers, AHCFM.

91. Peyton, *All for Her,* 63.

92. Ibid., 65.

93. Thomas Steiner, CSC, to Patrick Peyton, CSC, June 30, 1941, Steiner Papers, 08/07, AHCFI.

Chapter 2: The Mission Begins

1. Nativism and anti-Catholicism have played large roles in American Catholic history. This tragic story has been told in numerous outstanding monographs and essays. Some representative samples are: Ray Allen Billington, *The Protestant Crusade, 1800–1860: A Study of the Origins of American Nativism* (New York: Rinehart & Company, 1952); Sr. Marie Leonare Fell, *The Foundations of Nativism in American Textbooks, 1783–1860* (Washington, D.C.: Catholic University of America Press, 1941); James J. Kenneally, "The Burning of the Ursuline Convent: A Different View," *Records of the American Catholic Historical Society of Philadelphia* 90 (1979): 15–22; Sandra Yocum Mize, "Defending Roman Loyalties and Republican Values: The 1848 Italian Revolution in American Catholic Apologetics," *Church History* 60 (December 1991): 480–92; Tyler Anbinder, *Nativism and Slavery: The Northern Know Nothings and the Politics of the 1850s* (New York: Oxford University Press, 1992); Donald Kinzer, *An Episode in Anti-Catholicism: The American Protective Association* (Seattle: University of Washington Press, 1964).

2. *Longingua Oceani,* June 6, 1895, proclaimed, "It would be very erroneous to draw the conclusion that in America is to be sought the type of the most desirable status of the Church, or that it would be universally lawful or expedient for State and Church to be, as in America[,] dissevered and divorced."

3. Many outstanding monographs, books, and essays exist on the subject of Americanism. A sampling of the literature is: Thomas T. McAvoy, CSC, *The Great Crisis in American Catholic History, 1895–1900* (Chicago: Henry Regnery Company, 1957); Gerald P. Fogarty, SJ, *The Vatican and the Americanist Crisis: Denis J. O'Connell, American Agent in Rome, 1885–1903* (Rome: Gregorian University Press, 1974); Robert Emmett Curran, SJ, *Michael Augustine Corrigan and the Shaping of Conservative Catholicism in America, 1878–1902* (New York: Arno Press, 1978); Margaret Mary Reher, "Pope Leo XIII and Americanism'," *Theological Studies* 34 (1973): 679–89; Gerald Fogarty, "The Catholic Hierarchy in the United States between the Third Plenary Council and the Condemnation of Americanism," *U.S. Catholic Historian* 11, no. 3 (Summer 1993): 19–35; Thomas E. Wrangler, "Americanist Beliefs and Papal Orthodoxy: 1884–1889," *U.S. Catholic Historian* 11, no. 3 (Summer 1993): 37–51; Margaret Mary Reher, "The Church and the Kingdom of God in America: The Ecclesiology of the Americanists" (PhD dissertation: Fordham University, 1972).

4. Theological modernism is the United States is discussed most fully in R. Scott Appleby, *"Church" and Age Unite! The Modernist Impulse in American Catholicism* (Notre Dame, Ind.: University of Notre Dame Press, 1992).

5. Coined in or about 1905, the term "modernism" was intended as a pejorative description of certain scholarly trends that had developed in the Catholic Church during the last decade of Leo XIII's pontificate. These trends arose out of the conviction that Catholicism was incompatible with modernity. In practical application Modernists challenged two areas of Catholic teaching that were considered immutable. First, some contemporary European theologians, such as Alfred Loisy and George Tyrrell, SJ, coordinated by Baron Friedrich von Hügel, challenged the idea that Church doctrine had not developed through the Christian era. Scholars, using historical methods, postulated that many traditional beliefs of the Faith had experienced an evolution in their development. Second, the same historical-critical method was applied to the exegesis of Scripture. Thus, the long-standing belief that Moses alone was the author of the Pentateuch was challenged by new theories that postulated who, how, and why the various books of Old Testament Scripture were written. Books that describe modernism, its proponents, and its opponents include: Lester R. Kurtz, *The Politics of Heresy: The Modernist Crisis in Roman Catholicism* (Berkeley: University of California Press, 1986); Marvin O'Connell, *Critics on Trial: An Introduction to the Catholic Modernist Crisis* (Washington, D.C.: Catholic University of America Press, 1994); John Ratte, *Three Modernists: Alfred Loisy, George Tyrrell, William L. Sullivan* (New York: Sheed and Ward, 1967).

6. The death knell of American Catholic intellectual pursuit is described in Michael V. Gannon, "Before and After Modernism: The Intellectual Isolation of the American Priest," in *The Catholic Priest in the United States: Historical Investigations,* ed. John Tracy Ellis (Collegeville, Minn.: St. John's University Press, 1971): 293–383. A counteropinion is offered by Patrick Carey, "After *Testem Benevolentiae* and *Pascendi,*" *Catholic Southwest: A Journal of History and Culture* 7 (1996): 13–31.

7. William M. Halsey, *The Survival of American Innocence: Catholicism in an Era of Disillusionment, 1920–1940* (Notre Dame, Ind.: University of Notre Dame Press, 1980), 1, 64.

8. Anthony B. Smith, "American Catholicism and the Construction of a Public Tradition, 1932–1962" (PhD dissertation: University of Minnesota, 1995), 7, 8.

9. Gordon Edward Truitt, "A Historical and Theological Analysis of the Main Trends of the Catholic Theology of Prayer in the United States, 1940–1975" (PhD dissertation: Catholic University of America, 1982), 14.

10. John Tracy Ellis, "American Catholics and the Intellectual Life," *Thought* 30 (Autumn 1955): 351–88. For more information on the Catholic ghetto and its breakdown see Martin Marty, "The Catholic Ghetto and All the Other Ghettos," *Catholic Historical Review* 68 (1982): 184–205.

11. Joseph A. Tetlow, "American Catholic Spirituality," *New Catholic World* 225 (July–August 1982): 152–55.

12. John Manuel Lozano, CMF, *Grace and Brokenness in God's Country: An Exploration of American Catholic Spirituality* (New York: Paulist Press, 1991), 6–90.

13. Jean Leclercq, OSB, "The Distinctive Characteristics of Roman Catholic American Spirituality," *Louvain Studies* 9 (Spring 1983): 301–6.

14. Gordon Truitt, "Analysis of the Catholic Theology of Prayer in the United States," 25–30.

15. Popular devotions, defined as exercises in piety practiced by lay Christians, not only religious professionals, arose in the Church as a result of the codification of rites ordered by the Council of Trent. While devotions are not technically classified as liturgy Josef Jungmann has commented, "They were in every other respect part of the public worship of the Church." See Carl Dehne, "Roman Catholic Popular Devotions," *Worship* 49 (1975): 448–49, 452.

16. External manifestations of popular religiosity can be illustrated by the Italian custom of the procession on important feast days. The premier historian of popular religiosity in the American Church is Robert Orsi. See Orsi, *Madonna of 115th Street: Faith and Community in Italian Harlem, 1880–1950* (New Haven, Conn.: Yale University Press, 1985), and *Thank You, St. Jude: Women's Devotion to the Patron Saint of Hopeless Causes* (New Haven, Conn.: Yale University Press, 1996).

17. Quoted in Wilfrid Parsons, SJ, "Marian Devotion in the Early United States," *Marian Studies* 3 (1952): 241.

18. Quoted in Joseph Chinnici, OFM, "The Organization of the Spiritual Life: American Catholic Devotional Works, 1791–1866," *Theological Studies* 40 (June 1979): 249.

19. Thomas Kselman and Steven Avella, "Marian Piety and the Cold War in the United States," *Catholic Historical Review* 72 (1986): 407–12.

20. Ibid., 409–10.

21. Patrick Peyton, "The Family Rosary," *Catholic Charities Review* 27 (December 1943): 290.

22. "The Family Rosary," addendum to "Report on Family Rosary," contained in Patrick Peyton, CSC, to Edmund Gibbons, August 15, 1943, Family Rosary Papers, Archives Diocese of Albany (hereafter ADA), Albany, New York.

23. Gordon Truitt, "Analysis of the Catholic Theology of Prayer in the United States," 121.

24. "Family and the Home," Editorial, *America* 71 (May 6, 1944): 126.

25. Clare Booth Luce, "Anchor of the Christian Family," *Action Now* 5 (February 1952): 16.

26. U.S. Senate Resolution, September 4, 1932, National Catholic Welfare Conference (NCWC) General Administration Files, Box 99, Archives, Catholic University of America (hereafter ACUA), Washington, D.C.

27. Noted British essayist G. K. Chesterton in his usual unabashed style expressed a very different cause of the family crisis: "It cannot be too often repeated that what destroyed the family in the modern world was capitalism. No doubt, it might have been Communism, if Communism had ever had a chance, outside the semi-Mongolian wilderness where it actually flourishes. But, so far as we are concerned, what has broken up households, and encouraged divorces, and treated the old domestic virtues with more and more open contempt, is the epoch and power of Capitalism." See G. K. Chesterton, "Three Foes of the Family," *G. K.'s Weekly* 19 (August 2, 1934): 344.

28. Jeffrey Burns, *American Catholics and the Family Crisis, 1930–1962* (New York: Garland Publishing, 1988), 106–15.

29. In his presidential address before the 1940 convention of the American Catholic Sociological Society, on December 29, 1940, Paul Mundie stated, "It is

my belief that no problems of modern society are more serious than those surrounding family life." See Paul J. Mundie, "Family in Transition," *American Catholic Sociological Review* 2 (March 1941): 41.

30. Jeffrey Burns, *American Catholics and the Family Crisis*, 11–19, 89–105. On a more positive note the *Review* did outline five basic ideals that if achieved would begin to place the family on the correct path: an objective moral order, the superiority of rural life, Americanism, anti-contraception and anti-divorce, and the need for religious renewal.

31. Ibid., 19–28.

32. James M. Gillis, CSP, *The Catholic Church and the Home* (New York: Macmillan, 1928), 115; Charles Miltner, CSC, "Ideal Christian Home" (Sermon) *Homiletic and Pastoral Review* 30 (December 1929): 308; Karl J. Alter, "Restoring the Family Circle," *Catholic Mind* 49 (August 1951): 482.

33. Jeffrey Burns, *American Catholics and the Family Crisis*, 122–28.

34. Ibid., 128–30, 170–77, 213–20, 279–310. Father (later Cardinal) Josef Cardijn of Belgium was the architect of the "observe, judge, act" concept of Catholic Action, applying it in the work of his Young Christian Workers group. A complete history of the Christian Family Movement is given in Jeffrey Burns, *Disturbing the Peace: A History of the Christian Family Movement, 1949–1974* (Notre Dame, Ind.: University of Notre Dame Press, 1999).

35. The influence of the Industrial Revolution on the family was stated by the Catholic sociologist Paul Mundie in this way: The pre–Industrial Revolution era was characterized by "great stability and solidarity," a time when all contributed to the whole. Thus, families contributed an undivided wage. In the post–Industrial Revolution era, with the onset of factory life, family members contributed to a divided wage. Individualism overtook the communal family effort. Children in many ways became an economic liability. See Paul J. Mundie, "Family in Transition," 41.

36. Edgar Schmiedler, OSB, "Conserving the Family," *Catholic Action* 14 (January 1932): 12.

37. "The Christian Family: A Statement of the American Hierarchy," November 21, 1949, in *Catholic Mind* 48 (1950): 124.

38. Patrick Peyton, CSC, "Excerpts from Fr. Peyton's Family Rosary Crusade Talks," 09–17, Family Theater Papers, AHCFM.

39. Patrick Peyton, CSC, "An Hour with the Queen of Heaven," Radio Talk, June 14, 1946, 09–17, Family Theater Papers, AHCFM.

40. Patrick Peyton, CSC, *The Ear of God* (Garden City, N.Y.: Doubleday, 1951), 54.

41. Patrick Peyton, CSC, "Family Rosary Crusade," unpublished essay, June 1952, 01–13, Crusades, England, AHCFM.

42. Patrick Peyton, CSC, "Quotes from Speeches (Collected)," 06–09, Patrick Peyton Papers, AHCFM.

43. Patrick Peyton, CSC, "I Talked to Mary," *Extension* (reprint); "Presentation on the Family Rosary Crusade," (1949): 10.

44. Patrick Peyton, CSC, Sermon, n.d. [1946], 09–17, Family Theater Papers, AHCFM. See Patrick Peyton, *All for Her* (Hollywood, Calif.: Family Theater Publications, 1967), 68–71, and Jeanne Gosselin Arnold, *A Man of Faith* (Hollywood, Calif.: Family Theater, Inc., 1983), 26.

45. Patrick Peyton, CSC, to Thomas Peyton, CSC, November 8, 1942, 06–11, Patrick Peyton Papers, AHCFM.

46. Patrick Peyton, CSC, Speech to Catholic War Veterans, May 1948, 09–17, Family Theater Papers, AHCFM.

47. Patrick Peyton, CSC, to Edmund Gibbons, "Report on the Family Rosary," August 15, 1943, Family Rosary Papers, ADA. See also Patrick Peyton, CSC, "Family Rosary," *Catholic Educational Review* 41 (November 1943): 561.

48. Patrick Peyton, CSC, Sermon, n.d. [1944], 09–17, Family Theater Papers, AHCFM.

49. Patrick Peyton, CSC, to Christopher O'Toole, CSC, May 1, 1961, 428 (FR) Archives Holy Cross Generalate (hereafter AHCG), Rome, Italy; Arnold, *Man of Faith,* 27–28; Peyton, *All for Her,* 71.

50. Patrick Peyton, CSC, *All for Her,* 72; Peyton, "Report on the Family Rosary," *Homiletic and Pastoral Review* 44 (January 1944): 301; Patrick Peyton, CSC, to Henry Althoff, August 29, 1943, 06–02, Patrick Peyton Papers, AHCFM.

51. Letter of Obedience, July 23, 1942, 06–08, Patrick Peyton Papers, AHCFM.

52. Thomas Steiner, CSC, to Patrick Peyton, CSC, September 28, 1942, 10–04 Publications; Patrick Sullivan, CSC, Interview with Thomas Feeley, CSC, June 20, 1999, AHCFM; Jerome Lawyer, CSC, "James W. Connerton, CSC: Priest of the Congregation of Holy Cross," Personal Essay, April 14, 1985.

53. Francis Woods, "Bound by Gold Chains," unpublished manuscript, n.d. (1946), 71.

54. Marian feasts are celebrated throughout the liturgical year. Some of the principal ones are: January 1, Feast of Mary the Mother of God; March 25, the Annunciation; August 15, Assumption of Mary; September 8, Birthday of Mary; October 7, Feast of Our Lady of the Rosary; November 21, Feast of the Presentation; and December 8, the Immaculate Conception.

55. The Vincentian Institute was operated by the Brothers of Holy Cross, who taught the boys, and the Mercy Sisters, who taught the girls. The Brothers of Holy Cross helped stuff envelopes for these early mailings.

56. Patrick Peyton, CSC, "The Family Rosary Crusade," *Homiletic and Pastoral Review* 43 (May 1943): 716.

57. Ibid., 715; Patrick Peyton, *All for Her,* 76.

58. Henry Althoff to Patrick Peyton, CSC, August 25, 1943; Ildebrando Antoniutti to Peyton, CSC, September 23, 1944, 06–02, Patrick Peyton Papers, AHCFM.

59. Patrick Peyton, CSC, *All for Her,* 74–75.

60. Thomas Steiner, CSC, to Patrick Peyton, CSC, June 8, 1943, Holy Cross Camp, AHCFI; Patrick Peyton, CSC, *All for Her,* 80; Paul Waldschmidt, CSC, to James Connerton, CSC, November 22, 1961, 05–01, Correspondence Connerton, AHCFM; Patrick Peyton, CSC, to Albert Cousineau, CSC, September 4, 1944, 428 (FR) 14, AHCG.

61. Albert Cousineau, CSC, to Patrick Peyton, CSC, September 3, 1943, 428 (FR) 14, AHCG.

62. "Report of the Family Rosary Crusade for 1943–1944," n.d. [August 1944], 428 (FR) 14, AHCG.

63. "Saskatchewan Crusade," short essay in 01–06, Crusades, Canada, AHCFM; Francis Woods, "Bound by Gold Chains," 70. Woods was grateful to his ordinary

for the opportunity he had to work with Peyton: "I shall never forget your Excellency's great kindness to me, especially in allowing me the opportunity and privilege of working for the restoration of the Rosary to homes that need it so desperately today." See Francis Woods to Edmund Gibbons, November 30, 1952, Family Rosary File, ADA.

64. Patrick Peyton, CSC, *All for Her,* 78–79. Peyton spoke of Francis Woods as a man "[in] whose judgment I place great value and respect." Quoted in Jerome Lawyer, CSC, to Peyton, March 20, 1946, 06–02, Patrick Peyton Papers, AHCFM.

65. Patrick Peyton, CSC, to Sr. M. Attracta, OP, November 21, 1944, 06–02, Patrick Peyton Papers, AHCFM.

66. Patrick Peyton, CSC, to "Most Holy Father," May 1, 1945, 06–03, Patrick Peyton Papers, AHCFM.

67. As one example, Peyton wrote, "The family succeeds where there are apostles as concerned about it as you are. All I ask is that you keep up your enthusiasm and that you will place the hope of your success more in the Holy Hours of Adoration and the Rosary, than any other means." See Patrick Peyton, CSC, to Sr. Mary Austin, January 27, 1944, 06–04, Patrick Peyton Papers, AHCFM.

68. Patrick Peyton, CSC, to Thomas Steiner, CSC, July 25, 1944, and October 3, 1944, Steiner Papers, Family Rosary #1A, AHCFI.

69. Thomas Steiner, CSC, to Patrick Peyton, CSC, September 18, 1943, Steiner Papers, 08–07; Peyton to Steiner, October 3, 1944, Steiner Papers, Family Rosary #1A, AHCFI. Steiner wrote, "You may have every confidence that the spreading of the Family Rosary practice is going to have its effect. The world, including this country, is in such a chaotic state that only prayers can save it. The anti-religious and anti-Christian forces now at work can only be combated with prayer. The Rosary is the devotion that will save us, as it has done in the past. May God bless your efforts, and may Our Blessed Mother come to your aid in promoting this excellent and fruitful practice." It should be noted that Jeanne Arnold in *Man of Faith* suggests that Steiner merely tolerated Peyton's promotion of the rosary. See *Man of Faith,* 34.

70. Arnold, *Man of Faith,* 43–44; P. Peyton, CSC, to Edward Heston, CSC, February 20, 1948, 267.74 (FT), AHCG.

71. This depiction of the family rosary showed a family — father, mother, and four children — at home reciting the rosary. Prominently displayed are photos of two other sons, serving with the armed forces. Through the window overlooking this scene of devotion can be seen the Blessed Virgin Mary, surrounded by a heavenly light. Her arms are outstretched in a gesture of protection over the family, especially the sons in service. See *The Evangelist* (Albany diocesan newspaper), October 1, 1943; *Rosaverian* VII, March 15, 1944, Records of the College of St. Rose, Albany, New York.

72. Peyton, writing many years later, claimed that Steiner "gave carte blanche permission to preach the crusade message any place in the United States." See Patrick Peyton, CSC, to Thomas Barrosse, CSC, May 14, 1980, Patrick Peyton Personnel File, AHCFE.

73. Thomas Steiner, CSC, to Patrick Peyton, CSC, August 11, 1943; Peyton to Steiner, July 25, 1944, Steiner Papers Family Rosary #1A, AHCFI; "Report of the Family Rosary Crusade for 1943–1944," n.d. [August 1944], 428 (FR) 14, AHCG.

74. Patrick Peyton, CSC, 1944 Liturgical Calendar, 06–06, Patrick Peyton Papers; Peyton, Sermon, n.d. [1944], 09–17, Family Theater Papers, AHCFM.

75. Patrick Peyton, CSC, Sermon, n.d. [1944], 09–17, Family Theater Papers, AHCFM. In 1944 Peyton delivered a series of sermons that urged his audience to pray the family rosary. He gave a specific theme to each sermon: (1) Rosary, counter to the Devil, (2) Need for Mary to fight Satan, (3) Necessity of prayer (especially the rosary) to remedy the problems of life, (4) The rosary brings happiness and peace to homes, (5) The rosary allows us to show gratitude to God, (6) The rosary is the shortest and easiest fulfillment of our common vocation [of prayer], (7) The rosary brings home what it means to be a friend of Mary, (8) The intercession of Mary is of greater value than all others combined, (9) Welcoming Mary into your home, (10) Her consent (*fiat*) made her spokesperson [to God] for the human race, (11) The family rosary is the key that opens the door to Mary.

76. Patrick Peyton, CSC, "The Family Rosary Crusade," *Homiletic and Pastoral Review* 43 (May 1943): 713, 715; Peyton, "The Family Rosary," *Catholic Charities Review* 27 (December 1943): 288; Peyton, "They Must Say the Rosary," unpublished essay (draft), n.d. [1945], Steiner Papers, Family Rosary #1, AHCFI.

77. Patrick Peyton, CSC, to Edmund Gibbons, "Report on the Family Rosary," August 15, 1943, Family Rosary Papers, ADA. W. J. O'Neil, national president of the NCCM, publicized Peyton's appeal through *Catholic Action*.

78. Patrick Peyton, CSC, to Kerndt Healey, CSC, November 13, 1944, Steiner Papers, 08–07, AHCFI. The proposed broadcast never materialized, but Peyton never lost the idea of radio as a primary medium to promote his idea of family prayer.

79. "Family Rosary," Editorial, *Catholic Charities Review* 29 (June 1945): 62; "Family and the Home," Editorial, *America* 71 (May 6, 1944): 127. In a compilation of press comments one writer stated, "The Rosary must become a sword in the hands of Spiritual Crusaders — a weapon to be handled by old and young, in a word by the family. For it is the family which is most deeply involved in the world struggle."

80. "Report on the Family Rosary," n.d. [September 1943] 428 (FR) 14, AHCG.

81. Mother Abbess to Patrick Peyton, CSC, September 26, 1944, 06–04, Patrick Peyton Papers, AHCFM; "Rosary Campaign," *Ave Maria* 63 (June 22, 1946): 770.

82. Patrick Peyton, CSC, to Thomas Steiner, CSC, March 29, 1945, Family Rosary Papers, #1, AHCFI.

83. Donald Warren, *Radio Priest: Charles Coughlin, the Father of Hate Radio* (New York: Free Press, 1996).

84. Richard Gribble, CSC, *Guardian of America: The Life of James Martin Gillis, C.S.P.* (Mahwah, N.J.: Paulist Press, 1998): 96–98, 118–19.

85. "Establishment of Catholic Radio Bureau Announced by National Council of Catholic Men," *Catholic Action* 20 (December 1938): 15.

86. William C. Smith, "How to Produce Religious Radio Programs," *Catholic Action* 29 (January 1947): 17–18; "Some Notes on Catholic Radio Programs," *Catholic Action* 21 (November 1944): 19; "New Religious Program Begins on NBC Red Network: We Believe," *Catholic Action* 24 (July 1942): 24.

87. William Smith, "The Church of the Air," *Catholic Mind* 45 (January 1947): 15–18. It should be noted that not all Catholics were ready to give free license to radio. For example, some worried that religious messages would not be received well since the personality of preachers would not be manifest to listeners. James Gillis, CSP, feared that since radio was such a public medium people would not be as forceful as necessary, for fear of alienating people. He wrote, "There is . . . a warning for

those who use radio in the interest of religion. If we are meticulously careful to hurt no one's feelings; if we shy away from controversial topics, there is danger of lapsing into 'innocuous banality.' " See A. E. H. Swinstead, "Broadcasting Catholicism," *Blackfriars* 13 (December 1932): 743–53; James M. Gillis, CSP, "Radio and Religion," *Catholic World* 146 (October 1937): 89.

88. In August 1947 representatives of eighty-eight organizations interested in Catholic broadcasting met at Fordham University with the chief item of discussion being the formation of an association of Catholic broadcasters. William Smith headed a committee to investigate the question. The next year, 150 met at St. John's Seminary in Boston and formally inaugurated the Catholic Broadcasters' Association. Its purpose was mainly as a service medium for members. Its organ was called *Airtime*. See "Catholic Broadcasters Meet at Fordham, August 16–17, 1947," *Catholic Action* 29 (September 1947): 13; "CBA Charter Convention," *America* 79 (July 17, 1948): 339; Ella C. Clark, "Radio and Television are Your Business," *Catholic School Review* 58 (November 1958): 60.

89. "Report of the Family Rosary Crusade from 1943–1944," 428 (FR) 14, AHCG; Patrick Peyton, CSC, *All for Her,* 79–81.

90. *Variety* commented about *Evening Time:* "*Evening Time* makes a great improvement over earlier (15-minute) broadcasts....Recitation of the Rosary is still the basic idea, but music, musicians, script, and production have been added to give the feature smoother cohesion, wider appeal, and stronger listener pull." See "Radio Apostolate of the Family Rosary," 507.04 Family Rosary Papers, AHCFF. In 1946 *Evening Time* was moved to WSNY in Schenectady, but returned to Albany in late 1947. In 1948 the live broadcasts were discontinued, with tapes made and broadcast irregularly thereafter. See Paul D. McCann to Richard Gribble, CSC, August 19, 2000.

91. *The Catholic Hour* had broadcast a series entitled *The Rosary and the Rights of Man,* on October 16, 23, and 30, 1938. The three broadcasts, individually titled "Life" (October 16), "Liberty" (October 23), and "The Pursuit of Happiness" (October 30), demonstrated the connection between the basic rights of the Declaration of Independence and the rosary. This was an example of Catholicism's attempt to demonstrate its compatibility with American life. *The Catholic Hour* broadcast on the Third Sunday of Lent 1945 by Monsignor Sheen may have been the program's (or possibly the NCCM's) attempt to mollify Peyton.

92. Patrick Peyton, CSC, *All for Her,* 82–85; Peyton, "Father Peyton's First Program," *Catholic Digest* 15 (June 1951): 26.

93. Patrick Peyton, CSC, to Thomas Steiner, CSC, May 1, 1945, Family Rosary Papers #1, AHCFI.

94. Patrick Peyton, CSC, to Thomas Steiner, CSC, April 5, 1945, Steiner Papers 08–07, AHCFI.

95. Peyton told Crosby, "All I ask is that you will give such an important message on the Family Rosary that families who would otherwise not listen to a priest or anyone else [will], as a result of your talk, go down on their knees and practice the Family Rosary." See Patrick Peyton, CSC, to Bing Crosby, May 3, 1945, 10–04, Publications, AHCFM.

96. When the Constitutions of the Congregation of Holy Cross received approbation in 1857 it was mandated that the women's side of the Congregation be canonically separated from the men. Eventually three branches of women religious,

all claiming Basil Moreau as their founder, arose. The Marianites of Holy Cross (MSC) were French based and located more in the southern regions of the United States. The Sisters of Holy Cross (CSC) were Canadian based and ministered in France and in the eastern regions of the United States. The Sisters of the Holy Cross (CSC) were American based and centralized in the Midwestern United States. Today these three groups of sisters continue to minister in the geographic areas described.

97. Woods, "Bound by Gold Chains," 3–8; Peyton, *All for Her,* 88–89; Peyton, "Father Peyton's First Program," 27–28.

98. There is no extant data that shows why Peyton's original plan of a combination of mysteries was not used.

99. Mother's Day Radio Program Text, May 13, 1945, P98 Arm, AHCG.

100. Ibid.

101. Patrick Peyton, CSC, to Thomas Steiner, CSC, April 6, 1944, Steiner Papers, 08–07, AHCFI. Peyton was very clear that the May 13 broadcast success was the foundation to the rest of his ministry. Speaking of the program he once wrote, "It was the key that opened for F[amily] R[osary] C[rusade] the mass media that has been an essential element for bringing its message to the peoples of the earth." See Patrick Peyton, CSC, Memorandum, May 13, 1966, 267.74 (FT11) AHCG.

Chapter 3: *Family Theater of the Air*

1. Peyton originally asked that Bob Moher, CSC, and Bill Evans, CSC, be assigned to Family Rosary, but neither man even worked in the apostolate. See Patrick Peyton, CSC, to Thomas Steiner, CSC, March 29, 1945, and May 31, 1945. Steiner to Peyton, April 17, 1945, Family Rosary Papers #1, AHCFI.

2. "The Daily Family Rosary Apostolate," n.d. [1945], Steiner Papers Family Rosary #1A, AHCFI. The extant data is not clear as to why Gibbons was hesitant to allow expansion of the Congregation's efforts in Albany. Holy Cross came to Vincentian Institute in September 1935 and had served the diocese well.

3. Thomas Steiner, CSC, to Jerome Lawyer, CSC, October 20, 1945, Steiner Papers Family Rosary #1, AHCFI.

4. Lawyer's initial impressions of Family Rosary were positive: "I am grateful to Father Steiner for this appointment. At the time of receiving it, I think I would have preferred something more active, like parish work. However, I now see the wisdom in his judgment of giving me something that does not demand too much strength and energy. I sometimes feel I do not follow his advice of resting as much as I should. However, I do not hesitate to take off a day or so when I am not feeling well. I have become much more interested in the work and consider it second to no other work, except the...missions." Jerome Lawyer, CSC, to Christopher O'Toole, CSC, February 12, 1946, Family Rosary Papers #1, AHCFI.

5. Thomas Steiner, CSC, to Jerome Lawyer, CSC, October 20, 1945, Steiner Papers Family Rosary #1; Steiner to Mother M. Eucharia, IHM, January 11, 1947, Family Rosary Papers #2, AHCFI.

6. Thomas Steiner, CSC, to Patrick Peyton, CSC, September 20, 1947, Family Rosary Papers #3, AHCFI.

7. Patrick Peyton, CSC, to Thomas Steiner, CSC, January 26, 1948, Family Rosary Papers #3, AHCFI.

8. Patrick Peyton, CSC, "An Hour with the Queen of Heaven," Radio Talk, June 14, 1946, 09–17, Family Theater Papers, AHCFM.

9. Patrick Peyton, CSC, to Thomas Steiner, CSC, June 22, 1945, Family Rosary Papers #1, ACHFI. Peyton told Steiner that the bishop of Manchester, New Hampshire, Matthew Brady, suggested a weekly program that featured a message on family prayer from a member of the hierarchy or another prominent Catholic.

10. The ticket was apparently for Father John Tracy, but the nun misunderstood the name. Eileen Gerwin, Interview with Thomas Feeley, CSC, April 18, 1999; Patrick Peyton, CSC, Radio Interview (text), June 23, 1950, 09–17, Family Theater Papers, AHCFM.

11. Patrick Peyton, CSC, Sermon to Catholic War Veterans, May 1948, 09–17, Family Theater Papers, AHCFM.

12. Young's initial reaction to Peyton was one of sympathy. She remarked many years later, "I don't think I've ever felt so sorry for anyone in my life. He was so nervous. At the time our house was voluptuous, worldly with movie stars all over the place. I said, 'I know you want something; just tell me and I'll give it to you, if I can.' " See *The Evangelist* (clipping), June 18, 1992, 06–03; Patrick Peyton, CSC, to Jerome Lawyer, CSC, December 27, 1946, 06–02, Patrick Peyton Papers, AHCFM.

13. Patrick Peyton, CSC, *All for Her,* 103; Peyton, "Father Peyton and Family Theater," *Catholic School Journal* 47 (September 1947): 41a. The agreement that the stars signed stated: "In order to offer to our American families the protection which is necessary and fundamental against the dangers of the present age, and for the purposes of drawing down upon our country the special blessings of Almighty God, I pledge myself to do my part to cooperate for the realization of the project of a radio apostolate for the popularization of the practice of daily family prayer."

14. Joan Leslie Caldwell, Interview with James FitzPatrick, OMI, and Thomas Feeley, CSC, November 12, 1998; Joseph Campanella, Interview with Thomas Feeley, CSC, November 10, 1998; Ann Blyth, Interview with James FitzPatrick, OMI, and Thomas Feeley, CSC, November 14, 1998; Jack Wintz, OFM, "Jane Wyatt: Witness to Family Values," *St. Anthony Messenger* 105, no. 1 (June 1997): 22.

15. Helen M. Sherritt, "Peyton Power is Prayer," *Action Now* 4 (June 1951): 18.

16. Theodore Bonnet, "Father Peyton and God," *Family Digest* 8 (January 1953): 16.

17. Patrick Peyton, CSC, to Thomas Steiner, CSC, August 25, 1945, Family Rosary Papers #1, AHCFI.

18. Patrick Peyton, CSC, to Christopher O'Toole, CSC, August 23, 1945, Family Rosary Papers #1, AHCFI; Peyton to John Cantwell, September 15, 1945, Family Rosary, Family Theater File, Archives Archdiocese of Los Angeles (hereafter AALA), San Fernando, California. Peyton told Cantwell that he hoped to receive soon an answer from NBC on his request for air time.

19. Patrick Peyton, CSC, to Robert Fennell, September 12, 1945, 06–02, Patrick Peyton Papers, AHCFM.

20. Patrick Peyton, CSC, *All for Her* (Hollywood, Calif.: Family Theater Publications, 1967), 107–8. In early April 1946 Peyton reported that Mutual had agreed to give one half hour per week for one year — free, "provided that we, in our turn, take the responsibility, financially and otherwise, for producing a program that would rate amongst the finest in America, and a program not just of the Family Rosary, but rather to restore and popularize a lost notion in America — daily family prayer." See Peyton to Michael Gearin, June 8, 1946, 09–07, Family Theater Papers, AHCFM.

21. Jeanne Arnold, *Man of Faith* (Hollywood, Calif.: Family Theater, Inc., 1983), 68.

22. Patrick Peyton, CSC, to Thomas Steiner, CSC, December 20, 1945, Family Rosary Papers #1, AHCFI; Peyton to John Cantwell, December 20, 1945, Family Rosary, Family Theater File, AALA; Peyton to Steiner, January 7, 1946, Family Rosary Papers #1, AHCFI.

23. Jerome Lawyer, CSC, to Christopher O'Toole, April 4, 1946, Steiner Papers, Family Rosary #1, AHCFI. Lawyer also stated, "Sometimes I think it might be a good thing if we do not get everything we want in the way of radio time." It is interesting to note that Peyton apparently made no overtures and sought no assistance from leading Catholic radio people of the day. William C. Smith was radio director of the NCCM and might have provided significant help. Additionally, there is no extant data that shows Peyton was in communication with the Catholic Broadcasters of America seeking assistance for Family Theater.

24. Jerome Lawyer, CSC, to John Noll, May 21, 1946, 09–07, Family Theater Papers, AHCFM.

25. Patrick Peyton, CSC, to Jerome Lawyer, CSC, January 18, 1947, 06–02 Patrick Peyton Papers, AHCFM.

26. Patrick Peyton, CSC, to John Cantwell, July 30, 1946, Family Rosary, Family Theater File, AALA. In an interesting side note, Peyton, shortly after receiving the approval from Mutual, in the late summer of 1946 organized a meeting with other priests and religious who were interested in the promotion of Marian devotion. He wanted to look at the possibility of forming one unified organization, but others at the meeting turned down the idea because they feared the financial burden that Peyton's future radio ministry would place on them. Commenting on this series of events Peyton wrote, "I often think that this also was providential. Perhaps an organization would have been less trouble with fund raising, but its members would each have had a slightly different objective, and I think one of the great reasons for the success of Family Theater is that it has stuck to the straight line of selling family prayer and nothing else." See Patrick Peyton, CSC, *All for Her,* 112–13.

27. Patrick Peyton, CSC, to Thomas Steiner, CSC, December 16, 1946, Family Rosary Papers #1, AHCFI.

28. Dennis Roverato, Interview with author, August 9, 2000.

29. Patrick Peyton, CSC, to Family Rosary Staff, January 18, 1947, 06–01; Peyton to Francis Woods, January 11, 1947, 06–02, Patrick Peyton Papers, AHCFM.

30. *Our Sunday Visitor,* February 9, 1947, clipping found in UDIS 135/58, Archives of the University of Notre Dame (hereafter AUND), Notre Dame, Indiana.

31. Patrick Peyton, CSC, to J. T. Maloney, February 18, 1947, 01–06, Crusades, Canada, AHCFM.

32. Patrick Peyton, CSC, to Family Rosary Staff, January 18, 1947, 06–01, Patrick Peyton Papers, AHCFM. Peyton wrote of his joy that the 13th had been chosen: "The real reason is that it is the design of God and Our Lady as great things happen on the 13th during our age. It was [on] the 13th that the big Family Broadcast [*sic*] took place, and besides the 13th is my lucky day."

33. Jack Wintz, OFM, "Jane Wyatt," 18; Family Theater Publicity Department Initial Release, n.d. [February 1947], Family Rosary Papers #2, AHCFI. A synopsis of the first program is: "Jim and Mary's 'perfect' marriage comes to a tragic end. Passed over for a promotion at work Jim comes home late one evening and is intoxicated.

He insists upon driving his wife, Mary, who is pregnant and in labor, to the hospital in a driving rainstorm. An accident occurs leaving the unborn baby dead and Mary unable to bear more children. Jim bears tremendous guilt causing him to leave home to reevaluate his life." See Dennis Roverato to author, April 6, 2001.

34. Patrick Peyton, CSC, *All for Her,* 115; Patrick Peyton, CSC, to Thomas Steiner, CSC, February 24, 1947, found in PPC, Attymass, County Mayo, Ireland.

35. Patrick Peyton, CSC, to Thomas Steiner, CSC, February 24, 1947, found in PPC, Attymass, County Mayo, Ireland. The donation came from the provincial of the Redemptorist Order in Baltimore. An accompanying letter read, "We feel that you are indeed doing a great service in the interest of religion, the Church and our Lady." This letter is consistent with an earlier offer from the Redemptorists in June 1946 to sponsor one month of Family Theater broadcasts should the program be initiated. See Patrick Peyton, CSC, to Michael Gearin, CSSR, June 8, 1946, 09–07 Family Theater Papers, AHCFM.

36. Jerome Lawyer, CSC, to Albert Cousineau, CSC, April 24, 1947, 428 (FR) 14, AHCG.

37. Patrick Peyton, CSC, to Thomas Steiner, CSC, August 26, 1947, Family Theater Papers #3, AHCFI. *Family Theater of the Air* was one of two prominent religious programs broadcast from Los Angeles. In 1950 the *Rosary Hour,* sponsored by the Regina Coeli Association, was started. Within one year this program was syndicated on 230 radio stations throughout the United States. See Peter Conroy to Bishop Timothy Manning, January 25, 1951, Family Theater Papers, AALA.

38. Joseph Breig, "Father Peyton and the Family Theater," trans. of *L'Osservatore Romano,* July 3, 1947, found in Family Rosary Papers #3, AHCFI.

39. Patrick Peyton, CSC, to Jerome Lawyer, CSC, January 18, 1947, 06–02, Patrick Peyton Papers, AHCFM; Thomas Steiner, CSC, to Lawyer, November 26, 1947, Family Rosary Papers #3, AHCFI.

40. Joseph Breig, "Father Peyton and the Family Theater," found in Family Rosary Papers #3, AHCFI.

41. Members of the Sponsoring Committee included Basil Harris, chairman of the board for US Steamship Lines, New York; Joseph Breig, assistant editor, *Universe Bulletin,* Cleveland; James Conners of *Variety,* Albany; William Cotter, director of public relations for Union Carbide, New York; J. Peter Grace, president of W. R. Grace and Company, New York; Edgar Kobak, president of Mutual Broadcasting System, New York; Thomas Lewis, vice president and director of radio for Young and Rubican; Los Angeles' George Nelson, general manager WSNY, Schenectady; Spyros Skouras, president, Twentieth Century Fox, New York and Los Angeles; and Frank C. Walker, former postmaster general of the United States. Peyton's reputation in the industry was also enhanced through the Catholic Broadcasters' Association, which he led as president during 1949–50. See *The Tidings* (Los Angeles archdiocesan newspaper), August 5, 1949, clipping found in 01–06, Crusades, Canada, AHCFM.

42. Some of those who joined after 1948 were Don McNeill (host of the popular radio show *The Breakfast Club*), Claudette Colbert, Celeste Holm, Danny Thomas, Spencer Tracy, Branch Rickey (owner of the Brooklyn Dodgers), Tyrone Power, Lucille Ball, Grace Kelly, Charlton Heston, Clare Booth Luce, and Raymond Burr. It should be noted that Catholicism was not a prerequisite for participation. A large percentage of Hollywood personalities who agreed to help Peyton were Protestant or Jewish.

43. Patrick Peyton, CSC, Speech to Catholic War Veterans, May 1948, 09–17, Family Theater Papers, AHCFM.

44. Patrick Peyton, CSC, to Christopher O'Toole, CSC, July 29, 1946, Family Rosary Papers #1, AHCFI.

45. Family Theater Broadcasts, Complete Listing of Programs, property of Family Theater, Hollywood, Calif. Repeat performances were kept to a minimum, with as few as two in 1948, but as many as ten in 1952.

46. Dorothy Klock, "More Things Are Wrought," *Sign* 28 (October 1948): 47.

47. "The Story of the Family Rosary," n.d. [1954] 507.28; "Family Theater: Its Nature and Purpose," n.d. [1951], 507.02, Family Rosary Papers, AHCFE.

48. Patrick Peyton, CSC, Radio Interview, June 23, 1950, 09–17, Family Theater Papers, AHCFM.

49. Dorothy Klock, "An Afternote on the Family Theater," *Sign* 30 (October 1950): 65; "Father Peyton and the Family Rosary," unpublished essay, March 22, 1947, 09–17, Family Theater Papers, AHCFM.

50. Dorothy Klock, "More Things Are Wrought," 47.

51. Patrick Peyton, CSC, to Thomas Steiner, CSC, May 8, 1947, Family Rosary Papers #2, AHCFI.

52. Jerome Lawyer, CSC, to Thomas Steiner, CSC, December 29, 1947, Family Rosary Papers #3, AHCFI.

53. Quoted in "Radio Apostolate of the Family Rosary," 507.04, Family Rosary Papers, AHCFE.

54. "Family Theater — Its Nature and Purpose — 1947–1951," n.d., PPC, Attymass, County Mayo; Flyer, *The Triumphant Hour,* 507.04, Family Rosary Papers, AHCFE. Extant data shows that Peyton worked with Edward Heston, CSC, Procurator General for the Congregation in Rome, to have a section of the *Triumphant Hour* broadcast on Vatican Radio, but the effort failed. See Edward Heston, CSC, to Patrick Peyton, CSC, April 29, 1948, and May 7, 1948, 267.74 (FT1), AHCG.

55. "Family Theater — Its Nature and Purpose — 1947–1951," n.d., PPC, Attymass, County Mayo; Jerome Lawyer, CSC, Interview with author, May 4, 2000.

56. Family Theater Publicity Department, Initial Release, n.d. [February 1947], Family Rosary Papers #2, AHCFI. The *Augusta Chronicle* was pleased "to see some of [Hollywood's] principal stars...employing their talents in the cause of righteousness and morality."

57. Jeanne Miriam Johnson, CSJ, "Education to the Family Rosary" (MA thesis: Catholic University of America, 1950), 43.

58. "Family Theater: Its Nature and Purpose," n.d. [1951], 507.02, Family Rosary Papers; AHCFE; "Resolution to Father Patrick Peyton," July 5, 1949, 06–04 Patrick Peyton Papers, AHCFM.

59. Pope Pius XII to Patrick Peyton, CSC, January 14, 1948, 06–03, Patrick Peyton Papers, AHCFM.

60. Patrick Peyton, CSC, "I Talked to Mary," *Extension* (reprint); "Presentation on the Family Rosary Crusade," 1949, 507.34, Family Rosary Papers, AHCFE. The normal costs for a one-half hour radio show ran between $20,000 and $40,000. Average costs per show for Family Theater were: 1947–$2,011; 1948–$1,623; 1949 $1,499.

61. Thomas Steiner, CSC, to Patrick Peyton, CSC, July 31, 1948, Family Rosary Papers #4, AHCFI.

62. On May 3, 1948, the Eastern Vice-Province of Priests of the Congregation of Holy Cross was established. James Connerton, CSC, was appointed by the superior general, Albert Cousineau, CSC, as vice-provincial. In 1952 the Vice-Province received full provincial status. Patrick Peyton chose to be a member of the Eastern Province. Thus, Connerton became his provincial superior. See Patrick Peyton, CSC, to Albert Cousineau, CSC, February 15, 1949, Eastern Province Personnel File, AHCG.

63. James Connerton, CSC, to Francis McIntyre, January 19, 1949, Family Rosary File, AALA. McIntyre came to Los Angeles from New York in March 1948.

64. Jerome Lawyer, CSC, to Thomas Steiner, CSC, October 27, 1948, 507.10, Family Rosary Papers, AHCFE.

65. "Presentation on the Family Rosary Crusade," 1949, 507.38, Family Rosary Papers, AHCFE.

66. Articles of Incorporation, Family Rosary, February 1947, Family Rosary, Family Theater File, AALA; Meeting Minutes, Family Theater, Inc., April 10, 1947, Family Rosary Papers #2, AHCFI. In 1949 the board was increased from three to five members and reflected the new Eastern Province's control of the operation: James Connerton, CSC, president; Patrick Peyton, CSC, vice president; Francis Woods, vice president; Jerome Lawyer, CSC, secretary; and Raymond Finan, CSC, treasurer. See Meeting Minutes, Family Theater, Inc., June 30, 1949, 03–01, Corporation Papers, AHCFM.

67. Amended Articles of Incorporation, Family Theater, Inc., December 13, 1948, 03–01, Corporation Papers, AHCFM.

68. Meeting Minutes, Family Theater, Inc., November 7, 1948, 03–01, Corporation Papers; Dorothy Halloran, Interview with James FitzPatrick, OMI, September 30, 1997, AHCFM; "Presentation on the Family Rosary Crusade," 1949, 507.38, Family Rosary Papers, AHCFE.

69. James Connerton, CSC, to Patrick Peyton, CSC, December 29, 1948, Peyton to Connerton, December 13, 1948, 305.23, Connerton Provincial Papers, AHCFE. Connerton was the superior at Moreau Seminary, Notre Dame, when Peyton was a student.

70. James Connerton, CSC, to Jerome Lawyer, CSC, December 15, 1948, 507.10, Family Rosary Papers, AHCFE; Patrick Peyton, CSC, to Christopher O'Toole, CSC, May 8, 1947; Peyton to Thomas Steiner, CSC, May 8, 1947, Family Rosary Papers #2, AHCFI.

71. Francis Gartland, CSC, to Thomas Steiner, CSC, November 5, 1946, Family Rosary Papers #1, AHCFI; Patrick Peyton, CSC, Diary, 1945–48, 06–06, Patrick Peyton Papers, AHCFM; Thomas Steiner, CSC, to Albert Heinzer, CSC, January 23, 1948, Family Rosary Papers #3, AHCFI. Heinzer spent nine years at the parish before he too entered the Family Rosary ministry as director of the Family Theater office in Hollywood.

72. Jerome Lawyer, CSC, to Brother Bernard, CSC, March 3, 1949, 05–01, Correspondence, Lawyer, AHCFM.

73. Jerome Lawyer, CSC, to Robert Fennell, September 21, 1948, 06–02, Patrick Peyton Papers, AHCFM; John Murphy, CSC, Interview with Thomas Feeley, CSC, June 3, 1999.

74. Jerome Lawyer, CSC, to Robert Fennell, September 21, 1949, 06–02, Patrick Peyton Papers, AHCFM.

75. Jerome Lawyer, CSC, to John Murphy, CSC, February 21, 1950, and October 15, 1951, 05–01, Correspondence, Lawyer, AHCFM. Lawyer experienced Peyton as inconsistent in decision making. He would make a decision and then through the inspiration of prayer change his mind. This pattern was difficult for co-workers. Jerome Lawyer, CSC, Interview with author, June 1, 2000.

76. James McIntyre, Memorandum, January 12, 1949, Family Theater File, AALA; Raymond Finan, CSC, to Jerome Lawyer, CSC, November 30, 1948, 06–02, Patrick Peyton Papers, AHCFM.

77. Patrick Sullivan, CSC, Interview with Thomas Feeley, CSC, June 20, 1999, AHCFM; Jerome Lawyer, CSC, Interview with author, May 4, 2000. Lawyer stated, "Cardinal McIntyre wanted control on everything." The definitive biography of McIntyre is Francis J. Weber, *His Eminence of Los Angeles: James Francis Cardinal McIntyre*, 2 vols. (Santa Barbara, Calif.: McNally & Loftin, 1997). It is also interesting to note that in the early 1950s McIntyre asked Holy Cross to establish a parish in the area, ostensibly to root the community in the region and to provide a residence for community members who worked with Family Theater. It is likely that the archbishop also wanted the Congregation in a parish so he could hold more canonical control on the community's activities. The Eastern Province of Holy Cross turned down the offer, but in 1954 the Indiana Province established St. Francis Xavier parish in Burbank. The Congregation served the parish continually until July 1, 2000.

78. "Time for Family Prayer," November 14, 1948, 01–06, Crusades, Canada, AHCFM; Mother M. Eucharia to Thomas Steiner, CSC, January 20, 1947, Family Rosary Papers #2, AHCFI.

79. Thomas Steiner, CSC, to Patrick Peyton, CSC, March 10, 1948, Family Rosary Papers #3, AHCFI; Peyton, to James Connerton, CSC, August 7, 1948, 305.23, Connerton Provincial Papers, AHCFE; Grant Workman to Peyton, July 23, 1948, 06–01; Robert Fennell to Peyton, May 28, 1949, 06–02, Patrick Peyton Papers, AHCFM; Peyton to James McIntyre, December 2, 1948, Family Rosary, Family Theater File, AALA; M. J. McQueen, Interview with author, August 9, 2000. Mrs. Buchenau often invited Peyton to dinner at her Bel Air home. One evening when driving him back to Immaculata College she stopped at the Sunset Boulevard address and offered him the home.

80. Jeanne Johnson, CSJ, "Education to the Family Rosary," 33; Flyer, *The Road to Peace*, 507.04, Family Rosary Papers, AHCFE. Fox produced this picture without cost to Family Theater. It is interesting to note that Mutual seemed to be upset about Peyton's movement into television. Peyton warned Lawyer to be very attentive to requests from Mutual. Most probably Peyton feared some retribution and wanted to head off problems before they materialized. See Patrick Peyton, CSC, to Jerome Lawyer, CSC, February 7, 1951, 06–02, Patrick Peyton Papers, AHCFM.

81. *Variety,* November 23, 1951, found in P98 Arm, AHCG.

82. Patrick Peyton, CSC, to Timothy Manning, April 6, 1950, Family Theater File, AALA.

83. Church and secular reviews of *The Triumphant Hour* were extremely positive. One notable negative opinion was expressed by Archbishop McIntyre: "I have rather a strong conviction that it is not wise to present the Passion of Christ in action, or in voice either, on the stage or in the movies. The same would apply to

television. . . . I believe it is wise to be most careful in this regard." See James McIntyre to Patrick Peyton, CSC, April 10, 1950, Family Theater File, AALA.

84. Flyer, *The Joyful Hour,* 507.04, Family Rosary Papers, AHCFE. Always pressing further to promote his dream, Peyton engaged in a letter campaign in an attempt to get Pope Pius XII to appear in *The Joyful Hour* film saying one decade of the rosary. When the request for this particular film was rejected he continued to ask with the hope of capturing the Holy Father on tape. His efforts at the time remained unsuccessful. See Edward Heston, CSC, to Christopher O'Toole, CSC, October 29, 1950, 267.74 (FT11), and O'Toole to Pope Pius XII, September 28, 1950, 428 (FR) 8, AHCG.

85. Flyer, *Hill Number One,* 507.04, AHCFE. Another commentator wrote of *Hill Number One,* "Nothing of such spiritual beauty or such magnitude had been produced for television before, nor, it is said, had any television program ever reached so large an audience until that time." See Theodore Bonnet, "Father Peyton and God," *Family Digest* 8 (January 1953): 17.

86. "Family Theater: Its Nature and Purpose," n.d. [1951] 507.02, Family Rosary Papers, AHCFE.

87. Between 1951 and 1958 compiled statistics provide the following list of separate broadcasts for Peyton's films: *Triumphant Hour,* 157; *Joyful Hour,* 288; *Hill Number One,* 278; *That I May See,* 361, *World's Greatest Mother,* 672; *A Star Shall Rise,* 740; *Hound of Heaven,* 102.

88. Jack Gould, "What TV Is — and What It Might Be," *New York Times,* June 17, 1951.

89. Al Scalpone to Patrick Peyton, CSC, n.d. [1952], 06–02, Patrick Peyton Papers, AHCFM.

90. Edmund Gibbons to Patrick Peyton, CSC, April 18, 1952; Peyton to Gibbons, June 11, 1952, Family Rosary Papers, ADA.

91. Family Rosary Financial Statement, 310.1.60, Correspondence, Connerton, AHCFE. Between 1942 and 1948 Family Rosary's income was $129,224.68 and debits $120,360.94, yielding a net $8,863.74. Each Holy Cross religious affiliated with the Family Rosary ministry was at the outset (1945) required to submit $700 annually as an assessment for province maintenance. This figure steadily increased over the years. Holy Cross religious who worked with Peyton over the years have often commented how much he disliked submitting his assessment. He felt the province was taking money from Mary. Jerome Lawyer, CSC, to Thomas Steiner, CSC, May 8, 1946, Steiner Paper Family Rosary #1, AHCFI.

92. "W. P. Grace Thrives by Getting Complex," *Business Week,* January 25, 1958, 104–5, 107–8, 110, 112, 114, 116; J. Peter Grace, "Latin America — A Case Study in Self-Help," Speech to the Commonwealth Club of California, June 26, 1959, found in Richard Nixon, Vice Presidential Papers, Box 298, Grace File, National Archives, Pacific Branch (hereafter NAPB), Laguna Niguel, California.

93. Jerome Lawyer, CSC, Interviews with author, June 29, 2000, and May 4, 2000.

94. J. Peter Grace to Patrick Peyton, CSC, March 31, 1952, P98 Arm, AHCG.

95. Patrick Peyton, CSC, Diary, May 26–June 2, 1960, 06–06, Patrick Peyton Papers, AHCFM.

96. Production costs would have been much higher but many actors donated their services or worked for much less than their normal stipends. The loans for

each film were all obtained from Grace's bank with three men — Richard Moore, Joseph Wirth, and Thomas McDevitt — as persons on the accounts. See Meeting Minutes, Family Theater, Inc., January 15, 1951, and February 12, 1951, 03–01, Corporation Papers, AHCFM.

97. J. Peter Grace to Bishop Albert Fletcher, February 19, 1952, 06–06, Patrick Peyton Papers, AHCFM.

98. "Activities of the Family Rosary Crusade," June 1952, 507.40, Family Rosary Papers, AHCFE; Meeting Minutes, "Concerning Possible Family Foundation," February 12, 1952, 03–01, Corporation Papers, AHCFM.

99. Memorandum, Jerome Lawyer, CSC, to John Low and John Kirby, November 9, 1954, 05–01, Correspondence, Lawyer, AHCFM.

100. Al Scalpone to Patrick Peyton, CSC, n.d. [1952], 05–01, Correspondence, Lawyer, AHCFM.

101. Thomas F. O'Neill to Patrick Peyton, CSC, April 14, 1952, 09–05 Family Theater History, AHCFM.

102. Christopher O'Toole, CSC, Circular Letter #2, March 1, 1951, AHCG.

103. James Connerton, CSC, to Patrick Peyton, CSC, n.d. [Summer 1952], 507.09, Family Rosary Papers, AHCFE.

Chapter 4: The Crusade for Family Prayer

1. David O'Brien, *Public Catholicism* (New York: Macmillan, 1989). O'Brien uses the term "Public Catholicism" to refer to various models and understandings of the Church over history, but he views the 1950s as a period of great Catholic prosperity where its public practice and sensibility was enhanced. See pages 202–8 for details on the decade of the 1950s.

2. Will Herberg, *Protestant — Catholic — Jew* (Garden City, N.Y.: Doubleday & Company, 1960), 57. Herberg saw the 1950s as the period of breakout for American Catholicism from its self-constrained status of earlier generations. He wrote, "Catholicism in America today stands at its highest point of prestige and spiritual power. It is not hard to see why this should be so in this country as elsewhere in the Western world. In an age when the vacuities of 'rationalism' and unbelief have become so painfully evident, Catholicism presents the picture of a dynamic faith sure of itself and capable of preserving its substance and power despite elaborate institutionalization. In an age of spiritual chaos and disorientation, Catholicism stands forth as the keeper of an enduring tradition that has weathered the storms of the past and stands unshaken amidst the disasters of our time." See Will Herberg, "A Jew Looks at Catholicism," *Commonweal* 58 (May 22, 1953): 174.

3. Bryan T. Froehle and Mary L. Gautier, *Catholicism USA: A Portrait of the Catholic Church in the United States* (Maryknoll, N.Y.: Orbis Books, 2000), 3, 22; *The Official Catholic Directory* 1950 and 1960.

4. Robert Wuthnow, *After Heaven: Spirituality in America since the 1950s* (Berkeley: University of California Press, 1998), 25–26, 27, 32–34.

5. Patrick Allitt, *Catholic Intellectuals and Conservative Politics in America 1950–1985* (Ithaca, N.Y.: Cornell University Press, 1993), 17–48.

6. Ibid., 81–82.

7. John Tracy Ellis, "American Catholics and the Intellectual Life," *Thought* 30 (1955): 351–88. Ellis answered his own question, saying Catholic scholars were

insufficiently industrious and suffered from a "frequently self-imposed ghetto mentality" which kept them "from mingling as they should with their non-Catholic colleagues." See Philip Gleason, "A Half-Century of Change in Catholic Higher Education," *U.S. Catholic Historian* 19, no. 1 (Winter 2001): 7. George Shuster in 1925 and Robert Hutchins in 1937 had written about the absence of Catholic intellectual life in America, but it was Ellis's essay, originally given as a paper in May 1955 at a meeting of the Catholic Commission on Intellectual and Cultural Affairs, that initiated a storm of oral and printed responses and consequent plans of action.

8. John L. Thomas, SJ, *The American Catholic Family* (Englewood Cliffs, N.J.: Prentice Hall, 1956), 8; Quoted in Mario DiCesare, "Father Thomas on the American Catholic Family," *Christian Family* 52 (December 1957): 29.

9. Gerard Meath, OP, "Family Worship," *Blackfriars* 23 (May 1942): 174, 177.

10. Elaine T. May, *Homeward Bound: American Families in the Cold War Era* (New York: Basic Books, 1988), 9, 11; Arlene Skolnick, *Embattled Paradise: The American Family in an Age of Uncertainty* (New York: Basic Books, 1991), 53.

11. "The Christian Family: A Statement of the American Hierarchy," November 21, 1949, *Catholic Mind* 48 (1950): 124.

12. Karl Alter, "Restoring the Family Circle," *Catholic Mind* 49 (August 1951): 476.

13. Richard Cushing, "Christian Family Living," *Worship* 28 (December 1953): 10.

14. Patrick Peyton, CSC, Sermon n.d. [1951], 09–17, Family Theater Papers, AHCFM.

15. Jerome Lawyer, CSC, to Patrick Peyton, CSC, June 20, 1952, 05–01, Correspondence, Lawyer, AHCFM.

16. Patrick Peyton, CSC, to James Connerton, CSC, July 9, 1953, 507.09, Family Rosary Papers, AHCFE.

17. The Canon Law of 1917 under which the Church operated at the time required six finally professed religious, at least four of whom were ordained, in order to erect a *domus formata* and the appointment of a superior.

18. James Connerton, CSC, to Jerome Lawyer, CSC, December 15, 1948, 422.2, Correspondence Connerton, AHCG.

19. James Connerton, CSC, to Christopher O'Toole, CSC, February 15, 1956, 422.2, Correspondence Connerton, AHCG.

20. Strict geographic boundaries between provinces, including apostolic ventures and the recruitment of personnel, have always been less than definite, but it was clear that Family Theater's operations were outside the physical confines of the Eastern Province of Priests.

21. John Murphy, CSC, to Robert Fennell, September 13, 1950, 05–02, Correspondence, Lawyer, AHCFM.

22. Quoted in James Connerton, CSC, to Albert Cousineau, CSC, August 6, 1948, 422.2, Correspondence Connerton, AHCG.

23. John Murphy, CSC, Interview with Thomas Feeley, CSC, June 3, 1999, AHCFM.

24. "The Crusade for Family Prayer," n.d. [1952], 01–28, Crusades, General Reports, AHCFM.

25. Patrick Peyton, CSC, "Compilation of Quotes," 01–13, Crusades, England, AHCFM.

26. Patrick Peyton, CSC, to Albert Cousineau, CSC, May 7, 1946, 428 (FR) 14, AHCG.

27. Patrick Peyton, CSC, "A World at Prayer Is a World at Peace," Crusade Talk n.d. [1956], 01–26, Crusades, United States, 1949–68, AHCFM.

28. Jerome Lawyer, CSC, to James Connerton, CSC, February 12, 1951, 507.11, Family Rosary Papers, and May 7, 1951, 305.23, Provincial Papers, Connerton, AHCFE.

29. Patrick Peyton, CSC, *Father Peyton's Rosary Prayer Book* (Albany, N.Y.: Family Rosary, Inc., 1996), 2–3. Today the book continues to be popular. It has been revised four times since the original printing in 1953.

30. Patrick Peyton, CSC, Speech to Catholic War Veterans, May 1948, 09–17 Family Theater Papers; James Mannis, CSC, "Direct Appeal," February 13, 1957, 09–05, Family Theater History, AHCFM. See also Jeanne Johnson, CSJ, "Education to the Family Rosary," 53.

31. James P. McCardle to James Connerton, CSC, February 6, 1956, 507.09, Family Rosary Papers; "Family Rosary Crusade," *Catholic News,* September 27, 1952, found in 507.52, Family Rosary Papers, AHCFE.

32. Patrick Carroll, CSC, Editorial, *Ave Maria* 70 (October 1, 1949): 422.

33. "Father Peyton's Crusade," *America* 86 (February 16, 1952): 519.

34. List of Awards, 06–02, Patrick Peyton Papers; Joseph Quinn, CSC, to Jerome Lawyer, CSC, February 19, 1954, 05–01, Administration Papers, AHCFM. The three other former recipients of the Honorary Fourth Degree were: General Marshall Foch of France, Cardinal Desiré-François Mercier of Brussels, and Count Enrico Galeazzi, governor of Vatican City.

35. Pope Pius XII, *Ingruentium Malorum,* September 15, 1951.

36. Patrick Peyton, CSC, to John Murphy, CSC, November 8, 1951, 05–01, Correspondence, Murphy, AHCFM.

37. J. B. Montini to Patrick Peyton, CSC, July 3, 1952, 310.1.09, Connerton Provincial Correspondence, AHCFE.

38. Pope Pius XII to Patrick Peyton, CSC, November 2, 1955, 06–03, Patrick Peyton Papers, AHCFM. The pope wrote, "We have, on the occasion of the Marian year, drawn upon the treasury of the Church to enrich with further indulgences the pious Catholic practice of the family recitation of the Holy Rosary. . . . We renew our words of paternal encouragement to the ordinaries who are lending their zealous support to this most praiseworthy effort and, in like manner, to you beloved son, in your collaboration, when called upon by the Episcopal Shepherds of the flock of Christ, to assist them in the conduct of the Family Rosary Crusade."

39. Pope John XXIII to Patrick Peyton, CSC, May 1, 1959, Peyton Personnel File, AHCG.

40. Patrick Peyton, CSC, to Albert Cousineau, CSC, May 11, 1950, 428 (FR) 14; Peyton to Christopher O'Toole, CSC, September 22, 1950, 428 (FR) 28; "Unsigned" to Manuel Pereira, May 10, 1950, 428 (FR) 14, AHCG.

41. Celia Ruiz-Guinazu to Albert Cousineau, CSC, August 4, 1950, 428 (FR) 46, AHCG; "The Great Friends and Triumphs of Our Lady at the Family Rosary Crusade in Buenos Aires, Argentina," n.d. [1951] 06–06, Patrick Peyton Papers, AHCFM.

42. Patrick Peyton, CSC, to Christopher O'Toole, CSC, August 7, 1950, 428 (FR) 14, AHCG.

43. Juan Domingo Perón (1895–1974) was elected president of Argentina in 1946 and served until 1955. He pursued prolabor, pronationalist policies, helped by his wife Eva, who was affectionately known to the people as "Evita." In 1950 benefits to labor began to diminish and economic difficulties arose. Labor unrest, his excommunication by the Church, and the death of Evita weakened his government. At the same time a negative attitude toward the United States prevailed in the nation. This general situation made things difficult for a possible Family Rosary mission.

44. Christopher O'Toole, CSC, to James Connerton, CSC, September 2, 1950; O'Toole to Laurent Lapalne, CSC, October 4, 1950; O'Toole to Celina Ruiz-Guinazu, October 20, 1950, 428 (FR) 46, AHCG.

45. James Connerton, CSC, to Christopher O'Toole, CSC, September 12, 1950, and February 11, 1951, 428 (FR) 46, AHCG.

46. Christopher O'Toole, CSC, to Patrick Peyton, CSC, May 2, 1951, 428 (FR) 14, AHCG.

47. Patrick Peyton CSC, to Christopher O'Toole, CSC, November 15, 1950, 428 (FR) 46; Peyton to O'Toole, January 22, 1951, 428 (FR) 14, AHCG; Jerome Lawyer, CSC, to James Connerton, CSC, March 20, 1951, 507.11, Family Rosary Papers, AHCFE.

48. Archibald McDowell, CSC, to Christopher O'Toole, CSC, July 23, 1951; O'Toole to Celina Ruiz-Guinazu, June 28, 1951.

49. "Activities of the Family Rosary Crusade," June 1952, 507.40, Family Rosary Papers, AHCFE. McDowell initially lived with the Passionist Fathers, but logistically this was difficult for his work and, thus, after a short time he moved to a religious house of the Blessed Sacrament Fathers.

50. Archibald McDowell, CSC, to Patrick Peyton, CSC, October 11, 1951, 507.11, Family Rosary Papers, AHCFE.

51. Archibald McDowell, CSC, to Christopher O'Toole, CSC, July 23, 1951; O'Toole to McDowell, August 2, 1951, 428 (FR) 46, AHCG.

52. Archibald McDowell, CSC, to Christopher O'Toole, CSC, June 1, 1952, 428 (FR) 46, AHCG.

53. Christopher O'Toole, CSC, to Theodore Mehling, CSC, November 11, 1952.

54. Archibald McDowell, CSC, to Patrick Peyton, CSC, January 30, 1952; McDowell to Christopher O'Toole, April 5, 1952, 428 (FR) 46, AHCG; John Murphy, CSC, to Joseph Quinn, CSC, May 22, 1953, 05–01, Correspondence, Murphy, AHCFM. Even under the circumstances Peyton, who never wished to lose an opportunity to promote family prayer, wrote of the Argentine foundation, including the shrine, "I feel we should do everything possible not to let it [the foundation] go out of our hands, especially with the thought of a long range plan for the Family Rosary work in South America." See Patrick Peyton, CSC, to Jerome Lawyer, CSC, June 22, 1953, 05–01, Correspondence, Lawyer, AHCFM.

55. John Murphy, CSC, Interview with Thomas Feeley, CSC, June 3, 1999, AHCFM; Murphy, "Chronicle of Family Rosary, Inc., January 1, 1956–June 30, 1956," 507.07, Family Rosary Papers, AHCFM; John Murphy, CSC, to Christopher O'Toole, CSC, January 14, 1955; Hilary Paszek, CSC, to O'Toole, August 2, 1954, 428 (FR) 14, AHCG. The process of finding a satisfactory building for Family Rosary operations actually began in 1946, but little was done until the provincial pressed the issue.

56. Burke Harrington, "Report on Radio," *Ave Maria* 89 (January 17, 1959): 26.

57. Ibid., 25; E. C. Clark, "Radio and TV Are Your Business," *Catholic School Review*, 58 (November 1958): 60.

58. Don Sharkey, "This Is Your Mother: The Radio Rosary," *Ave Maria* 78 (October 17, 1953): 16.

59. Albert Heinzer, CSC, to Jerome Lawyer, CSC, and John Corr, CSC, May 15, 1961, 09–05, Family Theater Papers, AHCFM.

60. Radio Report, May 1961, 09–05, Family Theater History, AHCFM.

61. List of Awards, obtained at AHCFM; Patrick Peyton, CSC, to Edward Heston, CSC, December 31, 1955, 310.1.09, Correspondence Connerton, AHCFE; The American Legion Citation, February 14, 1957, 06–04, Patrick Peyton Papers, AHCFM.

62. Jerome Lawyer, CSC, to James Connerton, CSC, February 12, 1952, 507.11, Family Rosary Papers, AHCFE; Transcribed Telegram of Olive Ogilvy, September 29, 1953, 01–03, Crusades, Australia, AHCFM.

63. Patrick Peyton, CSC, to James Connerton, CSC, November 8, 1952, 310.1.09, Correspondence Connerton, AHCFE.

64. Joseph Quinn, CSC, to Jerome Lawyer, CSC, June 18, 1953, 05–01, Correspondence, Lawyer, AHCFM; Jeanne Arnold, *Man of Faith* (Hollywood, Calif.: Family Theater, Inc., 1983), 103–4.

65. Patrick Peyton, CSC, to James Connerton, CSC, November 8, 1952, 310.1.09, Connerton Correspondence, AHCFE.

66. "Chronicle of Family Theater, Inc., July 1, 1958, to June 30, 1959," 507.07, Family Rosary Papers, AHCFE.

67. Patrick Peyton, CSC, to Edward Heston, CSC, December 31, 1955, 507.09, Family Rosary Papers, AHCFE.

68. Marian Theater List of Programs, Family Theater Papers, Hollywood, Calif.; James Mannis to Edward Heston, CSC, February 13, 1957, 267.74 (FT1), AHCG; John Corr to Francis Woods, September 27, 1956, 05–01, Administration Papers, AHCFM. *Marian Theater* was broadcast weekly on Sunday afternoons from 2:00 to 2:30 p.m. (EST) and Saturday nights on the West Coast only from 8:00 to 8:30 p.m. The commercial nature of *Marian Theater* required some delicate maneuvering in order to keep *Family Theater of the Air* free to Family Theater. In an effort to keep possible opposition at bay, John Corr suggested that *Family Theater of the Air* and *Marian Theater* be kept separate in every way possible. Association of a commercial venture, *Marian Theater,* with the gratis *Family Theater of the Air* might be problematic. See John Corr, CSC, to Francis Woods, September 24, 1956, 05–01, Correspondence Corr, AHCFM. Peyton was hopeful that profit could be derived from the Marian Theater productions, but his goal was consistent with his overall mission: "The purpose of Marian Theater is to bring every heart and home in America a more thorough understanding of — and therefore a greater appreciation of — the great doctrines of our faith." See Press Release, n.d., [1956] found in 507.109, Family Theater Papers and Patrick Peyton, CSC, to Francis Woods, September 24, 1956, 05–01, Correspondence, Woods, AHCFM.

69. Marian Theater List of Programs, FTRH; Radio Report, May 1961, 09–05, Family Theater History, AHCFM.

70. Anthony Smith, "American Catholicism and Public Tradition," 95, 64–66. In 1952 "Life Is Worth Living" received an audience rating of 23.7, the highest ever attained in the pioneering days of television.

71. Ibid., 95. A very interesting study on the impact of Bishop Sheen on American culture is provided in: Mark Massa, *Catholics and American Culture: Fulton Sheen, Dorothy Day, and the Notre Dame Football Team* (New York: Crossroad, 1999), 82–101. Several books and dissertations have been written about Bishop Sheen. Christopher Owen Lynch, *Selling Catholicism: Bishop Sheen and the Power of Television* (Lexington: University Press of Kentucky, 1998); Kathleen Riley Fields, "Bishop Fulton J. Sheen: An American Catholic Response to the Twentieth Century" (PhD dissertation: University of Notre Dame, 1988); Fulton J. Sheen, *Treasure in Clay: The Autobiography of Fulton J. Sheen* (Garden City, N.Y.: Doubleday, 1980).

72. "Radio and TV Are Your Business," *Catholic School Review,* 60; "Catholic Hour: TV Success," *America* 102 (November 7, 1959): 145. For more information on Sheen's influence see Mark Massa, SJ, *Catholics and American Culture,* 82–101.

73. J. Peter Grace to Allen Dulles, November 24, 1958, 428 (FR) 14, AHCG; "Religious Films Available for Public Telecast," n.d. [1953] 01–01, Crusades, Africa; "Inspiration Please" Flyer, n.d., 09–02, Family Theater Papers, AHCFM. The entire list of twelve celebrities was Abraham Lincoln, Benjamin Franklin, Thomas Jefferson, Captain Mort Thompson, USMC (Okinawa Landing), Louis Pasteur, Francis of Assisi, Guglielmo Marconi, Teresa of Avila, Franz Josef Hadyn, Alexis Carroll, and Patrick Henry.

74. "Inspiration Please" Flyer, n.d., 09–02, Family Theater Papers, AHCFM.

75. Patrick Peyton, CSC, to James Connerton, CSC, July 9, 1953, 507.09, Family Rosary Papers, AHCFE; Peyton to Jerome Lawyer, CSC, and John Lynch, CSC, August 3, 1953, 03–01, Administrative Papers, AHCFM.

76. Patrick Peyton, CSC, to the Family Rosary Group, April 30, 1954, 03–01, Administrative Papers, AHCFM.

77. Radio Report, 1961, 09–05, Family Theater History, AHCFM.

78. Minutes of Meeting at Family Theater on Film Distribution, January 5, 1952, 09–07, Family Theater Papers, AHCFM. Many of the distributors were associated with the Catholic Church in local areas, but some were more generic companies.

79. "Chronicle of Family Theater, Inc., July 1, 1958, to June 30, 1959," 507.07, Family Rosary Papers, AHCFE; Meeting Minutes, Directors of Family Theater, Inc., July 31, 1959, 03–01, Corporation Papers, AHCFM.

80. Albert Heinzer, CSC, to James McIntyre, August 31, 1959, and October 1, 1959, Family Rosary, Family Theater File, AALA; George DePrizio, CSC, to Christopher O'Toole, CSC, March 4, 1960; Bernard Ransing, CSC, to DePrizio, March 11, 1960, 422.2, Correspondence, DePrizio, AHCG. Although McIntyre approved the basic plan he would not allow a chapel nor Eucharistic reservation in the building. His reasoning behind this refusal is not extant.

81. George DePrizio, CSC, to Christopher O'Toole, CSC, March 4, 1960, 422.2, Correspondence, DePrizio, AHCG.

82. Patrick Peyton, CSC, Diary, March 2, 1960, 06–06, Patrick Peyton Papers; "The Family Rosary Crusade — 1962," 01–05, Crusades, Brazil, AHCFM; James McIntyre to Patrick Peyton, CSC, July 31, 1961, Family Rosary, Family Theater File, AALA.

83. Patrick Peyton, CSC, *Ear of God,* 21.

84. Mary Jane McQueen, Interview with Thomas Feeley, CSC, November 1998, AHCFM.

85. Ann Blyth, Interview with James FitzPatrick, OMI, and Thomas Feeley, CSC, November 14, 1998, AHCFM.

86. Patrick Peyton, CSC, to Mary Peyton, January 27, 1949, 06–11, Patrick Peyton Papers, AHCFM. Peyton's colleague, John Murphy, asked him to slow down: "May God and Mary restrain your zeal while you are there so that you will store up energy. A burned out match can't set any fire, nor can a tired, weary, and worn out Father Pat." See John Murphy, CSC, to Patrick Peyton, CSC, June 8, 1956, 06–02, Patrick Peyton Papers, AHCFM.

87. Christopher O'Toole, CSC, Circular Letter #3, December 8, 1953, AHCG.

88. James Connerton, CSC, to Thomas Gill, May 31, 1955, 310.1.09, Correspondence, Connerton, AHCFE.

89. Patrick Peyton, CSC, to James Connerton, CSC, July 25, 1955, 507.09, Family Rosary Papers, AHCFE.

90. Jerome Lawyer, CSC, to Christopher O'Toole, CSC, July 27, 1956, 428 (FR) 8, AHCG.

91. George DePrizio, CSC, to Patrick Peyton, CSC, August 10, 1956, Patrick Peyton Personnel File; DePrizio, Circular Letter, September 15, 1958, 301.58.1, Provincial Chapter Papers, AHCFE.

92. It is very interesting and not readily explainable, but there is no extant data that shows any significant disagreements, arguments, or rifts between Peyton and Francis Woods, who was actually the first person to join the Crusade full time.

93. James Connerton, CSC, to Christopher O'Toole, CSC, December 12, 1955, 428 (FR) 14, AHCG. It should be noted that O'Toole did not agree with Connerton's observations. He wrote, "With regard to your control over the activities of the Family Rosary, I know that Father Peyton is most obedient and that he will follow readily any suggestions or directives that you give him." See Christopher O'Toole, CSC, to James Connerton, CSC, January 11, 1956, 428 (FR) 14, AHCG.

94. James Connerton, CSC, to Christopher O'Toole, CSC, January 30, 1956, 428 (FR) 14, AHCG.

95. John Murphy, CSC, to Jerome Lawyer, CSC, March 2, 1950, 02–01, Correspondence, AHCFM.

96. John Murphy, CSC, Interview with Thomas Feeley, CSC, June 3, 1999; Jerome Lawyer, CSC, Interview with author, June 29, 2000.

97. Francis Grogan, CSC, Interview with Thomas Feeley, CSC, June 2, 1999; James Mannis, CSC, Interview with Thomas Feeley, CSC, June 3, 1999, AHCFM.

98. Raymond Cour, CSC, Interview with Thomas Feeley, CSC, June 1999, AHCFM.

99. Jerome Lawyer, CSC, to John Murphy, CSC, February 7, 1951, and February 21, 1951, 02–01, Correspondence, AHCFM; Jerome Lawyer, CSC, Interview with author, May 4, 2000, June 1, 2000.

100. "The Family Rosary Crusade — 1962," 01–05, Crusades, Brazil, AHCFM.

101. Dennis Roverato, Interview with Thomas Feeley, CSC, October 28, 1998, AHCFM.

102. Joan Wiener, Interview with Thomas Feeley, CSC, November 1998; Mary Jane McQueen, Interview with Thomas Feeley, CSC, November 1998, AHCFM.

103. Patrick Peyton, CSC, to Jerome Lawyer, CSC, May 17, 1952, and June 3, 1953, 05–01, Correspondence, Lawyer; Peyton to Lawyer, John Murphy, CSC, Albert Heinzer, CSC, and Joseph Quinn, CSC, July 2, 1952, 05–01, Correspondence, Murphy, AHCFM.

104. Patrick Peyton, CSC, to Family Rosary Group, April 30, 1954, 03–01, Administrative Papers, AHCFM.

105. In general many of those who worked closely with Peyton, especially members of Holy Cross, have commented that his single-mindedness to Mary "blinded" him to the needs of others.

Chapter 5: The International Rosary Crusades

1. Many fine monographs exist that provide the history of revivalism in the United States. See, for example, Richard Owen Roberts, *New England Revivals: As They Existed at the Close of the Eighteenth and the Beginning of the Nineteenth Centuries* (Wheaton, Ill.: Wheaton College, 1980); Frank Lambert, *"Peddler in Divinity": George Whitefield and the Transatlantic Revivals, 1737–1770* (Princeton, N.J.: Princeton University Press, 1994); Richard M. Riss, *A Survey of 20th Century Revival Movements in North America* (Peabody, Mass.: Hendrickson, 1988); Marshall W. Fishwick, *Great Awakenings: Popular Religion and Popular Culture* (New York: Haworth Press, 1995); Charles E. Hambrick-Stowe, *Charles G. Finney and the Spirit of American Evangelicalism* (Grand Rapids, Mich.: William B. Eerdmans, 1996).

2. Representative biographies of Moody, Sunday, and McPherson include: James F. Findlay, *Dwight L. Moody, American Evangelist, 1837–1899* (Chicago: University of Chicago Press, 1969); Lyle W. Dorsett, *Billy Sunday and the Redemption of Urban America* (Grand Rapids, Mich.: William B. Eerdmans, 1991); Edith L. Blumhofer, *Aimee Semple McPherson: Everybody's Sister* (Grand Rapids, Mich.: William B. Eerdmans, 1993).

3. Jay P. Dolan, *Catholic Revivalism: The American Experience 1830–1890* (Notre Dame, Ind.: University of Notre Dame Press, 1998). Dolan's monograph is the authoritative account of this episode in American Catholic history.

4. Father William Mahoney, CSC, seems to have been the first Holy Cross priest to undertake parish missions in 1892. In 1912 extant records show that a residence was established and men assigned to the work.

5. "New Evangelist," *Time* 64 (October 25, 1964): 55–56.

6. John Pollock, *Billy Graham: Evangelist to the World* (San Francisco: Harper & Row, 1979), 221–25. Two additional biographies of Graham are Marshall Frady, *Billy Graham: A Parable of American Righteousness* (Boston: Little, Brown, 1979), and William Martin, *A Prophet with Honor: The Billy Graham Story* (New York: W. Morrow, 1991).

7. "New Crusade in Europe, Interview," *U.S. News & World Report* 37 (August 27, 1954): 86–87.

8. "New Evangelist," 55.

9. Ibid., 54.

10. "The Family Cruzade [*sic*]" n.d. 428 (FR); "Basic Reasons for Family Rosary Crusade," Sermon, April 30, 1950–June 4, 1950, 01–06, Crusades, Canada, AHCFM; "Family Rosary Crusade — Evaluation," April 1960, B428 (FR), AHCG.

11. J. T. Maloney to Jerome Lawyer, CSC, August 23, 1947; Lawyer to Maloney, September 10, 1947, 01–06, Crusades, Canada, AHCFM. The format for the Triduum was as follows: It began on Sunday evening with a hymn to Our Lady, followed by the rosary, litany of the Blessed Virgin Mary, a hymn to the Holy Spirit, and a talk, and closed with Benediction of the Blessed Sacrament. The same schedule was followed on Monday. On Tuesday Peyton held a holy hour with the Blessed Sacrament exposed. After Benediction he was available for confessions.

12. Thomas Steiner, CSC, to John T. Kidd, October 17, 1947, Family Rosary Papers #3, AHCFI. See also Jeanne Arnold, *Man of Faith* (Hollywood, Calif.: Family Theater, Inc., 1983), 82–84, and Patrick Peyton, CSC, *All for Her* (Hollywood, Calif.: Family Theater, Inc., 1967), 121–22, for summaries of this deal. The fact that Peyton initiated his international rosary crusade in Canada was not simply because the opportunity arose, but rather his belief that there was a need to protect that land. A clipping from the *Scrantonian* suggested: "Father Peyton said the reason why the first crusades were conducted in Canada was born of a glance he took at a newspaper cartoon, showing how the road of a possible World War III would come down from the North through Canada. Aware that radar stations and other methods of material defense were being spotted in Canada, Father Peyton decided that the 'spiritual defenses,' represented by the rosary, should start there." Additionally, the Marian Congress in Ottawa in 1947 suggested the recitation of the family rosary. This most assuredly would have impressed Peyton and told him that the nation was ready for his crusade. See the *Scrantonian,* n.d., and October 30, 1949, Scranton, Pennsylvania, clipping, 01–26, Crusades, Midwest USA, AHCFM.

13. Patrick Peyton, CSC, Radio Interview, June 23, 1950, 09–17, Family Theater Papers; John Murphy, CSC, Interview with Thomas Feeley, CSC, June 3, 1999, AHCFM; Murphy, Interview with author, October 24, 1999.

14. Andrew Mahoney to Patrick Peyton, October 4, 1947, 01–06, Crusades, Canada, AHCFM.

15. Jerome Lawyer, CSC, to John Cody, December 4, 1947, 01–06, Crusades, Canada, AHCFM; "Summary Sheet — London, Ontario, Crusade," n.d. 428 (FR) 45, AHCG. Thomas Steiner, CSC, asked Albert Heinzer, CSC, to take Woods's parish, St. Madeleine Sophie, in order to free the latter to work with Peyton on his first crusade.

16. John T. Kidd to Secular and Religious Clergy of the Diocese, February 25, 1948, 01–06, Crusades, Canada, AHCFM.

17. John T. Kidd, Pastoral Letter, n.d., quoted in "London, Canada Crusade," n.d. [1948], 01–06, Crusades, Canada, AHCFM.

18. Peyton's organization provided sample sermons that clergy might wish to use during the five-week period, although priests were free to preach on their own. This service became normative in the crusades throughout the world.

19. John T. Kidd to Secular and Religious Clergy, March 17, 1948, and March 18, 1948, 507.52, Family Rosary Papers, AHCFE.

20. Summary Sheet, London, Ontario, Crusade, n.d. [1948], 428 (FR) 45, AHCG.

21. George Godfrey to Francis Woods, January 29, 1948, 01–06, Crusades, Canada, AHCFM.

22. "London, Canada, Crusade," n.d. [1948], 01–06, Crusades, Canada, AHCFM.

23. *The Time for Family Prayer,* April 4, 1948, 01–06, Crusades, Canada, AHCFM.

24. Jeanne Arnold, *Man of Faith,* 84–85; "London, Canada, Crusade," n.d. [1948], 01–06, Crusades, Canada, AHCFM.

25. "London, Canada, Crusade," n.d. [1948] 01–06, Crusades, Canada, AHCFM.

26. Patrick Peyton, CSC, Speech to Catholic War Veterans, May 1948, 09–17, Family Theater Papers, AHCFM.

27. Francis Woods to John Cody, June 21, 1948, 01–06, Crusades, Canada, AHCFM.

28. Patrick Peyton, CSC, Crusade Calendar/Itinerary, 01–06, Crusades, Canada, AHCFM.

29. An *abbatia nullius* is an ecclesiastical structure used in certain rural areas where a monastery, priory, or similar religious community has established an institutional commitment.

30. Crusade Summary Sheet, n.d. [1954], 01–06, Crusades, Canada, AHCFM.

31. Quoted in Sr. Noel Marie, CSJ, "England Bows to Our Lady," *The Magnificat,* July 1951, clipping found in 01–13, Crusades, England, AHCFM.

32. Jerome Lawyer, CSC, to John Murphy, CSC, July 26, 1949, 02–01, Correspondence, AHCFM; Lawyer to James Connerton, CSC, October 21, 1949, 507.10, Family Rosary Papers, AHCFM. The hope that Murphy could better organize the crusade in a business manner came from two points. First, Murphy was a late vocation and had work experience before he entered Holy Cross. Second, it seems that the organization of the crusade in Saskatchewan was less than optimal: "Someday I'll sit down and write you a long letter telling you of the woes and tribulations of the Saskatchewan Family Rosary Crusade.... For the most part things have been going quite well though we are in the usual state of confusion and are always two days behind the deadlines." See Anonymous [Francis Woods] to Jerome Lawyer, CSC, September 13, 1948, 05–01, Correspondence, Woods, AHCFM.

33. Family Rosary General Information, n.d. [1950], 01–06, Crusades, Canada, AHCFM.

34. Patrick Peyton, CSC, "Plan of Organization of the Family Rosary Crusade," n.d. [1961], B428 (FR), AHCG.

35. "Family Rosary and Prayer Crusade," n.d., 428 (FR) 0, AHCG.

36. "Saskatchewan Crusade," n.d. [1948], 01–06, Crusades, Canada, AHCFM.

37. "Greatest Prayer Crusade Ever Launched Begins on Sunday," Press Release, August 30, 1950, 01–06, Crusades, Canada, AHCFM. The ecumenical tone of the crusades was noted by a secular journalist in an editorial: "The Family Rosary Crusade is sponsored by but not limited to the Roman Catholic Church. It makes its appeal to all who acknowledge the supremacy of God and believe that He works with and for those who put their trust in Him, and whose homes He rules.... For those to whom the invocation of saints seems akin or false in doctrinal implications, the Family Crusade urges merely that SOME form of daily family devotion, such as could be wholeheartedly adopted in every devout Protestant or Jewish household, be restored or begun as a spiritual bulwark in these anxious and troubled times." See "With One Accord," Editorial, *Vancouver Sun,* n.d. [1949], clipping in 01–06, Crusades, Canada, AHCFM.

38. Peyton set dates for crusades months and even over a year in advance. As his world recognition increased with more and more crusades being conducted, Peyton was besieged by bishops worldwide to bring the crusade to their diocese. He did his best to meet needs, but the requests always outnumbered what could be done. As mentioned in chapter 4, the cardinal archbishop of Buenos Aires asked for the crusade to come in October 1953, but Peyton had already arranged that he would be in Australia at the time. In this case a crusade was never held in Argentina, although many were conducted in other South American nations, including neighbors Chile and Brazil in the 1960s.

39. "Presentation on the Family Rosary Crusade," 1949, 507.38, Family Rosary Papers, AHCFE; "United States Security and the Power of Prayer," n.d. [1962], B428 (FR), AHCG; John Murphy, CSC, Interview with Thomas Feeley, CSC, June 3, 1999; Francis Grogan, CSC, Interview with Thomas Feeley, CSC, June 2, 1999, AHCFM.

40. "Family Rosary Pledge," n.d., 01–01, Crusades, Africa; Joseph Quinn, CSC, Interview with Thomas Feeley, CSC, March 16, 1999, AHCFM.

41. Booklet on Family Prayer, n.d. [1955], 428 (FR) 8, AHCG. Hoover's essay in *The Time* was titled "We Need God!"

42. Ibid.

43. Katharine Massam, *Sacred Threads: Catholic Spirituality in Australia 1922–1962* (Sydney, Australia: University of New South Wales Press, 1996), 101–2; Jeanne Johnson, CSJ, "Education to the Family Rosary," 51; Family Rosary Dioceses of Saskatchewan 1948 Handbook; "Family Rosary Crusade Hymn," 01–06, Crusades, Canada, AHCFM. The Crusade Prayer used in all the early crusades read: "Heavenly Father, we beg Thee in the name of Jesus Christ, Thy Son, to bless our family [*sic*] Rosary Crusade. Give us the courage and the grace to make the Daily Family Rosary Pledge and keep it faithfully. Amen." The lyrics to the Family Rosary Crusade Hymn were:

Verse 1:
O Queen of the Family Rosary, Queen of the perfect prayer,
help us spread this devotion to families everywhere.
The world we would encircle with ros'ry's golden chain,
that in all countries, homes and hearts the peace of God might reign.

Verse 2:
O Queen of the Family Rosary, be queen of homes once more,
and bless our every effort to fam'ly prayers restore.
The beads in loving fingers have powerful weapons been.
May they all evil forces crush, and bloodless victories win.

44. Jorge Canepa, CSC, Interview with author, June 18, 2000; John Murphy, CSC, Interview with author, October 29, 1999.

45. *Eastern Province Bulletin* 7, no. 2 (September 1964): 2; "Family Rosary and Prayer Crusades," n.d., 428 (FR), AHCG.

46. Jeanne Johnson, CSJ, "Educating to the Family Rosary," 48–50; "United States Security and the Power of the Rosary," n.d. [1962], B428 (FR), AHCG.

47. Joseph Quinn, CSC, Interview with Thomas Feeley, CSC, March 3, 1999, AHCFM.

48. Ibid.

49. Katharine Massam, *Sacred Threads*, 98; Workers' Handbook, Family Rosary Crusade Diocese of London [Ontario], 1948, 01–06, Crusades, Canada, AHCFM.

50. Workers' Handbook, Family Rosary Crusade Diocese of London [Ontario], 1948, 01–06, Crusades, Canada, AHCFM. See Patrick Peyton, CSC, *All for Her*, 131.

51. Crusade Summary — England, n.d. [1952], 01–13, Crusades, England; Patrick Peyton, CSC, *Ear of God*, 152.

52. Dorothy Halloran, Interview with author, July 20, 2000.

53. Patrick Peyton, CSC, to Francisco Munoz, OP, October 31, 1953, 01–24, Crusades, Philippines, AHCFM.

54. Joseph Quinn, CSC, to Jerome Lawyer, CSC, January 19, 1952, 02–01, Correspondence, AHCFM; Robert Rioux, CSC, to author, November 15, 2001. In 1952 Grace was working on a plan to obtain $1 million for Family Rosary. Grace wrote, "This would provide you with a wonderful capital and a nucleus for the whole movement." Quoted in John Murphy, CSC, to Jerome Lawyer, CSC, July 11, 1952, 05–01, Correspondence, Murphy, AHCFM.

55. In July 1955 Connerton came to Peyton asking that Quinn be released from the Family Rosary to become the vocation director for the province. He did not want to put Peyton in a bad position, but province members believed Quinn was the right man for the job at the time. Peyton did not like the idea, but eventually relented and released Quinn in September. He served in this position for two years. In 1957 Quinn returned to Family Rosary with Gerry Conmy, CSC, assigned as vocation director. The way Connerton tiptoed around Peyton in asking for Quinn gives further evidence that he feared acting against him in any way. See James Connerton, CSC, to Christopher O'Toole, CSC, July 5, 1955, and September 1, 1955, 422.2, Correspondence, Connerton, AHCG; James Connerton, CSC, to Patrick Peyton, CSC, and Joseph Quinn, CSC, August 6, 1955; Peyton to Connerton, August 21, 1955, 507.09, Family Rosary Papers, AHCFE; Christopher O'Toole, CSC, to George DePrizio, CSC, March 15, 1957; DePrizio to O'Toole, May 18, 1957, 422.2, Correspondence, DePrizio, AHCG.

56. "Activities of the Family Rosary Crusade," June 1952, 507.40, Family Rosary Papers, AHCFE.

57. "An English View of the Family Rosary," Condensed Article, 01–13, Crusades, England; "An Account of the Visit of Father Patrick Peyton, C.S.C., the Rosary Crusades to Upholland Carmel [Lancaster, England]," February 26, 1951, 01–13, Crusades, England, AHCFM.

58. George Gill, "Ireland Evaluates America's Father Peyton," July 1954, Press Release found in 01–20, Crusades, Ireland; *Geraldton Guardian*, December 17, 1953, 01–03, Crusades, Australia, AHCFM.

59. Joseph Quinn, CSC, Interview with Thomas Feeley, CSC, March 16, 1999; John Murphy, CSC, to Kitty and Michael Maloney, June 27, 1952, 06–11, Patrick Peyton Personal Papers, AHCFM.

60. "The Family Rosary — Protector of Family Life," Sermon, Family Rosary Crusade in Canada, April 20 to June 4, 1950, 01–06, Crusades, Canada, AHCFM.

61. Transcribed version of an article from the *Brisbane Evening Telegraph*, n.d. [September 1953], 01–03, Crusades, Australia, AHCFM.

62. Quoted in Theodore Bonnet, "Father Peyton and God," *Family Digest* 8 (January 1953): 17; Loretta Young Lewis, Interview with Thomas Feeley, CSC, November 13, 1998, AHCFM.

63. Report, English Crusade 1952, 01–13, Crusades, England, AHCFM.

64. Jarlath P. Burke, "Crusader with Rosary Beads," May 1, 1954, clipping found in 507.09, Family Rosary Papers, AHCFE.

65. Eileen Gerwin, Interview with Thomas Feeley, CSC, April 18, 1999, AHCFM.

66. *Geraldton Guardian,* December 17, 1953, 01–03, Crusades, Australia, AHCFM. One commentator stated of Peyton: "His message cannot be recorded in cold print: it is essentially a living message; it is the presence of the man which God's power seems to use to carry conviction and enthusiasm to all who hear him. And the most astonishing thing about it is the universal enthusiasm with which he is received." Report, England Crusade 1952, 01–13, Crusades, England, AHCFM.

67. "A Modern Apostle," *Oratory* (February 1956): 8.

68. Summary Report, English Crusade 1952, 01–13, Crusades, England, AHCFM.

69. A Sister of the Holy Infant Jesus to John Murphy, CSC, February 22, 1955, 01–19, Crusades, India, AHCFM.

70. J. Peter Grace to Christopher O'Toole, CSC, January 29, 1959, 428 (FR) 14, AHCG. There are several extant accounts of people who upon encountering Peyton were dramatically influenced by him. One example illustrates this. One day Peyton visited a nun, Sr. Mary Pius, who was sick in an Irish convent infirmary. Sister Mary told him she wanted to make a bargain with God. She asked God to send all the pains of soul, mind, and body destined for him to her so he could be well and strong to carry out his work. Peyton was aghast, but the nun was so insistent that he said, 'If God is happy about it I will agree.' He never saw the woman again, but heard that she had died several months later from intense suffering of mind and body." See "An Account of the Visit of Father Patrick Peyton, C.S.C., the 'Rosary Crusader,' to Upholland Carmel [Lancaster, England]," February 26, 1951, 01–13, Crusades, England, AHCFM.

71. Hafey gave Holy Cross $200,000 to establish King's College for the education of the children of coal miners in the region. The institution was founded in 1946 with James Connerton as the first president. A detailed history of King's College is provided in Donald Grimes, CSC, *Rooted in Hope: The First Fifty Years of King's College 1946–1996* (Wilkes-Barre, Pa.: King's College Press, 1998).

72. William Hafey to "Dearly Beloved in Christ," October 16, 1949, 01–26, Crusades, Scranton, AHCFM.

73. Patrick Peyton, CSC, to John Murphy, CSC, October 24, 1949, 05–01, Correspondence, Murphy, AHCFM.

74. *Scholastic,* October 27, 1950, University of Notre Dame, AUND.

75. Rosary Crusade Summary Sheet, AHCFM.

76. Ibid. A total of 218,000 attended the East Coast rallies.

77. Joseph Francis Rummel to Clergy, Archdiocese of New Orleans, January 30, 1952; News Release, n.d. [1952], 01–26, Crusades, New Orleans, AHCFM.

78. Cardinal Francis Spellman, Sermon, October 12, 1952, 01–26, Crusades, New York, AHCFM.

79. Francis Woods to Patrick Peyton, CSC, November 17, 1952, and November 25, 1952; J. Peter Grace to Patrick Peyton, CSC, November 20, 1952, 01–26, Crusades, New York, AHCFM.

80. Family Rosary Crusade Background Material and Sample Editorials, n.d. [May 31–July 5, 1953], 01–26, Crusades, United States, AHCFM.

81. Family Rosary Crusade, Ecclesiastical Provinces of Portland and Seattle, 1956; Northwest Family Rosary Crusade, Schedule of Rallies, November 7, 1956, 01–26, Crusades, United States, AHCFM.

82. James Byrne to Christopher O'Toole, CSC, October 8, 1956, 428 (FR) 14, AHCG.

83. P. W. Bartholme to Patrick Peyton, CSC, December 10, 1953; Peyton to Bartholme, January 9, 1953, 01–26, Crusades, United States, AHCFM.

84. Fact Sheet, n.d. [1958]; Resume of Family Rosary Crusade, Province of St. Paul, Minnesota, July–November 1958, 01–26, Crusades, United States, AHCFM.

85. Sr. Noel Marie, CSJ, "England Bows to Our Lady," *Magnificat,* July 1951, clipping found in 01–13, Crusades, England, AHCFM.

86. Patrick Peyton, CSC, to Gary Cooper, March 7, 1951, 01–13, Crusades, England, AHCFM.

87. News clipping, n.d. [February 1951], found in 507.52, Family Rosary Papers, AHCFE.

88. Thomas Flynn, Memorandum, n.d. [March 1951], 01–13, Crusades, England, AHCFM.

89. John Murphy, CSC, to Christopher O'Toole, CSC, February 26, 1951, 428 (FR) 14, AHCG.

90. Joseph McCormick, Address at Family Rosary Crusade, May 14, 1952, found in *The Fold* (June 1952): 12, 01–13, Crusades, England, AHCFM.

91. John Murphy, CSC, to Patrick Peyton, CSC, April 21, 1952, 05–01, Correspondence, Murphy, AHCFM.

92. Report, English Crusade 1952; Family Rosary Crusade — General Information, n.d. [1952], 01–13, Crusades, England, AHCFM.

93. Quoted in Summary Report, English Crusade, 1952, 01–13, Crusades, England, AHCFM.

94. "Father Peyton Captures England," *Ave Maria* 75 (June 21, 1952): 771.

95. Pope Pius XII to Bernard Cardinal Griffin, July 14, 1952, 06–02, Patrick Peyton Personal Papers, AHCFM. In the letter the pope also wrote, "Never before has the world been so sorely in need of prayer as at the present time, when a dangerous form of materialism tends to undermine man's relations with his creator and his fellowman and to destroy the sanctity of family life. The most powerful antidote against the evils that threaten human society is prayer, especially collective prayer.... And what form of collective prayer could be more simple and yet more efficacious than the Family Rosary, in which parents and children join together in supplicating the Eternal Father, through the intercession of their most loving Mother, meditating meanwhile on the most sacred mysteries of our faith? There is no surer means of calling down God's blessings upon the family and especially of preserving peace and happiness in the home than the daily recitation of the Rosary."

96. Sr. Noel Marie, CSJ, "England Bows to Our Lady," *The Magnificat,* July 1951, clipping found in 01–13, Crusades, England, AHCFM.

97. Quoted in Leonard Schweitzer, "Rosary Crusade in Britain," *Ave Maria* 76 (October 4, 1952): 423.

98. John Murphy, CSC, to Joseph Quinn, CSC, May 29, 1951, 02–01, Correspondence, AHCFM.

99. Family Rosary Crusade, Summary of Archdiocese of St. John's and St. George and Harbour Grace Dioceses, 1952, 01–06, Crusades, Canada, AHCFM.

100. Patrick Peyton, CSC, "Memorandum," June 12, 1956, 06–02, Patrick Peyton Papers, AHCFM.

101. Arthur Fox to "Reverend and Dear Father," November 5, 1953, 01–03, Crusades, Australia, AHCFM.

102. The first crusade in London, Ontario, required the use of French, but at least a significant percentage of the people understood English. In Málaga Peyton encountered his first totally non–English speaking crusade.

103. James Connerton, CSC, to Patrick Peyton, CSC, February 21, 1953, 507.60, Family Rosary Papers, AHCFM; Patrick Peyton, CSC, *All for Her,* 143–45; Jeanne Arnold, *Man of Faith,* 100.

104. Patrick Peyton, CSC, to James Connerton, CSC, August 29, 1953, 310.1.09, Connerton, Administrative Papers, AHCFE; Family Rosary Crusade Summary, 01–03, Crusades, Australia, AHCFM.

105. Patrick Peyton, CSC, to James Connerton, CSC, December 9, 1953, 310.1.09, Connerton Administrative Papers, AHCFE. As measured by fervor, attendance at the rallies, and numbers of pledges the crusade was a great success, yet at least one social historian of contemporary Australia is doubtful about the event's overall efficacy: "The oral history of the crusade reveals a clear collective memory of the visit of Father Peyton as a diocesan event, but not one which had any memorable impact on the prayer practices of many families. Rather than being the occasion of a dramatic change in devotion, the crusade reinforced established practices or strengthened resolves to continue the struggle to achieve the Catholic ideal." See Katharine Massam, *Sacred Threads,* 105.

106. Patrick Peyton, CSC, to James Connerton, CSC, April 10, 1954, 507.09, Family Rosary Papers, AHCFE.

107. Patrick Peyton, CSC, to James Connerton, CSC, July 9, 1953, 310.1.09, Connerton, Administrative Correspondence, AHCFE; Memorandum, n.d. [1954], 01–20, Crusades, Ireland, AHCFM.

108. Ed Murray, CSC, to John Lynch, CSC, June 6, 1954, 01–20, Crusades, Ireland, AHCFM.

109. Family Rosary Crusade Summary Sheet, 01–20, Crusades, Ireland, AHCFM; Group Interview with author, June 4, 2000.

110. George Gill, "Ireland Evaluates America's Father Peyton," July 1954, Press Release found in 01–20, Crusades, Ireland, AHCFM. Another relevant and illustrative comment was: "Ireland has given many great priests to the Church, men who gave their lives for Christ in every clime and in every land. Worthy of their traditions indeed is this modern crusader for the love of God, who is encircling the world with the Rosary of Mary." See Jarlath P. Burke, "Crusader with Rosary Beads," clipping found in 507.09, Family Rosary Papers, AHCFM.

111. Ed Murray, CSC, to Christopher O'Toole, CSC, May 25 [1954], 428 (FR) 14, AHCG.

112. Souvenir Newspaper, n.d. [1955], 01–19, Crusades, India, AHCFM; Joseph Quinn, CSC, to Christopher O'Toole, CSC, January 28, 1955, 428 (FR) 14, AHCG. Woods was sent by Peyton as a liaison to several places besides India, most prominently the African continent. See Francis Woods, "Survey Memo," n.d. [1955], 05–01, Correspondence, Woods, AHCFM.

113. "Father Peyton's Family Rosary Crusade in South and Southeast Asia, n.d. [1955], 01–19, Crusades, India, AHCFM.

114. Quoted in Joseph Quinn, CSC, to James Connerton, CSC, January 28, 1955, 428 (FR) 14, AHCG.

115. Joseph Quinn, CSC, to Christopher O'Toole, CSC, January 28, 1955, 428 (FR) 14, AHCG.

116. "Report from Pakistan," n.d. [1955], 01–19, Crusades, India, AHCFM.

117. Tom Gill to James Connerton, CSC, May 22, 1955, 507.09, Family Rosary Papers, AHCFE. Gill wrote in the same letter: "Father Peyton has stood up magnificently to his arduous journeys throughout the Union. He has endeared himself to one and all, and he has taught us that the Rosary is laden with love and peace and security, and we thank God that He made it possible for the Ambassador of His beloved Mother to visit Africa."

118. Family Rosary Crusade, Rallies Schedule 1955, 01–01, Crusades, Africa, AHCFM; Tom Gill to James Connerton, CSC, April 22, 1955, 310.1.09, Connerton, Administrative Correspondence, AHCFE.

119. Patrick Peyton, CSC, *All for Her*, 153.

120. Sisters of St. Peter to Reverend Father General [O'Toole], January 20, 1956, 428 (FR) 14, AHCG.

121. Souvenir Book, African Crusade 1955, 01–01, Crusades, Africa, AHCFM. John Cuneo, a Chicago businessman, agreed to offer $50,000 to help finance the African souvenir book. See Patrick Peyton, CSC, to John Cuneo, April 7, 1956, 01–01, Crusades, Africa, AHCFM.

122. Patrick Peyton, CSC, to James Connerton, CSC, December 18, 1954, 507.09, Family Rosary Papers, AHCFE; Peyton to Mario Macrionitis, February 25, 1956, 01–15, Crusades, Greece, AHCFM.

123. Patrick Peyton, CSC, "Report on Crusade Rallies in Albacete, Spain," October 9, 1957, 02–04, Correspondence, AHCFM. In 1957 Father Peyton was given two fifteen-acre adjoining parcels of land by the Urquijo and Infantado families for the purpose of continuing the mission of Family Rosary. The superior general, Christopher O'Toole, CSC, suggested that land should be used to build a novitiate or possibly a seminary. The basic plan was to have a house of formation to recruit men who would ultimately serve in Peyton's ministry. Spanish vocations in the late 1950s were plentiful, and it was reported that many who wished to enter seminaries were denied for lack of space. See Patrick Peyton, CSC, to Christopher O'Toole, CSC, July 6, 1957, July 24, 1957; O'Toole to Peyton, February 26, 1958; Peyton to O'Toole, March 8, 1958, 428 (FR) 14, AHCG.

124. John Murphy, CSC, to Patrick Peyton, CSC, May 23, 1956; "A Report about the Crusade in Greece," n.d. [1957], 01–15, Crusades, Greece; Emil De Smedt, "Reflections on the Family Rosary Crusade," n.d. [1959], 01–04, Crusades, Belgium. The detailed story of the production of these films is provided in chapter 6.

125. Francisco Munoz, OP, to Jerome Lawyer, CSC, July 29, 1953; Patrick Peyton, CSC, to Munoz, October 31, 1953; Munoz to John Murphy, CSC, April 13, 1954, 01–24, Crusades, Philippines, AHCFM.

126. Patrick Peyton, CSC, to Jerome Lawyer, CSC, November 2, 1959, 05–01, Correspondence, Lawyer, AHCFM.

127. Joseph Quinn, CSC, to Christopher O'Toole, CSC, February 8, 1960, 428 (FR) 14, AHCG; Patrick Peyton, CSC, "Diary of the Great Blessings of God and Our Lady on the Family Rosary Crusade in the Archdiocese of Manila," December 8, 1959, 06–06, Patrick Peyton Papers, AHCFM.

128. Patrick Peyton, CSC, to the Family Rosary Group, April 30, 1954, 05–01, Correspondence, AHCFM.

129. Patrick Peyton, "Report on Crusade in Albacete, Spain," October 9, 1957, 02–04, Office Correspondence, Europe, AHCFM.

130. John Murphy, CSC, to Patrick Peyton, CSC, April 21, 1952, 05–01, Correspondence, Murphy, AHCFM.

131. Christopher O'Toole, CSC, to Patrick Peyton, CSC, October 26, 1954, 428 (FR) 12, AHCG.

132. One example of a request for family assistance is found in Jerome Lawyer, CSC, to Beatrice Gallagher [Peyton's sister], May 12, 1949, 06–11, Patrick Peyton Personal Papers, AHCFM. He wrote, "I talked with Father Pat last night on the telephone and it seems that he is pretty tired. Will you try to get him to sleep in late every morning.... I have trouble getting him to sleep late, maybe you will be more successful than I am."

133. A rare example of Peyton admitting his need for rest came toward the end of the 1952 English crusade when he wrote to Jerome Lawyer, his religious superior: "I feel that in justice to the Cause Father Murphy and I and the girls need a real rest after this grind. It has been killing on the mind. We will be burnt out unless we get a chance to get over the strain completely. We feel...that we shouldn't do another tap of work after we finish here sometime in early August until September 1." See Patrick Peyton, CSC, to Jerome Lawyer, CSC, July 22, 1952, 05–01, Correspondence, Lawyer, AHCFM.

134. Patrick Peyton, CSC, to James Connerton, CSC, June 3, 1953, 507.09, Family Rosary Papers, AHCFE; John Murphy, CSC, Interview with Thomas Feeley, CSC, June 3, 1999; Joseph Quinn, CSC, Interview with Thomas Feeley, CSC, March 16, 1999, AHCFM.

135. "A Centenary Call to Family Prayer," 01–03, Crusades, Australia, AHCFM. An anecdote from a fellow Holy Cross religious illustrates the same idea. At the conclusion of a difficult crusade rally Peyton called the campaign group together: "Fr. Pat would insist we say the rosary right away. We never had a chance to converse with friends we would meet. He was single-minded and prayerful. He said the rosary I don't know how many times a day and we said it with him because that was the only thing we could do." See John Murphy, CSC, Interview with Thomas Feeley, CSC, June 3, 1999, AHCFM.

136. Joseph Quinn, CSC, Interview with Thomas Feeley, CSC, March 16, 1999, AHCFM.

137. One humorous anecdote about the practice of holy hours after rallies occurred in Barcelona, Spain. After the rally Joseph Quinn and Richard Sullivan,

provincial superior at the time, planned to go to a soccer contest, through the invitation of Jesús Garay, one of Spain's leading soccer players, who had arranged for the tickets. When informed that the two planned to attend the game Peyton argued, "But our Blessed Mother wants us to make that Holy Hour." Sullivan responded, "But Jesus wants us to go to the soccer match." See Joseph Quinn, CSC, Interview with Thomas Feeley, CSC, March 16, 1999, AHCFM.

138. Francis Grogan, CSC, Interview with Thomas Feeley, June 2, 1999, AHCFM.

139. "Family Rosary Crusade," Editorial, *America* 87 (September 27, 1952): 605.

Chapter 6: The Rosary Films

1. The fifteen radio shows of the mysteries of the rosary, sponsored by the CDA, were titled *The Story of the Holy Rosary*. In the cast were Ann Blyth, Ruth Hussey, Jeff Chandler, and Gene Lockhart. Musical selections were sung by Bing Crosby, Jo Stafford, Ann Blyth, Christopher Lynch, Marina Koshetz, Nan Merriman, and Jerome Hines. See Booklet, *Sixteen Half-Hour Radio Programs*, n.d. [1953], 09–02, Family Theater Papers, AHCFM.

2. Jerome Lawyer, CSC, "Report on Production of Father Peyton's Films in Madrid," 1956, PPC, Attymass, Ireland; John Murphy, CSC, Interview with Thomas Feeley, CSC, June 3, 1999, AHCFM. Peyton's first contact with the CDA in Cleveland was in 1943, but nothing was said at that time about the future radio programs.

3. Patrick Peyton, CSC, "Notes on Proposed Half-Hour Films on the Fifteen Mysteries of the Rosary," August 14, 1953, 428 (FR) 8, AHCG.

4. Ibid.; Patrick Peyton, CSC, to Jerome Lawyer, CSC, and John Lynch, CSC, August 3, 1953, 05–01, Correspondence, Lawyer, AHCFM.

5. Patrick Peyton, CSC, "Notes on Proposed Half-Hour Films on the Fifteen Mysteries of the Rosary," August 14, 1953, 428 (FR) 8, AHCG.

6. Patrick Peyton, CSC, *All for Her* (Hollywood, Calif.: Family Theater, Inc., 1967), 138–41; Jeanne Arnold, *Man of Faith* (Hollywood, Calif.: Family Theater, Inc., 1983), 104–07.

7. John Murphy, CSC, to Jerome Lawyer, CSC, October 17, 1953, 05–01, Correspondence, Lawyer, AHCFM.

8. Patrick Peyton, CSC, to Jerome Lawyer, CSC, and John Lynch, CSC, December 7, 1953, 05–01, Correspondence, Lawyer, AHCFM.

9. Edmund Murray, CSC, to Christopher O'Toole, May 25, [1954], 428 (FR) 14, AHCG.

10. Jerome Lawyer, CSC, "Report on Production of Father Peyton's Films in Madrid," 1956, PPC, Attymass, Ireland.

11. Patrick Peyton, CSC, "Report on Your Film Gift to Our Lady," Pentecost Season, 1954, 428 (FR) 8, AHCG.

12. Christopher O'Toole, CSC, to Theodore Mehling, CSC, August 17, 1953, 428 (FR) 8; Jerome Lawyer, CSC, to Christopher O'Toole, CSC, June 15, 1954, 428 (FR) 14, AHCG.

13. John Lynch, CSC, to Christopher O'Toole, CSC, Pentecost Season, 1954, 428 (FR) 8, AHCFM.

14. Patrick Peyton, CSC, to Jerome Lawyer, CSC, February 23, 1955, 05–01, Correspondence, Woods, AHCFM.

15. Patrick Peyton, CSC, "Report on Your Rosary Film Gift to Our Lady," Pentecost Season, 1954, 428 (FR) 8, AHCG.

16. "Notes on Proposed Half-Hour Films on the Fifteen Mysteries of the Rosary," August 14, 1953, 428 (FR) 8, AHCG.

17. Jerome Lawyer, CSC, "Report," October 20, 1956, 09–01, Family Theater Papers, AHCFM; John T. Kirby to Patrick Peyton, CSC, July 8, 1954, 428 (FR) 8, AHCG.

18. Francis Woods to Jerome Lawyer, CSC, n.d. [1954]; Lawyer to Patrick Peyton, CSC, August 10, 1955, 05–01, Correspondence, Lawyer, AHCFM.

19. Christopher O'Toole, CSC, to John Corr, CSC, December 12, 1955, 422.2, Correspondence, Connerton, AHCG.

20. Jerome Lawyer, CSC, to Francis Woods, March 23, 1955, 05–01, Correspondence, Woods, AHCFM.

21. Press Release, "The Mysteries of the Rosary," n.d. [1957]; Jerome Lawyer, Report, October 20, 1956, 09–01, Family Theater Papers, AHCFM. The only writer who had participated in *Family Theater of the Air* was John Kelley. Peyton had met Bennett during his New Zealand crusade of 1954. The local bishop released him to come to Hollywood and work on the project. He continued on and was a consultant in Spain during the filming before returning home.

22. Patrick Peyton, CSC, to Jerome Lawyer, CSC, July 23, 1955, 06–02, Patrick Peyton Papers, AHCFM. While several scripts proved difficult, the Coronation of Mary was by far the most problematic. Since the events celebrated in the mystery were not biblical, writers were perplexed on precisely how to illustrate both the story and its contemporary application. The situation became so perplexing that Lawyer suggested to Peyton that the Coronation not be a part of the fifteen-film set, but could be a standalone film that might be useful on Mother's Day. See Lawyer to Peyton, February 11, 1956, 06–02, Patrick Peyton Papers, AHCFM.

23. Jerome Lawyer, CSC, to Francis Woods and Joseph Quinn, CSC, January 24, 1955, 05–01, Correspondence, Lawyer, AHCFM.

24. Francis Woods to Jerome Lawyer, CSC, May 2, 1955, 05–01, Correspondence, Woods, AHCFM.

25. Jerome Lawyer, CSC, to John Murphy, CSC, November 16, 1955, 05–01, Correspondence, Lawyer, AHCFM.

26. The role of Christ was not greatly significant in the films because Church policy at the time would not allow the face of Christ to be seen on film, save a distant shot where one could not make out details.

27. Mary Jane McQueen, Diary, loaned to the author, May 18, 1956. McQueen (Buchenau at the time) wrote of Cantabella, "She is from the country, knows no English, and nothing about city life, cinemas or anything for that matter. Really, as someone on the set said today, her simplicity is 2000 years old."

28. Patrick Peyton, CSC, to James Connerton, CSC, April 10, 1956, 507.09, Family Rosary Correspondence, AHCFE; Peyton to Jerome Lawyer, CSC, August 2, 1956, 05–01, Correspondence, Lawyer; Peyton to John Murphy, CSC, April 7, 1956, 06–2, Patrick Peyton Papers, AHCFM.

29. Mary Jane McQueen, Diary, various dates, April to August 1956.

30. Ibid.; Jerome Lawyer, CSC, to Patrick Peyton, CSC, February 11, 1956, 06–02, Patrick Peyton Papers, AHCFM.

31. "Anecdotes," found in 06–03, Patrick Peyton Papers, AHCFM; Mary Jane McQueen, Diary, May 21, 1956.

32. George DePrizio, CSC, to Patrick Peyton, CSC, August 10, 1956, Patrick Peyton Personnel File, AHCFE; Christopher O'Toole to James Connerton, April 11, 1956, 422.2, Correspondence, Connerton, AHCG.

33. Jerome Lawyer, CSC, "Report on the Production of Father Peyton's Films in Madrid," 1956, PPC, Attymass, Ireland.

34. Patrick Peyton, CSC, to Jerome Lawyer, September 4, 1956, 05–01, Correspondence, Woods, AHCFM.

35. Breen was owed a favor from Count Enrico Galeazzi, governor of Vatican City. This relationship provided him entree into the Vatican music offerings.

36. Jerome Lawyer, CSC, to John Murphy, CSC, July 30, 1957, 05–01, Correspondence, Lawyer; Lawyer, "Report on Madrid Film Project," June 4, 1957, 09–01, Family Theater Papers, AHCFM.

37. R. Fontenelle to Pierre Marie Theas, March 19, 1957; George Roche, Memorandum, Visit of Rev. P. J. Peyton, December 18, 1957, 09–01, Family Theater Papers, AHCFM.

38. George Roche to Patrick Peyton, CSC, March 12, 1958, 09–01, Family Theater Papers, AHCFM; Peyton to John Murphy, CSC, April 28, 1958, 310.2.68, Provincial Papers, DePrizio, AHCFE. While extant data does not give complete answers as to why the films were not shown at Lourdes, one practical reason was that the dubbing process into French had not been completed by the time Peyton wanted to show the films.

39. Javier Echenique, "Mission of Mary in Madrid," n.d. [1958], 428 (FR) 14, AHCG.

40. Pope Pius XII to Patrick Peyton, April 4, 1958, found in Christopher O'Toole, CSC, Circular Letter #16, April 27, 1958, AHCG. In his letter the superior general personally described the films as "magnificent in conception, exquisitely beautiful in realization and most powerful in their import and influence." In succeeding years special screenings were set up for Popes John XXIII and Paul VI. The latter commented, "The fifteen films . . . that tell the story of the fifteen mysteries of the Rosary are indeed worthy of praise." See Philip Higgins, CSC, to Albert Heinzer, CSC, November 5, 1965, 05–01, Correspondence, Heinzer, AHCFM.

41. Patrick Peyton, CSC, "A Report on the Theater at Brussels," n.d. [1958], 09–01, Family Theater Papers, AHCFM; Peyton, *All for Her,* 167–69.

42. Although Dutch was suggested, the language needed was Walloon for the Belgian people.

43. The cheapest estimate Peyton had obtained for dubbing into any language was $20,000.

44. Paul Heymans to Patrick Peyton, CSC, August 20, 1957; Peyton to Heymans, September 1, 1957; Contract between Family Rosary Crusade and Commissioner General of *Civitas Dei,* November 18, 1957, 09–01, Family Theater Papers, AHCFM.

45. Jerome Lawyer, CSC, to John Murphy, CSC, September 19, 1957; Francis Woods to Patrick Peyton, CSC, November 29, 1957, 09–01, Family Theater Papers, AHCFM.

46. John Murphy, CSC, to Patrick Peyton, CSC, November 14, 1957, 06–02, Patrick Peyton Papers, AHCFM. The Code of Canon Law of 1917 gave clear rules

on the permissions needed for expenditure of funds. Several in Holy Cross believed Peyton to be operating independently of these rules.

47. Patrick Peyton, CSC, to Paul Heymans, February 27, 1958, 09–01, Family Theater Papers, AHCFM.

48. *Eastern Province Review* 1, no. 3 (September 1958): 3, AHCG; Questionnaire on the Projection of the Rosary Films in Brussels, n.d. [1958], 09–01, Family Theater Papers, AHCFM. The daily schedule of screenings was: Monday: Annunciation and Agony in the Garden; Tuesday: Visitation and Scourging at the Pillar; Wednesday: Nativity and Crowning with Thorns; Thursday: Presentation and Carrying of the Cross; Friday: Finding of Jesus in the Temple and the Crucifixion; Saturday: Resurrection and Ascension (12:00 noon to 3:00 p.m.), Descent of the Holy Spirit and Assumption (3:00 p.m. to 8:00 p.m.); Sunday: Schedule varied.

49. Patrick Peyton, CSC, to Christopher O'Toole, CSC, May 22, 1958, 428 (FR) 14, AHCG; Peyton, *All for Her,* 170–71; Jeanne Arnold, *Man of Faith,* 129–30.

50. Pope John XXIII to Patrick Peyton, CSC, November 27, 1959, 08–05, Albany Headquarters Correspondence, AHCFM. Mueller worked with Lawyer after the films were completed to get them dubbed into various languages.

51. Bernard Mullahy, CSC, to Albert Heinzer, CSC, June 9, 1959; Heinzer to Mullahy, July 1, 1959, 09–01, Family Theater Papers, AHCFM.

52. Patrick Peyton, CSC, to Jerome Lawyer, April 21, 1959, 05–01, Correspondence, Lawyer, AHCFM.

53. Patrick Peyton, CSC, to Bishop Francis Leipzig, May 31, 1957, 06–02, Patrick Peyton Papers; Report, n.d. [1957]; Peyton, Memorandum for Peter Grace and John Kirby, March 8, 1957, 09–01, Family Theater Papers, AHCFM.

54. Jerome Lawyer, CSC, "Report on Madrid Film Project," June 4, 1957, 09–01, Family Theater Papers; Lawyer to John Murphy, CSC, April 4, 1959, 05–01, Correspondence, Lawyer, AHCFM.

55. Joseph Breen Jr. to Albert Heinzer, CSC, n.d. [September 1958], 05–01, Correspondence, Heinzer; Breen to Heinzer, February 28, 1958, 09–01, Family Theater Papers, AHCFM.

56. Ulric Bell to Donald Henderson, September 3, 1958; John Springer to Donald Henderson, September 3, 1958, 09–01, Family Theater Papers, AHCFM. Springer's reaction was very positive, calling the films, "a remarkable achievement — terrifically impressive in its [*sic*] dramatic handling of the events depicted and surprisingly beautifully done." He suggested Fox acquire the films, edit them to a feature length, dub them into several languages, and then distribute them to theaters.

57. Joseph Breen Jr. to Albert Heinzer, CSC, n.d. [September 1958], 05–01, Correspondence, Heinzer, AHCFM.

58. Joseph Breen Jr. to Albert Heinzer, November 14, 1958, 09–01, Family Theater Papers; Patrick Peyton, CSC, to Albany Office, January 15, 1959, 06–02, Patrick Peyton Papers, AHCFM. Skouras may have made his decision based on opinions such as that of Alan Silverbach, who upon viewing the films in September wrote to Donald Henderson, "It [the films] will not have common appeal to people of other faiths throughout the world. I am sure it will be a most effective instrument for the Catholic Church and perhaps should be limited to that use." See Silverbach to Henderson, September 3, 1958, 09–01, Family Theater Papers, AHCFM.

59. Anonymous to Jerome Lawyer, CSC, February 5, 1959, 05–01, Correspondence, Lawyer, AHCFM.

60. Quoted in Frank Gartland, CSC, "Cardinal Cushing Backs Rosary Films," *Catholic Boy* 28, no. 2 (October 1959): 16–17. In 1959 Cushing founded the St. James Society, a group of Boston-based diocesan priests who, in response to Pope John XXIII's call for clerical assistance in Latin America, ministered in South America, principally in Peru.

61. *Knickerbocker News,* Albany, New York, clipping, September 1, 1959, found in 09–01, Family Theater Papers, AHCFM.

62. Press Release, October 1, 1959, Archdiocese of Boston, 09–01, Family Theater Papers; John Corr, CSC, to Patrick Peyton, CSC, November 8, 1959; Peyton to Corr, November 16, 1959, 06–02, Patrick Peyton Papers, AHCFM.

63. Jerome Lawyer, CSC, to John Corr, June 9, 1960, 05–01, Correspondence, Lawyer, AHCFM.

64. Conference Notes of Father Heinzer, Father Corr, and Joseph Breen Jr., May 22, 1957, 09–01, Family Theater Papers, AHCFM.

65. J. Peter Grace, Memorandum, March 7, 1960, FTH.

66. Family Rosary Crusade — Evaluation, April 1960, B428 (FR), AHCG.

67. Patrick Peyton, CSC, to Spyros Skouras, October 4, 1958, 09–01, Family Theater Papers, AHCFM.

68. John Corr, CSC, to George DePrizio, CSC, June 30, 1960, 09–01, Family Theater Papers, AHCFM.

69. Jerome Lawyer, CSC, to John Meehan, June 30, 1960, 09–01, Family Theater Papers, AHCFM.

70. Christopher O'Toole, CSC, to John Corr, CSC, October 8, 1960, 428 (FR) 14, AHCG.

71. Cardinal Richard Cushing to Patrick Peyton, CSC, September 26, 1959, 09–01, Family Theater Papers, AHCFM.

72. *Variety,* October 5, 1960, clipping; Donald Henderson to Albert Heinzer, CSC, March 15, 1961; Henderson to Jerome Lawyer, CSC, March 22, 1961, 09–01, Family Theater Papers, AHCFM.

73. Christopher O'Toole, CSC, to George DePrizio, June 19, 1961; John J. Meehan to Patrick Peyton, CSC, June 23, 1961, 428 (FR) 14, AHCG; Meehan to Peyton, July 28, 1961, 09–01, Family Theater Papers, AHCFM.

74. "Reasons Why We Should not Proceed in a Law Case with 20th Century Fox but Accept their First Offer of Settlement," n.d. [1962], 428 (FR) 14, AHCG.

75. Philip Higgins, CSC, to Albert Heinzer, CSC (Phone Transcription), March 21, 1962, 05–01, Correspondence, Heinzer, AHCFM.

Chapter 7: The Latin American Crusades

1. John Considine, MM, "The Struggle in Latin America," *Catholic Charities Review* 48 (January 1964): 25–26; Arthur McCormack, "The Catholic Church in South America," *Wiseman Review* 238 (Fall 1964): 232; Ronan Hoffman, OFM, "Latin America: The Church Meets the Challenge of Change," *Catholic World* 197 (June 1963): 165. In 1953 a conference of Catholic officials from throughout Latin America was held in Chimbote, Peru. The delegates published a statement on the "urgent necessity of restoring and revitalizing the Catholic traditions of Latin America." This conference was a catalyst to the organization of CELAM. See James Garneau, " 'Commandos for Christ': The Foundation of the Missionary Society of St. James the

Apostle and the Americanism of the 1950s and 1960s" (PhD dissertation: Catholic University of America, 2000), 71.

2. John Considine, MM, "The Pope's Program for Latin America," *Catholic Association for International Peace (CAIP) News* 23 (June 1962): 4; "Pope to Latin American Bishops," NCWC News Service, December 26, 1958, found in 02–04, Offices, Europe, AHCFM.

3. John Considine, MM, "The Struggle in Latin America," 65; Considine, "Who Is Winning in Latin America?" *Shield* 44 (December 1964–January 1965): 30.

4. John Considine, MM, "The Pope's Program for Latin America," 2.

5. Jaime Fonseca, "A Challenge to Catholics," *World Mission* 11 (September 1960), 15; Ronan Hoffman, OFM, "Latin America: The Church Meets the Challenge of Change," *Catholic World* 197 (June 1963): 171.

6. Ronan Hoffman, OFM, "SOS for Latin America," *Homiletic and Pastoral Review* 61 (July 1961): 967.

7. Bishop Manuel Larraín, "Latin America's Only Hope: An Interview," *Sign* 40 (February 1961): 36.

8. Ibid., 38.

9. Quoted in James O'Gara, "Uncertain Future," *Commonweal* 77 (November 16, 1962): 192. Another comment that illustrated the problem was published in *Look* magazine: "Before most Church members now alive are dead there will be as many Catholics in Latin America as in the rest of the world combined or there will be few, if any, Latin Americans left in the Church." See Leonard Gross, "The Catholic Church in Latin America: Its Poverty, Its Timidity, Its Failures, Its New Reformers," *Look* 26, no. 2 (October 9, 1962): 27.

10. Quoted in McCormack, "The Catholic Church in South America," 239.

11. Ibid., 243, 245, 237.

12. The history of the foundation of the St. James Society is provided in James Garneau, " 'Commandos for Christ': The Foundation of the Missionary Society of St. James the Apostle and the 'Americanism' of the 1950s and 1960s." Garneau speaks of the lack of clergy and the need for evangelization in Latin America as the two primary reasons for the Society's establishment. See pages 69–87.

13. The Latin American Bureau of the National Catholic Welfare Conference (NCWC), the precursor to the present National Conference of Catholic Bishops (NCCB) and the United States Catholic Conference (USCC), was originally established on April 9, 1929, and was suspended in November 1933. See Meeting Minutes for the Administrative Committee for the NCWC, November 14, 1933, NCWC Files, Archives, ACUA.

14. John Considine, MM, "The Pope's Program for Latin America," 1; Considine, "Mission to Latin America," *Perspectives* 6 (February 1961): 47.

15. Germain Lalande, CSC, Circular Letter #1, March 19, 1963, AHCG.

16. Robert J. Alexander, *Communism in Latin America* (New Brunswick, N.J.: Rutgers University Press, 1957), 27–29.

17. Ernst Halperin, "Decline of Communism in Latin America," *Atlantic* 215 (May 1965): 65–66.

18. Harry Schwartz, "Shadow over Latin America," *Commonweal* 66 (June 21, 1957): 295.

19. Ibid., 296; "How to Help Latin America," Editorial, *Christian Century* 78 (May 24, 1961): 644.

20. John Tierney, CPPS, "The Communist Plan for Latin America," *Nuntius Aulae* 45 (1963): 164.

21. "United States Security and the Power of Prayer," n.d. [1962], B428 (FR), AHCG.

22. List of Quotes, found in "Family Fortress," Family Theater Publication, n.d., 09–02, Family Theater Papers, AHCFM.

23. Douglas Hyde, "Communism in Latin America," *World Justice* 4 (September 1962): 16, 36.

24. "Communist Threat to Latin America," Editorial, *The Shield* 43 (October–November 1963): 13. One U.S. State Department official commented, "And what of moral and spiritual values which are the antithesis of Communism? They constitute a great bulwark of strength against Communist penetration of the Americas, which would destroy them if successful, although obviously they need to be reinforced by visible evidence of economic and social progress." See Roy R. Rubottom, Jr. "International Communism in Latin America: Statement, June 20, 1960," *United States Department of State Bulletin* 43 (July 11, 1960): 61. .

25. Quoted in Albert Heinzer, CSC, to Patrick Peyton, CSC, July 14, 1958, 05–01, Correspondence, Heinzer, AHCFM.

26. Quoted in "Communist Threat to Latin America," 13. *Christian Century* published a very different view concerning the Church's role as an antidote to Communism in Latin America: "Therefore look for the subversive beginnings of the Cuban Revolution not in Moscow — eager enough to be sure — but . . . in the indifferent Roman Catholic Church drawing its unconstitutional subsidy from the state while neglecting the people." See "How to Help Latin America," *Christian Century* 78 (May 24, 1961): 643–44.

27. Quoted in *Latin America: Pattern for the Sixties* found in "Communist Threat to Latin America," 11. A similar idea was offered by the British writer Douglas Hyde: "A lapsed-Catholic Latin America would be one that was wide open to Communism. One where Catholicism is largely normal can easily be disunited and is vulnerable to Communist attack. But a spiritually regenerated Latin America in which Catholics were playing their fullest part in the attempt to bring it right into the modern world would be one where the appeal of Communism might be expected soon to be a weakening force." See Douglas Hyde, "Communism in Latin America," 37.

28. Washington wrote (the address was never given orally) in his famous 1796 speech, "Against the insidious snare of foreign influence the jealousy of a free people ought to be constantly awake; since history and experience prove, that foreign influence is one of the most baneful woes of Republican government. . . . The great rule of conduct for us, in regard to foreign nations, is in extending our commercial relations, to have with them as little political connexion as possible."

29. The United States was involved with numerous actions in Latin America in the twentieth century. An excellent summary of U.S. foreign policy toward Latin America in this period is found in Cole Blasier, *The Hovering Giant: U.S. Responses to Revolutionary Change in Latin America 1910–1985* (Pittsburgh: University of Pittsburgh Press, 1985).

30. Quoted in Robert Pell, "Foreign Policies of Richard Milhous Nixon," *America* 104 (October 8, 1960): 42.

31. Arthur P. Whitaker, "Our Reaction to Communist Infiltration in Latin America: With Questions and Answers," *Annals of the American Academy of Political and Social Science* 330 (July 1960): 103, 111–12.

32. James Garneau, "Commandos for Christ," 18.

33. Quoted in J. Peter Grace, "It's Not Too Late in Latin America: Proposals for Action Now," 1961, Privately Published; Grace, "The Great Challenge of Latin America: Address, May 23, 1963," *Vital Speeches of the Day* 29 (August 1, 1963): 613.

34. J. Peter Grace, "The Great Challenge of Latin America: Address, May 23, 1963," 614.

35. Daniel M. Friedenberg, "Can the Alliance for Progress Work?" *Commentary* 34 (August 1962): 99–100.

36. Michael J. Heale, *American Anticommunism: Combating the Enemy Within, 1830–1970* (Baltimore: Johns Hopkins University Press, 1990), 122–90.

37. Ibid., 150, 170. Once McCarthy described his campaign against Communists as "a final, all-out battle between communistic atheism and Christianity."

38. Quoted in Ibid., 162.

39. J. Edgar Hoover, "The Home: Bulwark against Communism," *Family Digest* 19 (December 1963): 5–9.

40. Quoted in Richard Gribble, CSC, *Guardian of America: The Life of James Martin Gillis, C.S.P.* (Mahwah, N.J.: Paulist Press, 1998), 147.

41. Richard Gid Powers, *Not without Honor: The History of American Anticommunism* (New York: Free Press, 1995), 52.

42. John Cogley, "Two Fronts in the Same War," *Commonweal* 70 (September 18, 1959): 516; Jeremy York, "Peace, Communism, and American Catholics," *Ave Maria* 104 (July 2, 1966): 9–10. The historian Richard Gid Powers accurately summarized the Catholic attitude against Communism in 1933: "Because of their visceral anticommunism and because of their concern for the Catholic populations of Eastern Europe, especially Poland and Lithuania, American Catholics were the most outspoken critics of the American-Soviet alliance." See Powers, *Not without Honor,* 173.

43. Heale, *American Anticommunism,* 172.

44. Powers, *Not without Honor,* 51, 303.

45. "New Crusade in Europe, Interview," *U.S. News & World Report* 37 (August 27, 1954): 90. Although not a strong voice, it must be recognized that American Judaism also spoke out against Communism. Michael Heale suggests "Jews found in anticommunism a means of proving their American identity." See Heale, *American Anticommunism,* 173.

46. Patrick Peyton, Radio Talks, June 28, 1946, 09–17, Family Theater Papers, AHCFM.

47. Declan Flynn, OFM, "American Memories," No. 4 Faith and Films, n.d. [1951], clipping found in 507.92, Family Rosary Papers, AHCFE.

48. "An Explosion of Love," Interview of Patrick Peyton by Russell J. Huff, May 1960, 01–07, Crusades, Chile, AHCFM.

49. Jerome Lawyer, CSC, to John Corr, CSC, March 9, 1960, 05–01, Correspondence, Lawyer; James Mannis to Joseph Quinn, April 21, 1960, 01–07, Crusades, Chile, AHCFM.

50. Pope John XXIII to Patrick Peyton, CSC, May 1, 1959, 06–02, Patrick Peyton Papers, AHCFM.

51. Sr. Jeanne Miriam Johnson, CSJ, "Education to the Family Rosary" (MA thesis: Catholic University of America, 1950), 57; James Gillis, CSP, "Family Rosary Will Sweep World, 'Gates of Hell Shall Not Prevail,'" in *Time for Family Prayer,* November 14, 1948, 01–06, Crusades, Canada, AHCFM.

52. Editorial Broadcast over WEJL Radio, Scranton, Pennsylvania, September 13, 1961, 428 (FR), 14, AHCG.

53. Quoted in "The Family Rosary Crusade — 1962," 01–05, Crusades, Brazil, Recife, AHCFM.

54. Extant data does not indicate the source of this report, found in the General Archives of the Congregation of Holy Cross in Rome.

55. "United States Security and the Power of Prayer," B428 (FR) n.d. [1962], AHCG.

56. Norman Carignan to Peter Grace, Memorandum, July 31, 1961, 428 (FR) 14, AHCG.

57. Patrick Peyton, CSC, to Peter Grace, June 15, 1962, 08–05, Headquarters, Albany, AHCFM.

58. Christopher O'Toole, CSC, Circular Letter #1, September 15, 1950; *Eastern Province Review* 2, no. 2 (June 1959): 9; Germain Lalande, CSC, Circular Letter #1, March 19, 1963, AHCG.

59. "The Family Rosary Cruzade [*sic*]," n.d. 428 (FR) 0, AHCG.

60. Patrick Peyton, Generic Form Letter, June 1959, 05–01, Correspondence, Mary Buckley, AHCFM.

61. Patrick Peyton, CSC, Memorandum, July 24, 1958, 310.2.68, Provincial Papers, DePrizio, AHCFE.

62. John T. Kirby to Patrick Peyton, CSC, February 28, 1956; Peyton to Jerome Lawyer, CSC, and John Murphy, August 13, 1956, 06–02, Patrick Peyton Papers, AHCFM; Murphy to James Connerton, CSC, March 7, 1956, 310.1.45, Provincial Papers, Connerton, AHCFE.

63. Patrick Peyton, CSC, to John Corr, CSC, November 7, 1959, 06–02, Patrick Peyton Papers, AHCFM; J. Peter Grace, "It's Not Too Late in Latin America: Proposals for Action Now," Privately Published, 1961, 25.

64. Joseph Quinn, CSC, "Family Rosary Crusade Proposed Plan of Operation," April 9, 1961, 09–05, Family Theater Papers, AHCFM.

65. "Report of the Family Rosary Crusade," March–June 1963, 01–05, Crusades, Brazil, AHCFM; "United States Security and the Power of Prayer," n.d. [1962], B 428 (FR), AHCG.

66. Patrick Peyton, CSC, to Albert Heinzer, CSC, John Murphy, CSC, and Denis Sughrue, CSC, May 23, 1959, 06–02, Patrick Peyton Papers; Patrick Peyton to Fuensanta González et al. [Secular Missionaries], February 26, 1963, 01–05, Crusades, Brazil, Belo Horizonte, AHCFM.

67. Legal Agreement between Institute of Secular Missionaries and Family Rosary, n.d. [1963], 507.49, Family Rosary Papers, AHCFE. Beginning in 1961, through a verbal agreement, compensation, transportation, and supervision needs were worked out between Peyton and the missionaries. This 1963 contract made the earlier agreement legally binding. Peyton supplied residences for the missionaries: for those on the crusade, a renovated home owned by Peter Grace on his Manhasset,

New York, estate and for those in Hollywood a home in Woodland Hills, north of Los Angeles.

68. Patrick Peyton, CSC, to Bishop Carlos Brown, MM, June 5, 1958, 310.2.68, Provincial Papers, DePrizio, AHCFE.

69. Extant data has only five respondents, although there may have been more.

70. Bishop Carlos Brown, MM, to Patrick Peyton, CSC, June 26, 1958, 310.2.68, Provincial Papers, DePrizio, AHCFE.

71. Bishop Thomas Danehy, MM, to Patrick Peyton, CSC, July 6, 1958; Bishop Jorge Manrique to Peyton, July 14, 1958, 310.2.68, Provincial Papers, DePrizio, AHCFE.

72. Patrick Peyton, CSC, to George DePrizio, CSC, July 24, 1958 Peyton to DePrizio, August 13, 1958, 310.2.68 Provincial Papers, DePrizio, AHCFE. John actually sent the money in February 1959, but by that time other arrangements were being made to finance the entire Latin American crusade effort.

73. Patrick Peyton, CSC, Memorandum, n.d. [1959], 02–04, Offices, Europe, AHCFM. Peyton understood Grace to believe that the best hope to defeat Communism lay with the Church. In South America, where the Church was handicapped in its fight with Communism due to a lack of clergy, Grace believed from his first viewing that the films would be the catechetical tool to help the Church win its battle against the Red menace.

74. Peter Grace to Percy Gjertsen, July 12, 1960, 01–07, Crusades, Chile, AHCFM.

75. J. Peter Grace, Address at the World Trade Week Council, Dallas, Texas, May 19, 1958, found in Richard Nixon, Vice Presidential Papers, Box 298, Grace File, National Archives District Branch (hereafter NADB), Laguna Niguel, California.

76. J. Peter Grace to Richard Nixon, May 13, 1958, Richard Nixon, Vice Presidential Papers, Box 298, Grace File, NADB. Grace wrote that his agent John Moore had just returned from Latin America, "deeply moved by what you [Nixon] have done and convinced that you have opened the door to a new and better relationship with the Latin American countries, whose problems you see so clearly.... If we of the Grace organization can assist you in any way in following up on the work you have done on this trip, I want you to know that our people both here and in Latin America are completely at your disposal."

77. J. Peter Grace, "A Case Study in Self-Help," Speech to the Commonwealth Club of San Francisco, June 26, 1959, found in Richard Nixon, Vice Presidential Papers, Box 298, Grace File, NADB; Grace, "Excerpt from Memorandum," *Congressional Digest* 42 (March 1963): 89; Grace, "It's Not Too Late in Latin America," 46; *Congressional Record,* June 27, 1961, 10, 558–59.

78. Grace, "It's Not Too Late in Latin America," 28–33, 52–59.

79. Grace, "Excerpt from Memorandum," 89.

80. J. Peter Grace to Richard Nixon, April 8, 1958; Memorandum (Notes), Richard Nixon, Vice Presidential Papers, Box 298, Grace File, NADB.

81. Memorandum J. Peter Grace to J. D. J. Moore, July 26, 1958, 310.2.68, Provincial Papers, DePrizio, AHCFE.

82. Patrick Peyton, CSC, Memorandum, July 24, 1958, 310.2.68, Provincial Papers, DePrizio, AHCFE.

83. Peter Grace to Allen Dulles, November 24, 1958, 428 (FR) 14, AHCG. Grace promoted Peyton's crusade and especially the films as a means to defeat Communism in Latin America: "It seems to me that the most powerful way to fight Communism is with a positive answer that removes any semblance of a defensive position. The strongest bulwark against Communism is a belief in God — a strong belief in God. Communism cannot live in the same mind where there dwells a strong reliance on God. The family that prays together is banded together against Communism. Therefore, a crusade for family prayer is necessarily a crusade against Communism. What I have been searching for, and what I am sure you are searching for, is some force which will set fire to the minds and hearts of the abandoned peoples in the underdeveloped areas of the world, a force which will be so strong that Communism will not have a chance. I know of no other way to get into the highways and byways this, the only real fundamental answer to Communism, than through these beautiful pictures made by an organization which has achieved outstanding success in the fields of communication during the past thirteen years."

84. Vice President's Schedule, Wednesday, December 3, 1958, Richard Nixon, Vice Presidential Papers, Box 298, Grace File, NADB.

85. Allen Dulles to Richard Nixon, February 20, 1961; Nixon to J. Peter Grace, November 8, 1961, Richard Nixon, Vice Presidential Papers, Box 298, Grace File, NADB; Peggy Flood to Jerome Lawyer, December 4, 1958, 02–04, Offices, Europe, AHCFM; J. Peter Grace to Nixon, January 22, 1959, Richard Nixon, Vice Presidential Papers, Box 298, Grace File, NADB.

86. Patrick Peyton, CSC, to Christopher O'Toole, CSC, January 8, 1959, 428 (FR) 14; O'Toole to George DePrizio, CSC, April 26, 1961, 422.2, Correspondence, DePrizio, AHCG. Knowledge of the government source and its association with Peter Grace was known by several members of the Family Rosary team. One illustration is a letter from Denis Sughrue, CSC, to Albert Heinzer, CSC: "On this success [the Latin American Crusades] depends an amazing grant for further crusade work in South America. No doubt you are already acquainted with the magnanimous offer which came to Father Pat at Washington through the fine work of Peter Grace." See Sughrue to Heinzer, March 2, 1959, 05–01, Correspondence, Heinzer, AHCFM.

87. Peter Grace to John Coleman, July 19, 1974, 09–01, Family Theater Papers, AHCFM. Grace stated that the two people most associated with anti-Communism that he knew were Peyton and George Meany, the organized labor leader. Newspaper reporters Stephen Michaud and Hugh Aynesworth have written, "Grace's commitment to Peyton was absolute." See Michaud and Aynesworth, *"If You Love Me You Will Do My Will"* (New York: Signet, 1991), 106.

88. Sister Gerald Hartney, CSC, Interview with Thomas Feeley, CSC, June 16, 1999, AHCFM; Patrick Peyton, CSC, to George DePrizio, CSC, December 3, 1958, 310.2.68, DePrizio, Provincial Correspondence, AHCFE. Peyton wrote, "Having Peter Grace you have the beginning and the end. . . . Peter Grace commands the respect of all America."

89. Patrick Peyton, CSC, Report — Chilean Crusade, July 24 to August 15, 1960, 06–06, Patrick Peyton Papers, AHCFM.

90. Patrick Peyton, CSC, to Joseph Quinn, CSC, December 13, 1961, 01–24, Crusades, Philippines, AHCFM.

91. Patrick Peyton, CSC, to Christopher O'Toole, CSC, January 8, 1959, 428 (FR) 14, AHCG; Peyton to Mr. and Mrs. James McArdle, January 8, 1959, 02–04, Offices, Europe, AHCFM.

92. John Moore to Peter Grace, January 5, 1959, 02–04, Offices, Europe, AHCFM.

93. Thomas Doyle to Alfred Send, CSC, February 18, 1959; James F. McCloud to Patrick Peyton, CSC, March [*sic*–February] 28, 1959, 02–04, Offices, Europe, AHCFM.

94. Patrick Peyton, CSC, to Jerome Lawyer, CSC, May 10, 1959, 05–01, Correspondence, Lawyer, AHCFM.

95. Patrick Peyton, CSC, to Peter Grace, February 27, 1959, and March 10, 1959; Peyton to Rudolph Gomez, March 12, 1959, 02–04, Offices, Europe, AHCFM.

96. Konstantin Sergeevich Tarasow, *The C.I.A. in Latin America* (Moscow: Progress Publishers, 1984), 7–10.

97. *New York Times,* March 16, 1967, Editorial Page. During the 1960s the *Times* published numerous articles that described CIA involvement with private groups, several associated with Latin America. On February 15, 1967, the paper reported that "the agency provides clandestine aid to anticommunist labor unions, publications and radio and television stations." On February 15 and 16, 1967, it was reported that the CIA had been funding the United States National Student Association since 1952. Financial assistance was also provided to the International Student Conference of Leyden, Netherlands, the Independent Research Service of New York, the United States Youth Council of New York, and the World Assembly of Youth in Brussels. The February 18, 1967, issue of the *Times* revealed CIA financial assistance to the American Newspaper Guild of nearly $1 million to "help finance South American and other overseas activities." The money was to be used in "its [the Guild's] efforts combating Communist newspapers, unions and associations in South America." On February 22, 1967, the paper reported CIA financial assistance to the American Federation of State, County, and Municipal Employees. The *Times* stated, "The Union used agency funds for four and a half years — from 1959 until May 1964 to finance its overseas activities, mainly in Latin America." Confirmation of these financial deals is provided in Philip Agee, *Inside the Company: CIA Diary* (New York: Bantam Books, 1976). See also Angelyn Dries, OSF, *The Missionary Movement in American Catholic History* (Maryknoll, N.Y.: Orbis Books, 1998), 230.

98. Penny Lernoux, "C.I.A. Secret Missionaries," *Nation* 230 (April 26, 1980): 494.

99. Quoted in Angelyn Dries, *Missionary Movement,* 230.

100. Ibid., 231.

101. Ibid.

102. *New York Times,* February 27, 1980, A16. The Carter administration admitted that the CIA had continued using journalists, academics, and clergymen to obtain information, even though the practice had been forbidden since 1977.

103. Penny Lernoux, "C.I.A. Secret Missionaries," 496.

104. Ibid., 495.

105. Quoted in ibid.

106. Angelyn Dries, *Missionary Movement,* 230.

107. "How the C.I.A. Used the Churches," n.d., clipping from *Le Dossier* and found in 428 (FR) 14, AHCG.

108. James T. Fisher, *Dr. America: The Lives of Thomas A. Dooley, 1927–1961* (Amherst: University of Massachusetts Press, 1997), 155, 196–97.

109. Richard Cushing to Patrick Peyton, CSC, December 28, 1959; Summary Sheet, September 27, 1963; Richard Cushing to Peter Grace, June 20, 1963, 09–01, Family Theater Papers, AHCFM. Cushing wrote to Grace, hinting that the businessman was behind Peyton's work in Latin America: "I was happy to get a report on the work of Father Peyton in Latin America, but in all the publicity that Father Peyton has received for his project I haven't found any place where he made reference to the one who is helping more than all others to finance it."

110. Germain Lalande, CSC, to Howard Kenna, CSC, May 9, 1963; Patrick Peyton, CSC, to Lalande, May 28, 1963, 08–03, Headquarters, Albany, AHCFM.

111. There is no extant data to show that any money was received from Madden's bank.

112. Patrick Peyton, CSC, to Jerome Lawyer, CSC, January 13, 1959, 05–01, Correspondence, Lawyer. "The hinterlands" is a reference to the pilot program in La Serena, Chile.

113. Patrick Peyton, CSC, Memorandum, March 2, 1960, 06–06, Patrick Peyton Papers, AHCFM.

114. Manuel Larraín to Christopher O'Toole, CSC, March 1959, 01–07, Crusades, Chile, AHCFM.

115. "Operation Plan for the Family Rosary Crusade in Chile," August 15, 1959, to July 16, 1960, 01–07, Crusades, Chile, AHCFM.

116. Jorge Canepa, CSC, Interview with author, June 18, 2000; Alfred Silva Santiago to Patrick Peyton, CSC, October 20, 1959; Jorge Canepa, CSC, to Peyton October 24, 1959, 01–07, Crusades, Chile, AHCFM.

117. Statistics Sheet, n.d., 01–07, Crusades, Chile, AHCFM.

118. Joseph Quinn to Christopher O'Toole, February 8, 1960, 428 (FR) 14; Family Rosary Evaluation, April 1960, B428 (FR), AHCG; Terry Fellowes to John Corr, CSC, January 29, 1960, 01–07, Crusades, Chile; Joseph Quinn, CSC, to James Mannis, CSC, February 4, 1960, 00–01, Correspondence, Quinn, AHCFM.

119. "The World Family Rosary Crusade," Press Release, n.d. [1960], 01–07, Crusades, Chile, AHCFM.

120. Jorge Canepa, CSC, Interview with author, June 18, 2000.

121. Patrick Peyton, CSC, to Jerome Lawyer, CSC, April 9, 1960, 05–01, Correspondence, Lawyer, AHCFM.

122. Patrick Peyton, CSC, Diary, March 7 to April 29, 1960, 06–06, Patrick Peyton Papers, AHCFM. Frip Flanagan was an associate of Peter Grace.

123. "Yesterday We Heard Father Peyton," n.d. [1960], clipping found in 01–07, Crusades, Chile, AHCFM.

124. Joseph Quinn, CSC, to Robert Halderman, July 20, 1960, 01–07, Crusades, Chile, AHCFM.

125. Excerpts from Letters of Gratitude from the Bishops of Chile, October 25, 1960, 01–07, Crusades, Chile, AHCFM; Manuel Larraín to Christopher O'Toole, CSC, July 19, 1960, 428 (FR) 14, AHCG.

126. Patrick Peyton, CSC, to Bienvenido López, July 20, 1961, 05–01, Correspondence, Lopez, AHCFM.

127. Patrick Peyton, CSC, to John Meehan, March 27, [1961], 01–27, Crusades, Venezuela, AHCFM.

128. Walter Donnelly to Patrick Peyton, CSC, July 22, 1962, 08–05, Headquarters Correspondence, AHCFM.

129. Patrick Peyton, CSC, to Jerome Lawyer, CSC, March 13, 1961, 05–01, Correspondence, Lawyer, AHCFM. Peter Grace recognized Donnelly's contribution to Peyton's work in Venezuela: "You, Mrs. Donnelly and all your family have been unbelievably helpful in what is the most important and difficult task that Father Peyton has ever undertaken." See J. Peter Grace to Walter Donnelly, December 13, 1961, 08–05, Headquarters Correspondence, AHCFM.

130. Walter Donnelly to Peter Grace, May 9, 1961, 01–27, Crusades, Venezuela, AHCFM.

131. Joseph Quinn, CSC, to Philip Higgins, CSC, May 25, 1961, 01–27, Crusades, Venezuela, AHCFM.

132. "The Religious Meeting," *The Daily Journal,* July 19, 1961, clipping found in 01–27, Crusades, Venezuela, AHCFM.

133. Norman Carignan to John D. J. Moore, July 24, 1961, 01–27, Crusades, Venezuela, AHCFM.

134. Patrick Peyton, CSC, to Walter Donnelly, July 15, 1961, 08–05, Headquarters Correspondence, AHCFM. Similar ideas were expressed by Walter Donnelly when he wrote to Grace stating, "Please inform our friends," about the success of postcrusade family day celebrations held in Caracas on December 8, 1961, and December 8, 1962. See Patrick Peyton, CSC, to Francis Grogan, CSC, December 11, 1962, 05–01, Correspondence, Grogan; Walter Donnelly to Peter Grace (Cablegram), December 11, 1962, 08–05, Headquarters Correspondence, AHCFM.

135. Peter Grace to George DePrizio, CSC, August 23, 1961, 310.3.73, Provincial Correspondence, DePrizio, AHCFE; Grace to Christopher O'Toole, CSC, August 23, 1961; Norman Carignan to John Moore, July 24, 1961, 428 (FR) 46, AHCG.

136. Christopher O'Toole, CSC, to Peter Grace, September 5, 1961, 428 (FR) 14, AHCG.

137. Quoted in Peter Grace to Christopher O'Toole, CSC, August 23, 1961, 428 (FR) 46, AHCG.

138. Cardinal Humberto Quintero to Patrick Peyton, CSC, July 17, 1961, 01–27, Crusades, Venezuela, AHCFM.

139. Alejandro Fernández-Feo to Patrick Peyton, CSC, July 20, 1961, 01–27, Crusades, Venezuela, AHCFM. Numerous other comments about the Caracas crusade have been recorded. One highly illustrative statement came from Monsignor Reghezza, a pastor of a local parish in Caracas: "Venezuela is the key to the rise or fall of Latin America: if Venezuela falls to Communism... so will go Colombia, and Brazil will follow. The Crusade has within [itself] the power to leave a profound result in the masses, that at the moment, the masses are 'on the fence'; they can go quickly one way or the other—for Communism or against it. The Communists are not tired—they are busy, alert and keeping the air jittery by time-bombs here and there, always in American establishments—the 'hit and run' tactic." See Patrick Peyton, CSC, Diary of God's and Our Lady's Blessings on the Family Rosary Crusade in Caracas, n.d. [1961], 01–27, Crusades, Venezuela, AHCFM.

140. Patrick Peyton, CSC, to Norman Carignan, August 24, 1962, 01–05, Crusades, Brazil, AHCFM.

141. Christopher O'Toole, CSC, to Patrick Peyton, CSC, July 29, 1961, 428 (FR) 7, AHCG. More amplifying information on the political situation and Catholicism's influence in Brazil can be found in: Emanuel de Kadt, *Catholic Radicals in Brazil* (London: Oxford University Press, 1970).

142. Walter Donnelly to Patrick Peyton, CSC, October 10, 1961, 08–05, Headquarters Correspondence, AHCFM.

143. Patrick Peyton, CSC, to Walter Donnelly, October 2, 1961, 08–05; Peyton to Christopher O'Toole, CSC, October 2, 1961, 08–03, Headquarters Correspondence, AHCFM. On this date Peyton wrote, "There has been no word about the next Latin American Crusade." Grace was confident that a final decision would be made in three weeks.

144. In veiled language Peyton illustrated how the federal government decided where the Crusade would go. He wrote how Walter Donnelly had told Peyton that "Benefactor No. 2" is pleased with the Latin American work and it was hoped that Bogotá would be the Crusade's next stop, "but that Number 1 benefactor would have to be consulted." See Patrick Peyton, CSC, to Begonia Díaz, September 13, 1961, 06–02, Patrick Peyton Papers, AHCFM.

145. Patrick Peyton, CSC, to Peter Grace, February 29, 1962, 01–08, Crusades, Colombia; Peyton to Tere Aguinaco, March 3, 1962, 06–02, Patrick Peyton Papers; James Mannis, CSC, to Albert Heinzer, CSC, March 19, 1962, 05–01, Correspondence, Heinzer, AHCFM.

146. Patrick Peyton, CSC, to Peter Grace, July 13, 1962, 01–05, Crusades, Brazil, AHCFM.

147. Christopher O'Toole, CSC, to Patrick Peyton, CSC, May 8, 1962, 428 (FR) 14, AHCG. O'Toole had written Peyton earlier about his worries of Communism in the region: "Aside from the element of instructions in the Faith, family prayer, the unity of family life that comes from the activities of the Crusade, the power of Communism in all these areas has been considerably weakened." See O'Toole to Peyton, March 27, 1962, 428 (FR) 14, AHCG.

148. João Mohana, Testimony, included in Patrick Peyton, CSC, to Norman Carignan, August 24, 1962, 01–05, Crusades, Brazil, AHCFM.

149. The annual inflation in Brazil in 1949 was 12 percent, in 1959 26 percent, and in 1960 39.5 percent. See Rex A. Hudson, ed., *Brazil: A Country Study* (Washington, D.C.: Department of the U.S. Army, 1998).

150. William Blum, *Killing Hope: U.S. Military and C.I.A. Interventions since World War II* (Monroe, Mich.: Common Courage Press, 1995), 163–65; Clarence Hall, "The Country That Saved Itself," special feature, *Reader's Digest* special edition, November 1, 1964: 1–5.

151. Patrick Peyton, CSC, Family Rosary Report, n.d. [1962], 01–05, Crusades, Brazil, AHCFM. It is not clear if Peyton fully grasped the political situation in Brazil.

152. Patrick Peyton, CSC, to Norman Carignan, August 24, 1962, 01–05, Crusades, Brazil, AHCFM.

153. "History of Events during Preparations for Crusades in Brazil," n.d. [1962], 01–05, Crusades, Brazil, AHCFM.

154. The task of obtaining the necessary equipment was obviously a strain on all. In a comical release of energy, Joseph Quinn quipped about the difficulty of importing the necessary equipment: "If this doesn't work then I am going to see if Castro in Cuba can smuggle the equipment in when he is sending guns for the revolution in

Recife." See Joseph Quinn, CSC, to Begona Díaz, June 6, 1962, 01–05, Crusades, Brazil, AHCFM.

155. *Diario de Pernambuco,* September 23, 1962, clipping; "Interesting Information Gathered after the Grand Concentration at Recife," n.d. [1962], 01–05, Crusades, Brazil, AHCFM.

156. Quoted in Philip Higgins, CSC, to Albert Heinzer, CSC, May 10, 1963, 01–05, Crusades, Brazil, AHCFM.

157. Patrick Peyton, CSC, to Peter Grace, September 13, 1962, 01–05, Crusades, Brazil, AHCFM.

158. Patrick Peyton, CSC, to Walter Donnelly, August 21, 1962, 08–05, Headquarters Correspondence, AHCFM.

159. Patrick Peyton, CSC, to Walter Donnelly, August 23, 1962, 08–05, Headquarters Correspondence, AHCFM. Peyton reported that Grace was startled when confronted with such requests.

160. Patrick Peyton, CSC, to Walter Donnelly, August 23, 1962, 08–05, Headquarters Correspondence, AHCFM.

161. Patrick Peyton, CSC, to Peter Grace, July 13, 1962, 01–05, Crusades, Brazil, AHCFM. Peyton told Grace that the additional budget approved for Rio included thirty complete projector sets — $44,588.03; forty copies of the films — $46,700; dubbing costs — $8,000; operation costs — $60,000, for a total of $159,288.03.

162. Quoted in "Report of a Crusade," May 20 to December 20, 1962, 01–05, Crusades, Brazil, AHCFM.

163. Ibid.

164. Quoted in "Report of the Family Rosary Crusade in Rio de Janeiro," August 15 to December 24, 1962, 01–05, Crusades, Brazil, AHCFM.

165. Patrick Peyton, CSC, to Walter Donnelly, January 25, 1963, 08–05, Headquarters Correspondence, AHCFM.

166. Patrick Peyton, CSC, to Walter Donnelly, March 18, 1963, and April 6, 1963, 08–05 Headquarters Correspondence, AHCFM.

167. Patrick Peyton, CSC, to Walter Donnelly, June 11, 1963, 08–05, Headquarters Correspondence, AHCFM. The data is not clear if the New York meeting was held on June 6 or 7, 1962. Peyton did thank Donnelly for his efforts that brought some clarity to the crusade through 1964.

168. Patrick Peyton, CSC, to Unknown (Telegram), June 2, 1963, 01–05, Crusades, Brazil, AHCFM.

169. News clipping, n.d. [June 1963], 01–05, Crusades, Chile, AHCFM. Records are not consistent on attendance at the rally, ranging from 450,000 to 600,000.

170. H. Didonet, "The Films of the Family Rosary Crusade," in *Jornal do Dia,* November 30, 1963, found in 01–05, Crusades, Brazil, AHCFM.

171. Archbishop Vicente Scherer to Archbishop Dom Helder Camara, January 19, 1963, 01–05, Crusades, Brazil, AHCFM.

172. *Eastern Province Review* 7, no. 4 (December 1963): 2–3, AHCG.

173. Joseph Quinn, CSC, to Patrick Peyton, CSC, March 20, 1964, and March 27, 1964, 01–05, Crusades, Chile, AHCFM.

174. William Belyea, CSC, to Patrick Peyton, CSC, May 26, 1964, 01–05, Crusades, Brazil, AHCFM.

175. Clarence Hall, "The Country That Saved Itself," *Reader's Digest* special edition, November 1964, found in 01–05, Crusades, Brazil. It should be noted that

American involvement in the Brazilian coup has been suggested by some authors. William Blum, for example, claims that the military takeover in Brazil was "the culmination of a conspiratorial process in which the American embassy had been intimately involved." See William Blum, *Killing Hope,* 163–70. More amplifying information on the Brazilian coup of 1964 is found in Phyllis R. Parker, *Brazil and the Quiet Intervention, 1964* (Austin: University of Texas Press, 1979).

176. Patrick Peyton, CSC, to Peter Grace (Telegram), August 17, 1964, 01–05, Crusades, Brazil, AHCFM.

177. News clipping from *Folha de S. Paulo,* August 23, 1964, found in 01–28, Crusades, General, AHCFM. Following the great triumph of São Paulo the crusade concluded its almost three-year stay in Brazil with a small crusade, without the popular mission, in the Archdiocese of Curitaba. Conducted between November 3 and December 20, the rally drew 360,000. See Calendario de Ação, n.d. [1964], 01–05, Crusades, Brazil, AHCFM.

178. "United States Security and the Power of Prayer," n.d. [1962], B428 (FR), AHCG. One illustrative letter sent to Peyton after the April 1964 revolution stated, "A great miracle was realized in our country. And we all know that [it] was the Rosary that saved us!" See Celia Bretto de Azevedo to Patrick Peyton, CSC, June 2, 1961 [*sic*–1964], 01–05, Crusades, Brazil, AHCFM.

179. Raymond Cassel, CSC, "Father Patrick Peyton — The Power of the Family Rosary," unpublished essay found in 09–05, Family Theater Papers, AHCFM; Theodore Hesburgh, CSC, to Germain Lalande, CSC, October 7, 1964, 428 (FR) 14, AHCG.

180. Quoted in Joseph Quinn, CSC, to Patrick Peyton, CSC, August 26, 1964, 01–05, Crusades, Brazil, AHCFM.

181. Patrick Peyton, CSC, to Howard Kenna, CSC, July 13, 1964, Patrick Peyton Personnel File, AHCFE.

182. Richard Sullivan, CSC, to Germain Lalande, CSC, September 11, 1964, 422.2, Provincial Correspondence, Sullivan, AHCFE. This is a reference to the famous naval battle of 1571 when Christian forces defeated the Ottoman Turks at Lepanto through, it was believed, the intercession of the Our Lady of the Rosary.

183. Richard Sullivan, CSC, to Germain Lalande, CSC, November 3, 1964, 428 (FR) 14, AHCG.

184. Cardinal Carlo Confalonieri to Patrick Peyton, CSC, January 18, 1963, 01–05, Crusades, Brazil, AHCFM.

185. Philip Higgins, CSC, and Arthur McCormack, "Millions for Mary: Family Rosary Crusade in Latin America," *St. Joseph Magazine* 65 (October 1964): 31; Arthur McCormack, "The Catholic Church in South America," *Wiseman Review* 238 (Fall 1964): 252.

186. Quoted in Joseph Quinn, CSC, to Patrick Peyton, CSC, August 26, 1964; "Mysterious Force," news clipping from *A Gazeta,* August 6, 1964, found in 01–05, Crusades, Brazil, AHCFM.

187. George DePrizio, CSC, to Germain Lalande, CSC, December 28, 1962, 428 (FR) 14, AHCG.

188. Quoted in George DePrizio, CSC, Provincial Office Bulletin, February 2, 1963, 01–05, Crusades, Brazil, AHCFM.

189. Recall that Lalande's predecessor, Christopher O'Toole, was informed by Peyton at the outset of the effort by Peter Grace to gain U.S. government assistance

for the crusade. Thus, it is strange at the very least to realize that Lalande did not know of this situation. It is rather inconceivable that O'Toole would not have told Lalande this information upon assuming the duties of superior general.

190. Germain Lalande, CSC, to Richard Sullivan, CSC, September 28, 1964, 310.3.85, Provincial Papers, Sullivan, AHCFE.

191. Richard Sullivan, CSC, to Germain Lalande, CSC, October 5, 1964, 428 (FR) 14, AHCG.

192. Theodore Hesburgh, CSC, to Germain Lalande, CSC, October 7, 1964, 428 (FR) 14, AHCG.

193. Germain Lalande, CSC, to Theodore Hesburgh, CSC, October 28, 1964, 428 (FR) 14, AHCG.

194. Patrick Peyton, CSC, Memorandum, "Meeting in Rome of Fathers Lalande, Mullahy, and Peyton," October 24, 1964; Germain Lalande, CSC, "Meeting with Peyton and Mullahy," October 24, 1964, 428 (FR)14, AHCG.

195. Ibid. Peyton told Lalande that Billy Graham's Latin American revivals as well as the work of the Maryknoll religious community were also financed through the CIA.

196. Patrick Peyton, CSC, Memorandum, "Meeting in Rome of Fathers Lalande, Mullahy, and Peyton," October 24, 1964, 428 (FR) 14, AHCG. It should be noted that Lalande was also under pressure from the Vatican to speak with Peyton. Archbishop Dell'Acqua, from the Office of the Secretary of State, was quite concerned about the association of the Family Rosary Crusade with the revolution in Brazil, calling it "gravely serious for the Church." See Germain Lalande, CSC, to Richard Sullivan, CSC, October 29, 1965, 428 (FR) 14, AHCG.

197. Germain Lalande, CSC, to Richard Sullivan, CSC, January 5, 1965; Sullivan to Lalande, January 23, 1965, 428 (FR) 14, AHCG.

198. Germain Lalande, CSC, Notes of Meeting with Richard Sullivan, CSC, February 22, 1965; Lalande to Sullivan, March 18, 1965, 428 (FR) 14, AHCG. Lalande also told Sullivan that he was concerned about the fact that some Catholic organizations in Brazil, indirectly connected with the crusade, were using crusade funds for their own purposes. He wondered if these groups knew the source of the funds.

199. Germain Lalande, CSC, to Richard Sullivan, CSC, September 1, 1965, 428 (FR) 14, AHCG.

200. Ibid.

201. Germain Lalande, CSC, to Pope Paul VI, September 6, 1965, 428 (FR) 14, AHCG.

202. Richard Sullivan, CSC, to Germain Lalande, CSC, September 16, 1965; Lalande to Sullivan, September 27, 1965, 428 (FR) 14, AHCG. Extant correspondence provides a breakdown of monies received as required for the October 30 report. Between September 1959 and October 1965 a total of $996,450 was received via Peter Grace from the CIA. Additionally, $166,459.88 was received from stocks Grace held for a total of $1,192,909.88. See Joseph Quinn, CSC, to Richard Sullivan, CSC, October 19, 1965, 428 (FR) 14, AHCG.

203. Patrick Peyton, CSC, to Pope Paul VI, September 18, 1965, 428 (FR) 14, AHCG.

204. Germain Lalande, CSC, to Richard Sullivan, CSC, October 29, 1965, 428 (FR) 14, AHCG.

205. Germain Lalande, CSC, to Richard Sullivan, CSC, December 20, 1965, 428 (FR) 14, AHCG.

206. Germain Lalande, CSC, Minutes of Meeting with Richard Sullivan, CSC, Jerome Lawyer, CSC, Joseph Quinn, CSC, and Philip Higgins, CSC, April 25, 1966, 428 (FR) 14, AHCG.

207. Patrick Peyton, CSC, to Walter Donnelly, July 30, 1964, 08–05, Headquarters Correspondence, AHCFM; Germain Lalande, CSC, Notes of Meeting with Richard Sullivan, February 2, 1965, 428 (FR) 14, AHCG.

208. Peter Grace to "Unknown," June 28, 1965, 01–10, Crusades, Dominican Republic, AHCFM.

209. John Meehan to Peter Grace, February 25, 1965; Statistics Sheet, 01–10, Crusades, Dominican Republic, AHCFM.

210. Draft Account, June 28, 1965; Peter Grace to Unknown, June 28, 1965, 01–10, Crusades, Dominican Republic; Patrick Peyton, CSC, to Walter Donnelly, June 1, 1965, 08–05, Headquarters Correspondence, AHCFM. An excellent discussion of the morality of U.S. action in the Dominican Republic is provided in W. V. O'Brien, "International Law, Morality, and American Intervention," *Catholic World* 201 (September 1968): 388–93.

211. Meeting Minutes, Patrick Peyton and Two Cuban Bishops, March 30, 1965, 507.92, Family Rosary Papers, AHCFE; Peter Grace to "Unknown," June 28, 1965, 01–10, Crusades, Dominican Republic; Patrick Peyton, CSC, to Walter Donnelly, April 11, 1965, 08–05, Headquarters Correspondence, AHCFM.

212. Peter Grace to "Unknown," June 28, 1965, 01–10, Crusades, Dominican Republic, AHCFM.

213. John Meehan to Patrick Peyton, CSC, June 18, 1965, 01–10, Crusades, Dominican Republic. Meehan wanted to assist Peyton in any way possible. He wrote, "We want to do the very best we can for you so that you and your work can continue to flourish." Meehan wondered why the crusade had been sent to the Dominican Republic under the tense political conditions that existed and the long history of Church repression. Meehan also suggested that one reason the statistics were not as impressive in the Dominican Republic compared with previous places was the leadership of William Belyea, CSC, but he had to admit that Peyton was the one who made the decision to pull Quinn off this crusade and send him to Spain to lead operations there.

214. William Belyea, CSC, to Patrick Peyton, CSC, May 19, 1965, 01–23, Crusades, Panama, AHCFM.

215. William Belyea, CSC, to Patrick Peyton, CSC, June 25, 1965; Peyton to Belyea, June 23, 1965; "Rosary Crusade in Panama City," clipping from the *New York Journal-American,* August 11, 1965, 01–23, Crusades, Panama, AHCFM.

216. William Belyea, CSC, to Joseph Quinn, CSC, February 2, 1966, and June 20, 1966; Quito Report, n.d. [1966], 01–11, Crusades, Ecuador, AHCFM.

217. Guayaquil Report, n.d. [1966]; William Belyea, CSC, to Joseph Quinn, CSC, June 25, 1966, 01–11, Crusades, Ecuador.

218. Guayaquil Report, n.d. [1966], 01–11, Crusades, Ecuador, AHCFM.

219. Patrick Peyton, CSC, Minutes of Meeting in Salamanca, Spain, June 3, 1966, 05–01, Correspondence, Heinzer; William Belyea, CSC, to Joseph Quinn, CSC, June 8, 1966, 01–11, Crusades, Ecuador, AHCFM. The Missionaries did not believe conditions in Brazil allowed them to live their religious lives well. They did agree

to stay with the crusade in Spain, which was scheduled to conclude on January 31, 1967.

220. William Belyea, CSC, to Philip Higgins, CSC, August 8, 1966, 01–11, Crusades, Ecuador; Patrick Peyton, CSC, to Belyea, June 1, 1966, 05–01, Correspondence, Heinzer, AHCFM. Belyea wrote, "I am not leaving FRC in any spirit of anger. The pressure caught up with me and I realized I could no longer do this Crusade work." Peyton was grateful for Belyea's service, "The Crusade is the loser. You have been a gift of God and Mary to it — a tremendous enrichment of it — and your presence, your personality and your ability have given it a good image."

221. Joseph Quinn, CSC, to Richard Sullivan, CSC, October 19, 1965, 428 (FR) 14; "Popular Mission in South America," n.d. [1966], 428 (FR) 13, AHCG.

222. "United States Security and the Power of Prayer," n.d. [1962], B428 (FR), AHCG.

223. Post Crusade Plan, September 22, 1966, 507.46, Family Rosary Papers, AHCFE.

224. Patrick Peyton, CSC, Post Crusade Plan, April 6, 1966, 05–01, Correspondence, Heinzer, AHCFM.

225. Post Crusade Plan, September 22, 1966, 507.46, Family Rosary Papers, AHCFE. The five-year plan was: First Year: The Life of Christ and Family Prayer; Second Year: The Mass, Sacraments, and Family Prayer; Third Year: The Commandments and Family Prayer; Fourth Year: The Creed and Family Prayer; Fifth Year: Fruits of Prayer and Vocation.

226. Joseph Quinn, CSC, to Patrick Peyton, CSC, December 23, 1965, 06–02, Patrick Peyton Papers, AHCFM.

227. Richard Sullivan, CSC, to Patrick Peyton, CSC, January 4, 1966; Sullivan to Germain Lalande, CSC, January 12, 1966; Lalande to Sullivan, January 22, 1966, 428 (FR) 14, AHCG.

228. Germain Lalande, CSC, Meeting with Patrick Peyton, Richard Sullivan, Jerome Lawyer, Joseph Quinn, and Philip Higgins, April 25, 1966; Richard Sullivan, CSC, to Lalande, Memorandum, April 25, 1966; Sullivan to Peyton, April 28, 1966, 428 (FR) 14, AHCG.

229. Germain Lalande, CSC, Meeting with Richard Sullivan, June 20, 1966; Sullivan to Lalande, September 23, 1966, 428 (FR) 14, AHCG; Sullivan to Lalande, August 31, 1966, 422.2, Provincial Papers, Sullivan, AHCFE. Sullivan assured the general that all special aid to the crusade had been discontinued. Some left-over money was placed in a strong box and deposited in the Immigrants Bank of New York.

230. Jerome Lawyer, CSC, Interview with author, September 30, 2000.

Chapter 8: An Understudy Role

1. Hugh Donohoe to Patrick Peyton, CSC, February 1, 1960; "Father Peyton's Meeting with Bishop Donohoe," February 20, 1961; Joseph McGucken to Peyton, November 9, 1960, 01–26, Crusades, San Francisco, AHCFM.

2. John J. Mitty, Pastoral Letter, August 22, 1961, Family Rosary Crusade and Memory Book, Manuscripts A 93, Archives Archdiocese of San Francisco (hereafter AASF), Menlo Park, California.

3. Crusade Prayer, Family Rosary Crusade and Memory Book, Manuscripts A 93, AASF. The prayer was: "Heavenly Father, we beg Thee in the name of Jesus

Christ, Thy Son, to bless our Family Rosary Crusade. Holy Spirit of God, give us the courage, the grace and the enlightenment to make the Daily Family Rosary Pledge and keep it faithfully. Give us the help and the strength that we need to win families for Mary, so that through the Family Rosary, she and her Divine Son may reign in every home, bring special blessings to every family, and establish peace in the world. Amen."

4. Patrick Peyton, CSC, to Raymond Renwald, October 17, 1961, 01–26, Crusades, San Francisco, AHCFM.

5. Family Rosary Crusade in the Philippines, n.d. [1962]; "Some Points and Information for the Coming Family Rosary Crusade in 1961, n.d. [1960], 01–24, Crusades, Philippines, AHCFM.

6. Joseph Quinn to Bienvenido Lopez, July 21, 1960, 01–24, Crusades, Philippines, AHCFM. The ten archdioceses and dioceses that expressed interest in the crusade were: The archdioceses of Caceres, Cebu, and Jaro, and the dioceses of San Fernando, Sorsogon, Calbayog, Tagbilarau, Dumaguete, Malolos, and Imus.

7. Bienvenido Lopez to Patrick Peyton, CSC, August 29, 1960, 05–01, Correspondence, Lopez, AHCFM.

8. Bienvenido Lopez to Patrick Peyton, CSC, October 31, 1960; Peyton to Peter Grace, February 14, 1961, 05–01, Correspondence, Lopez; Joseph Quinn, CSC, to Peyton, December 15, 1961, 01–24, Crusades, Philippines, AHCFM.

9. Albert Heinzer, CSC, to James Reuter, SJ, n.d. [November 1960], 05–01, Correspondence, Heinzer; Patrick Peyton, CSC, to Albert Heinzer, November 9, 1960, 09–06, Family Theater Papers, AHCFM.

10. Memorandum to Family Rosary Crusade, United States, from Family Rosary Crusade in Manila, n.d. [March 1962], 05–01, Correspondence, Mannis, AHCFM.

11. Gertie Lally, Bridie Doherty, Genevieve Campion, Pearl Buckley, and Anne O'Sullivan were Irish women who assisted the works of Family Rosary, beginning in early 1960. In 1961 they assisted in the Philippines and the Hollywood office. See Albert Heinzer to Patrick Peyton, CSC, March 26, 1962, 06–02, Patrick Peyton Papers; Peyton to Colin Conlon, March 3, 1962, 01–24, Crusades, Philippines, AHCFM.

12. Family Rosary Crusades in the Philippines, n.d. [1962], 01–24, Crusades, Philippines, AHCFM.

13. Francis Grogan, CSC, to Patrick Peyton, CSC, May 1, 1962, 05–01, Correspondence, Grogan, AHCFM.

14. Tere Aguinaco to Francis Grogan, CSC, January 8, 1963; Grogan to Aguinaco, February 14, 1963; Grogan to Patrick Peyton, CSC, February 19, 1963, 05–01, Correspondence, Grogan, AHCFM.

15. "The Popular Mission of the Family Rosary Crusade in the Far East," n.d. 01–24, Crusades, Philippines; Harold Seer to Patrick Peyton, CSC, April 30, 1963, 04–07, Development, Raskob, AHCFM.

16. Jose Borces to Philip Higgins, CSC, April 11, 1964, and May 4, 1964; Bienvenido Lopez to Patrick Peyton, CSC, n.d. [June 1964], 05–01, Correspondence, Lopez, AHCFM.

17. Jose Borces to Patrick Peyton, CSC, July 18, 1964; Peyton, Memorandum, December 16, 1964, 06–02, Patrick Peyton Papers, AHCFM.

18. Patrick Peyton, CSC, Memorandum, December 16, 1964, 06–02, Patrick Peyton papers; Joseph Quinn, CSC, to Philip Higgins, CSC, August 9, 1965, 05–01, Correspondence, Quinn, AHCFM; Arlene LaCava, "Reporter Backstage," n.d. [1964], 507.109, Family Rosary Papers, AHCFE. Speaking of Grace, Peyton wrote, "He solved [the] problem in his usual spontaneous generosity when it is anything connected with Our Blessed Mother and Her Rosary."

19. Tere Aguinaco to Patrick Peyton, CSC, January 29, 1963; Peyton to James McArdle, April 24, 1963, 01–25, Crusades, Spain, AHCFM. Oriol committed himself to give $150,000 to support the popular mission and the crusade that would follow.

20. Germain Lalande to Pope Paul VI, September 6, 1965; Lalande Meeting with Monsignor Angelo Dell'Acqua, October 14, [1965], 428 (FR) 14, AHCG. Dell'Acqua, secretary to Cardinal Amleto Cicognani, Vatican secretary of state, was concerned about government financing. Lalande reported, "Monsignor said that he has nothing against the Spanish government, but that one must guard against making the work of a religious institution such as the Crusade subservient to the political aims of a government." On the same subject Peyton held a meeting with two of the government contacts who "promised to obtain money in the same way it is being obtained in South America." See Tere Aguinaco to Francis Grogan, CSC, January 8, 1963, 05–01, Correspondence, Grogan, AHCFM.

21. Patrick Peyton, CSC, to Germain Lalande, CSC, April 19, 1963; "Drawing Room Apostolate," February 17, 1964, 05–01, Correspondence, Grogan, AHCFM.

22. Patrick Peyton, CSC, to Javier Echenique, March 8, 1963, 01–25, Crusades, Spain, AHCFM.

23. Patrick Peyton to Angel Delclaux, December 5, 1963, 01–25, Crusades, Spain, AHCFM.

24. Francis Grogan, CSC, to Patrick Peyton, CSC, February 20, 1964, 05–03, Reorganization Papers, AHCFM.

25. Bernard Mullahy, CSC, to Richard Sullivan, CSC, June 15, 1964, 310.3.85, Correspondence, Provincial, Sullivan, AHCFE.

26. "Father Peyton's Report from Madrid," June 15, 1964, 06–06, Patrick Peyton Papers, AHCFM.

27. Calendar of Events, n.d., 01–25, Crusades, Spain, AHCFM.

28. Meeting Minutes, Focolare and CSC, Madrid, March 4, 1965, 507.95, Family Rosary Papers, AHCFE. The Focolare, a religious movement founded in 1943 by Chiara Lubich and approved by the Vatican in 1962, has a number of branches within a larger movement. There are celibate communities of men and women who follow the evangelical counsels but do secular work, married people who identify with the ideals of the movement, young people, and a priestly fraternity. The movement's general idea is to transform the world through the observance of Gospel ideals.

29. Patrick Peyton, CSC, to Ralph Carpenter, CSP, October 17, 1961, 01–26, Crusades, San Francisco, AHCFM.

30. Report on the Trip of Bienvenido Lopez and Francis Grogan, CSC, May–June 1962, 05–01, Correspondence, Grogan, AHCFM.

31. Carmen Amann to Francis Grogan, CSC, May 5, 1963, 05–01, Correspondence, Grogan; Patrick Peyton, CSC, to Mercedes Lopez Vela, March 29, 1968; "Reporter Backstage," n.d. [1968], 06–02, Patrick Peyton Papers, AHCFM.

32. Provincial Chapter Report 1967, 507.46, Family Rosary Papers, AHCFE; Patrick Peyton, CSC, to Maria Luisa Luca de Tena, December 4, 1961, 05–01, Correspondence, Peyton, AHCFM.

33. Summary Sheet, October 26, 1962, 09–06, Family Theater Papers; Denis Sughrue, CSC, to Albert Heinzer, CSC, March 20, 1962, 05–01, Correspondence, Heinzer, AHCFM.

34. Twentieth Anniversary Program, September 8, 1962, 09–06, Family Theater Papers, AHCFM; Richard Nixon to J. Peter Grace, September 17, 1962, Richard Nixon, Vice Presidential Papers, 298 Grace File, NADB.

35. Provincial Office Bulletin, September 1962, AHCG; clipping *Los Angeles Herald Examiner* September 9, 1962, found in PPC, Attymass, County Mayo, Ireland.

36. Pope Paul VI to Patrick Peyton, CSC, September 13, 1963, 428 (FR) 14, AHCG.

37. Richard Sullivan, CSC, to Patrick Peyton, CSC, June 3, 1962, 06–02; *Tidings* (Los Angeles archdiocesan newspaper), April 24, 1964, clipping found in 06–04, Patrick Peyton Papers, AHCFM.

38. Benziger Brothers to Patrick Peyton, CSC, November 16, 1961, 10–05, Publications; Tom Lewis to Peyton, August 13, 1965, 09–01, Family Theater Papers; Joseph Quinn, CSC, to Peyton, July 11, 1966, 06–02, Patrick Peyton Papers, AHCFM.

39. Arlene LaCava, "Reporter Backstage," n.d. [1967], 507.109, Family Rosary Papers, AHCFE.

40. Patrick Peyton, CSC, to Mrs. Michael [Beatrice] Gallagher, June 2, 1965, 06–11, Patrick Peyton Papers, AHCFM.

41. Patrick Peyton, CSC, to Mary Peyton, December 1, 1961, September 9, 1964, September 24, 1964, 06–11, Patrick Peyton Papers, AHCFM.

42. James McArdle to Albert Heinzer, CSC, January 18, 1963, 310.2.72, Provincial Correspondence, DePrizio, AHCFE; Bernard Mullahy, CSC, to Richard Sullivan, CSC, June 15, 1964, 428 (FR) 14, AHCG.

43. Patrick Peyton, CSC, to Edward Donnelly, May 27, 1969, 06–02, Patrick Peyton Papers, AHCFM.

44. Eastern Province Reporter, March 1969, AHCG; John Gurley to Pat Spanbauer, February 9, 1969, 05–01, Correspondence, Gurley, AHCFM.

45. Stephen G. Michaud and Hugh Aynesworth, *"If You Love Me You Will Do My Will"* (New York: Signet, 1991), 75–80; Peter Grace, "Survey of Sarita K. East Affair," 267.74 (FTC), AHCG.

46. Grace and Leo wanted to see the creation of a foundation that would be managed by the best businessmen and allowed to earn more money. Then certain causes, universal in nature, such as the Family Rosary Crusade, would be permanent recipients of the income from the foundation. See Patrick Peyton, CSC, to Jerome Lawyer, CSC, May 7, 1960, 05–01, Correspondence, Lawyer, AHCFM.

47. Patrick Peyton, CSC, to Jerome Lawyer, CSC, May 7, 1960, 05–01, Correspondence, Lawyer, AHCFM.

48. Ibid.

49. Patrick Peyton, CSC, Diary, May 26–June 2, 1960, 06–06, Patrick Peyton Papers, AHCFM.

50. Michaud and Aynesworth, *"If You Love Me,"* 106, 108–12; Patrick Peyton, CSC, Diary, May 26–June 2, 1960, 06–06, Patrick Peyton Papers, AHCFM.

51. Patrick Peyton, CSC, Diary, May 26–June 2, 1960, 06–06, Patrick Peyton Papers, AHCFM. Peyton wrote: "That really was a day to be remembered in the history of the Family Rosary Crusade, and a great gift from Our Blessed Mother — a security won by Her for the crusade. Unless Sarita changes it by another codicil, which she has the right to do before she dies, the Crusade will have the security that all of us have been longing for and praying for throughout the years."

52. Patrick Peyton, CSC, to Francis Grogan, August 27, 1963, 05–01, Correspondence, Grogan.

53. Jerome Lawyer, CSC, to John Corr, CSC, June 9, 1960, 05–01, Correspondence, Lawyer, AHCFM.

54. Patrick Peyton, CSC, to Peter Grace, July 10, 1960, 04–08, Development, AHCFM.

55. Michaud and Aynesworth, *"If You Love Me,"* 144–46; State of Texas, 79th District Court, April 19, 1961, Plaintiff Petition, 04–08, Development, AHCFM.

56. Peter Grace to Edward Heston, CSC, June 6, 1961, 267.74 (FTC), AHCG.

57. Peter Grace to Christopher O'Toole, CSC, May 1, 1961; O'Toole to Grace, May 6, 1961, 428 (FR) 7, AHCG.

58. Christopher O'Toole, CSC, to Patrick Peyton, CSC, August 3, 1961, 428 (FR) 7; Memorandum to Archbishop Pietro Palazzini, June 7, 1961, 267.74 (FTC), AHCG.

59. Philip Higgins, CSC, to Albert Heinzer, CSC, November 30, 1961, 05–01, Correspondence, Heinzer, AHCFM. As one example of Peyton keeping abreast of the Sarita East case, Higgins writes, "Word from John Meehan in New York has it that Father Peyton is in confinement all day today, out at Shelterrock Road, going over the papers on the Sarita East problem."

60. Christopher O'Toole, CSC, to Patrick Peyton, CSC, May 8, 1962, 428 (FR) 14, AHCG.

61. Memorandum, June 8, 1962, included in Peter Grace to Edward Heston, CSC, June 8, 1962, 428 (FR) 7, AHCG.

62. Michaud and Aynesworth, *"If You Love Me,"* 180–83.

63. Peter Grace to Pope Paul VI, July 12, 1963, 267.74 (FTC), AHCG.

64. Michaud and Aynesworth, *"If You Love Me,"* 274.

65. Ibid., 297–346.

Chapter 9: Reorganization, Restructure, and Frustration

1. Family Rosary Crusade — Evaluation, April 1960, B428 (FR), AHCG.

2. When the Eastern Province of Priests was established certain religious had to choose which province they would join. The superior general outlined a plan that would allow a religious native of the east, but working in the Midwest or west to join what became the Indiana Province. Conversely, those native to the west or Midwest but working in the east could join the new Eastern Province. Although Peyton emigrated to Scranton, he considered his American maturity to have been gained during his time at Notre Dame. He had to decide which province to join and chose the East since the headquarters for Family Rosary was in Albany. His brother Tom, who was in a similar situation, remained with the Indiana Province as he was from the Midwest and working in the same region.

3. Patrick Peyton, CSC, "Plan of Organization of the Family Rosary Crusade," n.d. [1961], B428 (FR), AHCG.

4. George DePrizio, CSC, to Christopher O'Toole, CSC, February 2, 1961, 428 (FR) 14, AHCG.

5. Jerome Lawyer, CSC, to Patrick Peyton, CSC, September 20, 1960, 05–03, Reorganization Papers, AHCFM.

6. See Sharon Holland, "Religious House According to Canon 608," *Jurist* 50 (1990): 529–52, for a complete discussion of *domus formata*.

7. Family Rosary Crusade — Evaluation, April 1960, B428 (FR), AHCG; Jerome Lawyer, CSC, to Peter Grace, April 28, 1960, 05–03, Reorganization Papers, AHCFM.

8. John Meehan and Maria Luisa Luca de Tena to Patrick Peyton, CSC, November 29, 1960, 05–03, Reorganization Papers, AHCFM.

9. Germain Lalande, CSC, to George DePrizio, CSC, February 16, 1963, 422.2, Provincial Files, DePrizio, AHCG. A report this same year listed the personnel needs for the Family Rosary Crusade: Manila, 3; Latin America, 8; Madrid, 3; Nairobi, 3; Albany, 4; Hollywood, 3, for a total of 24. See The Family Rosary, n.d. [1963], 310.2.74, Provincial Papers, DePrizio, AHCFE.

10. Jerome Lawyer, CSC, pointed out this failure: "If I can point to any weakness in you as a leader, it is your lack of visiting headquarters." See Jerome Lawyer, CSC, to Patrick Peyton, CSC, September 20, 1960, 05–03 Reorganization Papers, AHCFM.

11. Ibid.

12. George DePrizio, CSC, to Christopher O'Toole, CSC, February 20, 1961, 428 (FR) 14, AHCG.

13. Christopher O'Toole, CSC, to George DePrizio, CSC, February 24, 1962, 428 (FR) 14, AHCG.

14. Christopher O'Toole, CSC, to George DePrizio, CSC, February 23, 1961, 428 (FR) 14, AHCG.

15. Bernard Mullahy, CSC, to Richard Sullivan, CSC, June 15, 1964, 310.3.85, Provincial Papers, Sullivan, AHCFE.

16. Richard Sullivan, CSC, to Bernard Mullahy, CSC, June 23, 1964, 310.3.85, Provincial Papers, Sullivan, AHCFE.

17. Patrick Peyton, CSC, to Joseph Quinn, CSC, October 11, 1966, 05–01, Correspondence Connerton, AHCFM.

18. Germain Lalande, CSC, to Richard Sullivan, CSC, March 18, 1965, 428 (FR) 14, AHCG.

19. Jerome Lawyer, CSC, to James Connerton, CSC, September 14, 1964, "Lawyer and Connerton Correspondence in the Reorganization of Family Rosary," B428 (FR), AHCG.

20. Jerome Lawyer, CSC, to James Connerton, CSC, October 7, 1964, "Lawyer and Connerton Correspondence in the Reorganization of Family Rosary," B428 (FR), AHCG.

21. Jerome Lawyer, CSC, to James Connerton, CSC, October 27, 1964, "Lawyer and Connerton Correspondence in the Reorganization of Family Rosary," B428 (FR), AHCG.

22. Ibid.

23. James Connerton, CSC, to Patrick Peyton, CSC, "Lawyer and Connerton Correspondence in the Reorganization of Family Rosary," B428 (FR), AHCG. A district is an organizational status below that of province. In the evolution and growth of the Holy Cross community districts were often established when sufficient personnel were engaged in ministry in a specific geographical region. Today, the Congregation of Holy Cross has districts in East and West Africa, Chile, Brazil, and Peru.

24. Jerome Lawyer, CSC, to James Connerton, CSC, November 20, 1964, 507.126, Family Rosary Papers, AHCFE. At the outset of the study Lawyer had suggested several options for reorganization of the Crusade: creation of a province or vice-province dedicated to the Crusade, establishment of a district or vicariate, appointing Peyton to the Provincial Council or as superior of a *domus formata,* placing the Crusade directly under the general, or placing Family Rosary directly under the Holy Father. See Jerome Lawyer, CSC, to James Connerton, CSC, September 14, 1964, "Lawyer and Connerton Correspondence in the Reorganization of Family Rosary," B428 (FR), AHCG.

25. Notes of Meeting between Germain Lalande, CSC, and Richard Sullivan, CSC, February 20–22, 1965, 428 (FR) 14, AHCG.

26. Family Rosary Meeting at Provincial House, Bridgeport, Connecticut, April 12, 1965, 507.103, Family Rosary Papers, AHCFE; "Report of April 13–14, 1965, Meeting," 428 (FR) 14, AHCG.

27. Provincial Council Meeting Minutes, April 19, 1965; Richard Sullivan, CSC, to Germain Lalande, CSC, May 21, 1965, 428 (FR) 14, AHCG. Sullivan originally suggested that George DePrizio, CSC, be appointed superior, but Lawyer told Sullivan, "a great conflict would arise between the Superior and Father Peyton as it did between himself and Father Peyton."

28. Germain Lalande, CSC, to Richard Sullivan, CSC, September 1, 1965, 428 (FR) 14, AHCG. Lalande stated that his intention in not setting up a district structure for the Family Rosary Crusade was "to avoid a purely personal government both with regard to authority to be exercised over subjects and to the administration of material matters," and not to paralyze the Crusade's operation.

29. Ibid. Recall that this discussion on reorganization was being held at the same time that the Eastern provincial and General Administrations were dealing with the ramifications of the revelation that CIA money was supporting the Latin American crusades. Most assuredly the superior general was concerned about gaining control over Peyton's efforts.

30. Patrick Peyton, CSC, to "Dear Fathers," Feast of the Epiphany 1961, 05–03, Reorganization Papers, AHCFM.

31. John Corr, CSC, and Jerome Lawyer, CSC, to All Family Rosary Officers, April 10, 1961, 05–03, Reorganization Papers, AHCFM. It is interesting to note that the provincial, George DePrizio, CSC, was not too keen at the outset on a plan of reorganization, stating, "We do not want Father Peyton or his work to suffer in any way."

32. Patrick Peyton, CSC, "Plan of Organization of the Family Rosary Crusade," November 21, 1961, B428 (FR), AHCG.

33. Ibid.

34. Albert Heinzer, CSC, to Patrick Peyton, CSC, March 8, 1966, 428 (FR) 14, AHCG.

35. Philip Higgins, CSC, to William Persia, October 5, 1966, 05–01, Correspondence, Persia, AHCFM; Patrick Peyton, CSC, to Joseph Quinn, CSC, Philip Higgins, CSC, and James Connerton, CSC, March 17, 1966, 428 (FR) 14, AHCG.

36. Peter Grace to Patrick Peyton, CSC, February 1, 1966, 05–03, Reorganization Papers, AHCFM.

37. William E. Hill & Company, Inc., "Family Rosary Crusade Organization," June 6, 1966, 507.46, Family Rosary Papers, AHCFE.

38. Al Scalpone, "Centralization Report," September 1966, 507.46, Family Rosary Papers, AHCFE.

39. Patrick Peyton, CSC, to Cardinal Francis Spellman, May 31, 1960, 09–05, Family Theater Papers, AHCFM.

40. Ellwood E. Keiser, CSP, *The Spiritual Journey of a Showbusiness Priest* (Mahwah, N.J.: Paulist Press, 1996), 20.

41. Family Rosary Crusade Evaluation, April 1960, B428 (FR), AHCG. In 1958 MBS passed into the hands of Alexander Gutterman, who resigned as president in February 1959 after being convicted of conspiracy and fraud, leaving the network in debt. At this point Albert G. McCarthy Jr. and Associates gained control. They put MBS through bankruptcy and paid its debts, but it continued to lose money. Thus, in 1960 Minnesota Mining and Manufacturing (3M) purchased MBS for an estimated $1.3 to 1.5 million.

42. Peyton claimed there were two principal reasons that *Family Theater* of the Air ceased operations: (1) shortage of funds and (2) the mortal blow that television inflicted upon radio programs. See Patrick Peyton, CSC, to Jeanne Bates, February 2, 1960, 09–02, Family Theater Papers, AHCFM.

43. Family Rosary Crusade Evaluation, April 1960, B428 (FR), AHCG.

44. Ibid.

45. Ibid. John Corr, CSC, to Patrick Peyton, CSC, May 26, 1960, 06–02, Patrick Peyton Papers; James Mannis, CSC, to Albert Heinzer, CSC, January 19, 1962, 05–01, Correspondence, Heinzer, AHCFM. Peyton did not like to be referred to as "another Billy Graham," an appellation he often received because Graham's press coverage was so much greater.

46. Family Rosary Crusade Evaluation, April 1960, B428 (FR), AHCG.

47. Leonard Hunt to Patrick Peyton, CSC, July 19, 1960, 09–07 Family Theater Papers, AHCFM.

48. Patrick Peyton, CSC, to Albert Heinzer, CSC, October 11, 1963, 09–15, Family Theater Papers, AHCFM. Peter Grace commented that in order for Family Rosary to move forward it was necessary for the organization to become as powerful in television as it once was in radio. In order to accomplish this goal he believed a New York City office was necessary. See Peter Grace, "Evolution of the Family Rosary Crusade Organization," March 7, 1960, "Family Rosary Confidential File," AHCFE.

49. Patrick Peyton, CSC, Memorandum Meeting with John O'Neil, April 22, 1965, 09–02, Family Theater Papers, AHCFM.

50. Peter Grace to Patrick Peyton, CSC, February 1, 1966, 05–03 Reorganization Papers, AHCFM. Grace wrote of the dilemma of Family Theater: "It is impossible to predict the results of the Family Rosary Crusade or the results of any of your efforts. Time and time again miracles have been performed, but it seems that the Family Theater in Hollywood, for at least ten years, has been left out of the

miracle orbit. Actually since Madrid in the early 1950s there have been no successes by Family Theater in the creative field which would lead anyone to predict, on a 'prudent man' basis, that there is any reason to devote money to Family Theater for producing creative TV or motion picture films in Hollywood."

51. Patrick Peyton, CSC, Albert Heinzer, CSC, and John Gurley, CSC, to Richard Sullivan, CSC, February 15, 1969, 05–01, Correspondence, Rioux, AHCFM.

52. Dennis Roverato, Interview with author, August 9, 2000, AHCFM.

53. "Planning Dinnerman's Meetings," n.d. [Fall 1960], 04–03, Development, AHCFM.

54. James Mannis, CSC, to Patrick Corcoran, September 19, 1963, 04–01, Development, AHCFM.

55. Patrick Peyton, CSC, to Fred Fox, October 7, 1968; Al Scalpone to Peyton, January 27, 1967; "The M of Florida," n.d. [June 1967], 04–12, Development, AHCFM.

56. Jerome Lawyer, CSC, to Denis Sughrue, CSC, June 15, 1964; Albert Heinzer, CSC, to Harry John, November 4, 1963, and December 14, 1964, 09–06, Family Theater, AHCFM.

57. James Mannis, CSC, to Patrick Peyton, CSC, April 8, 1965, 06–02, Patrick Peyton Papers, AHCFM. One interesting counternote to Grace's continued assistance was voiced by Tere Aguinaco, one of the Spanish secular missionaries, who commented about Grace, "What a pity that we have to depend so much on 'Mr. Money' in order to carry out our projects." See Tere Aguinaco to Francis Grogan, CSC, March 5, 1963, 05–01, Correspondence, Grogan, AHCFM.

58. Family Rosary Crusade — Evaluation, April 1960, B428 (FR), AHCG; Marian Theater Release, September 1962, 09–02, Family Theater Papers; Albert Heinzer, CSC, to Pat Spanbauer, February 1, 1963, 05–01, Correspondence, Heinzer, AHCFM.

59. AFTRA, "Pension and Welfare Fund," September 3, 1957, 05–01, Correspondence, Heinzer; Albert Heinzer, CSC, to Lawrence Dobkin, October 19, 1960, 09–02; Heinzer to Patrick Peyton, CSC, Jerome Lawyer, CSC, and John Corr, CSC, May 15, 1961, 09–07, Family Theater Papers, AHCFM.

60. Patrick Peyton, CSC, to Jeanne Bates, February 27, 1960, 09–02, Family Theater Papers, AHCFM. Peyton began to pay royalties on March 3, 1960. Many of the writers did return their checks in donations.

61. Management Meeting, Hollywood Office, April 4, 1962, 05–01, Correspondence, Mannis; Patrick Peyton, CSC, to Joseph Quinn, CSC, October 25, 1967, 05–01, Correspondence, Quinn, AHCFM.

62. Radio Report, May 1961, 09–05, Family Theater Papers, AHCFM; Tom Lewis, "The Priest Who Won Hollywood for Our Lady," *Our Lady's Digest* 21 (May–June 1966): 16.

63. Philip Higgins, CSC, to Albert Heinzer, CSC, December 16, 1966; Heinzer to Patrick Peyton, CSC, February 9, 1967, 05–01, Correspondence, Heinzer, AHCFM.

64. Jack Wintz, OFM, "Family Theater at 50: Father Patrick Peyton Remembered," *St. Anthony Messenger* 105, no. 1 (June 1997): 17.

65. James Connerton, CSC, to Philip Higgins, CSC, June 23, 1964, 05–01, Correspondence, Higgins; Patrick Peyton, CSC, to Albert Heinzer, CSC, January 15, 1963, 05–01, Correspondence, Heinzer, AHCFM.

66. Lourdes Report, February 17, 1964, 09–01, Family Theater Papers, AHCFM.

67. Patrick Peyton, CSC, to Philip Higgins, CSC, and Francis Grogan, CSC, September 16, 1964, 09–01, Family Theater Papers; Robert Rioux, CSC, to William Persia, CSC, April 6, 1966, 05–01, Correspondence, Persia; Persia to Higgins, February 13, 1967, 09–01, Family Theater Papers, AHCFM.

68. *Variety,* December 23, 1964, clipping found in 267.74 (FT) 2, AHCG.

69. James Connerton, CSC, to Terry Fellowes, June 13, 1963, 05–01, Correspondence, Connerton, AHCFM.

70. *Variety,* December 23, 1964, clipping found in 267.74 (FT) 2, AHCG. Several attempts were made to reedit *The Redeemer.* Joseph Breen Jr., the director of the original rosary films, agreed that parts of some of the films might be found objectionable by some people or groups. The Jewish concern over *The Redeemer* was voiced by Julius Schatz, director of community service for the Jewish Congress: "I can assure you that there was a unanimous feeling that this film, in its overall presentation, is a distortion of historical fact, misrepresents theological dogma and practice, and does great violence in stereotyping and exaggerating the role of Jews in the crucifixion." See Julius Schatz to Martin Weldon, December 24, 1963, 09–02, Family Theater Papers, AHCFM.

71. Lester Gutterman to Jewish Community Relations Council, April 6, 1945, 507.34, Family Rosary Papers, AHCFE. Gutterman said further, "In so doing, it [the film] does gross and serious violence to the hopeful spirit with which Jews the world over have viewed the events taking place at the Vatican Council. The unfair and, by many present-day Christian standards, untrue portrayal of the crucifixion, is bound to have an anti-Semitic impact on many who see this film. Its wide commercial distribution is destined to do a great disservice to interreligious relations generally and to Catholic-Jewish relations specifically."

72. Patrick Peyton, CSC, to Terry Fellowes, January 14, 1965, 09–01, Family Theater Papers, AHCFM.

73. Tom Lewis to John Meehan, February 23, 1965, 507.34, Family Rosary Papers, AHCFE.

74. Albert Heinzer, CSC, to Archbishop Leo Binz, April 1, 1966, 09–01, Family Theater Papers, AHCFM.

75. Listing of Movie Showings, November 12, 1965, 507.34, Family Rosary Papers, AHCFE.

76. Movie Review, *Corpus Christi Post,* October 17, 1965, clipping found in 267.74 (FT2), AHCG.

77. *Congressional Record,* 89th Congress, March 10, 1966.

78. James Mannis, CSC, to Albert Heinzer, CSC, June 28, 1965, 05–01, Correspondence, Heinzer, AHCFM; Provincial Chapter Report 1967, 507.46, Family Rosary Papers, AHCFE.

79. Albert Henizer, CSC, to Kenneth Thomson, November 13, 1963, 05–01, Correspondence, Heinzer; Heinzer to Patrick Peyton, CSC, December 26, 1963, 06–02, Patrick Peyton Papers, AHCFM.

80. *Reporter Backstage,* n.d. [1968], clipping found in 267.74 (FT2), AHCG. The six films and their featured stars were: *The Word Was "Yes,"* with Jeanne Crain, *The Sound of Praise,* with Dolores Hope, *Prime Time,* with Jane Wyatt, *Final Encounter,* with Frankie Avalon, *The Unlikliest Place,* with Stephen McNally, and *The Promise,* with Bing Crosby and Frankie Avalon.

81. Patrick Peyton, CSC, to Donald McGannon, March 27, 1964, 09–02, Family Theater Papers, AHCFM.

82. James Connerton, CSC, to Albert Hartigan, December 13, 1963, 05–01, Correspondence, Connerton; Management Meeting Minutes, Hollywood Office, April 4, 1962, 05–01, Correspondence, Mannis, AHCFM.

83. Pat Spanbauer to James Mannis, August 19, 1964, 05–01, Correspondence, Higgins, AHCFM; Provincial Chapter Report 1967, 507.46, Family Rosary Papers, AHCFE.

84. Patrick Peyton, CSC, to Albert Heinzer, CSC, May 23, 1964; Maria Luisa Luca de Tena to Arthur Bellaire, February 13, 1963, 09–02, Family Theater Papers, AHCFM.

85. Hathaway Watson to Maria Luisa Luca de Tena, June 20, 1963; Luca de Tena to Francis Grogan, CSC, May 17, 1963, 09–02, Family Theater Papers, AHCFM.

86. Maria Luisa Luca de Tena to Patrick Peyton, CSC, September 3, 1963, 09–02, Family Theater Papers, AHCFM.

87. List of Psalm Films, n.d., 09–02, Family Theater Papers, AHCFM. The thirty psalms that were used for films were: 1, 2, 3, 4, 6, 7, 8, 17, 28, 21, 22, 24, 29, 37, 41, 50, 54, 61, 62, 83, 85, 99, 102, 112, 113, 120, 125, 132, 138(1), 138(2).

88. Albert Henizer, CSC, to Joseph Geuer, CSC, October 13, 1964, 05–01, Correspondence, Higgins, AHCFM. In the film a soldier is seen on a deserted beach. As he shares his chocolate bar with a seagull, the soldier is shot. His death fall is depicted in slow motion as the words of the Psalm are heard, "Why are you sad, my soul, sighing within me? Hope in God I shall praise Him again." *The Soldier* also captured the "Award for Exceptional Merit" granted by the Philadelphia International Festival of Short Films in November 1971.

89. News Release, April 4, 1967, 09–02, Family Theater Papers, AHCFM; *Reporter Backstage,* n.d. [1967], clipping found in 507.109, Family Rosary Papers, AHCFE. The five films that were used to create *The Promise* were *The Soldier* (Psalm 41), *The Lord Is My Shepherd* (Psalm 23), *His Dwelling Place* (Psalm 83), *The Escape* (Psalm 1), and *Once Upon a Morning* (Psalm 138[2]).

90. Patrick Peyton, CSC, Memorandum, Meeting with John O'Neal, April 22, 1965, 09–02, Family Theater Papers, AHCFM.

91. Patrick Peyton, CSC, to Tom Lewis, February 25, 1965; Edward Stanley to Peyton, July 23, 1965, 09–02, Family Theater Papers, AHCFM.

92. Memorandum, Meeting between Albert Heinzer, CSC, James Reuter, SJ, and Al Scalpone, June 6, 1961, 09–06, Family Theater Papers, AHCFM.

93. Anonymous, "Patrick Peyton," unpublished essay, March 2, 1960, 06–06, Family Theater Papers, AHCFM.

94. Albert Henizer, CSC, to Patrick Peyton, CSC, January 15, 1962, and January 16, 1962, 05–01, Correspondence, Mannis, AHCFM.

95. "Outline for a Series of Family Theater Television Programs," n.d. [1964], 09–02, Family Theater Papers, AHCFM.

96. Joseph Breen Jr. to Albert Heinzer, CSC, December 2, 1957, 05–01, Correspondence, Heinzer, AHCFM.

97. Progress Report Development of a Motion Picture Series on the Principles of the Ten Commandments, December 15, 1963, 507.50, Family Theater Papers,

AHCFE; Patrick Peyton, CSC, to Misioneros, February 26, 1963, 01–05, Crusades, Brazil, AHCFM.

98. Progress Report Development of a Motion Picture Series on the Principles of the Ten Commandments, November 18, 1963, 09–02, Family Theater Papers.

99. Maria Luisa Luca de Tena to Tom Lewis, October 18, 1965, 09–02, Family Theater Papers, AHCFM.

100. Patrick Peyton, CSC, to Tom Lewis, February 15, 1967, 09–02, Family Theater Papers, AHCFM. Some of the prepared scripts were: "One Came Back" by James Sweeney (seventh commandment), "Two Gladiators" by Walter Doniger (fifth commandment), "A Time to Love" by Gerry Day (sixth commandment), "Mirror of Bronze" by Eugene Poire (tenth commandment).

101. Patrick Peyton, CSC, to Jackie Gleason, February 26, 1966, Family Theater Papers, FTH.

102. Patrick Peyton, CSC, Memorandum to Peter Grace, April 11, 1966, 267.74 (FT11), AHCG.

103. Patrick Peyton, CSC, Memorandum to Joseph Quinn, CSC, Philip Higgins, CSC, Albert Heinzer, CSC, and James Connerton, CSC, 267.74 (FT11), AHCG.

104. The council consisted of Joseph Quinn, CSC, James Connerton, CSC, Philip Higgins, CSC, and Albert Heinzer, CSC.

105. Patrick Peyton, CSC, Memorandum to Joseph Quinn, CSC, Philip Higgins, CSC, Albert Heinzer, CSC, and James Connerton, CSC, 267.74 (FT11), AHCG.

106. Edward Heston, CSC, to Patrick Peyton, CSC, September 27, 1966, 267.74 (FT11), AHCG; Patrick Peyton, CSC, to Pope Paul VI, October 1, 1966, Family Theater Papers, FTH.

107. Preliminary Outline for Christmas Eve, "Prayer for Peace" Broadcast, n.d. [August 1966], 428 (FR) 14, AHCG.

108. John Gurley, CSC, to Gary MacEoin, November 11, 1969, 01–16, Crusades, Guatemala, AHCFM.

109. Patrick Peyton, CSC, to "Associates within the Framework of Family Theater," Holy Week 1969, 05–01, Correspondence, Gurley, AHCFM.

Chapter 10: Renewal and New Directions

1. Many fine historical sources on Vatican II have been published. A representative sample follows: Robert McAfee Brown, *Observer in Rome: A Protestant Report on the Vatican Council* (Garden City, N.Y.: Doubleday, 1964); Anthony J. Cernera, ed., *Vatican II: The Continuing Agenda* (Fairfield, Conn.: Sacred Heart University Press, 1997); Henri de Lubac, SJ, "The Church in Crisis," *Theology Digest* 17 (1969): 312–25; Dennis M. Doyle, *The Church Emerging from Vatican II: A Popular Approach to Contemporary Catholicism* (Mystic, Conn.: Twenty-Third Publications, 1992); Adrian Hastings, ed., *Modern Catholicism: Vatican II and After* (New York: Oxford University Press, 1991); Christopher Hollis, *The Achievements of Vatican II* (New York: Hawthorn Books, 1967); Rene Latourelle, ed., *Vatican II Assessment and Perspectives Twenty-Five Years After (1962–1987)*, 5 vols. (New York: Paulist Press, 1988); Timothy G. McCarthy, *The Catholic Tradition: Before and After Vatican II 1878–1993* (Chicago: Loyola University Press, 1994); Timothy E. O'Connell, ed., *Vatican II: An American Appraisal* (Wilmington, Del.: Michael Glazier, 1986); John W. O'Malley, SJ, "Developments, Reforms, and Two Great Reformations: Towards a Historical Assessment of Vatican II," *Theological Studies*

44 (1983): 373–406; Joseph Ratzinger, *Theological Highlights of Vatican II* (New York: Paulist Press, 1966); Xavier Rynne, *Vatican Council II* (Maryknoll, N.Y.: Orbis Books, 1999); Edward Schillebeeckx, OP, *The Real Achievement of Vatican II* (New York: Herder and Herder, 1967); Alberic Stacpoole, ed., *Vatican II Revisited by Those Who Were There* (Minneapolis: Winston Press, 1986); Herbert Vorgrimler, ed., *Commentary on the Documents of Vatican II*, 5 vols. (New York: Herder and Herder, 1969).

2. Karl Rahner, SJ, *Theological Investigations,* vol. 20, *Concern for the Church* (London: Darton, Longman, and Todd, 1981), 77–89, esp. 82–84.

3. The volume of material associated with the American civil rights movement is staggering. Some representative significant sources are Herbert Aptheker, *Anti-Racism in U.S. History: The First Two Hundred Years* (New York: Greenwood Press, 1992); Joseph Barndt, *Dismantling Racism: The Continuing Challenge to White America* (Minneapolis: Augsburg Press, 1991); Jack Bloom, *Class, Race, and the Civil Rights Movement* (Bloomington: Indiana University Press, 1987); Rhoda Lois Blumberg, *Civil Rights: The 1960s Freedom Struggle* (Boston: Twayne Publishers, 1984); Kenneth B. Clark, "The Civil Rights Movement: Momentum and Organization" *Daedalus* 95 (Winter 1966): 595–625; John Hope Franklin, *The Color Line: Legacy for the Twenty-First Century* (Columbia: University of Missouri Press, 1993); David J. Garrow, *Protest at Selma: Martin Luther King and the Voting Rights Act of 1965* (New Haven, Conn.: Yale University Press, 1978); Henry Hampton and Steve Fayer (with Sarah Flynn), *Voices of Freedom: An Oral History of the Civil Rights Movement from the 1950s through the 1980s* (New York: Bantam Books, 1990). Herbert Hill and James E. Jones, *Race in America: The Struggle for Equality* (Madison: University of Wisconsin Press, 1993); Peter B. Levy, ed., *Documentary History of the Modern Civil Rights Movement* (Westport, Conn.: Greenwood Press, 1992); Harvard Sitkoff, *The Struggle for Black Equality, 1954–1992* (New York: Hill and Wang, 1993).

4. The literature associated with American involvement in Vietnam is abundant. A few representative books on the subject are Peter A. Poole, *Eight Presidents and Indochina* (Huntington, N.Y.: R. E. Krieger Publishing Company, 1978); Robert D. Schulzinger, *A Time for War: The United States and Vietnam, 1941–1975* (New York: Oxford University Press, 1997); Allan R. Millett, *A Short History of the Vietnam War* (Bloomington: Indiana University Press, 1978); James W. Mooney and Thomas R. West, eds., *Vietnam: A History and Anthology* (St. James, N.Y.: Brandywine Press, 1994); Marilyn Blatt Young, *The Vietnam Wars, 1945–1990* (New York: Harper Collins, 1991).

5. Robert Wuthnow, *After Heaven,* 70–73, 57, 41.

6. Philip Gleason, "In Search of Unity: American Catholic Thought, 1920–1960," *Catholic Historical Review* 65 (1979): 186.

7. Unquestionably, the primary example of the breakdown in ecclesiastical authority came in the wake of the 1968 publication of *Humanae Vitae,* Pope Paul VI's encyclical letter which continued the Church's traditional stance against artificial forms of birth control. The negative reaction to the pope's letter was heightened when it was revealed that the majority opinion of the Papal Birth Control Commission, established by John XXIII and continued by Paul VI, recommended some modification in the Church's teaching in this area. The priest-sociologist Andrew Greeley argues that *Humanae Vitae* was the principal catalyst to upheaval in the

American Church, manifest most significantly by losses from the priesthood and religious life. See Andrew Greeley, "American Catholics — Ten Years Later," *Critic* 33 (January–February 1975): 14–21; "*Humanae Vitae* and the Sense of the Faithful: Some Questions for Theologians," *Critic* 35 (September 1977): 14–25. For a full history and analysis of the Papal Birth Control Commission and *Humanae Vitae* see Robert McClory, *Turning Point: The Inside Story of the Papal Birth Control Commission and How Humanae Vitae Changed the Life of Patty Crowley and the Future of the Church* (New York: Crossroad, 1995).

8. Gleason, "In Search of Unity," 186–89.

9. Andrew Greeley, "Changing Styles of Catholic Spirituality," *Homiletic and Pastoral Review* 67 (April 1967): 558–65.

10. Ibid.

11. Karl Rahner, SJ, "Family Prayer and the Home," unpublished essay, 507.34.3, Family Rosary Papers, AHCFE.

12. Two especially fine monographs that describe in detail specific popular devotional practices in the United States are Robert Orsi, *The Madonna of 115th Street: Faith and Community in Italian Harlem, 1880–1950* (New Haven, Conn.: Yale University Press, 1985), and Orsi, *Thank You, St. Jude: Women's Devotion to the Patron Saint of Hopeless Causes* (New Haven, Conn.: Yale University Press, 1996).

13. Austin Flannery, OP, ed., *Vatican Council II: The Conciliar and Post Conciliar Documents* (Northport, N.Y.: Costello Publishing Company, 1992), *Sacrosanctum Concilium* no. 13.

14. Carl Dehne, "Roman Catholic Popular Devotions," *Worship* 49 (1975): 452–54.

15. Andrew Greeley, "Popular Devotions: Friend or Foe?" *Worship* 33 (October 1959): 570.

16. Edward Schillebeeckx, OP, *Mary, Mother of the Redemption* (New York: Sheed and Ward, 1964), 168.

17. Gary MacEoin, "Has the Rosary Survived the Council?" *Ave Maria* 104 (July 9, 1966): 12.

18. Patrick Peyton, CSC, to Cardinal James Francis McIntyre, May 15, 1964, Rosary-Family Theater File, AALA.

19. Gary MacEoin, "Has the Rosary Survived the Council?" 104; Patrick Peyton, CSC, "Mary, Family Prayer, and Vatican II," unpublished manuscript, 09–17, Family Theater Papers, AHCFM.

20. Patrick Peyton, CSC, to Cardinal Leo Joseph Suenens, September 23, 1965, 428 (FR) 14, AHCG. Peyton wrote, "It would be very wonderful to see the Council at its last session confirm the beauty and the necessity of family prayer. Trusting in your own conviction of the importance of this goal, I humbly ask you to help accomplish it."

21. Vatican II Intervention, Leo Josef Suenens, September 29, 1965, PPC, Attymass, County Mayo, Ireland.

22. Vatican II Intervention, Bishop Erbert Bednorz, September 30, 1965, PPC, Attymass, County Mayo, Ireland.

23. Austin Flannery, OP, ed., *Vatican Council II, Gaudium et Spes,* no. 48.

24. Ibid., *Apostolicam Actuositatem,* no. 11.

25. Germain Lalande, CSC, to Richard Sullivan, CSC, December 20, 1965, 428 (FR) 14, AHCG. One side note to Peyton's efforts in Rome is an anecdote told by

Robert Pelton, CSC. When the council ended there was a cocktail social hour hosted by the Belgian College and attended by all the major bishops and theologians of the council. Peyton arrived late to the party and said to Pelton upon entering, "Glory be to God! Here I am in the presence of the giants of the Church and they are coming to see things my way." Robert Pelton, CSC, Interview with author, June 15, 2000, AHCFM.

26. Patrick Peyton, CSC, to Joseph Quinn, CSC, October 25, 1965, 06–02, Patrick Peyton Papers; Film Schedule, n.d. [November 1965], 05–03, Reorganization Papers, AHCFM.

27. Patrick Peyton, CSC, to Richard Sullivan, CSC, October 22, 1965, 05–03, Reorganization Papers; Joseph Quinn, CSC, to Robert Rioux, CSC, June 27, 1967, 05–01, Correspondence, Rioux, AHCFM; "The Catholic Universe Bulletin," 92(45), February 16, 1966, clipping found in 428 (FR) 0, AHCG. Several of the essays planned were actually written. Topics included: the Holy Christian Family, the Family Rosary, Family in the Liturgy, Family in the Apostolate, Marriage and the Family, Mary and the Family, and Family Rosary Crusade.

28. Mark McGrath, CSC, to Renato Poblete, SJ, October 4, 1965, 05–03, Reorganization Papers, AHCFM; Germain Lalande, CSC, to Richard Sullivan, CSC, September 27, 1965, 428 (FR) 14, AHCG.

29. Richard Sullivan, CSC, to Patrick Peyton, CSC, July 22, 1964, Patrick Peyton Personnel File, AHCFE; Robert Pelton, CSC, Interview with author, June 15, 2000, AHCFM.

30. Mark McGrath, CSC, to Renato Poblete, SJ, October 4, 1965; Patrick Peyton, CSC, to Richard Sullivan, CSC, September 28, 1965, 05–03, Reorganization Papers, AHCFM; Peyton to Sullivan, September 27, 1965, Patrick Peyton Personnel File, AHCFE.

31. Patrick Peyton, CSC, to Mother Mary Magdalena [Buckley], October 26, 1965, 05–01, Correspondence, Buckley, AHCFM.

32. Renato Poblete, SJ, "Report of Study of Family Rosary Crusade," November 1965, 507.105, Family Rosary Papers, AHCFE. The bishops chosen were distributed geographically: two from the Philippines, two from South Africa, five from East Africa, three from Australia, three from Canada, six from the United States, five from Panama, six from Brazil, two from Venezuela, and three from Chile.

33. Patrick Peyton, CSC, "Family Rosary Crusade — Self-Study Program," October 25 to November 27, 1965, 05–03, Reorganization Papers, AHCFM.

34. Renato Poblete, SJ, "Report of Study of Family Rosary Crusade," November 1965, 507.105, Family Rosary Papers, AHCFE.

35. Minutes of Meeting at Belgian College, November 11, 1965, 05–03, Reorganization Papers, AHCFM.

36. Summary of Meeting on the Crusade, November 11, 1965, 05–03, Reorganization Papers, AHCFM.

37. Renato Poblete, SJ, "Report of the Study of Family Rosary Crusade," November 1965, 507.105, Family Rosary Papers, AHCFE.

38. Ibid.

39. Ibid.

40. Program, "An International Conference on the Theological Issues of Vatican II," March 20–26, 1966, University of Notre Dame, 05–03, Reorganization Papers, AHCFM.

41. Resolutions Document, March 30, 1966, 267.74 (FT11), AHCG.

42. Joseph Quinn, CSC, to William Persia, CSC, April 12, 1966, 05–01, Correspondence, Persia, AHCFM.

43. Gary MacEoin, "Has the Rosary Survived the Council?" 14; Eastern Provincial Office Bulletin, May 1966, AHCG.

44. Gary MacEoin, "Has the Rosary Survived the Council?" 14

45. Peyton received many letters that were critical of the decision to change the Crusade's name. One letter stated, "We did not think you would succumb to those liberals who were trying to dishonor the Blessed Mother before the Second Vatican Council began." See Mr. and Mrs. Paul O'Leary to Patrick Peyton, CSC, May 30, 1966, 06–02, Patrick Peyton Papers, AHCFM.

46. Resolutions Document, March 30, 1966, 267.74 (FT11), AHCG.

47. Joseph Quinn to Jerome Lawyer, Memorandum, January 6, 1967, 267.74 (FT)2, AHCG.

48. Ibid. Quinn hoped that renewal would once again place Family Rosary in its place of prominence. He wrote to Peyton informing him that one of the theologians at Salamanca, Rev. Manuel Useros, believed "that our Crusade could be the leading mission activity in the whole Church today." For Quinn, and Peyton as well, this was the goal. See Joseph Quinn, CSC, to Patrick Peyton, CSC, November 13, 1967, 05–01, Correspondence, Quinn, AHCFM.

49. Joseph Quinn, CSC, to Patrick Peyton, CSC, June 14, 1966; Peyton to Quinn, August 22, 1967, 06–02, Patrick Peyton Papers, AHCFM. The Milwaukee crusade, described later in this chapter, was the first scheduled crusade after Vatican II and the revision of all materials.

50. William Persia, CSC, to Patrick Peyton, CSC, July 8, 1967, 05–01, Correspondence, Persia; James Mannis, CSC, Interview with Thomas Feeley, CSC, June 3, 1999, AHCFM.

51. Patrick Peyton, CSC, to William Cousins, July 7, 1959, 01–26, Crusades, Milwaukee, AHCFM. Peyton had plans to visit Indonesia, Japan, and Hawaii.

52. Ibid., Cousins to "Fathers/Monsignors," February 19, 1968, 01–26, Crusades, Milwaukee, AHCFM.

53. Patrick Peyton, CSC, Speech to Serra Club, May 10, 1958, 05–01, Correspondence, Rioux, AHCFM.

54. Campaign for Family Prayer, n.d. [1968], 01–26, Crusades, Milwaukee, AHCFM.

55. Joseph Quinn, CSC, to William Cousins, December 15, 1967, 01–26, Crusades, Milwaukee, AHCFM.

56. William Cousins to "Fathers/Monsignors," February 19, 1968, 01–26, Crusades, Milwaukee, AHCFM.

57. Patrick Peyton, CSC, to Joseph Quinn, CSC (Transcribed Telephone Conversation), January 5, 1967, 05–01, Correspondence, Quinn; Peyton to William Cousins, March 3, 1967, 01–26, Crusades, Milwaukee, AHCFM. Cousins obtained two hundred thousand rosaries from the rosary factory in Dublin, supervised by Bridie Doherty.

58. Patrick Peyton, CSC, to Joseph Quinn, CSC, March 3, 1967, 01–26, Crusades, Milwaukee, AHCFM.

59. Some Observations on the Inter-Confessional Dimensions of the Campaign for Family Prayer, n.d. [1968]; Kenneth Knoespel to "Pastor," April 18, 1968, 01–26, Crusades, Milwaukee, AHCFM.

60. Ibid.

61. "Excerpts from Father Peyton's Talks in Milwaukee," n.d. [1968], PPC, Attymass, County Mayo, Ireland.

62. Patrick Peyton, CSC, Speech, April 3, 1968, 05–01, Correspondence, Rioux, AHCFM.

63. Joseph Quinn, CSC, to Patrick Peyton, CSC, February 28, 1968, 05–01, Correspondence, Quinn, AHCFM.

64. Albert Heinzer, CSC, to Philip Higgins, CSC, March 11, 1968, 05–01, Correspondence, Heinzer, AHCFM. The overall cost of the crusade was $120,000, most of which was given by private donations, including Charles Miller of the Miller Brewing Company.

65. *Milwaukee Journal,* May 13, 1968, clipping found in 01–26, Crusades, Milwaukee, AHCFM.

66. *Milwaukee Sentinel,* May 15, 1968, clipping found in 01–26, Crusades, Milwaukee; William Cousins to Gary MacEoin, October 1, 1969, 05–01, Correspondence, Gurley, AHCFM.

67. *Milwaukee Journal,* May 13, 1968, clipping found in 01–26, Crusades, Milwaukee, AHCFM; Eastern Provincial Office Bulletin, May 1968, AHCG.

68. F. Bleidorn to William Cousins, April 4, 1968, 01–26, Crusades, Milwaukee, AHCFM. The priest wrote, "If the streets of Milwaukee are littered with the bodies of rioters in July, and if some historian asks what the religious people were doing at that time, and if our greatest public display of activity is the final rally, then the historian might well say the Church people were busy holding a big party — another case of 'fiddling while Rome burns.' "

69. Lawrence S. Brey to Patrick Peyton, CSC, April 14, 1968, 01–26, Crusades, Milwaukee, AHCFM.

70. William Cousins to Gary MacEoin, October 1, 1969, 05–01, Correspondence, Gurley, AHCFM.

71. Albert Henizer, CSC, to Patrick Peyton, CSC, February 29, 1968, 05–01, Correspondence, Heinzer; "Reporter Backstage," n.d. [1968], 06–02, Patrick Peyton Papers; Peyton to William Cousins, August 3, 1967, 01–26, Crusades, Milwaukee, AHCFM.

72. In a letter to the provincial Quinn wrote, "I feel a more priestly work will be much more fulfilling. [I] guess all of us — Jerry [Lawyer], John Murph[y], John Corr and the others come to the limit of our endurance. But I have left without bitterness and will always pray for the success of the work." See Joseph Quinn, CSC, to Richard Sullivan, CSC, July 22, 1968, Quinn File, FTH.

73. Richard Sullivan, CSC, to Patrick Peyton, CSC, July 12, 1969, 01–16, Crusades, Guatemala, AHCFM.

74. John Gurley, CSC, to Gary MacEoin, November 11, 1969, 01–16, Crusades, Guatemala, AHCFM.

75. Remote Background of the Family Rosary Crusade in Central America and Guatemala, n.d. [1969]; Patrick Peyton, CSC, "Guatemala Crusade and Projected Results for the Future," November 8, 1969, 01–16, Crusades, Guatemala, AHCFM.

76. Schema of the Organization of the Crusade, n.d. [1970], 01–21, Crusades, Mexico, AHCFM.

77. Remote Background of the Family Rosary Crusade in Central America and Guatemala, n.d. [1969], 01–16, Crusades, Guatemala.

78. John Gurley, CSC, to Gary MacEoin, November 11, 1969, 01–16, Crusades, Guatemala, AHCFM.

79. Pastoral Letter of Guatemalan Bishops, November 9, 1969, 01–16, Crusades, Guatemala, AHCFM. The bishops additionally stated in their letter: "The greatest values we have is [*sic*] for a new appreciation of the spiritual and human values of justice and peace. Everything that denies any of the fundamental human rights; everything that divides families, peoples and nations into castes or social levels; everything that violates the supreme dignity of man, subjugating him either to the power of force, of wealth or of strange ideologies, is opposed to justice and peace. Consequently, our world is seen to be influenced by such values in the economic, social, political, cultural, familial, and religious orders."

80. Cardinal Mario Casariego, Speech, December 7, 1969, 01–16, Crusades, Guatemala, AHCFM.

81. Remote Background of the Family Rosary Crusade in Central America and Guatemala, n.d. [1969]; John Gurley, CSC, to Robert Rioux, CSC, February 19, 1970, 01–16, Crusades, Guatemala, AHCFM. Tensions between bishops and their priests throughout Central America were centered about drawing sides on the issues associated with the poor. In general the hierarchy favored the traditional stance of the Church, which had stood for the status quo and the needs of the favored classes. The clergy, on the other hand, become more and more advocates for the poor and downtrodden, especially in the area of land reform. This situation was best exemplified in El Salvador in the 1970s and 1980s. The assassination of Archbishop Oscar Romero, a bishop who became an advocate for the poor, on March 24, 1980, by a government death squad, crystallized the problem in peoples' minds.

82. Calendar of Events, n.d. [1971], 01–12, Crusades, El Salvador, AHCFM.

83. Robert Rioux, CSC, to Germain Lalande, CSC, May 13, 1970, 428 (FR) 14, AHCG.

84. The Crusade for Family Prayer and the Celebration in the Archdiocese of Mexico City, D.F., 1974–75, 01–21, Crusades, Mexico, AHCFM.

85. The Crusade was accompanied by a pilgrimage to the Holy Land. Similar annual pilgrimages were conducted through the sponsorship of the Crusade for Family Prayer from 1971 through 1974. See Holy Land Pilgrimage Brochures 1971 to 1974, 507.35, Family Rosary Papers, AHCFE.

86. John Gurley to Hanna Nazzal, February 3, 1971, 01–17, Crusades, Holy Land, AHCFM.

87. Hanna Nazzal to Patrick Peyton, CSC, July 19, 1971, 01–17, Crusades, Holy Land, AHCFM.

Chapter 11: Patrick Peyton and the Rosary in Eclipse

1. Bernard Donahue, OSF, "Developing a Crisis Model of American Catholicism," *Jurist* 35 (Spring–Summer 1975): 323; T. P. Mahoney, "Impressions of American Catholicism." *Catholic Mind* 74 (November 1975): 22; "The Catholic Church in the United States Today," *Catholic Mind* 72 (November 1974): 11.

2. The historian Richard Hofstader wrote, "In the post–Vatican II period . . . Catholics, with few exceptions, have indeed been more shaped by their American environment than they have reciprocally influenced it." Quoted in John A. Coleman, SJ, "American Bicentennial, Catholic Crisis." *America* 134 (June 26, 1976): 552.

3. Ibid.

4. Ibid., 551.

5. Richard John Neuhaus, *The Catholic Moment: The Paradox of the Church in the Postmodern World* (San Francisco: Harper & Row, 1987). Neuhaus's thesis is that the American Church had the opportunity to seize the moment and make a significant impact in America, but failed to adequately take advantage of the opportunity presented.

6. John Tracy Ellis, "American Catholicism, 1953–1979: A Notable Change," *Thought* 54 (June 1979): 119, 125.

7. Paula Kane, "American Madonnas: Perspectives on Mary since the 1940s," Paper delivered at the Cushwa Center for the Study of American Catholicism, the University of Notre Dame, March 2000. A detailed description of the various Marian splinter groups that formed after Vatican II, many of which were associated with the Traditionalist (schismatic) Archbishop Lefebvre wing, is provided in Michael Cuneo, *The Smoke of Satan: Conservative and Traditionalist Dissent in Contemporary American Catholicism* (New York: Oxford University Press, 1997).

8. *The Evangelist* (Albany Diocesan Newspaper), September 14, 1972, 07–1, Families for Prayer, AHCFM. Jeanne Arnold, *Man of Faith,* 226–27.

9. Patrick Peyton, CSC, "Family Rosary Novena," January 30 to March 23, 1972, Family Rosary–Family Theater Papers, AALA.

10. Patrick Peyton, CSC, "Statement," n.d. [1980], 07–2, Families for Prayer, AHCFM.

11. Raymond Cassel, CSC, to "Nicholas," June 30, 1971; Cassel to John Gurley, CSC, November 14, 1971, 05–01, Correspondence, Cassel, AHCFM.

12. In a series of letters between Raymond Cassel, CSC, and John Gurley, CSC, the question of Peyton's control of operations was a major topic. It is clear from the correspondence that Cassel made up his mind that he wanted to get away from Family Theater and day-to-day contact with Peyton. Gurley was more settled but did feel that Peyton was a solo operator who used Holy Cross religious for his own needs. Gurley once wrote, "I personally think that it's at last time for Peyton to become part of the human race and [the] Holy Cross Community." Equally passionately Cassel opined, "Once again I have the feeling of Peyton squeezing out that last drop, then throwing away an empty shell on the ground who's no good for anything else." See Raymond Cassel, CSC, to John Gurley, CSC, Good Friday, 1970, and September 5, 1970, 05–01, Correspondence, Cassel, AHCFM.

13. Jeanne Arnold, *Man of Faith* (Hollywood, Calif.: Family Theater, Inc., 1983), 230–32; Dennis Roverato, Interview with author, August 9, 2000.

14. Press Release, December 22, 1970, 507.109, Family Theater Papers, AHCFE; John Gurley, CSC, to Raymond Cassel, CSC, September 24, 1971, 05–01, Correspondence, Cassel, AHCFM.

15. News Release, n.d. [1971], 09–02, Family Theater Papers, AHCFM. The seven programs featured: (1) Archbishop William Baum of Washington, D.C., and Cardinal Stephan Kim of Seoul, Korea, (2) Cardinal John Carberry of St. Louis and Giacomo Beltritti, patriarch of Jerusalem, (3) Bishop Vincent McCauley, CSC, of Fort

Portal, Uganda, (4) Archbishop Mark McGrath, CSC, of Panama and Archbishop Francis Arinze of Ontisha, Nigeria, (5) Archbishop Leo Christopher of St. Paul, Minnesota, (6) Cardinal Leo Suenens of Malines-Brussels, Belgium, and Rev. Bernard Häring, CSSR, of Rome, and (7) Cardinal John Krol of Philadelphia and Bishop Francis Thuan of South Vietnam.

16. 1972–73 Report of Activities of Father Patrick Peyton's Crusade for Family Prayer, n.d. [1973], 507.94, Family Rosary Papers; Family Theater Memo, n.d. [1972], 310.4.65, Provincial Papers, Hogan; Summary Sheet, n.d. [1974], 507.67, Family Rosary Papers, AHCFE; Patrick Peyton to Jose Dutriz, January 31, 1973, 09–14, Family Theater Papers, AHCFM.

17. *Matter of Faith,* n.d. Flyer; Brooklyn *Tablet,* clipping, December 11, 1969, 09–02, Family Theater Papers, AHCFM.

18. Vincent J. Ryan, "Fr. Peyton, Abp. Sheen on TV Mother's Day," *Twin Circle,* 7, no. 19 (May 18, 1973).

19. Patrick Peyton, CSC, to Richard Sullivan, CSC, October 30, 1969, 01–16, Crusades, Guatemala, AHCFM. The complete committee was: Theodore Hesburgh, CSC, Colonel Frank Borman, Hubert Humphrey, R. Sargent Shriver, Ambassador Lloyd Hand (chief of protocol at the White House), Mrs. George Romney, George Putnam (Los Angeles television newscaster and media personality), Ed Sullivan, and Mr. and Mrs. Bing Crosby.

20. The complete list of programs broadcast is: May 6, Bishop F. A. Marrocco of Peterborough, Canada; May 13, Bishop Sheen; May 20, Archbishop P. Pocock of Toronto; May 27, Bishop Emmett Carter of London, Ontario; June 3, Marshall McLuhan; June 10, Malcolm Muggeridge June 17; Cardinal Leo Josef Suenens; June 24, Cardinal John Wright of Pittsburgh; July 1, General Carlos Romulo (Philippine army commander); July 18, Father Matthew F. Morry, OP, professor at Providence College; July 15, Mrs. Rose Kennedy. See *Catholic Register,* Peterborough, Canada, April 28, 1973, clipping found in 09–02 Family Theater Papers. Some of the people interviewed but not broadcast were: Father Pedro Arrupe, SJ, superior general of the Society of Jesus; Bishop John J. Scanlon of Honolulu, a leader in the Reverence for Life Program; Bishop Gerald Carter, chairman of the International Committee for English in the Liturgy (ICEL).

21. Peter Grace, "Evolution of Family Rosary Crusade Organization," March 7, 1960, Family Rosary Confidential File; 1972–73 Report of Father Peyton's Crusade for Family Prayer," n.d. [1973], 507.94, Family Rosary Papers, AHCFE.

22. Frank P. Cawl to "Dear Parent Agencies," December 28, 1971; Report on Outdoor Advertising Campaign, July 1, 1972, 507.116, Family Rosary Papers, AHCFE.

23. Vincent J. Ryan, "Fr. Peyton, Abp. Sheen on TV Mother's Day," *Twin Circle* 7, no. 19 (May 18, 1973).

24. Report to the Grace Foundation on Multi-Media Campaign of Family Theater Production, April 1977, 507.99, Family Rosary Papers; Report to the Grace Foundation on the Third Phase of Multi-Media Campaign, July 1979, 310.5.103, Provincial Papers, Ribando, AHCFE; Albert Henizer, CSC, to Allen Rupley, June 2, 1980, 09–02, Family Theater Papers, AHCFM. In 1980, for example, the Grace Foundation gave Family Theater $20,000 for the billboard campaign.

25. Report to the Grace Foundation on the Second Phase of Multi-Media Campaign, July 1978, 310.5.104, Provincial Papers, Ribando, AHCFE.

26. Family Rosary Papers; Report to the Grace Foundation on the Third Phase of Multi-Media Campaign, July 1979, 310.5.103, Provincial Papers, Ribando, AHCFE. The audio portion of the spot in the 1979 campaign year was: "So why not ask God into your home...a simple prayer will do it. And remember the family that prays together stays together."

27. Raymond Cassel, CSC, to John Gurley, CSC, June 19, 1969, 05–01, Correspondence, Cassel, AHCFM.

28. Frank Fahey, Interview with Michael Heraghty, July 19, 1993, found in PPC, Attymass, County Mayo, Ireland. Fahey additionally stated, "I don't think he would have wanted anything to take away from the main mission or focal point of the organization, which was the rosary and family prayer."

29. Peter Grace to John Coleman, July 19, 1974, 09–01, Family Theater Papers; Grace to Patrick Peyton, CSC, June 1, 1987, 09–14, Family Theater Papers, AHCFM.

30. Jack Haley to Patrick Peyton, CSC, October 9, 1969, 03–03, All for Her Fund, AHCFM; Dennis Roverato, Interview with author, August 9, 2000.

31. All for Her Trust, n.d. [1970], 03–03, All for Her Fund, AHCFM.

32. Patrick Peyton, CSC, to John Gurley, CSC, January 12, 1970, 01–16, Crusades, Guatemala; Antonio Oriol to Peyton, July 20, 1970; Peter Grace to Peyton January 15, 1970; Cardinal Rufino Santos to Patrick Peyton, CSC, May 14, 1971, 03–03, All for Her Fund, AHCFM. The community of the Little Sisters of the Poor, with whom Peyton would later establish a special relationship, was one religious order that pledged one Hail Mary. See Sister Marguerite to Patrick Peyton, CSC, Peyton Personnel File, AHCG.

33. Benjamin H. Swig to Patrick Peyton, CSC, 03–03, All for Her Papers, 03–03, All for Her Fund; Patrick Peyton, CSC, to John Gurley, CSC, January 12, 1970, 01–16, Crusades, Guatemala, AHCFM.

34. Patrick Peyton, CSC, to Thomas Barrosse, CSC, July 8, 1980; Barrosse to Peyton, September 9, 1980, Patrick Peyton Personnel File, AHCG.

35. Patrick Peyton, CSC, to Thomas Barrosse, CSC, May 14, 1980, Patrick Peyton Personnel File, AHCG.

36. The composition of the Finance Committee was J. Peter Grace, chair, Thomas Doyle, and Joseph Quinn, CSC, with Patrick Peyton, CSC, and Albert Heinzer, CSC, as *ex officio* members. Monies for the All for Her Fund continue to this day to arrive, although the original goal was exceeded in the early 1980s. As one side note, in 1992 the Sarita Kenedy East Foundation agreed to make an annual contribution of $200,000 for ten years to celebrate the two thousandth birthday of Christ. See Meeting Minutes, Board of Directors of Family Rosary, Inc., April 28, 1992, 05–01, Correspondence, Farrell, AHCFM.

37. Family Rosary Crusade, Summary Account, n.d. [1970], 05–04, Administration Reports, AHCFM.

38. Patrick Peyton, CSC, to Richard Sullivan, CSC, October 30, 1969, 03–03, All for Her Fund; Peyton to John Gurley, CSC, February 4, 1975, 06–02, Patrick Peyton Papers, AHCFM; Provincial Bulletin n.d. [May 1979].

39. John Gurley, CSC, to Archbishop Adolfo Tortolo, September 5, 1972, and September 21, 1972, 01–02, Crusades, Argentina, AHCFM.

40. Luis Armijos, Diary Entries, August 26–30, 1973; Crusade Summary Sheet, n.d. [1983], 01–02, Crusades, Argentina, AHCFM.

41. Juan Rodolfo Laise to Patrick Peyton, CSC, February 19, 1977, 01–02, Crusades, Argentina, AHCFM.

42. Andrew Schierhoff to Patrick Peyton, CSC, August 15, 1974; John Gurley, CSC, to Schierhoff, January 20, 1975; Memorandum, Luis Camacho Hidalgo, March 17, 1978; Cruzada de Oración en Familia, En Bolivia, May 5, 1978, 01–31, Crusades, Bolivia, AHCFM.

43. Crusade for Family Prayer, January 1980; Jorge Hurtado to John Gurley, CSC, January 2, 1980; *El Deber* (Newspaper clipping), October 7, 1979, found in 01–31, Crusades, Bolivia, AHCFM.

44. Crusade for Family Prayer in Latin America, February 26, 1981, 02–06, Offices, South America, AHCFM.

45. Crusade for Family Prayer, Inc., By-Laws, September 13, 1971, 03–03, Crusade for Family Prayer, AHCFM.

46. William Ribando, CSC, to John Gurley, CSC, November 4, 1975; Ribando to Directors of Family Rosary and Family Theater, n.d. [1977], 310.5.105, Provincial Papers, Ribando, AHCFE

47. William Ribando, CSC, "Proposed Restructuring of Family Rosary, Family Theater and the Crusade for Family Prayer," June 3, 1976, 510.20, Families for Prayer, AHCFM. Ribando's plan was very close to the restructuring plan that was actually implemented in 1990. See chapter 13 for more information on this reorganization effort.

48. William Ribando, CSC, to Donald Haycock, CSC, and Walter Reilly, CSC, May 4, 1977, 310.5.105, Provincial Papers, Ribando, AHCFE.

49. Charles Miller and Thomas Doyle to Thomas Barrosse, CSC, December 4, 1980, 07–02, Families for Prayer, AHCFM.

50. Patrick Peyton, CSC, "A Genesis of 'The Messiah,'" December 1975; Gene Kelly to Peyton, August 7, 1973; Michael Frankovich to Peyton, August 1, 1973, 09–01, Family Theater Papers, AHCFM.

51. Thomas Donlan, OP, "Fr. Peyton, Rossellini Team for 'The Messiah,'" n.d. [1974], clipping found in 09–01, Family Theater Papers, AHCFM. Some of Rossellini's most noteworthy film credits were: *Socrates, Augustine of Hippo, The Age of the Medici, Descartes, The American Revolution,* and *The Industrial Revolution.* According to Tag Gallagher, Rossellini and Peyton met in Houston, Texas, in the fall of 1973. See Tag Gallagher, *The Adventures of Roberto Rossellini: His Life and Films* (New York: Da Capo Press, 1998), 664.

52. Quoted in *Chicago Tribune,* September 14, 1975, clipping found in 09–01, Family Theater Papers, AHCFM.

53. John Meehan to Peter Grace, November 15, 1973, 09–01, Family Theater Papers, AHCFM; Dennis Roverato, Interview with author, August 9, 2000.

54. Patrick Peyton, CSC, "A Genesis of 'The Messiah,'" December 1975, 09–01, Family Theater Papers, AHCFM.

55. Patrick Peyton, CSC, to Frank J. Lewis Foundation, August 15, 1974, 09–01, Family Theater, AHCFM.

56. Thomas Donlan, OP, "Fr. Peyton, Rossellini Team for 'The Messiah,'" n.d. [1974], clipping; Crux of the News, September 1, 1975, found in 09–01, Family Theater Papers, AHCFM.

57. *Crux of the News,* September 1, 1975, found in 09–01, Family Theater Papers, AHCFM.

58. Patrick Peyton, CSC, to Roberto Rossellini, May 2, 1975, 09–01, Family Theater Papers, AHCFM.

59. Al Scalpone to "Whom it May Concern," February 12, 1976; "The Messiah Project," n.d., 09–01, Family Theater Papers, AHCFM. Rossellini claimed that $1.5 million of his share would be provided by the Italian government as part of its support for the arts.

60. John Meehan to Peter Grace, Memorandum, November 15, 1973, 09–01, Family Theater Papers, AHCFM.

61. Harry John to Don Gallagher, January 14, 1974; John Miller to John, April 18, 1974, 09–01 Family Theater Papers, AHCFM.

62. Extant data does not say why DeRance agreed to support the project, but previous history would indicate that Peyton's powerful persuasive ability must have won the day with Harry John and his foundation.

63. Thomas Doyle to Patrick Peyton, CSC, October 18, 1973; Summary Sheet, Messiah Mailing, n.d. [1976], 09–01, Family Theater Papers, AHCFM; Frank Fahey, Interview with Michael Heraghty, July 19, 1993, PPC, Attymass, County Mayo, Ireland.

64. J. Peter Grace to John Meehan, Memorandum, April 17, 1975, 09–01 Family Theater Papers, AHCFM.

65. Macario Palanca to Patrick Peyton, CSC, December 28, 1973; Rosalind Farber to Patrick Paton [*sic*], September 16, 1974; Peyton to Harry John, July 14, 1974, 09–01, Family Theater Papers, AHCFM. The offer from Palanca was to give Family Theater $100,000 for the distribution rights in the Far East. There is no extant reason given for inaction, especially at a time when Peyton was looking for financial backing, but most probably he believed that the film would be a great success and $100,000 would be a small fee for what Palanca would ultimately receive in box office revenues.

66. John Meehan to Patrick Peyton, CSC, April 14, 1975, 09–01, Family Theater Papers, AHCFM. Meehan suggested that, due to the nature of the film, a Catholic-only distribution, possibly through local bishops, might be the best avenue to use. It was thought that Catholic groups and individuals would have a greater interest in promoting the film. After the film was completed it was viewed by representatives of Universal Pictures but their "reaction was coldly polite and we haven't heard from them since." See Al Scalpone to Lawrence McKay, February 25, 1976, 09–01, Family Theater Papers, AHCFM.

67. Patrick Peyton, CSC, to Mary Buckley, RSM, January 6, 1975, 05–01, Correspondence, Buckley; John Meehan to Peter Grace, January 13, 1975, 09–01, Family Theater Papers, AHCFM.

68. Sister M. Macrina to Mary Buckley, RSM, Match 13, 1975, 05–01, Correspondence, Buckley, AHCFM.

69. Patrick Peyton, CSC, "The Messiah: An Authentic Film Biography of Jesus Christ," n.d. 09–01, Family Theater Papers, AHCFM.

70. Patrick Peyton, CSC, to Mary Buckley, RSM, February 5, 1975, Correspondence, Buckley, AHCFM.

71. *Crux of the News,* September 1, 1975, found in 428 (FR) 8, AHCG; Roberto Rossellini to Patrick Peyton, CSC, Draft Document, n.d. [December 1973], 09–01, Family Theater Papers, AHCFM. Rossellini commented to Peyton, "In all the recent films I have made I never worked from a treatment or script. In these last twelve

years I have, let us say, abandoned cinema fiction and attempted to develop a new means of educating through film. I try to relate the subject of my films accurately based on documents.... This is what I want to do with 'The Messiah.' "

72. Al Scalpone to "Whom It May Concern," February 2, 1976, 09–01, Family Theater Papers; Patrick Peyton, CSC, to Mary Buckley, RSM, November 6, 1975, and November 22, 1975, 05–01, Correspondence, Buckley, AHCFM.

73. Patrick Peyton, CSC, to Mary Buckley, RSM, November 7, 1975, and November 22, 1975, 05–01, Correspondence, Buckley, AHCFM. Peyton commented about his first impressions of *The Messiah:* "The first emotion was how thrilled and grateful I was when I saw the picture moving past the half-hour, the hour, the two hours — until the end without causing me alarm. How much more thrilled I was when I couldn't keep back the tears that came. The last scene of our Blessed Mother moved me so much that I could not speak to Rossellini except through tears." See Patrick Peyton, CSC, to Josefina Bayot, January 2, 1976, 09–14, Family Theater Papers, AHCFM.

74. Al Scalpone to "Whom It May Concern," February 2, 1976, 09–01, Family Theater Papers, AHCFM; Patrick Peyton, CSC, to Thomas Barrosse, CSC, January 6, 1976, 428 (FR) 8, AHCG.

75. Report, February 19, 1976, 510.20, Families for Prayer; Thomas Donlan, OP, to Patrick Peyton, CSC, October 17, 1975, 09–01, Family Theater Papers, AHCFM; *Variety,* May 10, 1978, clipping found in 428 (FR) 0, AHCG.

76. "Two Films of Christ Neglect His Divinity," *Wanderer,* March 11, 1976, clipping found in 09–01, Family Theater Papers, AHCFM; "Rossellini's Neo-Realistic New Testament," *Herald Tribune,* February 25, 1976, clipping found in 510.20, Families for Prayer, AHCFE.

77. Herb A. Lightman, review in *American Cinematographer,* quoted in Al Scalpone to "Whom It May Concern," February 2, 1976, 09–01, Family Theater Papers, AHCFM.

78. Points for Jack Meehan, January 20, 1976, 09–01, Family Theater Papers, AHCFM.

79. Patrick Peyton, CSC, "A Genesis of the 'The Messiah,' " December 1975, 09–01, Family Theater Papers, AHCFM; Peyton to Thomas Barrosse, CSC, January 6, 1976, 428 (FR) 8, AHCG. Peyton told Barrosse it appeared that Rossellini had been given a stipend of $400,000 for his services, four times the agreed-upon payment.

80. Rough Draft Letter to Archbishop Giovanni Benelli, n.d. [1976]; Al Scalpone to "Whom It May Concern," February 2, 1976, 09–01, Family Theater Papers, AHCFM.

81. Patrick Peyton, CSC, to Patricia Spanbauer, April 27, 1976, 09–01, Family Theater Papers, AHCFM.

82. Patrick Peyton, CSC, to Norbert Rans, MM, April 6, 1976, 09–01, Family Theater Papers, AHCFM.

83. Points for Jack Meehan, January 20, 1976, 09–01, Family Theater Papers, AHCFM.

84. John Gurley, CSC, to Roberto Rossellini, April 2, 1976; Summary of Meeting Between Father Gurley and Roberto Rossellini, March 27, 1976, 09–01, Family Theater Papers, AHCFM.

85. Albert Heinzer, CSC, to Harry John, July 9, 1976; Civil Court Summons, July 9, 1976; Heinzer to Patrick Peyton, CSC, John Gurley, CSC, Mary Buckley, RSM, and Ed Fox, November 3, 1977, 09–01, Family Theater Papers, AHCFM. Rossellini family members decided after the director's death not to pursue the case and, thus, Family Theater paid an undisclosed amount of money to Orizzonte in 2000. The DeRance Foundation obtained rights to *Messiah* in return for its cancellation of the $1.5 million it was owed by Family Theater. The film was released with subtitles by Santa Fe Productions, headed by Bruno John, in 1998. Bruno John, Interview with author, February 14, 2002.

86. Dinner Program, September 10, 1972; Thirty-Fifth Anniversary Booklet, n.d. [1977]; Golden Jubilee Pamphlet, 1942–92, n.d. [1992], 06–04, Patrick Peyton Papers, AHCFM.

87. The Eucharistic Congress's theme was "The Eucharist and the Hunger of the Human Family." Presentations were given on the hungers for God, bread, freedom and justice, truth, understanding, peace, and Jesus, the bread of life. See Joseph Bernardin, "Spirituality and the Catholic Church in America," *Chicago Studies* 15 (Spring 1976): 9.

88. Patrick Peyton, CSC, to Frank Fahey, 510.55, Families for Prayer, AHCFE; G. E. De Salinier, M.D., to Patrick Peyton, CSC, November 24, 1976, 06–08, Patrick Peyton Papers, AHCFM.

89. Beatrice Gallagher to Patrick Peyton, CSC, January 8, 1977, 09–13, Family Theater Papers, AHCFM. Peyton's sister believed her brother's heart attack was a sign from Mary that she wanted him to rest.

90. News clipping, May 12, 1978, Rosary Hour File, AALA; Robert Yates, M.D., to Roger Waters, M.D., March 17, 1980; Doctor's Report, September 20, 1978, 06–08, Patrick Peyton Papers, AHCFM; William Ribando, CSC, to John Gurley, CSC, July 6, 1978, 510.19, Families for Prayer, AHCFE.

91. Dorothy Halloran, Interview with James FitzPatrick, OMI, September 30, 1997, AHCFM; Mary Buckley, RSM, to William Ribando, CSC, October 2, 1978, 310.5.103, Provincial Papers, Ribando, AHCFE. Halloran claims that Peyton's bout with ill health changed his manner of dealing with people. She stated, "I think maybe having the heart attack made him think more of his own mortality and he thought more about other people."

Chapter 12: Families for Prayer

1. "The Diocesan Crusades," n.d. [1970]; Patrick Peyton, CSC, to Albert Heinzer, CSC, February 21, 1971, 05–01, Correspondence, Gurley, AHCFM.

2. It is certain that while Peyton's public pronouncements may have suggested a more post–Vatican II approach to prayer, in his heart the family rosary could never be replaced. His inability to find interior conversion was a significant factor in the lack of progress of the Crusade since the organization ran on the charismatic enthusiasm that Peyton brought to his ministry.

3. "Proposal for a National Program of Families for Prayer," n.d. [1972], 507.43; "Time for Prayer," Spring 1972, 507.35, Family Rosary Papers, AHCFE.

4. Families for Prayer General Handbook, n.d. [1972]; Bishop Louis E. Gelineau, Statement, October 4, 1972, 07–01, Families for Prayer, AHCFM.

5. "Proposal for a National Program of Families for Prayer," n.d. [1972], 507.43, AHCFM.

6. Families for Prayer General Handbook, n.d. [1972]; Families for Prayer Parish Program, n.d. [1972], 07–01, Families for Prayer, AHCFM.

7. Ibid.

8. "Proposal for a National Program of Families for Prayer," n.d. [1972], 507.43, AHCFM.

9. Ibid.

10. Press Release, n.d. [September 1972], 06–04, Patrick Peyton Papers; Patrick Peyton, CSC, to John Gurley, CSC, Memorandum, May 14, 1972, 07–01, Families for Prayer, AHCFM.

11. "News from the Diocese of Providence," November 24, 1972; "Family Prayer Rally in Providence Begins Father Peyton's Crusade throughout North America," clipping from the *Evangelist* (Albany, New York), n.d. [November 1972], 07–01, Families for Prayer, AHCFM.

12. Patrick Peyton, CSC, to Charles P. O'Donnell, November 29, 1972, 07–01, Families for Prayer, AHCFM.

13. Calendar of Events, Archdiocese of St. Louis, n.d. [1973]; *Fort Wayne News Sentinel,* May 20, 1974, clipping found in 07–01, Families for Prayer, AHCFM.

14. Alfred Méndez, CSC, to Raymond Cassel, CSC, October 2, 1973, 05–01, Correspondence, Gurley; General Calendar of Crusade for Family Prayer, Diocese of Ponce, January to June 1975, 07–01, Families for Prayer, AHCFM; Patricia Spanbauer to Robert McDonnell, CSC, December 6, 1976, 510.178, Families for Prayer, AHCFE.

15. Calendar of Events, Diocese of Joliet, n.d. [1973], 07–01, Families for Prayer, AHCFM; Frank Fahey, Interview with Michael Heraghty, July 19, 1993, PPC, Attymass, County Mayo, Ireland.

16. John Gurley, CSC, to William Ribando, CSC, May 7, 1981, 310.5.106, Provincial Papers, Ribando; Families for Prayer Report to the Board of Directors, February 8, 1980, 510.34a, Families for Prayer, AHCFE.

17. Patrick Peyton, CSC, Documentation of the Relationship between the Family Rosary and Families for Prayer, March 3, 1990, 507.128, Family Rosary Papers, AHCFE.

18. Mary Buckley, RSM, to William Ribando, CSC, May 11, 1981, 507.189, Family Rosary Papers, AHCFE.

19. John Gurley, CSC, to Cardinal Timothy Manning, April 11, 1978, Rosary Hour File, AALA.

20. Families for Prayer, Summary Report, n.d., 510.40, Families for Prayer, AHCFE; Proposal for National Program of Families for Prayer, n.d. [1973], FTH.

21. Families for Prayer, Leadership Team, 07–02, Families for Prayer, AHCFM.

22. Patrick Peyton, CSC, to John Gurley, CSC, January 28, 1977, 09–13, Family Theater Papers, AHCFM.

23. Families for Prayer, Into the Future, n.d., 510.119; William Ribando, CSC, to John Gurley, CSC, May 9, 1979, 510.178, Families for Prayer, AHCFE.

24. Assessment of FFP's Growth Rate, Appendix I, n.d. [1981], 510.14, Families for Prayer, AHCFE.

25. John Gurley, CSC, to Frank Fahey, January 17, 1976, 510.55, Families for Prayer, AHCFE; Patrick Peyton, CSC, to "Peggy," n.d. [May 1977], 428 (FR) 14, AHCG.

26. Families for Prayer, "Report to the Board of Directors," February 8, 1980, 510.34a, Families for Prayer; Families for Prayer Staff to "Dear Father," January 1979, 310.5.103, Provincial Papers, Ribando, AHCFE.

27. William Ribando, CSC, to John Gurley, CSC, July 21, 1978, 510.19; Ribando to Gurley, November 19, 1979, and June 18, 1980, 510.178, Families for Prayer; Ribando to Mary Buckley, RSM, July 18, 1981, 310.5.106, Provincial Papers, AHCFE.

28. Families for Prayer, "Report to the Board of Directors," February 8, 1990, 510.34a, Families for Prayer; Review Sheet, n.d. [1980], 310.5.106, Provincial Papers, Ribando, AHCFE. When depreciation and overhead were added the FFP debt between 1976 and 1980 was over $500,000.

29. William Ribando, CSC, Interview with author, February 23, 2001.

30. Patrick Peyton, CSC, Documentation on the Relationship between the Family Rosary and Families for Prayer, March 3, 1990, 507.128, AHCFE.

31. Patrick Peyton, CSC, to Hugh T. Tunney, September 19, 1980, Patrick Peyton Personnel File, AHCG.

32. Patrick Peyton, CSC, "One Solution to the Problem of Fr. G.," n.d. [1980], 07–02, Families for Prayer, AHCFM.

33. Patrick Peyton, CSC, "The Problem of Albany and Father Gurley," n.d. [1980], 07–02, Families for Prayer, AHCFM. Peyton wrote of Gurley, "The incompetence of Fr. G is exemplified in — his overall behavior — silent — uncommunicative — unilateral in decision making — seeks no counsel — no priorities — no delegation." See Patrick Peyton, CSC, "One Solution to the Problem of Fr. G.," n.d. [1980], 07–02, Families for Prayer, AHCFM. It is very interesting to see that the very side of Gurley that Peyton seemed to dislike was precisely what several members of Holy Cross who worked with him closely saw in the rosary priest.

34. This is the opinion of William Ribando, CSC. See William Ribando, CSC, Interview with author, February 23, 2001.

35. John Gurley, CSC, to William Ribando, CSC, May 7, 1981, 310.5.106, Provincial Papers, Ribando, AHCFE.

36. Ibid.

37. William Ribando, CSC, Interview with Thomas Feeley, June 4, 1999. Ribando stated that the Family Rosary ministry must be continued after Peyton's death and that action against Gurley would jeopardize this. It was his opinion that the work needed to develop in lines not exclusive to the rosary. This was what led him to consult with the Provincial Council.

38. William Ribando, CSC, to Thomas Barrosse, CSC, March 6, 1981, 310.5.106, Provincial Papers, Ribando, AHCFM; "Proposed Solution to the Present Crusade for Family Prayer, Inc. Controversy," June 1981, 428 (FR) 14, AHCG. The Provincial Council felt J. Peter Grace had too much control in the Crusade for Family Prayer operation. The council also recommended that Sr. Mary Buckley be removed from her position, but the provincial at this time did not press this issue.

39. William Ribando, CSC, to Patrick Peyton, CSC, March 21, 1981, 507.189, Family Rosary Papers, AHCFE. The letter read in part: "You [Peyton] are to move immediately to give control of the control board of the apostolate, Crusade for Family Prayer, back to Holy Cross. This could be achieved either by amending the bylaws to increase the membership of the board with three more Holy Cross Fathers or resignations of several people could be requested. This must be accomplished by

a special meeting within fifteen days.... You are not to interfere in any way with the direction or management of the work [of] Families for Prayer or *Together.* If there should be any attempt to fire Fr. John Gurley from the apostolates, your own retirement to Notre Dame would be immediately enforced by Church mandate. The same steps would be taken if, regretfully, you were not to accept and implement the other directives."

40. William Ribando, CSC, to Patrick Peyton, CSC, 310.6.180, Provincial Papers, Callahan, AHCFE.

41. Grace acknowledged that Peyton was individualistic and was "very hard to work with because he might say something one day and have a different idea later," but that was part of the magic of the man. Grace admitted that he could "never resist any request from Father Peyton" for he knew the request was centered about his devotion to the Blessed Mother. One typical comment, made at the time of this crisis, illustrates Grace's devotion to Peyton: "Father Peyton is divinely inspired through our Blessed Mother and I have seen him say things that everybody thinks are nuts and then it happens and it comes true." See Annual Meeting of the Board of Directors of the Crusade for Family Prayer, Inc., August 21, 1981; J. Peter Grace to Thomas Barrosse, CSC, April 2, 1981, 07–02, Families for Prayer, AHCFM.

42. J. Peter Grace to Thomas Barrosse, CSC, April 2, 1981, and April 16, 1981, 07–02, Families for Prayer, AHCFM.

43. J. Peter Grace to William Ribando, CSC, three letters, April ?, 1981, 310.5.106, Provincial Papers, Ribando, AHCFE. Many years after this affair Ribando reflected on Grace's outburst: "I felt that Fr. Peyton allowed Mr. Grace to be his hit man on me and the provincial administration in general. I didn't appreciate it. I wasn't edified by it. I felt it was an unfortunate incident." See William Ribando, CSC, Interview with Thomas Feeley, CSC, June 4, 1999.

44. William Ribando, CSC, to Peter Grace, April 27, 1981, 310.5.106, Provincial Papers, Ribando, AHCFE.

45. William Ribando, CSC, to Cardinal Terence Cooke, April 9, 1981; Ribando to Archbishop Pio Laghi, April 10, 1981, 310.5.106, Provincial Papers, Ribando, AHCFE.

46. Joseph Callahan, CSC, to Thomas Barrosse, CSC, May 22, 1981, 310.5.125, Provincial Papers, Ribando, AHCFE.

47. John Gurley, CSC, to William Ribando, CSC, May 7, 1981, 310.5.106, Provincial Papers, Ribando, AHCFE.

48. John Gurley, CSC, Memorandum, May 22, 1981, 310.5.106, Provincial Papers, Ribando, AHCFE.

49. In 1980 the Board of Directors for the Crusade for Family Prayer, Inc., based in New York City, The Family Rosary, Inc., based in Albany, and Family Theater, Inc., was constituted by George DePrizio, CSC, John Gurley, CSC, Bartley MacPhaidin, CSC, Patrick Peyton, CSC, William Ribando, CSC, J. Peter Grace, Thomas Doyle, Charles Miller, and Sister Mary Buckley.

50. Thomas Barrosse, CSC, to William Ribando, CSC, April 15, 1981, 310.5.106, Provincial Papers, Ribando, AHCFE.

51. Patrick Peyton, CSC, to William Ribando, CSC, May 8, 1981, 507.189, Family Rosary Papers, AHCFE.

52. Thomas Barrosse, CSC, Memorandum, May 27, 1981, 310.5.126, Provincial Papers, Ribando, AHCFE.

53. J. Peter Grace to Thomas Barrosse, CSC, April 2, 1981, 07–02, Families for Prayer, AHCFM.

54. *Together,* June 15–21, 1981, and July 27–August 1, 1981, 07–02, Families for Prayer, AHCFM. The June 15 essay stated further: "His [Jesus'] command: 'Eat this bread and drink this wine, for they are my flesh and blood,' needs some translation. At times we all speak in exaggerated language, in order to make a point. For example, when a person is embarrassed and says, 'I could just die,' she does not literally mean that she wants to die. She means, 'I am just so embarrassed,' or 'I couldn't be more embarrassed.' And so it is with Jesus telling us to eat the bread that is his flesh. By saying that he means, 'Take this bread, for through my power it contains my very life. If you eat it, it will be the same as though you were to eat my flesh. By eating this bread, you absorb into yourself my living Presence." The July 27–August 1 issue stated, "The Gospel accounts tell us that Jesus called together his closest followers to share the Passover for the last time. *It is supposed* [emphasis added] that at the moment when the unleavened bread was blessed and passed, Jesus spoke the word, 'This is my body.' Later, at the end of the meal, when the wine was blessed and shared, *Jesus is thought to have said* [emphasis added] 'This is my Blood.' "

55. Peter Cups, SSS, to Patrick Peyton, CSC, August 3, 1981, 07–02, Families for Prayer, AHCFM.

56. *Wanderer,* July 30, 1981, clipping found in 07–02, Families for Prayer, AHCFM.

57. J. Peter Grace to Thomas Barrosse, CSC, August 20, 1981, 07–02, Families for Prayer, AHCFM.

58. Meeting Minutes, Board of Directors, Crusade for Family Prayer, August 21, 1981, Patrick Peyton Personnel File, AHCG.

59. Provincial Council Meeting Minutes, November 13–14, 1981, 310.5.126, Provincial Papers, Ribando, AHCFE. There is no extant data indicating that this initial discussion went any further than this first meeting. The tension on both sides was apparent, but even for the council to threaten pulling its sponsorship and Peyton to consider another religious sponsor is a significant comment.

60. Bartley MacPhaidin, CSC, to Members of the Board, November 23, 1981, 310.5.126, Provincial Papers, Ribando, AHCFE.

61. Peyton was scheduled for a minor surgical procedure and said, therefore, he could not sign the final agreement until he had recovered. Ribando ordered Peyton not to leave the county until he signed the agreement. The provincial claimed that Peyton's delay in signing was an attempt to extend his influence into Families for Prayer by having one of his people placed on the board. However, the tactic failed as the original board members for Families for Prayer were William Ribando, CSC, John Gurley, CSC, Ken Silvia, CSC, and John Corr, CSC.

62. Certificate of Incorporation, Families for Prayer, Inc., April 26, 1982, Families for Prayer, ADA.

63. Lease Agreement, n.d. [1982], 510.33; Minutes of Board Meeting for Families for Prayer, Inc., May 2, 1983, 510.119, Families for Prayer, AHCFE. The plan called for liquidation of the debt in 9.5 years, terminating on December 31, 1992.

64. Peter Grace to Thomas Barrosse, CSC, March 15, 1983, 422.2, Ribando Papers, AHCG.

65. Joseph Callahan, CSC, to Thomas Barrosse, CSC, August 24, 1983, 310.6.01, Provincial Papers, Callahan, AHCFE; Barrosse to Patrick Peyton, CSC, March 31, 1983, Patrick Peyton Personnel File, AHCG.

66. Meeting Minutes, Board of Directors of Families for Prayer, October 17, 1983; Joseph Callahan, CSC, to John Gurley, CSC, January 5, 1985, 310.6.73, Provincial Papers, Callahan; Thomas Doyle to J. Peter Grace, December 5, 1984, 507.79, Family Rosary Papers, AHCFE.

67. Meeting Minutes, Board of Directors for Families for Prayer, January 9, 1987, and June 6, 1987, 310.6.73, Provincial Papers, Callahan, AHCFE.

68. Families for Prayer, Inc., Balance Sheet, September 8, 1989, 510.117, Families for Prayer, AHCFE.

69. David Farrell, CSC, to Claude Grou, CSC, October 6, 1989; Erin O'Grady-Parent to Farrell, April 2, 1990, 510.117, Families for Prayer, AHCFE.

70. William Ribando, CSC, Interview with Thomas Feeley, CSC, June 4, 1999.

Chapter 13: Renewal and Encores

1. Quoted in Rodger Van Allen, "Memories and Hopes: Questions on American Catholicism," *Commonweal* 106 (June 8, 1979): 326–28.

2. David O'Brien, "Catholic Consciousness: The Public Consequences of Denominational Disputes," in *Uncivil Religion: Interreligious Hostility in America,* ed. Robert N. Bellah and Frederick Greenspan (New York: Crossroad, 1987), 165–67. O'Brien stated that the Catholic subculture collapsed due to the convergence of three major streams of change: (1) The social composition and location of Catholics changed. Catholics had moved from being an immigrant working-class people who saw themselves as a minority to a highly Americanized Church in which they were full participants. (2) As freedom became more and more an internal experience, religion tended to accommodate the culture in which it found itself. (3) This freedom that Catholics experienced as voluntarism is confined largely to the private side of life, which locates the Church even more fully as one specialized institution among many.

3. See Van Allen, "Memories and Hopes: Questions on American Catholicism," 326–28.

4. See Joseph A. Varacelli, "The Future of U.S. Catholicism," *Ecumenist* 20 (July–August 1982): 71.

5. James W. Malone, "Reporting the Life of the Church in the 1980s," *Origins* 14 (November 1, 1984): 314–15.

6. Although the preponderance of opinions during this period in the literature speak of a mini-renaissance of Catholic life in the 1980s there were dissenting opinions. John McDermott wrote that, in his opinion, American Catholicism's large numbers (50 million) are only "a facade that masks both weakness and decay. The American Catholic community, viewed as a whole, viewed as a social movement, is remarkably weak, passive and ineffective." See John M. McDermott, "The Weakness of American Catholicism," *Chicago Studies* 28 (April 1989): 79–88. Interestingly, in an interview with *U.S. Catholic* in 1981 David O'Brien stated that he felt that Americans were weak, choosing to follow the dictates of Rome than to think for themselves. While not wholly original in thought the two pastoral letters of 1983 and 1986 certainly demonstrated that the bishops were willing to take a stand and one that was not popular with many, especially with respect to "Economic Justice

for All." See "American Catholics: Just Who Do You Think You Are?" Interview with David O'Brien, *U.S. Catholic* 46 (April 1981): 6–11.

7. Allan Figueroa Deck, SJ, *The Second Wave: Hispanic Ministry and the Evangelization of Cultures* (New York: Paulist Press, 1989), 1; Archbishop Patrick Flores, "The Opportunity Hispanics Provide for the Church," *Origins* 10 (September 11, 1980): 202.

8. C. Gilbert Romero, "Self-Affirmation of the Hispanic Church," *Ecumenist* 23 (March–April 1985): 39–42; María García, "Hispanic-Americans: A Vital Presence within the American Church," *Catechist* 13 (April 1980): 43. One writer claimed that in 1980 as many as 5 million Hispanics had been to date proselytized by various evangelical sects. See Frank Ponce, "The U.S. Church's Hispanic Catholics," *Origins* 10 (September 11, 1980): 199.

9. John C. Blackwell, "The Hispanic Presence," *Homiletic and Pastoral Review* 85 (December 1984): 28.

10. "Background on the Bishops' Family Plan," *Origins* 8, no. 1 (May 25, 1978): 8.

11. Patrick Peyton, CSC, Memorandum, June 8, 1979, 06–06, Patrick Peyton Papers, AHCFM.

12. Patrick Peyton, CSC, to Archbishop John Quinn, February 25, 1980, 07–02, Families for Prayer, AHCFM; Peyton to Quinn, May 14, 1980, Patrick Peyton Personnel File, AHCG.

13. "Notes to Help Create the Message that Cardinal Sin Will Make on His Own as He Reports to the Philippine Hierarchy in January," n.d. [1984], 09–17, Family Theater Papers, AHCFM.

14. Sample Introductory Letter, n.d., 10–01, Publications, AHCFM. See "The Message to Christian Families," *Origins* 10, no. 21 (November 6, 1980): 324.

15. Golden Jubilee Pamphlet, 1942–92, 06–04, Patrick Peyton Papers; J. Peter Grace, Memorandum, February 17, 1979, 09–17, Family Theater Papers; Patrick Peyton, CSC, Memorandum, June 8, 1979, 06–06, Patrick Peyton Papers, AHCFM.

16. Pope John Paul II, Worldwide TV Broadcast, June 6, 1987, 10–01, Publications, AHCFM. The pope continued to provide his support for Peyton until the latter's death. On the occasion of Family Rosary's forty-fifth anniversary the pope wrote Peyton, "I am happy to know that you personally will celebrate this year as the crowning of your lifelong efforts to promote devotion to Mary through the Family Rosary Crusade. I fully share your hope that this time of special devotion to Mary will encourage many to take up or return to the daily Family Rosary." See Pope John Paul II to Patrick Peyton, CSC, February 25, 1987, 10–01, Publications, AHCFM.

17. Patrick Peyton, CSC, "A Global Crusade," July 11, 1980, 09–13, Family Theater Papers, AHCFM.

18. Al Scalpone to Patrick Peyton, CSC, Memorandum, October 31, 1983, 09–15, Family Theater Papers, AHCFM.

19. Patrick Peyton, CSC, "The Family Crusade" Presentation to Thomas Barrosse, CSC, n.d. [1980], 428 (FR) 12, AHCG.

20. Jeanne Arnold, *Man of Faith* (Hollywood, Calif.: Family Theater, Inc., 1983), 256–59; Dennis Roverato to Thomas Barrosse, September 23, 1980, Patrick Peyton, CSC, Personnel File, AHCG.

21. Arnold, *Man of Faith,* 256–59.

22. Ibid.; Patrick Peyton, CSC, to Harry John, January 21, 1983, 507.79, Family Rosary, AHCFE.

23. Proposal from Family Theater to the John D. and Catherine MacArthur Foundation, n.d. [1981], 507.79, Family Rosary Papers, AHCFE.

24. Flyers, n.d., 507.34.4; *New York Daily News,* October 3, 1982, 507.65, Family Theater Papers, AHCFE; Fact Sheet, October 22, 1982, Patrick Peyton Personnel File, AHCG.

25. Arnold, *Man of Faith,* 291; President's Newsletter 25 (3) (November 1981), UDIS 146/41, AUND; Flyer, n.d., "The Annunciation," 507.122, Family Theater Papers, AHCFE.

26. Flyers, n.d., 09–02, Family Theater Papers, AHCFM; Fact Sheets, n.d. 428 (FR) 8, AHCG. While Father Peyton was generating his new films Paulist Father Ellwood Keiser produced *The Fourth Wise Man,* starring Martin Sheen and Alan Arkin and aired on March 30, 1985, over ABC. Keiser stated that a changed attitude at national networks toward religious programming made its national broadcast possible. Keiser also obtained a sponsor, Bristol-Myers. See James P. Breig, "Catholic Productions on ABC a First for the Church," *Our Sunday Visitor* 73 (March 24, 1985): 19.

27. Family Theater Awards, 1947–87, December 31, 1987, 507.122, Family Rosary, AHCFE.

28. Archbishop Robert Sanchez to Patrick Peyton, October 21, 1981, 01–26, Crusades, United States; Flyer, "Rosary Sunday," October 15, 1989, 08–04, Headquarters, Albany, AHCFM; *Catholic Bulletin,* St. Paul, Minnesota, May 5, 1983, clipping found in 507.72, Family Rosary Papers, AHCFE.

29. Patrick Peyton, CSC, to Peter Grace, February 2, 1983, 507.79, Family Rosary Papers, AHCFE.

30. "The Family Rosary Crusade in Peru," April 3, 1984, 05–01, Correspondence, DePrizio, AHCFM.

31. Arnold, *Man of Faith,* 248; Cardinal Jaime Sin, Pastoral Letter, March 22, 1978; Patrick Peyton, CSC, to John Gurley, CSC, 09–13, Family Theater Papers, AHCFM.

32. Liam Devine to Patrick Peyton, CSC, May 16, 1981; Peyton to Devine, June 18, 1981, 02–02, Offices, Philippines, AHCFM.

33. Pamphlets and Programs, Various, 1981, 02–02, Offices, Philippines, AHCFM.

34. Summary Essay, n.d., 02–02, Offices, Philippines, AHCFM.

35. Patrick Peyton to Archbishop Ricardo Vidal, December 15, 1984, 02–02, Offices, Philippines, AHCFM.

36. Patrick Peyton to Mr. and Mrs. Alejandro Melchor, December 15, 1984, 02–02, Offices, Philippines, AHCFM.

37. Patrick Peyton, CSC, to Albert Heinzer, CSC, and Dennis Roverato, Memorandum, August 29, 1985, 02–02, Offices, Philippines, AHCFM; Peyton to Joseph Callahan, CSC, December 13, 1985, 310.6.178, Provincial Papers, Callahan, AHCFE.

38. Patrick Peyton, CSC, to Thomas Barrosse, CSC, November 4, 1985, Patrick Peyton Personnel File, AHCG.

39. Patrick Peyton, CSC, Address, December 8, 1985, 02–02, Offices, Philippines, AHCFM.

40. Report of the Family Rosary Crusade, n.d. [December 1985], 02–02, Offices, Philippines, AHCFM.

41. Luis Nepomuceno, "Of Rosaries and Tanks," Essay found in 02–02, Offices, Philippines, AHCFM. On February 7, 1986, Marcos was elected to a fourth term as president. Only days later, however, Defense Minister Juan Ponce Enrile and Armed Forces Chief of Staff Lt. General Fidel Ramos led forces against Marcos. Cardinal Jaime Sin, who had generally been quiet concerning the Marcos regime, chose this time, however, to rally his bishops, priests, and religious in a three-day effort of prayer to topple the government. The *Los Angeles Times* reported in its February 27, 1986, issue, "The Cardinal's mobilization of the devout Philippine masses was key to the victory."

42. Patrick Peyton, CSC, to Leon Hontiveros and J. Walter Thompson, March 30, 1986, Patrick Peyton Personnel File, AHCG.

43. Patrick Peyton, CSC, Sample Introductory Letter, n.d., 10–01, Publications, AHCFM.

44. Patrick Peyton, CSC, Memorandum, n.d. [1987], 10–01, Publications, AHCFM.

45. Joseph Callahan, CSC, to Board of Directors of the Sarita Kenedy East Foundation, December 8, 1986, 310.6.176, Provincial Papers, Callahan, AHCFE.

46. Patrick Peyton, CSC, A Plan to Carry the Family Rosary Crusade Message into the 21st Century and Beyond, n.d. [1989], 06–02, Patrick Peyton Papers; Patrick Peyton, CSC, Memorandum, n.d. [1987], 10–01, Publications, AHCFM.

47. Patrick Peyton, CSC, Memorandum, n.d. [1989], Patrick Peyton Personnel File, AHCG.

48. Patrick Peyton, CSC, to J. Neville Ward, January 25, 1985; Peyton, Sample Introductory Letter, n.d. 10–01, Publications, AHCFM.

49. Patrick Peyton, CSC, Memorandum, n.d. [1989], Patrick Peyton Personnel File, AHCG; Peyton, A Plan to Carry the Family Rosary Crusade Message into the 21st Century and Beyond, n.d. [1989], 06–02, Patrick Peyton Papers, AHCFM. Eight hundred handbooks were mailed by May 16, 1990. Of the 25 percent who responded to Peyton's handbook package very few stated that they would pledge to offer a crusade as outlined in the manual. See Dorothy Halloran, Interview with James FitzPatrick, September 30, 1997.

50. Proclamation, Synod of Bishops in Rome, October 1987, 10–01, Publications, AHCFM. The cardinals who signed this particular proclamation were Luigi Dadaglio, president of the Central Committee for the Marian Year; Josef Tomko, prefect of the Congregation for the Evangelization of Peoples; Edward Pironio, president of the Pontifical Commission of the Laity; Bernadin Gantin, prefect of the Congregation of Bishops; Edouard Gagnone, president of the Pontifical Commission for the Family; Antonio Innocenti, prefect of the Congregation of the Clergy; D. Simon Lourdusamy, prefect of the Congregation for Oriental Churches; and William Baum, prefect for the Congregation for Catholic Education.

51. Patrick Peyton, CSC, Memorandum, n.d. [1989], The Rosary File, AALA.

52. Patrick Peyton, CSC, A Plan to Carry the Family Rosary Crusade Message into the 21st Century and Beyond, n.d. [1989], 06–02, Patrick Peyton Papers; Progress Report, March 12, 1989, 10–01, Publications, AHCFM.

53. Statement of the Mexican Hierarchy, October 19, 1989, 10–01, Publications, AHCFM.

54. Testimonies Regarding the Family Rosary Crusade and the Handbook, n.d. [1989], 05–01, Correspondence, Farrell, AHCFM; Archbishop Roger Mahoney to Stephen Blaine, December 4, 1988, The Rosary File, AALA.

55. Donald Montrose to Patrick Peyton, CSC, May 16, 1988, 06–02, Patrick Peyton Papers, AHCFM.

56. Golden Jubilee Pamphlet, 1942–92, 06–04, Patrick Peyton Papers, AHCFM.

57. Albert Heinzer, CSC, to Allan S. Rupley, April 17, 1982, 09–02, Family Theater Papers; Heinzer, "Outdoor and TV Spot Campaign," 09–13, Family Theater Papers, AHCFM.

58. Martin J. Neeb to Albert Heinzer, CSC, April 9, 1985, 507.60, Family Rosary Papers, AHCFE.

59. Meeting Minutes, Board of Directors of Family Rosary, Inc., April 28, 1992, 05–01, Correspondence, Farrell, AHCFM.

60. Patrick Peyton, CSC, Documentation on the Relationship Between the Family Rosary Crusade and Families for Prayer, March 3, 1990, 507.75, Family Rosary Papers, AHCFE; Dorothy Halloran, Interview with James FitzPatrick, September 30, 1997, AHCFM.

61. Meeting Minutes of Combined Boards of the Crusade for Family Prayer, Family Rosary, and Family Theater, June 13, 1980, 507.91, Family Rosary Papers, AHCFE; Contract, May 1983, 10–03, Publications, AHCFM.

62. Proclamation, January 9, 1984, 06–08, Patrick Peyton Papers, AHCFM.

63. News Release, n.d. [October 1989], 06–04, Patrick Peyton Papers, AHCFM. The citation read: "Father Peyton, you have heeded the challenge, and continue to do what He tells you. She has let you become her instrument. She is proud of the way in which you and the Family Rosary Crusade have integrated theology, spirituality, and the evangelization apostolate." See Award Citation, October 6, 1989, 05–01, Correspondence, Farrell, AHCFM.

64. Dennis Roverato, Interview with Thomas Feeley, CSC, October 28, 1998, AHCFM.

65. John Gurley died at age fifty of a heart attack on March 4, 1990, only a few months after the dissolution of Families for Prayer.

66. Joseph Callahan, CSC, to "USA Provincials," Memorandum, May 24, 1983, 310.6.178, Provincial Papers, Callahan, AHCFE.

67. Patrick Peyton, CSC, to Peter Grace, June 15, 1984, 507.189, Family Rosary Papers, AHCFE.

68. Sr. M. Gerald Hartney, CSC, to Patrick Peyton, CSC, February 19, 1990, 05–01, Correspondence, Farrell, AHCFM.

69. Sr. M. Gerald Hartney, CSC, to David Farrell, CSC, October 26, 1990, 05–01, Correspondence, Farrell; Hartney, Interview with Thomas Feeley, CSC, June 16, 1999, AHCFM.

70. Hartney's recommendation was for the two New York–based corporations — the Crusade for Family Prayer and Family Rosary, Inc. — to become one entity.

71. Sr. M. Gerald Hartney, CSC, "Rationale for Restructuring the Corporations of Family Rosary," June 1, 1990, 05–01, Correspondence, Farrell, AHCFM.

72. Ibid.

73. Claude Grou, CSC, to Patrick Peyton, CSC, April 19, 1990, Patrick Peyton Personnel File, AHCG; Family Rosary, Inc., Corporate Structure, July 1991,

507.190, Family Rosary Papers, AHCFE. The reconstituted boards were: (1) Corporate Board: President, Patrick Peyton, CSC; Members, Claude Grou, CSC, David Farrell, CSC, Richard Warner, CSC, Sr. Gerald Hartney, CSC, J. Peter Grace, and J. P. Bolduc; (2) Family Rosary Board of Directors: Honorary Chairman, Patrick Peyton, CSC, President; David Farrell, CSC; Members, George DePrizio, CSC, Thomas Doyle, Paul Pagnucci, Rev. Kevin Farrell, Jacquelyn Norris; (3) Family Theater Board of Directors: Honorary Chairman, Patrick Peyton, CSC; President, David Farrell, CSC; Members, J. Frank Marias Sr., Gerald Hartney, CSC, Albert Heinzer, CSC, Bob Smith, Carl Karcher, Dr. Charles Miller, and Mary Jane McQueen.

74. Claude Grou, CSC, to Patrick Peyton, CSC, April 19, 1990, Patrick Peyton Personnel File, AHCG.

75. Patrick Peyton, CSC, to Mary Buckley, RSM, Feast of the Visitation [1981], 05–01, Correspondence, Buckley, AHCFM. Peyton lauded Buckley's contribution to his ministry on numerous occasions. Another typical comment was, "You are the greatest. Our Lady knows this. You have measured your love for Her and for the Family Rosary with your life." See Peyton to Buckley, May 21, 1980, 05–01, Correspondence, Buckley, AHCFM.

76. Patrick Peyton, CSC, "Christmas Newsletter," 1991, 06–04, Patrick Peyton Papers, AHCFM; *Eastern Province Bulletin,* February 1992, AHCG.

77. News Release, June 3, 1992; Minutes, Corporation Members, Family Rosary, Inc., June 15, 1992, 05–01, Correspondence, Farrell, AHCFM; Dennis Roverato, Interview with author, August 9, 2000.

78. News Release, December 23, 1991; Patrick Peyton, CSC, to Dear _____ (General Letter), Easter 1992, 05–01, Correspondence, Farrell, AHCFM.

79. News Release, December 22, 1992, 05–01, Correspondence, Farrell, AHCFM.

80. Fiftieth Anniversary Booklet, 1997, FTH.

81. Pope John Paul II to Patrick Peyton, CSC, February 11, 1992, 06–02, Patrick Peyton Papers, AHCFM.

82. Jack Wintz, OFM, "Family Theater at 50: Father Patrick Peyton Remembered," *St. Anthony Messenger* 105, no. 1 (June 1997): 17. It should be noted that in 1996 Peyton was posthumously recognized by UNDA-USA, the National Association of Catholic Broadcasters, receiving its Gabriel Award for Personal Achievement. The citation acknowledged him as "a pioneer in producing radio and TV programs to uplift the human spirit."

83. News clipping, n.d. [1991], 06–04, Patrick Peyton Papers; News Release, June 3, 1992, 05–01, Correspondence, Farrell; Dorothy Halloran to Justin Joos, OFM Cap., October 13, 1992, 08–05, Headquarters, Albany, AHCFM. Bishops sent numerous requests to Family Rosary in Albany for more rosaries even after they had received a shipment. One such appeal from Jura Jezerinac, auxiliary bishop of Zagreb, Yugoslavia, is illustrative: "Presently there is a great need for the rosaries. Till now we have distributed approximately 250,000. And still there is a need for more." See John Griswold to Robert Klein, October 26, 1992, 05–01, Farrell Correspondence, AHCFM.

84. Kermit Pins, M.D., to Patrick Peyton, CSC, January 13, 1988, 06–08, Patrick Peyton Papers; Mary Jane Buchenau McQueen, Interview with Thomas Feeley, November 1998; Sr. Mary Anthony, "Last Days of Fr. Patrick Peyton," n.d.

[1992], 09–15, Family Theater Papers, AHCFM; *Eastern Province Bulletin,* January 1992, AHCG.

85. Archbishop John P. Foley, Statement, June 4, 1992; Claude Grou, CSC, Message of the Superior General of the Death of Father Patrick Peyton, CSC, Peyton Personnel File, AHCG.

86. William Ribando, CSC, Interview with Thomas Feeley, CSC, June 4, 1999, AHCFM.

Epilogue

1. Quoted in Mary Ann Walsh, "Father Patrick Peyton," *Our Sunday Visitor Magazine* 71 (May 30, 1982): 10; Patrick Peyton, CSC, Spiritual Journal, November 23, 1967, 09–17, Family Theater Papers, AHCFM.

2. Patrick Peyton, CSC, Speech at Nazareth, May 24, 1971, 01–18, Crusades, Honduras, AHCFM.

3. Patrick Peyton, CSC, Memorabilia, General, 06–07, Patrick Peyton Papers, AHCFM.

4. Patrick Peyton, CSC, Spiritual Journal, November 23, 1967, 09–17, Family Theater Papers, AHCFM. Peyton once wrote: "It [*sic*] could say a thousand times over: that the Family Rosary Crusade personnel will be effective instruments for Her wishes and will and service, to the degree that they find their happiness with Her and their compensation in praying to Her and spending their time filled with an awareness of Her personality and Her warm friendship for service and love and affection." See Patrick Peyton, CSC, to Denis Sughrue, CSC, May 25, 1959, 05–01, Correspondence, Sughrue, AHCFM.

5. Patrick Peyton, CSC, Memorandum, July 24, 1958, 02–04, Offices, Europe, AHCFM; Peyton, "Reflections on the Family Rosary Crusade," January 27, 1980, PPC, Attymass, County Mayo, Ireland. The same idea is expressed in a letter to John Gurley, CSC: "I always beg Our Lady to be the one responsible for the direction of the Crusade, to be its leader, to be its decision maker, to select its priorities and to choose its options." See Peyton to Gurley, Memorandum, December 14, 1976, 07–01, Families for Prayer, AHCFM.

6. Patrick Peyton, CSC, Spiritual Journal, November 24, 1967, 09–17, Family Theater Papers, AHCFM; quoted in "Family Rosary and Prayer Crusades," n.d., 428 (FR) 0, AHCG. One example of how Peyton prayed to Mary to intercede and make things happen is: "I need you now to win two hundred TV stations for The Prince of Peace Series. Please pray for this intention to be realized. It must be done. Please Mary do it.... Please do it, dearest Mary. I need your prayers for this."

7. Patrick Peyton, CSC, to John Murphy, CSC, July 14, 1956, 05–01, Correspondence, Thomas Sullivan, AHCFM.

8. Patrick Peyton, CSC, to Jerome Lawyer, CSC, June 14, 1952, 05-01, Correspondence, Lawyer, AHCFM.

9. Joseph Quinn, CSC, Interview with Thomas Feeley, CSC, March 16, 1999, AHCFM. George DePrizio in his funeral oration quoted Peyton, "Total surrender to Mary is the secret of my happiness, my security. It will be yours, too, if you ask Her." George DePrizio, CSC, Homily, June 8, 1992, 09–15, Family Theater Papers, AHCFM.

10. Sister Marie Anne, LSP, Interview with Thomas Feeley, CSC, November 3, 1998, AHCFM.

11. John Murphy, CSC, Homily, June 7, 1992, 09–15, Family Theater Papers, AHCFM. Another longtime colleague on the crusade, Joseph Quinn, CSC, held a similar view: "He [Peyton] was certainly secure in his belief that he had been blessed by our Blessed Mother with a miracle. He was also secure in his belief that this apostolate had begun through our Blessed Mother, and all his successes made him even more convinced that his work was the will of God and of our Blessed Mother for him and for the needs of the people throughout the world." See Joseph Quinn, Interview with Thomas Feeley, CSC, March 16, 1999, AHCFM.

12. James McCardle to James Connerton, CSC, February 6, 1956, 507.09, Family Rosary Papers, AHCFM.

13. Loretta Young, Interview with James FitzPatrick, OMI, and Thomas Feeley, CSC, November 13, 1998, AHCFM.

14. Francis Grogan, CSC, Interview with Thomas Feeley, CSC, June 2, 1999, AHCFM.

15. Patrick Peyton, CSC, Sermon, n.d. [1946], 09–17, Family Theater Papers, AHCFM. Joan Wiener, another close friend of Peyton over the years, commented, "It [Peyton's spirituality] was never devotion to Mary alone. It was always, 'Mary will bring us to her Son.' Everything he said or did focused on that." See Joan Wiener, Interview with Thomas Feeley, CSC, September 10, 1998, AHCFM.

16. Patrick Peyton, CSC, to Mr. and Mrs. Michael McCable, March 15, 1966, 09–17, Family Theater Papers, AHCFM.

17. Patrick Peyton, CSC, "40 Hours Devotion," Sermon, n.d. [1944], 09–17, Family Theater Papers, AHCFM.

18. Patrick Peyton, CSC, "Thoughts on Prayer," n.d., 09–17, Family Theater Papers, AHCFM.

19. Comment of Father Dacian Dee, OFM, Cap. Quoted in Jeanne Arnold, *Man of Faith* (Hollywood, Calif: Family Theater, Inc., 1983), 245.

20. Robert Smith, Interview with James FitzPatrick, OMI, and Thomas Feeley, CSC, November 18, 1998; Sr. Mary Anthony, LSP, Interview with Thomas Feeley, CSC, June 15, 1999, AHCFM.

21. Patrick Peyton, CSC, Quotes from Speeches (Collected), 06–09, Patrick Peyton Papers; Peyton, "Thoughts on the Rosary," 09–17, Family Theater Papers, AHCFM.

22. Patrick Peyton, CSC, "Reflections on the Family Rosary," Reprint from *Our Family,* found in Patrick Peyton Personnel File, AHCFE.

23. Patrick Peyton, CSC, "The Family Rosary Crusade," Presentation to Thomas Barrosse, CSC, n.d. [1980], 428 (FR) 12, AHCG; "A Crusading Priest Puts His Message on the Screen, *Chicago Tribune,* September 20, 1975, clipping found in 09–01, Family Theater Papers, AHCFM.

24. Patrick Peyton, CSC, Untitled Crusade Talk, 01–26, Crusades, New York, AHCFM.

25. Patrick Peyton, CSC, "Reflections on the Family Rosary," Reprint from *Our Family,* found in Patrick Peyton Personnel File, AHCFE.

26. Patrick Peyton, CSC, "Family Rosary Crusade," *Homiletic and Pastoral Review* 43 (May 1943): 715.

27. Patrick Peyton, CSC, "Reflections on the Family Rosary," Reprint from *Our Family,* found in Patrick Peyton Personnel File; Peyton, Untitled Essay, n.d. [1948], 01–13, Crusades, Canada, AHCFE.

28. Peyton's more ecumenical spirit is most evident after Vatican II, but there is evidence that he possessed this basic view on prayer at a much earlier date. In a radio interview in June 1950 he stated, "Everyone has his or her favorite prayers. If a family is of the Protestant faith or the Jewish faith, they should pray together too, using the prayers that they feel are best suited for them." See Patrick Peyton, Radio Interview, June 23, 1950, 09–17, Family Theater Papers, AHCFM.

29. Quoted in Francis Grogan, CSC, Interview with Thomas Feeley, CSC, June 2, 1999, AHCFM.

30. Frank Fahey, Interview with Michael Heraghty, July 19, 1993, PPC, Attymass, County Mayo, Ireland.

31. Joseph Quinn, CSC, Interview with Thomas Feeley, CSC, March 16, 1999, AHCFM.

32. William Ribando, CSC, Interview with author, February 23, 2001.

33. James Mannis, CSC, Interview with Thomas Feeley, CSC, June 3, 1999; John Murphy, CSC, Homily, June 7, 1992, 09–15, Family Theater Papers, AHCFM.

34. Kenneth D. Chisholm to Patrick Peyton, CSC, November 7, 1969, 05–01, Correspondence, Rioux, AHCFM.

35. Patrick Peyton, CSC, Memorandum, n.d. [1980], 07–02, Families for Prayer, AHCFM.

36. Dorothy Halloran, Interview with Thomas Feeley, CSC, September 2, 1998, AHCFM.

37. Dennis Roverato, Interview with author, August 9, 2000; John Murphy, CSC, Interview with Thomas Feeley, CSC, June 3, 1999, AHCFM.

38. Ann Blyth, Interview with James FitzPatrick, OMI, and Thomas Feeley, CSC, November 14, 1998.

39. The superior general, Germain Lalande, CSC, as one example of support for Peyton wrote to the Eastern Priests' provincial, George DePrizio, CSC: "I thank God for the good He chooses to accomplish through the instrumentality of Father Peyton. In these decades Father Peyton is to your Province and the Congregation as a whole what, in his time, Brother Andre was to Holy Cross in Canada and to the whole Congregation. These are men whose message and influence escape geographical bounds." Quoted in Provincial Office Bulletin, February 2, 1963, AHCG.

40. John Murphy, CSC, Interview with Thomas Feeley, CSC, June 3, 1999, AHCFM.

41. Mary Jane Buchenau McQueen, Interview with Thomas Feeley, CSC, November 1998, AHCFM.

42. Dorothy Halloran, Interview with Thomas Feeley, CSC, September 2, 1998; Dennis Roverato, Interview with Thomas Feeley, CSC, October 28, 1998, AHCFM.

43. Ann Blyth, Interview with James FitzPatrick, OMI, and Thomas Feeley, CSC, November 14, 1998, AHCFM; Dennis Roverato, Interview with author, August 9, 2000.

44. Margaret O'Brien, Interview with James FitzPatrick, OMI, and Thomas Feeley, CSC, November 16, 1998; Dennis Roverato, Interview with Feeley, October 28, 1998, AHCFM.

45. Dorothy Halloran, Interview with Thomas Feeley, CSC, September 2, 1998, AHCFM.

46. Ibid.; Joan Wiener, Interview with Thomas Feeley, CSC, September 10, 1998, AHCFM.

47. Group Interview with author, June 3, 2000, PPC, Attymass, County Mayo, Ireland. Peyton's ability to command attention was illustrated by one story. Once he was invited to speak in the ballroom of a major Dublin hotel. People were milling about and speaking softly as others gave speeches from the rostrum, but as soon as Peyton rose to speak an eerie silence descended upon the assembled group. People wanted to hear a man whom they perceived to fervently believe what he was saying.

48. Dennis Roverato, Interview with Thomas Feeley, CSC, October 28, 1998, AHCFM.

49. Ibid.

50. Gigi Perreau, Interview with James FitzPatrick, OMI, and Thomas Feeley, CSC, November 15, 1998, AHCFM.

51. Timothy McCarthy, "How Father Peyton Got the Rosary to Fly," *Catholic Digest* 58 (October 1994): 60.

52. Joseph Campanella, Interview with Thomas Feeley, CSC, November 10, 1998, AHCFM.

53. Quoted in Provincial Office Bulletin, February 2, 1963, AHCG.

54. Gigi Perreau, Interview with James FitzPatrick, OMI, and Thomas Feeley, CSC, November 15, 1998, AHCFM.

55. Anecdotes, 06–03, Patrick Peyton Papers, AHCFM.

56. Joseph Campanella, Interview with Thomas Feeley, CSC, November 10, 1998; Patrick Peyton, CSC, Audio Tape, AHCFM.

Bibliography

Primary Sources

Archival Sources

AALA   Archives Archdiocese of Los Angeles, San Fernando, California
Family Rosary Papers

AASF   Archives Archdiocese of San Francisco, Menlo Park, California
Rosary Rally San Francisco 1961 Papers

ACUA   Archives The Catholic University of America, Washington, D.C.
National Catholic Welfare Conference Papers

ADA   Archives Diocese of Albany, Albany, New York
Family Rosary Papers

AHCFE   Archives Holy Cross Fathers Eastern Province, North Easton, Massachusetts

     Family Rosary Papers, Provincial Papers for James Connerton, CSC, George DePrizio, CSC, Richard Sullivan, CSC, William Hogan, CSC, William Ribando, CSC, Joseph Callahan, CSC, and David Farrell, CSC, Provincial Council Papers, Provincial Chapter Papers, Families for Prayer

AHCFI   Archives Holy Cross Fathers Indiana Province, Notre Dame, Indiana

     Family Rosary Papers; Provincial Papers of Thomas Steiner, CSC

AHCFM   Archives Holy Cross Family Ministries, North Easton, Massachusetts

     Crusades, Offices, Corporation, Development, Administration (Correspondence), Patrick Peyton Papers, Families for Prayer, Worldwide Headquarters, Family Theater

AHCG   Archives Holy Cross Generalate, Rome, Italy

     Family Rosary Papers; Patrick Peyton Papers; Correspondence Files of Superior General with James Connerton, CSC, George DePrizio, CSC, Richard Sullivan, CSC, William Hogan, CSC, William Ribando, CSC, Joseph Callahan, CSC, and David Farrell, CSC

AUND   Archives of the University of Notre Dame, Notre Dame, Indiana

FTH   Archives Family Theater, Hollywood, Calif. (Records now have been transferred to Archives of Holy Cross Family Ministries, North Easton, Massachusetts)

               Family Theater of the Air Papers

NAPB   National Archives Pacific Branch, Laguna Niguel, California

               Richard Nixon, Pre-Presidential Papers

PPC   Patrick Peyton Centre, Attymass, County Mayo, Ireland

               Uncatalogued material in file cabinets

Books and Articles

Peyton, Patrick, CSC. *All for Her.* Hollywood, Calif. Family Theater Publications, 1967.

———. *The Ear of God.* Garden City, N.Y.: Doubleday, 1951.

———. "Ear of God — Excerpt with Title: Father Peyton's First Program." *Catholic Digest* 15 (June 1951): 25–28.

———. *Family Prayer.* New York: Benziger Brothers, Inc., 1964.

———. "Family Rosary." *Catholic Charities Review* 27 (December 1943): 285–91.

———. "The Family Rosary." *St. Joseph Magazine* (July 1956): ii–viii, 55.

———. "The Family Rosary Circle." *St. Joseph Magazine* (September 1956): ii–iii, 52–53.

———. "Family Rosary Crusade." *Homiletic and Pastoral Review* 43 (May 1943): 713–17.

———. "Family Theater of the Air: Photographs." *Catholic Digest* 13 (June 1949): 97–112.

———. "Father Peyton and Family Theater." *Catholic School Journal* 47 (September 1947): 40a–41a.

———. "Father Peyton's First Program." *Catholic Digest* 15 (June 1951): 25–28.

———. "Father Peyton's Own Story." *The Messenger of the Sacred Heart* 83 (5) (May 1948): 16–24.

———. "Fiesta of Stars." *Catholic Digest* 15 (August 1951): 97–102.

———. "First Family Christmas." *Ave Maria* 74 (November 24, 1951): 661.

———. "I Talked to Mary." *Extension* 43 (June 1948): 10–11.

———. "The Meaning of the Rosary." *Catholic Layman* 79 (December 1965): 26–28.

———. "Mine Was a Happy Home." *Our Lady's Digest* 21 (October 1956): 123–30.

———. "Report on the Family Rosary." *Homiletic and Pastoral Review* 44 (January 1944): 300–02.

Secondary Sources

Adolorata, Sister M. "Family Rosary School Play." *Catholic School Journal* 47 (October 1947): 288–89.

Agee, Philip. *Inside the Company: CIA Diary.* New York: Bantam Books, 1976.

Alexander, Robert Jackson. *Communism in Latin America*. New Brunswick, N.J.: Rutgers University Press, 1957.

Allitt, Patrick. *Catholic Intellectuals and Conservative Politics in America 1950–1985*. Ithaca, N.Y.: Cornell University Press, 1993.

Alter, Karl J. "Restoring the Family Circle." *Catholic Mind* 49 (August 1951): 476–82.

"American Catholics: Just Who Do You Think You Are?" Interview with David O'Brien. *U.S. Catholic* 46 (April 1981): 6–11.

"Apostolate of the Air: Catholic Programs in the United States." *Missionary* 45 (March 1931): 86–88.

Arnold, Jeanne Gosselin. *A Man of Faith*. Hollywood, Calif.: Family Theater, Inc., 1983.

Baldwin, Robert F. "The Rosary Priest." *Our Sunday Visitor* 80 (August 11, 1991): 5.

Belloc, Hilaire. "Family as a Unit." *Sign* 18 (April 1938): 21–22.

Bemis, Samuel I. "Way to Stop the Reds in Latin America." *U.S. News & World Report* 47 (December 28, 1959): 77–80.

Berger, Florence S. "The Psalms and Family Prayer." *North American Liturgical Week Proceedings* 22 (1961): 192 96.

Berle, Adolf A. "Alliance for Progress vs. Communism: Remarks, April 24, 1961." *United States Department of State Bulletin* 44 (May 22, 1961): 763–64.

Bernardin, Joseph. "Spirituality and the Catholic Church in America." *Chicago Studies* 15 (Spring 1976): 5–11.

Blackwell, John C. "The Hispanic Presence." *Homiletic and Pastoral Review* 85 (December 1984): 28–32.

Blum, William. *Killing Hope: U.S. Military and C.I.A. Interventions since World War II*. Monroe, Mich.: Common Courage Press, 1995.

Blunt, H. F. *Mary's Garden of Roses*. New York: P. J. Kenedy and Sons, 1939.

Bonnet, Theodore. "Father Peyton and God." *Family Digest* 8 (January 1953): 16–17.

Bourgeois, Lawrence L. "Keeping the Family Together." *Grail* 39 (November 1957): 41–46.

Breig, James P. "Catholic Productions on ABC a First for the Church." *Our Sunday Visitor* 73 (March 24, 1985): 19.

Breig, Joseph. "Combating Communism." *Catholic Mind* 60 (April 1962): 28–30.

———. "Father Peyton: 25 Years After." *Ave Maria* 103 (May 28, 1966): 30.

———. *Life With My Mary*. Milwaukee: Bruce Publishing Company, 1955.

Brophy, Liam. "Modern Assaults on the Family: Where Secularist Planners and Marxists Are at One." *Social Justice Review* 53 (September 1960): 148–50.

Burghardt, Walter. "American Church and American Theology: Response to an Identity Crisis." *Catholic Theological Society of America Proceedings* 28 (1973): 1–14.

"Burning Question: Spiritual and Social Fortification of the Home." *Catholic Charities Review* 28 (November 1944): 247.

Burns, Jeffrey M. *American Catholics and the Family Crisis, 1930–1962*. New York: Garland Publishing, 1988.

Byrnes, L. M. "Bringing the Family Back to Christ." *National Catholic Education Association Proceedings* (1944): 284–88.

Cabell, C. P. "U.S. Intelligence: Principal Forces upon International Communism." *Vital Speeches of the Day* 25 (November 1, 1958): 60–62.

Callahan, William R. "Lifestyle of the American Catholic Church." *New Catholic World* 216 (January–February 1973): 33–37.

Carol, Juniper B. *Mariology,* 3 vol. Milwaukee: Bruce Publishing Company, 1961.

Carroll, Patrick J., CSC. Editorial. *Ave Maria* 70 (October 1, 1949): 422.

————. Editorial. *Ave Maria* 67 (May 29, 1948): 678.

Cassel, Raymond J. "My Favorite Priest: Father Patrick Peyton, CSC." *Homiletic and Pastoral Review* 93 (October 1992): 70–71.

Cassidy, J. F. *The Old Irish Love of the Blessed Virgin Mary.* Dublin: M. H. Gill and Son, 1933.

"Catching Fire: President Kennedy's Three-Day Visit." *Time* 78 (December 29, 1961): 21.

"Catholic Broadcasters Meet at Fordham, August 16–17, 1947." *Catholic Action* 29 (September 1947): 13.

"The Catholic Church in the United States Today." *Catholic Mind* 72 (November 1974): 9–16.

"The Catholic Hour: Cream to Walsh." *Sign* 40 (September 1960): 28–30.

"Catholic Hour to Inaugurate Unusual Series on the Rosary." *Catholic Action* 20 (October 1938): 5.

"Catholic Hour: TV Success." *America* 102 (November 7, 1959): 145.

"CBA Charter Convention." *America* 79 (July 17, 1948): 339.

Cheadle, P. "Experience in Family Spirituality." *Torch* 43 (November 1959): 16–19.

Chesterton, G. K. "Three Foes of the Family (Capitalism, Communism, and Fascism)." *G.K.'s Weekly* 19 (August 2, 1934): 344–45.

Chinnici, Joseph, OFM. "The Catholic Community at Prayer, 1926–1976." Working Paper Presented at the Cushwa Center for the Study of American Catholicism, University of Notre Dame, April 2000.

————. *Living Stones: The History and Structure of Catholic Spiritual Life in the United States.* New York: Macmillan, 1989.

————. "The Organization of the Spiritual Life: American Catholic Devotional Works, 1791–1866." *Theological Studies* 40 (June 1979): 229–55.

Chinnici, Joseph, OFM, and Angelyn Dries, eds. *Prayer and Practice in the Catholic Community.* Maryknoll, N.Y.: Orbis Books, 2000.

"The Christian Family: A Statement of the American Hierarchy," November 21, 1949. *Catholic Mind* 48 (1950): 124.

"The Christian Family Today." *Furrow* 35 (June 1984): 402–05.

"C.I.A. Recruitment and the Church." *Christian Century* 113, no. 9 (March 13, 1996): 285–86.

Clark, Denis J. "The Irish Catholics: A Postponed Perspective" in Randall M. Miller and Thomas D. Marzik, eds. *Immigrants and Religion in Urban America.* Philadelphia: Temple University Press, 1977.

Clark, E. C. "Radio and Television Are Your Business." *Catholic School Review* 58 (November 1958): 60–64.

Coffey, Mary Kean. "Beading a Path Down the Interstate." *Liguorian* 81 (July 1993): 26–27.

Cogley, John. "Two Fronts in the Same War." *Commonweal* 70 (September 18, 1959): 516.

Coleman, John A., SJ. "American Bicentennial, Catholic Crisis." *America* 134 (June 26, 1976): 551–56.

Collins, Mary, OSB. "Liturgical Methodology and the Cultural Evolution of Worship in the United States." *Worship* 49 (February 1975): 85–102.

"A Complex Task." *Commonweal* 72 (May 13, 1960): 163–64.

"Communist Threat to Latin America." *The Shield* 43 (October–November 1963): 11–13.

Concannon, Helena Walsh. *The Queen of Ireland.* Dublin: M. H. Gill and Son, 1938.

Connell, Francis J. "Rosary on the Radio: May Indulgences Be Gained?" *American Ecclesiastical Review* 125 (July 1951): 63–64.

Considine, John J., MM, "Mission to Latin America." *Perspectives* 6 (February 1961): 45–49.

———. "The Pope's Program for Latin America." *Catholic Association for International Peace (CAIP) News* 23 (June 1962): 1–6.

———. "The Struggle in Latin America." *Catholic Charities Review* 48 (January 1964): 23–28.

———. "Who Is Winning in Latin America?" *The Shield* 44 (December 1964– January 1965): 10–11, 30.

Cooke, Bernard J. "The Vatican and the U.S. Church." *America* 156 (October 18, 1986): 206–08.

Corish, Patrick J. *The Irish Catholic Experience.* Wilmington, Del.: Michael Glazier, 1985.

"Crusade in Latin America." *View* 26 (May 1962): 7–10.

Curran, Dolores. *Family Prayer.* Cincinnati: St. Anthony Messenger Press, 1983.

Curran, William, OP. "Rosary Today." *Dominicana* 21 (September 1936): 175–78.

Cushing, Richard J. "Christian Family Living." *Worship* 28 (December 1953): 7–15.

Daly, Mary T. "Family Rosary Does Fit In." *America* 84 (October 14, 1950): 45–48.

David, M. G. "Have No Fear, Mary, Our Mother Is Praying." *Praise* 4, no. 4 (1985): 6.

David, Sister M. "Family Rosary." *Catholic School Journal* 49 (May 1949): 170.

DeBlanc, Irving A. "Facts and Family Life." *Ave Maria* 83, no. 25 (June 23, 1956): 11–13, 29–30.

Deck, Allan Figueroa, SJ. *The Second Wave: Hispanic Ministry and the Evangelization of Cultures.* New York: Paulist Press, 1989.

"Defending Latin America." *Commonweal* 71 (March 18, 1960): 663–64.

DeFossa, Marie Louise and Jacques. "Family Prayer." *Lumen Vitae* 7 (April 1952): 221–26.

Dehne, Carl. "Roman Catholic Popular Devotions." *Worship* 49 (1975): 446–60.

de Kadt, Emanuel. *Catholic Radicals in Brazil.* London: Oxford University Press, 1970.

Delaney, John (Frederic Frars, pseudonym). "Sanctify the Family by the Family Retreat." *America* 71 (1944): 117–19.

DiCesare, Mario. "Father Thomas on the American Catholic Family." *Christian Family* 52 (December 1957): 28–30.

Dimock, Giles. "The Rosary: A Spirit-Filled Prayer." *New Covenant* 20 (May 1991): 15–16.

"Disintegration of the Family Today." *Ave Maria* 95 (April 28, 1962): 17.

Dolan, Jay P. "American Catholics and Modernity." *Cross Currents* 31 (Summer 1981): 150–62.

Donahue, Bernard, OSF. "Developing a Crisis Model of American Catholicism." *Jurist* 35 (Spring–Summer 1975): 323–34.

Donovan, Joseph P. "One Way of Restoring the Family: Devotion to the Eucharist." *Homiletic and Pastoral Review* 43 (December 1942): 256–59.

Dorsett, Lyle W. *Billy Sunday and the Redemption of Urban America.* Grand Rapids, Mich.: William B. Eerdmans, 1991.

Dorzweiler, Edwin, OFM Cap. "Prayer in the Home." *Catholic Home Journal* 50 (September 1950): 2.

Dougan, E. "The Christian Concept of Family Life." *Christus Rex* 14 (April 1960): 75–91.

"Doyles' Family Rosary." *Ave Maria* 71 (May 6, 1950): 549.

Dries, Angelyn. *The Missionary Movement in American Catholic History.* Maryknoll, N.Y.: Orbis Books, 1998.

Dulles, Allen W. "Analysis of Communist Techniques for Conquest: Address, August 9, 1962." *Vital Speeches of the Day* 28 (October 1, 1962): 743–47.

Dulles, Avery, SJ. *"Sensus Fidelium."* *America* 155 (November 1, 1986): 240–42, 263.

Ebel, John B. "Christian Home — A Little Church." *Orate Fratres* 21 (September 7, 1947): 445–51.

Eberhardt, A. B. "Are Our Homes Truly Catholic?" *Ave Maria* 54 (December 27, 1941): 807–09.

Egan, John. "The Leadership Role of the Roman Catholic Church in Pluralistic America." *Catholic Mind* 78 (April 1980): 23–32.

Ellard, Gerald, SJ. "The American Scene, 1926–1951." *Orate Fratres* 25 (October 1951): 500–08.

Ellis, John Tracy. "American Catholicism, 1953–1979: A Notable Change." *Thought* 54 (June 1979): 113–31.

"Establishment of Catholic Radio Bureau Announced by National Council of Catholic Men." *Catholic Action* 20 (December 1938): 15.

"Evaluating Graham." *Newsweek* 39 (April 28, 1952): 84–85.

"Families in Crisis." *America* 108 (January 12, 1963): 32–33.

"Family Crusade: Salvatorian Crusade for Catholic Family Life." *Clergy Review* 32 (October 1949): 287–88.

"Family and the Home." *America* 71 (May 6, 1944): 126–27.

Family Life Bureau, NCWC. "The Family Life Bureau of the NCWC: Its Origins, Functions, and Purposes." Washington, D.C.: NCWC, 1947.

"Family Rosary." *America* 74 (October 6, 1945): 15.

"Family Rosary." *Ave Maria* 58 (October 23, 1943): 514.

"Family Rosary." *Catholic Charities Review* 27 (June 1943): 166–67.

"Family Rosary." *Catholic Charities Review* 29 (June 1945): 162.

"Family Rosary." *Catholic Educational Review* 41 (November 1943): 561–62.

"Family Rosary." *Catholic Worker* 10 (November 1943): 4.

"Family Rosary Crusade." *America* 87 (September 27, 1952): 603.

"Family Rosary Crusade." *Tablet* 199 (April 19, 1952): 318.

"Family Rosary: Dialogue for Senior Girls." *Sower* 185 (October 1952): 94–99.

"Family Rosary for Victory." *Ave Maria* 57 (March 6, 1943): 290.

"Father Peyton's Crusade." *America* 86 (February 16, 1952): 519.

"Fr. Peyton Captures England." *Ave Maria* 75 (June 21, 1952): 771–72.

"Father Patrick Peyton... A Modern Apostle." *The Oratory* (February 1956): 7–9.

"Father Peyton and Family Theater." *Catholic School Journal* 47 (September 1947): 40a–41a.

"Father Peyton Marches On." *Ave Maria* 74 (November 3, 1951): 548.

"Father Peyton's Rosary Stars." *Ave Maria* 69 (May 7, 1949): 578.

Faupel, Luke, OFM. "Catholics and Broadcasting." *Christus Rex* 19 (January–March 1968): 10–17.

Felix, Robert H. "The Family in the Twentieth Century." *Catholic Charities Review* 50 (June 1966): 6–14.

Fennell, Desmond. "The Myth of the Irish: A Failure of American Catholic Scholarship." In *The Changing Face of Catholic Ireland,* ed. Desmond Fennell, 121–34. London: Geoffrey Chapman, 1968.

Findlay, James F. *Dwight L. Moody, American Evangelist, 1837–1899.* Chicago: University of Chicago Press, 1969.

Fisher, James T. *The Catholic Counterculture in America, 1933–62.* Chapel Hill: University of North Carolina Press, 1989.

———. *Dr. America: The Lives of Thomas A. Dooley, 1927–1961.* Amherst: University of Massachusetts Press, 1997.

Fitzpatrick, J. "Why Your Family Should Pray." *Liguorian* 52 (October 1964): 22–27.

Flores, Patrick. "The Opportunity Hispanics Provide for the Church." *Origins* 10 (September 11, 1980): 201–3.

Flynn, Thomas E. "Family Rosary Crusade in England." *American Ecclesiastical Review* 125 (September 1951): 161–65.

———. "Family Rosary Crusade: Father Peyton's Secret." *Clergy Review* 35 (May 1951): 289–93.

Fogarty, Gerald, SJ. "American Conciliar Legislation, Hierarchical Structure and Priest-Bishop Tension." *Jurist* 32 (Summer 1972): 400–409.

———. "Catholicism and American Culture." *Catholic Mind* 71 (January 1973): 12–18.

Fonseca, Jaime. "A Challenge to Catholics." *World Mission* 11 (September 1960): 15–31.

"For Family Prayer: Great Meeting in Wembley Stadium." *Tablet* 200 (August 2, 1952): 94.

Friedenberg, Daniel M. "Can the Alliance for Progress Work?" *Commentary* 34 (August 1962): 93–101.

Gallagher, Michael. "Catholicism in the Movies: Then and Now." *Columbia* 69 (June 1989): 10–12.

Gallagher, Tad. *The Adventures of Roberto Rossellini: His Life and Films.* New York: Da Capo Press, 1998.

Gallup, George G., Jr. "*U.S. Catholic* Polls George Gallup: Interview." *U.S. Catholic* 42 (October 1977): 28–32.

García, María de Los Angeles. "Hispanic-Americans: A Vital Presence within the American Church." *Catechist* 13 (April 1980): 42–43.

Garneau, James. " 'Commandos for Christ': The Foundation of the Missionary Society of St. James the Apostle and the Americanism of the 1950s and 1960s."
PhD dissertation: Catholic University of America, 2000.

Garnett, Sadie A. "Prayer or Poison?" *Catholic Home Journal* 48 (March 1948): 3.

Gartland, Frank, CSC. "Cardinal Cushing Backs Rosary Films." *Catholic Boy* 28,
no. 2 (October 1959): 15–18.

Gent, George. "Crisis for Religious Programs." *Sign* 44 (April 1965): 44–45.

Gillis, James M., CSP. *The Catholic Church and the Home.* New York: Macmillan,
1928.

———. "Radio and Religion." *Catholic World* 146 (October 1937): 88–93.

Gleason, Philip. "A Half-Century of Change in Catholic Higher Education." *U.S.
Catholic Historian* 19, no. 1 (Winter 2001): 1–19.

———. "In Search of Unity: American Catholic Thought, 1920–1960." *Catholic
Historical Review* 65 (1979): 185–205.

Goff, Philip. "We Have Heard the Joyful Sound: Charles E. Fuller's Radio Broadcast
and the Rise of Modern Evangelicalism." *Religion and American Culture* 9,
no. 1 (1999): 67–95.

Goodier, A. "Ireland: Today and Tomorrow." *Month* 159 (June 1932): 481–89.

Gordon, Michael, ed. *The Family in Social-Historical Perspective.* New York:
St. Martin's Press, 1977.

Grace, J. Peter. "Excerpt from Memorandum." *Congressional Digest* 42 (March
1963): 87, 89, 91.

———. "Great Challenge of Latin America: Address, May 23, 1963." *Vital Speeches
of the Day* 29 (August 1, 1963): 613–16.

———. "It's Not Too Late in Latin America: Proposals for Action Now." Privately
published pamphlet, 1961.

———. "United States Business Responds." *Annals of the American Academy of
Political and Social Science* 334 (March 1961): 143–47.

Greeley, Andrew. "Changing Styles of Catholic Spirituality." *Homiletic and Pastoral
Review* 67 (April 1967): 557–65.

———. "Popular Devotions: Friend or Foe?" *Worship* 33 (October 1959): 569–73.

Gross, Leonard. "The Catholic Church in Latin America: Its Poverty, Its Timidity,
Its Failures, Its New Reformers." *Look* 26, no. 2 (October 9, 1962): 27–35.

Halberstadt, Walter. "How to Make the Rosary a Family Affair." *Liguorian* 69
(October 1981): 10–13.

Hall, Clarence. "The Country That Saved Itself." Special Feature. *Readers' Digest*
(November 1, 1964): 1–24.

Halperin, E. "Decline of Communism in Latin America." *Atlantic* 215 (May 1965):
65–70.

Harrington, Bruce. "Report on Radio." *Ave Maria* 89 (January 17, 1959): 24–26.

Haynes, Renee. "Family, the Pivot." *Blackfriars* 23 (May 1942): 184–89.

Heale, Michael J. *American Anticommunism: Combating the Enemy Within, 1830–
1970.* Baltimore: Johns Hopkins University Press, 1990.

Heffron, Edward J. "Threat to Religious Broadcasting." *America* 84 (February 3,
1951): 117–19.

Hennesey, James, SJ. "Square Peg in a Round Hole: On Being Roman Catholic in
America." 84 (December 1973): 167–95.

Henry, H. T. "Rosary." *Homiletic and Pastoral Review* 39 (October 1938): 3–11.

Higgins, Philip, CSC, and Arthur McCormack. "Millions for Mary: Family Rosary Crusade in Latin America." *St. Joseph Magazine* 65 (October 1964): 30–34.

Hoffman, Ronan, OFM. "Latin America: The Church Meets the Challenge of Change." *Catholic World* 197 (June 1963): 164–71.

———. "SOS for Latin America." *Homiletic and Pastoral Review* 61 (July 1961): 965–70.

"Hollywood Triumphant Hour: Father Peyton's Family Rosary Hour." *Ave Maria* 71 (April 27, 1950): 485.

Hoover, J. Edgar. "American Freedom's Champion: Address, October 18, 1960." *Vital Speeches of the Day* 27 (January 15, 1961): 197–200.

———. "The Home: Bulwark against Communism." *Family Digest* 19 (December 1963): 5–9.

"Hoover Urges Family Prayer." *Ave Maria* 67 (January 27, 1948): 133.

Horowitz, Irving L. "Michigan State and the C.I.A.: A Dilemma for Social Science." *Bulletin of the Atomic Sciences* 22 (September 1966): 26–29.

"How to Help Latin America." *Christian Century* 78 (May 24, 1961): 643–44.

Huber, M. J. "How to Pray the Family Rosary." *Liguorian* 49 (May 1961): 45–50.

Hyde, Douglas. "Communism in Latin America." *World Justice* 4 (September 1962): 14–37.

Johnson, Jeanne Miriam, CSJ. "Education to the Family Rosary." MA thesis: Catholic University of America, 1950.

Johnson, Kathryn A. "A Question of Authority: Friction in the Catholic Family Movement, 1948–1962." *Catholic Historical Review* 86, no. 2 (April 2000): 217–41.

Johnson, Lyndon B. "Challenge of the Americas: Address, April 15, 1966." *Vital Speeches of the Day* 32 (May 1, 1966): 418–20.

Johnston, George S. "A Civilization of Love: Some Notes on John Paul II's Letter to Families." *Crisis* 12 (December 1994): 34–38.

Jones, Arthur. "Same Old C.I.A. Out to Fix Image." *National Catholic Reporter* (April 26, 1996): 1–5.

Joos, Jan. "Religious Television in 1968." *Christ to the World* 14, no. 4 (1969): 337–46.

Jorgensen, T. N., SJ. "Rosary and the Eucharist." *Review for Religious* 6 (May 15, 1947): 129–40.

"Joyful Hour Program." *Ave Maria* 69 (January 8, 1949): 35.

Juliana, L. "Our Family and the Rosary." *Family Digest* 13 (October 1957): 16–18.

Kalvoda, Josef. "Communist Strategy in Latin America." *Yale Review* 50 (September 1960): 32–41.

Kavanagh, Aidan, OSB. "Spirituality in the American Catholic Church: An Evaluative Essay." In *Contemporary Catholicism in the United States,* ed. Philip Gleason, 197–214. University of Notre Dame Press, 1969.

Keenan, Desmond J. *The Catholic Church in Nineteenth-Century Ireland: A Sociological Study.* Dublin: Gill and Macmillan, 1983.

Keiser, Ellwood E., CSP. "Memories of a Priest Filmmaker: Excerpts from a Hollywood Priest." *St. Anthony Messenger* 99 (August 1991): 16–21.

———. *The Spiritual Journey of a Showbusiness Priest.* Mahwah, N.J.: Paulist Press, 1996.

Kerwin, J. "The McCarthy Era in Perspective." *Critic* 23 (April–May 1965): 55–61.

Keyser, Leo, and Barbara Keyer. *Hollywood and the Catholic Church: The Image of Roman Catholicism in American Movies.* Chicago: Loyola University Press, 1984.

Klock, Dorothy. "An Afternote on the Family Theater." *Sign* 30 (October 1950): 64–65.

———. "More Things Are Wrought." *Sign* 28 (October 1948): 47.

———. "Triumphant Hour." *Sign* 30 (March 1951): 65.

Knoll, Aloysius, OFM Cap. "Harbinger of Peace: The Family Rosary." *Catholic Home Journal* 51 (October 1951): 3.

Kselman, Thomas, and Steven Avella. "Marian Piety and the Cold War in the United States." *Catholic Historical Review* 72 (1986): 403–24.

Langan, John P., SJ. "The Debate Begins: the Bishops and the Bottom Line." *Commonweal* 111 (November 2–16, 1984): 586–92.

Larkin, Emmet. "Church and State in Ireland in the Nineteenth Century." *Church History* 31 (1962): 295–306.

———. "The Devotional Revolution in Ireland." *American Historical Review* 77 (1972): 625–52.

"Latin America to Date." *Commonweal* 83 (March 4, 1966): 628–29.

"Latin American Crusade for Renewal: Family Rosary Crusade." *Mary Today* 57 (March 1966): 2–7.

Larraín Errázuriz, Manuel. "Latin America's Only Hope: An Interview." *Sign* 40 (February 1961): 36–39.

"Leaking Ship." *Newsweek* 66 (December 27, 1965): 25–26.

Leckey, Dolores R. "The Rosary Time of My Life." *Catholic Digest* 47 (October 1983): 57–58.

Leclercq, Jean, OSB. "The Distinctive Characteristics of Roman Catholic American Spirituality." *Louvain Studies* 9 (Spring 1983): 295–306.

Lernoux, Penny. "C.I.A. Secret Missionaries." *Nation* 230 (April 26, 1980): 494–96.

Lewis, Tom. "The Priest Who Won Hollywood for Our Lady." *Our Lady's Digest* 21 (May–June 1966): 12–18.

———. "Why Radio Needs an Angel." *America* 63 (April 27, 1940): 75–76.

Lippmann, Walter. *The Communist World and Ours.* Boston: Little and Brown, 1959.

Long, Christina G. "Father Peyton Is Still the Rosary Priest." *Catholic Digest* 48 (October 1984): 58–62.

Lozano, John M., CMF. *Grace and Brokenness in God's Country: An Exploration of American Catholic Spirituality.* New York: Paulist Press, 1991.

Luce, Clare Booth. "Anchor of the Christian Family." *Action Now* 5 (February 1952): 15–16.

Lunn, Arnold. "The Rosary and the Modern Mind." *Ave Maria* 44 (October 3, 1936): 417–21.

Lynch, James, SJ. "The Redeemer." *Sacred Heart Messenger* 100 (February 1966): 4–5, 59–60.

MacEoin, Gary. "Has the Rosary Survived the Council?" *Ave Maria* 104 (July 9, 1966): 12–14.

Magan, J. W. "Catholic Devotion Wins Radio Acclaim: Sacred Heart Program." *America* 67 (July 25, 1942): 428–29.

Maher, Michael, ed. *Irish Spirituality.* Dublin: Veritas Publications, 1981.

Mahoney, T. P. "Impressions of American Catholicism." *Catholic Mind* 74 (November 1975): 16–24.

Malone, James. "Reporting the Life of the Church in the 1980s." *Origins* 14 (November 1, 1984): 313–15.

Marchetti, Victor, and John D. Marks. *The C.I.A. and the Cult of Intelligence.* New York: Alfred A. Knopf, 1974.

Marek, J. J., CSC. "The Family Rosary." *Ave Maria* 93 (May 13, 1961): 9–11.

Martin, Martha. "The Man Who Made Hollywood Pray (Abridged)." *Catholic Digest* 12 (June 1948): 27–32.

Marty, Martin E. "The Catholic Ghetto and All the Other Ghettos." *Catholic Historical Review* 68 (1982): 184–205.

Massa, Mark, SJ. *Catholics and American Culture: Fulton Sheen, Dorothy Day, and the Notre Dame Football Team.* New York: Crossroad, 1999.

Massam, Katharine. *Sacred Threads: Catholic Spirituality in Australia 1922–1962.* Sydney, Australia: University of New South Wales Press, 1996.

Mathews, J. A. "Living Faith and Fruitful Living: Father, Education, Etc." *Catholic Mind* 33 (February 8, 1933): 51–58.

May, Elaine Tyler. *Homeward Bound: American Families in the Cold War Era.* New York: Basic Books, 1988.

Maynard, Theodore. "The Spiritual Heritage of America." *Spiritual Life* 2 (December 1956): 235–44.

McAvoy, Thomas T., CSC., ed. *Roman Catholicism and the American Way of Life.* Notre Dame, Ind.: University of Notre Dame Press, 1960.

McCann, Patricia. "A Lifetime with the Rosary." *Catholic Digest* 55 (June 1991): 17–18.

McCarthy, Timothy A. "How Father Peyton Got the Rosary to Fly." *Catholic Digest* 58 (October 1994): 55–60.

McCawley, Pat K. "Dial 1040: Your Rosary Hour." *Family Digest* 22 (October 1966): 41–44.

McCormack, Arthur. "The Catholic Church in South America." *Wiseman Review* 238 (Fall 1964): 226–60.

McDermott, Edwin, SJ. "Family Bill of Rights." *Catholic Mind* 45 (June 1947): 337–41.

McDermott, John Michael. "The Weakness of American Catholicism." *Chicago Studies* 28 (April 1989): 79–88.

McGinnis, H. C. "Dad, Priest of the Family." *Extension* 41 (June 1946): 6–7.

McGowan, Raymond A. "Catholic Action and the Family." *NCWC Review* 12 (January 20, 1930): 31.

———. "Changing World and the Family." *NCWC Review* 12 (January 1930): 7–8.

McSherry, Maria. "Why Don't You Start the Block Rosary?" *Ave Maria* 72 (August 19, 1950): 247–48.

Meath, Gerard, OP. "Family Worship." *Blackfriars* 23 (May 1942): 173–78.

Meekison, Mary Frances. "Recipe for a Home." *Ave Maria* 64 (October 5, 1946): 440.

"Message of Hope." *Catholic Preview of Entertainment* (September–October 1958): 9–12.

Michaud, Stephen G., and Hugh Aynesworth. *"If You Love Me You Will Do My Will."* New York: Signet, 1991.

"Millions Are Praying More." *Hibernia* 19, no. 1 (Autumn 1954): 7–8.

Miltner, Charles C., CSC. "Ideal Christian Home." *Homiletic and Pastoral Review* 30 (December 1929): 306–11.

Monagle, Robert. "Lost: The American Family." *Family Digest* 8 (August 1953): 41–43.

Moriarity, David, OP. "A Family Prayer." *Dominicana* 30 (Autumn 1945): 183–87.

"Movement for Revival of Family Rosary." *Catholic Action* 25 (April 1943): 17.

Mueller, Victoria E. "Home as an Institution for Religious Instruction." *Journal of Religious Instruction* 13 (April 1943): 590–600.

Mundie, Paul J. "Family in Transition." *American Catholic Sociological Review* 2 (March 1941): 41–45.

Myers, Rawley. "American Spirituality." *Homiletic and Pastoral Review* 78 (December 1977): 59–62.

"National Crusade of Prayer." *Tablet* 161 (May 20, 1933): 640.

Nelly, Una. "Prayer in Irish Spirituality." *Furrow* 39 (July 1988): 429–41.

"New Crusade in Europe, Interview." *U.S. News & World Report* 37 (August 27, 1954): 82–90.

"New Evangelist." *Time* 64 (October 25, 1964): 54–60.

"New Evangelist Arrives." *Life* 27 (November 21, 1949): 97–98.

"New Religious Program Begins on NBC Red Network." *Catholic Action* 24 (July 1942): 24–25.

"Next Decade in Latin America: Interview of Larraín Errázuriz." *Catholic World* 192 (February 1961): 278–85.

Niblo, Fred, Jr. "Family Theater's Passion Play." *Family Digest* (April 1966): 46–51.

Nieberdig, Velma. "Priceless Ingredient: Religion." *Catholic Home Journal* 45 (April 1945): 8–9.

Nixon, Richard M. "Nixon's Latest Word on Foreign Policy: Address, November 24, 1957." *U.S. News & World Report* 43 (December 6, 1957): 110–11.

Noel Marie, Sister. "England Bows to Our Lady." *The Magnificat* (July 1951): 118–20.

———. "Family Rosary." *Journal of Religious Instruction* (*Catholic Educator*) 15 (May 1945): 752–54.

"Non-Catholics and the Rosary Crusade." *Tablet* 200 (August 9, 1952): 116.

Noonan, Daniel P. *The Catholic Communicators: Portraits of Father Charles E. Coughlin, Archbishop Fulton J. Sheen, Pope John Paul II, Mother Angelica, Father Patrick Peyton, Mother Teresa.* Huntington, Ind.: Our Sunday Visitor: 1990.

Norwood, Allen. "Rosary Crime Fighters." *Catholic Digest* 58 (October 1994): 61–63.

O'Brien, David. "Catholic Contentiousness: The Public Consequences of Denominational Disputes." In *Uncivil Religion: Interreligious Hostility in America,* ed. Robert Bellah and Frederick Greenspan, 156–80. New York: Crossroad, 1987.

———. "Toward an American Catholic Church." *Cross Currents* 31 (Winter 1981–82): 457–73.

O'Dea, Thomas F. *American Catholic Dilemma.* New York: Sheed and Ward, 1958.

O'Dwyer, Peter. *Towards a History of Irish Spirituality.* Blackrock, Ireland: Columba Press, 1995.

O'Gara, James. "Uncertain Future." *Commonweal* 77 (November 16, 1962): 192.

"Old Fashioned Home." *Ave Maria* 32 (November 1, 1930): 563.

"On Fighting Communism: Vatican Decree on Communism." *America* 101 (May 2, 1959): 268–69.

Ong, Walter J., SJ. *American Catholic Crossroads: Religious-Secular Encounters in the Modern World.* N.J.: Macmillan Company, 1959.

Oswald, R. "The Church: Protector of the Family." *Altar and Home* 25 (April 1958): 28–32.

Oxton, Charles. "Father Peyton's Family Theater: A New Look." *Catholic Preview of Entertainment* 5 (November 1961): 8–12.

Parker, Phyllis R. *Brazil and the Quiet Intervention, 1964.* Austin: University of Texas Press, 1979.

Parsons, Wilfrid, SJ. "Marian Devotion in the Early United States." *Marian Studies* 3 (1952): 236–50.

Pattison, B. A. "Papal Concern about the Family." *Homiletic and Pastoral Review* 59 (December 1958): 270–72.

Pell, Robert. "Foreign Policies of Richard Milhous Nixon." *America* 104 (October 8, 1960): 38–42.

Pennington, Basil. "The Rosary: An Ancient Prayer for All of Us." *Our Sunday Visitor Magazine* 72 (October 23, 1983): 3.

Pepler, Conrad, OP. "Worship and Family Life." *Blackfriars* 20 (September 1939): 655–66.

Peter, Robert. "Communist Priests in South America." *National Review* 17 (October 5, 1965): 876.

"Plan for Family Spirituality." *Ave Maria* 89 (May 23, 1959): 16–17.

Pollock, John. *Billy Graham: Evangelist to the World.* San Francisco: Harper & Row, 1979.

Ponce, Frank. "The U.S. Church's Hispanic Catholics." *Origins* 10, no. 12 (September 11, 1980): 194–201.

Powers, Joshua B. "What About South America?" *Friar* 26 (July–August 1966): 14–20.

Powers, Richard Gid. *Not without Honor: The History of American Anticommunism.* New York: Free Press, 1995.

"Prayer and Family Life." *Life of the Spirit* 14 (October 1959): 146–51.

Purcell, M. "New Religious Film: The Fifteen Mysteries of the Rosary." *Messenger of the Sacred Heart* 92 (May 1957): 20–25.

Quinn, Edward. "Mass or Elite?" *Clergy Review* 37 (December 1952): 726–31.

Raddatz, Leslie. "Hollywood's Priestly Producers." *Notre Dame Magazine* 15, no. 2 (Summer 1987): 48–49.

Ramirez, Ricardo. "The Time for the Church to Act is Now: Interview" *Extension* 80 (July 1985): 20–22.

Ranelagh, John. *The Agency: The Rise and Decline of the C.I.A.* New York: Simon and Schuster, 1986.

Reed, Ruth V. "Constructive Influence Affecting American Family Life." *American Catholic Sociological Review* 7 (December 1946): 273–76.

Reilly, Ruth W. "Family Rosary." *Ave Maria* 90 (September 12, 1959): 9–11.

Reinhold, H. A. "Family Communion." *Orate Fratres* 16 (January 1942): 126–29.

Rigol, Peter N., SJ. "Bolivia, Catholicism or Communism." *World Mission* 12 (September 1961): 89–97.

Roche, Douglas J. "Christ to Marx Step by Step: Why a Latin American Left the Church for the Communist Party." *Sign* 41 (June 1962): 23–26, 70.

Roche, James, SJ. "Mary Is Alive!" *Immaculata* (May 1970): 5–8.

Romero, C. Gilbert. "Self-Affirmation of the Hispanic Church." *Ecumenist* 23 (March–April 1985): 39–42.

Rooney, Richard L., SJ. "Family Rosary Crusade." *Action Now* 4 (March 1951): 26–29.

"Rosary Broadcast." *Ave Maria* 67 (January 3, 1948): 2.

"Rosary Campaign." *Ave Maria* 63 (June 22, 1946): 770.

"Rosary Crusade." *Ave Maria* 79 (January 9, 1954): 5–6.

"The Rosary Crusade." *Tablet* 200 (July 5, 1952): 15.

"Rosary Crusade in England." *Ave Maria* 75 (May 31, 1952): 677.

"Rosary Crusade in England." *Tablet* (July 12, 1952): 38.

"Rosary Crusade: A Pastoral Letter from Cardinal Griffin." 199 (June 28, 1952): 526.

"Rosary Crusade in Canada." *Ave Maria* 72 (September 30, 1950): 418.

Rosser, Donna C. "The Family Rosary in the Real World." *Catholic Digest* 57 (January 1993): 109–11.

Roll, Bertin, OFM Cap. "Christian Mother's Page: Family Prayers." *Catholic Home Journal* 51 (May 1951): 29.

Rubottom, Roy R., Jr. "International Communism in Latin America: Statement, June 20, 1960." *United States Department of State Bulletin* 43 (July 11, 1960): 60–64.

———. "Toward Better Understanding between United States and Latin America." *Annals of the American Academy of Political and Social Science* 330 (July 1960): 116–23.

———. "Vice President's Visit to South America in Perspective: Statement before Subcommittee on Latin America, June 3, 1958." *United States Department of State Bulletin* 38 (June 30, 1958): 1104–9.

Russell, W. H. "American Spirituality." *Spiritual Life* 2, no. 4 (December 1956): 227–34.

Ryan, Liam. "The Changing Irish Family." *Furrow* 45 (April 1994): 212–20.

Sable, Martin Howard. *Communism in Latin America*. Los Angeles: University of California Press, 1968.

Schmiedler, Edgar, OSB. "Building Vital Families from Within." *Homiletic and Pastoral Review* 35 (November 1934): 219–24.

———. "Catholic Action and the Family." *Homiletic and Pastoral Review* 35 (November and December 1934): 214–24, 305–12.

———. "Conserving the Family." *Catholic Action* 14 (January 1932): 12–13.

———. "Father Peyton's Rosary Prayer Book." *American Benedictine Review* 5 (Summer 1954): 159–60.

Schurmann, Franz. *The Foreign Politics of Richard Nixon: The Grand Design*. Berkeley: Institute of International Studies, University of California Press, 1987.

Schwartz, Harry. "Shadow over Latin America." *Commonweal* 66 (June 21, 1957): 295–98.

Schweitzer, Leonard J. "Rosary Crusade in Britain." *Ave Maria* 76 (October 4, 1952): 423–27.

Sharkey, Don. "This Is Your Mother." *Ave Maria* 78 (October 17, 1953): 16.

———. "This Is Your Mother: The Radio Rosary." *Ave Maria* 78 (October 24, 1953): 16

Shaw, Paul V. "Ambassador Steven's Mission." *New Republic* 145 (July 3, 1961): 14–15.

Sherritt, Helen M. "Peyton Power is Prayer." *Action Now* 4 (June 1951): 18–20.

Sherry, Gerard E. "Father Patrick Peyton: Crusading for the Rosary." *Our Sunday Visitor* 76 (December 13, 1987): 3.

Shriver, R. Sargent, Jr. "Some Issues for the 1980s." *Catholic World* 79 (January 1981): 10–18.

Shriver, W. H. "Radio and Television: Programs on Communism over the Catholic Hour and We the People." *Catholic World* 171 (September 1950): 467–68.

Skolnick, Arlene. *Embattled Paradise: The American Family in an Age of Uncertainty.* New York: Basic Books, 1991.

Smith, Anthony B. "American Catholicism and the Construction of a Public Tradition, 1932–1962." PhD dissertation: University of Minnesota, 1995.

———. "Sinner, Judge, and Cavalryman: John Ford and Popular American Catholicism." In *American Catholic Tradition: Resources for Renewal,* ed. Sandra Yocum Mize. Maryknoll, N.Y.: Orbis Books, 1997.

Smith, William C. "Church of the Air." *Catholic Mind* 45 (January 1947): 15–18.

———. "How to Get Radio Time." *Catholic Action* 28 (October 1946): 14–15.

———. "How to Produce Religious Radio Programs." *Catholic Action* 29 (January 1947): 17–18.

———. "Radio Production Problems." *Catholic Action* 20 (February 1947): 18–20, 22.

"Some Notes on Catholic Radio Programs." *Catholic Action* 21 (November 1944): 18–20.

Sparr, Arnold. *To Promote, Defend and Redeem: The Catholic Literary Revival and the Cultural Transformation of American Catholicism, 1920–1960.* New York: Greenwood Press, 1990.

Springer, John L. "What Makes a Happy Family?" *Catholic Digest* 21 (February 1957): 42–46.

"The State of the Church in America." *Our Sunday Visitor Magazine* 68 (October 7, 1979): 3–5; (October 14, 1979): 3–5, 20–22.

Stevenson, Adlai. E. "Alliance for Progress: A Road Map to New Achievements: Report to the Secretary of State, July 24, 1961." *United States Department of State Bulletin* 45 (August 21, 1961): 311–16.

Stickley, J. M. "This Was a Man Sent From God." *American Mercury* 79 (October 1954): 21–22.

" 'Stomach' Appeal Not Latin American Key, Priest Says." *Catholic Association for International Peace News* 24 (July–August 1963): 11–12.

"Story of Allen Dulles and the C.I.A." *U.S. News & World Report* 48 (May 23, 1960): 25.

"Suspicion and the C.I.A." *Commonweal* 84 (May 13, 1966): 214.

Swinstead, A. E. H. "Broadcasting Catholicism." *Blackfriars* 13 (December 1932): 743–53.

Tansey, A. "Supersalesman for the Family Rosary." *Family Digest* 17 (October 1961): 6–11.

Tarasow, Konstantin S. *The C.I.A. in Latin America.* Moscow: Progress Publishers, 1984.

Taves, Ann. *The Household of Faith: Roman Catholic Devotions in Mid-Nineteenth-Century America.* Notre Dame, Ind.: University of Notre Dame Press, 1986.

Tetlow, Joseph A., SJ. "American Catholic Spirituality." *New Catholic World* 225 (July–August 1982): 152–55.

———. "The Second Half-Generation." *New Catholic World* 223 (September–October 1980): 196–200.

Thomas, John L., SJ. *The American Catholic Family.* Englewood Cliffs, N.J.: Prentice Hall, 1956.

———. "The American Catholic Family." In *Contemporary Catholicism in the United States,* ed. Philip Gleason, : 215–38. Notre Dame, Ind.: University of Notre Dame Press, 1969.

———. "Family in American Society." *Family Digest* 12 (February 1957): 1–6.

Thompson, Thomas A., SM, and Jack Alton Wintz, OFM. "The Rosary a Gospel Prayer." *St. Anthony Messenger* 96 (May 1989): 34–38.

Tierney, John, CPPS. "The Communist Plan for Latin America." *Nuntius Aulae* 45 (1963): 163–76.

"Time of Decision in Latin America." *Tablet* 216 (May 26, 1962): 509.

"Tribute to Father Peyton." *Ave Maria* 76 (July 26, 1952): 98.

Trisco, Robert. "American Catholicism: The Voice of Conscience and Culture." *Columbia* 55 (April 1975): 6–15.

———, ed. *Catholics in America 1776–1976.* Washington, D.C.: United States Catholic Conference, 1976.

Truitt, Gordon Edward. "A Historical and Theological Analysis of the Main Trends of the Catholic Theology of Prayer in the United States, 1940–1975." PhD dissertation: Catholic University of America, 1982.

Ulanar, John G. "Can the Family Survive the 20th Century?" *Family Digest* 24 (January 1969): 7–12.

Valentry, D. "One Family and the Rosary." *Family Digest* 12 (May 1957): 41–44.

Van Allen, Rodger. "Memories and Hopes: Questions on American Catholicism." *Commonweal* 106 (June 8, 1979): 326–28.

Varacelli, Joseph A. "The Future of U.S. Catholicism." *Ecumenist* 20 (July–August 1982): 71–75.

"Vatican II on the Family." *Columbia* 46 (January 1966): 44.

Walsh, Mary Ann. "Father Patrick Peyton." *Our Sunday Visitor Magazine* 71 (May 30, 1982): 10–12.

Warner, Marina. *Alone of All Her Sex: The Myth and Cult of the Virgin Mary.* New York: Pocket Books, 1976.

Weber, Francis J. *His Eminence of Los Angeles: James Francis Cardinal McIntyre.* Santa Barbara, Calif.: McNally and Loftin, 1997.

Weigel, George S. "American Catholicism: A Moment of Hope and Opportunity." *National Catholic Reporter* 65 (February 5, 1989): 10.

———. *Catholicism and the Renewal of American Democracy.* Mahwah, N.J.: Paulist Press, 1989.

Whitaker, Arthur P. "Our Reaction to Communist Infiltration in Latin America." *Annals of the American Academy of Political and Social Science* 330 (July 1960): 103–15.

"Why Free Time for Religious Broadcasts?" *Catholic Action* 24 (July 1942): 25.

Wintz, Jack, OFM. "Family Theater at 50: Father Patrick Peyton Remembered." *St. Anthony Messenger* 105, no. 1 (June 1997): 16–21.

———. "Jane Wyatt: Witness to Family Values." *St. Anthony Messenger* 105, no. 1 (June 1997): 22–23.

Woods, Francis F. "Bound by Gold Chains." Unpublished manuscript, n.d. [1946], PPC, Attymass, County Mayo, Ireland.

Wuthnow, Robert. *After Heaven: Spirituality in America since the 1950s.* Berkeley: University of California Press, 1998.

York, Jeremy. "Peace, Communism, and American Catholics." *Ave Maria* 104 (July 2, 1966): 8–11.

Yzermans, V. A. "C.B.A. Comes of Age." *Crosier* 34 (November 1959): 9–15.

Index

Richard Gribble, CSC is a priest in the Congregation of Holy Cross. A 1975 graduate of the U.S. Naval Academy, Father Gribble has served in parish ministry and as a college professor. Presently, Father Gribble holds a position as Associate Professor of Religious Studies at Stonehill College and is the author of 15 books of history and spirituality and over 170 articles.

Of Related Interest

Mark Massa, S.J.
CATHOLICS AND AMERICAN CULTURE
Fulton Sheen, Dorothy Day,
and the Notre Dame Football Team

While in the early years of the twentieth century Catholics in America were for the most part distrusted outsiders with respect to the dominant culture, by the 1960s the mainstream of American Catholicism was in many ways "the culture's loudest and most uncritical cheerleader." Mark Massa explores the rich irony in this postwar transition, beginning with the heresy case of Leonard Feeney, examining key figures such as Fulton Sheen, Thomas Merton, and John F. Kennedy, and concluding with a look at the University of Notre Dame and the transformed status of American Catholic higher education.

Pope John Paul II
Edited by Carl J. Moell, S.J.
HOLY FATHER, SACRED HEART
The Complete Collection of John Paul II's Writings
on the Perennial Catholic Devotion

Pope John Paul II has given the devotion to the Sacred Heart a special place in his spiritual life and public ministry for decades. In *Holy Father, Sacred Heart,* Carl J. Moell, drawing from his experience working with the Society of Jesus in Rome, gathers together every teaching the Holy Father has proclaimed regarding this most intimate of Catholic devotions. From the Pope's speeches before audiences of millions, to his personal prayers and writings, *Holy Father, Sacred Heart* is the perfect treasury for everyone devoted to the Sacred Heart of Jesus Christ.

crossroad

Of Related Interest

Michael Crosby
SOLANUS CASEY
The Official Account
of a Virtuous American Life

"This volume makes public the simple yet awesome facts of a man whose relationship with God was so profound that his prayers could help heal people."   —*New York Times*

In 1995, Pope John Paul II bestowed on Bernard (Solanus) Casey the title of Venerable, making him the first male born in the U.S. to be elevated to this position. This true story of an American saint, excerpted from the official 1300-page canonization document, is both a moving spiritual biography and an inside look at the canonization process.

crossroad